ACCOUNTING

THE
BASIS
FOR
BUSINESS
DECISIONS

THE
BASIS
FOR
BUSINESS
DECISIONS

1962

ACCOUNTING

THE BASIS FOR BUSINESS DECISIONS

WALTER B. MEIGS, *Ph.D., C.P.A.*
Professor of Accounting and Head, Department of Accounting,
University of Southern California

CHARLES E. JOHNSON, *Ph.D., C.P.A.*
Professor of Accounting and Head, Department of Accounting
and Business Statistics, University of Oregon

McGraw-Hill **BOOK COMPANY**   NEW YORK SAN FRANCISCO TORONTO LONDON

Preface

The first course in accounting attempts to meet the needs of students who have elected or plan to elect accounting as a major, students of business administration who need a good understanding of accounting as a background for a business career, and students in other social science and professional areas who will find the ability to use accounting data intelligently a valuable accomplishment. This book is designed to serve the needs and interests of all three groups.

In developing the material in this book, consideration has been given to a number of modern trends in accounting instruction:

Selection of subject matter. In recent years the subject matter of accounting has broadened, and new areas clamor for admission to the list of topics standard for an introductory course. Indeed, it has been proposed at one time or another that almost every facet of accounting be included in the introductory text. We have avoided the temptation to make perfunctory comment on the widest variety of material in order to be able to point to its inclusion in the book. The topics chosen have been treated at an introductory level, but each topic has been given sufficient coverage to enable the student to gain a useful degree of understanding of the subject matter.

The first five chapters give an overview of the accounting cycle. In Chapters 6 to 9, on accounting for sales, purchases, and cash transactions, the issues of internal control are emphasized. The problem of valuation receives considerable attention in the chapters on specific classes of assets and liabilities, and the special problems that arise in accounting for partnership and corporate ownership equity are thoroughly covered in Chapters 15 to 20. The functional classification of expenses and its relation to expense analysis and allocation are discussed in Chapter 24. An introductory consideration of direct costing and the issues raised by this approach to cost determination appears in Chapter 26, on cost accounting. Chapter 27 contains a discussion of the way in which income taxes influence business decisions and the relation between accounting income and taxable income. Chapter 28, on analysis of financial statements, includes a discussion of fund-flow information and how such data can be developed without the use of traditional extensive working-paper techniques. Because of the importance of advanced planning in the control of business operations, a full chapter, Chapter 29, is devoted to budgeting and the use of budget data by management. These examples are illustrative of the attempt to give the introductory student a wide-angle view of today's accounting problems, with sufficient depth and focus to make the exposure meaningful.

Emphasis on the use and interpretation of accounting data. Accounting data are used by business managers, investors, governmental agencies, and every citizen who is interested in questions of public policy which turn, in part at least, on accounting information. In the past perhaps undue attention has been given in the introductory course to the viewpoint of investors and the public, and too little to the managerial viewpoint. At present there are some who would apparently swing the pendulum of accounting instruction far over to the managerial side, devoting primary if not sole attention to the use of accounting data by management. We feel that none of the pertinent viewpoints should be slighted in an introductory text. Careful attention is given to the effect of various business transactions on financial statements and to the problems that arise in interpreting accounting information from the viewpoint of investors and the public. An equal amount of attention is devoted to the ways in which accounting data can serve management in controlling and planning business operations.

A reasonable perspective on procedures. The major objective of a first course in accounting is to foster an understanding of accounting and the way it serves in developing useful information about economic organizations. We believe that some attention to procedure is necessary if a student is to gain reasonable facility in dealing with and interpreting accounting data. Accordingly, procedural matters are not neglected, but discussion of some purely technical procedures has been omitted and discussion of procedural details minimized. For example, the coverage of prepayments and accruals is arranged so as to avoid the issue of reversing entries, a purely technical bookkeeping procedure. The essential features of special journals and control accounts are covered clearly but compactly in a single chapter, which is sufficient for understanding, but does not belabor the point. Material on payroll accounting procedures and the voucher system is placed in the latter half of the text, and may be omitted in a course if desired. Problem material is balanced; the instructor who wishes to give minimum attention to procedure and the one who wants to place relatively more weight on this area will both find problem material suitable to their objectives.

Emphasis on accounting theory. We believe that the logic and theory underlying accounting are not a separate topic but an integral part of any discussion of accounting problems. Accordingly, as each topic is developed, there is consideration of the nature of the problem and the reasoning behind the accounting procedures designed to cope with it. At the same time, to the extent appropriate in an introductory discussion, the student is made aware of differences between theory and accounting practice and the reasons for the differences.

Complete package of instructional aids. A comprehensive set of instructional aids is provided. Some of these are included in the text; others are published separately.

Discussion questions. A series of questions designed as a basis for classroom discussion and to aid the student in testing his understanding of the text material is given at the end of each chapter.

Problem material with time and difficulty ratings. Two sets of problems for each chapter, Group A and Group B problems, are included in the text. The problems in the two groups are of similar difficulty, require about the same solution time, and can be worked on similar accounting forms. Instructors may thus choose problems from both groups or may alternate, using Group A problems in one year or in one class and Group B problems in another.

Working papers. Working papers for the problem material are published separately from the text. Partially filled-in accounting work sheets are available for Group A problems; on these work sheets headings and some preliminary data have been entered. Specially designed blank accounting forms suitable for both Group A and Group B problems are also available.

Practice sets. Two practice sets have been prepared. One is for use with material in the first half of the book; the other, for use with material in the second half of the book. Each practice set consists of two separate items: the narrative of transactions and the solution forms.

Study guide. Written by Lyle H. McIff of Utah State University, the study guide makes available to the enterprising student an aid in mastering accounting principles. Specially designed to accompany the text, it contains for each chapter: (1) an informal discussion of the chapter's objectives; (2) an outline of the important points; (3) objective questions for review, with answers included to help the student evaluate his understanding of the subject; and (4) short exercises, with answers. The study guide will be found useful also in classroom discussion and for examination review.

The authors are indebted to the following persons who reviewed the manuscript and made many helpful suggestions: Dean O. J. Curry, North Texas State College; and Profs. Irving K. Christiansen, John Carroll University; Robert K. Jaedicke, Stanford University; Elzy V. McCullough, Louisiana State University; Thomas M. Dickerson, Western Reserve University; Catherine E. Miles, Georgia State College of Business Administration; Raymond C. Dein, University of Nebraska; Emanuel Grody, East Los Angeles Junior College; Raymond R. Orie, University of Pittsburgh; T. E. Fitzgerald, Temple University; Phil Loprinzi, University of Portland; Othel D. Westfall, The University of Oklahoma, and Dennis Gordon, University of Akron.

Walter B. Meigs
Charles E. Johnson

Contents

accounts. Purchases journal. Cash receipts journal. Posting the cash receipts journal. Cash payments journal. Posting the cash payments journal. The general journal. Showing the source of postings in ledger accounts. The running balance form of account. Ledger accounts. Proving the ledgers. Variations in special journals. Direct posting from invoices.

check register. Special considerations of the voucher register. As a subsidiary ledger. Handling purchase returns and allowances. Making partial payments. Issuing notes payable. Correcting errors in the voucher register. Presentation of liability in the balance sheet. A "voucher system" without vouchers. Appraisal of the voucher system. Payroll accounting. Deductions from earnings of employees. Payroll records and procedures. Payroll taxes on the employer.

1

Accounting: the basis for business decisions

Accounting has often been called the "language of business" because people in the business world—owners, managers, bankers, salesmen, attorneys, engineers, investors—use accounting terms and concepts to describe the events that make up the existence of businesses of every kind. The analogy between learning accounting and learning a language is not perfect, but the similarities are significant. You will find that many of the terms used in accounting have meanings that differ from the meanings attached to the same words in ordinary nonaccounting usage. It is usually true that as a person gains familiarity with a language he begins to understand better the country in which that language is spoken and the customs and actions of people who speak it. Similarly, as you gain a knowledge of accounting you will increase your understanding of the way businesses operate and the way in which business decisions are made. Finally, a language is a man-made means of communication; languages change gradually to meet the changing needs of society. Accounting, too, is a man-made art, one in which changes and improvements are continually being made in the process of communicating business information.

THE PURPOSE AND NATURE OF ACCOUNTING

The underlying purpose of accounting is to provide financial information about any economic entity, usually a business enterprise. This information is needed by a business manager to help him plan and control the activities of his organization. It is also needed by outsiders—owners, creditors, investors, and the public—who have supplied money to the business or who have some other interest that will be served by information about its financial position and operating results.

If someone gave you the task of making a record of what went on in a business enterprise and you knew nothing about the way in which this was ordinarily done, you would, after a little experimentation, probably arrive at a system somewhat similar to that which has evolved in accounting.

First, you would find it necessary to create some systematic record of business transactions, in terms of money. In essence, a business is a collection of economic resources devoted to a particular purpose or goal. An orderly description of these resources, their source, and the way in which they are employed to promote a growth in value would be the natural starting point in fulfilling your assignment. Goods and services are purchased and sold; credit is extended to customers, debts are incurred, cash is received and expended—these are typical of the events you would record. It would soon be obvious that not all business events can be described in monetary terms. You would probably not be able to show in your record such significant happenings as the appointment of a new chief executive or the signing of a labor contract, except as these happenings in turn affected future business transactions.

Once you had compiled a narrative record of events as they occurred, you would find it advisable to sort various transactions and events into related groups or categories. In science the systematic classification of animals, minerals, and plants into categories based upon a scheme of natural relationship is the first step in gaining a greater understanding of natural phenomena. Classification would serve your purpose equally well by enabling you to reduce a mass of detail into compact and usable form. For example, grouping all transactions in which cash is received or paid out would be a logical step in developing useful information about the cash position of the company.

In order to be helpful to anyone, the information you have recorded and classified would have to be summarized in the form of a report or statement, that is, a concise picture of the significant findings gleaned from your detailed records. You would probably attempt to show where the business stood at the time of your report, and the process by which it had arrived at this position.

These three rather natural and logical steps—recording, classifying, and summarizing—form the basic process by which accounting data are created. Accounting as we know it today has evolved over a period of several hundred years. During this time certain rules, conventions, and procedures have become accepted as standard. Some of these rules are simply traditional and, like driving on the right side of the road, operate to reduce confusion. Others follow logically from the objectives which accounting is designed to attain. Knowing the rules of accounting construction is a prerequisite to understanding the way accounting data are developed and what they mean.

Accounting extends beyond the process of *creating* data. The ultimate objective of accounting is the *use* of these data, their analysis and interpretation. A good accountant is always concerned with the significance of the figures he has produced. He looks for meaningful relationships between events and financial results; he studies the effect of various alternatives; and he searches for significant trends that may throw some light on what will happen in the future.

Interpretation and analysis are not the sole province of the accountant. If managers, investors, and creditors are to make effective use of accounting information, they too must have some understanding of how the figures were put together and what they mean. Strangely enough, an important part of this understanding is to recognize clearly the limitations of accounting reports. A business manager, an investor, or a creditor who lacks training in accounting may fail to appreciate the extent to which accounting data are based upon estimates rather than upon precisely accurate measurements.

Persons with little knowledge of accounting may also fail to understand the difference between accounting and bookkeeping. *Bookkeeping* means the recording of transactions, the record-making phase of accounting. The recording of transactions tends to be mechanical and repetitive; it is only a small part of the field of accounting and probably the simplest part. A person might become a reasonably proficient bookkeeper in a few weeks or months; to become a professional accountant, however, requires several years of study and experience.

The work of accountants

In terms of career opportunities, the field of accounting may be divided into three areas:

1. Private businesses employ accountants to perform accounting functions ranging all the way from bookkeeping to designing accounting systems, preparing various reports and statements, and interpreting the results. The chief accounting officer of a private business of any size is usually called the *controller*, in recognition of the fact that one of the primary uses of accounting data is to aid in controlling business operations. The controller manages the work of the accounting staff. He is also a part of the management team charged with the task of running the business, setting its objectives, and seeing that these objectives are met.

2. *Certified public accountants* are independent professional persons, comparable to physicians or lawyers, who offer accounting services to clients for a fee. The CPA certificate is a license to practice granted by the state on the basis of a rigorous examination and evidence of practical experience. Although the CPA performs a wide variety of accounting-related services, his principal function is to review the accounting records of a business concern and issue a report in which he expresses his professional opinion as to the fairness and dependability of the financial state-

ments. Persons outside the business, who rely upon financial statements for information, attach considerable importance to the CPA's report because they know that it represents the conclusions of an independent expert who has made a thorough review of the accounting records.

The public accounting profession is relatively young; it began in England and dates in the United States from about 1896 when the first CPAs were licensed by the State of New York. In recent years the profession has expanded tremendously because of the increasing demand for accounting services. In addition to auditing, the CPA renders many other services to his clients. He is often called upon to prepare or assist in the preparation of income tax returns, and to design and install accounting systems. He also acts as a consultant on a wide variety of financial and business problems. Among the factors responsible for the spectacular growth of professional accounting have been the increasing size and complexity of business corporations, the growing interest of the general public in stock ownership, the increasing complexity of income and other forms of taxation, and the broadening of governmental interest in and regulation of business activity.

3. A third field of accounting is governmental and institutional accounting. The officers and elected representatives of the Federal, state, and local governments rely on financial information to help them direct the affairs of their agencies just as do the executives of private corporations. Many of the taxes levied by government are based upon accounting results, and governmental units find it advisable to employ accountants to verify tax information submitted by individuals and businesses.

Many governmental accounting problems are similar to those applicable to private industry. In other respects, however, accounting for governmental affairs requires a somewhat different approach because the objective of earning a profit is absent from public affairs. Universities, hospitals, churches, and other nonprofit institutions also follow a pattern of accounting that is similar to governmental accounting.

The work of an accountant employed by a governmental unit or nonprofit enterprise is similar in nature to that performed by both the controller and the public accountant. Many CPAs are in fact employed in this field. Government auditors review the accounting records of various departments and subdivisions and of private businesses who hold government contracts, in much the same way as do independent public accountants. Internal revenue agents perform auditing functions in examining income tax returns and the accounting data on which they are based. Accountants are employed by the Securities and Exchange Commission to aid in a critical review of the financial statements of corporations which offer securities for sale to the investing public.

Specialized phases of accounting
All business concerns, large and small, in every kind of industry, find it necessary to record transactions and prepare periodic financial statements

from accounting records. Within this area of general accounting, or in addition to it, a number of specialized phases of accounting have developed. Among the more important of these are:

Design of accounting systems. Although the same basic accounting principles are applicable to all types of businesses, each enterprise requires an individually tailored set of accounting forms, records, and reports to fit its particular needs. Designing an accounting system and putting it into operation is thus a specialized phase of accounting. With the advent of various accounting machines and electronic data-processing equipment, the problems that arise in creating an effective accounting system have become increasingly complex. On the other hand, once the system is devised and working, machines take much of the drudgery out of the bookkeeping process. Machine accounting methods also make it possible to compile data that would be too costly to gather by hand methods, and they increase materially the speed with which reports can be made available to management.

Cost accounting. Knowing the cost of a particular product, a manufacturing process, or any business operation is vital to the efficient management of that business. The phase of accounting particularly concerned with collecting and interpreting cost data has come to be known as *cost accounting.* Determining the cost of anything is not as simple as it appears at first glance, because the term "cost" has many meanings and different kinds of costs are useful for different purposes.

Budgeting. A budget is a plan of financial operations for some future period, expressed in accounting terms and designed to facilitate comparison between plans and actual results. A budget is thus an attempt to preview accounting results before the actual transactions have taken place. A budget is a particularly valuable tool in the controller's kit because it provides each element of the business with a specific goal, and because it gives management a means of measuring the efficiency of performance throughout the company.

Tax accounting. The primary source of revenue to the Federal government, and an important source for many state governments, is a tax on the income of individuals and businesses. The computation of taxable income is closely related to the problem of measuring the operating income of a business. As income tax rates have gone up and the determination of taxable income has become more complex, both internal and professional accountants have devoted more time to the problems of taxation. Tax accounting includes planning business operations in order to minimize the impact of taxes, as well as the computation of taxable income and preparation of tax returns.

Auditing. No matter how carefully an accounting system is designed and the records are kept, the results should be reviewed periodically to verify their reasonableness and to see that the system is working satisfactorily. An audit is a systematic process of examining financial statements, accounting records, and the underlying data for these purposes. Auditing may be *internal,* which means that it is done by employees of the organization; or it may be *external,* which means that it is done by CPAs who represent a viewpoint independent of the company whose records are being reviewed.

Two primary business objectives

The management of every business must keep foremost in its thinking two primary objectives. The first is to earn a profit. The second is to have on hand sufficient funds to pay debts as they fall due.

A business is a collection of resources committed by an individual or group of individuals, who hope that the investment will increase in value. Investment in any given business, however, is only one of a number of alternative investments available. If a concern does not earn as great a profit as might be obtained from alternative investments, its owners will be well advised to sell or terminate the business and invest elsewhere. A firm that continually operates at a loss will quickly exhaust its resources and be forced out of existence. Therefore, in order to operate successfully and to survive, the owners or managers of an enterprise must direct the business in such a way that it will earn a reasonable profit.

Business concerns that have sufficient funds to pay their debts promptly are said to be solvent. In contrast, a firm which finds itself unable to meet its obligations as they fall due is called insolvent. Solvency must also be ranked as a primary objective of any enterprise, since a firm that is insolvent will be forced by its creditors to close its doors.

Profits and solvency are of course not the only objectives of businessmen. There are many others, such as providing jobs for people, creating new and improved products, providing more goods and services at a lower cost. It is clear, however, that a business cannot hope to accomplish these things unless it meets the two basic tests of survival—operating profitably and staying solvent.

Accounting as the basis for management decisions

How does a business executive know whether his company is earning profits or incurring losses? How does he know whether the company is solvent or insolvent, and whether it will probably be solvent, say, a month from today? The answer to both these questions in one word is *accounting.* Not only is accounting the process by which the profitability and solvency of a firm can be measured, but it provides information needed as a basis for making business decisions that will enable management to guide the firm on a profitable and solvent course.

Stated simply, managing a business is a matter of deciding what should be done, seeing to it that the means are available, and getting people employed in the business to do it. At every step in this process management is faced with alternatives, and every decision to do something or to refrain from doing something involves a choice. Successful managers must make the right choice in at least a majority of situations. In most cases the probability that a good decision will be made depends on the amount and validity of the information that the manager has about the alternatives and their consequences. It is seldom true that all the information needed is either available or possible to obtain. Often a crystal ball in good working order would be helpful. As a practical matter, however, information which flows from the accounting records, or which can be developed by special analysis of accounting data, constitutes the basis on which a wide variety of business decisions should be made. What price should the firm set on its products? If production is increased, what effect will this have on product costs? Will it be necessary to borrow from the bank? How much will costs increase if a pension plan is established for employees? Is it more profitable to produce and sell product A or product B? Shall a given part be made or be bought from suppliers? Should an investment be made in new equipment? All these are examples of decisions that should depend, in part at least, upon accounting information. It might be reasonable to turn the quesiton around and ask: What business decisions could be intelligently made without the use of accounting information? Examples would be hard to find.

In a very small business (a hamburger stand, for example) it is possible that the owner could get along with very little in the way of accounting records. This is not because he does not need information on which to base decisions, but simply because he might be able to keep the necessary information in his head. If he could keep in mind the terms of his rental agreement with the landlord, the bills for food and utility services, the size of his bank account, and other such matters, he might get by with very little in the way of written records.

It is safe to say that business on any scale larger than our hypothetical hamburger stand could hardly exist without accounting records. In large-scale business undertakings such as the manufacture of automobiles, or the operation of nationwide chains of retail stores, and even in enterprises much smaller than these, the top executives cannot possibly have close physical contact with and knowledge of the details of operations. Consequently, these executives must depend to an even greater extent than the small businessman upon information provided by the accounting system.

FINANCIAL STATEMENTS: THE STARTING POINT IN THE STUDY OF ACCOUNTING

The preparation of financial statements is not the first step in the accounting process, but it is a convenient point to begin the study of accounting. The financial statements are the means of conveying to management and to interested outsiders a concise picture of the profitability and financial condition of the business. Since these statements are in a sense the end product of the accounting process, the student who acquires a clear understanding of the content and meaning of financial statements will be in an excellent position to appreciate the purpose of the earlier steps of recording and classifying business transactions.

There are two major financial statements, the balance sheet and the statement of income. Together, these two statements (each a page or less in length) summarize all the information contained in the hundreds or thousands of pages comprising the detailed accounting records. In this introductory chapter and in Chapter 2, we shall explore the nature of the balance sheet, or statement of financial condition, as it is sometimes called. Once we have become familiar with the form and arrangement of the balance sheet and with the meaning of technical terms such as assets, liabilities, and owners' equity, it will be as easy to read and understand a report on the financial condition of a business as it is for an architect to read the blueprint of a proposed building.

After we have gained some skill in reading (and preparing) a balance sheet, we shall round out our introduction to financial statements in Chapter 3 by a similar study of the income statement, which tells the story of profits or losses experienced by the firm. Then, having acquired a speaking acquaintance with financial statements, we shall in the next few chapters examine the recording procedures and other accounting processes which make possible the preparation of concise summary reports.

The balance sheet

The purpose of a balance sheet is to show the financial condition of a business as of a particular date. Every business prepares a balance sheet at the end of the year, and many concerns prepare one at the end of each month. A balance sheet consists of a listing of the assets and liabilities of a business and of the owner's equity. The following balance sheet portrays the financial condition of the Roberts Real Estate Company at September 30.

BALANCE
SHEET
REFLECTS
FINANCIAL
CONDITION
AT A
SPECIFIC
DATE

ROBERTS REAL ESTATE COMPANY
Balance Sheet
September 30, 19___

Assets		Liabilities & Owner's Equity	
Cash	$ 7,800	Liabilities:	
Accounts receivable	1,200	Accounts payable	$ 7,800
Land	5,000	Owner's equity:	
Building	12,000	James Roberts, capital	20,000
Office equipment	1,800		
	$27,800		$27,800

Notice that the balance sheet sets forth in its heading three items: (1) the name of the business, (2) the name of the statement "Balance Sheet," and (3) the date of the balance sheet. Below the heading is the body of the balance sheet, which consists of three distinct elements: assets, liabilities, and the owner's equity. The remainder of this chapter is largely devoted to making clear the nature of these three elements.

The illustrated balance sheet refers only to the affairs of the business unit known as the Roberts Real Estate Company, and not to the personal affairs of the owner, James Roberts. Mr. Roberts may have a personal bank account, investments in government bonds, a cattle ranch, and other property, but since these personal belongings are not a part of his real estate brokerage business, they are not included in the balance sheet of this business unit. A balance sheet and an income statement are intended to portray the financial condition and the operating results of a single business entity. If the owner intermingles his personal affairs with the transactions of the business, the resulting financial statements will be misleading and will fail to describe the business fairly.

If a man owns two businesses, such as a lumber mill and a drugstore, he should have a completely separate set of accounting records for each. Separate financial statements should also be prepared for each business, thus providing information on the progress and success of each venture.

To summarize this aspect of accounting, we may say that a separate set of accounting records is needed for each business entity, and the affairs of the owner are not to be intermingled with the affairs of the business. By observing these conventions, we shall be able to develop accounting information measuring the financial condition and profitability of each business venture.

Assets. In general, assets are economic resources which are owned by a business. Assets may have definite physical character, such as buildings, machinery, or merchandise. On the other hand, some assets exist not in physical or tangible form, but in the form of valuable legal claims or rights; examples are amounts due from customers, government bonds, and patent rights.

One of the most basic, and at the same time most controversial, problems in accounting is the assignment of dollar values to the assets of a business. Two kinds of assets cause little difficulty. Cash and amounts due from customers represent funds that either are available for expenditure or will be available in the near future (when the customers pay their accounts). The amount of cash on hand is a clear statement of the dollars that are available for expenditure. The amount that customers owe the business (after taking into account that some receivables may prove uncollectible) represents the dollars that will be received in the near future.

Other assets such as land, buildings, merchandise, and equipment represent economic resources that will be used in producing income for the business. The prevailing accounting view is that such assets should be accounted for on the basis of the dollars that have been invested in these resources, that is, the cost incurred in acquiring such property or property rights. In accounting terms, therefore, the "value" or "valuation" of an asset ordinarily means the cost of that asset.

For example, let us assume that a business buys a tract of land for use as a building site, paying $40,000 in cash. The amount to be entered in the accounting records as the value of the asset will be the cost of $40,000. Ten years later (if we assume a booming real estate market) a fair estimate of the sales value of the land might be $100,000. Although the market price or economic value of the land has risen greatly, the accounting value as shown by the accounting records and by the annual balance sheet would continue unchanged at the cost of $40,000.

In reading a balance sheet, it is important to bear in mind that the dollar amounts listed do not indicate the prices at which the assets could be sold, nor the prices at which they could be replaced. One useful generalization to be drawn from this discussion is that a balance sheet does not show "how much a business is worth."

It is appropriate to ask *why* accountants do not change the recorded values of assets to correspond with changing market prices for these properties. One reason is that the land and building used to house the business are acquired for use and not for resale; in fact, these assets cannot be sold without disrupting the business. The balance sheet of a business is prepared on the assumption that the business is a continuing enterprise, a "going concern." Consequently, the present estimated prices at which the land and buildings could be sold are not of particular importance since these properties are not available for sale.

Another reason for using cost rather than market values in accounting for assets is the need for a definite, factual basis. The cost of land, buildings, and many other assets purchased for cash can be rather definitely determined. Estimated market values, on the other hand, for assets such as land and buildings, are not factual and definite; market values are constantly changing and are largely a matter of personal opinion. Of course cost and value are ordinarily the same at the date of acquisition of an asset, because the buyer would not pay more than the asset was worth and the seller would not take less than current market value. The bargaining process which results in a sale serves to establish both the current market value of the property and the cost to the buyer. With the passage of time, however, the current market value of assets is likely to differ considerably from the cost recorded in the owner's accounting records.

Although the cost of many assets can be determined in a definite manner as the result of a cash purchase, the measurement of cost in some cases may be rather difficult. For example, when a factory machine is purchased, a question arises as to whether the cost basis of the machine should include (1) the charges for transporting, installing, and testing it, and (2) the salary paid the purchasing agent and engineering employees, who may have devoted considerable time to making a choice among various competing machines on the market. Another common example is that of a manufacturing concern which constructs a building for its own use. Identifying and measuring all the cost elements to be included in the total cost of the building will require many borderline decisions.

The wide changes in the purchasing power of the dollar in recent years have raised serious doubts as to the adequacy of the conventional cost basis in accounting for assets. Proposals for adjusting recorded dollar amounts to reflect changes in the value of the dollar are receiving increasing attention. Accounting concepts are not as exact and unchanging as many persons assume; to serve the needs of a fast-changing economy, accounting concepts and methods must also undergo continuous evolutionary change.

The problem of valuation of assets is one of the most complex in the entire field of accounting. The problem is merely being introduced at this point; in later chapters we shall explore carefully some of the valuation principles applicable to the major types of assets.

Liabilities. Liabilities are debts. All business concerns have liabilities; even the largest and most successful companies find it convenient to purchase merchandise and supplies on credit rather than to pay cash at the time of each purchase. The liability arising from the purchase of goods or services on credit (on time) is called an *account payable,* and the person or company to whom the account payable is owed is called a *creditor.* These terms are applicable to the personal affairs of individuals as well as to business concerns. For example, when a college freshman opens a charge account at the Campus Clothing Store and buys a new suit on credit, he is thereby incurring a liability, an account payable. He could properly refer to the Campus Clothing Store as a creditor and to himself as a debtor. Among the more common types of liabilities that may be owed by a business are accounts payable, notes payable, and taxes payable.

Business concerns frequently find it desirable to borrow money as a means of supplementing the funds invested by owners. The borrowing of money may enable the business to expand more rapidly. The borrowed funds may, for example, be used to buy merchandise which can be sold at a profit to the firm's customers. Or, the borrowed money might be used to buy new and more efficient machinery, thus enabling the company to turn out a larger volume of products at lower cost. When a business borrows money for any reason, a liability is incurred and the lender becomes a creditor of the business. The form of the liability when money is borrowed is usually a *note payable,* a formal written promise to pay a certain amount of money, usually with interest, at a definite future time. An account payable, as contrasted with a note payable, does not involve the issuance of a formal written promise to the creditor. When a business has both notes payable and accounts payable, the two types of liabilities are shown separately in the balance sheet. The sequence in which these two liabilities are listed is not important. A figure showing the total of the liabilities may also be inserted, as shown by the illustration on the next page.

ONE OF KEY
FIGURES ON
BALANCE
SHEET IS
TOTAL
LIABILITIES

WESTSIDE CLEANING SHOP
Balance Sheet
December 31, 1962

Assets		*Liabilities & Owner's Equity*	
Cash	$ 1,500	Liabilities:	
Accounts receivable ...	3,000	Notes payable	$ 6,000
Land	7,000	Accounts payable ...	4,000
Building	15,000	Total liabilities ...	$10,000
Office equipment	1,000	Owner's equity:	
Delivery equipment ...	2,500	J. R. Crane, capital	20,000
	$30,000		$30,000

The creditors have claims against the assets of the business, usually not against any particular asset but against the assets in general. The claims of the creditors are liabilities of the business and have priority over the claims of owners. Creditors are entitled to be paid in full even if such payment should exhaust the assets of the business, leaving nothing for the owner. The issue of valuation, which poses so many difficulties in accounting for assets, is a much smaller problem in the case of liabilities, because the amounts of most liabilities are definitely stated.

Owner's equity. The owner's equity in a business is equal to the total assets minus the liabilities. The equity of the owner is a residual claim; as the owner of the business he is entitled to whatever remains after the claims of the creditors are fully satisfied. For example:

The Westside Cleaning Shop has total assets of	*$30,000*
And total liabilities amounting to	*10,000*
Therefore, the owner's equity must equal	*$20,000*

Suppose that the Westside Cleaning Shop borrows $1,000 from a bank. After recording the additional asset of $1,000 in cash and recording the new liability of $1,000 owed to the bank, we would have the following:

The Westside Cleaning Shop now has total assets of	*$31,000*
And total liabilities are now	*11,000*
Therefore, the owner's equity still is equal to	*$20,000*

It is apparent that the total assets of the business were increased by the act of borrowing money from a bank, but the increase in total assets was exactly offset by an increase in liabilities, and the owner's equity remained unchanged. The owner's equity in a business is not increased by the incurring of liabilities of any kind.

The owner's equity in a business comes from two sources:

1. Investment by the owner
2. Earnings from profitable operation of the business

Only the first of these two sources of owner's equity is considered in this chapter. The second source, an increase in owner's equity through earnings of the business, will be discussed in Chapter 2.

The balance sheet equation. One of the fundamental characteristics of every balance sheet is that the total figure for assets always equals the total figure for liabilities and owners' equity. This agreement or balance of total assets with total equities is one reason for calling this statement of financial condition a *balance sheet.* But *why* do total assets equal total equities? The answer can be given in one short paragraph, as follows:

The dollar totals on the two sides of the balance sheet are always equal because these two sides of the statement are merely two views of the same business property. The listing of assets shows us what things the business owns; the listing of liabilities and owners' equity tells us who supplied these resources to the business and how much each group supplied. Everything that a business owns has been supplied to it by the creditors or by the owners. Therefore, the total claims of the creditors plus the claims of the owners equal the total assets of the business.

The equality of assets on the one hand and of the claims of the creditors and the owners on the other hand is expressed in the equation:

**FUNDA-
MENTAL
ACCOUNTING
EQUATION**

$$Assets = liabilities + owners' \; equity$$
$$\$27,800 = \$7,800 + \$20,000$$

The amounts listed in the equation were taken from the balance sheet illustrated on page 8. A balance sheet is nothing more than a detailed statement of this equation. To emphasize this relationship, the balance sheet is presented again for comparison with the above equation.

**ASSETS =
LIABILITIES
+ OWNER'S
EQUITY**

ROBERTS REAL ESTATE COMPANY
Balance Sheet
September 30, 19___

Assets		Liabilities & Owner's Equity	
Cash	$ 7,800	Liabilities:	
Accounts receivable	1,200	Accounts payable	$ 7,800
Land	5,000	Owner's equity:	
Building	12,000	James Roberts, capital	20,000
Office equipment	1,800		
	$27,800		$27,800

Regardless of whether a business grows or contracts, this equality between the assets and the claims against the assets is always maintained. Any increase in the amount of total assets is necessarily accompanied by an equal increase on the other side of the equation, that is, by an increase in either the liabilities or the owner's equity. Any decrease in total assets is necessarily accompanied by a corresponding decrease in liabilities or owner's equity. The continuing equality of the two sides of the balance sheet can best be illustrated by taking a brand new business as an example and observing the effects of various transactions upon the balance sheet.

Effects of business transactions upon the balance sheet

Assume that James Roberts, a licensed real estate broker, decided to start a real estate business of his own, to be known as the Roberts Real Estate Company. The operations of the business consist of obtaining listings of houses being offered for sale by owners, advertising these houses, and showing them to prospective buyers. The listing agreement signed with each owner provides that the Roberts Real Estate Company shall receive at the time of sale a commission equal to 5% of the sales price.

The new business was begun on September 1, when Mr. Roberts deposited $20,000 in a bank account in the name of the business, the Roberts Real Estate Company. The initial balance sheet of the new business then appeared as follows:

ROBERTS REAL ESTATE COMPANY
Balance Sheet
September 1, 19___

Assets		Owner's Equity	
Cash	$20,000	James Roberts, capital	$20,000

Observe that the interest of the owner in the assets is designated on the balance sheet by the caption, James Roberts, Capital. The word *capital* is the traditional accounting term used in describing the equity of the proprietor.

Purchase of an asset for cash. The next transaction entered into by the Roberts Real Estate Company was the purchase of land suitable as a site for an office. The price for the land was $7,000 and payment was made in cash on September 3. The effect of this transaction on the balance sheet was twofold: first, cash was decreased by the amount paid out, and second, a new asset, Land, was acquired. After this exchange of cash for land, the balance sheet appeared as follows:

ROBERTS REAL ESTATE COMPANY
Balance Sheet
September 3, 19__

Assets		Owner's Equity	
Cash	$13,000	James Roberts, capital	$20,000
Land	7,000		
	$20,000		$20,000

Purchase of an asset and incurring of a liability. On September 5 an opportunity arose to buy a complete office building which had to be moved to permit the construction of a freeway. A price of $12,000 was agreed upon, which included the cost of moving the building and installing it upon the Roberts Company's lot. Mr. Roberts considered this a very fortunate purchase as the building was in excellent condition and would have cost approximately $20,000 to build.

The terms of the $12,000 purchase provided for an immediate cash payment of $5,000 and payment of the balance of $7,000 within 90 days. Cash was decreased $5,000, but a new asset, Building, was recorded at cost in the amount of $12,000. Total assets were thus increased by $7,000 but the total of liabilities and owner's equity was also increased as a result of recording the $7,000 account payable as a liability. After this transaction had been recorded, the balance sheet appeared as follows:

ROBERTS REAL ESTATE COMPANY
Balance Sheet
September 5, 19__

Assets		Liabilities & Owner's Equity	
Cash	$ 8,000	Liabilities:	
Land	7,000	Accounts payable	$ 7,000
Building	12,000	Owner's equity:	
		James Roberts, capital	20,000
	$27,000		$27,000

Notice that the building appears in the balance sheet at $12,000, its cost to the Roberts Real Estate Company. The estimate of $20,000 as the probable cost to construct such a building is irrelevant. Even if someone should offer to buy the building from the Roberts Company for $20,000 or more, this offer, if refused, would have no bearing on the balance sheet. Accounting records are intended to provide a historical record of *costs* actually incurred; therefore, the $12,000 price at which the building was purchased is the amount to be recorded.

Sale of an asset. After the office building had been moved to the Roberts Company's lot, Mr. Roberts decided that the lot was much larger than was needed. The adjoining business, Carter's Drugstore, wanted more room for a parking area so, on September 10, the Roberts Company sold the unused part of the lot to Carter's Drugstore for a price of $2,000. The sales price was computed at the same amount per foot as the Roberts Company had paid for the land, so there was neither a profit nor a loss on the sale. No down payment was required but it was agreed that the full price would be paid within three months. By this transaction a new asset in the form of an account receivable was acquired, but the asset Land was decreased by the same amount; consequently, there was no change in the amount of total assets. After this transaction, the balance sheet appeared as follows:

NO CHANGE
IN TOTALS
BY SELLING
LAND ON
CREDIT

ROBERTS REAL ESTATE COMPANY
Balance Sheet
September 10, 19___

Assets		Liabilities & Owner's Equity	
Cash	$ 8,000	Liabilities:	
Accounts receivable	2,000	Accounts payable	$ 7,000
Land	5,000	Owner's equity:	
Building	12,000	James Roberts, capital	20,000
	$27,000		$27,000

In the illustration thus far, the Roberts Real Estate Company has an account receivable from only one debtor, and an account payable to only one creditor. As the business grows, the number of debtors and creditors will increase, but the Accounts Receivable and Accounts Payable accounts will continue to be used. The additional records necessary to show the amount receivable from each debtor and the amount owing to each creditor will be explained in Chapter 8.

Purchase of an asset on credit. A complete set of office furniture and equipment was purchased on credit from General Equipment, Inc., on September 14. The amount of the transaction was $1,800, and it was agreed that payment should be made later. As the result of this trans- action the business owned a new asset, Office Equipment, but it had also incurred a new liability. The increase in total assets was exactly offset by the increase in liabilities. After this transaction the balance sheet appeared as follows:

ROBERTS REAL ESTATE COMPANY
Balance Sheet
September 14, 19___

Assets		Liabilities & Owner's Equity	
Cash	$ 8,000	Liabilities:	
Accounts receivable ...	2,000	Accounts payable ...	$ 8,800
Land	5,000	Owner's equity:	
Building	12,000	James Roberts, capital	20,000
Office equipment	1,800		
	$28,800		$28,800

Collection of an account receivable. On September 20, cash in the amount of $800 was received as partial settlement of the account receivable from Carter's Drugstore. This transaction caused cash to increase and the accounts receivable to decrease by an equal amount. In essence, this transaction was merely the exchange of one asset for another of equal value. Consequently, there was no change in the amount of total assets. After this transaction was completed the balance sheet appeared as shown below:

ROBERTS REAL ESTATE COMPANY
Balance Sheet
September 20, 19___

Assets		Liabilities & Owner's Equity	
Cash	$ 8,800	Liabilities:	
Accounts receivable ...	1,200	Accounts payable ...	$ 8,800
Land	5,000	Owner's equity:	
Building	12,000	James Roberts, capital	20,000
Office equipment	1,800		
	$28,800		$28,800

Payment of a liability. On September 30 Mr. Roberts paid $1,000 in cash to General Equipment, Inc. This payment caused a decrease in cash and an equal decrease in liabilities. Therefore the totals of assets and equities were still in balance. The balance sheet appeared as on page 18 after this transaction.

ROBERTS REAL ESTATE COMPANY
Balance Sheet
September 30, 19___

Assets		Liabilities & Owner's Equity	
Cash	$ 7,800	Liabilities:	
Accounts receivable	1,200	Accounts payable	$ 7,800
Land	5,000	Owner's equity:	
Building	12,000	James Roberts, capital	20,000
Office equipment	1,800		
	$27,800		$27,800

The transactions which have been illustrated for the month of September were merely preliminary to the formal opening for business of the Roberts Real Estate Company on October 1. During September no sales were arranged by the company and no commissions were earned. Since we have assumed that the business had no revenues and no expenses during September, the owner's equity at September 30 is shown in the above balance sheet at $20,000, unchanged from the original investment by Mr. Roberts on September 1. September was a month devoted exclusively to organizing the business, and not to regular operations. In succeeding chapters we shall continue the example of the Roberts Real Estate Company by illustrating operating transactions and considering how the net income of the business can be determined.

SINGLE PROPRIETORSHIPS, PARTNERSHIPS, AND CORPORATIONS

The business used as an illustration in this chapter is a *single proprietorship,* a business owned by one person; therefore, the owner's equity section consists of only one item, the equity of the proprietor, James Roberts. If the business were a partnership of two or more persons, we would use the caption Partners' Equity instead of Owner's Equity and would list under that caption the amount of each partner's equity. If the business were organized as a corporation, the owners would be called stockholders, and the caption to be used would be Stockholders' Equity. It is not customary in a corporation balance sheet to show separately the equity of each stockholder. The equity of all the stockholders as a group is shown, and this ownership equity is divided into two amounts: (1) Capital Stock, the amount of the original investment, and (2) Retained Earnings, the amount of earnings (or losses) accumulated since the formation of the corporation.

These three methods of showing the ownership equity on the balance sheet may be illustrated as follows:

For a Single Proprietorship

Owner's equity:
   John Smith, capital .... $ 30,000

For a Partnership

Partners' equity:
   William Abbott, capital $25,000
   Raymond Barnes, capital 40,000
     Total capital .... $ 65,000

For a Corporation

Stockholders' equity:
   Capital stock $1,000,000
   Retained earnings 278,000
     Total capital $1,278,000

The preceding illustration of the ownership equity of a corporation shows that $1,000,000 of capital was invested in the corporation by stockholders, and that through profitable operation of the business an additional $278,000 of earned capital has been accumulated. The corporation has chosen to retain this $278,000 in the business rather than to distribute these earnings to the stockholders as dividends. The total earnings of the corporation may have been considerably more than $278,000, because any earnings which were paid to stockholders as dividends would not appear on the balance sheet. The term "retained earnings" describes only the earnings which were *not* paid out in the form of dividends. Although stockholders naturally like to receive dividends, the retaining of earnings in the business may enable the corporation to acquire additional operating properties, to expand the scope of operations, and thereby to enjoy larger future earnings.

Corporations are required by state laws to maintain a distinction between capital stock and retained earnings; the reasons underlying this requirement will be considered in a later chapter. In a single proprietorship, capital earned through profitable operations and retained in the business is merely added to the amount of the original invested capital and a single figure is shown for the owner's equity. A similar procedure is followed in a partnership, each partner's capital being increased by his share of the retained earnings. There is no theoretical reason why the balance sheet for a single proprietorship or a partnership should not show each owner's equity divided into two portions: the amount originally invested, and the earnings retained in the business, but customarily this separation is not made for an unincorporated business.

USE OF ACCOUNTING DATA BY OUTSIDERS

Another function of accounting is to provide annual or quarterly reports to outsiders who have an interest in the affairs of the business. The balance sheet is one of the financial statements prepared at regular intervals for management and owners and also distributed to bankers, creditors, credit agencies, investors, government agencies, and other outsiders. In large corporations quarterly and annual balance sheets are designed especially for use by outsiders; more frequent and detailed internal reports are prepared for use by management.

Through careful study of the balance sheet, it is possible for the outsider with training in accounting to obtain a fairly complete understanding of the financial condition of the business and to become aware of significant changes in financial condition that have occurred since the date of the preceding balance sheet. Bear in mind, however, that financial statements have limitations. As stated earlier, only those factors which can be reduced to monetary terms appear in the balance sheet. Let us consider for a moment some important business factors which are not set forth in financial statements. Some companies have a record of good relations with labor unions, freedom from strikes, and mutual respect between management and employees. Other companies have been plagued by frequent and bitter labor disputes. The relationship between a company and a union of its employees is certainly an important factor in the successful operation of the business, but it is not mentioned in the balance sheet. Perhaps a new competing store has just opened for business across the street; the prospect of intensified competition in the future will not be described in the balance sheet.

Bankers

Bankers who have loaned money to a business concern or who are considering making such a loan will be vitally interested in the balance sheet of the business. By studying the amount and kinds of assets in relation to the amount and payment dates of the liabilities, the banker can form an opinion as to the ability of the concern to pay its debts promptly. The banker gives particular attention to the amount of cash and of other assets (such as accounts receivable) which will soon be converted into cash; he compares the amount of these assets with the amount of liabilities falling due in the near future. The banker is also interested in the amount of the owner's equity, as this ownership capital serves as a protecting buffer between the banker and any losses which may befall the business. Bankers are seldom, if ever, willing to make a loan unless the balance sheet and other information concerning the prospective borrower offer reasonable assurance that the loan can and will be repaid promptly at the maturity date.

Creditors

Another important group making constant use of balance sheets consists of the credit managers of manufacturing and wholesaling firms, who must decide whether prospective customers are to be allowed to buy merchandise on credit. The credit manager, like the banker, studies the balance sheets of his customers for the purpose of appraising their debt-paying ability. Credit agencies such as Dun and Bradstreet make a business of obtaining financial statements from virtually all business concerns and appraising their debt-paying ability. The conclusions reached by these credit agencies are available to businessmen willing to pay for credit reports about prospective customers.

Others interested

In addition to owners, managers, bankers, and merchandise creditors, other groups making use of accounting data include governmental agencies, employees, investors, and writers for business periodicals. Some very large corporations have more than a half million stockholders; these giant concerns send copies of their annual financial statements to each of these many owners. In recent years there has been a definite trend toward wider distribution of financial statements to all interested persons, in contrast to the attitude of a generation or more ago when many companies regarded their financial statements as confidential matter.

The purpose of this recital is to show the student the extent to which a modern industrial society depends upon accounting. Even more important, however, is a clear understanding at the outset of your study of this subject that accounting does not exist just for the sake of keeping a record, or in order to fill out social security records, income tax returns, and various other regulatory reports. These are but auxiliary functions. The prime and vital purpose of accounting, and the function which makes it a part of the fascination of business, is to aid in the choice among alternatives that faces everyone who plays a part in the business world.

QUESTIONS

1. In broad general terms, what is the purpose of accounting?
2. Not all of the significant happenings in the life of a business can be expressed in monetary terms and entered in the accounting records. List two examples of significant events affecting a business which could not be satisfactorily entered in its accounting records.
3. Distinguish between bookkeeping and accounting.
4. What is the principal function of a certified public accountant?
5. Cost accounting may be regarded as a specialized phase of accounting utilized

by virtually every kind of industry. List four other specialized phases of accounting of comparable importance.

6. Information available from the accounting records provides a basis for making many business decisions. List five examples of business decisions requiring the use of accounting data.

7. State briefly the purpose of a balance sheet.

8. Define assets. List five examples.

9. Roger Kent, owner of the Kent Company, was offered $100,000 for the land and building occupied by his business. He had acquired these assets five years ago at a price of $75,000. Mr. Kent refused the offer of $100,000 but is inclined to believe that the land and buildings should be listed at the higher valuation on the balance sheet in order to show more accurately "how much the business is worth." Do you agree? Explain.

10. State the balance sheet equation.

11. Indicate the effect of each of the following transactions upon the total assets of a business by use of the appropriate phrase: "Increase total assets," "decrease total assets," "no change in total assets."

    a. Purchase of office equipment for cash
    b. Payment of a liability
    c. Borrowing money from a bank
    d. Investment of cash by owner
    e. Purchase of a delivery truck at a price of $2,500, terms $500 cash and the balance payable in 20 equal monthly installments
    f. Sale of land for cash at a price equal to its cost
    g. Sale of land on account (on credit) at a price equal to its cost
    h. Sale of land for cash at a price in excess of its cost
    i. Sale of land for cash at a price below its cost
    j. Collection of an account receivable

12. State precisely what information is contained in the heading of a balance sheet.

PROBLEMS

Group A

    1A-1. *Instructions.* From the information given below, prepare a balance sheet for the Forrester Company as of December 31, 1962.

        Data

Accounts receivable	$12,800
Accounts payable	12,300
Building	17,600
Cash	7,200
Land	8,000
K. G. Murray, capital	35,700
Office equipment	2,400

    1A-2. *Instructions.* Show the effect of business transactions upon the balance sheet by preparing a new balance sheet after each transaction.

Data
1962
Apr. 1.   Mr. Raymond Grant deposited $15,000 cash in a bank account in the
name of the business, the Pacific Travel Service.
Apr. 2.   Land was purchased for $7,000 cash.
Apr. 6.   A prefabricated building was purchased at a cost of $8,000 to serve
as an office. A cash payment of $3,000 was made; the balance was to
be paid within 60 days.
Apr. 10. The Pacific Travel Service acquired office equipment at a cost of
$2,000, paying $500 in cash and agreeing to pay the remainder within
30 days.
May 11.   The balance of $1,500 owed on the office equipment was paid in cash.

1A-3. Each of the following balance sheets was prepared immediately after the completion of a transaction:

(1)

VIEWPARK BOWLING ALLEY
Balance Sheet
May 1, 1962

Assets		*Owner's Equity*	
Cash	$30,000	Charles Black, capital	$30,000

(2)

VIEWPARK BOWLING ALLEY
Balance Sheet
May 2, 1962

Assets		*Owner's Equity*	
Cash	$28,500	Charles Black, capital	$30,000
Land	1,500		
	$30,000		$30,000

(3)

VIEWPARK BOWLING ALLEY
Balance Sheet
May 13, 1962

Assets		*Liabilities & Owner's Equity*	
Cash	$17,500	Liabilities:	
Land	1,500	Accounts payable	$ 5,000
Building	16,000	Owner's equity:	
		Charles Black, capital	30,000
	$35,000		$35,000

(4)   **VIEWPARK BOWLING ALLEY**
                                              Balance Sheet
                                              May 20, 1962

	Assets		**Liabilities & Owner's Equity**	
Cash	$12,500	*Liabilities:*		
Land	1,500	*Accounts payable*	$ 8,000	
Building	16,000	*Owner's equity:*		
Equipment	8,000	*Charles Black, capital*	30,000	
	$38,000		$38,000	

(5)   **VIEWPARK BOWLING ALLEY**
                                              Balance Sheet
                                              May 31, 1962

	Assets		**Liabilities & Owner's Equity**	
Cash	$ 9,500	*Liabilities:*		
Land	1,500	*Accounts payable*	$ 5,000	
Building	16,000	*Owner's equity:*		
Equipment	8,000	*Charles Black, capital*	30,000	
	$35,000		$35,000	

Instructions. Explain fully the nature of each of these indicated transactions. (For example, the transaction leading to the balance sheet of May 1 could be described as follows: "Mr. Charles Black on May 1 invested $30,000 in cash and started the business of Viewpark Bowling Alley.")

1A-4. *Instructions.* Prepare a balance sheet as of March 1, 1962, based on the data given below for the Martin Insurance Agency.

Also prepare a new balance sheet after each of the transactions.

Data

Accounts payable	$ 2,200
Building	14,650
Office equipment	5,450
J. B. Martin, capital	28,700
Cash	?
Land	9,000

Mar. 2.   One-third of the land was sold to a parking lot operator at a price of $3,000. A down payment of $500 in cash was received and the buyer promised to pay the remainder within 10 days.

Mar. 3.   A cash payment of $250 was made to a creditor.

Mar. 11. Cash in the amount of $2,500 was received from the buyer of the land, in final settlement of the transaction negotiated on March 2.

1A-5. On September 1, 19___, Mr. Leon Robertson deposited $48,000 cash in a bank account as a preliminary step toward purchasing the assets of the Viewpark Theater for $90,000. The purchase price included land valued at $29,000, building at $54,500, and projection equipment at $6,500. A down payment of $10,000 was made from the bank account on September 1, and Mr. Robertson agreed to pay the balance within six months. The theater was renamed Campus Theater, and after substantial remodeling was opened for business late in September.

On December 23, 19___, Mr. Robertson had a fatal traffic accident and was pronounced dead on arrival at a local hospital. Mr. Jackson, a certified public accountant, was called in to determine the financial condition of the Campus Theater.

Mr. Jackson found that the records kept by the late Mr. Robertson were rather skimpy. He was able to determine, however, that a partial payment of $20,000 had been made on the account payable resulting from the purchase of the theater. He also found that the remodeling of the building had been completed at a cost of $19,000. In order to help pay for the work on the building, Mr. Robertson had invested an additional $2,000 in the business. Projection equipment had been purchased at a cost of $3,000, of which only $1,000 had been paid. The bank balance as of December 23 was $13,340.

Mr. Jackson decided to prepare a balance sheet based on the information he had gathered, before going further with his analysis.

Instructions

a. Based on the information in the first paragraph, prepare a balance sheet as of September 1, 19___.

b. Prepare a balance sheet as of December 23, 19___.

c. Compute the amount of change in the owner's equity from September 1 to December 23 and state the reason or reasons for this change.

1A-6. Because of the illness of the only accountant employed by the Pomona Company, the owner, Mr. Ralph Davis, requested a clerk to prepare a balance sheet of the business as of December 31, 1962. Mr. Davis explained that the accounting records were complete except for three recent events: (1) he had just invested an additional $1,000 cash in the business; (2) he had removed from the business and made a gift to his son of a new typewriter which had cost $300; and (3) he had just received a cash offer of $20,000 for the land and $50,000 for the building. He had refused this offer because of the impracticability of moving the business. Mr. Davis pointed out that no entry had been made in the accounting records for any of these events. He added as an afterthought that the business had not yet paid for the typewriter although the liability had been recorded.

The clerk examined the ledger and found that the Land account had a balance of $16,000; the Building account a balance of $37,650, and the Cash account a balance of $4,860. He was somewhat puzzled over the procedures to be followed, but finally produced the following balance sheet, using the balances shown in the ledger for accounts payable, notes payable, accounts receivable, cash, delivery equipment, and office equipment. This balance sheet is unsatisfactory in several respects.

THE POMONA COMPANY
Balance Sheet
December 31, 1962

Accounts payable	$13,660	Building	$50,000
Office equipment	2,900	Land	20,000
Equity of owner	60,140	Accounts receivable	900
Cash	4,860	Delivery equipment	2,900
		Notes payable	7,760
	$81,560		$81,560

Instructions. Prepare a revised balance sheet in proper form.

Group B

1B-1. *Instructions.* Use the data to prepare a balance sheet for the Swanson Company as of December 31 of the current year.

Data

Robert Swanson, capital	$64,400
Office equipment	1,800
Accounts receivable	18,600
Accounts payable	6,300
Cash	8,400
Land	14,000
Building	31,500
Delivery equipment	3,400
Note payable to bank	7,000

1B-2. *Instructions.* Show the effect of business transactions upon the balance sheet by preparing a new balance sheet after each of the transactions listed below has been completed.

Data

(1) On July 1, Mr. James Plant deposited $10,000 cash in a bank account in the name of the business, the Automobile Repair Shop.

(2) On July 2, purchased land at $3,500 and workroom at $3,000, paying cash.

(3) On July 5, purchased tools at a cost of $1,200. A cash payment of $600 was made. The balance was to be paid in 30 days.

(4) On July 6, purchased a towing truck at a cost of $2,600. A cash payment of $1,200 was made, and it was agreed that the balance should be paid within 60 days.

(5) On August 4, the account payable relating to the purchase of tools made July 5 was paid in cash.

1B-3. *Instructions.* By studying the successive balance sheets in the series shown below, determine what transactions have taken place. Prepare a list of these transactions by date of occurrence. (For example, the transaction leading to the balance sheet of June 1, 19___, could be described as follows: "On June 1, 19___,

Mr. Howard Brown invested $20,000 in cash and started the business of Valley Miniature Golf Course.'')

Data

(1)

VALLEY MINIATURE GOLF COURSE
Balance Sheet
June 1, 19___

Assets		Owner's Equity	
Cash	$20,000	Howard Brown, capital	$20,000

(2)

VALLEY MINIATURE GOLF COURSE
Balance Sheet
June 3, 19___

Assets		Liabilities & Owner's Equity	
Cash	$ 5,000	Liabilities:	
Land	30,000	Accounts payable	$15,000
		Owner's equity:	
		Howard Brown, capital ...	20,000
	$35,000		$35,000

(3)

VALLEY MINIATURE GOLF COURSE
Balance Sheet
June 6, 19___

Assets		Liabilities & Owner's Equity	
Cash	$ 2,000	Liabilities:	
Land	30,000	Accounts payable	$16,000
Equipment	4,000	Owner's equity:	
		Howard Brown, capital ...	20,000
	$36,000		$36,000

(4)

VALLEY MINIATURE GOLF COURSE
Balance Sheet
June 8, 19___

Assets		Liabilities & Owner's Equity	
Cash	$ 1,200	Liabilities:	
Land	30,000	Accounts payable	$16,000
Equipment	4,800	Owner's equity:	
		Howard Brown, capital ...	20,000
	$36,000		$36,000

(5) **VALLEY MINIATURE GOLF COURSE**
Balance Sheet
July 6, 19___

Assets		Liabilities & Owner's Equity	
Cash	$ 700	**Liabilities:**	
Land	30,000	Accounts payable	$15,500
Equipment	4,800	**Owner's equity:**	
		Howard Brown, capital ...	20,000
	$35,500		$35,500

1B-4. *Instructions.* Prepare a balance sheet as of May 1 based on the data in (1); prepare a new balance sheet after transactions for each of the following days have been completed.

Data

(1) The balance sheet data (listed alphabetically) for Universal Tabulating Service as of May 1, 19___, were:

Accounts payable	$20,000
Accounts receivable	1,900
Building	60,000
Business machines	55,000
Cash	12,500
Land	15,000
Notes payable	24,000
John Jones, capital	?

(2) On May 5, Mr. Jones invested an additional $20,000 in cash in the business. A cash payment of $12,000 was made to the holders of the notes payable, reducing the amount of these obligations to $12,000.

(3) On May 8, made a cash payment of $5,000 in partial settlement of the accounts payable.

(4) On May 10, collected $900 cash applicable to the accounts receivable.

(5) On May 11, purchased tabulating supplies at a cost of $600, to be paid in 30 days. Tabulating supplies were also purchased from another supplier for cash in the amount of $200.

1B-5. On May 15, 19___, Mr. Richard Disney deposited his savings of $20,000 in a bank account in preparation to purchasing the assets of Niagara Falls Cruise Company for $40,000. The company was engaged in making regular boat trips from and around Niagara Falls, N.Y. The purchase price of $40,000 included an inland vessel valued at $39,500 and office equipment valued at $500. Mr. Disney made a down payment of $18,000 on May 15 from the cash deposited in the bank and signed a promissory note for the balance of the purchase price. The vessel was rechristened *Imperial,* and the business renamed Imperial Cruise. *Imperial* was put into service on June 1, following the opening of the tourist season on Decoration Day.

On September 5, after the close of the tourist season, Mr. Disney engaged the services of Mr. Peter Mitchell, a public accountant, to summarize the results of operations for Imperial Cruise for the season.

The only records kept by Mr. Disney for Imperial Cruise were memorandum notes written on the check stubs. From that source, Mr. Mitchell learned that Mr. Disney had made an additional investment of $10,000 in cash and that certain improvements had been added to the vessel at a cost of $6,000. Payment had been made in full for the improvements after the completion of work. Mr. Mitchell also found that three monthly payments of $1,000 each had been made on the promissory note issued at the time of purchasing the business. Early in the season a portable ticket stand had been built at a cost of $1,000, and a promissory note for that amount had been signed and given to the builder. As of September 5, $750 had been paid on this $1,000 note. The bank balance was $3,061 as of September 5.

Mr. Disney informed Mr. Mitchell that he made a practice of paying all his bills immediately upon receipt, and that as of September 5 all bills for the season had been paid. During his engagement, Mr. Mitchell did not come across any incoming bills. Before he proceeded further, Mr. Mitchell decided to prepare a balance sheet as of September 5, based on the information he had gathered.

Instructions

a. Use the information in the first paragraph as a basis for preparing a balance sheet dated May 15, 19___.

b. Prepare a balance sheet as of September 5, 19___.

c. Explain the sources of increase in owner's equity, by comparing the two balance sheets prepared.

1B-6. The balance sheet data for Young Auto Wash Service as of April 1, 19___, were:

Accounts payable	*$ 4,500*
Accounts receivable	*400*
Building	*30,000*
Cash	*1,500*
Equipment	*12,000*
Land	*20,000*
Notes payable	*10,500*
Arthur Young, capital	*?*

During the next few weeks the following transactions occurred:

Apr. 10. Mr. Young invested an additional $5,000 in cash in the business. The accounts payable were paid in full. (No payment was made on the note payable.)

Apr. 15. One half of the land was sold at cost. A down payment of $4,000 was received, and the buyer agreed to pay the balance in 60 days.

Apr. 19. Washing supplies were purchased at a cost of $1,000, to be paid in 10 days. Washing supplies were also purchased for cash in the amount of $250 from another car-washing concern which was going out of business. These supplies, if purchased through normal channels, would have cost $500.

Instructions

a. Prepare a balance sheet as of April 1, 19___.

b. Prepare a balance sheet as of April 19, 19___.

2

Recording changes in financial condition

Many business concerns have several hundred or even several thousand business transactions each day. It would obviously be impracticable to prepare a balance sheet after each transaction, and it is quite unnecessary to do so. Instead, the many individual transactions are recorded in the accounting records, and, at the end of the month or other accounting period, a balance sheet is prepared from these records.

The use of accounts for recording transactions

The accounting records include a separate page for each item that appears in the balance sheet. For example, a separate record is kept for the asset Cash, showing all the increases and decreases in cash which result from the many transactions in which cash is received or paid. A similar record is kept for every other asset, for every liability, and for each component of the ownership equity. The form of record used to record increases and decreases in a single balance sheet item is called an *account,* or sometimes a *ledger account.* All of these separate accounts are usually kept in a loose-leaf binder, and the entire group of accounts is called a *ledger.*

THE LEDGER

Ledger accounts are a means of accumulating information needed by management in directing the business. For example, by maintaining a Cash account, management can keep track of the amount of cash available for meeting payrolls and for making current purchases of merchandise. This record of cash is also useful in planning future operations, and in advance planning of applications for bank loans. The development of the annual budget requires estimating in advance the expected receipts and payments of cash; these estimates of cash flow are naturally based to some extent on the ledger accounts showing past receipts and payments.

In its simplest form, an account has only three elements: (1) a title, consisting of the name of the particular asset, liability, or owners' equity; (2) a left side, which is called the *debit* side; and (3) a right side, which is called the *credit* side. This form of account, illustrated below, is called a T account because of its resemblance to the letter T. More complete forms of accounts will be illustrated later.

T ACCOUNT: A LEDGER ACCOUNT IN SIMPLIFIED FORM

Title	
Left or debit side	*Right or credit side*

Debit and credit entries

An amount recorded on the left or debit side of an account is called a *debit,* or a *debit entry;* an amount entered on the right or credit side is called a *credit,* or a *credit entry.* Accountants also use the words *debit* and *credit* as verbs. The act of recording a debit in an account is called *debiting* the account; the recording of a credit is called *crediting* the account.

Students beginning a course in accounting often have preconceived but erroneous notions about the meanings of the terms *debit* and *credit.* For example, to some people unacquainted with accounting, the word *credit* may carry a more favorable connotation than does the word *debit.* Such connotations have no validity in the field of accounting. Accountants use *debit* to mean an entry on the left-hand side of an account, and *credit* to mean an entry on the right-hand side. The student should therefore regard *debit* and *credit* as simple equivalents of left and right, without any hidden or subtle implications.

To illustrate the recording of debits and credits in an account, let us **LIST OF** go back to the cash transactions of the Roberts Real Estate Company. The **CASH** various receipts and payments of cash in this business during September **TRANS-** appear in the following list:
ACTIONS

Date		Explanation	Cash	
			Receipts	Payments
Sept.	1	Invested cash in business	$20,000	
	3	Purchased land for cash		$ 7,000
	5	Made down payment on building		5,000
	20	Collected an account receivable	800	
	30	Paid a liability		1,000
		Total	$20,800	$13,000

When these cash transactions are recorded in an account, the receipts are listed in vertical order on the debit side of the account and the payments are listed on the credit side. The dates of the transactions may also be listed, as shown in the following illustration:

CASH
TRANS-
ACTIONS
ENTERED IN
LEDGER
ACCOUNT

		Cash		
9/1		*20,000*	*9/3*	*7,000*
9/20	*7,800*	*800*	*9/5*	*5,000*
		20,800	*9/30*	*1,000*
				13,000

Notice that the total of the cash receipts, $20,800, is in small-type figures so that it will not be mistaken for a debit entry. The total of the cash payments (credits), amounting to $13,000, is also in small-type figures to distinguish it from the credit entries. These *footings,* or memorandum totals, are merely a convenient step in determining the amount of cash on hand at the end of the month. The difference in dollars between the total debits and the total credits in an account is called the *balance.* If the debits exceed the credits the account has a *debit balance;* if the credits exceed the debits the account has a *credit balance.* In the illustrated Cash account, the debit total of $20,800 is larger than the credit total of $13,000, therefore the account has a debit balance. By subtracting the credits from the debits ($20,800 − $13,000), we determine that the balance of the Cash account is $7,800. This debit balance is noted on the debit (left) side of the account. The balance of the Cash account represents the amount of cash owned by the business on September 30; in a balance sheet prepared at this date, Cash in the amount of $7,800 would be listed as an asset.

Debit balances in asset accounts. In the preceding illustration of a cash account, increases were recorded on the left or debit side of the account and decreases were recorded on the right or credit side. The increases were greater than the decreases and the result was a debit balance in the account.

All asset accounts normally have debit balances; as a matter of fact, the ownership by a business of cash, land, or any other asset indicates that the increases (debits) to that asset have been greater than the decreases (credits). It is hard to imagine an account for an asset such as land having a credit balance, as this would indicate that the business had disposed of more land than it had acquired and had reached the impossible position of having a negative amount of land.

The balance sheets previously illustrated in Chapter 1 showed all the

**ASSET
ACCOUNTS
NORMALLY
HAVE DEBIT
BALANCES**

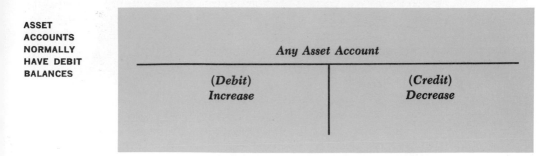

Any Asset Account

(Debit)	*(Credit)*
Increase	*Decrease*

assets on the left side of the balance sheet. The fact that assets are located on the left side of the balance sheet is a convenient means of remembering the rule that an increase in an asset is recorded on the *left* (debit) side of the account, and also with the idea that an asset account has a debit (left-hand) balance.

Credit balances in liability and owners' equity accounts. Next we must consider the method of recording increases and decreases in the amounts that comprise the right-hand side of the balance sheet, that is, the liabilities and the owners' equity. Increases in liability and owners' equity accounts are recorded by credit entries and decreases in the accounts are recorded by debits.

The relationship between entries in these accounts and their position on the balance sheet may be summed up as follows: (1) liabilities and

**LIABILITY
ACCOUNTS
AND
OWNERS'
EQUITY
ACCOUNTS
NORMALLY
HAVE
CREDIT
BALANCES**

*Any Liability Account
or Owners' Equity Account*

(Debit)	*(Credit)*
Decrease	*Increase*

owners' equity belong on the *right* side of the balance sheet; (2) an increase in a liability or an owners' equity account is recorded on the *right* side of the account; and (3) liability and owners' equity accounts have credit (*right-hand*) balances.

The diagram on page 34 emphasizes again the relationship between the position of an account in the balance sheet and the method of recording an increase or decrease in the account. The accounts used are those previously shown in the balance sheet (page 8) prepared for the Roberts Real Estate Company.

**DIAGRAM OF
BALANCE
SHEET
ACCOUNTS**

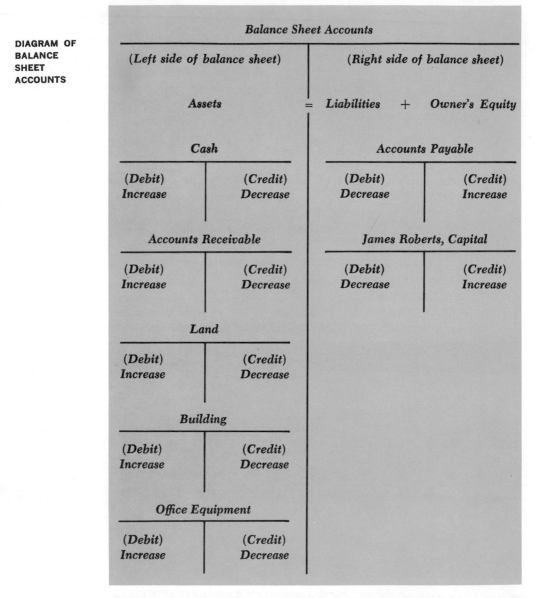

Balance Sheet Accounts

(Left side of balance sheet) | *(Right side of balance sheet)*

Assets = *Liabilities* + *Owner's Equity*

Cash

(Debit)	*(Credit)*
Increase	*Decrease*

Accounts Receivable

(Debit)	*(Credit)*
Increase	*Decrease*

Land

(Debit)	*(Credit)*
Increase	*Decrease*

Building

(Debit)	*(Credit)*
Increase	*Decrease*

Office Equipment

(Debit)	*(Credit)*
Increase	*Decrease*

Accounts Payable

(Debit)	*(Credit)*
Decrease	*Increase*

James Roberts, Capital

(Debit)	*(Credit)*
Decrease	*Increase*

**MECHANICS
OF DEBIT
AND CREDIT**

Concise statement of the rules of debit and credit. The rules of debit and credit, which have been explained and illustrated in the preceding sections, may be concisely summarized as follows:

Asset Accounts	*Liability & Owners' Equity Accounts*
Increases are recorded by debits	*Increases are recorded by credits*
Decreases are recorded by credits	*Decreases are recorded by debits*

Equality of debits and credits. Every business transaction affects two or more accounts. *Double-entry bookkeeping,* which is the system in almost universal use, takes its name from the fact that equal debit and credit entries are made for every transaction. If only two accounts are affected (as in the purchase of land for cash) one account, Land, is debited, and the other account, Cash, is credited for the same amount. If more than two accounts are affected by a transaction, the sum of the debit entries must be equal to the sum of the credit entries. This situation was illustrated when the Roberts Real Estate Company purchased a building for a price of $12,000. The $12,000 debit to the asset account, Building, was exactly equal to the total of the $5,000 credit to the Cash account plus the $7,000 credit to the liability account, Accounts Payable. Since every transaction results in an equal amount of debits and credits in the ledger, it follows that the total of all debit entries in the ledger is equal to the total of all the credit entries.

Recording transactions in ledger accounts: illustration

The procedure for recording transactions in ledger accounts will be illustrated by using the September transaction of the Roberts Real Estate Company. Each transaction will first be analyzed in terms of increases and decreases in assets, liabilities, and owner's equity. Then we shall follow the rules of debit and credit in entering these increases and decreases in T accounts. Asset accounts will be shown on the left side of the page; liability and owner's equity accounts on the right side. For convenience in following the transactions into the ledger accounts, the letter used to identify a given transaction will also appear opposite the debit and credit entries for that transaction. This use of identifying letters is for illustrative purposes only and is not used in actual accounting practice.

**RECORDING
AN
INVESTMENT
IN THE
BUSINESS**

Transaction a. Mr. Roberts invested $20,000 cash in the business on September 1.

Analysis	Rule	Entry
The asset Cash was increased	Increases in assets are recorded by debits	Debit: Cash, $20,000
The owner's equity was increased	Increases in owner's equity are recorded by credits	Credit: James Roberts, Capital, $20,000

Cash		James Roberts, Capital
9/1 (a) 20,000		9/1 (a) 20,000

Transaction b. On September 3, the Roberts Real Estate Company purchased land for cash in amount of $7,000.

Analysis	Rule	Entry
The asset Land was increased	Increases in assets are recorded by debits	Debit: Land, $7,000
The asset Cash was decreased	Decreases in assets are recorded by credits	Credit: Cash, $7,000

	Cash		
9/1	20,000	9/3	(b) 7,000

	Land	
9/3	(b) 7,000	

Transaction c. On September 5, the Roberts Real Estate Company purchased a building from X Company at a total price of $12,000. The terms of the purchase required a cash payment of $5,000 with the remainder of $7,000 payable within 90 days.

Analysis	Rule	Entry
A new asset, Building, was acquired	Increases in assets are recorded by debits	Debit: Building, $12,000
The asset Cash was decreased	Decreases in assets are recorded by credits	Credit: Cash, $5,000
A new liability, Accounts Payable, was incurred	Increases in liabilities are recorded by credits	Credit: Accounts Payable, $7,000

	Cash				Accounts Payable		
9/1	20,000	9/3	7,000			9/5	(c) 7,000
		9/5	(c) 5,000				

	Building	
9/5	(c) 12,000	

Transaction d. On September 10, the Roberts Real Estate Company sold a portion of its land on credit to Carter's Drugstore for a price of $2,000. The land was sold at its cost, so there was no gain or loss on the transaction.

SALE OF LAND ON CREDIT

Analysis	Rule	Entry
A new asset, Accounts Receivable, was acquired	Increases in assets are recorded by debits	Debit: Accounts Receivable, $2,000
The asset Land was decreased	Decreases in assets are recorded by credits	Credit: Land, $2,000

Accounts Receivable

9/10 (d) 2,000	

Land

9/3 7,000	9/10 (d) 2,000

PURCHASE OF AN ASSET ON CREDIT

Transaction e. On September 14, the Roberts Real Estate Company purchased office equipment on credit from General Equipment, Inc., in the amount of $1,800.

Analysis	Rule	Entry
A new asset, Office Equipment, was acquired	Increases in assets are recorded by debits	Debit: Office Equipment, $1,800
A new liability, an account payable, was incurred	Increases in liabilities are recorded by credits	Credit: Accounts Payable, $1,800

Office Equipment

9/14 (e) 1,800	

Accounts Payable

	9/5 7,000
	9/14 (e) 1,800

ACCOUNT
RECEIVABLE
COLLECTION *Transaction f.* On September 20, cash of $800 was received as partial collection of the account receivable from Carter's Drugstore.

Analysis	Rule	Entry
The asset Cash was increased	*Increases in assets are recorded by debits*	*Debit: Cash, $800*
The asset Accounts Receivable was decreased	*Decreases in assets are recorded by credits*	*Credit: Accounts Receivable, $800*

Cash

9/1	20,000	9/3	7,000
9/20 (f)	800	9/5	5,000

Accounts Receivable

9/10	2,000	9/20 (f)	800

PAYMENT
OF A
LIABILITY *Transaction g.* A cash payment of $1,000 was made on September 30 in partial settlement of the amount owing to General Equipment, Inc.

Analysis	Rule	Entry
The liability Accounts Payable was decreased	*Decreases in liabilities are recorded by debits*	*Debit: Accounts Payable, $1,000*
The asset Cash was decreased	*Decreases in assets are recorded by credits*	*Credit: Cash, $1,000*

Cash | *Accounts Payable*

9/1	20,000	9/3	7,000			9/5	7,000
9/20	800	9/5	5,000	9/30 (g) 1,000		9/14	1,800
		9/30 (g) 1,000					

Standard form of the ledger account

The standard form of ledger account provides for more information than the T accounts used in preceding illustrations. The only change from the T account to a formal ledger account is the addition of special rulings, as shown by the following illustration:

STANDARD
FORM OF
LEDGER
ACCOUNT

		Title of Account				*Account No. ( )*		
Date	*Explanation*	*Ref*	*Amount*	*Date*	*Explanation*	*Ref*	*Amount*

Notice that each side of the account has identical columns as follows:

Date column. The date of the transaction is listed here.

Explanation column. This column is needed only for unusual items, and in most companies is seldom used.

Ref (Reference) column. The page number of the journal on which the transaction is recorded is listed in this column, thus making it possible to trace ledger entries back to their source.

Amount column. The amount of the entry is entered here.

The headings for these columns are usually not printed on ledger paper, although paper with column headings is also available. Since T accounts provide the basic elements of a ledger account, they are used in this text in preference to the standard form of account to achieve simplicity in illustrating accounting principles and procedures.

Numbering of ledger accounts

Accounts are generally arranged in the ledger in the same order as they appear in the balance sheet, and an identification number is assigned to each account. In the following list of accounts, certain numbers have not been assigned; these numbers are held in reserve so that additional accounts can be inserted in a loose-leaf ledger in balance sheet sequence whenever such new accounts become necessary. In this illustration, the numbers from 1 to 29 are used exclusively for asset accounts; numbers from 30 to 49 are reserved for liabilities; and numbers in the 50s signify owner's equity accounts.

SYSTEM FOR
NUMBERING
LEDGER
ACCOUNTS

Account title	*Account number*
Assets:	
Cash	*1*
Accounts receivable	*5*
Land	*20*
Building	*22*
Office equipment	*25*
Liabilities:	
Accounts payable	*30*
Owner's equity:	
James Roberts, capital	*50*

In large businesses with many more accounts, a more elaborate numbering system would be needed. Some companies use a four-digit number for each account; each of the four digits carries special significance as to the classification of the account.

THE JOURNAL

In our description of accounting procedures thus far, emphasis has been placed on the analysis of transactions in terms of debits and credits to ledger accounts. Although transactions could be entered directly in ledger accounts in a very small business, it is much more convenient and efficient in all businesses, large or small, to record transactions first in a journal, and later to transfer the debits and credits to ledger accounts. The *journal,* or *book of original entry,* is a chronological record, showing for each day the debits and credits from transactions; it also may include explanatory information concerning transactions. At convenient intervals the debits and credits in the journal are transferred to the accounts in the ledger; as we have already seen, the ledger accounts serve as the basis from which the balance sheet and other accounting reports are prepared.

The unit of organization for the journal is the transaction, whereas the unit of organization for the ledger is the account. By making use of both a journal and a ledger, we can achieve several advantages which are not possible when transactions are recorded directly in ledger accounts:

1. *The journal shows all information about a transaction in one place and also provides an explanation of the transaction.* In a journal entry, the debits and credits for a given transaction are recorded together, but when the transaction is recorded in the ledger, the debits and credits are entered in different accounts. Since a ledger may contain hundreds of accounts, it would be very difficult to locate all the facts about a particular transaction by looking in the ledger. The journal is the record which shows the complete story of a transaction in one entry.

2. *The journal provides a chronological record of all the events in the life of a business.* If we want to look up the facts about a transaction of some months or years back, all we need is the date of the transaction in order to locate it in the journal.

3. *The use of a journal helps to prevent errors.* If transactions were recorded directly in the ledger, it would be very easy to make errors such as omitting the debit or the credit, or entering the debit twice or the credit twice. Such errors are not likely to be made in the journal, since the offsetting debits and credits appear together for each transaction. It is of course possible to forget to transfer a debit or credit from the journal to a ledger account, but such an error can be detected by tracing the entries in the ledger accounts back to the journal. If a business of any size were to follow the practice of recording transactions directly in ledger accounts without using a journal, it would be virtually impossible to locate an error such as the omission of a debit or credit.

The general journal: illustration of entries

Many businesses maintain several types of journals. The nature of operations and the volume of transactions in the particular business determine the number and type of journals needed. The simplest type of journal, and the one with which we are concerned in this chapter, is called a *general journal.* It has only two money columns, one for debits and the other for credits; it may be used for all types of transactions.

The process of recording a transaction in a journal is called *journalizing* the transaction. To illustrate the use of the general journal, we shall now journalize the transactions of the Roberts Real Estate Company which have previously been discussed.

SEPTEMBER JOURNAL ENTRIES FOR ROBERTS REAL ESTATE COMPANY

General Journal					(Page 1)
Date		Account titles and explanation	LP	Debit	Credit
19__					
Sept.	1	Cash	1	20,000	
		James Roberts, Capital	50		20,000
		Invested cash in the business.			
	3	Land	20	7,000	
		Cash	1		7,000
		Purchased land for office site.			
	5	Building	22	12,000	
		Cash	1		5,000
		Accounts Payable	30		7,000
		Purchased building to be moved to our lot. Paid part cash; balance payable within 90 days to X Company.			
	10	Accounts Receivable	2	2,000	
		Land	20		2,000
		Sold the unused part of our lot at cost to Carter's Drugstore. Due within three months.			
	14	Office Equipment	25	1,800	
		Accounts Payable	30		1,800
		Purchased office equipment on credit from General Equipment, Inc.			
	20	Cash	1	800	
		Accounts Receivable	2		800
		Collected part of receivable from Carter's Drugstore.			

General Journal					(Page 1)
Date		Account titles and explanation	LP	Debit	Credit
19__					
Sept.	30	Accounts Payable	30	1,000	
		Cash	1		1,000
		Made partial payment of the liability to General Equipment, Inc.			

Efficient use of a general journal requires two things: (1) ability to analyze the effect of a transaction upon assets, liabilities, and owners' equity; and (2) familiarity with the standard form and arrangement of journal entries. Our primary interest is in the analytical phase of journalizing; the procedural steps can be learned quickly by observing the following points in the illustrations of journal entries shown above and on the preceding page.

1. The year, month, and day of the first entry on the page are written in the date column. The year and month need not be repeated for subsequent entries until a new page or a new month is begun.

2. The name of the account to be debited is written on the first line of the entry and is customarily placed at the extreme left next to the date column. The amount of the debit is entered on the same line in the left-hand money column.

3. The name of the account to be credited is entered on the line below the debit entry and is indented, that is, placed about 1 inch to the right of the date column. The amount credited is entered on the same line in the right-hand money column.

4. A brief explanation of the transaction is usually begun on the line immediately below the title of the account. The explanation need not be indented.

5. A blank line is usually left after each entry. This spacing causes each journal entry to stand out clearly as a separate unit and makes the journal easier to read.

6. An entry which includes more than one debit or more than one credit (such as the entry on September 5) is called a *compound journal entry*. Regardless of how many debits or credits are contained in a compound journal entry, all the debits are customarily entered before any credits are listed.

7. The LP (ledger page) column just to the left of the debit money column is left blank at the time of making the journal entry. When the debits and credits are later transferred to ledger accounts, the numbers of the ledger accounts are listed in this column to provide a convenient cross reference with the ledger.

Posting

The process of transferring the debits and credits from the journal to the proper ledger accounts is called *posting*. Each amount listed in the debit column of the journal is posted by entering it on the debit side of an account in the ledger, and each amount listed in the credit column of the journal is posted to the credit side of a ledger account.

The mechanics of posting may vary somewhat with the preferences of the individual bookkeeper. For example, the debits and credits may be posted in the sequence shown in the journal, or all the debits on a journal page may be posted first. The following sequence is commonly used:

1. Locate in the ledger the first account named in the journal entry.

2. Enter in the debit column of the ledger account the amount of the debit as shown in the journal.

3. Enter the date of the transaction in the ledger account.

4. Enter in the Reference column of the ledger account the number of the journal page from which the entry is being posted.

5. The recording of the debit in the ledger account is now complete; as evidence of this fact, return to the journal and enter in the LP (ledger page) column the number of the ledger account or page to which the debit was posted.

6. Repeat the posting process described in the preceding five steps for the credit side of the journal entry.

In businesses having a large volume of transactions the posting of ledger accounts is performed by especially designed machines which speed up the work and reduce errors. Although posting is not difficult, it does require alertness and concentration if errors are to be avoided. The most common types of errors in posting include the following: (1) posting a debit as a credit, or vice versa; (2) posting to the wrong account; (3) posting the wrong amount; (4) omitting a posting; and (5) posting an item twice.

Entering the journal page number in the ledger account and listing the ledger page in the journal provide a cross reference between these two records. The audit of accounting records always requires looking up some journal entries to obtain more information about the amounts listed in ledger accounts. A cross reference between the ledger and journal is therefore essential to efficient audit of the records. Another advantage gained from entering in the journal the number of the account to which a posting has been made is to provide evidence throughout the posting work as to which items have been posted. Otherwise, any interruption in the posting might leave the bookkeeper uncertain as to what had been posted.

Illustration. The journal entry for the first transaction of the Roberts Real Estate Company is repeated at this point to illustrate the posting process. Note especially that the numbers of the ledger accounts are entered in the reference column of the journal.

NOTE THE
POSTING
REFERENCES
IN THE
JOURNAL

Journal					(Page 1)
19__					
Sept.	1	Cash	1	20,000	
		James Roberts, Capital ..	50		20,000

The two ledger accounts affected by this entry appear as follows after the posting has been completed; notice that the reference column of each account contains the number 1, indicating that the posting was made from page 1 of the journal.

NOTE THE
POSTING
REFERENCES
IN THE
LEDGER

Cash						(Account No. 1)
19__						
Sept.	1		1	20,000		

James Roberts, Capital						(Account No. 50)
			19__			
			Sept.	1	1	20,000

Computing balances of ledger accounts

The computation of the balance of the Cash account was illustrated earlier in this chapter, but a concise statement of a commonly used procedure for computing the balance of an account containing several entries may be useful at this point.

1. Add the debits in the account and insert the total in small figures just below the last entry in the debit column.

2. Add the credits in the account and insert the total in small figures just below the last entry in the credit column.

3. Compute the difference between the debit total and the credit total. If the account has a debit balance, enter this amount as a small figure to the left of the last debit entry; if the account has a credit balance, enter this amount to the left of the last credit entry.

Ledger accounts after posting

After all the September transactions have been posted, the ledger of the Roberts Real Estate Company appears as shown on page 45. The accounts are arranged in the ledger in balance sheet order, that is, assets first, followed by liabilities and owner's equity.

LEDGER SHOWING SEPTEMBER TRANS-ACTIONS

Cash (Account No. 1)

19__ Sept.	1		1	20,000	19__ Sept.	3		1	7,000
	20	7,800	1	800		5		1	5,000
				20,800		30		1	1,000
									13,000

Accounts Receivable (Account No. 2)

19__ Sept.	10	1,200	1	2,000	19__ Sept.	20		1	800

Land (Account No. 20)

19__ Sept.	3	5,000	1	7,000	19__ Sept.	10		1	2,000

Building (Account No. 22)

19__ Sept.	5		1	12,000					

Office Equipment (Account No. 25)

19__ Sept.	14		1	1,800					

Accounts Payable (Account No. 30)

19__ Sept.	30		1	1,000	19__ Sept.	5		1	7,000
						14	7,800	1	1,800
									8,800

James Roberts, Capital (Account No. 50)

					19__ Sept.	1		1	20,000

THE TRIAL BALANCE

Since equal dollar amounts of debits and credits are entered in the accounts for every transaction recorded, the sum of all the debits in the ledger must be equal to the sum of all the credits. If the computation of account balances has been accurate, it follows that the total of the accounts with debit balances must be equal to the total of the accounts with credit balances.

Before using the account balances to prepare a balance sheet, it is desirable to *prove* that the total of accounts with debit balances is in fact equal to the total of accounts with credit balances. This proof of the equality of debit and credit balances is called a *trial balance*. A trial balance is a two-column schedule listing the names and balances of all the accounts in the order in which they appear in the ledger; the debit balances are listed in the left-hand column and the credit balances in the right-hand column. The totals of the two columns should agree. A trial balance taken from the ledger of the Roberts Real Estate Company appears below:

TRIAL
BALANCE AT
MONTH-END
PROVES
LEDGER IS
IN BALANCE

ROBERTS REAL ESTATE COMPANY
Trial Balance
September 30, 19___

Cash	$ 7,800	
Accounts receivable	1,200	
Land	5,000	
Building	12,000	
Office equipment	1,800	
Accounts payable		$ 7,800
James Roberts, capital		20,000
	$27,800	$27,800

Uses and limitations of the trial balance

The trial balance provides proof that the ledger is in balance. The agreement of the debit and credit totals of the trial balance gives assurance that:

1. Equal debits and credits have been recorded for all transactions.
2. The debit or credit balance of each account has been correctly computed.
3. The addition of the account balances in the trial balance has been correctly performed.

Suppose that the debit and credit totals of the trial balance do not agree. This situation indicates that one or more errors has been made.

Typical of such errors are: (1) the entering of a debit as a credit, or vice versa; (2) arithmetical mistakes in balancing accounts; (3) clerical errors in copying account balances into the trial balance; (4) listing a debit balance in the credit column of the trial balance, or vice versa; and (5) errors in addition of the trial balance.

The preparation of a trial balance does not prove that transactions have been correctly analyzed and recorded in the proper accounts. If, for example, a receipt of cash were erroneously recorded by debiting the Land account instead of the Cash account, the trial balance would still balance. Also, if a transaction were completely omitted from the ledger, the error would not be disclosed by the trial balance. In brief, the trial balance proves only one aspect of the ledger, and that is the equality of debits and credits.

Despite these limitations, the trial balance is a useful device. It not only provides assurance that the ledger is in balance, but it also serves as a convenient steppingstone for the preparation of financial statements. As explained in Chapter 1, the balance sheet is a formal statement showing the financial condition of the business, intended for distribution to managers, owners, bankers, and various outsiders. The trial balance, on the other hand, is merely a working paper, useful to the accountant but not intended for distribution to others. The balance sheet and other financial statements can be prepared more conveniently from the trial balance than directly from the ledger, especially if there are a great many ledger accounts.

QUESTIONS

1. Explain precisely what is meant by each of the phrases listed below. Whenever appropriate, indicate whether the left or right side of an account is affected and whether an increase or decrease is indicated.

    a. A debit of $200 to the Cash account —
    b. Credit balance —
    c. Credit side of an account
    d. A debit of $600 to Accounts Payable
    e. Debit balance
    f. A credit of $50 to Accounts Receivable
    g. The Land account was debited

2. What relationship exists between the position of an account on the balance sheet and the rules for recording increases in that account?

3. Certain accounts normally have *debit balances* and other types of accounts normally have *credit balances*. State a rule indicating the position on the balance sheet of each such group of accounts.

4. For each of the following transactions, indicate whether the account in parentheses should be debited or credited, and give the reason for your answer.

a. Purchased a typewriter on credit, promising to make payment in full within 30 days. (Accounts Payable)

b. Purchased land for cash. (Cash)

c. Sold an old, unneeded typewriter on 30-day credit. (Office Equipment)

d. Obtained a loan of $5,000 from a bank. (Cash)

e. James Brown began the business of Brown Sporting Goods Shop by depositing $20,000 cash in a bank account in the name of the business. (James Brown, Capital)

5. What is a T account? How does it differ from a ledger account?

6. Compare and contrast a journal and a ledger.

7. During the first week of an accounting course, one student expressed the opinion that a great deal of time could be saved if a business would record transactions directly in ledger accounts rather than entering transactions first in a journal and then posting the debit and credit amounts from the journal to the ledger. Student B agreed with this view but added that such a system should not be called double-entry bookkeeping since each transaction would be entered only once. Student C disagreed with both A and B. He argued that the use of a journal and a ledger was more efficient than entering transactions directly in ledger accounts. Furthermore, he argued that the meaning of double-entry bookkeeping did not refer to the practice of maintaining both a journal and ledger.

Evaluate the statements made by all three students.

8. Which step in the recording of transactions requires greater understanding of accounting principles: (*a*) the entering of transactions in the journal, or (*b*) the posting of entries to ledger accounts?

9. What purposes are served by the preparation of a trial balance?

PROBLEMS

Group A

2A-1. *Instructions.* Analyze the transactions, then enter in T accounts.

Data

(1) On April 1, Mr. Henry Holmes deposited $25,000 cash in a bank account in the name of the business, the Atlas Travel Service.

(2) On April 2, land was acquired for $12,000 cash.

(3) On April 3, a prefabricated building was purchased from Ez-Built Supply Company at a cost of $8,000. A cash payment of $6,000 was made. The balance was to be paid within 30 days.

(4) On April 4, office equipment was purchased from Modern Office Equipment Company at a cost of $4,000. A down payment of $1,000 was made in cash. A promissory note was issued for the balance.

(5) On May 3, the balance due Ez-Built Supply Company was paid.

Note: The type of analysis to be made is illustrated by the following example, using item (1) above.

(1) (a) The asset Cash was increased. Increases in assets are recorded by debits. Debit Cash $25,000.

(b) The owner's equity was increased. Increases in owner's equity are recorded by credits. Credit Henry Holmes, Capital $25,000.

2A-2. *Instructions.* Journalize the transactions, then post to ledger accounts.

Data. The account titles used and the account numbers are:

Cash	*11*
Accounts receivable	*15*
Land	*21*
Building	*22*
Office equipment	*23*
Accounts payable	*35*
Note payable	*41*
Richard Stuart, capital	*51*

19___

Sept. 1.   Mr. Richard Stuart, a certified public accountant, deposited $15,000 cash in a bank account in the name of his accounting firm, Richard Stuart, CPA.

Sept. 2.   Purchased land for $15,000 and the building on the lot for $12,000. A cash payment of $10,000 was made, and a promissory note was issued for the balance.

Sept. 3.   Bought a typewriter for $250, paying cash.

Sept. 4.   Purchased an adding machine and filing cabinets from Utility Equipment Company at a cost of $1,350. A cash down payment of $350 was made, the balance to be paid in two equal installments due September 14 and October 14.

Sept. 5.   Two-thirds of land purchased on September 2 was sold for $10,000 to Barnes Grocery Store. Barnes Grocery Store made a cash down payment of $5,000 and agreed to pay the balance within 15 days.

Sept. 14.   Paid Utility Equipment Company $500 cash as the first installment due on office equipment.

Sept. 20.   Collected $5,000 cash from Barnes Grocery Store, in full settlement of transaction negotiated on September 5.

2A-3. *Instructions.* Based on the following transactions of the Downtown Parking System,

   a. Prepare journal entries.
   b. Post to ledger accounts and determine their balances.
   c. Prepare a trial balance as of March 31, 19___.

   Data. The account titles and the account numbers to be used are as follows:

Cash	*1*
Land	*17*
Building	*18*
Office equipment	*19*
Accounts payable	*21*
Notes payable	*27*
John Jones, capital	*31*

19___

Mar. 1.   Mr. Jones deposited $60,000 cash in a bank account in the name of the business, the Downtown Parking System.

Mar. 2. Acquired land from Safety Insurance Agency at a cost of $41,200. Agreed to pay the entire amount within 10 days.

Mar. 3. Acquired additional land at a cost of $16,000. A cash payment of $4,000 was made and a promissory note was issued for the balance.

Mar. 4. Purchased a small portable building for $600 cash.

Mar. 5. Purchased an electric time-punch clock for $125 in cash.

Mar. 6. Purchased a cash register from American Cash Register Company at a cost of $1,200. A cash down payment of $200 was made, the balance to be paid in equal installments due March 16, March 26, April 26, and May 26.

Mar. 11. Paid Safety Insurance Agency $41,200 cash in full settlement of the transaction negotiated on March 2.

Mar. 16. Paid American Cash Register Company $250, the amount of the payment due today.

Mar. 18. Purchased a storage cabinet for $75 cash.

Mar. 26. Paid American Cash Register Company $250, the amount of the second installment payment.

2A-4. The Baldwin Company, a partnership owned by Roger Baldwin and Charles Baldwin, had the following ledger accounts at October 31, 1962:

Cash			*Notes Payable*	
8,650.20	3,410.00			7,000.00

Accounts Receivable			*Accounts Payable*	
50.00	3,210.00		1,101.00	150.60
810.00				320.00
21,480.00				3,700.60

Land			*Taxes Payable*	
12,000.00			345.50	845.50

Building			*Mortgage Payable*	
29,500.00				20,000.00

Furniture & Fixtures			*Roger Baldwin, Capital*	
5,400.00				10,000.00
300.00				12,000.00

Delivery Equipment			*Charles Baldwin, Capital*	
3,800.00	800.00			10,000.00
				12,000.00

Instructions

a. Compute the account balances and prepare a trial balance as of October 31, 1962.

b. Prepare a balance sheet as of October 31, 1962.

2A-5. The account balances at October 31 for Park Lane Playhouse are listed below in alphabetical order:

Accounts payable	$ 1,275
Accounts receivable	200
Building	25,250
Cash	1,200
Land	12,000
Lighting equipment	3,770
Notes payable	15,000
Notes receivable	350
Office equipment	1,575
Stage equipment	4,825
Taxes payable	350
Thomas Ragan, capital	32,545

Instructions

a. Prepare a trial balance.

b. Prepare a balance sheet.

2A-6. *Instructions.* Based on the following transactions for radio station KLST,

a. Prepare journal entries.

b. Post to ledger accounts.

c. Prepare a trial balance as of October 31, 19___.

d. Prepare a balance sheet.

Data. The account titles used and their account numbers are:

Cash	11
Accounts receivable	15
Land	21
Building	22
Transmitter	23
Broadcasting equipment	24
Record library	25
Notes payable	31
Accounts payable	32
Sidney Tilden, capital	51

19___

Oct. 1. A charter was granted to Mr. Sidney Tilden for the organization and operation of radio station KLST. Mr. Tilden invested $40,000 cash.

Oct. 2. Purchased land at a cost of $13,000 from Suburb Development Company. A cash down payment of $1,000 was made, and a promissory note was signed for the balance.

Oct. 3. Purchased a transmitter at a cost of $25,000 from Radio Technicians, Inc. A cash down payment of $15,000 was made. The balance was to be paid in monthly installments of $500, beginning October 18.

Oct. 4. Erected an office and broadcasting building at a cost of $18,000, paying cash.

Oct. 5. Purchased a turntable at a cost of $450 from Hi-fi Music Center, paying cash.

Oct. 6. Purchased a tape recorder at a cost of $1,250 from Hi-fi Music Center, paying cash.

Oct. 9. Purchased a record library at a cost of $3,750 from Hi-fi Music Center. A cash payment of $1,750 was made, with the balance to be paid within 30 days.

Oct. 11. Sold part of record library to Community Recreation Center, cost $250, selling price $250. Community Recreation Center agreed to pay the whole amount in 30 days.

Oct. 18. Paid $500 cash to Radio Technicians, Inc., as the first installment due this day.

Oct. 25. Purchased some additional records from Hi-fi Music Center at a cost of $1,125, to be paid within 30 days.

2A-7. The trial balance for Speedy Delivery Service at October 31, 1962, was as follows:

SPEEDY DELIVERY SERVICE
Trial Balance
October 31, 1962

Account no.			
11	Cash	$ 3,515	
12	U.S. government bonds	2,500	
15	Accounts receivable	4,890	
21	Land	22,000	
22	Building	36,000	
24	Delivery trucks	28,000	
26	Office equipment	1,320	
31	Notes payable		$25,000
33	Accounts payable		4,000
35	Property taxes payable		675
41	Jack Norton, capital		68,550
		$98,225	$98,225

The transactions were as follows:

1962

Nov. 1. Paid $675 to the county government for property taxes due this day.

Nov. 2. Paid $400 in partial settlement of accounts payable.

Nov. 3. Purchased a typewriter for $250 cash.

Nov. 5. Collected $775 cash from Downtown Department Store (applicable to Accounts Receivable).

Nov. 6. Purchased a new truck at a cost of $3,800 from Tiger Motor Company. A cash down payment of $800 was made. A promissory note was issued for the balance to be paid in monthly installments of $300, beginning December 6.

Nov. 7.   Collected $850 cash from Alpha Furniture Store (applicable to Accounts Receivable).

Nov. 18. Sold United States government bonds for cash, $2,500.

Nov. 25. Sold one-half of land to Downtown Department Store as their new site for a warehouse, selling price $11,000. Downtown Department Store agreed to pay within 30 days.

Instructions

a. Transfer the October 31 balances to ledger accounts.
b. Prepare journal entries (page 20 of journal) for the month of November.
c. Post to ledger accounts.
d. Prepare a trial balance as of November 30, 1962.
e. Prepare a balance sheet.

Group B

2B-1. *Instructions.* Analyze the transactions given below in terms of increases and decreases in assets, liabilities, and owner's equity. After preparing this written analysis for each transaction, make the appropriate debit and credit entries in T accounts.

Data

(1) On March 1, Mr. Jack Anthony deposited $60,000 cash in a bank account in the name of the business, Anthony Investment Service.

(2) On March 2, purchased land at $14,000 and office building at $40,000 paying cash.

(3) On March 4, purchased office equipment from Downtown Furniture Store at a cost of $3,000. A cash payment of $1,200 was made, the balance to be paid in 30 days.

(4) On March 5, purchased some additional office equipment from First Business Machine Company at a cost of $2,000. A cash down payment of $500 was made and a promissory note was issued for the balance.

(5) On April 4, the amount due Downtown Furniture Store was paid in cash.

Note: Refer to problem 2A-1 for an illustration of the type of analysis to be made.

2B-2. *Instructions.* Journalize the transactions, then post to ledger accounts.

Data. The account titles and numbers are:

Cash	*11*
Accounts receivable	*12*
Land	*15*
Building	*16*
Automobiles	*17*
Office equipment	*18*
Accounts payable	*21*
Notes payable	*22*
George Burton, capital	*31*

19__

Oct. 1.   Mr. George Burton deposited $100,000 cash in a bank account in the name of the business, Burton Car Rental System.

Oct. 2. Purchased land for $15,000 and building on the lot for $35,000. A cash payment of $20,000 was made, and a promissory note issued for the balance.

Oct. 3. Purchased 20 new automobiles at $2,200 each from Ace Motor Company. A cash down payment of $24,000 was made, the balance to be paid in 30 days.

Oct. 4. Sold one automobile to one of the company's employees at cost. The employee paid $1,000 in cash and agreed to pay the balance within 30 days.

Oct. 5. One automobile proved to be defective and was returned to Ace Motor Company. The amount due the company was reduced by $2,200.

Oct. 10. Purchased a cash register and office desks for $1,800, paying cash.

Oct. 25. Paid $7,800 cash to Ace Motor Company.

2B-3. Owen's Barbershop was started on January 1, 19___, and had the transactions given below for the month of January. The account titles and numbers used were as follows:

Cash *10*
Barbershop supplies *12*
Land *14*
Building *15*
Barbershop equipment *16*
Notes payable *20*
Accounts payable *21*
Alex Owen, capital *30*

19___
Jan. 1. Mr. Alex Owen deposited $25,000 cash in a bank account in the name of the business, Owen's Barbershop.

Jan. 2. Purchased land for $12,000 and building on the lot for $22,000. A cash down payment of $20,000 was made, and a promissory note was issued for the balance.

Jan. 3. Purchased three barbershop chairs from Swivel Chairs, Inc., at $600 each. A cash payment of $1,000 was made, with the balance to be paid within 10 days.

Jan. 4. Paid cash of $1,150 to have mirrors and cabinets installed in shop.

Jan. 5. Paid $300 cash for miscellaneous barbershop supplies.

Jan. 6. Mr. Owen made an additional investment in the business of $4,000 in cash.

Jan. 12. Paid Swivel Chairs, Inc., $800 cash in full settlement of account.

Jan. 15. Borrowed $10,000 from the Continental National Bank, issuing a promissory note.

Jan. 28. Paid $14,000 cash in settlement of the note issued on January 2.

Instructions
a. Journalize the above transactions.
b. Post to ledger accounts, and determine their balances.
c. Prepare a trial balance as of January 31, 19___.

2B-4. The Fleetwood Stenographic Service is located in a downtown office building and provides typing, duplicating, and other stenographic services to the tenants of the building and to other clients. The company is a partnership, owned and operated by Robert Fleetwood and Stuart Fleetwood. As of June 30, 19___, the ledger accounts contained entries as follows:

Cash			Accounts Payable	
2,036.65	260.00		165.00	870.00
132.00	165.00		81.00	640.00
150.00	81.00		410.00	537.15
	410.00			260.00

Accounts Receivable			Taxes Payable	
132.00	132.00		165.00	946.00
227.00	150.00		95.00	
1,265.00				
62.50				
260.00				

Office Supplies			Robert Fleetwood, Capital	
300.00				4,500.00
350.00				

Office Equipment			Stuart Fleetwood, Capital	
5,620.00				4,500.00

Delivery Equipment	
2,000.00	

Instructions

a. Determine the account balances and prepare a trial balance as of June 30, 19___.

b. Prepare a balance sheet.

2B-5. The National Market Research Company was organized to gather information on consumer behavior on behalf of its clients. The following alphabetical list shows the account balances at August 31, 19___:

Accounts payable	$ *2,585.40*
Accounts receivable	*1,690.00*
Automobiles	*5,400.00*
Cash	*3,325.60*
Furniture & fixtures	*2,102.10*
Garage building	*2,300.00*
Land	*15,000.00*
Notes payable	*20,000.00*
Office building	*35,000.00*
Office machines	*2,650.00*
Office supplies	*115.50*
Taxes payable	*645.00*
United States government bonds	*4,000.00*
William Hawley, capital	*?*

Instructions

a. Rearrange the above data and prepare a trial balance.

b. Prepare a balance sheet.

2B-6. The Western Riding Stable was started on May 1, 19___, renting saddle horses to the general public. The transactions given below occurred in May. The account titles and numbers used are:

Cash	*1*
Accounts receivable	*3*
Land	*4*
Building	*5*
Horses	*6*
Notes payable	*11*
Accounts payable	*13*
Fred Healy, capital	*19*

19___

May 1. Mr. Fred Healy deposited $30,000 cash in a bank account in the name of the business, Western Riding Stable.

May 2. Purchased land for $15,000 and a prefabricated building on the lot for $12,000. A cash payment of $20,000 was made, and a promissory note was issued for the balance.

May 3. Purchased 20 horses at $350 each from Jackson Ranch. A cash payment of $5,000 was made, the balance to be paid in 10 days.

May 4. One of the horses purchased was too wild for horseback riding purposes, and was returned to Jackson Ranch. The amount due the ranch was reduced by $350.

May 5. Sold the prefabricated building on the lot to Rainbow Construction Company at cost. The buyer was responsible for the removal of the building. A cash down payment of $8,000 was received and the buyer agreed to pay the remainder within 30 days.

May 6. A stable was erected at a cost of $8,500, paid in cash.

May 8. Purchased five horses at $380 each from Star Ranch. Payment in full was to be made in 30 days.

May 12. Paid Jackson Ranch the amount due.

May 18. Mr. Healy made an additional investment in the business of $10,000 in cash.

May 28. Paid $1,000 cash to Star Ranch to apply on account.

Instructions

a. Journalize the above transactions.
b. Post to ledger accounts, and determine the balances.
c. Prepare a trial balance as of May 31, 19___.
d. Prepare a balance sheet.

2B-7. The Downtown Tabulating Service offers services in accounting and statistical data processing to business clients. The account balances at January 31, 19___, were as follows:

Trial Balance
January 31, 19___

1	Cash	$13,115
3	Accounts receivable	12,885
8	Supply of business forms	1,120
21	Land	10,000
23	Building	24,000
25	Furniture & fixtures	4,000
27	Business machines	60,000
29	Delivery equipment	3,200
41	Notes payable	25,000
43	Accounts payable	3,600
45	Taxes payable	125
50	George Smith, capital	?

The following transactions were completed during the month of February:

19___

Feb. 1. Paid in full a liability to Business Forms, Inc., of $100.

Feb. 2. Collected in full an account receivable of $625 from Johnson Store.

Feb. 3. Purchased a supply of business forms from Business Forms, Inc., at a cost of $350, to be paid within 30 days.

Feb. 4. Purchased a computer from Modern Business Corporation at a cost of $20,000; a cash payment of $3,000 was made, the balance to be paid within 10 days.

Feb. 6. Mr. Smith made an additional investment of $15,000 in cash in the business.

Feb. 8. Collected an account receivable of $1,300 from Statistical Research Associates.

Feb. 10. Made a cash payment of $7,000 to Modern Business Corporation in partial payment of the liability created by the purchase of February 4. Issued a note payable for the balance of $10,000.

Feb. 28. Paid in full the liability of $350 to Business Forms, Inc.

Instructions

a. Journalize the above transactions.

b. Transfer the amounts given as of January 31 to the ledger accounts, post the February entries, and determine the new balances.

c. Prepare a trial balance as of February 28, 19___.

d. Prepare a balance sheet.

3

Measuring business income

The earning of net income, or profits, is the chief goal of most business concerns. The individual who organizes a small business of his own does so with the hope and expectation that the business will operate at a profit, thereby increasing his equity in the business. In other words, profit is an increase in the owner's equity resulting from operation of the business. From the standpoint of the individual firm, profitable operation is essential if the firm is to succeed, or even to survive.

Profits may be retained in the business to finance expansion, or they may be withdrawn by the owner or owners. Some of the largest corporations have become large by retaining their profits in the business and using these profits for purposes of growth: retained profits may be used, for example, to acquire new plant and equipment, to carry on research leading to new and better products, and to extend sales operations into new territories. A satisfactory rate of business profits is generally associated with high employment, an improving standard of living, and a strong, expanding national economy.

Since the drive for profits underlies the very existence of business concerns, it follows that a most important function of an accounting system is to provide information about the profitability of the business. Before we can measure the profits of a business, we need to establish a sharp, clear meaning for *profits*. The word is used in somewhat different senses by economists, lawyers, and the general public. Perhaps for this reason, accountants prefer to use the alternative term *net income*, and to define this term very carefully. At this point, we shall adopt the technical accounting term "net income" in preference to the less precise term "profits."

In Chapter 1, accounting was referred to as the "language of business," and some of the key words of this language such as *assets, liabilities,* and *owners' equity*, were introduced. In the present chapter we want to establish clear working definitions for *revenue, expenses,* and *net income.* Very concisely stated, *revenue minus expenses equals net income.* To understand why this is true and how the measurements are made, let us begin with the meaning of revenue.

Revenue

When a business renders services to its customers or delivers merchandise to them, it either receives immediate payment in cash or acquires an account receivable which will be collected and thereby become cash within a short time. The revenue for a given period consists of the inflow of cash and receivables from sales made in that period. For any single transaction, the amount of revenue is a measurement of the asset values received from the customer.

Not all receipts of cash represent revenue; for example, as shown in Chapter 1, a business may obtain cash by borrowing from a bank. This increase in cash is offset by an increase in liabilities in the form of a note payable to the bank. The owners' equity is not changed by the borrowing transaction. Collection of an account receivable is another example of a cash receipt that does not represent revenue. The act of collection causes an increase in the asset, cash, and a corresponding decrease in another asset, accounts receivable. The amount of total assets remains unchanged, and, of course, there is no change in liabilities or owners' equity.

As another example of the distinction between revenue and cash receipts, let us assume that a business begins operations in March and makes sales of merchandise and/or services to its customers in that month as follows: sales for cash, $25,000; sales on credit (payable in April), $15,000. The revenue for March is $40,000, the total amount of cash received or to be received from the month's sales. When the accounts receivable of $15,000 are collected during April, they must not be counted as revenue a second time.

Revenue causes an increase in owners' equity. The inflow of cash and receivables from customers increases the total assets of the company; on the other side of the accounting equation, the liabilities do not change, but the owners' equity is increased to match the increase in total assets. Bear in mind, however, that not every increase in owners' equity comes from revenue. As illustrated in Chapter 1, the owners' equity is increased by the investment of assets in the business by the owners.

Expenses

Expenses represent the cost of the goods and services used up or consumed in the process of obtaining revenue. Examples include salaries paid employees, charges for newspaper advertising and for telephone service, and the wearing out (depreciation) of the building and office equipment. All these items are necessary to attract and serve customers and thereby to obtain revenue. Expenses are sometimes referred to as the "cost of doing business," that is, the cost of the various activities necessary to carry on a business.

Expenses cause the owners' equity to decrease. Revenue may be regarded as the positive factor in creating net income, expenses as the negative factor. The relationship between expenses and revenue is a significant one; the expenses of a given month or other period are incurred in order to generate revenue in that same period. The salaries earned by sales employees waiting on customers during July are applicable to July revenues and should be treated as July expenses, even though these salaries may not actually be paid to the employees until sometime in August.

As previously explained, revenues and cash receipts are not one and the same thing; similarly, expenses and cash payments are not identical. Examples of cash payments which are not expenses of the current period include the purchase of an office building for cash, the purchase of merchandise for later sale to customers, the repayment of a bank loan, and withdrawals of cash from the business by the owners. In deciding whether a given item should be regarded as an expense of the current period, it is often helpful to pose the following questions:

1. Does the alleged "expense" relate to revenue of the current period?
2. Does the item in question reduce the owners' equity?

Withdrawals by the owner

The owner of an unincorporated business invests money in the enterprise and devotes all or part of his time to its affairs in hopes that the business will earn a profit. The owner does not receive interest on the money he invests nor a salary for his personal services. His incentive, rather than interest or salary, is the increase in owner's equity that will result if the business earns a net income.

An owner of an unincorporated business usually makes withdrawals of cash from time to time, for his personal use. These withdrawals are in anticipation of profits and are not regarded as an expense of the business. The withdrawal of cash by the owner is like an expense in one respect; it reduces the owner's equity. However, expenses are incurred for the purpose of generating revenue, and a withdrawal of cash by the owner does not have this purpose. From time to time the owner may also make additional investments in the business. The investment of cash and the withdrawal of cash by the owner may be thought of as exact opposites: the investment does not represent revenue; the withdrawal does not represent an expense. Investments and withdrawals of cash affect only balance sheet accounts and are not reflected in the income statement.

Since a withdrawal of cash reduces the owner's equity, it *could be* recorded by debiting the owner's capital account (James Roberts, Capital, in our example). However, a clearer record is created if a separate *drawing account* (James Roberts, Drawing) is debited to record all amounts withdrawn. The drawing account is also known as a *personal account.*

Debits to the owner's drawing account are required for any of the following transactions:

1. Withdrawals of cash.

2. Withdrawals of other assets. The owner of a clothing store, for example, may withdraw merchandise for his personal use. The debit to the drawing account would be for the cost of the goods withdrawn.

3. Payment of the owner's personal bills out of company funds.

The disposition of the drawing account when financial statements are prepared will be illustrated later in this chapter.

The income statement

A series of balance sheets prepared at monthly or yearly intervals will indicate whether the owner's equity in a business is increasing or decreasing. A more complete picture of operating results is needed, however, for effective management of a business and intelligent planning of future operations. The financial statement which shows the amount and kind of revenues, the amount and kind of expenses, and the resulting net income (or net loss) is called an *income statement.* Alternative titles for this important financial statement include *profit and loss statement, operating statement,* and *statement of operations.* The illustration of the Roberts Real Estate Company presented in Chapters 1 and 2 is now continued by showing the income statement for the month of October.

INCOME
STATEMENT
SHOWS
RESULTS OF
OPERATIONS
FOR THE
MONTH

ROBERTS REAL ESTATE COMPANY
Income Statement
For the Month Ended October 31, 19___

Sales commissions earned		*$1,880*
Expenses:		
Advertising expense	*$210*	
Office salaries expense	*700*	
Telephone expense	*48*	
Depreciation expense: building	*50*	
Depreciation expense: office equipment	*15*	*1,023*
Net income		*$ 857*

This income statement shows that the revenue during October exceeded the expenses of the month, thus producing a net income of $857. The methods used in developing this financial statement will be explained in the remainder of this chapter.

Relating revenue and expenses to time periods

Although the assets and liabilities of a going business concern are in a process of constant change, the balance sheet, like a photographer's snapshot, serves to "stop the action" momentarily and to show the financial position of the business at a given date. An income statement, on the other hand, shows the results of operations over a *period of time.* In fact, the concept of income is meaningless unless it is related to a period of time. For example, if a businessman says, "My business produces net income of $5,000," the meaning is not at all clear; it could be made clear, however, by relating the income to a time period, such as "$5,000 a week," "$5,000 a month," or "$5,000 a year."

The accounting period. Every business concern prepares a yearly income statement, and most businesses prepare quarterly and monthly income statements as well. Management needs to know from month to month whether revenues are rising or falling, whether expenses are being held to the level anticipated, and how net income compares with the net income of the preceding month and with the net income of the corresponding month of the preceding year. The term *accounting period* means the span of time covered by an income statement. It may consist of a month, a quarter of a year, a half year, or a year.

Many income statements cover the calendar year ended December 31, but an increasing number of concerns are adopting an annual accounting period ending with a month other than December. Generally a business finds it more convenient to end its annual accounting period during a slack season rather than during a time of peak activity. Any 12-month accounting period adopted by a business is called its *fiscal year.* The fiscal year selected by the Federal government for its accounting measurements begins on July 1 and ends 12 months later on June 30.

Transactions affecting two or more accounting periods. The operation of a business entails an endless stream of transactions, many of which begin in one accounting period but affect several succeeding periods. Fire insurance policies, for example, are commonly issued to cover a period of three years. In this case, the apportionment of the cost of the policy by months is an easy matter. If the policy covers three years (36 months) and costs, for example, $360, the expense each month of maintaining insurance is $10.

Not all transactions can be so precisely divided by accounting periods. The purchase of a building, furniture and fixtures, machinery, a typewriter, or an automobile provides benefits to the business over all the years in which such an asset is used. No one can determine in advance exactly how many years of service will be received from such long-lived assets. Nevertheless, in measuring the net income of a business for a period of one year or less, the accountant must estimate what portion of the cost of the building and similar long-lived assets is applicable to the current year. Since the apportionments for these and many other transactions which overlap two or more accounting periods are in the nature of estimates rather than precise measurements, it follows that income statements should be regarded as useful approximations of annual income rather than as absolutely accurate determinations.

The only time period for which the measurement of net income can be absolutely accurate is the entire life span of the business. When a business concern sells all its assets, pays its debts, and ends its existence, it would then theoretically be possible to determine with precision the net income for the time period from the date of organization to the date of dissolution. Such a theoretically precise measurement of net income would, however, be too late to be of much practical use to the owners or managers of the business. The practical needs of business enterprise are well served by income statements of reasonable accuracy that tell managers and owners each month, each quarter, and each year the results of business operation.

Rules of debit and credit for revenue and expenses

Our approach to revenue and expenses has stressed the fact that revenue increases the owners' equity, and expenses decrease the owners' equity. The rules of debit and credit for recording revenue and expenses follow this relationship, and therefore the recording of revenue and expenses in ledger accounts requires only a slight extension of the rules of debit and credit presented in Chapter 2. The rule previously stated for recording increases and decreases in owners' equity was as follows:

> Increases in owners' equity are recorded by credits.
> Decreases in owners' equity are recorded by debits.

This rule is now extended to cover revenue and expense accounts:

> Revenue increases owners' equity; therefore revenue is recorded by a credit.
> Expenses decrease owners' equity; therefore expenses are recorded by debits.

Ledger accounts for revenue and expenses

During the course of an accounting period a great many revenue and expense transactions occur in the average business. To classify and summarize these numerous transactions, a separate ledger account is maintained for each major type of revenue and expense. For example, almost every business maintains accounts for Advertising Expense, Telephone Expense, and Office Salaries Expense. At the end of the period, all the advertising expenses appear as debits in the Advertising Expense account. The debit balance of this account represents the total advertising expense of the period and is listed as one of the expense items in the income statement.

Revenue accounts are usually much less numerous than expense accounts. A small business such as the Roberts Real Estate Company in our continuing illustration may have only one or two types of revenue, such as commissions earned from arranging sales of real estate, and commissions earned from the rental of properties in behalf of clients. In a business of this type the revenue accounts might be called Sales Commissions

Earned and Rental Commissions Earned. For physicians and attorneys conducting a professional practice, the revenue account is often called Fees. Businesses which sell merchandise of any kind rather than services generally use the term Sales for the revenue account.

Recording revenue and expense transactions: illustration. The organization of the Roberts Real Estate Company during September has already been described. The illustration is now continued for October, during which month the company earned commissions by selling several residences for its clients. Bear in mind that the company does not own any residential property; it merely acts as a broker or agent for clients wishing to sell their houses. A commission of 5% of the sales price of the house is charged for this service. During October the company not only earned commissions but also incurred a number of expenses.

Notice that each illustrated transaction which affects an income statement account also affects a balance sheet account. This pattern is consistent with our previous discussion of revenue and expenses. In recording revenue transactions, we shall debit the assets received and credit a revenue account. In recording expense transactions, we shall debit an expense account and credit the asset Cash, or perhaps a liability account if payment is to be made later. The transactions for October were as follows:

Oct. 1.   Paid $120 for publication of newspaper advertising describing various houses offered for sale.

ADVERTISING
EXPENSE
INCURRED
AND PAID

Analysis	*Rule*	*Entry*
The cost of advertising is an expense	*Expenses decrease the owner's equity and are recorded by debits*	*Debit: Advertising Expense, $120*
The asset Cash was decreased	*Decreases in assets are recorded by credits*	*Credit: Cash, $120*

Oct. 6.   Earned and collected a commission of $750 by selling a residence previously listed by a client.

REVENUE
EARNED
AND
COLLECTED

Analysis	*Rule*	*Entry*
The asset Cash was increased	*Increases in assets are recorded by debits*	*Debit: Cash, $750*
Revenue was earned	*Revenue increases the owner's equity and is recorded by a credit*	*Credit: Sales Commissions Earned, $750*

Oct. 16.   Newspaper advertising was ordered at a price of $90, payment to be made within 30 days.

ADVERTISING EXPENSE INCURRED BUT NOT PAID

Analysis	Rule	Entry
The cost of advertising is an expense	Expenses decrease the owner's equity and are recorded by debits	Debit: Advertising Expense, $90
An account payable, a liability, was incurred	Increases in liabilities are recorded by credits	Credit: Accounts Payable, $90

Oct. 20.   A commission of $1,130 was earned by selling a client's residence. The sales agreement provided that the commission would be paid in 60 days.

REVENUE EARNED, TO BE COLLECTED LATER

Analysis	Rule	Entry
An asset in the form of an account receivable was acquired	Increases in assets are recorded by debits	Debit: Accounts Receivable, $1,130
Revenue was earned	Revenue increases the owner's equity and is recorded by a credit	Credit: Sales Commissions Earned, $1,130

Oct. 30.   Paid salaries of $700 to office employees for services rendered during October.

SALARIES EXPENSE INCURRED AND PAID

Analysis	Rule	Entry
Salaries of employees are an expense	Expenses decrease the owner's equity and are recorded by debits	Debit: Office Salaries Expense, $700
The asset Cash was decreased	Decreases in assets are recorded by credits	Credit: Cash, $700

Oct. 30.   A telephone bill for October amounting to $48 was received. Payment was required by November 10.

TELEPHONE EXPENSE INCURRED, TO BE PAID LATER

Analysis	Rule	Entry
The cost of telephone service is an expense	Expenses decrease the owner's equity and are recorded by debits	Debit: Telephone Expense, $48
An account payable, a liability, was incurred	Increases in liabilities are recorded by credits	Credit: Accounts Payable, $48

Oct. 30. Mr. Roberts withdrew $600 cash for his personal use.

WITHDRAWAL OF CASH BY OWNER

Analysis	Rule	Entry
Withdrawal of assets by the owner decreases owner's equity	Decreases in owner's equity are recorded by debits	Debit: James Roberts, Drawing, $600
The asset Cash was decreased	Decreases in assets are recorded by credits	Credit: Cash, $600

The journal entries to record the October transactions are as follows:

OCTOBER JOURNAL ENTRIES FOR ROBERTS REAL ESTATE COMPANY

			Journal			(Page 2)
19__						
Oct.	1	Advertising Expense		70	120	
		Cash		1		120
		Paid for newspaper advertising.				
	6	Cash		1	750	
		Sales Commissions Earned . .		61		750
		Earned and collected commission by selling residence for client.				
	16	Advertising Expense		70	90	
		Accounts Payable		30		90
		Ordered newspaper advertising; payable in 30 days.				
	20	Accounts Receivable		2	1,130	
		Sales Commissions Earned . .		61		1,130
		Earned commission by selling residence for client; commission to be received in 60 days.				

			Journal			(Page 2)
19__						
Oct.	30	Office Salaries Expense	72	700		
		Cash	1			700
		Paid office salaries for October.				
	30	Telephone Expense	74	48		
		Accounts Payable	30			48
		To record liability for October tele-				
		phone service.				
	30	James Roberts, Drawing	51	600		
		Cash	1			600
		Withdrawal of cash by owner.				

The ledger of the Roberts Real Estate Company after the October transactions have been posted is now illustrated. For all accounts with more than one entry, the totals and month-end balances are noted in small-type figures. The accounts appear in the ledger in financial statement order as follows:

Balance sheet accounts
  Assets
  Liabilities
  Owner's equity
Income statement accounts
  Revenue
  Expenses

POSTING OCTOBER TRANS-ACTIONS TO LEDGER ACCOUNTS   To conserve space in this illustration, several ledger accounts appear on a single page. In actual practice, however, each account occupies a separate page in the ledger.

					Cash					(1)
19__						19__				
Sept.	1			1	20,000	Sept.	3		1	7,000
	20	7,800		1	800		5		1	5,000
					20,800		30		1	1,000
Oct.	6	7,130		2	750					13,000
					21,550	Oct.	1		2	120
							30		2	700
							30		2	600
										14,420

Accounts Receivable   (2)

19__					19__				
Sept.	10	1,200	1	2,000	Sept.	20		1	800
Oct.	20	2,330	2	1,130					
				3,130					

Land   (20)

19__					19__				
Sept.	3	5,000	1	7,000	Sept.	10		1	2,000

Building   (22)

19__									
Sept.	5		1	12,000					

Office Equipment   (25)

19__									
Sept.	14		1	1,800					

Accounts Payable   (30)

19__					19__				
Sept.	30		1	1,000	Sept.	5		1	7,000
						14	7,800	1	1,800
									8,800
					Oct.	16		2	90
						30	7,938	2	48
									8,938

James Roberts, Capital   (50)

					19__				
					Sept.	1		1	20,000

James Roberts, Drawing   (51)

19__									
Oct.	30		2	600					

Sales Commissions Earned   (61)

					19__				
					Oct.	6		2	750
						20		2	1,130
									1,880

	Advertising Expense						(70)
19__ Oct. 1 16		2 2	120 90 2 1 0				

	Office Salaries Expense						(72)
19__ Oct. 30		2	700				

	Telephone Expense						(74)
19__ Oct. 30		2	48				

Trial balance

After the October transactions have been posted from the journal to the ledger accounts, the next step in the accounting cycle is to prepare a trial balance from the ledger. As explained in Chapter 2, a trial balance is not a financial statement but merely an accounting work paper which serves two purposes. First, it proves that the ledger is in balance, with equal debit and credit totals. Secondly, it facilitates the preparation of the balance sheet and the income statement by bringing together in concise fashion all the account balances which comprise these two financial statements.

PROVING
THE
EQUALITY
OF DEBITS
AND
CREDITS

ROBERTS REAL ESTATE COMPANY
Trial Balance
October 31, 19__

Cash	$ 7,130	
Accounts receivable	2,330	
Land	5,000	
Building	12,000	
Office equipment	1,800	
Accounts payable		$ 7,938
James Roberts, capital		20,000
James Roberts, drawing	600	
Sales commissions earned		1,880
Advertising expense	210	
Office salaries expense	700	
Telephone expense	48	
	$29,818	$29,818

Recording depreciation at the end of the period

The preceding trial balance includes all the October expenses requiring cash payments such as salaries, advertising, and telephone service, but it does not include any depreciation expense. Although depreciation expense does not require a monthly cash outlay, it is nevertheless an inevitable and continuing expense. Failure to make an entry for depreciation expense would result in understating the total expenses of the period and consequently in overstating the net income.

Building. The office building purchased by the Roberts Real Estate Company at a cost of $12,000 is estimated to have a useful life of 20 years. The purpose of the $12,000 expenditure was to provide a place in which to carry on the business and thereby to obtain revenue. After 20 years of use the building will be worthless and the original cost of $12,000 will have been entirely consumed. In effect, the company has purchased 20 years of "housing services" at a total cost of $12,000. A portion of this cost expires during each year of use of the building. If we assume that each year's operations should bear an equal share of the total cost (straight-line depreciation), the annual depreciation expense will amount to 1/20 of $12,000, or $600. On a monthly basis, depreciation expense is $50 ($12,000 cost ÷ 240 months). There are alternative methods of spreading the cost of a depreciable asset over its useful life, some of which will be considered in Chapter 13.

RECORDING DEPRECIA-TION OF THE BUILDING

The journal entry to record depreciation of the building during October follows:

19—					
Oct.	31	Depreciation Expense: Building	76	50	
		Accumulated Depreciation: Building	23		50
		To record depreciation for October.			

After this entry has been posted, the three accounts relating to the building and its depreciation will appear as follows:

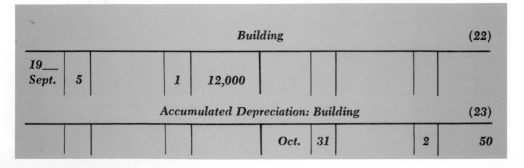

				Building					(22)
19—									
Sept.	5		1	12,000					

				Accumulated Depreciation: Building					(23)
					Oct.	31		2	50

Depreciation Expense: Building					(76)				
19__ Oct.	31		2	50					

The depreciation expense account will appear in the income statement for October along with the other expenses of salaries, advertising, and telephone expense. The Accumulated Depreciation: Building account will appear in the balance sheet as a deduction from the Building account, as shown by the following illustration of a partial balance sheet:

ROBERTS REAL ESTATE COMPANY
Partial Balance Sheet
October 31, 19__

Building (at cost)	$12,000	
Less: Accumulated depreciation	50	$11,950

Notice that the end result of crediting the Accumulated Depreciation: Building account is the same as if the credit had been made to the asset account, Building; that is, the net amount shown on the balance sheet for the building is reduced from $12,000 to $11,950. Although the credit side of a depreciation entry could logically be made directly to the asset account, it is customary and more efficient to record such credits in a separate account entitled Accumulated Depreciation. The original cost of the asset and the total amount of depreciation recorded over the years can more easily be determined from the ledger when separate accounts are maintained for the asset and for the accumulated depreciation.

Office equipment. Depreciation on the office equipment of the Roberts Real Estate Company must also be recorded at the end of October. This equipment cost $1,800 and is assumed to have a useful life of 10 years. Monthly depreciation expense on the straight-line basis is, therefore, $15, computed by dividing the cost of $1,800 by the useful life of 120 months. The journal entry is as follows:

RECORDING
DEPRECIA-
TION OF
OFFICE
EQUIPMENT

19__ Oct.	31	Depreciation Expense: Office Equipment	78	15	
		Accumulated Depreciation: Office Equipment	26		15
		To record depreciation for October.			

After this entry has been posted, the three ledger accounts relating to office equipment and its depreciation will appear as follows:

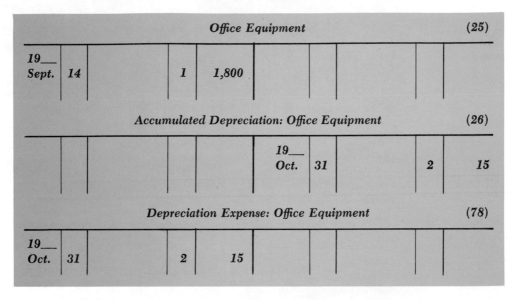

				Office Equipment						**(25)**
19__ Sept.	14		*1*	1,800						

				Accumulated Depreciation: Office Equipment						**(26)**
					19__ Oct.	31			*2*	15

				Depreciation Expense: Office Equipment						**(78)**
19__ Oct.	31		*2*	15						

No depreciation was recorded on the building and office equipment for September, the month in which these assets were acquired, because regular operations did not begin until October. Generally, depreciation is not recognized until the business begins active operation and the assets are placed in use. Accountants often use the expression "matching costs and benefits" to convey the idea of writing off the cost of an asset to expense during the time periods in which the business enjoys the use of the property.

The journal entry by which depreciation is brought on the books at the end of the month is called an *adjusting entry.* The adjustment of certain asset accounts and related expense accounts is a necessary step at the end of each accounting period so that the information presented in the financial statements will be as accurate and complete as possible. In the next chapter, adjusting entries will be shown for some other matters in addition to depreciation.

The adjusted trial balance

After all the necessary adjusting entries have been made at the end of the period, an adjusted trial balance is prepared. The adjusted trial balance provides assurance that the ledger is still in balance after the posting of the adjusting entries; it also provides a complete listing of the account balances to be used in preparing the financial statements. The following illustration shows the trial balance before adjustments as well as the adjusted trial balance.

TRIAL
BALANCE
AND
ADJUSTED
TRIAL
BALANCE

ROBERTS REAL ESTATE COMPANY
Trial Balances
October 31, 19___

	Before adjustments		After adjustments	
Cash	$ 7,130		$ 7,130	
Accounts receivable	2,330		2,330	
Land	5,000		5,000	
Building	12,000		12,000	
Accumulated depreciation:				
Building				$ 50
Office equipment	1,800		1,800	
Accumulated depreciation:				
Office equipment				15
Accounts payable		$ 7,938		7,938
James Roberts, capital		20,000		20,000
James Roberts, drawing ...	600		600	
Sales commissions earned .		1,880		1,880
Advertising expense	210		210	
Office salaries expense	700		700	
Telephone expense	48		48	
Depreciation expense:				
Building			50	
Depreciation expense:				
Office equipment			15	
	$29,818	$29,818	$29,883	$29,883

The adjusted trial balance contains both balance sheet accounts and income statement accounts. In preparing the financial statements at October 31, the asset, liability, and owner's equity accounts in the adjusted trial balance are arranged to form a balance sheet; the revenue and expense accounts in the adjusted trial balance are used to prepare an income statement.

Financial statements

The income statement for October was presented earlier in this chapter; it is shown again at this point along with the balance sheet to illustrate how the information for these two financial statements is taken from the adjusted trial balance.

INCOME
STATEMENT
FOR
OCTOBER

ROBERTS REAL ESTATE COMPANY
Income Statement
For the Month Ended October 31, 19___

Sales commissions earned		$1,880
Expenses:		
Advertising expense	$210	
Office salaries expense	700	
Telephone expense	48	
Depreciation expense: building	50	
Depreciation expense: office equipment	15	1,023
Net income		$ 857

BALANCE
SHEET AT
OCTOBER 31:
REPORT
FORM

ROBERTS REAL ESTATE COMPANY
Balance Sheet
October 31, 19___

Assets

Cash		$ 7,130
Accounts receivable		2,330
Land		5,000
Building	$12,000	
Less: accumulated depreciation	50	11,950
Office equipment	$ 1,800	
Less: accumulated depreciation	15	1,785
		$28,195

Liabilities and Owner's Equity

Liabilities:		
Accounts payable		$ 7,938
Owner's equity:		
James Roberts, capital, October 1, 19___	$20,000	
Net income for October	$857	
Less: withdrawals	600	
Increase in capital	257	
James Roberts, capital, October 31, 19___		20,257
		$28,195

Previous illustrations of balance sheets have been arranged in the *account form;* that is, with the assets on the left side of the page and the liabilities and owner's equity on the right side. This illustrated balance sheet is shown in *report form*, that is, with the liabilities and owner's equity sections listed below rather than to the right of the asset section. Both the account form and the report form are widely used.

The relationship between the income statement and the balance sheet is shown in the owner's equity section of the balance sheet. The owner's original capital investment of $20,000 was increased by reason of the $857 net income earned during October, making a total equity of $20,857. This equity was decreased, however, by the owner's withdrawal of $600 in cash at the end of October, leaving a final balance of $20,257.

In the Roberts Real Estate Company illustration, we have shown the two common ways in which the owner's equity in a business may be increased: (1) investment of cash or other assets by the owner, and (2) operating the business at a profit. There are also two ways in which the owner's equity may be decreased: (1) withdrawal of assets by the owner, and (2) operating the business at a loss.

Closing the books

Revenue and expense accounts are closed at the end of each accounting period by transferring their balances to a summary account called Income Summary. When the credit balances of the revenue accounts and the debit

REVENUES MINUS EXPENSES EQUAL NET INCOME

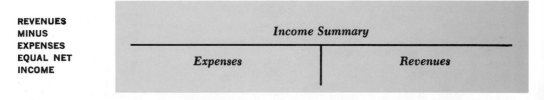

balances of the expense accounts have been transferred into one summary account, the balance of this Income Summary will be the net income or net loss for the period. If the revenues (credit balances) exceed the expenses (debit balances), the Income Summary account will have a credit balance representing net income. Conversely, if expenses exceed revenues, the Income Summary will have a debit balance representing net loss.

As previously explained, all debits and credits in the ledger are posted from the journal; therefore, the closing of revenue and expense accounts requires the making of journal entries and the posting of these journal entries to ledger accounts. A journal entry made for the purpose of closing a revenue or expense by transferring its balance to the Income Summary account is called a *closing entry*. This term is also applied to the journal entries (to be explained later) used in closing the Income Summary account and the owner's drawing account into the capital account.

A principal purpose of the year-end process of closing the revenue and expense accounts is to reduce their balances to zero. Since the revenue and expense accounts provide the information for the income statement of a *given accounting period,* it is essential that these accounts have zero balances at the beginning of each new period. The closing of the books has the effect of wiping the slate clean and preparing the accounts for the recording of revenues and expenses during the succeeding accounting period.

It is common practice to close the books only once a year, but for illustration, we shall now demonstrate the closing of the books of the Roberts Real Estate Company at October 31 after one month's operation.

Closing entries for revenue accounts. Revenue accounts have credit balances. Closing a revenue account, therefore, means transferring its credit balance to the Income Summary account. This transfer is accomplished by a journal entry debiting the revenue account in an amount equal to its credit balance, with an offsetting credit to the Income Summary account. The only revenue account of the Roberts Real Estate Company is Sales Commission Earned, which had a credit balance of $1,880 at October 31. The journal entry necessary to close this account is as follows:

CLOSING A REVENUE ACCOUNT

19__					
Oct.	31	Sales Commissions Earned	61	1,880	
		Income Summary	53		1,880
		To close the Sales Commissions Earned account.			

After this closing entry has been posted, the two accounts affected will appear as follows:

Sales Commissions Earned (61)

19__					19__				
Oct.	31		3	1,880	Oct.	6		2	750
						20		2	1,130
				1,880					1,880

Income Summary (53)

					19__				
					Oct.	31		3	1,880

The Sales Commission Earned account is now closed and has a zero balance. The equal totals on both sides of the account and the ruling of the account (double lines under the totals) show that it has no balance.

When account balances were computed for use in preparing a trial balance, small figures were placed in the ledger account to show the totals and balances. After an account has been ruled as shown in this illustration, there is no longer any need for these small figures and they may be erased.

Closing entries for expense accounts. Expense accounts have debit balances. Closing an expense account means transferring its debit balance to the Income Summary account. The journal entry to close an expense account, therefore, consists of a credit to the expense account in an amount equal to its debit balance, with an offsetting debit to the Income Summary account.

There are five expense accounts in the ledger of the Roberts Real Estate Company. Five separate journal entries could be made to close these five expense accounts, but the use of one compound journal entry is an easier, more efficient, timesaving method of closing all five expense accounts.

19__					
Oct.	31	Income Summary	53	1,023	
		Advertising Expense	70		210
		Office Salaries Expense	72		700
		Telephone Expense	74		48
		Depreciation Expense:			
		Building	76		50
		Depreciation Expense: Office			
		Equipment	78		15
		To close the expense accounts.			

After this closing entry has been posted, the Income Summary account and the five expense accounts will appear as follows:

Income Summary									(53)
19__					19__				
Oct.	31		3	1,023	Oct.	31		3	1,880

Advertising Expense									(70)
19__					19__				
Oct.	2		2	120	Oct.	31		3	210
	16		2	90					
				210					210

Office Salaries Expense (72)

19__					19__					
Oct.	30		2	700	Oct.	31		3	700

Telephone Expense (74)

19__					19__					
Oct.	30		2	48	Oct.	31		3	48

Depreciation Expense: Building (76)

19__					19__					
Oct.	31		2	50	Oct.	31		3	50

Depreciation Expense: Office Equipment (78)

19__					19__					
Oct.	31		2	15	Oct.	31		3	15

Ruling closed accounts. The ruling of the closed accounts should be studied closely. The ruling process was similar for the Sales Commission Earned account and the Advertising Expense account because both these accounts contained more than one entry on a side. A single ruling was placed on the same line across the debit and credit money columns. The totals were entered just below this single ruling and a double ruling was drawn below the totals. The double ruling was also placed across the date columns and the reference columns in order to establish a clear separation between the transactions of the period just ended and the entries to be made in the following period. All the expense accounts except Advertising Expense contained only one debit entry: In ruling an account with only one debit and one credit, it is not necessary to enter totals; the double lines may be placed just below the debit and credit entries.

Closing the income summary account. The five expense accounts have now been closed and the total amount formerly contained in these accounts appears on the debit side of the Income Summary account. The commissions earned during October appear on the credit side of the Income Summary account. Since the credit entry of $1,880 representing October revenue is larger than the debit of $1,023 representing October expenses, the account has a credit balance of $857—the net income for October.

The net income of $857 earned during October causes the owner's equity to increase. The credit balance of the Income Summary account is, therefore, transferred to the owner's capital account by the closing entry:

NET INCOME
EARNED
INCREASES
THE
OWNER'S
EQUITY

	19__ Oct.	31	*Income Summary* .... *James Roberts, Capital* .... *To close the Income Summary account* *for October by transferring the net in-* *come to the owner's capital account.*	53 50	857	857

After this closing entry has been posted, the Income Summary account has a zero balance, and the net income earned during October appears in the owner's capital account as shown below:

Income Summary **(53)**

19__ Oct.	31 31		3 3	1,023 857	19__ Oct.	31		3	1,880
				1,880					1,880

James Roberts, Capital **(50)**

					19__ Sept. Oct.	1 31		1 3	20,000 857

In our illustration the business has operated profitably with revenues in excess of expenses. Not every business is so fortunate; if the expenses of a business are larger than its revenue, the Income Summary account will have a debit balance. In this case, the closing of the Income Summary account will require a debit to the owner's capital account and an off-setting credit to the Income Summary account. The owner's equity will, of course, be reduced by the amount of the loss debited to his capital account.

Notice that the Income Summary account is used only at the end of the period when the books are being closed. The account has no entries and no balance except during the process of closing the books at the end of the accounting period.

Closing the owner's drawing account. As explained earlier in this chapter, withdrawals of cash or other assets by the owner are not considered as an expense of the business and, therefore, are not taken into account in determining the net income for the period. Since drawings by the owner do not constitute an expense, the owner's drawing account is not closed into the Income Summary account but directly to the owner's capital account. The following journal entry serves to close the drawing account in the ledger of the Roberts Real Estate Company at October 31.

DRAWING ACCOUNT IS CLOSED TO OWNER'S CAPITAL ACCOUNT						
	19__					
	Oct.	*31*	*James Roberts, Capital*	*50*	*600*	
			James Roberts, Drawing	*51*		*600*
			To close the drawing account.			

After this closing entry has been posted, the drawing account will have a zero balance, and the amount withdrawn by Mr. Roberts during October will appear as a deduction or debit entry in his capital account, as shown below:

James Roberts, Drawing						*(51)*
19__				*19__*		
Oct.	*30*		*2*	*600*	*Oct.*	*31*		*3*	*600*

James Roberts, Capital						*(50)*
19__				*19__*		
Oct.	*31*		*3*	*600*	*Sept.*	*1*		*1*	*20,000*
					Oct.	*31*		*3*	*857*

Summary of closing procedure. Let us now summarize briefly the procedure of closing the books.

1. Close the various revenue and expense accounts by transferring their balances into the Income Summary account.

2. Compute the balance of the Income Summary account. (If revenues exceed expenses, the account will have a credit balance, indicating the business has earned net income. If expenses exceed revenues, the account will have a debit balance, indicating the business has operated at a net loss.)

3. Close the Income Summary account by transferring its balance into the owner's capital account.

DIAGRAM
SHOWING
THE
CLOSING
OF THE
BOOKS
4. Close the drawing account into the owner's capital account. (The balance of the owner's capital account in the ledger will now be the same as the amount of capital appearing in the balance sheet.)

The closing of the books may be illustrated graphically as follows:

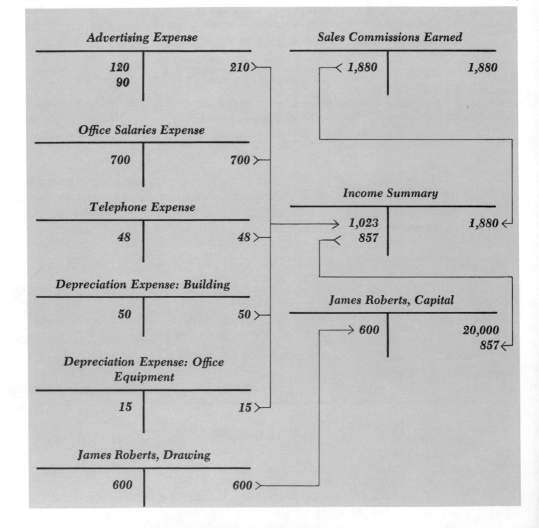

Balancing and ruling balance sheet accounts

The closing and ruling of income statement accounts at the end of the accounting period has been explained and illustrated. In addition, some bookkeepers find it convenient to balance and rule any balance sheet accounts (such as Cash) which have numerous debit and credit entries. The purpose of this optional procedure is to begin the new accounting period with a single figure showing clearly the balance of the account. Balancing

**RULING A
BALANCE
SHEET
ACCOUNT** is unnecessary for accounts with only one entry or entries on only one side. The balancing procedure is now illustrated for the Cash account for the Roberts Real Estate Company at the end of September.

Cash									(1)	
19__ Sept.	1		1	20,000	19__ Sept.	2		1	7,000
	20		1	800		5		1	5,000
						30		1	1,000
									13,000
						30	Balance	√	7,800
				20,800					20,800
19__ Oct.	1	Balance	√	7,800					

The sequence of steps used in balancing the Cash account is as follows:

1. Enter the balance of the account and the date on the side having the smaller total. Write the word "Balance" in the explanation column to make clear that this amount was not posted from the journal. A check mark may be placed in the reference column for the same purpose. With the balance added to the smaller side of the account, the debit and credit totals will agree.

2. Rule the debit and credit money columns with a single rule. Then record the debit and credit totals on the same line.

3. Rule the account by placing double lines through the date columns, reference columns, and money columns. In the new accounting period it will not be necessary to refer to information above the double-line ruling.

4. Bring down the balance of the account just below the double lines on the side that had the larger total. Write the word "Balance," so that this amount will not be mistaken for an entry posted from the journal, and place a check mark in the reference column. The date to be used for this new balance is the first of the following month.

Ledger accounts after closing the books

After the adjusting, closing, and ruling of the accounts at October 31, the ledger of the Roberts Real Estate Company appears as follows. Note that the balance sheet accounts are placed first in the ledger and that these accounts are still open, with the exception of the Drawing account. The balance sheet accounts are followed by the income statement accounts, all of which have been closed and ruled.

Cash   (1)

19__					19__				
Sept.	1		1	20,000	Sept.	2		1	7,000
	20		1	800		5		1	5,000
						30		1	1,000
									13,000
						30	Balance	√	7,800
				20,800					20,800
19__					19__				
Oct.	1	Balance	√	7,800	Oct.	1		2	120
	6		2	750		30		2	700
						30		2	600
									1,420
						31	Balance	√	7,130
				8,550					8,550
19__									
Nov.	1	Balance	√	7,130					

Accounts Receivable   (2)

19__					19__				
Sept.	10		1	2,000	Sept.	20		1	800
						30	Balance	√	1,200
				2,000					2,000
19__									
Oct.	1	Balance	√	1,200					
	20		2	1,130					
				2,330					

Land   (20)

19__					19__				
Sept.	3		1	7,000	Sept.	10		1	2,000
						30	Balance	√	5,000
				7,000					7,000
19__									
Oct.	1	Balance	√	5,000					

Building   (22)

19__				
Sept.	5		1	12,000

Accumulated Depreciation: Building   (23)

					19__ Oct.	31		2	50

Office Equipment   (25)

19__ Sept.	14		1	1,800					

Accumulated Depreciation: Office Equipment   (26)

					19__ Oct.	31		2	15

Accounts Payable   (30)

19__ Sept.	30		1	1,000	19__ Sept.	5		1	7,000
						14		1	1,800
	30	Balance	√	7,800					
				8,800					8,800
					19__ Oct.	1	Balance	√	7,800
						16		2	90
						30		2	48
									7,938

James Roberts, Capital   (50)

19__ Oct.	31		3	600	19__ Sept.	1		1	20,000
	31	Balance	√	20,257	Oct.	31		3	857
				20,857					20,857
					19__ Nov.	1	Balance	√	20,257

James Roberts, Drawing   (51)

19__ Oct.	30		2	600	19__ Oct.	31		3	600

Income Summary (53)

19__					19__				
Oct.	31		3	1,023	Oct.	31		3	1,880
	31		3	857					
				1,880					1,880

Sales Commissions Earned (61)

19__					19__				
Oct.	31		3	1,880	Oct.	6		2	750
						20		2	1,130
				1,880					1,880

Advertising Expense (70)

19__					19__				
Oct.	2		2	120	Oct.	31		3	210
	16		2	90					
				210					210

Office Salaries Expense (72)

19__					19__				
Oct.	30		2	700	Oct.	31		3	700

Telephone Expense (74)

19__					19__				
Oct.	30		2	48	Oct.	31		3	48

Depreciation Expense: Building (76)

19__					19__				
Oct.	31		2	50	Oct.	31		3	50

Depreciation Expense: Office Equipment						(78)	
19__ Oct.	31		2	15	19__ Oct.	31	3	15

After-closing trial balance

After the revenue and expense accounts have been closed, it is desirable to take an *after-closing trial balance,* which of course will consist solely of balance sheet accounts. There is always the possibility that an error in posting the closing entries may have upset the equality of debits and credits in the ledger. The after-closing trial balance, or *post-closing trial balance* as it is often called, gives assurance that the books are in balance and ready for the recording of the transactions of the new accounting period. The after-closing trial balance of the Roberts Real Estate Company follows:

ONLY THE BALANCE SHEET ACCOUNTS REMAIN OPEN

ROBERTS REAL ESTATE COMPANY
After-closing Trial Balance
October 31, 19__

Cash	$ 7,130	
Accounts receivable	2,330	
Land	5,000	
Building	12,000	
Accumulated depreciation: building		$ 50
Office equipment	1,800	
Accumulated depreciation: office equipment		15
Accounts payable		7,938
James Roberts, capital		20,257
	$28,260	$28,260

QUESTIONS

1. What is the meaning of the term *revenue?* Does the receipt of cash by a business indicate that revenue has been earned? Explain.

2. Henry Bowman & Associates, a firm of real estate brokers, had the following transactions during June. Which of these transactions represented revenue to the firm during the month of June? Explain.

    a. Arranged a sale of an apartment building owned by a client, James Robbins. The commission for making the sale was $2,000, but this amount would not be received until July 20.

    b. Collected cash of $1,500 from an account receivable. The receivable originated in April from services rendered to a client.

    c. Borrowed $4,000 from the National Bank, to be repaid in three months.

    d. Collected $150 from a dentist to whom Bowman & Associates rented part of its building. This amount represented rent for the month of June.

    e. Henry Bowman invested an additional $2,000 cash in the business.

3. What is the meaning of the term *expenses?* Does the payment of cash by a business indicate that an expense has been incurred? Explain.

4. A business had the following transactions, among others, during January. Which of these transactions represented expenses for January? Explain.

    a. Paid $300 salary to a salesman for time worked during January. ✓ yes

    b. Paid $60 for gasoline purchases for the delivery truck during January. yes

    c. Purchased a typewriter for $300 cash. no

    d. Paid $2,000 in settlement of a loan obtained three months earlier. no

    e. The owner withdrew $500 from the business for his own use. no

    f. Paid a garage $200 for automobile repair work performed in November. yes

5. The Torino Company, owned by Robert Gennaro, completed its first year of operation on December 31, 1962. State the proper heading for the first annual income statement.

6. Does a well-prepared income statement provide an exact and precise measurement of net income for the period, or does it represent merely an approximation of net income? Explain.

7. How does depreciation expense differ from other operating expenses?

8. Assume that a business acquires a delivery truck at a cost of $3,600. Estimated life of the truck is four years. State the amount of depreciation expense per year and per month. Give the adjusting entry to record depreciation on the truck at the end of the first month, and explain where the accounts involved would appear in the financial statements.

9. Supply the missing figures in the following independent cases:

    a. *Net income for the year* $11,400
           Owner's equity at beginning of year   22,500
           Owner's equity at end of year   33900
           Owner's drawings during the year   7,200

    b. *Owner's equity at end of year* $33,300   33,300
           Owner's drawings during the year   6,700   6,700
           Net income for the year   18,300   26,606
           Owner's equity at beginning of year   ———

    c. *Owner's drawings during the year*   ———
           Owner's equity at end of year $38,700
           Net income for the year   7,700
           Owner's equity at beginning of year   46,400

    d. *Net income for the year*   ———
           Owner's equity at end of year $25,600
           Owner's equity at beginning of year   22,500
           Owner's drawings during the year   7,200

e. *Owner's equity at beginning of year* $48,600
    Owner's equity at end of year   58,000
    Additional investment by owner during the year 16,000
    Net income   ————
    Owner's drawings for the year   4,800

PROBLEMS

Group A

3A-1. The May transactions of the Bryan Travel Service are listed below.

(1) On May 1, Bryan Travel Service paid $150 for an advertisement in the Travel section of the *Sunday Tribune.*

(2) On May 2, Bryan Travel Service arranged a round-the-world trip for Mr. and Mrs. Henry Benson. A commission of $400 cash was collected from the steamship company.

(3) On May 3, fly-now-pay-later European trips were arranged for several clients. The Transatlantic Airway System agreed to pay Bryan Travel Service a commission of $550 for services rendered, payment to be made as soon as arrangements were confirmed.

(4) On May 8, another advertisement was placed in the *Sunday Tribune* for $200, payment to be made in 30 days.

(5) On May 15, Mr. Henry Arthur, owner of Bryan Travel Service, withdrew $300 from the business for personal use.

(6) On May 18, cash in the amount of $550 was collected from the Transatlantic Airway System.

Instructions. Analyze each transaction, and then prepare the necessary journal entry.

The following will illustrate an analysis, using (1) above:

(1) (a) Advertising is an operating expense. Expenses are recorded by debits. Debit Advertising Expense $150.

(b) The asset Cash was decreased. Decreases in assets are recorded by credits. Credit Cash $150.

3A-2. *Instructions.* From the information given in the transactions:

a. Prepare journal entries.

b. Post to ledger accounts.

c. Prepare a trial balance as of April 30, 19___.

Data. The account titles to be used and the account numbers are as follows:

Cash	*1*
Land	*15*
Building	*16*
Notes payable	*27*
Accounts payable	*29*
Robert Miller, capital	*31*
Robert Miller, drawing	*32*
Admissions revenue	*41*
Advertising expense	*51*
Film rental expense	*52*
Light & power expense	*53*
Salaries expense	*54*

19___

Apr. 1. Mr. Robert Miller invested $25,000 cash in a bank account in the name of the business, the Campus Cinema.

Apr. 2. Purchased land, $12,500, and theater building, $27,500, paying cash of $20,000 and signing a note payable for the balance of $20,000.

Apr. 3. Arranged with the *Daily Tribune* for newspaper advertising for the month of April at a total price of $400, payable before May 10.

Apr. 4. Arranged with AAA Studio for a two-week showing of their recent production at a total rental of $1,000. A cash payment of $500 was made, the balance to be paid after the run was over.

Apr. 5. Various advertising expenses for the promotion of "Gala Opening Night" amounted to $250 and were paid in cash.

Apr. 10. The box office cash receipts for the first week amounted to $1,350.

Apr. 15. Paid $450 to employees for services rendered during the first half of April.

Apr. 17. The box office cash receipts for the second week amounted to $1,005.

Apr. 18. Paid AAA Studio $500, the balance due on the showing just ended.

Apr. 19. Arranged with Douglas Bros. Studio for a 12-day showing of their recent production at a total rental of $600. A cash payment of $300 was made, the balance to be paid after the run was over.

Apr. 24. The box office cash receipts for the third week amounted to $935.

Apr. 30. Paid $450 to employees for services rendered during the second half of April.

Apr. 30. The light and power bill from A&P Power Company amounted to $250, to be paid before May 10.

Apr. 30. Paid the Douglas Bros. Studio $300, the balance due on the showing just ended.

Apr. 30. The box office receipts for the last week of April amounted to $945.

Apr. 30. Mr. Miller withdrew $550 from the business for personal use.

3A-3. The Theater Parking System operates a parking lot in a downtown location. The ledger includes the following accounts:

	Account no.
Cash	*10*
Land	*17*
Notes payable	*20*
Accounts payable	*21*
Sam Morris, capital	*31*
Sam Morris, drawing	*32*
Parking fees	*41*
Advertising expense	*51*
Lighting expense	*52*
Salaries expense	*53*

The transactions for the organization of the business and its operation during the month of May were as follows:

May 1. Mr. Sam Morris deposited $22,000 cash in a bank account in the name of the business, the Theater Parking System.

May 2.   Purchased land for $28,400. Of this total cost, the sum of $18,400 was paid in cash. A non-interest-bearing note payable was issued for the balance of $10,000.

May 3.   Arranged with the Playbill Printing Company for a regular advertisement in the Playbill at a monthly cost of $50. Paid for advertising during May by check, $50.

May 4.   An arrangement was made with the Playgoer Restaurant for free parking privileges for their customers. Playgoer Restaurant agreed to pay $150 monthly, payable in advance. Cash was collected for the month of May.

May 15. Parking receipts for the first half of the month were $603.

May 31. Paid $350 to the parking attendant for services rendered during the month.

May 31. Electricity bill from the A&P Power Company amounted to $35, to be paid before June 10.

May 31. Parking receipts for the second half of the month amounted to $577.

May 31. Mr. Morris withdrew $400 for personal use.

Instructions
a. Journalize these transactions.
b. Post to ledger accounts.
c. Prepare a trial balance.
d. Prepare an income statement and a balance sheet in report form.

3A-4. The following adjusted trial balance of the Alpha Insurance Agency shows the accounts arranged in alphabetical order:

ALPHA INSURANCE AGENCY
Adjusted Trial Balance
June 30, 19___

Accounts payable		$ 275.15
Accounts receivable	$ 225.35	
Accumulated depreciation: building		100.00
Accumulated depreciation: office equipment		80.00
Advertising expense	150.00	
Building	15,000.00	
Cash	2,400.00	
Commissions earned		1,850.00
Depreciation expense: building	50.00	
Depreciation expense: office equipment	40.00	
Land	12,200.00	
Lighting expense	125.15	
Notes payable		9,000.00
Office equipment	3,600.00	
Peter Parnell, capital		23,752.88
Peter Parnell, drawing	400.00	
Salaries expense	800.00	
Telephone expense	67.53	
	$35,058.03	$35,058.03

Instructions

a. Prepare an adjusted trial balance with the accounts arranged in the customary sequence of ledger accounts.

b. Prepare an income statement for the month ended June 30, 19___.

c. Prepare a balance sheet in report form.

3A-5. *Instructions.* Based on the trial balance and other data, prepare the following:

a. Adjusting entries

b. An adjusted trial balance

c. An income statement for the month ended July 31, 19___

d. A balance sheet in report form

Data

QUICKIE AUTO-WASH SERVICE
Trial Balance
July 31, 19___

Cash	$ 1,355.15	
Accounts receivable	36.00	
Land	21,500.00	
Building	24,000.00	
Accumulated depreciation: building		$ 600.00
Equipment	9,000.00	
Accumulated depreciation: equipment		450.00
Notes payable		22,000.00
Accounts payable		617.89
Leonard Fain, capital		32,051.39
Leonard Fain, drawing	450.00	
Revenue from wash service		3,316.25
Advertising expense	125.00	
Detergent expense	118.00	
Salaries expense	2,200.00	
Water expense	251.38	
	$59,035.53	$59,035.53

Other data

(1) The building was acquired January 2 of the current year; estimated useful life was 20 years.

(2) The equipment was acquired on January 2 of the current year; estimated useful life was 10 years.

3A-6. *Instructions.* From the trial balance and supplementary data given, prepare

a. Adjusting entries

b. Adjusted trial balance

c. Income statement for the month ended August 31, 19___

d. Balance sheet

e. Closing entries

f. After-closing trial balance

Data. The Appreciation Investment Service offers investment counseling and brokerage service to its clients.

APPRECIATION INVESTMENT SERVICE
Trial Balance
August 31, 19___

Cash	$ 9,177	
Marketable securities	8,322	
Accounts receivable	2,026	
Land	23,000	
Building	24,000	
Accumulated depreciation: building		$ 700
Equipment	9,600	
Accumulated depreciation: equipment		700
Furniture	3,600	
Accumulated depreciation: furniture		210
Notes payable		20,000
Wayne Tippe, capital		56,005
Wayne Tippe, drawing	600	
Commissions earned		9,860
Advertising expense	350	
News service expense	400	
Salaries expense	6,150	
Telephone expense	250	
	$87,475	$87,475

Other data. Building, equipment, and furniture were all acquired on January 2 of the current year. The useful life of the building was estimated at 20 years; of equipment, at 8 years; of furniture, at 10 years.

3A-7. The Arrow Moving Service was organized on September 1 by Mr. Paul Ryder to provide transcontinental transportation of household goods. During September the following transactions occurred:

19___

Sept. 1. Mr. Paul Ryder deposited $100,000 cash in a bank account in the name of the business, the Arrow Moving Service.

Sept. 2. Purchased land $25,000 and building $36,000, paying cash.

Sept. 3. Purchased four trucks from Ball Motor at a cost of $10,800 each. A cash down payment of $20,000 was made, the balance to be paid by November 10.

Sept. 4. Purchased office equipment for cash, $2,400.

Sept. 5. Moved furniture for Mr. and Mrs. John Chambers from New York City to Los Angeles for $1,685. Collected $485 in cash; balance to be paid within 30 days.

Sept. 8. Moved furniture for Mr. and Mrs. Daniel Knight from San Francisco to Philadelphia for $2,005. Collected $605 in cash; balance to be paid within 30 days.

Sept. 9. Moved furniture for Mr. William White from Chicago to St. Louis for $1,230. Cash collected.

Sept. 15. Paid salaries to drivers for the first half of month, $1,510.

Sept. 20. Moved furniture for various clients for a total of $2,700. Cash collected in full.

Sept. 30.   Salaries expense for the second half of September amounted to $1,325.

Sept. 30.   Received a gasoline bill for the month of September from Atlantic Oil Company in the amount of $1,750 to be paid before October 10.

Sept. 30.   Received bill of $125 for repair work on trucks during September by Ace Motor Company.

Sept. 30.   Mr. Ryder withdrew $600 cash for his personal use.

Other data. Mr. Ryder estimated the useful life of the building at 20 years, of trucks at 4 years, and of equipment at 10 years.

Instructions

a. Prepare journal entries. (Number journal pages to permit cross reference to ledger.)

b. Post to ledger accounts. (Number ledger accounts to permit cross reference to journal.)

c. Prepare a trial balance as of September 30, 19___.

d. Prepare adjusting entries and post to ledger accounts.

e. Prepare an adjusted trial balance.

f. Prepare an income statement for the month ended September 30, 19___.

g. Prepare a balance sheet.

h. Prepare closing entries, post to ledger accounts, and rule off accounts having zero balances.

i. Prepare an after-closing trial balance.

Group B

3B-1.   The September transactions of Plant Motors, an automobile repair shop, are:

(1) On September 1, paid $50 cash for newspaper advertising.

(2) On September 2, made repairs to car of J. M. Jones and collected in full the charge of $185. (Credit Repair Service Revenue.)

(3) On September 8, at request of National Insurance, Inc., made repairs on car of Roger Sands. Sent bill for $245 for services rendered to National Insurance, Inc.

(4) On September 15, placed advertisement in *Daily News* at cost of $60, payment to be made in 30 days.

(5) On September 25, received a check for $245 from National Insurance, Inc.

(6) On September 30, Mr. James Plant, owner of Plant Motors, withdrew $250 from the business for his personal use.

Instructions. Write an analysis of each transaction and then prepare the necessary journal entry. An example of the type of analysis desired is as follows:

(1) (a) Advertising is an operating expense. Expenses are recorded by debits. Debit Advertising Expense $50.

(b) The asset Cash was decreased. Decreases in assets are recorded by credits. Credit Cash $50.

3B-2.   *Instructions.* Based on the following transactions,

a. Prepare journal entries.

b. Post to ledger accounts.

c. Prepare a trial balance as of September 30, 19___.

Data. The account titles and the account numbers to be used are:

Cash	*11*
Helicopter	*17*
Spare parts	*18*
Accounts payable	*21*
John Hyland, capital	*31*
John Hyland, personal	*32*
Admissions revenue	*41*
Maintenance expense	*52*
Gasoline expense	*53*
Salaries expense	*54*
Advertising expense	*55*

19__

Sept. 1. Mr. John Hyland deposited $30,000 cash in a bank account in the name of the business, the Helicopter Sight-seeing Service.

Sept. 3. Purchased a helicopter for $22,000 and spare parts for $2,000, paying cash.

Sept. 4. Paid $400 cash for an advertisement in the *Sunday News.*

Sept. 10. Cash receipts from passengers for the first ten days amounted to $1,150.

Sept. 11. Paid $200 to Aero Maintenance Service for maintenance and repair service for September.

Sept. 15. Paid $600 to employees for services rendered during the first half of September.

Sept. 20. Cash receipts from passengers for the second ten days amounted to $1,350.

Sept. 22. Placed another advertisement in the *Sunday News* for $425, to be paid before October 10.

Sept. 30. Paid $600 to employees for services rendered during the second half of September.

Sept. 30. Received a gasoline bill from Aero Gas Company amounting to $375, to be paid before October 10.

Sept. 30. Mr. Hyland withdrew $700 from the business for his personal use.

Sept. 30. Cash receipts from passengers for the last ten days of September amounted to $1,750.

3B-3. The Collegian Trio was organized on April 1, 19__, by Mr. James Ellington, to provide music at social functions. The following transactions were for the month of April. Note: James Ellington was the sole owner of the business; the other members of the Trio were salaried employees and had no equity in the enterprise.

19__

Apr. 1. Mr. Ellington deposited $1,500 cash in a bank account in the name of the business, the Collegian Trio.

Apr. 2. Purchased musical instruments from Musik, Incorporated, for $1,500. Cash down payment of $750 was made, the balance to be paid in 60 days.

Apr. 3. Retained Music Booking Service as exclusive agents for the Collegian Trio. The arrangement called for a flat $50 monthly retainer fee plus

10% of gross fees earned, to be paid on the last day of every month. The $50 retainer fee was paid this day. (Debit Promotion Expense.)

Apr. 10. Fees from appearances before various organizations for the first ten days amounted to $550. Cash was collected.

Apr. 15. Purchased a used station wagon for $1,000, paying cash.

Apr. 20. Fees from appearances for the second ten days amounted to $500. Cash was collected.

Apr. 28. Signed an agreement with Hilltop Country Club to provide music for the regular Saturday dances and also at other parties (not to exceed two per month) scheduled by the club. The agreement covered a period of six months beginning May 1, and provided for a maximum cost to the club of $750 monthly. The agreement was arranged by Music Booking Service.

Apr. 30. Paid gasoline bill for the month, $45.

Apr. 30. Paid $600 to the two employee-members in the Trio for their services rendered during the month.

Apr. 30. Fees from appearances for the last ten days of April amounted to $520. Cash was collected.

Apr. 30. Paid Music Booking Service 10% of the gross fees earned during the month.

Apr. 30. Mr. Ellington withdrew $300 for his personal use.

Instructions

a. Journalize the above transactions. (Number journal pages, to permit cross reference to ledger.)

b. Post to ledger accounts. (Number accounts consecutively, beginning with No. 11.)

c. Prepare a trial balance as of April 30, 19___.

3B-4. Gray Music Conservatory was organized on January 1, 19___, offering instruction to students of music. The following list of account balances on January 31, 19___, is in alphabetical order.

Accounts payable	$ 110
Accounts receivable	35
Accumulated depreciation: building	25
Accumulated depreciation: musical instruments	50
Advertising expense	75
Bruce Gray, capital	10,000
Bruce Gray, drawing	400
Building	15,000
Cash	777
Depreciation expense: building	25
Depreciation expense: musical instruments	50
Land	5,000
Musical instruments	3,000
Notes payable	14,000
Salaries expense	600
Telephone expense	12
Tuition revenue	824
Utilities expense	35

Instructions

a. Prepare a trial balance, rearranging the above accounts in the customary sequence of ledger accounts.

b. Prepare an income statement for the month ended January 31, 19___, and a balance sheet in report form.

3B-5. The trial balance for Pico Auto Repair Shop on March 31, 19___, and other pertinent data are presented below. This repair business was organized on January 1, 19___.

PICO AUTO REPAIR SHOP
Trial Balance
March 31, 19___

Cash	$ 695	
Accounts receivable	200	
Land	3,500	
Building	9,600	
Accumulated depreciation: building		$ 80
Repair equipment	2,100	
Accumulated depreciation: repair equipment ..		70
Notes payable		6,000
Accounts payable		150
Lee Davis, capital		10,000
Lee Davis, personal	400	
Repair services revenue		1,025
Advertising expense	20	
Repair parts expense	150	
Utilities expense	35	
Wages expense	625	
	$17,325	$17,325

Other data

(1) The useful life of the building was estimated at 20 years.

(2) The useful life of repair equipment was estimated at five years.

Instructions

a. Prepare adjusting entries needed at March 31.

b. Prepare an adjusted trial balance.

c. Prepare an income statement for the month ended March 31, 19___, and a balance sheet in report form.

3B-6. John Jackson received his D.D.S. degree in June, 19___, and set up his own dental practice on July 1. A trial balance as of July 31, 19___, and other data are shown below.

JOHN JACKSON, D.D.S.
Trial Balance
July 31, 19___

Cash	$ 1,180	
Government bonds	300	
Accounts receivable	500	
Land	5,000	
Building	9,000	
Dental equipment	4,320	
Office equipment	2,400	
Notes payable		$12,640
Accounts payable		125
John Jackson, capital		9,500
John Jackson, drawing	500	
Professional fees earned		2,070
Building maintenance expense	35	
Dental supplies expense	175	
Electricity expense	15	
Salaries expense	850	
Telephone expense	60	
	$24,335	$24,335

Other data. The useful life of the building was estimated at 15 years; of dental equipment, 6 years; of office equipment, 10 years.

Instructions
a. Prepare adjusting entries at July 31.
b. Prepare an adjusted trial balance at July 31.
c. Prepare an income statement, and a balance sheet in report form.
d. Prepare closing entries.
e. Prepare an after-closing trial balance.

3B-7. Thomas Stewart, M.D., after several years with a hospital, set up his own practice on July 1, 19___. The following transactions were for the month of July:

19___
July 1.   Thomas Stewart deposited $6,000 cash in a bank account in the name of his practice, Thomas Stewart, M.D.
July 1.   Paid office rent for the month, $250.
July 2.   Purchased medical instruments from Medic Manufacturing Company at a cost of $8,640. A cash down payment of $4,000 was made, the balance to be paid in 60 days.
July 3.   Purchased office equipment at a cost of $1,200, paying cash.
July 4.   Retained by Queen Nursery School as a medical consultant at a monthly fee of $30. Fee for the month of July was collected in cash.
July 10.   Cash fees from patients for the first ten days amounted to $325.
July 12.   Treated Mr. Jeffrey Jefferson, fees amounting to $35 to be paid by August 10.

July 15.   Paid Mrs. Charles Young, R.N., her salary for the first half of the
           month, $200.
July 20.   Cash fees from patients for the second ten days amounted to $360.
July 28.   Treated Mr. Gregory Holmes, who paid $10 cash and agreed to pay
           the balance of $40 by September 1.
July 30.   Cash fees from patients from July 21 to July 30 amounted to $415.
           This figure did not include Mr. Holmes's payment on July 28.
July 31.   Paid Mrs. Young $200, her salary for the second half of the month.
July 31.   Received a bill of $185 from Medical Supplies Company, representing
           the amount of medical supplies used during the month. (Debit Medical
           Supplies Expense.)
July 31.   Paid telephone bill for the month, $15.
July 31.   Dr. Stewart withdrew $600 for his personal use.

Other data. Dr. Stewart estimated the useful life of medical instruments at
8 years, of office equipment at 10 years.

Instructions

a. Journalize the above transactions. (Number journal pages to permit
cross reference to ledger.)

b. Post to ledger accounts. (Number ledger accounts to permit cross reference to journal.)

c. Prepare a trial balance as of July 31, 19___.

d. Prepare adjusting entries and post to ledger accounts.

e. Prepare an adjusted trial balance.

f. Prepare an income statement, and a balance sheet in report form.

g. Prepare closing entries, post to ledger accounts, and rule off accounts
having zero balances.

h. Prepare an after-closing trial balance.

4

End-of-period adjustments

Management makes many important decisions on the basis of information reported in financial statements. Decisions to expand production, to borrow money, to acquire new plant and equipment, and to pay dividends are typical of the key moves made in reliance upon the information shown in the income statement and balance sheet. Groups other than management also take action based upon this information. Investors decide to buy or sell securities after a close study of financial statements. Bankers approve or reject applications for loans after intensive study of the financial statements of companies seeking credit. To serve the needs of management, investors, bankers, and other groups, financial statements must be as complete and accurate as possible. The balance sheet must contain all the assets and liabilities at the close of business on the last day of the period. The income statement must contain all the revenue and expenses applicable to the period covered but must not contain any revenue or expenses relating to the following period. In other words, a precise cutoff of transactions at the end of the period is essential to the preparation of accurate financial statements.

APPORTIONING TRANSACTIONS BETWEEN ACCOUNTING PERIODS

Some business transactions are begun and completed within a single accounting period, but many other transactions are begun in one accounting period and concluded in a later period. For example, a building purchased this year may last for 25 years; during each of those 25 years a fair share of the cost of the building should be recognized as expense. The making of adjusting entries to record the depreciation expense applicable to a given accounting period was illustrated in the preceding chapter. Let us now consider some other transactions which overlap two or more accounting periods and therefore require adjusting entries.

It is customary for fire insurance policies to cover a period of three years. The premium for the entire policy is paid in advance and the total amount paid is recorded as an asset. By means of adjusting entries at the end of each accounting period, one-third of the total premium is charged to expense each year. In other words, a payment for insurance protection in the future is an asset, but as the insurance protection is received the asset becomes expense. The accounting theory underlying this practice is similar to that described in Chapter 3, in which an office building was described as a "bundle of housing services" to be received over the life of the building. A principal difference between apportioning the cost of the building and apportioning the cost of the fire insurance policy to the periods benefited is that the useful life of the building is difficult to estimate, whereas the life of the fire insurance policy is known exactly. However, both examples illustrate the point that assets include costs incurred for the benefit of future periods, and that these assets become expense over the periods of their usefulness.

Another common situation in which adjusting entries are required relates to the wages paid employees. Assume that employees are paid each Friday for the week ending that day, and assume further that the last day of the month falls on Wednesday. A month-end balance sheet should show among the liabilities the amount owed to employees for work performed on Monday, Tuesday, and Wednesday, the last three days of the month. The income statement for the month must also include the wages expense for the three workdays since the last payday.

Office supplies are often purchased in sufficient quantities to last for several months. For example, let us say that supplies sufficient to last for three months are purchased on January 1 at a cost of $600. It would not be reasonable to show the entire $600 as an expense in the January income statement and to show no supplies expense in the income statements for February and March. To do so would cause the net income for January to be understated and the net income for February and March to be overstated. The $600 paid for supplies benefits the business during the three months the supplies are *used*. The element of expense is associated with the using of supplies rather than with the act of purchase or of payment. In the language of the accountant, *the cost of $600 expires and becomes expense as the supplies are used.* The unused supplies on hand at the end of each month should appear on the balance sheet as an asset because they represent *unexpired costs* which will provide benefits to the business in future periods.

PRINCIPAL TYPES OF TRANSACTIONS
REQUIRING ADJUSTING ENTRIES

The various kinds of transactions requiring adjusting entries at the end of the period may be classified into the following groups:

1. Recorded costs which must be apportioned between two or more accounting periods. Example: the cost of a building.

2. Recorded revenue which must be apportioned between two or more accounting periods. Example: commissions collected in advance for services to be rendered in future periods.

3. Unrecorded expenses. Example: wages earned by employees after the last payday in an accounting period.

4. Unrecorded revenue. Example: commissions earned but not yet collected or billed to customers.

To demonstrate these various types of adjusting entries, the illustration of the Roberts Real Estate Company will be continued for November.

Recorded costs apportioned between accounting periods

When a business concern makes an expenditure that will benefit more than one period, the amount is usually debited to an asset account. At the end of each period which benefits from the expenditure, an appropriate portion of the cost is transferred from the asset account to an expense account.

Insurance. On November 1, the Roberts Real Estate Company paid $180 for a three-year fire insurance policy covering the building. This expenditure was debited to an asset account by the following journal entry:

<table>
<tr><td>EXPENDI-
TURE FOR
INSURANCE
POLICY
RECORDED
AS ASSET</td><td>*Unexpired Insurance* *180*
    Cash *180*
Purchased three-year fire insurance policy.</td></tr>
</table>

Since this expenditure of $180 will protect the company against fire loss for three years, the cost of protection each year is $\frac{1}{3}$ of $180, or $60. The insurance expense applicable to each month's operations is $\frac{1}{12}$ of the annual expense, or $5. In order that the accounting records for November show insurance expense of $5, the following adjusting entry is required at November 30:

<table>
<tr><td>PORTION
OF ASSET
EXPIRES
(BECOMES
EXPENSE)</td><td>*Insurance Expense* *5*
    Unexpired Insurance *5*
To record insurance expense for November.</td></tr>
</table>

This adjusting entry serves two purposes: (1) it apportions the proper amount of insurance expense to November operations, and (2) it reduces the asset account so that the correct amount of unexpired insurance will appear in the balance sheet at November 30. After this adjusting entry has been posted, the two ledger accounts relating to insurance are:

ASSET AND EXPENSE ACCOUNTS FOR INSURANCE

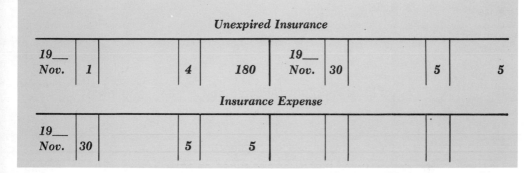

One of the best ways to gain an understanding of adjusting entries is to analyze each adjustment by considering its effect on the financial statements, and also by visualizing the errors which would exist in these statements if the adjustment were not made. What would be the effect on the income statement for November if the above adjustment were not made? The expenses would be understated by $5 and consequently the net income would be overstated $5. The balance sheet would also be affected by failure to make the adjustment: the assets would be overstated by $5 and so would the owner's equity. The overstatement of the owner's equity would result from the overstated amount of net income transferred to Mr. Roberts's capital account when the books were closed at November 30.

Office supplies. On November 2, the Roberts Real Estate Company purchased a sufficient quantity of stationery and other office supplies to last for several months. The cost of the supplies was $240, and this amount was debited to an asset account by the following journal entry.

EXPENDITURE FOR OFFICE SUPPLIES RECORDED AS ASSET

Office Supplies	*240*	
Cash		*240*
Purchased office supplies.		

No entries were made during November to record the day-to-day usage of office supplies, but on November 30 a careful count was made of the supplies still on hand. This count, or physical inventory, showed unused supplies with a cost of $200. It is apparent, therefore, that supplies costing $40 were used during November. An adjusting entry is made on the basis of the November 30 count, debiting an expense account $40 (the cost of supplies consumed during November), and reducing the asset account by $40 to show that only $200 worth of office supplies remained on hand at November 30.

<table>
<tr><td rowspan="4">PORTION OF
SUPPLIES
USED
REPRESENTS
EXPENSE</td><td>*Office Supplies Expense* .... 40</td><td></td></tr>
<tr><td>*Office Supplies* ....</td><td>40</td></tr>
<tr><td>*To record consumption of office supplies in November.*</td><td></td></tr>
</table>

The two ledger accounts affected now appear as follows:

Office Supplies

| 19__
Nov. | 2 | | 4 | 240 | 19__
Nov. | 30 | | 5 | 40 |

Office Supplies Expense

| 19__
Nov. | 30 | | 5 | 40 | | | | | |

The Office Supplies account will appear in the balance sheet as an asset; the Office Supplies Expense account will be shown in the income statement. How would failure to make this adjustment affect the financial statement? In the income statement for November, the expenses would be understated by $40 and the net income overstated by the same amount. Since the overstated amount for net income in November would be transferred into the owner's capital account in the process of closing the books, the owner's equity section of the balance sheet would be overstated by $40. Assets would, of course, also be overstated because Office Supplies would be listed at $40 too much.

Depreciation of building. The November 30 journal entry to record depreciation of the building used by the Roberts Real Estate Company is exactly the same as the October 31 entry explained in Chapter 3.

<table>
<tr><td rowspan="5">COST OF
BUILDING IS
GRADUALLY
CONVERTED
TO
EXPENSE</td><td>*Depreciation Expense: Building* .... 50</td><td></td></tr>
<tr><td>*Accumulated Depreciation: Building* ....</td><td>50</td></tr>
<tr><td>*To record depreciation for November.*</td><td></td></tr>
</table>

This allocation of depreciation expense to November operations is based on the following facts: the building cost $12,000 and is estimated

END-OF-PERIOD ADJUSTMENTS **105**

RELATED ACCOUNTS FOR BUILDING AND DEPRECIATION
to have a useful life of 20 years (240 months). Using the straight-line method of depreciation, the portion of the original cost which expires each month is $\frac{1}{240}$ of $12,000, or $50. After the adjusting entry has been posted, the ledger accounts for the building, the accumulated depreciation, and the depreciation expense appear as follows:

Building

19—			1	12,000						
Sept.	5									

Accumulated Depreciation: Building

					19—					
					Oct.	31		2		50
					Nov.	30		5		50

Depreciation Expense: Building

19—					19—					
Oct.	31		2	50	Oct.	31		3		50
Nov.	30		5	50						

The Accumulated Depreciation: Building account now has a credit balance of $100 as a result of the October and November credits of $50 each. The book value of the building is $11,900, that is, the original cost of $12,000 minus the accumulated depreciation of $100. The term *book value* means the net amount at which an asset is shown in the accounting records, as distinguished from its market value. *Carrying value* is an alternative term, with the same meaning as book value.

Depreciation of office equipment. The November 30 adjusting entry to record depreciation of the office equipment is the same as the entry for depreciation a month earlier, as shown in Chapter 3.

COST OF OFFICE EQUIPMENT IS GRADUALLY CONVERTED TO EXPENSE

Depreciation Expense: Office Equipment 15
   Accumulated Depreciation: Office Equipment . . 15
To record depreciation for November.

Original cost of the office equipment was $1,800, and the estimated useful life was 10 years (120 months). Depreciation each month under the straight-line method is therefore $\frac{1}{120}$ of $1,800, or $15. After this adjusting entry has been posted, the asset account, the accumulated depreciation account, and the depreciation expense account appear as:

RELATED
ACCOUNTS
FOR OFFICE
EQUIPMENT
AND DEPRE-
CIATION

Office Equipment								
19__ Sept.	14		1	1,800				

Accumulated Depreciation: Office Equipment								
				19__ Oct.	31		2	15
				Nov.	30		5	15

Depreciation Expense: Office Equipment							
19__ Oct.	31		2	15	*19__* Oct.	31		3	15
Nov.	30		5	15				

What is the book value of the office equipment at this point? Original cost of $1,800 minus accumulated depreciation of $30 leaves a book value of $1,770.

What would be the effect on the financial statements if the adjusting entries for depreciation of the building and office equipment were omitted at November 30? In the income statement the expenses would be understated by $65 ($50 depreciation of building and $15 depreciation of office equipment), and net income for the month would be overstated by $65. In the balance sheet the assets would be overstated by $65; the owner's equity would be overstated the same amount because of the $65 overstatement of the net income added to the capital account. If depreciation had not been recorded in either October or November, the overstatement in the balance sheet at November 30 would, of course, amount to $130 with respect both to assets and to owner's equity.

Recorded revenue apportioned between accounting periods

On November 1, Mr. James Fortune, a client of the Roberts Real Estate Company, asked Mr. Roberts to accept the responsibility of managing a considerable amount of rental properties. The duties consisted of keeping the buildings rented, arranging for repairs, and collecting rents which were to be deposited in Mr. Fortune's bank account. It was agreed that $100 a month would be a reasonable fee to the Roberts Real Estate Company for its services. Since Mr. Fortune was leaving the country on an extended trip, he paid the company for six months' service in advance at the time of signing the agreement. The journal entry to record the transaction on November 1 was as follows:

COMMISSION
COLLECTED
BUT NOT
YET EARNED

Cash *600*
        Unearned Rental Commissions *600*
*Collected in advance six months' commissions for man-
agement of Fortune properties.*

Notice that no service had been performed for the customer at the
time the $600 was received. As emphasized in Chapter 3, not every re-
ceipt of cash represents revenue. In this case the receipt of cash represented an advance payment by the customer which obligated the Roberts
Real Estate Company to render services in the future. Revenue is earned
only by the *rendering* of services to a customer, or the *delivering* of goods
to him. A portion of the agreed services (1/6, to be exact) will be rendered
during November, but it would be unreasonable to regard the entire $600
as revenue of that month. The commission is earned gradually over a
period of six months as the Roberts Real Estate Company performs the
required services. The $600 collected in advance is therefore credited to
an *unearned revenue* account at the time of its receipt. Some accountants
prefer the alternative term *deferred revenue*. At the end of each month,
an amount of $100 will be transferred from unearned revenue to an earned
revenue account by means of an adjusting entry. The first in this series of

ENTRY TO
RECOGNIZE
EARNING OF
A PART OF
COMMISSION

transfers will be made at November 30 as follows:

Unearned Rental Commissions *100*
        Rental Commissions Earned *100*
*Commission earned from Fortune property management
in November.*

LEDGER
ACCOUNTS
FOR COM-
MISSIONS
UNEARNED
AND
EARNED

After this adjusting entry has been posted, the ledger accounts are:

Unearned Rental Commissions								
19__					19__			
Nov.	30			5	100	*Nov.*	1			4	600

Rental Commissions Earned								
					19__			
					Nov.	30			5	100

The $500 credit balance remaining in the Unearned Rental Commis-
sions account represents an obligation to render $500 worth of services
in future months; therefore, it belongs on the balance sheet in the liability

section. An unearned revenue account differs from other liabilities since it will ordinarily be settled by the rendering of services rather than by making a cash payment, but it is nevertheless a liability. The Rental Commissions Earned account is shown in the income statement as revenue for the month.

What would be the effect on the financial statements of omitting the adjustment of the Unearned Rental Commissions account at November 30? In the income statement, the revenue earned in November would be understated by $100, and consequently the net income would also be understated $100. In the balance sheet, the liabilities would be overstated $100 by showing Unearned Rental Commissions at $600 rather than $500; the owner's equity would be understated by $100 because of the understatement of net income added to the capital account at November 30.

Unrecorded expenses

Adjusting entries are necessary at the end of each accounting period to record any expenses which have been incurred but not recognized in the accounts. Salaries of employees and interest on borrowed money are common examples of expenses which accumulate day by day but which may not be recorded until the end of the period. These expenses are said to *accrue*, that is, to grow or accumulate.

Accrual of interest. On November 1, the Roberts Real Estate Company borrowed the sum of $1,000 from a bank. Banks require every borrower to sign a *promissory note*, that is, a formal, written promise to repay the amount borrowed plus interest at an agreed future date. (Various forms of notes in common use, the calculation of interest, and the accounting problems involved will be discussed more fully in Chapter 10.) The note signed by Mr. Roberts, with certain details omitted, is shown on page 109.

The note payable is a liability of the Roberts Real Estate Company, similar to an account payable but different in that a formal written promise to pay is required and interest is charged on the amount borrowed. A Notes Payable account is credited when the note is issued; the Notes Payable account will be debited three months later when the note is paid. Interest accrues throughout the life of the note payable, but it is not payable until the note matures on February 1. From the viewpoint of the bank making the loan, the note signed by Mr. Roberts is an asset, a note receivable. The revenues earned by banks consist largely of interest charged borrowers.

The journal entry made on November 1 to record the borrowing of $1,000 from the bank was as follows:

ENTRY WHEN BANK LOAN IS OBTAINED		
Cash	*1,000*	
Notes Payable		*1,000*
Obtained three-month, 6% loan from bank.		

NOTE PAYABLE ISSUED TO BANK

$1,000   Los Angeles, California   November 1, 19__

Three months .... after date .... I .... promise to pay

to the order of .... American National Bank

-------One thousand and no/100------- .... dollars

for value received, with interest at .... 6 per cent

Roberts Real Estate Company

By *James Roberts*

No payment of interest was made during November, but one month's interest expense, or $5 ($1,000 $\times$ 0.06 $\times$ $\frac{1}{12}$), was incurred during the month. The following adjusting entry is made at November 30 to charge November operations with one month's interest expense and also to record the amount of interest owed to the bank at the end of November.

ENTRY FOR INTEREST EXPENSE INCURRED IN NOVEMBER

Interest Expense 5
    Interest Payable 5
To record interest expense applicable to November.

RELATED ACCOUNTS FOR NOTE PAYABLE AND INTEREST

After this adjusting entry has been posted, the ledger accounts for notes payable, interest payable, and interest expense appear as follows:

Notes Payable

					19__ Nov.	1		4	1,000

Interest Payable

					19__ Nov.	30		5	5

Interest Expense

19__ Nov.	30		5	5					

The debit balance in the Interest Expense account will appear in the November income statement; the credit balances in the Interest Payable and Notes Payable accounts will be shown in the balance sheet as liabilities. These two liability accounts will remain on the books until the maturity date of the loan, at which time a cash payment to the bank will wipe out both the Notes Payable account and the Interest Payable account.

What would be the effect on the financial statements if the adjustment for accrued interest were omitted at November 30? In the income statement, the expenses would be understated $5, with the result that net income would be overstated by that amount. In the balance sheet, the liabilities would be understated $5 because of the omission of interest payable. The owner's equity would be overstated $5 because of the overstatement in the amount of the November net income added to the capital account.

Accrual of salary. On November 19, Mr. Roberts hired a salesman whose duties were to call on property owners and secure listings of property for sale or rent. The agreed salary was $75 a week for a five-day work week, payable each Friday; payment for the first week was made on Friday, November 24.

Assume that the last day of the accounting period, November 30, fell on Thursday. The salesman had worked four days since being paid the preceding Friday and therefore had earned $60 (⅘ × $75). In order that this $60 of November salary expense be reflected in the accounts before the financial statements are prepared, an adjusting entry is necessary at November 30.

SALARIES
EXPENSE
INCURRED
BUT UNPAID
AT NOVEM-
BER 30

Sales Salaries Expense 60	
Sales Salaries Payable	60
To record salary expense and related liability to salesman for last four days' work in November.	

LIABILITY
AND
EXPENSE
ACCOUNTS
FOR
SALARIES

After this adjusting entry has been posted, the ledger accounts appear as follows:

Sales Salaries Payable

				19__ Nov.	30	5	60

Sales Salaries Expense

19__ Nov.	24		4	75			
	30		5	60			

The debit balance in the Sales Salaries Expense account will appear as an expense in the November income statement; the credit balance in the Sales Salaries Payable account is the amount owing to the salesman for work performed during the last four days of November and will appear among the liabilities on the balance sheet at November 30.

The next regular payday for the salesman will be Friday, December 1, which is the first day of the new accounting period. Since the books were adjusted and closed on November 30, all the revenue and expense accounts have zero balances at the beginning of business on December 1. The payment of a week's salary to the salesman will be recorded by the following entry on December 1:

PAYMENT OF SALARIES INCURRED IN TWO ACCOUNTING PERIODS

Sales Salaries Payable	*60*	
Sales Salaries Expense	*15*	
Cash		*75*
Paid weekly salary to salesman.		

Notice that the net result of the November 30 accrual entry has been to split the salesman's weekly salary expense between November and December. Four days of the work week fell in November, so four days' pay, or $60, was recognized as November expense. One day of the work week fell in December so $15 was recorded as December expense.

What would be the effect on the financial statements if the adjusting entry to accrue sales salaries at November 30 were omitted? In the income statement, the expenses would be understated by $60, and as a result, net income would be overstated by that amount. In the balance sheet, liabilities would be understated by $60 through the omission of Sales Salaries Payable, and the owner's equity would be overstated $60 because of the error in November net income added to the capital account.

No accrual entry is necessary for office salaries in the Roberts Real Estate Company because Mr. Roberts regularly pays the office employees on the last working day of the month.

Unrecorded revenue

The treatment of unrecorded revenue is similar to that of unrecorded expenses. Any revenue which has been earned but not recorded during the accounting period should be recognized in the accounts by means of an adjusting entry, debiting an asset account and crediting a revenue account. *Accrued revenue* is a term often used to describe revenue which has been accumulating during the period but which has not been recorded prior to the closing date.

On November 16, the Roberts Real Estate Company entered into a management agreement with Henry Clayton, the owner of several office buildings. The company agreed to manage the Clayton properties for a commission of $80 a month, payable on the fifteenth of each month. No entry is made in the accounting records at the time of signing the contract, because no services have yet been rendered and no change has occurred in assets or liabilities. The managerial duties were to begin immediately, but the first monthly commission would not be received until December 15. The following adjusting entry is therefore necessary at November 30:

ENTRY FOR COMMISSIONS EARNED BUT UNCOLLECTED

Rental Commissions Receivable 40	
Rental Commissions Earned	40
To record revenue accrued from services rendered Henry Clayton during November.	

After this adjusting entry has been posted, the two ledger accounts affected appear as follows:

LEDGER ACCOUNTS

Rental Commissions Receivable

19___								
Nov.	30		5	40				

Rental Commissions Earned

			19___				
			Nov.	30		5	100
				30		5	40

The debit balance in the Rental Commissions Receivable account will be shown in the balance sheet as an asset. The credit balance of the Rental Commission Earned account, including earnings from both the Fortune and Clayton contracts, will appear in the November income statement.

The collection of the first monthly commission from Mr. Clayton will occur in the next accounting period (December 15, to be exact). One-half of this $80 cash receipt represents collection of the asset account, Rental Commissions Receivable, created at November 30 by the adjusting entry. The other half of the $80 cash receipt represents revenue earned during December; this should be credited to the December revenue account for Rental Commissions Earned. The entry on December 15 is as follows:

COLLECTION OF COMMISSION APPLICABLE TO TWO ACCOUNTING PERIODS

Cash 80	
Rental Commissions Receivable	40
Rental Commissions Earned	40
Collected commission for month ended December 15.	

The net result of the November 30 accrual entry has been to divide the revenue from managing the Clayton properties between November and December in accordance with the timing of the services rendered. What would be the effect on the financial statements if the adjusting entry to accrue commissions earned at November 30 were omitted? In the income statement, the revenue would be understated by $40 and consequently net income would be understated by that amount. In the balance sheet, assets would be understated through the omission of Rental Commissions Receivable, and the owner's equity would be understated $40 because of the understatement of November net income added to the capital account.

RELATIONSHIP OF ADJUSTING ENTRIES
TO THE ENTIRE ACCOUNTING PROCESS

To give an over-all picture of adjusting entries and to show their relationship to the rest of the accounting process, a complete illustration of the November transactions of the Roberts Real Estate Company is now presented. The illustration is divided into the following sections:

1. A journal page containing entries for the November operating transactions
2. A trial balance showing the balances of ledger accounts after the journal entries for operating transactions had been posted
3. A journal page containing the *adjusting entries* required at the end of the month

NOVEMBER ENTRIES WITH EXCEPTION OF MONTH-END ADJUST-MENTS

4. An *adjusted trial balance* showing the balances of the ledger accounts after the *adjusting entries* had been posted
5. Financial statements that are prepared from the *adjusted trial balance*

Journal entries for November operating transactions

		Journal		*(Page 4)*
19___				
Nov.	1	*Unexpired Insurance*	*180*	
		Cash		*180*
		Purchased three-year fire insurance policy.		
	1	*Cash*	*600*	
		Unearned Rental Commissions		*600*
		Collected in advance six months' commissions for management of Fortune properties.		

		Journal		(Page 4)

19__				
Nov.	1	Cash	1,000	
		Notes Payable		1,000
		Obtained three-month loan from bank, 6% per annum.		
	2	Office Supplies	240	
		Cash		240
		Purchased office supplies.		
	8	Accounts Payable	48	
		Cash		48
		Paid the October telephone bill.		
	14	Accounts Payable	90	
		Cash		90
		Paid October advertising bill.		
	17	Cash	1,828	
		Sales Commissions Earned		1,828
		Earned and collected commissions on sales.		
	24	Sales Salaries Expense	75	
		Cash		75
		Paid weekly salary to salesman.		
	25	Advertising Expense	425	
		Cash		425
		Paid for November newspaper advertising.		
	26	James Roberts, Drawing	500	
		Cash		500
		Withdrawal by proprietor.		
	30	Office Salaries Expense	400	
		Cash		400
		Paid office salaries for November.		
	30	Telephone Expense	65	
		Accounts Payable		65
		To record telephone expense for November.		

Trial balance before adjustments. The following trial balance was prepared from the ledger after all transactions for November had been posted, but before any adjusting entries had been recorded.

FIVE
KINDS OF
ACCOUNTS
IN THIS
TRIAL
BALANCE

ROBERTS REAL ESTATE COMPANY
Trial Balance
November 30, 19___

Cash	$ 8,600	
Accounts receivable	2,330	
Unexpired insurance	180	
Office supplies	240	
Land	5,000	
Building	12,000	
Accumulated depreciation: building		$ 50
Office equipment	1,800	
Accumulated depreciation: office equipment		15
Notes payable		1,000
Accounts payable		7,865
Unearned rental commissions		600
James Roberts, capital		20,257
James Roberts, drawing	500	
Sales commissions earned		1,828
Advertising expense	425	
Office salaries expense	400	
Sales salaries expense	75	
Telephone expense	65	
	$31,615	$31,615

ADJUST-
MENTS
MAKE
REVENUE
AND
EXPENSE
ACCOUNTS
COMPLETE
AND UP TO
DATE

Journal entries for end-of-period adjustments. The adjusting entries previously explained in this chapter are now presented as a group.

		Journal		*(Page 5)*
19___				
Nov.	30	Insurance Expense	5	
		Unexpired Insurance		5
		To record insurance expense for November.		
	30	Office Supplies Expense	40	
		Office Supplies		40
		To record consumption of office supplies during November.		
	30	Depreciation Expense: Building	50	
		Accumulated Depr.: Building		50
		To record depreciation for November.		
	30	Depreciation Expense: Office Equipment	15	
		Accumulated Depr.: Office Equipment		15
		To record depreciation for November.		
	30	Unearned Rental Commissions	100	
		Rental Commissions Earned		100
		Commissions earned for Fortune property management in November.		

Journal				(Page 5)
19__ Nov.	30	Interest Expense	5	
		Interest Payable		5
		Interest expense accrued during November.		
	30	Sales Salaries Expense	60	
		Sales Salaries Payable		60
		To record salary expense and related liability to sales-man for last four days' work in November.		
	30	Rental Commissions Receivable	40	
		Rental Commissions Earned		40
		To record revenue earned from services rendered Henry Clayton in November.		

Adjusted trial balance. The following adjusted trial balance was pre-pared from the ledger after the adjusting entries of November 30:

THESE
AMOUNTS
WILL
APPEAR IN
FINANCIAL
STATEMENTS

ROBERTS REAL ESTATE COMPANY
Adjusted Trial Balance
November 30, 19__

Cash	$ 8,600	
Accounts receivable	2,330	
Rental commissions receivable	40	
Unexpired insurance	175	
Office supplies	200	
Land	5,000	
Building	12,000	
Accumulated depreciation: building		$ 100
Office equipment	1,800	
Accumulated depreciation: office equipment ...		30
Notes payable		1,000
Accounts payable		7,865
Interest payable		5
Sales salaries payable		60
Unearned rental commissions		500
James Roberts, capital		20,257
James Roberts, drawing	500	
Sales commissions earned		1,828
Rental commissions earned		140
Advertising expense	425	
Office supplies expense	40	
Office salaries expense	400	
Sales salaries expense	135	
Telephone expense	65	
Depreciation expense: building	50	
Depreciation expense: office equipment	15	
Interest expense	5	
Insurance expense	5	
	$31,785	$31,785

As previously explained, the trial balance and the adjusted trial balance are not financial statements and are not intended for use by management or outsiders. Trial balances are merely working tools used by the accountant to prove the equality of debits and credits in the ledger and to assemble the information which will appear in the financial statements.

Financial statements. *Income statement.* The following income statement was prepared by using the balances of the revenue and expense accounts in the adjusted trial balance.

ROBERTS REAL ESTATE COMPANY
Income Statement
For the Month Ended November 30, 19___

Revenue:

Sales commissions earned	$1,828
Rental commissions earned	140
Total revenue	$1,968

Expenses:

Advertising	$425	
Office supplies	40	
Office salaries	400	
Sales salaries	135	
Telephone	65	
Depreciation: building	50	
Depreciation: office equipment	15	
Interest	5	
Insurance	5	
Total expenses		1,140
Net income		$ 828

This income statement shows that the revenues during November exceeded the expenses and that the company earned a net income for the month. The form and arrangement of an income statement are the same, regardless of whether the final figure represents net income or a net loss.

Balance sheet and statement of owner's equity. The balance sheets previously illustrated have shown in the owner's equity section the changes during the month caused by the owner's withdrawals and by the net income or loss from operation of the business. A separate statement, illustrated on page 118, is sometimes used to show changes in the owner's equity during the period. When a separate statement is used, only the ending amount of the owner's capital account is shown in the balance sheet. The separate statement showing changes in the owner's equity may be used with either the account form or the report form of balance sheet. In this illustration, the report form of balance sheet is used.

ROBERTS REAL ESTATE COMPANY
Statement of Owner's Equity
For the Month Ended November 30, 19___

James Roberts, capital, Nov. 1, 19___		$20,257
Add: Net income for November	$828	
Less withdrawals	500	
Increase in capital		328
James Roberts, capital, Nov. 30, 19___		$20,585

ROBERTS REAL ESTATE COMPANY
Balance Sheet
November 30, 19___

Assets

Cash		$ 8,600
Accounts receivable		2,330
Rental commissions receivable		40
Unexpired insurance		175
Office supplies		200
Land		5,000
Building	$12,000	
Less: accumulated depreciation	100	11,900
Office equipment	$ 1,800	
Less: accumulated depreciation	30	1,770
		$30,015

Liabilities and Owner's Equity

Liabilities:		
Notes payable	$ 1,000	
Accounts payable	7,865	
Interest payable	5	
Sales salaries payable	60	
Unearned rental commissions	500	
Total liabilities		$ 9,430
Owner's equity:		
James Roberts, capital		$20,585
		$30,015

Effect of adjusting entries on the financial statements

The effect of each adjusting entry on the financial statements has already been pointed out in explaining the individual adjustments. However, the importance of the adjusting entries in developing a complete picture of the revenues and expenses may be better appreciated by considering the illustrated income statement as a whole. If the adjustments had not been made, an income statement prepared from the ledger accounts would have given a very different and a very misleading picture of the results achieved by the business during November. The entire amount of rental commissions earned was set up by an adjusting entry. Also the expense accounts for office supplies, depreciation, interest, and insurance were created by adjusting entries, and the sales salaries expense account was increased by an adjusting entry. In summary, we can say that the adjusting entries played a large part in developing the statement showing the operating results for the month.

The impact of adjustments on the balance sheet was also substantial. The asset accounts for rental commissions receivable, unexpired insurance, and office supplies were all created or changed in amount by adjusting entries. In addition, accumulated depreciation, or asset valuation accounts, were increased by the month-end adjustments. Three of the five liability accounts were created or changed by adjusting entries, and of course the owner's capital account was affected because it included the November net income, which was computed after giving effect to the adjustments.

The purpose of adjusting entries is to make possible the preparation of accurate and complete financial statements. Since the balance sheet and the income statement are merely a rearrangement of the amounts in the adjusted trial balance, it is clear that adjusting entries are an essential step in producing statements that reflect fairly the financial condition and operating results.

LOCATING ERRORS

In the illustrations given thus far, the trial balances have all been in balance. Every accounting student soon discovers in working problems, however, that errors are easily made which prevent trial balances from balancing. The lack of balance may be the result of a single error or a combination of several errors. An error may have been made in adding the trial balance columns or in copying the balances from the ledger accounts. If the preparation of the trial balance has been accurate, then the error may lie in the accounting records, either in the journal or in the ledger accounts. What is the most efficient approach to locating the error or errors? There is no single technique which will give the best results every time, but the following procedures, done in sequence, will often save considerable time and effort in locating errors.

1. Prove the addition of the trial balance columns by adding these columns in the opposite direction from that previously followed.

2. If the error does not lie in addition, next determine the exact amount by which the schedule is out of balance. The amount of the discrepancy is often a clue to the source of the error. If the discrepancy is divisible by 9, this suggests either a transposition error or a "slide." For example, assume that the cash account has a balance of $2,175, but in copying the balance into the trial balance the figures are transposed and written as $2,157. The resulting error is $18, and like all transposition errors is divisible by 9. Another common error is the "slide," or incorrect placement of the decimal point, as when $2,175.00 is copied as $21.75. The resulting discrepancy in the trial balance will also be an amount divisible by 9.

To illustrate another method of using the amount of a discrepancy as a clue to locating the error, assume that the Telephone Expense account has a *debit* balance of $34, but that it is erroneously listed in the *credit* column of the trial balance. This will cause a discrepancy of two times $34, or $68, in the trial balance totals. Since such errors as recording a debit in a credit column are not uncommon, it is advisable, after determining the discrepancy in the trial balance totals, to scan the columns for an amount equal to exactly one-half of the discrepancy. It is also advisable to look over the transactions for an item of the exact amount of the discrepancy. An error may have been made by recording the debit side of the transaction and forgetting to enter the credit side.

3. Trace each balance of a ledger account into the trial balance, making sure that it has been entered in the correct column.

4. Recompute the balance of each ledger account.

5. Trace all postings from the journal to the ledger accounts. As this is done, place a check mark in the journal and in the ledger after each figure verified. When the operation is completed, look through the journal and the ledger for unchecked amounts. In tracing postings, be alert not only for errors in amount but also for debits entered as credits, or vice versa.

QUESTIONS

1. The Property Management Company manages office buildings and apartment buildings for various owners who wish to be relieved of this responsibility. The revenues earned for this service are credited to Management Fees Earned. On December 1, the company received a check for $1,200 from a client, James Thurston, who was leaving for a six-month stay abroad. This check represented payment in advance for management of Mr. Thurston's real estate properties during the six months of his absence. Explain how this transaction would be recorded, the adjustment, if any, to be made at December 31, and the presentation of this matter in the year-end financial statements.

2. At the end of 1962, the adjusted trial balance of the Black Company showed the following account balances, among others: Depreciation Expense: Building, $1,580; Building, $31,600; Accumulated Depreciation: Building, $11,060. Assuming that straight-line depreciation has been used, what length of time do these facts suggest that the Black Company has owned the building?

3. The weekly payroll for salesmen of the Ryan Company amounts to $1,250. All salesmen are paid up to date at the close of business each Friday. If December 31 falls on Wednesday, what year-end adjusting entry is needed?

4. The Marvin Company purchased a three-year fire insurance policy on August 1 and debited the entire cost of $540 to Unexpired Insurance. The books were not adjusted or closed until the end of the year. Give the adjusting entry at December 31.

5. The net income reported by the Haskell Company for 1962 was $18,300, and the capital account of the owner, J. B. Haskell, stood at $36,000. However, the company had failed to recognize that interest amounting to $150 had accrued on a note payable to the bank. State the corrected figures for net income and for the owner's equity. In what other respect was the balance sheet of the company in error?

6. Office supplies on hand in the Melville Company amounted to $642 at the beginning of the year. During the year additional office supplies were purchased at a cost of $1,561 and charged to Inventory of Office Supplies. At the end of the year a physical count showed that supplies on hand amounted to $742. Give the adjusting entry needed at December 31.

7. The X Company at December 3 recognized the existence of certain unexpired costs which would provide benefits to the company in future periods. Give examples of such unexpired costs and state where they would be shown in the financial statements.

PROBLEMS

Group A

4A-1. *Instructions.* For each of the transactions for Variety Showcase, prepare a journal entry as of the transaction date, and an adjusting entry as of April 30, the end of a fiscal period.

Data

(1) On April 1, purchased a five-year fire insurance policy for $900.

(2) On April 1, purchased a public address system for $2,400. The useful life was estimated at five years.

(3) On April 2, tickets for Drama Subscription Series were sold for a total of $4,500. The series consisted of five different plays, scheduled to be presented as follows: Play A, April 10–17; play B, April 20–27; play C, May 4–10; play D, May 14–20; and play E, May 24–30.

(4) On April 3, purchased make-up supplies for $750. A physical count on April 30 showed unused supplies amounting to $380.

(5) On April 4, an agreement was reached with Miss Jane Roberts to give

six solo performances, April 28 to May 3, inclusive. Compensation was arranged at 20% of total box-office receipts for the six performances, to be paid in one lump sum after the sixth performance. Box office receipts for three performances ending April 30 amounted to $2,750. (Note: No entry is needed on April 4.)

(6) On April 15, borrowed $6,000 from the First National Bank, to be repaid two months later, plus interest computed at 6% a year. A promissory note was signed.

4A-2. *Instructions.* Based on the trial balance and other data, prepare adjusting entries. The firm closes its books every month.

Data

OLYMPIC STORAGE AND MOVING SERVICE
Trial Balance
May 31, 19___

Cash	$ 3,250	
Unexpired insurance	1,440	
Inventory of office supplies	125	
Trucks	8,400	
Accumulated depreciation: trucks		$ 700
Office equipment	1,320	
Accumulated depreciation: office equipment		44
Notes payable		4,000
Interest payable		80
Unearned storage fees		180
Olin Pick, capital		9,327
Olin Pick, drawings	425	
Storage fees earned		645
Moving service fees earned		2,655
Gasoline expense	485	
Rent expense	545	
Office salaries	350	
Drivers' salaries expense	1,255	
Telephone expense	36	
	$17,631	$17,631

Other data

(*a*) The monthly insurance expense amounted to $90.

(*b*) The amount of office supplies on hand, based on a physical count on May 31, was $47.

(*c*) Trucks were purchased on January 2 of the current year. The useful life was estimated at four years.

(*d*) Office equipment was purchased on January 2 of the current year. The useful life was estimated at 10 years.

(*e*) A $4,000 note was signed on January 2 as partial payment for trucks purchased. The liability was to be paid six months later, plus interest computed at 6% a year.

(*f*) Certain clients chose to pay several months' storage fees in advance.

Based on individual service records, it was determined that $125 of such fees was still unearned as of May 31.

(g) Based on individual service records, it was further determined that several clients neglected to send in their storage fees for the month of May, amounting to $65.

(h) Salaries earned by drivers but not paid amounted to $145.

4A-3. *Instructions.* Based on the trial balance and other data at June 30:

   a. Prepare adjusting entries.

   b. Post to ledger accounts.

   c. Prepare an adjusted trial balance.

   Data. The fiscal year of the Advance Advertising Agency ended on May 31.

ADVANCE ADVERTISING AGENCY
Trial Balance
June 30, 19___

Account
no.

11	*Cash*	$ 4,235	
14	*Prepaid rent*	1,800	
15	*Unexpired insurance*	576	
16	*Inventory of advertising supplies*	735	
17	*Inventory of office supplies*	110	
21	*Office equipment*	4,320	
22	*Accumulated depreciation: office equipment*		$ 225
31	*Accounts payable*		150
32	*Notes payable*		1,000
38	*Unearned advertising layout design fees*		1,500
41	*J. J. Johnson, capital*		8,776
42	*J. J. Johnson, drawings*	500	
51	*Advertising layout design fees earned*		1,800
52	*Advertising space commissions earned*		1,225
61	*Office salaries expense*	2,400	
		$14,676	$14,676

Other data

(1) The monthly rent was $450.

(2) The unexpired insurance was for a three-year fire insurance policy purchased on February 1 of the current year for $648.

(3) Based on a physical count on June 30, advertising supplies on hand amounted to $440, and office supplies on hand amounted to $25.

(4) Office equipment was purchased on January 2 of the current year. The useful life was estimated at eight years.

(5) Accrued interest expense on note payable amounted to $5 for the month of June.

(6) Fees considered as earned for miscellaneous advertising layout designs done as of June 30, which had not been billed or recorded, amounted to $1,325.

Of this amount, the sum of $775 was for clients who had made advance payments.

(7) Salaries earned by employees but not paid amounted to $240.

The additional ledger accounts (and account numbers) required by the adjusting entries are as follows:

13   *Advertising layout design fees receivable*
34   *Interest payable*
35   *Office salaries payable*
62   *Rent expense*
63   *Insurance expense*
64   *Advertising supplies expense*
65   *Office supplies expense*
66   *Depreciation expense: office equipment*
67   *Interest expense*

4A-4. The trial balances of Southern Insurance Agency before and after the posting of adjusting entries are shown below:

SOUTHERN INSURANCE AGENCY
Trial Balance
July 31, 19___

	Before adjustments		After adjustments	
Cash	$3,105		$3,105	
Commissions receivable			15	
Prepaid rent	600		400	
Inventory of office supplies	215		45	
Office equipment	2,400		2,400	
Accumulated depreciation: office equip.		$ 120		$ 140
Accounts payable		200		200
Note payable		1,500		1,500
Salaries payable				25
Interest payable				6
Unearned commissions		175		95
Samuel Gordon, capital		3,745		3,745
Samuel Gordon, drawings	300		300	
Commissions earned		1,485		1,580
Salaries expense	605		630	
Rent expense			200	
Office supplies expense			170	
Depreciation expense: office equipment			20	
Interest expense			6	
	$7,225	$7,225	$7,291	$7,291

Instructions. Determine what adjusting entries were made, and prepare these adjusting entries.

4A-5. *Instructions.* From the information given, prepare the following:

    a. Adjusting entries required at August 31

    b. An adjusted trial balance

    c. An income statement for the month ended August 31

    d. A balance sheet in report form

Data

PREVIEW THEATER
Trial Balance
August 31, 19___

Cash	$ 3,075	
Prepaid insurance	290	
Prepaid film rental	2,200	
Prepaid advertising	475	
Land	12,000	
Building	24,000	
Accumulated depreciation: building		$ 1,400
Notes payable		5,000
Unearned concessions revenue		1,500
Jack Owen, capital		31,725
Jack Owen, drawing	500	
Admissions revenue		3,500
Salaries expense	585	
	$43,125	$43,125

Other data

(1) A three-year fire insurance policy was purchased on January 2 of the current year for $360.

(2) Film rental expense for the month of August amounted to a total of $1,650.

(3) Advertising expense for the month amounted to $250.

(4) Building was purchased on January 2 of the current year. The useful life was estimated at 10 years.

(5) Interest expense on notes payable amounted to $25 for the month of August.

(6) Mr. John Brown, concessionaire, reported that net income from concessions for August amounted to $1,200. Preview Theater's share was 25%, as per agreement. This agreement also provided for semiannual advance payments by Mr. Brown based on estimates of future sales.

(7) Salaries earned by employees but not paid amounted to $115.

4A-6. The Downtown Window Cleaning Service, which was organized on September 1, carried out the following transactions during the month:

Sept. 1. Mr. Robert Chambers deposited $10,000 cash in a bank account in the name of the business, the Downtown Window Cleaning Service.

Sept. 1. Signed a lease for an office with monthly rent of $100. Rent for three months was paid in advance.

Sept. 1. Purchased a three-year insurance policy for $504.

Sept. 1. Purchased ladders and other equipment for a total of $2,400. A cash down payment of $1,400 was made, and a two-month note bearing interest at 6% per year was given for the balance. The equipment was estimated to have a useful life of 10 years.

Sept. 2. Purchased 100 one-minute spot radio advertisements from radio station KXQZ at $2.50 per spot announcement. The station was to report, at the end of each month, the number of spot announcements presented in that month.

Sept. 2. Purchased washing supplies for $520, paying cash.

Sept. 3. Signed a contract with the Midwestern Bank for window washing services for its office building at $75 per week. The bank paid $500 in advance.

Sept. 14. Cash received for services for the first two-week period amounted to $1,850, exclusive of the payment from the Midwestern Bank.

Sept. 14. Biweekly wages to employees amounted to $1,135.

Sept. 28. Cash received for services for the second two-week period amounted to $1,775.

Sept. 28. Biweekly wages to employees amounted to $1,030.

Sept. 30. Mr. Chambers withdrew $450 for personal use.

Other data

(1) A statement from radio station KXQZ noted that 44 one-minute spot announcements were made during September.

(2) Based on a physical count on September 30, the cost of washing supplies on hand amounted to $145.

(3) A statement was sent to the Midwestern Bank stating that five weekly services were rendered during the month of September.

(4) Services rendered to clients too late to be billed amounted to $125.

(5) Salaries earned by employees but not paid amounted to $95.

Instructions

a. Prepare journal entries for all the September transactions and post to ledger accounts. (Number journal pages and ledger accounts to permit cross reference.)

b. Prepare a trial balance as of September 30.

c. Prepare adjusting entries and post to ledger accounts. (Adjusting entries are required for rent, insurance, depreciation, and interest as well as for the items indicated by the data for adjustments.)

d. Prepare an adjusted trial balance.

e. Prepare financial statements.

f. Prepare closing entries, post to ledger accounts, and rule the accounts having zero balances.

g. Prepare an after-closing trial balance.

4A-7. *Instructions.* From the information given below concerning the Snow Summit Ski Resort, prepare the adjusting entries required at December 31.

Data

(1) Accrued property taxes, $725.

(2) Accrued wages payable, $1,100.

(3) Interest receivable on United States government bonds owned, $82.

(4) A tractor had been obtained on December 5 from Equipment Rentals, Inc., at a daily rate of $8. No rental payment had yet been made. Continued use of the tractor was expected through the month of January.

(5) A six-month bank loan in the amount of $15,000 had been obtained on November 1 at an annual interest rate of 6%. No interest expense recorded.

(6) A portion of the land owned had been leased to a riding stable at a yearly rental of $2,400. One year's rent was collected in advance at the date of the lease (December 16) and credited to Unearned Rental Revenue.

(7) Another portion of the land owned had been rented on December 1 to a service station operator at an annual rate of $1,800. No rent had as yet been collected from this tenant.

(8) On December 31, the Snow Summit Ski Resort signed an agreement to lease a truck from Gray Drive Ur-Self Company for the next calendar year at a rate of 20 cents for each mile of use.

(9) Depreciation on the ski lodge for the period ended December 31 was $800.

Group B

4B-1. *Instructions.* For each of the paragraphs from (1) through (7), write first the journal entry (if one is required) to record the transaction and secondly the adjusting entry, if any, required at October 31, the end of a fiscal period.

Data. Community Music Festival had the following transactions in October:

(1) On October 1, paid rent for six months at $200 per month.

(2) On October 1, purchased portable lighting equipment for $2,400. The useful life was estimated at four years.

(3) On October 2, season tickets to the Community Music Festival were sold for a total of $4,800. Four different programs were included in the festival, scheduled to be presented as follows: Program No. 1, October 15–16; Program No. 2, October 29–30; Program No. 3, November 5–6; and Program No. 4, November 19–20.

(4) On October 5, an agreement was reached with Mr. Peter Payne, allowing him to sell refreshments in the theater. In return for this privilege, Mr. Payne agreed to pay 5% of his gross receipts to the management within three days after the conclusion of each program.

(5) On October 6, four *Program Notes,* one for each of the four programs, were printed at a total cost of $380. Cash was paid.

(6) On October 19, received from Mr. Payne cash in the amount of $23.62, representing 5% of refreshment sales of $472.40 at Program No. 1.

(7) On October 31, Mr. Payne reported that total refreshment sales at Program No. 2 amounted to $503.60.

4B-2. *Instructions.* Based on the trial balance at December 31 and other data, prepare the adjusting entries needed at December 31, 1962.

Data. Glamour Photographic Salon was organized on January 1, 1962, and the first closing of the books was set for December 31.

GLAMOUR PHOTOGRAPHIC SALON
Trial Balance
December 31, 1962

Cash	$ 640	
Unexpired insurance	240	
Inventory of photographic films	1,505	
Inventory of chemical supplies	922	
Cameras	4,800	
Lighting equipment	840	
Notes payable		$ 3,000
Unearned wedding portrait fees		745
Eastman Cliffton, capital		2,119
Eastman Cliffton, drawing	3,325	
Fees earned		12,460
Rent expense	2,400	
Salaries expense	3,120	
Telephone expense	320	
Water and light expenses	212	
	$18,324	$18,324

Other data

(*a*) The insurance policy purchased at the beginning of business covered a period of three years.

(*b*) The amount of photographic films on hand on December 31 was valued at $225.

(*c*) The amount of chemical supplies on hand on December 31 was valued at $380.

(*d*) Cameras were purchased on January 1. The useful life was estimated at five years.

(*e*) Lighting equipment was purchased on January 1. The useful life was estimated at five years.

(*f*) A six-month bank loan was obtained on November 1 in the amount of $3,000, with interest at 6% per year.

(*g*) Customers ordering wedding portraits were requested to pay the estimated fees in advance. Based on individual orders, it was determined that $425 of these orders were unfilled on December 31.

(*h*) Salary earned by an assistant but not yet paid amounted to $80 on December 31.

4B-3. Western Market Research Service was organized on January 1, 19___, to render services in the Pacific Coast area. The firm closed its books every month. The following is the trial balance on April 30.

WESTERN MARKET RESEARCH SERVICE
Trial Balance
April 30, 19___

Cash	$ 1,947	
Prepaid rent	1,500	
Prepaid computer service expense	2,520	
Inventory of office supplies	285	
Office equipment	1,920	
Accumulated depreciation: office equipment		$ 48
Accounts payable		411
Unearned market research contracts		6,200
Unearned packaging design contracts		2,440
N. N. Nelson, capital		4,123
N. N. Nelson, personal	500	
Market research fees earned		415
Packaging design fees earned		202
Office salaries expense	350	
Research salaries expense	4,220	
Telephone expense	185	
Travel expense	412	
	$13,839	$13,839

Other data
(a) The monthly rent was $375.
(b) During the month, eight hours of computer time were used, at $120 per hour.
(c) Office supplies on hand on April 30 amounted to $35.
(d) Office equipment was purchased on January 1. The useful life was estimated at 10 years.
(e) Services rendered and chargeable to Unearned Market Research Contracts and Unearned Packaging Design Contracts during the month were $3,120 and $1,815, respectively.
(f) Market research services rendered for other clients and not yet billed amounted to $1,240.
(g) Salaries earned by researchers but not paid amounted to $320 on April 30.

Instructions
a. Prepare adjusting entries.
b. Prepare an adjusted trial balance.

4B-4. Trial balances of Electronic Tabulating Service before and after the posting of adjusting entries are shown below:

ELECTRONIC TABULATING SERVICE
Trial Balances
December 31, 19___

	Before adjustments Dr.	Cr.	After adjustments Dr.	Cr.
Cash	$ 2,711		$ 2,711	
Tabulating service fees receivable			665	
Prepaid office rent	2,400			
Prepaid accounting machine rental	2,400		1,800	
Inventory of office supplies	1,151		527	
Office equipment	3,600		3,600	
Accumulated depreciation: office equipment		$ 360		$ 720
Accounts payable		1,432		1,432
Notes payable		7,200		7,200
Interest payable				18
Salaries payable				161
Unearned tabulating service fees		1,875		440
James Mast, capital		3,051		3,051
James Mast, drawings	4,425		4,425	
Tabulating service fees earned		14,504		16,604
Maintenance expense	105		105	
Salaries expense	11,012		11,173	
Telephone expense	618		618	
Office rent expense			2,400	
Accounting machine rental expense			600	
Office supplies expense			624	
Depreciation expense: office equipment			360	
Interest expense			18	
	$28,422	$28,422	$29,626	$29,626

By comparison of the two trial balances, it is possible to determine what year-end adjusting entries were made.

Instructions. Write out these adjusting entries.

4B-5. Mr. Stanley Preston organized his own engineering consulting firm on July 1, 1962. At December 31, 1962, when the books were to be closed for the first time, the following trial balance was prepared.

PRESTON ENGINEERING CONSULTING SERVICE
Trial Balance
December 31, 1962

Cash	$ 7,030	
Prepaid office rent	6,000	
Prepaid professional dues	270	
Inventory of drafting supplies	1,000	
Drafting equipment	4,800	
Notes payable		$ 3,000
Unearned consulting service fees		11,000
Stanley Preston, capital		13,600
Stanley Preston, drawing	4,200	
Consulting service fees earned		8,400
Salaries expense	11,500	
Miscellaneous expense	1,200	
	$36,000	$36,000

Other data

(*a*) Office rent for one year was paid on July 1, when the lease was signed.

(*b*) A three-year membership in a professional engineering society had been paid for on July 1 in the amount of $270.

(*c*) Drafting supplies on hand on December 31 amounted to $120.

(*d*) Drafting equipment was purchased on July 1. The useful life was estimated at 10 years.

(*e*) Accrued interest expense on notes payable was $30 as of December 31.

(*f*) A number of clients obtained during the first six months of the company's operations had made advance payments for consulting services to be rendered over a considerable period. As of December 31, value of services rendered and chargeable against Unearned Consulting Service Fees $8,500.

(*g*) Services rendered and chargeable to other clients amounted to $1,100 as of December 31. No entries had yet been made to record the services performed for these clients.

(*h*) Salaries earned by staff engineers but not yet paid amounted to $500 on December 31.

Instructions

a. Prepare adjusting entries as of December 31, 1962.

b. Prepare an adjusted trial balance. (Note: You may find the use of T accounts helpful in computing the account balances after adjustments.)

c. Prepare an income statement for the six-month period ended December 31, 1962, a statement of owner's equity, and a balance sheet.

4B-6. Spencer Brown, after several years with a leading architect, set up his own office on April 1, 19___, known as Brown and Associates, Architects. The following transactions occurred in April:

Apr. 1.   Spencer Brown deposited $10,000 cash in a bank account in the name of the firm, Brown and Associates, Architects.

Apr. 1.   Signed a lease for an office, monthly rent at $250. Rent for six months was paid at the time of signing.

Apr. 1. Purchased drafting equipment for $6,000. A cash down payment of $4,000 was made and a non-interest-bearing note issued for the balance. The equipment was estimated to have a useful life of 10 years.

Apr. 1. Purchased a one-year insurance policy for $180; cash was paid.

Apr. 2. Signed a design contract with Mr. and Mrs. Theodore Dillon for $1,800. Mr. Dillon paid the full amount at the time of signing. It was estimated that the design might take several months to complete.

Apr. 3. Purchased drafting supplies at a total cost of $500; cash was paid.

Apr. 4. Signed a design contract with Mr. and Mrs. Charles Walker for $250; cash was collected. It was estimated that the design would take three to five days to complete.

Apr. 8. Signed a contract with Mr. and Mrs. Randolph Taylor for a design of their new home, the total fee being 5% of the estimated construction cost of $50,000. No payment was to be made until the services had been performed.

Apr. 16. Paid staff architects the semimonthly salaries of $600.

Apr. 25. Signed a design contract with Mr. and Mrs. John Hartman for $2,200. Mr. Hartman paid $1,100 at the time of signing. The tentative completion date for the design was set at June 30.

Apr. 26. Mr. Brown withdrew $400 for personal use.

Apr. 30. Paid the following expenses in cash: telephone, $35; electricity, $40.

Other data

(1) Services rendered and chargeable to various uncompleted contracts as of April 30 were as follows:

Services chargeable to	Amount of services rendered
Dillon	$750
Taylor	550
Hartman	400

(2) Drafting supplies on hand on April 30 amounted to $320.

(3) The semimonthly salaries of $600 earned by staff architects were not paid until May 1.

(Note: In addition to the above, adjusting entries are required to recognize rent expense, depreciation expense, and insurance expense.)

Instructions

a. Prepare journal entries and post to ledger accounts. (Supply numbers for journal pages and ledger accounts to permit cross referencing.)

b. Prepare a trial balance as of April 30.

c. Prepare adjusting entries at April 30 and post to ledger accounts.

d. Prepare an adjusted trial balance.

e. Prepare an income statement for the month ended April 30, a separate statement showing changes in owner's equity during the period, and a balance sheet.

f. Prepare closing entries, post to ledger accounts, and rule the accounts having zero balances.

g. Prepare an after-closing trial balance.

5

The work sheet

The nature of the work necessary at the end of an accounting period has been explained in the preceding chapters. This work includes construction of a trial balance, journalizing and posting of adjusting entries, preparation of financial statements, and journalizing and posting of closing entries. So many details are involved in these end-of-period procedures that it is easy to make errors. Once these errors are recorded in the journal and the ledger accounts, considerable time and effort must be wasted in correcting them. Both the journal and the ledger are formal, permanent records kept in ink or prepared on bookkeeping machines. One way of avoiding errors in the permanent accounting records and also of simplifying the work to be done at the end of the period is to use a *work sheet.*

Purpose of the work sheet

A work sheet is a large columnar sheet of paper, especially designed to organize and arrange in a convenient systematic form all the accounting data required at the end of the period. The work sheet is not a part of the permanent accounting records; it is prepared in pencil by the accountant for his own convenience. If an error is made on the work sheet, it may be erased and corrected much more easily than an error in the formal accounting records. Furthermore, the work sheet is so designed as to minimize errors by automatically bringing to light many types of discrepancies which might otherwise be entered in the journal and posted to the ledger accounts.

The work sheet may be thought of as a testing ground on which the ledger accounts are adjusted, balanced, and arranged in the general form of financial statements. The satisfactory completion of a work sheet provides considerable assurance that all the details of the end-of-period accounting procedures have been properly brought together. After this point has been established, the work sheet then serves as the source or guidebook from which the formal financial statements are prepared and the adjusting and closing entries are made in the journal.

The work sheet is *not* a financial statement and is not distributed to bankers, stockholders, or any one else. It is a working tool of the accountant, prepared by him for his own convenience in organizing the end-of-period procedures and as an aid in preparing the financial statements. The work sheet does not replace any accounting record or any financial statement. It represents an informal, preliminary working out of the financial statements and of the adjusting and closing entries to be made in the journal and ledger. Incidentally, some accountants prefer the term *working papers* rather than work sheet.

Sequence of accounting procedures

In a very small business with a simple accounting system consisting of perhaps only 15 or 20 accounts, working papers are not essential although they may be used. The sequence of accounting procedures when working papers are not used has already been described. A brief restatement of these procedures follows:

1. Record all transactions in the journal as they occur.
2. Post debits and credits from the journal entries to the proper ledger accounts.
3. Take a trial balance of the ledger to prove the equality of debits and credits.
4. Enter adjusting entries in the journal and post these adjustments to ledger accounts.
5. Take an adjusted trial balance from the ledger to prove again the equality of debits and credits.
6. Prepare financial statements, consisting of an income statement and a balance sheet.
7. Enter closing entries in the journal and post these entries to ledger accounts. These entries will clear the revenue and expense accounts, making them ready for the events of the succeeding period; they will also transfer the net income or loss of the completed period to the owner's capital account.
8. Prepare an after-closing trial balance to prove that the ledger is still in balance.

In a larger business concern or in any business which maintains a considerable number of accounts or makes numerous adjusting entries, the use of a work sheet will save time and labor. Since the work sheet includes a trial balance, adjusting entries in preliminary form, and an adjusted trial balance, the use of the work sheet will modify the sequence of accounting procedures as follows:

1. Record all transactions in the journal as they occur.
2. Post debits and credits from the journal entries to the proper ledger accounts.

3. Prepare the work sheet. (The work sheet includes a trial balance of the ledger.)

4. Prepare financial statements, consisting of an income statement and a balance sheet.

5. Using the work sheet as a guide, enter the adjusting and closing entries in the journal. Post these entries to ledger accounts.

6. Prepare an after-closing trial balance to prove that the ledger is still in balance.

Notice that the first two procedures, consisting of the journalizing and posting of transactions during the period, are the same regardless of whether a work sheet is to be used at the end of the period.

The accounting cycle. The above sequence of accounting procedures constitutes a complete accounting process, which is repeated in the same order in each accounting period. The regular repetition of this standardized set of procedures is often referred to as the *accounting cycle.*

In most business concerns the books are closed only once a year; for these companies the accounting cycle is one year in length. For purposes of illustration in a textbook, it is convenient to assume that the entire accounting cycle is performed within the time period of one month. The completion of the accounting cycle is always the occasion for closing the revenue and expense accounts and preparing financial statements.

Preparing the work sheet

Starting point. The November transactions and adjusting entries of the Roberts Real Estate Company were explained in Chapter 4; the account balances and adjusting entries will now be used again to illustrate the preparation of a work sheet. The starting point for this illustration is a trial balance of the ledger at November 30 before any adjustments have been made.

BEGIN WORK
SHEET
WITH
LEDGER
BALANCES
BEFORE
ADJUSTMENT

ROBERTS REAL ESTATE COMPANY
Trial Balance
November 30, 19___

Cash	$ 8,600	
Accounts receivable	2,330	
Unexpired insurance	180	
Office supplies	240	
Land	5,000	
Building	12,000	
Accumulated depreciation: building		$ 50
Office equipment	1,800	
Accumulated depreciation: office equipment		15
Notes payable		1,000
Accounts payable		7,865
Unearned rental commissions		600

James Roberts, capital		20,257
James Roberts, drawing	500	
Sales commissions earned		1,828
Advertising expense	425	
Office salaries expense	400	
Sales salaries expense	75	
Telephone expense	65	
	$31,615	$31,615

Notice that this unadjusted trial balance does not show the correct end-of-month balances for such balance sheet accounts as Unexpired Insurance, Office Supplies, Accumulated Depreciation, and Unearned Rental Commissions. Neither does it show the correct amount of revenue and expense, since such accounts as Interest Expense, Depreciation Expense, and Rental Commissions Earned do not appear at all. Numerous adjusting entries are necessary in order to produce correct, current balances for use in the financial statements. However, this unadjusted trial balance is the starting point in the preparation of the work sheet.

Illustration of procedures. A commonly used form of work sheet with the appropriate headings for the Roberts Real Estate Company is illustrated on page 137. Notice that the heading of the work sheet consists of three parts: (1) the name of the business, (2) the title Work Sheet, and (3) the period of time covered. The body of the work sheet contains five pairs of money columns, each pair consisting of a debit and a credit column. The procedures to be followed in preparing a work sheet will now be illustrated in five simple steps.

1. *Enter the ledger account balances in the Trial Balance columns.* The titles and balances of the ledger accounts at November 30 are copied into the Trial Balance columns of the work sheet, as illustrated on page 137. In practice these amounts may be taken directly from the ledger. It would be a duplication of work to prepare a trial balance as a separate schedule and then to copy this information into the work sheet. As soon as the account balances have been listed on the work sheet, these two columns should be added and the totals entered.

Accounting problems requiring the use of work sheets often present the basic information in the form of a trial balance, including debit and credit totals. It is unwise to *copy* the trial balance totals on the work sheet; instead, the totals should be established by adding the amounts on the work sheet. This precaution will bring to light any errors which may have been made in copying the individual account balances.

2. *Enter the adjustments in the Adjustments columns.* The work sheet as it appears after the completion of the Adjustments columns is illustrated on page 139. Bear in mind that adjustments are made on the work sheet *before* they are entered in the journal and posted to ledger accounts.

ROBERT'S REAL ESTATE COMPANY
Work Sheet
For the Month Ended November 30, 19___

	Trial balance		Adjustments		Adjusted trial balance		Income statement		Balance sheet	
	Dr	Cr	Dr	Cr	Dr	Cr	Dr	Cr	Dr	Cr
Cash	8,600									
Accounts receivable	2,330									
Unexpired insurance	180									
Office supplies	240									
Land	5,000									
Building	12,000									
Accumulated depreciation: bldg.		50								
Office equipment	1,800									
Accumulated depreciation: off. equip.		15								
Notes payable		1,000								
Accounts payable		7,865								
Unearned rental commissions		600								
James Roberts, capital		20,257								
James Roberts, drawing	500									
Sales commissions earned		1,828								
Advertising expense	425									
Office salaries expense	400									
Sales salaries expense	75									
Telephone expense	65									
	31,615	31,615								

The information underlying the adjustments for the Roberts Real Estate Company has already been explained in Chapter 4 but is restated briefly at this point in terms of the entries to be made on the work sheet.

a. The $180 debit balance in the asset account Unexpired Insurance represents a payment for 36 months of insurance protection, beginning November 1. On November 30, therefore, 1/36 of this amount, or $5, has expired and should be transferred to Insurance Expense. Since the account Insurance Expense does not appear in the trial balance, it is written on the first available line below the trial balance totals. The adjustment is made by entering $5 in the Adjustments debit column for Insurance Expense and $5 in the Adjustments credit column on the line for Unexpired Insurance. As a cross reference, the debit and credit parts of the adjustment are keyed together by placing the letter *a* to the left of each amount. An explanation of the adjustment appears at the bottom of the work sheet, identified by the letter *a.*

b. A count of the office supplies on hand was made at November 30; this count showed unused office supplies of $200. The debit balance of the Office Supplies account in the trial balance is $240; therefore, we may assume that supplies with a cost of $40 were used during November. The adjustment consists of debiting Office Supplies Expense and crediting Office Supplies for $40. Since Office Supplies Expense does not appear in the trial balance, it must be written on a line below the trial balance totals. The related debit and credit of $40 are identified by the letter *b.* An explanation of the adjustment, also identified by the letter *b,* is placed at the bottom of the work sheet.

c. Depreciation of the building during November amounted to $50, computed by dividing the cost of $12,000 by the estimated useful life of 240 months. The required adjustment is a debit to Depreciation Expense: Building and a credit to Accumulated Depreciation: Building. Since the account Depreciation Expense: Building does not appear in the trial balance, it must therefore be written below the trial balance totals.

d. Depreciation of office equipment during November amounted to $15. Depreciation Expense: Office Equipment is therefore debited $15 in the Adjustments debit column and Accumulated Depreciation: Office Equipment is credited $15 in the Adjustments credit column. The account Depreciation Expense: Office Equipment is written below the trial balance totals.

e. The $600 credit balance in the liability account, Unearned Rental Commissions, represents an advance payment by a client, James Fortune, for six months' services in managing his rental properties, beginning November 1. On November 30, therefore, 1/6 of the amount advanced, or $100, has been earned and should be transferred to Rental Commissions Earned, a revenue account. The adjustment is made by debiting Unearned Rental Commissions $100 in the Adjustments debit column and crediting Rental Commissions Earned in the Adjustments credit column. This latter account is written on a line below the trial balance totals.

ROBERTS REAL ESTATE COMPANY
Work Sheet
For the Month Ended November 30, 19___

	Trial balance Dr	Trial balance Cr	Adjustments Dr	Adjustments Cr	Adjusted Trial balance Dr	Adjusted Trial balance Cr	Income statement Dr	Income statement Cr	Balance sheet Dr	Balance sheet Cr
Cash	8,600									
Accounts receivable	2,330									
Unexpired insurance	180			(a) 5						
Office supplies	240			(b) 40						
Land	5,000									
Building	12,000									
Accumulated depreciation: bldg.		50		(c) 50						
Office equipment	1,800									
Accumulated depreciation: off. equip.		15		(d) 15						
Notes payable		1,000								
Accounts payable		7,865								
Unearned rental commissions		600	(e) 100							
James Roberts, capital		20,257								
James Roberts, drawing	500									
Sales commissions earned		1,828								
Advertising expense	425									
Office salaries expense	400									
Sales salaries expense	75		(g) 60							
Telephone expense	65									
	31,615	31,615								
Insurance expense			(a) 5							
Office supplies expense			(b) 40							
Depreciation expense: bldg.			(c) 50							
Depreciation expense: off. equip.			(d) 15							
Rental commissions earned				(e) 100						
				(h) 40						
Interest expense			(f) 5							
Interest payable				(f) 5						
Sales salaries payable				(g) 60						
Rental commissions receivable			(h) 40							
			315	315						

° Adjustments: (a) portion of insurance cost which expired during November; (b) office supplies used; (c) depreciation of building during November; (d) depreciation of office equipment during November; (e) earned 1/6 of the commission collected in advance on the Fortune properties; (f) interest expense accrued during November on note payable; (g) salesman's salary for last four days of November; (h) rental commission accrued on Clayton contract in November.

f. At November 30 the interest accrued on the note payable to the bank amounted to $5. This accrual represents an increase in expenses and an increase in liabilities. The adjustment is made by debiting Interest Expense $5 and crediting Interest Payable. Neither of these accounts appears on the trial balance so each must be written on lines available below the trial balance totals.

g. The salary owed the salesman at November 30 amounted to $60, computed at $15 a day for the four days since the last payday during November. This increase in expenses and liabilities is recorded by debiting Sales Salaries Expense $60 and crediting Sales Salaries Payable. The latter account does not appear in the trial balance, so it is written on a line below the trial balance totals.

h. On November 16 the Roberts Real Estate Company began the management of rental properties owned by Henry Clayton at an agreed monthly commission of $80. No payment was received from Clayton during November, but half of the monthly commission of $40 had been earned by the rendering of services during the last half of November. To record the increase in assets and increase in revenue, an adjustment is made debiting Rental Commissions Receivable and crediting Rental Commissions Earned. The account, Rental Commissions Earned, has already been written below the trial balance totals and credited for $100 in the recording of adjustment *e*; the present credit entry of $40 to this account is placed in the Adjustments credit column on the blank line just below the previous credit of $100. (Some accountants leave one or more blank lines between accounts on the work sheet so that additional debits or credits required in the adjustment process may be inserted in the proper position without crowding two figures into a single line.) The account Rental Commissions Receivable does not appear in the trial balance and must be added below the trial balance totals.

After all the adjustments have been entered in the Adjustments columns, this pair of columns must be totaled. Proving the equality of debit and credit totals tends to prevent arithmetical errors from being carried over into other columns of the work sheet.

The procedures described in this section for writing the titles of additional accounts below the trial balance totals are widely used, but other procedures are also common. An alternative procedure preferred by some accountants is to determine in advance what additional accounts will be required by the adjustments; these accounts (without amounts) can then be included in appropriate sequence in the body of the trial balance.

3. *Enter the account balances as adjusted in the Adjusted Trial Balance columns.* The work sheet as it appears after completion of the Adjusted Trial Balance columns is illustrated on page 141. Each account balance in the first pair of columns is combined with the adjustment, if any, in the second pair of columns, and the combined amount is entered in the Adjusted Trial Balance columns. This process of combining the items on each line throughout the first four columns of the work sheet

ENTER THE ADJUSTED AMOUNTS IN COLUMNS 5 AND 6 OF WORK SHEET

ROBERTS REAL ESTATE COMPANY
Work Sheet
For the Month Ended November 30, 19___

	Trial balance		Adjustments *		Adjusted trial balance		Income statement		Balance sheet	
	Dr	Cr	Dr	Cr	Dr	Cr	Dr	Cr	Dr	Cr
Cash	8,600				8,600					
Accounts receivable	2,330				2,330					
Unexpired insurance	180			(a) 5	175					
Office supplies	240			(b) 40	200					
Land	5,000				5,000					
Building	12,000				12,000					
Accumulated depreciation: bldg.		50		(c) 50		100				
Office equipment	1,800				1,800					
Accumulated depreciation: off. equip.		15		(d) 15		30				
Notes payable		1,000				1,000				
Accounts payable		7,865				7,865				
Unearned rental commissions		600	(e) 100			500				
James Roberts, capital		20,257				20,257				
James Roberts, drawing	500				500					
Sales commissions earned		1,828				1,828				
Advertising expense	425				425					
Office salaries expense	400				400					
Sales salaries expense	75		(g) 60		135					
Telephone expense	65				65					
	31,615	31,615								
Insurance expense			(a) 5		5					
Office supplies expense			(b) 40		40					
Depreciation expense: bldg.			(c) 50		50					
Depreciation expense: off. equip.			(d) 15		15					
Rental commissions earned				(e) 100 / (h) 40		140				
Interest expense			(f) 5		5					
Interest payable				(f) 5		5				
Sales salaries payable				(g) 60		60				
Rental commissions receivable			(h) 40		40					
			315	315	31,785	31,785				

* Explanatory notes relating to adjustments are the same as on page 139.

requires horizontal addition and/or subtraction. It is called *crossfooting,* in contrast to the addition of items in a vertical column, which is called *footing* the column.

For example, the Office Supplies account is seen to have a debit balance of $240 in the Trial Balance columns. This $240 debit amount is combined with the $40 credit appearing on the same line in the Adjustments column; the combination of a $240 debit with a $40 credit produces an adjusted debit amount of $200 in the Adjusted Trial Balance debit column. As another example, consider the Office Supplies Expense account. This account had no balance in the Trial Balance columns but shows a $40 debit in the Adjustments debit column. The combination of a zero starting balance and a $40 debit adjustment produces a $40 debit amount in the Adjusted Trial Balance.

Many of the accounts in the trial balance are not affected by the adjustments made at the end of the month; the balances of these accounts (such as Cash, Land, Building, or Notes Payable in the illustrated work sheet) are entered in the Adjusted Trial Balance columns in exactly the same amounts as shown in the Trial Balance columns. After all the accounts have been extended into the Adjusted Trial Balance columns, this pair of columns is totaled to prove that no arithmetical errors have been made up to this point.

4. *Extend each amount in the Adjusted Trial Balance columns into the Income Statement columns or into the Balance Sheet columns.* Assets, liabilities, and the owner's capital and drawing accounts are extended into the Balance Sheet columns; revenue and expense accounts are extended to the Income Statement columns. The process of extending amounts horizontally across the work sheet should begin with the account at the top of the work sheet, which is usually Cash. The cash figure is extended to the Balance Sheet debit column. Then the accountant goes down the work sheet line by line, extending each account balance to the appropriate Income Statement or Balance Sheet column. The likelihood of error is much less when each account is extended in the order of its appearance on the work sheet, than if accounts are extended in random order.

The extension of amounts horizontally across the work sheet is merely a sorting of the accounts making up the Adjusted Trial Balance into the two categories of income statement accounts and balance sheet accounts. The work sheet as it appears after completion of this sorting process is illustrated on page 143. Notice that each amount in the Adjusted Trial Balance columns is extended to one and only one of the four remaining columns.

5. *Total the Income Statement columns and the Balance Sheet columns. Enter the net income or net loss as a balancing figure in both pairs of columns, and again compute column totals.* The work sheet as it appears after this final step is shown on page 144.

The net income or net loss for the period is determined by computing the difference between the totals of the two Income Statement

EXTEND
EACH
ADJUSTED
AMOUNT TO
COLUMNS
FOR INCOME
STATEMENT
OR BALANCE
SHEET

ROBERTS REAL ESTATE COMPANY
Work Sheet
For the Month Ended November 30, 19___

	Trial Balance		Adjustments *		Adjusted trial balance		Income statement		Balance sheet	
	Dr	Cr	Dr	Cr	Dr	Cr	Dr	Cr	Dr	Cr
Cash	8,600				8,600				8,600	
Accounts receivable	2,330				2,330				2,330	
Unexpired insurance	180			(a) 5	175				175	
Office supplies	240			(b) 40	200				200	
Land	5,000				5,000				5,000	
Building	12,000				12,000				12,000	
Accumulated depreciation: bldg.		50		(c) 50		100				100
Office equipment	1,800				1,800				1,800	
Accumulated depreciation: off. equip.		15		(d) 15		30				30
Notes payable		1,000				1,000				1,000
Accounts payable		7,865				7,865				7,865
Unearned rental commissions		600	(e) 100			500				500
James Roberts, capital		20,257				20,257				20,257
James Roberts, drawing	500				500				500	
Sales commissions earned		1,828				1,828		1,828		
Advertising expense	425				425		425			
Office salaries expense	400				400		400			
Sales salaries expense	75		(g) 60		135		135			
Telephone expense	65				65		65			
	31,615	31,615								
Insurance expense			(a) 5		5		5			
Office supplies expense			(b) 40		40		40			
Depreciation expense: bldg.			(c) 50		50		50			
Depreciation expense: off. equip.			(d) 15		15		15			
Rental commissions earned				(e) 100 (h) 40		140		140		
Interest expense			(f) 5		5		5			
Interest payable				(f) 5		5				5
Sales salaries payable				(g) 60		60				60
Rental commissions receivable			(h) 40		40				40	
			315	315	31,785	31,785				

* Explanatory notes relating to adjustments are the same as on page 139.

ROBERTS REAL ESTATE COMPANY
Work Sheet
For the Month Ended November 30, 19___

	Trial Balance Dr	Trial Balance Cr	Adjustments Dr	Adjustments Cr	Adjusted trial balance Dr	Adjusted trial balance Cr	Income statement Dr	Income statement Cr	Balance sheet Dr	Balance sheet Cr
Cash	8,600				8,600				8,600	
Accounts receivable	2,330				2,330				2,330	
Unexpired insurance	180			(a) 5	175				175	
Office supplies	240			(b) 40	200				200	
Land	5,000				5,000				5,000	
Building	12,000				12,000				12,000	
Accumulated depreciation: bldg.		50		(c) 50		100				100
Office equipment	1,800				1,800				1,800	
Accumulated depreciation: off. equip.		15		(d) 15		30				30
Notes payable		1,000				1,000				1,000
Accounts payable		7,865				7,865				7,865
Unearned rental commissions		600	(e) 100			500				500
James Roberts, capital		20,257				20,257				20,257
James Roberts, drawing	500				500				500	
Sales commissions earned		1,828				1,828		1,828		
Advertising expense	425				425		425			
Office salaries expense	400				400		400			
Sales salaries expense	75		(g) 60		135		135			
Telephone expense	65				65		65			
	31,615	31,615								
Insurance expense			(a) 5		5		5			
Office supplies expense			(b) 40		40		40			
Depreciation expense: bldg.			(c) 50		50		50			
Depreciation expense: off. equip.			(d) 15		15		15			
Rental commissions earned				(e) 100 (h) 40		140		140		
Interest expense			(f) 5		5		5			
Interest payable				(f) 5		5				5
Sales salaries payable				(g) 60		60				60
Rental commissions receivable			(h) 40		40				40	
			315	315	31,785	31,785	1,140	1,968	30,645	29,817
Net income							828			828
							1,968	1,968	30,645	30,645

* Explanatory notes relating to adjustments are the same as on page 139.

columns. In the illustrated work sheet, the credit column total is the larger and the excess represents net income:

Income Statement credit column total (revenues) $1,968
Income Statement debit column total (expenses) 1,140

Difference: net income for period .... $ 828

Notice on the work sheet that the net income of $828 is entered in the Income Statement *debit* column as a balancing figure and also on the same line as a balancing figure in the Balance Sheet *credit* column. The caption Net Income is written in the space for account titles to identify and explain this item. New totals are then computed for both the Income Statement columns and the Balance Sheet columns. Each pair of columns is now in balance.

The reason for entering the net income of $828 in the Balance Sheet credit column is that the net income accumulated during the period in the revenue and expense accounts causes an increase in the owner's equity. If the balance sheet columns did not have equal totals after the net income had been recorded in the credit column, the lack of agreement would indicate that an error had been made in the work sheet.

Let us assume for a moment that the month's operations had produced a loss rather than a profit. In that case the Income Statement debit column would exceed the credit column. The excess of the debits (expenses) over the credits (revenues) would have to be entered in the credit column in order to bring the two Income Statement columns into balance. The incurring of a loss would decrease the owner's equity; therefore, the loss would be entered as a balancing figure in the Balance Sheet debit column. The Balance Sheet columns would then have equal totals.

Self-balancing nature of the work sheet. Why does the entering of the net income or net loss in one of the Balance Sheet columns bring this pair of columns into balance? The answer is short and simple. All the accounts in the Balance Sheet columns have November 30 balances with the exception of the owner's capital account, which still shows the October 31 balance. By bringing in the current month's net income or loss as an addition to or deduction from the October 31 capital, the capital account is brought up to date as of November 30. The Balance Sheet columns now prove the familiar proposition that assets are equal to the total of liabilities and owner's equity.

Uses for the work sheet

Preparing financial statements. Preparing the formal financial statements from the work sheet is an easy step. All the information needed for both the income statement and the balance sheet has already been sorted and arranged in convenient form in the work sheet. The income statement shown below contains the amounts listed in the Income Statement columns of the work sheet.

ROBERTS REAL ESTATE COMPANY
Income Statement
For the Month Ended November 30, 19___

DATA TAKEN
FROM
INCOME
STATEMENT
COLUMNS
OF WORK
SHEET

Revenue:		
Sales commissions earned		$1,828
Rental commissions earned		140
Total revenue		$1,968

Expenses:		
Advertising	$425	
Office supplies	40	
Office salaries	400	
Sales salaries	135	
Telephone	65	
Insurance	5	
Depreciation: building	50	
Depreciation: office equipment	15	
Interest	5	
Total expenses		1,140
Net income		$ 828

The following balance sheet contains the amounts listed in the Balance Sheet columns of the work sheet.

ROBERTS REAL ESTATE COMPANY
Balance Sheet
November 30, 19___

DATA TAKEN
FROM
BALANCE
SHEET
COLUMNS
OF WORK
SHEET

Assets

Cash		$ 8,600
Accounts receivable		2,330
Rental commissions receivable		40
Unexpired insurance		175
Office supplies		200
Land		5,000
Building	$12,000	
Less: accumulated depreciation	100	11,900
Office equipment	$ 1,800	
Less: accumulated depreciation	30	1,770
		$30,015

Liabilities and Owner's Equity

Liabilities:
Notes payable	$ 1,000
Accounts payable	7,865
Sales salaries payable	60
Interest payable	5
Unearned rental commissions	500
Total liabilities	$ 9,430

Owner's equity:

James Roberts, capital, Nov. 1, 19__ ...	$20,257	
Net income for November $828		
Less: withdrawals 500		
Increase in capital during November ...	328	
James Roberts, capital, Nov. 30, 19__ ...		20,585
		$30,015

Making adjusting entries. After the financial statements have been prepared from the work sheet at the end of the period, the ledger accounts are adjusted to bring them into agreement with the statements. As indicated in the sequence of accounting procedures on page 134, the work sheet is prepared before the ledger accounts are adjusted. After the work sheet and the financial statements have been completed, it is still necessary to enter the end-of-period adjustments in the accounting records. This is an easy step because the adjustments have already been computed on the work sheet. The amounts appearing in the Adjustments columns of the work sheet and the related explanations at the bottom of the work sheet provide all the necessary information for the adjusting entries, as shown below, which are first entered in the journal and then posted to the ledger accounts.

ADJUSTMENTS ON WORK SHEET ARE ENTERED IN JOURNAL

		Journal		_(Page 5)_
19__				
Nov.	30	Insurance Expense	5	
		Unexpired Insurance		5
		Insurance expense for November.		
	30	Office Supplies Expense	40	
		Office Supplies		40
		Office supplies used during November.		
	30	Depreciation Expense: Building	50	
		Accumulated Depreciation: Building		50
		Depreciation for November.		

			Journal		*(Page 5)*
19__					
Nov.	30	*Depreciation Expense: Office Equipment*		*15*	
		Accumulated Depreciation: Office Equipment .			*15*
		Depreciation for November.			
	30	*Unearned Rental Commissions*		*100*	
		Rental Commissions Earned			*100*
		Earned 1/6 of commission collected in advance for management of the properties owned by James Fortune.			
	30	*Interest Expense*		*5*	
		Interest Payable			*5*
		Interest expense accrued during November on note payable.			
	30	*Sales Salaries Expense*		*60*	
		Sales Salaries Payable			*60*
		To record expense and related liability to salesman for last four days' work in November.			
	30	*Rental Commissions Receivable*		*40*	
		Rental Commissions Earned			*40*
		To record the receivable and related revenue earned for managing properties owned by Henry Clayton.			

Making closing entries. When the income statement and balance sheet have been prepared from the work sheet, the revenue and expense accounts have served their purpose for the current period and should be closed. These accounts will then have zero balances and will be ready for the recording of revenue and expenses during the next fiscal period.

The journalizing and posting of closing entries were illustrated in Chapter 3. The point to be emphasized now is that the completed work sheet provides in convenient form all the information needed to make the closing entries. The preparation of closing entries from the work sheet may be summarized as follows:

1. To close the accounts listed in the Income Statement credit column, debit the revenue accounts and credit Income Summary.

2. To close the accounts listed in the Income Statement debit column, debit Income Summary and credit the expense accounts.

3. To close the Income Summary account, transfer the balancing figure in the Income Statement columns of the work sheet ($828 in the illustration) to the owner's capital account. A profit is transferred by debiting Income Summary and crediting the capital account; a loss is transferred by debiting the capital account and crediting Income Summary.

4. To close the owner's drawing account, debit the capital account and credit the drawing account. Notice on the work sheet that the account, James Roberts, Drawing, is extended from the Adjusted Trial Balance debit column to the Balance Sheet debit column. It does not appear in the Income Statement columns because a withdrawal of cash by the owner is not regarded as an expense of the business.

CLOSING
ENTRIES
DERIVED
FROM WORK
SHEET

The closing entries at November 30 are as follows:

		Journal		*(Page 6)*
19__				
Nov.	30	Sales Commissions Earned	1,828	
		Rental Commissions Earned	140	
		Income Summary		1,968
		To close the revenue accounts.		
	30	Income Summary	1,140	
		Advertising Expense		425
		Office Salaries Expense		400
		Sales Salaries Expense		135
		Telephone Expense		65
		Insurance Expense		5
		Office Supplies Expense		40
		Depreciation Expense: Building		50
		Depreciation Expense: Office Equipment		15
		Interest Expense		5
		To close the expense accounts.		
	30	Income Summary	828	
		James Roberts, Capital		828
		To close the Income Summary account.		
	30	James Roberts, Capital	500	
		James Roberts, Drawing		500
		To close the owner's drawing account.		

Preparing monthly financial statements without closing the books. Many companies which close their books only once a year nevertheless prepare *monthly* financial statements for managerial use. These monthly statements are prepared from work sheets, but the adjustments indicated on the work sheets are not entered in the accounting records and no closing entries are made. Under this plan, the time-consuming operation of journalizing and posting adjustments and closing entries is performed only at the end of the fiscal year, but the company has the advantage of monthly financial statements.

Summary

In summary, we may say that a work sheet serves several purposes:

1. All the adjusting entries and closing entries are worked out in preliminary form on the work sheet before being entered in the permanent accounting records. This approach tends to prevent errors.

2. The preparation of the balance sheet and the income statement is facilitated because all the required information is assembled and organized on the work sheet.

3. The self-balancing nature of the work sheet provides a safeguard against various types of errors which may be made in performing the end-of-period procedures. (Of course the work sheet also includes trial balance columns, which indicate whether the ledger is in balance before the accounts are adjusted.)

4. Through the use of a work sheet, monthly financial statements can be prepared even though the books are closed only once a year.

QUESTIONS

1. In performing the regular end-of-period accounting procedures, does the preparation of the work sheet precede or follow the posting of adjusting entries to ledger accounts? Why?

2. The Adjustments columns of the work sheet for Davis Company contained only three adjustments, as follows: depreciation of building, $2,000; expiration of insurance, $300; and salaries accrued at year-end, $900. If the Trial Balance columns showed totals of $100,000, what would be the totals of the Adjusted Trial Balance columns?

3. Should the Adjusted Trial Balance columns be totaled before or after the adjusted amounts are carried to the Income Statement and Balance Sheet columns?

4. In extending adjusted account balances from the Adjusted Trial Balance columns to the Income Statement and Balance Sheet columns, is there any particular sequence to be followed in order to minimize the possibility of errors? Explain.

5. Do the totals of the balance sheet ordinarily agree with the totals of the Balance Sheet columns of the work sheet?

6. Is a work sheet ever prepared when there is no intention of closing the books? Explain.

7. In extending the amounts in the Adjusted Trial Balance columns of a work sheet, a bookkeeper made the following errors:

    a. Extended the Salaries Payable account to the Income Statement credit column.

    b. Extended the Commissions Earned account to the Balance Sheet debit column.

    c. Extended the Advertising Expense account to the Balance Sheet debit column.

Which (if any) of these errors would necessarily be discovered in the process of completing the work sheet? Explain.

PROBLEMS

Group A

5A-1. Fairview Golf Course obtains revenue from greens fees and also from a contract with a concessionaire who sells refreshments on the premises. The books are closed at the end of each calendar year; at December 31, 19___, the ledger contained the following balances:

Cash	$ 9,000	
Prepaid insurance	1,800	
Prepaid advertising	900	
Land	150,000	
Equipment	40,000	
Accumulated depreciation: equipment		$ 8,000
Notes payable		40,000
Unearned revenue from concessions		5,000
James Cross, capital		51,250
James Cross, drawing	11,000	
Revenue from greens fees		214,500
Advertising expense	4,500	
Water expense	9,400	
Salaries expense	71,150	
Repairs and maintenance expense	17,000	
Miscellaneous expense	4,000	
	$318,750	$318,750

Other data

(*a*) Insurance expired during the year, $600.

(*b*) The $900 balance in the Prepaid Advertising account represents a payment made for advertisements to appear in six monthly issues of a magazine. The first of the six advertisements appeared in the December issue. All other advertising expenditures during the year were charged directly to expense.

(*c*) Accrued interest expense on notes payable, $350.

(*d*) The $5,000 balance in Unearned Revenue from Concessions represents an advance payment received under the contract with the concessionaire. The contract provides that Fairway Golf Course is entitled to 10% of the concession sales. Concession sales to December 31 totaled $45,000. (Credit Revenue from Concessions with the portion earned by Fairview Golf Course.)

(*e*) Salaries earned by employees but unpaid at December 31 amounted to $850.

(*f*) The equipment is being depreciated on the basis of estimated useful life of 10 years.

Instructions. Prepare working papers.

5A-2. *Instructions.* Based on the trial balance and other data, prepare a work sheet for the month ended October 31, 19___.

BRANDON SERVICE COMPANY
Trial Balance
October 31, 19___

Cash	$ 7,958	
Prepaid rent	500	
Prepaid insurance	462	
Prepaid advertising	500	
Inventory of supplies	600	
Equipment	10,500	
Accumulated depreciation: equipment		$ 1,070
Notes payable		6,500
Unearned revenue		1,000
Robert Brandon, capital		11,075
Robert Brandon, drawing	400	
Revenue from services		3,125
Salaries expense	1,850	
	$22,770	$22,770

Other data

(a) The monthly rent expense was $100.

(b) Insurance expense for the month, $14.

(c) Advertising expense for the month, $175.

(d) Cost of supplies on hand, based on physical count on October 31, $395.

(e) Depreciation expense on equipment, $130 per month.

(f) Accrued interest expense on notes payable, $30.

(g) Salaries earned by employees but not yet paid, $125.

(h) Services amounting to $225 were rendered during October for customers who had paid in advance. This portion of the Unearned Revenue account should be regarded as earned as of October 31.

5A-3. *Instructions.* Based on the trial balance and other data, prepare

    a. A work sheet for the month ended October 31, 19___

    b. An income statement

    c. A statement of owner's equity

    d. A balance sheet

Data. Additional accounts needed for adjustments are included in the body of the trial balance.

NATIONAL ADVERTISING AGENCY
Trial Balance
October 31, 19___

Cash	$ 3,756	
Advertising layout design fees receivable		
Prepaid rent	1,800	
Unexpired insurance	504	
Inventory of advertising supplies	805	
Inventory of office supplies	150	
Office Equipment	4,320	

Accumulated depreciation: office equipment ...		$ 405
Notes payable		500
Accounts payable		200
Interest payable		
Office salaries payable		
Unearned advertising layout design fees		1,000
J. J. Johnson, capital		9,105
J. J. Johnson, drawing	500	
Advertising layout design fees earned		1,835
Advertising space commissions earned		1,290
Office salaries expense	2,500	
Rent expense		
Insurance expense		
Advertising supplies expense		
Office supplies expense		
Depreciation expense: office equipment		
Interest expense		
	$14,335	$14,335

Other data

(a) The monthly rent was $450.

(b) Insurance expense for the month amounted to $18.

(c) Based on a physical count on October 31, the amount of advertising supplies on hand was $507; the amount of office supplies on hand was $42.

(d) Office equipment was purchased on January 2 of the current year. Its useful life was estimated at eight years.

(e) Interest expense on notes payable amounted to $2 for the month of October.

(f) Fees considered as earned for advertising layout designs done as of October 31, which had not been billed or recorded, amounted to $1,475, of which $655 were for clients who had made advance payments.

(g) Salaries earned by employees but not yet paid amounted to $220.

5A-4. State Storage and Moving Service had the following trial balance at November 30. Assume that the company closes its books monthly.

STATE STORAGE AND MOVING SERVICE
Trial Balance
November 30, 19___

Cash	$ 11,500	
Unexpired insurance	1,700	
Office supplies	1,850	
Trucks	84,000	
Accumulated depreciation: trucks		$ 17,500
Office equipment	13,200	
Accumulated depreciation: office equipment .		1,100
Unearned moving service fees		2,250
Arthur Ryan, capital		96,050
Arthur Ryan, drawing	4,250	

Storage fees earned		7,150
Moving service fees earned		22,450
Gasoline expense	6,180	
Rent expense	5,450	
Office salaries expense	4,200	
Drivers' salaries expense	13,750	
Telephone expense	420	
	$146,500	$146,500

Other data

(*a*) The insurance expense for November amounted to $900.

(*b*) The amount of office supplies on hand, based on a physical count on November 30, was $1,080.

(*c*) Trucks were purchased on January 2 of the current year. The useful life was estimated at four years.

(*d*) Office equipment was purchased on January 2 of the current year. The useful life was estimated at 10 years.

(*e*) Moving services amounting to $2,050 were rendered on the last day of November too late to be billed. Of this total, the sum of $1,300 pertained to clients who had made advance payment.

(*f*) Salaries earned by office employees but not paid amounted to $550; salaries earned by drivers but not paid amounted to $1,550.

Instructions. Prepare

a. A work sheet for the month ended November 30

b. An income statement

c. A balance sheet showing the detail of changes in proprietor's capital

Group B

5B-1. *Instructions.* Based on the trial balance and other data, prepare a work sheet for the year ended December 31, 1962.

Data. Barker Engineering Consulting Service closes its books at the end of the calendar year.

BARKER ENGINEERING CONSULTING SERVICE
Trial Balance
December 31, 1962

Cash	$ 6,720	
Marketable securities	10,000	
Prepaid office rent	9,000	
Prepaid dues and subscriptions	240	
Inventory of drafting supplies	1,250	
Drafting equipment	4,800	
Accumulated depreciation: drafting equipment .		$ 960
Notes payable		5,000
Unearned consulting fees		38,000
J. B. Barker, capital		18,000
J. B. Barker, drawing	8,400	

Consulting fees earned		*4,500*
Salaries expense	*25,000*	
Telephone and telegraph expense	*450*	
Miscellaneous expense	*600*	
	$66,460	*$66,460*

Other data

(*a*) On January 1, 1962, the account Prepaid Office Rent had a balance of $3,000, representing the prepaid rent for the months January to June, 1962, inclusive. On July 1, 1962, the lease was renewed and office rent for one year at $500 per month was paid in advance.

(*b*) Dues and subscriptions expired during the year in the total amount of $75.

(*c*) A count of drafting supplies on hand was made at December 31; the cost of the unused supplies was $400.

(*d*) The useful life of the drafting equipment had been estimated as 10 years from the date of acquisition.

(*e*) Accrued interest on notes payable amounted to $25 at the year-end.

(*f*) Consulting services valued at $32,400 were rendered during the year for clients who had made payment in advance.

(*g*) It is the custom of the firm to bill clients only when consulting work is completed, or, in the case of prolonged engagements, at six-month intervals. At December 31, engineering services valued at $1,800 had been rendered to clients but not yet billed. No advance payments had been received from these clients.

(*h*) Salaries earned by staff engineers but not yet paid amounted to $550 at December 31.

5B-2. Modern Research Service was organized on January 1, 19___, to render statistical, mathematical, and data-processing services to business organizations. To conserve capital, the firm decided not to purchase an electronic computer but to arrange to use electronic computers at a nearby computer center by paying an hourly rate. The books of the firm were closed each month. At August 31, the ledger contained the following information prior to the making of adjustments.

Cash	*$41,620*
Research fees receivable	
Prepaid office rent	*22,500*
Prepaid computer rental expense	*27,600*
Inventory of office supplies	*3,000*
Office equipment	*19,200*
Accumulated depreciation: office equipment	*1,120*
Notes payable	*10,000*
Accounts payable	*3,650*
Interest payable	
Salaries payable	
Unearned research fees	*89,500*
N. N. Nelson, capital	*58,430*
N. N. Nelson, drawing	*5,000*
Research fees earned	*10,350*

Office salaries expense	*3,500*
Research salaries expense	*43,100*
Telephone expense	*2,100*
Travel expense	*5,430*
Office rent expense	
Computer rental expense	
Office supplies expense	
Depreciation expense: office equipment	
Interest expense	

Other data

(*a*) The amount in the Prepaid Office Rent account represented office rent for six months paid in advance on August 1 when the lease was renewed.

(*b*) During August, 110 hours of computer time were used at a cost of $120 an hour.

(*c*) Office supplies on hand on August 31 were determined by count to amount to $550.

(*d*) Office equipment was estimated to have a useful life of 10 years from date of purchase.

(*e*) Accrued interest on notes payable amounted to $40 on August 31.

(*f*) Services to clients amounting to $59,800 performed during August were chargeable against the Unearned Research Fees Account.

(*g*) Services to clients who had not made advance payments and had not been billed amounted to $14,500 at August 31.

(*h*) Salaries earned by research staff but not paid amounted to $3,400 on August 31.

Instructions

a. Prepare a work sheet for the month ended August 31, 19___.

b. Prepare an income statement and a balance sheet that contains the details of changes in the owner's equity.

5B-3. Island Flying Service offers air service for visitors to a famous island resort. The company was organized on September 1, 1962, and follows the policy of closing its books each month. At December 31, 1962, the following trial balance was prepared from the ledger.

ISLAND FLYING SERVICE
Trial Balance
December 31, 1962

Cash	*$ 80,700*	
Prepaid hangar rental expense	*15,000*	
Prepaid insurance	*13,200*	
Prepaid maintenance expense	*6,000*	
Spare parts	*18,000*	
Airplanes	*220,000*	
Accumulated depreciation: airplanes		*$ 26,400*
Unearned passenger revenue		*10,000*

John Green, capital		302,000
John Green, drawing	7,000	
Passenger revenue earned		50,600
Gasoline expense	4,100	
Salaries expense	23,500	
Advertising expense	1,500	
	$389,000	$389,000

Other data

(*a*) Monthly hangar rent amounted to $500.

(*b*) Insurance expense for December was $1,100.

(*c*) All necessary maintenance work was provided by Ryan Air Services at a fixed charge of $2,000 a month. Service for three months had been paid for in advance on December 1.

(*d*) Spare parts used in connection with maintenance work amounted to $1,250 during the month.

(*e*) At the time of purchase the remaining useful life of the airplanes, which were several years old, was estimated at 4,000 hours of flying time. During December, total flying time amounted to 230 hours.

(*f*) The Chamber of Commerce purchased 1,000 special tickets for $10,000. Each ticket allowed the holder one flight normally priced at $15. During the month 240 tickets had been tendered.

(*g*) Salaries earned by employees but not paid amounted to $1,000 at December 31.

Instructions

a. Prepare a work sheet for the month ended December 31, 1962.

b. Prepare an income statement and a balance sheet that includes the details of changes in owner's equity.

c. Prepare adjusting and closing entries.

5B-4. Bayside Theater closes its books each month. At September 30, the trial balance and other data given below were available for adjusting and closing the books.

BAYSIDE THEATER
Trial Balance
September 30, 19___

Cash	$ 28,900	
Prepaid advertising	5,000	
Prepaid film rental	24,000	
Office supplies	750	
Land	25,000	
Building	75,000	
Accumulated depreciation: building		$ 1,250
Projection equipment	30,000	
Accumulated depreciation: projection equip-ment		2,500
Notes payable		10,000

Accounts payable		*2,450*
Robert Miller, capital		*153,000*
Robert Miller, drawing	*5,500*	
Revenue from admissions		*36,750*
Salaries expense	*8,750*	
Light, heat, & power	*3,050*	
	$205,950	*$205,950*

Other data

(*a*) Advertising expense for the month, $3,550.

(*b*) Film rental expense for the month, $18,400.

(*c*) Amount of office supplies on hand as of September 30, based on a physical count, $150.

(*d*) Depreciation expense on building, $250 per month; on projection equipment, $500 per month.

(*e*) Accrued interest on notes payable, $50.

(*f*) The company's share of revenue from concessions for September, as reported by concessionaire, $3,050. Check should be received by October 5.

(*g*) Salaries earned by employees but not paid, $1,050.

Instructions. Prepare

a. A work sheet for the month ended September 30

b. An income statement

c. A statement of proprietor's capital

d. A balance sheet

e. Adjusting and closing entries

6

Accounting for purchases and sales of merchandise

The preceding five chapters have illustrated step-by-step the complete accounting cycle for a business rendering personal services. The illustrations thus far have been based on a real estate brokerage business, but the financial statements and accounting records illustrated would apply equally well to other commercial concerns rendering personal services, as, for example, laundries, beauty shops, theaters, golf courses, and taxicab companies. The illustrated financial statements and accounting records would also be appropriate for professional firms such as those engaged in the practice of law, architecture, or public accounting. All these service-type enterprises obtain their revenues by charging customers a fee or commission for the services rendered. In measuring the profitability of a service-type business, the accountant compares the total commissions or fees earned during a given time period with the total operating expenses applicable to that same period.

In contrast to the service-type business, there are a great many companies which obtain revenue by buying and selling goods. These companies are often referred to as merchandising or trading enterprises; they may be engaged in either the retail or wholesale distribution of merchandise. The retailer buys goods from the wholesaler, or in some cases directly from the manufacturer, and then sells these goods to consumers at retail prices. Shoe stores, supermarkets, filling stations, and department stores are familiar, everyday examples of retail businesses. The wholesaler buys goods from manufacturers, farmers, and importers, and sells to retailers or to large-scale consumers. Businessmen in both retail and wholesale trade often use the terms *vendors* and *suppliers* in referring to the companies from which they buy goods.

Accounting cycle for a merchandising business

In this chapter we shall study the accounting cycle for a merchandising business. To a considerable extent, the accounting records and procedures of a merchandising business are the same as those for a business rendering personal services. In both types of business, transactions are recorded in journals and posted to ledger accounts. At the end of the period, both the service-type firm and the merchandising concern compute the balances of the ledger accounts and list these balances on a work sheet. Both types of business prepare financial statements from the completed work sheet, and both enter adjusting and closing entries in the journal and post these entries to the accounts. The preparation of an after-closing trial balance completes the cycle for both the service-type firm and the merchandising business. Although the accounting concepts and methods described in the preceding chapters are nearly all applicable to a merchandising business, some additional accounts and techniques are needed in accounting for purchases and sales of merchandise.

Accounting for sales of merchandise

If merchandising concerns are to succeed or even to survive, they must, of course, sell their goods at prices higher than they pay to the vendors or suppliers from whom they buy. The selling prices charged by a retail store must cover three things: (1) the cost of the merchandise to the store; (2) the operating expenses of the business such as advertising, store rent, and salaries of salesmen; and (3) a net income to the owner of the business. These three elements of successful merchandising are emphasized in the income statement of a merchandising business illustrated on page 162.

The nature of revenue earned by selling services to customers has been discussed in preceding chapters. The sale of merchandise, like the sale of services, is recorded by debiting Cash or Accounts Receivable and crediting a revenue account. The title for this revenue account is Sales, and it appears as the first item on the income statement.

When a business sells merchandise to its customers, it either receives immediate payment in cash or acquires an account receivable which will soon become cash. As explained in Chapter 3, the inflow of cash and receivables from customers represents the revenue for the period. The entry to record the sale of merchandise consists of a debit to an asset account and a credit to the Sales account, as shown by the following example:

JOURNAL
ENTRY FOR
CASH SALE

Cash *100*
    Sales *100*
To record the sale of merchandise for cash.

If the sale was not a cash transaction but called for payment at a later date, the entry would be:

JOURNAL
ENTRY FOR
SALE ON
CREDIT

Accounts Receivable *100*
   Sales *100*
To record the sale of merchandise on credit; payment due
within 30 days.

    The debits to Cash and to Accounts Receivable require no explanation; these debits clearly record increases in assets. But what is the nature of the $100 credit to the Sales account? Let us assume that the merchandise sold in this example had cost the business $60. The credit to the Sales account could then be regarded as representing two elements: (1) a decrease in the amount of merchandise owned, $60; and (2) a gain or increase in the owner's equity of $40. In accounting terminology, we could say that the *cost of goods sold* was $60 and the *gross profit* on the sale was $40. (Both these terms are considered more fully later in this chapter.) Most businesses, however, do not find it practicable to divide the amount of the sales price between cost and gross profit at the time of recording the sale. It is much more convenient to regard the entire amount of the sales price as revenue and to credit this amount to the Sales account. The question of a division between cost of goods sold and gross profit is postponed until the end of the accounting period. At that time the total cost of all merchandise sold will be subtracted from the amount in the Sales account to determine the gross profit for the period.

    Revenue from the sale of merchandise is usually considered as earned in the period in which the merchandise is delivered to the customer, even though payment in cash is not received for a month or more after the sale. Consequently, the revenue earned in a given accounting period may differ considerably from the cash receipts of that period.

    The amount and trend of sales are watched very closely by management, investors, and others interested in the progress of a company. A rising volume of sales is evidence of growth and suggests the probability of an increase in earnings. A declining trend in sales, on the other hand, is often the first signal of reduced earnings and of financial difficulties ahead. The amount of sales for each year is compared with the sales of the preceding year; the sales of each month may be compared with the sales of the preceding month and also with the corresponding month of the preceding year. These comparisons bring to light significant trends in the volume of sales. The financial pages of newspapers regularly report on the volume and trend of sales for corporations with public-owned stock.

Income statement for a merchandising business

An income statement for a retail sporting goods store will now be illustrated to show how net income is determined in a business which derives its entire revenue from selling merchandise. We shall assume that the business of the Campus Sports Shop consists of buying sports equipment from manufacturers and selling this merchandise to college students. To keep the illustration reasonably short, we shall use a smaller number of expense accounts than would generally be employed.

NOTE THE
DISTINCTION
BETWEEN
COST OF
GOODS
SOLD AND
OPERATING
EXPENSES

CAMPUS SPORTS SHOP
Income Statement
For the Month Ended September 30, 19___

Sales		$10,000
Cost of goods sold:		
Inventory, Sept. 1	$ 4,400	
Purchases	9,100	
Cost of goods available for sale	$13,500	
Deduct: inventory, Sept. 30	7,500	
Cost of goods sold		6,000
Gross profit on sales		$ 4,000
Operating expenses:		
Salaries	$ 2,230	
Advertising	450	
Telephone	60	
Depreciation	40	
Insurance	20	
Total operating expenses		2,800
Net income		$ 1,200

Analyzing the income statement. How does this income statement compare in form and content with the income statement of the service-type business presented in the preceding chapters? The most important change is the inclusion of the section entitled Cost of Goods Sold. Notice how large the Cost of Goods Sold is in comparison with the other figures on the statement. The cost of the merchandise sold during the month amounts to $6,000, or 60% of the month's sales of $10,000. Another way of looking at this relationship is to say that for each dollar the store receives by selling goods to customers, the sum of 60 cents represents a recovery of the cost of the merchandise. This leaves a gross profit of 40 cents from each sales dollar, out of which the store must pay its operating expenses. In our illustration the operating expenses for the month were $2,800, that is, 28% of the sales figure of $10,000. Therefore, the gross profit of 40 cents contained in each dollar of sales was enough to cover the operating expenses of 28 cents and leave a net income of 12 cents.

Of course the percentage relationship between sales and cost of sales will vary from one type of business to another, but, in all types of merchandising concerns, the cost of goods sold is one of the largest elements in the income statement. Accountants, bankers, and businessmen in general have the habit of mentally computing percentage relationships when they look at financial statements. Formation of this habit will be helpful throughout the study of accounting, as well as in many business situations.

In analyzing an income statement, it is customary to compare each item in the statement with the amount of sales. These comparisons are easier to make if we express the data in percentages as well as in dollar amounts. If the figure for sales is regarded as 100%, then every other item or subtotal on the statement can conveniently be expressed as a percentage of sales. The cost of goods sold in most types of business will be between 60% and 80% of sales. Conversely, the gross profit on sales (excess of sales over cost of goods sold) will usually vary between an upper limit of 40% and a lower limit of 20% of sales. Numerous exceptions may be found to such a sweeping generalization, but it is sufficiently valid to be helpful in visualizing customary relationships on the income statement.

Appraising the adequacy of net income. The income statement for the Campus Sports Shop illustrated above shows that a net income of $1,200 was earned during the month of September. Should this be regarded as an excellent showing, a fair profit, or only a mediocre return? Before reaching a conclusion, let us consider what this item of net income represents in an unincorporated business.

First, let us make the reasonable assumption that the owner of the Campus Sports Shop, Robert Riley, works full time as manager of the business. It is not customary, however, to include any compensation for the personal services of the owner among the expenses of the business. One reason for not including among the expenses a salary to the owner-manager is the fact that he would be in a position to set his own salary at any amount he chose. The use of an arbitrarily chosen, unrealistic salary to the proprietor would tend to destroy the significance of the income statement as a device for measuring the earning power of the business. Another reason may be that in the proprietor's own thinking he is not working for a salary when he manages his own business but is investing his time in order to make a profit. The net income of the Campus Sports Shop must, therefore, be considered in part as the equivalent of a salary earned by the owner. If we assume that the owner, Robert Riley, could obtain employment elsewhere as a store manager at a salary of $600 a month, then we can reasonably regard $600 of the net income earned by the Campus Sports Shop as compensation to Riley for his personal services during the month.

Secondly, it is necessary to recognize that Riley, as owner of this small business, has invested his own funds, amounting to, say, $20,000. If, as an alternative to starting his own business, he had invested this $20,000 capital in high-grade securities, he might be receiving investment income of perhaps $100 a month.

After deducting from the $1,200 reported net income of the Campus

Sports Shop an imputed monthly salary of $600 to the owner and an estimated return on invested capital of $100, we have left a "pure profit" of $500. In judging the adequacy of this amount, we must bear in mind that this residual element of profit is the all-important incentive which induced Riley to risk his savings in a new business venture. The residual profit may also be regarded as the reward for the time and effort which an owner must spend in planning, financing, and guiding a business, apart from the routine aspects of day-to-day management. Moreover, the earning of $1,200 net income in one month provides no assurance that a similar profit, or for that matter any profit, will be forthcoming in another month. It would be somewhat rash to form an opinion about the adequacy of earning power of a business on the basis of only a short period of operating experience.

Economists often use the word "profit" to mean the residual pure profit remaining after deducting from the net income estimated amounts to compensate the proprietor for his personal services and the use of his capital. Confusion over the meaning of technical terms is a major difficulty faced by the accountant in conveying to economists and businessmen the results of his analysis of business operations.

Inventory of merchandise and cost of goods sold

In the illustrated income statement on page 162, the inventory of merchandise and the cost of goods sold are important new concepts which require careful attention. An inventory of merchandise consists of the goods on hand and available for sale to customers. In the Campus Sports Shop, the inventory consists of golf clubs, tennis racquets, and skiing equipment; in a pet shop the inventory might include puppies, fish, and parakeets. Inventories are acquired through the purchase of goods from wholesalers, manufacturers, or other suppliers. A company's inventory is increased by the purchase of goods from suppliers and decreased by the sale of goods to customers. The cost of the merchandise sold during the month appears in the income statement as a deduction from the sales of the month. The merchandise which is *not sold* during the month constitutes the inventory of merchandise on hand at the end of the accounting period and is included in the balance sheet as an asset. The ending inventory of one accounting period is, of course, the beginning inventory of the following.

How can the businessman determine, at the end of the month or year, the quantity and the cost of the goods remaining on hand? How can he determine the cost of the goods sold during the period? These amounts must be determined before either a balance sheet or an income statement can be prepared. In fact, the determination of inventory value and of the cost of goods sold may be the most important single step in measuring the profitability of a business.

There are two alternative approaches to the determination of inventory and of cost of goods sold, namely, the *periodic inventory method* and the *perpetual inventory method.* Business concerns which sell merchandise of high unit value, such as automobiles or television sets, generally use a perpetual inventory system. This system requires the keeping of records showing the cost of each article sold. At the end of the accounting period, the total cost of goods sold is easily determined by adding the costs recorded from day to day for the individual units sold. The perpetual inventory system is described in more detail in Chapters 12 and 26.

The periodic inventory method. The great majority of businesses, however, do not maintain perpetual inventory records; they rely instead upon a periodic inventory (a count of merchandise on hand) to determine the inventory at the end of the accounting period and the cost of goods sold during the period. The periodic inventory system may be concisely summarized as follows:

1. A physical count of merchandise on hand is made at the end of each accounting period.

2. The cost value of this inventory is computed by multiplying the quantity of each item by an appropriate unit cost. A total cost figure for the entire inventory is then determined by adding the costs of all the various types of merchandise.

3. The *cost of goods available for sale* during the period is determined by adding the amount of the inventory at the beginning of the period to the amount of the purchases during the period.

4. The *cost of goods sold* is computed by subtracting the inventory at the end of the period from the cost of goods available for sale. In other words, the difference between the cost of goods available for sale and the amount of goods remaining unsold at the end of the period is presumed to have been sold.

A simple illustration of the above procedures for determining the cost of goods sold follows:

**USING THE
PERIODIC
INVENTORY
METHOD**

Beginning inventory (determined by count)	$1,000
Add: purchases	1,800
Cost of goods available for sale	$2,800
Deduct: ending inventory (determined by count)	1,200
Cost of goods sold	$1,600

The periodic inventory system is the method we shall be working with throughout most of this book. Because of the importance of the process for determining inventory and cost of goods sold, we shall now consider in more detail the essential steps in using the periodic inventory system.

Taking a physical inventory. When the periodic inventory system is in use, there is no day-to-day record of the cost of goods sold. Neither is there any day-to-day record of the amount of goods unsold and still on hand. At the end of the accounting period, however, it is necessary to determine the cost of goods sold during the period and also the amount of unsold goods on hand. The figure for cost of goods sold is used in determining the profit or loss for the period, and the value of the merchandise on hand at the end of the period is included in the balance sheet as an asset.

To determine the cost of the merchandise on hand, a physical inventory is taken. The count of merchandise should be made after the close of business on the last day of the accounting period if possible. It is difficult to make an accurate count during business hours while sales are taking place; consequently, the physical inventory is often taken in the evening or on Sunday. After all goods have been counted, the proper cost price must be assigned to each article. The assignment of a cost price to each item of merchandise in stock is often described as *pricing the inventory*. Inventories of merchandise are usually valued at cost for accounting purposes, although some alternative bases will be discussed in Chapter 12, as well as alternative methods of determining cost.

Computing the cost of goods sold. The taking of a physical inventory at the end of the accounting period is a major step toward computing the cost of goods sold during the period. Let us illustrate the computation of cost of goods sold by considering the first year of operation for a new business. We can reasonably assume that there was no beginning inventory of merchandise at the inception of the enterprise. During the first year, the purchases of merchandise totaled $50,000. These purchases constituted the goods available for sale. A physical count of merchandise was made on December 31; the quantities shown as on hand were multiplied by unit cost prices, and a total cost for the inventory was computed as $10,000. If goods costing $50,000 were available for sale during the year and goods costing $10,000 remained unsold at year-end, then the cost of goods sold must have been $40,000, as summarized below:

COMPUTING COST OF GOODS SOLD IN FIRST YEAR	*Inventory at beginning of period* .... $ *000*
	Purchases *50,000*
	Cost of goods available for sale *$50,000*
	Deduct: inventory at end of period *10,000*
	Cost of goods sold *$40,000*

The merchandise on hand at the close of business December 31 of the first year is, of course, still on hand on January 1 of the second year. As previously stated, the *ending* inventory of one year is the *beginning* inventory of the following year. To continue our example, let us assume that in the second year of operation purchases amounted to $75,000 and the inventory of goods on hand at the end of the second year was determined by the taking of a physical inventory that amounted to $25,000. The cost of goods sold during the second year would be computed as follows:

COMPUTING
COST OF
GOODS
SOLD IN
SECOND
YEAR

Inventory at beginning of second year	$10,000
Purchases	75,000
Cost of goods available for sale	$85,000
Deduct: inventory at end of second year	25,000
Cost of goods sold	$60,000

Dependability of the periodic inventory method. In computing the cost of goods sold by the periodic inventory method, we are making a somewhat dangerous assumption that all goods not sold during the year will be on hand at the end of the year.

Referring to the above example, let us assume that, during the second year of operations, shoplifters stole $1,000 worth of merchandise from the store without being detected. The cost of goods available for sale is still $85,000, and the final inventory is still $25,000, but the cost of goods sold is not actually $60,000. The $60,000 difference between goods available for sale and goods in final inventory is composed of two distinct elements: cost of goods sold, $59,000, and cost of goods stolen, $1,000. However, under the periodic inventory method, the loss of goods by theft would not be apparent, and the cost of goods sold would erroneously be shown in the income statement as $60,000. A method of disclosing inventory shortages of this type is explained in Chapter 12.

Another possible source of error in the figure for cost of goods sold lies in mistakes made in taking the physical inventory at the end of the year. Referring again to the example on page 166, let us assume that a certain group of merchandise was overlooked during the count made on December 31. The cost of the goods overlooked and accidentally omitted from the count was $5,000. In other words, the ending inventory was counted and listed as $25,000 instead of the correct amount of $30,000. Understating the ending inventory by $5,000 will cause the cost of goods sold to be overstated by $5,000, because the cost of goods sold is determined by subtracting the ending inventory from the cost of goods available for sale. The effect of this $5,000 error in the physical inventory at year-end is illustrated below:

EFFECT OF
ERROR IN
PHYSICAL
INVENTORY
ON COST
OF GOODS
SOLD

	Based on understated ending inventory	Based on corrected ending inventory
Inventory at beginning of year	$10,000	$10,000
Purchases	75,000	75,000
Cost of goods available for sale	$85,000	$85,000
Deduct: inventory at end of year	25,000	30,000
Cost of goods sold	$60,000	$55,000

The essential point to remember from this illustration is that any error in counting or pricing the inventory will cause a corresponding error in the cost of goods sold. Furthermore, since the cost of goods sold is used in computing the net income for the period, any error in the cost of goods sold figure will cause an error of the same amount in the net income reported for the period.

To demonstrate the relationship of the inventory figure to the determination of net income, the above example of a $5,000 error in the ending inventory is now continued by assuming that the sales for the year amounted to $100,000 and the operating expenses to $30,000. The following schedule shows that the $5,000 error in the ending inventory caused the net income (as well as the cost of goods sold) to be in error by $5,000.

EFFECT OF ERROR IN PHYSICAL INVENTORY ON NET INCOME

	Based on understated ending inventory	Based on corrected ending inventory
Net sales	*$100,000*	*$100,000*
Cost of goods sold	*60,000*	*55,000*
Gross profit on sales	*$ 40,000*	*$ 45,000*
Expenses	*30,000*	*30,000*
Net income	*$ 10,000*	*$ 15,000*

This illustration shows that an understatement of the ending inventory will cause an understatement of the same amount in the net income. Conversely, an overstatement of the ending inventory will cause an overstatement of the same amount in the net income. Fraud cases in which an unscrupulous manager attempted to deceive an absentee owner, stockholders, bankers, or income tax authorities have often involved the purposeful misstatement of inventories as a means of reporting a misleading amount of net income. This is one reason why outsiders who must rely upon financial statements of a business usually insist that these statements be audited by an independent firm of certified public accountants.

These possibilities of error in using the periodic inventory method are not described with any intention of discrediting this system of accounting for merchandise. The businessman should, however, be aware of the assumptions implicit in this method of computing the cost of goods sold.

Accounting for merchandise purchases

The purchase of merchandise for resale to customers is recorded by debiting an account called Merchandise Purchases. This title is often shortened to the single word Purchases. The Purchases account is used *only* for merchandise acquired for resale; assets acquired for use in the business (such as a delivery truck, a typewriter, or office supplies) are recorded by debiting the appropriate asset account, not the Purchases account. Only merchandise acquired for resale is entered in the Purchases account because this account is used in computing the cost of goods sold. The journal entry to record a purchase of merchandise is illustrated as follows:

JOURNAL
ENTRY FOR
PURCHASE
OF MER-
CHANDISE

Purchases	*1,000*	
Accounts Payable (or Cash)		*1,000*
Purchased merchandise from ABC Supply Co.		

At the end of the accounting period, the balance accumulated in the Purchases account represents the total cost of merchandise purchased during the period. This amount is used in preparing the income statement. The Purchases account has then served its purpose and it is closed to the Income Summary account. Since the Purchases account is closed at the end of each period, it has a zero balance at the beginning of each succeeding period.

Transportation-in. The cost of merchandise acquired for resale logically includes any transportation charges necessary to place the goods in the purchaser's place of business. To illustrate this point, let us assume that the manager of an electrical appliance store has the alternative of buying electric stoves locally at $200 apiece or of buying the identical stoves from a vendor in a distant city at $180 each. If he buys the stoves from the more distant supplier, however, he will have to pay freight charges of $20 for each stove. With which supplier should he place the order?

In comparing the two alternatives, the manager will surely regard the charges for transportation as part of the cost of the stoves. In other words, the delivered cost of the stoves is $200 each, regardless of which source of supply is used. In more general terms, we may say that the cost of merchandise includes the amount paid the vendor plus any transportation charges for delivery of the goods.

In some lines of business it is customary for the manufacturer to pay the cost of shipping merchandise to the retailer's store. Of course the manufacturer tries to set the price of the goods high enough to cover the transportation charges as well as all his other costs. Consequently, the cost of merchandise to the purchaser normally includes the cost of transporting the goods, regardless of whether he pays the freight charges directly to the railroad or merely pays the seller a sufficiently high price to cover the cost of delivering the goods.

A separate ledger account is used to accumulate transportation charges on merchandise purchased. An account title commonly used is Transportation-in; alternative titles include Freight-in and Freight on Purchases. The journal entry to record the payment of transportation charges on inbound shipments of merchandise is as follows:

JOURNALIZ-
ING TRANS-
PORTATION
CHARGES
ON PUR-
CHASES
OF MER-
CHANDISE

> *Transportation-in* *169.50*
>   *Cash (or Accounts Payable)* *169.50*
> *Air freight charges on merchandise purchased from*
> *Miller Brothers, Kansas City.*

Since transportation charges are part of the delivered cost of merchandise purchased, the Transportation-in account is combined with the Purchases account in the income statement to determine the cost of goods available for sale. The inclusion of transportation-in in the income statement is illustrated below.

TRANSPOR-
TATION-IN:
AN ELEMENT
OF COST OF
GOODS
AVAILABLE
FOR SALE

Partial Income Statement
For the Year Ended December 31, 19___

Sales		*$100,000*
Cost of goods sold:		
Inventory, Jan. 1	*$22,000*	
Purchases	*$60,500*	
Transportation-in	*2,500*	*63,000*
Cost of goods available for sale	*$85,000*	
Deduct: inventory, Dec. 31	*20,000*	
Cost of goods sold		*65,000*
Gross profit on sales		*$ 35,000*

One reason for using a separate ledger account for Transportation-in rather than debiting these charges directly to the Purchases account is to provide management with a clear record of the amount expended each period for inbound transportation. A knowledge of the amount and trend of each significant type of cost is a necessary first step if management is to control costs effectively. For example, detailed information concerning transportation costs would be important to management in making decisions between rail and air transportation, or in deciding whether to order in carload lots rather than in smaller quantities.

Transportation charges on inbound shipments of merchandise must not be confused with transportation charges on outbound shipments of goods to customers. Freight charges and other expenses incurred in making deliveries to customers are regarded as selling expenses; these outlays are debited to a separate account entitled Transportation-out, and are not included in the cost of goods sold.

Purchases returns and allowances. When merchandise purchased from suppliers is found to be unsatisfactory the goods may be returned to the seller, or a request may be made for an allowance on the price. A return of goods to the vendor is recorded as follows:

<table>
<tr><td>JOURNAL
ENTRY FOR
RETURN OF
GOODS TO
SUPPLIER</td><td>*Accounts Payable* *1,200*
    Purchases Returns and Allowances *1,200*
To charge Marvel Supply Co. for the cost of goods
returned.</td></tr>
</table>

Sometimes when the purchaser of merchandise finds the goods not entirely satisfactory, he may agree to keep the goods in consideration for a reduction or allowance on the original purchase price. The entry to record such an allowance is essentially the same as that for a return.

<table>
<tr><td>JOURNAL
ENTRY FOR
PRICE
ALLOWANCE
ON DEFEC-
TIVE GOODS
PURCHASED</td><td>*Accounts Payable* *360*
    Purchases Returns and Allowances *360*
Obtained allowance on price of merchandise purchased
from XY Company, because of defects in the goods.</td></tr>
</table>

The effect of the debit side of each of these entries is to reduce the liability to the supplier. In some cases a cash refund might be obtained; under these circumstances the debit portion of the entry would be to Cash rather than to Accounts Payable.

The effect of the credit to Purchases Returns and allowances is the same as if the Purchases account itself were reduced by a credit. In the income statement, the credit balance of the Purchases Returns and Allowances account is deducted from the debit balance of the Purchases account to arrive at the net purchases, as illustrated below.

<table>
<tr><td>SHOWING
PURCHASE
RETURNS
IN THE
INCOME
STATEMENT</td><td>*Cost of goods sold:*
  Inventory, Jan. 1 .... *$32,900*
  Purchases *$51,500*
    Deduct: purchases returns & allowances .. *1,200*
  Net purchases *$50,300*
  Transportation-in *3,100*   *53,400*
  Cost of goods available for sale .... *$86,300*</td></tr>
</table>

The use of a Purchases Returns and Allowances account rather than the recording of returns by direct credits to the Purchases account is advisable because the books then show both the total amount of the purchases and the amount of purchases which required adjustment or return. Management is interested in the percentage relationship of goods returned to total goods purchased, because the returning of merchandise for credit is a time-consuming, costly process. Excessive returns suggest that the purchasing department should look for more dependable sources of supply.

The Inventory account

As previously mentioned, all purchases of merchandise for resale are recorded by debiting the Purchases account. At the end of the period, the Purchases account is closed by transferring its balance to the Income Summary account. However, in making this transfer, we must recognize that not all the merchandise purchased has been sold; the unsold merchandise must be counted and listed at its cost value and an entry made to record this inventory in the ledger. This step assures that the inventory will be included as an asset on the balance sheet and will also be used in the income statement in computing the cost of goods sold.

Let us use again the example of a new business which begins operations sometime during the year 1962. Since it is a new business, there is no beginning inventory of merchandise. During 1962 several purchases of merchandise for resale are made; the total amount of these purchases is $50,000. Some of these goods are sold, but a considerable stock of merchandise is on hand at the end of the first year of operations. The taking of a physical inventory on December 31, 1962, reveals a stock of goods with a cost value of $10,000. The journal entry to bring this inventory on the books is as follows:

RECORDING THE ENDING INVENTORY

```
1962
Dec. 31   Inventory  ........................ 10,000
                Income  Summary  ...........           10,000
          To record the ending inventory.
```

To understand the reason for this entry, we must bear in mind that the entire amount of the year's purchases of merchandise has been transferred to the Income Summary account by the closing of the Purchases account. Now by debiting Inventory and crediting Income Summary, we are recognizing that a portion of this merchandise remains as an asset to be carried forward to the next period when it will be offered for sale. In other words, most of the merchandise purchased during a given year is sold in that year and thus becomes a cost of obtaining that year's revenue. However, some portion of the year's purchases remains unsold at the year-end; it therefore represents an unexpired cost (or asset) to be used to obtain revenue in the following period.

The Inventory account is set up at the end of the first year of operations; no other entry will be made in the Inventory account until the end of 1963, the second accounting period. Throughout the year 1963, the Inventory account does not show the amount of goods currently on hand; it shows the cost of goods which *were* on hand at the beginning of 1963.

At December 31, 1963, the end of the second year, the Inventory account still contains the debit balance of $10,000, representing the stock of merchandise on hand at the beginning of the year. This beginning inventory balance is now closed into the Income Summary account:

```
1963
Dec. 31   Income Summary .................. 10,000
                Inventory ................            10,000
          To close the beginning inventory into
          Income Summary.
```

Since the Inventory, Purchases, Transportation-in, and Purchases Returns and Allowances accounts, taken as a group, contain the cost of all goods available for sale during the year, it is logical that all these accounts should be closed into the Income Summary. The Income Summary account then contains the cost of goods available for sale during the year.

The ending inventory amounting to, say, $25,000, is determined by counting and pricing the goods on hand at the end of 1963. This ending inventory is recognized as an asset and brought on the books by an entry debiting Inventory and crediting Income Summary, thus removing from the Income Summary account the cost of the *unsold* goods and leaving as a net debit in the account the cost of goods sold during the year. The entry at the end of the second year to record the ending inventory is as follows:

```
1963
Dec. 31   Inventory ...................... 25,000
                Income Summary ...........            25,000
          To record the ending inventory.
```

Illustration of periodic inventory method

The October transactions of the Campus Sports Shop will now be used to illustrate the accounting cycle for a business using the periodic inventory

CAMPUS SPORTS SHOP
After-closing Trial Balance
September 30, 19___

Cash	$ 2,800	
Inventory	7,500	
Unexpired insurance	200	
Land	3,000	
Building	10,000	
Accumulated depreciation: building		$ 960
Accounts payable		2,600
Robert Riley, capital ......·...............		19,940
	$23,500	$23,500

system of accounting for merchandise. The starting point for this illustration is an after-closing trial balance prepared on September 30. As explained in Chapter 3, an after-closing trial balance is prepared at the end of each period to prove that the ledger is in balance *after* the books have been adjusted and closed. Since this trial balance was prepared after the books were closed for September, it contains balance sheet accounts only.

The amount of inventory listed in the above after-closing trial balance had been determined on September 30 by counting the merchandise on hand and pricing it at cost.

Recording sales of merchandise. Sales of sports equipment during October amounted to $10,025. All sales were for cash, and each sales transaction was rung up on a cash register. At the close of each day's business, the total sales for the day were computed by pressing the total key on the cash register. As soon as each day's sales were computed, a separate journal entry could have been prepared and posted to the Sales account in the ledger. To keep this illustration reasonably short, however, we shall make only two journal entries, each of which represents one-half of the month's sales. These summary journal entries for sales are as follows:

<table>
<tr><td>SALES FOR
FIRST
HALF OF
OCTOBER</td><td>19__
Oct. 15 Cash 5,025
          Sales   5,025
          To record sales for first half of Ocober.</td></tr>
</table>

<table>
<tr><td>SALES
FOR LAST
HALF OF
OCTOBER</td><td>19__
Oct. 31 Cash 5,000
          Sales   5,000
          To record sales from October 16 to 31.</td></tr>
</table>

In actual practice, daily entering of cash sales in the journal is desirable in order to minimize the opportunity for errors or dishonesty by employees in handling the cash receipts. In Chapter 8 a procedure will be described which provides a daily record of sales and cash receipts yet avoids the making of an excessive number of entries in the Cash account and Sales account.

Recording sales returns and allowances. On October 27 a customer returned some unsatisfactory merchandise and was given a refund of $46. Another customer complained on October 28 of a slight defect in an article he had recently purchased and was given a refund of $10, representing half of the original price. The journal entries to record these returns and allowances were as follows:

RETURNS
AND ALLOW-
ANCES

19__			
Oct. 27	*Sales Returns and Allowances*	*46*	
	Cash		*46*
	Make refund for merchandise returned by customer.		
Oct. 28	*Sales Returns and Allowances*	*10*	
	Cash		*10*
	Allowance to customer for defect in merchandise.		

Other transactions. During October other transactions were as follows :

Oct. 2.   Paid for newspaper advertising for October, $250.

Oct. 10.   Purchased merchandise from Miller Company costing $7,300. Payment to be made in 30 days.

Oct. 11.   Paid $200 in transportation charges for delivery to store of merchandise purchased from Miller Company.

Oct. 12.   Returned to Miller Company a portion of the goods purchased on October 10. Cost of the goods returned was $600.

Oct. 15.   Paid salaries for first half of October, $1,000.

Oct. 19.   Purchased merchandise for cash from Swingline Manufacturing Company in amount of $800.

Oct. 29.   Paid for October telephone service, $50.

Oct. 30.   Paid salaries for last half of month, $1,000.

Oct. 30.   Cash withdrawn by owner, $300.

Oct. 31.   Paid accounts payable in amount of $2,600.

OCTOBER
TRANS-
ACTIONS

Journal entries for all October transactions are now presented in chronological order.

19__				
Oct.	*2*	*Advertising Expense*	*250*	
		Cash		*250*
		Paid for October newspaper advertising.		
	10	*Purchases*	*7,300*	
		Accounts Payable		*7,300*
		Purchased merchandise from Miller Co.		
		Payment due in 30 days.		

19__				
Oct.	11	Transportation-in	200	
		Cash		200
		Freight charges on inbound merchandise.		
	12	Accounts Payable	600	
		Purchase Returns and Allowances		600
		Returned merchandise to vendor.		
	15	Salaries Expense	1,000	
		Cash		1,000
		Paid salaries for first half of October.		
	15	Cash	5,025	
		Sales		5,025
		To record sales for first half of October.		
	19	Purchases	800	
		Cash		800
		Purchased merchandise from Swingline Mfg. Co.		
	27	Sales Returns and Allowances	46	
		Cash		46
		Made refund for merchandise returned by customer.		
	28	Sales Returns and Allowances	10	
		Cash		10
		Allowance to customer for defect in merchandise.		
	29	Telephone Expense	50	
		Cash		50
		Paid for September telephone service.		
	30	Salaries Expense	1,000	
		Cash		1,000
		Paid salaries for last half of month.		
	30	Robert Riley, Drawing	300	
		Cash		300
	31	Cash	5,000	
		Sales		5,000
		To record sales for last half of October.		
	31	Accounts Payable	2,600	
		Cash		2,600
		Paid creditors.		

Work sheet for a merchandising business. After the October transactions of the Campus Sports Shop had been posted to ledger accounts, the work sheet illustrated on page 179 was prepared. The first step in the preparation of the work sheet was, of course, the listing of the balances of the ledger accounts in the Trial Balance columns. In studying this work sheet, notice that the Inventory account in the Trial Balance debit column still shows a balance of $7,500, the cost of merchandise on hand at the end of September. No entries were made in the Inventory account during October despite the various purchases and sales of merchandise. The significance of the Inventory account in the trial balance is that it shows the amount of merchandise with which the Campus Sports Shop began operations for the month of October.

Adjustments on the work sheet. Only two adjustments were necessary at October 31, one to record depreciation of the building and the other to record the insurance expense for the month. If an adjustment affects an account not listed in the trial balance, the account title is written below the trial balance totals and the amount is entered on the same line in the Adjustments columns. For example, the adjustment for depreciation in the amount of $40 required a debt to the Depreciation Expense account which did not appear in the trial balance. Similarly, the adjustment to record the expiration during October of $20 of the prepaid insurance premium required a debit to Insurance Expense. This account also was written in below the trial balance totals. The Adjustments columns were then totaled to prove the equality of the adjustment debits and credits. This last step may be omitted until the work sheet is completed. If all remaining columns balance, it will not be necessary to make this test of accuracy.

Omission of Adjusted Trial Balance columns. In the work sheet previously illustrated in Chapter 5, page 144, the amounts in the Trial Balance columns were combined with the amounts listed in the Adjustments columns and then extended into the Adjusted Trial Balance columns. When there are only a few adjusting entries, many accountants prefer to omit the Adjusted Trial Balance columns and to extend the trial balance figures (as adjusted by the amounts in the Adjustments columns) directly to the Income Statement or Balanced Sheet columns. This procedure is used in the work sheet for the Campus Sports Shop.

Recording the ending inventory on the work sheet. The key points to be observed in this work sheet are (1) the method of recording the ending inventory and (2) the method of handling the various accounts making up the cost of goods sold.

After the close of business on October 31, Mr. Riley and his assistants took a physical inventory of all merchandise in the store. The cost of the entire stock of goods was determined to be $9,000. This ending inventory, dated October 31, does not appear in the trial balance; it is therefore written on the first available line below the trial balance totals. The amount of $9,000 is listed in the Income Statement credit column and also in the Balance Sheet debit column. By entering the ending inventory in the Income Statement *credit* column, we are in effect deducting it from the total of the beginning inventory, the purchases, and the transportation-in, all of which are extended from the trial balance to the Income Statement *debit* column.

One of the functions of the Income Statement columns is to bring together all the accounts involved in determining the cost of goods sold. The accounts with debit balances are the beginning inventory, the purchases, and the transportation-in; these accounts total $15,800. Against this total, the two credit items of purchases returns, $600, and ending inventory, $9,000, are offset. The three merchandising accounts with debit balances exceed in total the two with credit balances by an amount of $6,200; this amount is the cost of goods sold, as shown in the income statement on page 180.

The ending inventory is also entered in the Balance Sheet debit column, because this inventory of merchandise on October 31 will appear as an asset in the balance sheet bearing this date.

Completing the work sheet. When all the accounts on the work sheet have been extended into the Income Statement or Balance Sheet columns (and the ending inventory has been entered), the final four columns should be totaled. The net income of $1,409 is computed by subtracting the Income Statement debit column from the Income Statement credit column. This same amount of $1,409 can also be obtained by subtracting the Balance Sheet credit column from the Balance Sheet debit column. To balance out the four columns, the amount of the net income is entered in the Income Statement debit column and on the same line in the Balance Sheet credit column. (The proof of accuracy afforded by the self-balancing nature of the work sheet was explained in Chaper 5.) Final totals are determined for the Income Statement and Balance Sheet columns, and the work sheet is complete.

Financial statements. The work to be done at the end of the period is much the same for a merchandising business as for a service-type firm. First, the work sheet is completed; then, financial statements are prepared from the data in the work sheet; next, the adjusting and closing entries are entered in the journal and posted to the ledger accounts; and finally, a post-closing trial balance is prepared. This completes the periodic accounting cycle.

The income statement for a merchandising business may be regarded as consisting of three sections: (1) the sales revenue section, (2) the cost of goods sold section, and (3) the operating expense section. The following income statement and balance sheet were prepared from the work sheet on page 179. Notice particularly the arrangement of items in the cost of goods sold section of the income statement; this portion of the income statement shows in summary form most of the essential accounting concepts covered in this chapter.

CAMPUS SPORTS SHOP
Work Sheet
For the Month Ended October 31, 19___

	Trial balance Dr	Trial balance Cr	Adjustments° Dr	Adjustments° Cr	Income statement Dr	Income statement Cr	Balance sheet Dr	Balance sheet Cr
Cash	6,569						6,569	
Inventory, September 30	7,500				7,500			
Unexpired insurance	200			(b) 20			180	
Land	3,000						3,000	
Building	10,000						10,000	
Accumulated depreciation: bldg.		960		(a) 40				1,000
Accounts payable		6,700						6,700
Robert Riley, capital		19,940						19,940
Robert Riley, drawing	300						300	
Sales		10,025				10,025		
Sales returns & allowances	56				56			
Purchases	8,100				8,100			
Purchase returns & allowances		600				600		
Transportation-in	200				200			
Advertising expense	250				250			
Salaries expense	2,000				2,000			
Telephone expense	50				50			
	38,225	38,225						
Depreciation expense: bldg.			(a) 40		40			
Insurance expense			(b) 20		20			
			60	60				
Inventory, October 31						9,000	9,000	
					18,216	19,625	29,049	27,640
Net income					1,409			1,409
					19,625	19,625	29,049	29,049

° Adjustments: (a) depreciation of building during October; (b) insurance premium expired during October.

CAMPUS SPORTS SHOP
Income Statement
For the Month Ended October 31, 19___

Revenue from sales:

Sales	$10,025	
Deduct: sales returns & allowances	56	
Net sales		$9,969

Cost of goods sold:

Merchandise inventory, Oct. 1		$ 7,500	
Purchases	$8,100		
Deduct: purchase returns & allowances	600	7,500	
Transportation-in		200	
Cost of goods available for sale		$15,200	
Deduct: merchandise inventory, Oct. 31		9,000	
Cost of goods sold			6,200
Gross profit on sales			$3,769

Operating expenses:

Salaries	$ 2,000	
Advertising	250	
Telephone	50	
Depreciation	40	
Insurance	20	
Total operating expenses		2,360
Net income		$1,409

CAMPUS SPORTS SHOP
Balance Sheet
October 31, 19___

Assets

Cash		$ 6,569
Merchandise inventory		9,000
Unexpired insurance		180
Land		3,000
Building	$10,000	
Less: accumulated depreciation	1,000	9,000
		$27,749

Liabilities and Owner's Equity

Liabilities:
Accounts payable . . . . $ 6,700
Owner's equity:
Robert Riley, capital, Sept. 30 . . . . $19,940
Net income for October $1,409
Less: withdrawals 300
Increase in capital 1,109
Robert Riley, capital, Oct. 31 21,049
$27,749

Closing entries. The entries used in closing revenue and expense accounts have been explained in preceding chapters. The only new elements in this illustration of closing entries for a trading business are the entries showing the elimination of the beginning inventory and the recording of the ending inventory. The beginning inventory is cleared out of the Inventory account by a debit to Income Summary and a credit to Inventory. A separate entry could be made for this purpose, but we can save time by making one compound entry which will debit the Income Summary account with the balance of the beginning inventory and with the balances of all temporary proprietorship accounts having debit balances. The *temporary proprietorship accounts* are those which appear in the income statement. As the name suggests, the temporary proprietorship accounts are used during the period to accumulate temporarily the increases and decreases in the proprietor's equity resulting from operation of the business.

CLOSING
TEMPORARY
PROPRIETOR-
SHIP
ACCOUNTS
WITH DEBIT
BALANCES

Oct. 31   Income Summary 18,216
Inventory 7,500
Purchases 8,100
Sales Returns and Allowances . . . 56
Transportation-in 200
Advertising Expense 250
Salaries Expense 2,000
Telephone Expense 50
Depreciation Expense 40
Insurance Expense 20
To close out the beginning inventory and
the temporary proprietorship accounts
having debit balances.

Note that the above entry closes all the operating expense accounts as well as the accounts used to accumulate the cost of merchandise sold, and also the Sales Returns and Allowances account. Although the Sales

Returns and Allowances account has a debit balance, it is not an expense account. In terms of account classification, it belongs in the revenue group of accounts because it serves as an offset to the Sales account and appears in the income statement as a deduction from Sales.

To bring the ending inventory on the books after the stock taking on October 31, we could make a separate entry debiting Inventory and crediting the Income Summary account. It is more convenient, however, to combine this step with the closing of the Sales account and any other temporary proprietorship accounts having credit balances, as illustrated in the following closing entry.

CLOSING TEMPORARY PROPRIETOR- SHIP ACCOUNTS WITH CREDIT BALANCES	*Oct. 31 Inventory* .... 9,000 *Sales* .... 10,025 *Purchase Returns and Allowances* ..... 600 *Income Summary* .... *To record the ending inventory and to close all temporary proprietorship accounts having credit balances.*	*19,625*

The remaining closing entries serve to transfer the balance of the Income Summary account to the owner's capital account, and to close the drawing account, as follows:

CLOSING THE INCOME SUMMARY ACCOUNT AND OWNER'S DRAWING ACCOUNT	*Oct. 31 Income Summary* .... 1,409 *Robert Riley, Capital* .... *To close the Income Summary account.* *Oct. 31 Robert Riley, Capital* .... 300 *Robert Riley, Drawing* .... *To close the Drawing account.*	*1,409* *300*

Summary of merchandising transactions and related accounting entries

The transactions regularly encountered in merchandising operations and the related accounting entries may be concisely summarized as follows:

CUSTOMARY JOURNAL ENTRIES RELATING TO MER- CHANDISE	*Transactions during the period:* Purchase merchandise for re- sale. Incur transportation charges on merchandise purchased for resale.	*Related accounting entries:* Debit Purchases; credit Cash or Accounts Payable. Debit Transportation-in; credit Cash or Accounts Payable.

Return unsatisfactory merchandise to the supplier, or obtain a reduction from the original price.	Debit Cash or Accounts Payable; credit Purchase Returns and Allowances.
Sell merchandise to customers.	Debit Cash or Accounts Receivable; credit Sales.
Permit customers to return merchandise, or grant them a reduction from original price.	Debit Sales Returns and Allowances; credit Cash or Accounts Receivable.

Inventory procedures at end of period:

Transfer the balance of the beginning inventory to the Income Summary.	Debit Income Summary; credit Inventory.
Take a physical inventory of goods on hand at the end of the period, and price these goods at cost.	Debit Inventory; credit Income Summary.

Summary of inventory methods available to management

The management of a merchandising business must decide whether to maintain continuous day-to-day records of the merchandise inventory on hand (the perpetual inventory system), or to rely upon the periodic inventory system described in this chapter. Perpetual inventory records are appropriate for merchandise of high unit cost; these continuous "book inventories" give management current detailed information on the amount of capital invested in inventory and on the adequacy of the supply of goods being offered for sale to customers.

A dealer in new automobiles, for example, will record the receipt of a shipment of new cars from the factory by debiting Inventory and crediting Accounts Payable. In support of the Inventory account he will fill out a separate inventory card for each car received, showing its serial number and its cost. The total of the costs shown on these cards will equal the amount in the Inventory account. When an automobile is sold, the dealer will debit a Cost of Sales account in the ledger and credit the Inventory account for the cost of that particular car. The inventory card will be removed from the file showing cars on hand. This method of accounting for merchandise is known as a perpetual inventory system because it shows the quantity and cost of goods in inventory from day to day. The cost of each car purchased is immediately added to the inventory and the cost of each car sold is promptly removed from the inventory. The cost of cars sold is accumulated in a Cost of Sales account in the ledger as rapidly as sales occur. The determination of the gross profit on sales is a simple step when both a Sales account and a Cost of Sales account are maintained on this current basis.

As a contrast to the example of the automobile dealer, let us consider the problem of determining the cost of goods sold in a drugstore. Assume that a customer buys a chocolate sundae, a bottle of aspirin, and a package of razor blades. It would obviously be impracticable to keep a separate inventory card for each of these small items; it would also be impracticable to make an entry recording the cost of each small item sold. The cost of performing so much bookkeeping work on these low-priced items would be greater than the profit from their sale. In every business it is necessary to select accounting procedures that will be efficient and economical for the kind of products being handled. Accounting for merchandise by using a perpetual inventory system is usually desirable for businesses which sell high-priced articles such as automobiles; it is generally less appropriate in businesses handling a large volume of low-priced articles. The latter type of business is more likely to use the periodic inventory system.

Under the periodic inventory method, the accounting records do not show the amount of merchandise on hand from day to day during the accounting period. Additions to the stock of merchandise by purchases from suppliers are recorded as they occur, but reductions in the inventory caused by selling goods to customers are not measured or recognized in the accounts until the end of the period. On the last day of the period the cost of merchandise on hand is determined by counting all goods in stock and valuing them at the appropriate cost prices. The cost of goods sold during the period is then determined by adding the inventory amount at the beginning of the period to the cost of goods purchased during the period and deducting from this total the ending inventory of merchandise.

QUESTIONS

1. During October the Lee Company made sales of merchandise on account amounting to $40,000, of which $38,000 remained uncollected at October 31. Sales for cash during the month amounted to $10,000, and an additional $33,000 was received from customers in payment for goods sold to them in prior months. Also, during October, the Lee Company borrowed $12,000 cash from the First National Bank. What was the total revenue for October?

2. Will a store that sells all merchandise at prices in excess of cost necessarily report a net profit for the year?

3. Compute the amount of cost of goods sold, given the following account balances: beginning inventory $11,000, purchases $43,000, purchase returns and allowances $1,500, transportation-in $500, and ending inventory $12,000.

4. During 1962 Darnley Corporation purchased merchandise costing $100,000. State the cost of goods sold under each of the following alternative assumptions:

  a. No beginning inventory; ending inventory $20,000
  b. Beginning inventory $30,000; no ending inventory
  c. Beginning inventory $18,000; ending inventory $26,000
  d. Beginning inventory $29,000; ending inventory $25,000

5. Given the following data, determine the amount of purchases for the period.

Cost of goods sold	*$121,000*
Transportation-in	*1,890*
Beginning inventory	*43,640*
Purchase returns and allowances	*2,310*
Ending inventory	*38,500*
Sales	*182,650*

6. During the taking of physical inventory at December 31, merchandise stored in a warehouse was overlooked and therefore omitted from the inventory. Assuming the cost of the inventory merchandise in the warehouse was $6,000, what were the effects of the error on the income statement and the balance sheet?

7. During the taking of physical inventory at December 31, 1962, certain merchandise which cost $2,500 was counted twice and the inventory was therefore overstated by $2,500. What was the effect of this error on the cost of goods sold? On net income for 1962?

8. A transposition error made in compiling the year-end inventory caused an understatement of $9,000 in inventory. The error was not discovered, and the company prepared an income statement showing a net loss for the year of $5,500. State the correct figure to reflect the operating results for the year.

9. Zenith Company uses the periodic inventory method and maintains its accounting records on a calendar-year basis. Does the beginning or the ending inventory figure appear in the trial balance prepared from the ledger on December 31?

PROBLEMS

Group A

6A-1. *Instructions.* Prepare journal entries for the selected transactions of the Winchester Wholesale Company, which uses the periodic inventory method.

  Data

May 4. Sold merchandise to George V. Hatch on open account, $826.

May 5. Purchased merchandise on 30-day credit from Bruce Corporation, $2,324.

May 9. George V. Hatch returned for credit $20 of the merchandise purchased on May 4.

May 10. Transportation charges on merchandise purchased from Bruce Corporation in the amount of $18 were paid by check today.

May 12. Sold merchandise for cash to Williams Company, $2,128.

May 17. Purchased office equipment on open account from Candor Corporation, $248.

May 19. Purchased merchandise for cash, $97.

May 24. Sold merchandise for cash, $174.

May 26. Refunded $25 to a customer who had made a cash purchase on May 24.

May 26. Sold merchandise to Hailey Company on open account, $163.

May 26. Paid transportation charges on sale to Hailey Company, $12.

May 28. Purchased merchandise on open account from Simpson & Company, $410.

May 29.   Returned for credit $105 of merchandise purchased from Simpson & Company.

May 30.   Purchased stationery and other office supplies for cash, $242.

6A-2. The Trent Company maintains its accounting records on the basis of a fiscal year ending June 30. After all necessary adjustments had been made at June 30, 1963, the adjusted trial balance appeared as follows:

TRENT COMPANY
Adjusted Trial Balance
June 30, 1963

Cash	$ 13,624	
Accounts receivable	32,010	
Inventory (June 30, 1962)	31,400	
Prepaid insurance	640	
Supplies	1,240	
Furniture and fixtures	14,870	
Accumulated depreciation: furn. and fix.		$ 974
Accounts payable		7,800
Notes payable		5,000
Robert Trent, capital		48,500
Sales		281,620
Sales returns and allowances	2,365	
Purchases	189,382	
Purchase returns and allowances		1,820
Transportation-in	13,508	
Salaries and wages expense	37,652	
Rent expense	6,000	
Depreciation expense	974	
Supplies expense	1,225	
Insurance expense	824	
	$345,714	$345,714

Other data

The inventory on June 30, 1963, as determined by count, amounted to $36,992.

Instructions

a. Prepare an income statement for Trent Company for the year ended June 30, 1963.

b. Prepare the necessary journal entries to close the books on June 30, 1963.

c. Assume that the ending inventory of $36,992 was overstated $2,500 as a result of double counting part of the goods on hand at June 30, 1963. Prepare a list of the items in the income statement which are incorrect as a result of the overstatement, and list in a second column the corrected figures.

6A-3. After several years of managerial experience in retailing, A. C. Norton opened his own retail store on January 1, 1962. He had saved $20,000 over a period of years and had received an inheritance of $60,000, all of which he invested in the new business. Before taking this step, Norton had given considerable thought to the alternative of continuing in his present position, which paid a salary of $9,000 a year, and investing his capital in high-grade securities, which he estimated would provide an average return of 4% on the amount invested.

This trial balance was taken from the records at December 31, 1962.

NORTON COMPANY
Trial Balance
December 31, 1962

Cash	$ 3,438	
Accounts receivable	8,720	
Inventory	24,500	
Supplies	1,980	
Prepaid insurance	474	
Land	25,000	
Building	48,000	
Equipment	10,000	
Accounts payable		$ 23,690
Notes payable		8,000
A. C. Norton, capital		80,000
A. C. Norton, drawing	6,000	
Sales		164,440
Sales returns and allowances	2,310	
Purchases	106,520	
Purchase returns and allowances		2,364
Transportation-in	5,860	
Selling commissions	5,852	
Delivery expense	2,170	
Salaries and wages	27,160	
Property taxes	510	
	$278,494	$278,494

The December 31, 1962, inventory by physical count was $26,220.

Other data
(a) Accrued property taxes, $940.
(b) Supplies on hand, $360.
(c) Insurance expired during year, $212.
(d) Depreciation rates: 2 1/2% on buildings; 10% on equipment.

Instructions
a. Prepare working papers for the year ended December 31, 1962.
b. Prepare the necessary adjusting journal entries at December 31, 1962.
c. Prepare the journal entries required to close the books as of December 31, 1962.
d. Prepare a schedule comparing the adequacy of net income from the business for the year 1962 with the income Norton would have received by continuing as a salaried manager and investing his capital in securities. State your opinion based on this comparative schedule.

6A-4. The Richardson Company operates a small but fashionable clothing shop and makes about 90% of its sales on a charge account basis. The financial condition of the company on April 30, 19___, is reflected in the following balance sheet.

RICHARDSON COMPANY
Balance Sheet
April 30, 19___

Assets

Current assets:

Cash	$11,000	
City of X bonds	6,000	
Accounts receivable	23,000	
Inventory	39,300	
Prepaid insurance	1,080	
Total current assets		$ 80,380

Fixed assets:

Equipment	$60,000	
Less: accumulated depreciation	18,000	
Total fixed assets		42,000
Total assets		$122,380

Liabilities and Proprietorship

Liabilities:

Accounts payable	$21,200	
Accrued taxes payable	3,800	
Total liabilities		$ 25,000

Proprietorship:

E. M. Richardson, capital		97,380
Total liabilities & proprietorship		$122,380

The transactions for the month of May are listed below.

May 1.	Paid store rent for May, $1,250.
May 4.	Summary of cash sales, May 1 to 4 inclusive, $310.
May 6.	Sales of merchandise on account, $2,757.
May 8.	Payments on accounts payable, $6,437.
May 11.	Summary of weekly cash sales, $285.
May 12.	Paid one-half of the accrued taxes.
May 13.	Sales of merchandise on account, $3,416.
May 15.	Purchased two-year insurance policy, $624.
May 18.	Summary of weekly cash sales, $296.
May 18.	Purchases of merchandise for cash, $1,650.
May 20.	Collections on open accounts, $15,680.
May 20.	Sales of merchandise on account, $3,340.
May 23.	Purchased merchandise on account from Becker Company, $7,821.

May 25. Summary of weekly cash sales, $342.
May 26. Sales commissions for May were paid, $2,800.
May 31. Sales of merchandise on account, $2,760.
May 31. Summary of weekly cash sales, $198.
May 31. Sales returns and allowances during May amounted to $732; purchase returns and allowances, $226; transportation charges on goods purchased, $660. All returns pertain to goods sold on credit; all transportation charges were paid in cash.

Other data
(*a*) Of the prepaid insurance on April 30, $648 is still prepaid at May 31. For the policy purchased May 15, the expiration of premium for half a month should be recognized.
(*b*) Depreciation is at the rate of 10% per annum.
(*c*) May taxes accrued amounted to $220.
(*d*) The inventory by physical count was $42,560 at May 31.

Instructions
a. Enter the balance sheet figures for April 30 in the ledger.
b. Journalize and post all May transactions to the ledger.
c. Prepare necessary working papers.
d. Prepare the financial statements.
e. Prepare the adjusting entries and post to the ledger.
f. Prepare closing journal entries, post to ledger accounts, and rule the nominal accounts.
g. Prepare an after-closing trial balance.

Group B

6B-1. Listed below are the transactions of the Ready-Mix Cement Company for the month of August. The company closes its books annually on December 31.
Aug. 2. Purchased merchandise on account from Sharp Supply Company, $482.
Aug. 2. Paid monthly rent on building, $300.
Aug. 5. Cash sale of merchandise, $1,216.
Aug. 7. Purchased equipment on account from Darby Company, $583.
Aug. 8. Sold merchandise on account to Field Construction Company, $1,792.
Aug. 10. Purchased merchandise for cash, $2,221.
Aug. 10. Returned $120 of defective equipment to Darby Company for credit.
Aug. 13. Sold merchandise on account to A. K. Smith, $1,128.
Aug. 15. Granted a $22 allowance to A. K. Smith on merchandise delivered on Aug. 13, because of minor defects discovered in the merchandise.
Aug. 18. Agreed to cancel the account receivable from Field Construction Company in exchange for their services in erecting an additional garage on company property.
Aug. 25. Paid balance due Darby Company.
Aug. 29. Cash sale of merchandise, $174.
Aug. 31. Paid salaries and wages for the month, $1,520.
Aug. 31. Paid Holmes Service Station $624 for gasoline and oil used by delivery trucks during the month. No prior entry had been made for these purchases, which were made daily.

Instructions. Journalize the above transactions.

6B-2. An alphabetical listing of the account balances of Clark's Clothing Store after its second complete year of operations is shown below. All necessary adjustments as of December 31 have been recorded and posted.

Accounts receivable	$ 14,398.46
Accounts payable	9,642.80
Accrued property taxes payable	498.66
Accumulated depreciation: equipment	1,656.00
Cash	5,361.27
Delivery expense	1,964.80
Depreciation expense	687.13
Equipment	6,871.30
Insurance expense	481.72
Inventory, January 1	20,460.22
J. L. Clark, capital	29,052.72
J. L. Clark, drawing	1,440.00
Notes receivable	2,500.00
Notes payable	3,000.00
Prepaid insurance	162.96
Property taxes	758.20
Purchases	107,473.00
Purchase returns and allowances	3,846.74
Rent expense	6,000.00
Salaries and wages expense	30,402.70
Sales	168,561.42
Sales returns and allowances	4,356.27
Selling commissions	7,428.55
Supplies	864.16
Supplies expense	685.40
Transportation-in	3,962.20

The inventory, determined by count at December 31, was $18,756.32.

Instructions
a. Prepare the income statement for the year ended December 31.
b. Prepare all necessary journal entries to close the books at December 31.

6B-3. The trial balance of Latham Company was prepared from the records of the company on June 30, 19___, the close of its fiscal year.

LATHAM COMPANY
Trial Balance
June 30, 19___

Cash	$ 4,722
Notes receivable	1,200
Accounts receivable	9,467
Inventory, beginning	35,660
Prepaid insurance	620
Office supplies	463
Land	12,680

Buildings	34,500	
Accumulated depreciation: buildings		$ 6,900
Equipment	8,550	
Accumulated depreciation: equipment		1,728
Accounts payable		7,956
A. R. Latham, capital		76,107
A. R. Latham, drawing	2,400	
Sales		152,632
Sales returns and allowances	3,134	
Purchases	118,455	
Purchase returns and allowances		1,824
Transportation-in	2,049	
Salaries and wages expense	12,473	
Property taxes expense	774	
	$247,147	$247,147

Other data

(*a*) The buildings are being depreciated over a 20-year useful life, and the equipment over a 15-year useful life.

(*b*) Accrued salaries payable as of June 30 were $2,630.

(*c*) Examination of policies showed $268 prepaid insurance on June 30.

(*d*) Supplies on hand at June 30 were estimated to amount to $182.

(*e*) Inventory of merchandise on June 30 was $23,240.

Instructions

a. Prepare the working papers at June 30, 19___.

b. Prepare an income statement for the year.

c. Prepare adjusting entries.

d. Prepare closing journal entries.

6B-4. The adjusted trial balance of Cook Company for the year ended December 31, 19___, is shown below. An inventory taken on December 31 amounted to $24,600. The following adjustments have been made to the original trial balance figures:

(*a*) Depreciation of buildings, $2,400; delivery equipment, $1,280.

(*b*) Accrued salaries: office, $642; salesmen's, $834.

(*c*) Insurance expired, $150.

(*d*) Store supplies used, $800.

COOK COMPANY
Adjusted Trial Balance
December 31, 19___

Cash	$ 7,040
Accounts receivable	10,700
Inventory, January 1	19,000
Store supplies	540
Prepaid insurance	300
Land	34,400

Buildings	50,000	
Accumulated depreciation: buildings		$ 12,500
Delivery equipment	14,000	
Accumulated depreciation: delivery equipment		5,600
Notes payable		2,900
Accounts payable		8,150
Accrued salaries payable		1,476
L. C. Cook, capital		100,994
L. C. Cook, drawing	4,200	
Sales		143,000
Sales returns and allowances	1,810	
Purchases	109,300	
Purchase returns and allowances		1,300
Salesmen's salaries expense	8,000	
Advertising expense	1,200	
Delivery expense	2,500	
Depreciation expense: delivery equipment ..	1,280	
Rent expense	2,200	
Office salaries expense	6,100	
Depreciation expense: buildings	2,400	
Insurance expense	150	
Store supplies expense	800	
	$275,920	$275,920

Instructions
a. Prepare working papers, starting with the unadjusted trial balance.
b. Prepare financial statements.
c. Prepare adjusting journal entries.
d. Prepare closing journal entries.

7

Control procedures in a merchandising business

Our discussion of a merchandising business in Chapter 6 emphasized the steps of the accounting cycle, especially the determination of cost of goods sold and the preparation of financial statements. In the present chapter we shall round out this discussion by considering methods by which management maintains control over purchases and sales transactions.

Business papers

Carefully designed business papers and procedures for using them are necessary to ensure that all transactions are properly authorized and recorded. To illustrate this point in a somewhat exaggerated manner, let us assume that every employee in a large department store was authorized to purchase merchandise for the store and that no standard forms or procedures had been provided to keep track of these purchases. The result would undoubtedly be many unwise purchases, confusion as to what had been ordered and received, shortages of some types of merchandise and an oversupply of other types. The opportunity for fraud by dishonest employees, as well as for accidental errors, would be unlimited under such a haphazard method of operation.

Each step in ordering, receiving, and making payment for merchandise purchases should be controlled and recorded. A similar approach is necessary to establish control over the sales function. For a very small business in which the owner participates actively in all phases of operation, his personal observation of transactions is a substitute to some extent for accounting controls. In a larger business, protection against errors, fraud, and wasteful duplication of effort rests largely upon business papers, accounting procedures, and proper delegation of duties to various departments and employees. As indicated in Chapter 1, accounting is more than a means of measuring business income. Accounting is also a tool of management, essential in controlling day-to-day operations and in planning future actions.

Purchasing procedures

In small retail businesses, the owner or manager may personally perform the purchasing function by placing orders with sales representatives of wholesalers and manufacturers. These sales representatives make regular visits to the store and may carry catalogues and samples to illustrate the products offered.

The owner-manager of a small store is sufficiently familiar with his stock of merchandise to know what items need to be replenished. He may keep a notebook record of items to be ordered, writing down each day any items which he observes to be running low. In some instances orders may be placed by telephone. When the sales representative of a wholesaler or manufacturer visits the store, he writes up the order in his order book. A copy of the order, showing the quantities and prices of all items ordered, is left with the store owner.

Purchase orders. In many businesses and especially in large organizations, the buying company uses its own purchase order forms. A purchase order of the Zenith Company issued to Adams Manufacturing Company is illustrated below.

SERIALLY NUMBERED ORDER FOR MER-CHANDISE

PURCHASE ORDER

ZENITH COMPANY

10 Fairway Avenue
San Francisco, California

Order No.

999

To: Adams Manufacturing Company

19 Union Street

Kansas City, Missouri

Date Nov. 10, 1961

Ship via Jones Truck Co.

Terms: 2/10; n/30

Please enter our order for the following:

Quantity	Description	Price	Total
15 sets	Model S irons	$60.00	$900.00
50 dozen	X3Y Shur-Par golf balls	7.00	350.00

Zenith Company

By *D. D. McCarthy*

In large companies in which the functions of placing orders, receiving merchandise, and making payment are lodged in separate departments, several copies of the purchase order are usually prepared, each on a different color paper. The original is sent to the supplier; this purchase order is his authorization to deliver the merchandise and to submit a bill based on the prices listed. In a departmentalized business, carbon copies of the purchase order are usually routed to the purchasing department, accounting department, receiving department, and finance department.

Notice that the illustrated purchase order bears a serial number, 999. When purchase orders are serially numbered, there can be no doubt as to how many orders have been issued. Each department authorized to receive copies of purchase orders should account for every number in the series, thus guarding against the loss or nondelivery of any document. As a control device, serial numbers are used for many types of business papers.

Where merchandise is ordered by telephone, a formal written purchase order should nevertheless be prepared and sent to the supplier to confirm the verbal instructions. Orders for office equipment, supplies, and other assets as well as merchandise should also be in writing to avoid misunderstanding and to provide a permanent record of the action taken.

The issuance of a purchase order does not call for any debit or credit entries in the accounting record of either the prospective buyer or seller. The company which receives an order does not consider for accounting purposes that a sale has been made until the merchandise is delivered. At that point ownership of the goods changes, and both buyer and seller should make accounting entries to record the transaction.

Invoices. The supplier (vendor) mails an invoice to the purchaser at the time of shipping the merchandise. An invoice contains a description of the goods being sold, the quantities, prices, credit terms, and method of shipment. The illustration on page 196 shows an invoice issued by Adams Manufacturing Company in response to the previously illustrated purchase order from Zenith Company.

From the viewpoint of the seller, an invoice is a *sales invoice;* from the buyer's viewpoint it is a *purchase invoice.* The invoice is the basis for an entry in the accounting records of both the seller and the buyer because it evidences the transfer of ownership of goods. At the time of issuing the invoice, the seller makes an entry debiting accounts receivable and crediting sales. The buyer, however, does not record the invoice as a liability until he has made a careful verification of the transaction, as indicated in the following section.

Verification of invoice by purchaser. Upon receipt of an invoice, the purchaser should verify the following aspects of the transaction:

1. The invoice agrees with the purchase order as to prices, quantities, and other provisions.

2. The invoice is arithmetically correct in all extensions of price times quantity and in the addition of amounts.

3. The goods covered by the invoice have been received and are in satisfactory condition.

ADAMS MANUFACTURING COMPANY
19 Union Street
Kansas City, Missouri

Sold to Zenith Company

         10 Fairway Avenue

         San Francisco, Calif.

Shipped to Same

Terms 2/10; n/30

Invoice No. 777

Invoice date Nov. 15, 1961

Your Order No. 999

Date shipped Nov. 15, 1961

Shipped by Jones Truck Co.

Quantity	Description	Price	Amount
15 sets	Model S irons	$60.00	$900.00
50 dozen	X3Y Shur-Par golf balls	7.00	350.00
			$1,250.00

The task of verifying purchase invoices is usually assigned to the accounting department, although in some concerns the purchasing department may share in this work. In the following discussion it is assumed that purchase invoices and other documents relating to the purchase are sent to the accounting department for verification.

Evidence that the merchandise has been received in good condition must be obtained from the receiving department. It is the function of the receiving department to receive all incoming goods, to inspect them as to quality and condition, and to determine the quantities received by counting, measuring, or weighing. The receiving clerk may record the quantities and date of receipt on his copy of the purchase order and then forward this document to the accounting department, where it can be compared with the purchase invoice. Some companies require the receiving department to prepare a separate receiving report for each shipment received; this report is sent to the accounting department for use in verifying the invoice.

The verification of the invoice in the accounting department is accomplished by comparing the purchase order, the invoice, and the receiving report. Comparison of these documents establishes that the goods described in the invoice were actually ordered, have been received in good condition, and were billed at the prices specified in the purchase order. To ensure that this comparison of documents is made in every case and that the arithmetical accuracy of the invoice is proved, it is customary to require an invoice approval sheet such as that shown below to be attached to each invoice and initialed by the employees performing each step in the verification work. Some companies prefer to use a rubber stamp imprint of this form to place the verification data directly on the vendor's invoice.

When these verification procedures have been completed, the invoice is recorded as a liability by an entry debiting the Purchases account and crediting an account payable in the name of the vendor.

Errors in invoices. The procedures just described normally lead up to the payment of an invoice; these systematic routines give the purchaser of merchandise assurance that he is actually getting what he pays for. Sometimes, however, these verification procedures reveal that an invoice should not be paid, or at least, not paid in full. The verification procedures may disclose that the invoice contains an arithmetical error, or that a wrong price was used. Some of the goods listed in the invoice may not have been included in the shipment or may be of unsatisfactory quality, broken, or damaged. In such cases a *debit memorandum* is prepared and sent to the vendor, informing him that his account is being debited (reduced) on the books of the buyer, and explaining the circumstances.

Debit and credit memoranda. To illustrate the use of a debit memorandum, let us assume that Zenith Company receives another shipment

SEVERAL EMPLOYEES PARTICIPATE IN VERIFICATION OF A PURCHASE INVOICE

Invoice Approval Form

Invoice No. 777   Date Nov. 15, 1961

Purchase order No. 999   Date Nov. 1, 1961
Vendor Adams Manufacturing Co.

Invoice compared with purchase order as to:
    Description of goods   *L.B.A.*
    Quantities   *L.B.A.*
    Prices   *L.B.A.*
    Discount terms   *L.B.A.*
    Transportation charges   *L.B.A.*

Receiving report compared with purchase order   *D.L.W.*
and invoice as to quantities

Invoice verified as to:
    Extensions   *R.A.*
    Footings   *R.A.*

Approved for payment   *J.R.K.*

Paid by check No. 2116   Date Nov. 25, 1961

of merchandise from Adams Manufacturing Company and a related invoice dated November 18 in the amount of $1,000. However, some of the goods with a value of $450 were badly damaged when received and cannot be accepted. Zenith Company therefore wishes to return the damaged goods and to pay only $550 of the $1,000 amount billed. One method would be to record the purchase as $550 and send a check for that amount to the supplier accompanied by a letter explaining the situation. To record the transaction as a $550 purchase, however, would not provide a clear and complete picture of the events. A better procedure is to record the invoice in its full amount and to make a second entry recording the return of the damaged merchandise. The debit memorandum shown below should be prepared in two or more copies and the original sent to the vendor.

ENTRIES FOR PURCHASE AND PURCHASE RETURN

The duplicate copy of the debit memorandum serves as a basis for an entry in the buyer's accounting records showing the return of the goods and a corresponding reduction in the liability to the vendor. The two entries to record the purchase invoice and the debit memorandum are as follows:

Nov. 18	*Purchases*	*1,000*	
	Accounts Payable		*1,000*
	To record invoice from Adams Manufacturing Company.		
Nov. 19	*Accounts Payable*	*450*	
	Purchase Returns and Allowances		*450*
	To record return of damaged merchandise to Adams Manufacturing Company. See our debit memo No. 42.		

DEBIT MEM-ORANDUM REDUCES LIABILITY TO VENDOR

ZENITH COMPANY
10 Fairway Avenue
San Francisco, California

Debit memorandum No. 42

To: Adams Manufacturing Company   Date: Nov. 19, 1961

       19 Union Street

       Kansas City, Missouri

We debit your account as follows:

Return of merchandise. Fifty DLX gloves arrived badly damaged and are being returned via Jones Truck Co. collect. Your invoice No. 825, dated November 18, 1960..................................$450.00

CREDIT
MEMO-
RANDUM
ISSUED BY
SELLER OF
GOODS

ADAMS MANUFACTURING COMPANY
19 Union Street
Kansas City, Missouri

Credit
memorandum
No. 102

To: Zenith Company

Date: Nov. 22, 1961

10 Fairway Avenue

San Francisco, Calif.

We credit your account as follows:

Merchandise returned, 50 DLX gloves,
our invoice No. 825 ....$450.00

The supplier, upon being informed of the return of the damaged merchandise will issue the *credit memorandum* shown above as evidence that the account receivable from the purchaser is being credited (reduced).

ENTRY
RECORDING
CREDIT
MEMO

The entry on the part of Adams Manufacturing Company at the time of issuing this credit memorandum would be as follows:

Nov. 22   *Sales Returns and Allowances* *450*
              Accounts Receivable *450*
          To record return by Zenith Company of damaged merchandise. See our credit memo No. 102.

This credit memorandum, when received by the Zenith Company, will be filed with the original invoice and the carbon copy of the debit memorandum. These documents represent evidence supporting the entries in the accounts.

As an alternative to the method described, the Zenith Company instead of issuing a debit memorandum might have notified the supplier informally of the damaged merchandise and waited for the supplier's credit memorandum to serve as the basis for the entry reducing the liability. Another alternative would have been to delay making any entry for the purchase until both the invoice and the credit memorandum were on hand. The essential point, however, is that the Purchases Returns and Allowances account should be used rather than merely showing the purchase as a $550 transaction. The accounting records will then provide management with information on the amount and frequency of purchase returns. This information is helpful in analyzing and controlling operating expenses.

In summary, we may say that debit and credit memoranda are used to make adjustments between buyer and seller when (1) goods are received in damaged condition, (2) goods are received in excess of quantities ordered, (3) the quantities of goods received are less than the quantities specified in the invoice, and (4) the invoice contains erroneous prices or arithmetical errors of any kind.

Trade discounts. Manufacturers and wholesalers in many lines of industry publish annual catalogues in which their products are listed at retail prices. Substantial reductions from the *list prices* shown in the catalogue are offered to dealers and other large-scale purchasers. These reductions from the list prices (often as much as 30 or 40%) are called trade discounts. The rate of discount may vary considerably by type of product, and the entire schedule of discounts may be revised as price levels and market conditions fluctuate. To publish a new catalogue every time the price of one or more products changes would be an expensive practice; the issuance of a new schedule of trade discounts is much more convenient and serves just as well in revising actual selling prices.

Trade discounts may also be used as a means of offering different prices to different classes of customers. A manufacturer of automobile repair parts, for example, may issue different schedules of discounts to wholesalers and to garages.

Trade discounts are not recorded in the accounting records of either the seller or the buyer. A sale of merchandise is recorded at the actual selling price and the trade discount is merely a device for computing the actual sales price. From the viewpoint of the company purchasing goods, the significant price is not the list price but the amount which must be paid, and this amount is recorded as the cost of the merchandise.

To illustrate the use of a trade discount, assume that the Martin Manufacturing Company sells goods to Austin Auto Repair at a list price of $100 with a trade discount of 30%. Martin Manufacturing Company would record the sale by the following entry:

NEITHER
SELLER . . .

Accounts Receivable	70	
Sales		70

The entry by Austin Auto Repair to record the purchase would be:

. . . NOR
BUYER
RECORDS
TRADE
DISCOUNTS

Purchases	70	
Accounts Payable		70

Because trade discounts are not recorded in the accounts, they should be clearly distinguished from the cash discounts discussed later in this chapter.

Credit terms

A manufacturer or wholesaler may extend liberal credit to certain of his customers yet demand immediate payment from other customers. Obviously a retail store known to be in strong financial condition will find it easy to buy goods on credit, whereas a store tottering on the brink of insolvency may find that suppliers insist upon immediate cash payment for merchandise.

If the agreement between the buyer and seller calls for immediate payment, the invoice will usually bear the term "cash" or "net cash." Most sales of goods by manufacturers and wholesalers, however, are made on credit, and the arrangements for payment, or *credit terms,* are precisely stated on the invoice. If credit is allowed for a period of 30 days, the invoice may bear the symbol "n/30," which is read "net 30 days" and means that the customer must make payment within 30 days from the date of the invoice. The word "net" in this expression means the full amount of the invoice less any trade discount.

The length of the credit period offered varies considerably in different lines of business, as well as in accordance with the credit standing of the individual customer. For merchandise of a type that is likely to be resold quickly, credit terms are often 30 days or less. For goods that normally move slowly, credit terms of 60 or 90 days are not uncommon. In these cases, the invoice would show the terms as "n/60" or "n/90." In some industries, it is customary for invoices to become payable 10 days after the end of the month in which the sale occurs. Such invoices bear the expression "10 EOM." These credit terms are especially convenient for the small business in which the owner wishes to pay all the bills on a given day of the month or within a few days after the beginning of each month.

Cash discounts. Manufacturers and wholesalers generally offer a cash discount to encourage their customers to pay invoices before expiration of the credit period. For example, the credit terms may be "2% 10 days, net 30 days"; these terms mean that the authorized credit period is 30 days, but that the customer may deduct 2% of the amount of the invoice if he makes payment within 10 days. On the invoice these terms would appear in the abbreviated form "2/10, n/30"; this expression is read "2, 10, net 30." The selling company regards a cash discount as a *sales discount;* the buyer calls the discount a *purchase discount.*

To illustrate the application of a cash discount, assume that Adams Manufacturing Company sells goods to the Zenith Company and issues a sales invoice for $1,000 dated November 3 and bearing the terms 2/10, n/30. If Zenith Company mails its check in payment on or before November 13, it is entitled to deduct 2% of $1,000, or $20, and settle the obligation for $980. If Zenith Company decides to forego the discount, it may postpone payment for an additional 20 days until December 3 but must then pay $1,000.

Reasons for cash discounts. From the viewpoint of the seller, the acceptance of $980 in cash as full settlement of a $1,000 account receivable represents a $20 reduction in the amount of revenue earned. By making this concession to induce prompt payment, the seller collects accounts receivable more quickly and is able to use the money collected to buy additional goods. A greater volume of business can be handled with a given amount of invested capital if this capital is not tied up in accounts receivable for long periods. There is also less danger of accounts receivable becoming uncollectible if they are collected promptly; in other words, the older an account receivable becomes, the greater becomes the risk of nonpayment.

Is it to the advantage of the Zenith Company to settle the $1,000 invoice within the discount period and thereby save $20? The alternative is for Zenith to conserve cash by postponing payment for an additional 20 days. The question may therefore be stated as follows: Does the amount of $20 represent a reasonable charge for the use of $980 for a period of 20 days? Definitely not; this charge is the equivalent of an annual interest rate of about 36%. (A 20-day period is approximately 1/18 of a year; 18 times 2% amounts to 36%.) Most businesses are able to borrow money from banks at an annual interest rate of 6% or less. Well-managed business, therefore, generally pay all invoices within the discount period even though this policy necessitates borrowing from banks in order to have the necessary cash available.

Since buyers generally take advantage of all cash discounts offered and sellers are well aware of this fact, it may be argued that the "real price" of the goods in our example is $980 rather than $1,000. The amount of $980 is the amount Adams Manufacturing Company expects to collect and also the amount that Zenith Company expects to pay. From this viewpoint, the discount of $20 may logically be regarded as a "penalty" to be charged the occasional customer who, because of carelessness or a tight cash position, fails to pay invoices promptly.

Recording sales discounts. Sales of merchandise are generally recorded at the full selling price without regard for the cash discount being offered. The discount is not reflected in the seller's accounting records until payment is received. Continuing our illustration of a sale of merchandise by Adams Manufacturing Company for $1,000 with terms of 2/10, n/30, the entry to record the sale on November 3 is as shown by the following:

SALE
ENTERED
AT FULL
PRICE

Nov. 3	*Accounts Receivable* *1,000*	
	Sales	*1,000*
	To record sale to Zenith Company,	
	terms 2/10, n/30.	

Assuming that payment is made by Zenith Company on November 13, the last day of the discount period, the entry by Adams to record collection of the receivable is as follows:

SALES
DISCOUNT
RECORDED
AT TIME OF
COLLECTION

Nov. 13 Cash 980
           Sales Discount 20
                  Accounts Receivable   1,000
           To record collection from Zenith Company
           of invoice of November 3 less 2% cash
           discount.

As previously explained, the allowing of a cash discount reduces the amount received from sales. On the income statement, therefore, the sales discount appears as a deduction from sales, as shown below:

TREATMENT
OF SALES
DISCOUNT
ON THE
INCOME
STATEMENT

Partial Income Statement		
Sales		*$189,788*
Deduct: Sales returns and allowances	*$4,462*	
Sales discount	*3,024*	*7,486*
Net sales		*$182,302*

Recording purchase discounts. On the books of the Zenith Company, the purchase of merchandise on November 3 was recorded at the gross amount of the invoice, as shown by the following entry:

PURCHASE
ENTERED
AT FULL
PRICE

Purchases 1,000
       Accounts Payable   1,000
To record purchase from Adams Manufacturing Com-
pany, terms 2/10, n/30.

When the invoice was paid on November 13, the last day of the discount period, the payment was recorded as follows:

PURCHASE
DISCOUNT
RECORDED
WHEN
PAYMENT
MADE

Accounts Payable 1,000
       Purchase Discounts   20
       Cash   980
To record payment to Adams Manufacturing Company
of invoice of November 3, less 2% cash discount.

The effect of the discount was to reduce the cost of the merchandise to the Zenith Company. The credit balance of the Purchase Discounts account should therefore be deducted in the income statement from the debit balance of the Purchases account, as shown in the following partial income statement of the Zenith Company:

Partial Income Statement

Net sales			$99,960
Deduct: Cost of goods sold:			
Inventory Jan. 1, 19__		$15,000	
Purchases	$60,000		
Transportation-in	5,102		
Delivered cost of purchases	$65,102		
Deduct: Purchase returns			
and allowances	$2,100		
Purchase discounts	1,100	3,200	
Net purchases		61,902	
Cost of goods available for sale		$76,902	
Deduct: Inventory Dec. 31, 19__		14,000	
Cost of goods sold			62,902
Gross profit on sales			$37,058

Since the Purchase Discount account is deducted from Purchases in the income statement, a question naturally arises as to whether the Purchase Discount account is really necessary. Why not reduce the amount of purchases at the time of taking a discount by crediting Purchases rather than crediting Purchase Discounts? The answer is that management needs to know the amount of discounts taken. The Purchase Discounts account supplies this information. Any decrease in the proportion of purchase discounts to purchases carries the suggestion that the accounts payable department is becoming inefficient. That department has the responsibility of paying all invoices within the discount period, and management should be informed of failure by any department to follow company policies consistently. If management is to direct the business effectively, it needs to receive from the accounting system information indicating the level of performance in every department.

Some companies have chosen to regard purchase discounts as a form of nonoperating revenue. Instead of deducting purchase discounts from purchases in the income statement, these companies show purchases at the gross amount as listed on the invoices and place the Purchase Discounts account as an item of Other Revenue near the end of the income statement. Under this method the merchandise purchased by Zenith Company on November 3 would be reported as having cost $1,000; the excess of this so-called "cost" over the $980 actually paid would be considered as a gain realized through prompt payment. This method has no theoretical justification and is gradually disappearing. It is objectionable because it inflates the reported figure for purchases and thereby distorts the income statement. Furthermore, to report a gain or increase in owners' equity merely by reason of purchasing merchandise is absurd. If profits could really be achieved in this manner, a business might as well close its doors to customers and devote all its energies to buying more and more goods.

Alternative method: recording invoices at net price. As previously stated, most well-managed companies have a firm policy of taking all purchase discounts offered. These companies may prefer the alternative method of recording purchase invoices at the net amount after discount rather than at the gross amount as previously described. For example, in our illustration of a $1,000 invoice bearing terms of 2/10, n/30, the entry for the purchase could be made as follows:

ENTRY FOR PURCHASE: NET-PRICE METHOD	*Nov. 3* *Purchases* 980	
	Accounts payable	*980*
	To record purchase invoice from Adams Manufacturing Company less 2% cash discount available.	

Assuming that the invoice is paid within 10 days, the entry for the payment is as follows:

ENTRY FOR PAYMENT: NET-PRICE METHOD	*Nov. 13* *Accounts Payable* 980	
	Cash	*980*
	To record payment of $1,000 invoice from Adams Manufacturing Company less 2% cash discount.	

Through oversight or carelessness, the purchasing company may occasionally fail to make payment of an invoice within the 10-day discount period. If such a delay occurred in paying the invoice from Adams Manufacturing Company, the full amount of the invoice would have to be paid rather than the recorded liability of $980. The journal entry to record the late payment on, say, December 3, is as follows:

ENTRY FOR PAYMENT AFTER DISCOUNT PERIOD: NET-PRICE METHOD	*Dec. 3* *Accounts Payable* 980	
	Purchase Discounts Lost 20	
	Cash	*1,000*
	To record payment of invoice and loss of discount by delaying payment beyond the discount period.	

Under this method the cost of goods purchased is properly recorded at $980, and the additional payment of $20 caused by failure to pay the invoice promptly is placed in a special expense account designed to attract the attention of management. The gross-price method of recording invoices previously described shows the amount of purchase discounts *taken* each period; the net-price method now under discussion shows the amount of purchase discounts *lost* each period. The latter method has the advantage of drawing the attention of management to a breakdown in prescribed operating routines. The fact that a purchase discount has been taken does not require attention by management, but a discount lost because of inefficiency in processing accounts payable does call for managerial investigation. Under the net-price method of recording invoices, the purchases discount account is eliminated and the amount of routine bookkeeping work is held to a minimum.

As previously suggested, inefficiency and delay in paying invoices should not be concealed by adding the penalty of lost discount to the cost of merchandise purchased. The purchases should be stated at the net price available by taking cash discount; the Purchase Discounts Lost account should be shown in the income statement as an expense in the section headed Operating Expenses.

Mechanics of handling approved invoices. The procedures for proper verification of a purchase invoice were described earlier in this chapter. After a purchase invoice has been approved for payment, it should be filed in a manner which assures that the required payment date will not be overlooked. For example the invoice of November 3 from Adams Manufacturing Company could be placed in a "tickler file," a file with index cards bearing dates. Since this invoice must be paid by November 13 to take advantage of the cash discount, the invoice is filed in front of the index card for November 13. On that date the invoice is removed from the tickler file and sent to the cashier. The cashier prepares a check for $980 payable to Adams Manufacturing Company, enters the check number on the invoice approval form, and forwards both documents to the treasurer. The treasurer signs the check, mails it, and marks the invoice "Paid." The invoice and the attached approval sheet are then returned to the accounting department and placed in an alphabetical file of paid invoices.

Sales procedures

The procedures for controlling and recording sales will necessarily vary from one business to another, depending upon the nature and size of the business. The following description of sales procedures should therefore be regarded as a generalized pattern subject to many variations.

In retail stores many sales are made for cash. After the customer has selected the merchandise desired, the sales clerk rings up the sale on a cash register, wraps the merchandise, and hands it to the customer along with a sales slip printed by the cash register. When the entire transaction is handled by one clerk in this manner, a possibility exists that a dishonest employee may withhold cash received and attempt to conceal his theft by not ringing up the sale or by ringing up a lesser amount. However some simple precautions can be taken to guard against such fraud and against accidental errors as well. For example, the cash register should be so located that the customer as well as supervisors can see the amount rung up. Also clerks should be required to ring up a sale before wrapping the merchandise. This practice ensures that the customer will be present to observe the recording of the sale. At the close of business each day, the total sales as shown by the cash register are entered in the accounting records by debiting Cash and crediting Sales.

In retail stores which make sales on credit, each salesclerk is supplied with a book of serially numbered sales tickets. For each sale on account, the clerk fills out a sales ticket in duplicate and obtains approval of the customer's credit from the credit department. One copy of the sales ticket is given to the customer with the merchandise; another copy is sent to the accounting department, where it is recorded by an entry debiting the account receivable from the customer and crediting Sales. Since the sales tickets are serially numbered, it is possible to account for all tickets used and thus make sure that all credit sales have been recorded.

Most orders in retail stores are received orally from customers, but in manufacturing and wholesaling companies written orders are customary. These written sales orders come through the mail from the company's staff of traveling salesmen and directly from customers. The first step in processing the order usually is to obtain the approval of the credit department as to the customer's credit rating. If credit approval is obtained, a sales invoice may be prepared in three or more copies.

The first carbon copy of the sales invoice is sent to the stock room; there the merchandise ordered is assembled and sent with this copy of the invoice to the shipping department. When the shipping department has finished packing and shipping the merchandise, the employee in charge signs the invoice, records the date of shipment, and sends the invoice to the accounting department. As an alternative, the data identifying the shipment may be placed on a separate document to accompany the invoice to the accounting department.

While this assembling, packing, and shipping of goods is taking place, a second carbon copy of the invoice is being carefully examined in the accounting department to make sure that the prices, credit terms, and all extensions and footings are correct. This copy of the invoice is also compared with the customer's order to determine that these two documents are in agreement as to quantities, prices, and other details.

When the first carbon of the sales invoice arrives from the shipping department showing that the goods have been sent to the customer, the accounting department places this invoice in a file called a shipping record. Now that the accounting department has written evidence that the goods have been shipped, it places its own verified copy of the invoice in a sales binder or register and makes a journal entry debiting the account receivable from the customer and crediting Sales. The original copy of the invoice is mailed to the customer promptly after the goods have been shipped. As previously mentioned, the set of procedures which has been described represents merely one of many alternative methods of processing sales orders.

Monthly statements to customers. In addition to sending an invoice to the customer for each separate sales transaction, some concerns send each customer a statement at the end of the month. The customer's statement is similar to a ledger account and is sometimes called a statement of account. It shows the balance receivable at the beginning of the month, the charges for sales during the month, the credits for payments received or goods returned, and the balance receivable from the customer at the end of the month. A statement sent by Zenith Company to one of its customers at the end of November appears in the illustration on page 209.

Upon receipt of a monthly statement from a vendor, the customer should make a detailed comparison of the purchases and payments shown on the statement with the corresponding entries in his accounts payable records. Any differences in the invoiced amounts, payments, or balance owed should be promptly investigated. Frequently the balance shown on the statement will differ from the balance of the customer's accounts payable record because shipments of merchandise and letters containing payments are in transit at month-end. These in-transit items will have been recorded by the sender but will not yet appear on the other party's records.

Internal control

In this chapter some systematic procedures for controlling the purchase and sale of merchandise have been described. These procedures place particular emphasis upon the subdivision of duties within the company so that no one person or department handles a transaction completely from beginning to end. When duties are divided in this manner, the work of one employee serves to verify that of another and any errors made are quickly disclosed. The duties performed by each employee are so interrelated with the duties of other persons that it is very difficult for a fraudulent action to be concealed without collusion by two or more employees. The likelihood of fraud or of undetected errors is much less than if one employee were responsible for all aspects of a transaction.

Another method of achieving internal control, in addition to the subdivision of duties, consists of having the printer include serial numbers on such documents as purchase orders, sales invoices, and checks. The use of serial numbers makes it possible to account for all documents. In other words, if a sales invoice is misplaced or concealed, the break in the sequence of numbers will call attention to the discrepancy.

To illustrate the development of internal control through subdivision of duties, let us review the procedures for a sale of merchandise on account by a wholesaler. The sales department of the company is responsible for securing the order from the customer; the credit department must approve the customer's credit before the order is filled; the stock room assembles the goods ordered; the shipping department packs and ships the goods; and the accounting department records the transaction. Each department receives written evidence of the action of the other departments and reviews the documents describing the transaction to see that

MONTHLY
STATEMENT
SUMMARIZ-
ING TRANS-
ACTIONS
WITH
CUSTOMER

Statement

ZENITH COMPANY

10 Fairway Avenue
San Francisco, California

In account with: Date: Nov. 30, 1961

John D. Graham
210 Moranda Lane
Santa Barbara, Calif.

Date	Our invoice no.	Charges	Credits	Balance due
Oct. 31	Balance forwarded			125.40
Nov. 8	4127	81.00		206.40
10			125.40	81.00
21	4352	62.50		143.50

Accounts are payable on tenth of month following purchase

the actions taken correspond in all details. The shipping department, for instance, does not release the merchandise until after the credit department has approved the customer as a credit risk. The accounting department does not record the sale until it has received documentary evidence that (1) the goods were ordered, (2) the extension of credit was approved, and (3) the merchandise has been shipped to the customer.

Assume for a moment, as a contrast to this procedure, that a single employee were permitted to secure the customer's order, approve the credit terms, get the merchandise from the stock room, deliver the goods to the customer, prepare the invoice, enter the transaction in the accounting records, and perhaps, even collect the account receivable. If this employee made errors, such as selling to poor credit risks, forgetting to enter the sale in the accounting records, or perhaps delivering more merchandise to the customer than he was charged for, no one would know the difference. By the time such errors came to light, substantial losses would have been incurred.

If one employee is permitted to handle all aspects of a transaction, the danger of fraud is also increased. Studies of fraud cases suggest that a considerable number of individuals may be tempted into dishonest acts if given complete control of company property. Most of these persons, however, would not engage in fraud if doing so required collaboration with another employee. Losses through employee dishonesty occur in a variety of ways; merchandise may disappear, payments by customers may be withheld, suppliers may be overpaid with a view to kickbacks to employees, and lower prices may be allowed to favored customers. The opportunities for fraud are almost endless if all aspects of a sale or purchase transaction are concentrated in the hands of one employee.

Because internal control rests so largely upon the participation of several employees in each transaction, it is apparent that strong internal control is more easily achieved in large organizations than in small ones. In a small business with only one or two office employees, such duties as the issuance of purchase orders, approval of credit, and maintenance of accounting records may necessarily have to be performed by the same employee. In later chapters numerous suggestions will be made for strengthening internal control in small organizations.

A description of internal control solely in terms of the prevention of fraud and the detection of errors represents too narrow a concept of this managerial technique. The building of a strong system of internal control is an accepted means of increasing operational efficiency. Broadly defined, internal control includes the plan of organization and all measures taken by a business to safeguard assets, to ensure reliability in accounting data, to promote operational efficiency, and to encourage compliance with company policies.

In appraising the merits of various internal control procedures, the question of their cost cannot be ignored. Too elaborate a system of internal control may entail greater operating costs than are justified by the protection gained. For this reason among others, the system of internal control must be tailored to meet the requirements of the individual business. In most organizations, however, proper subdivision of duties and careful design of accounting procedures will provide a basis for adequate internal control and at the same time will contribute to economical and efficient operation.

Classified financial statements

The financial statements illustrated up to this point have been rather short and simple because of the limited number of transactions and accounts used in these introductory chapters. Now let us look briefly at a more comprehensive and realistic balance sheet for a merchandising business. A full understanding of all the items on this balance sheet may not be possible until our study of accounting has progressed further, but a bird's-eye view of a fairly complete balance sheet is nevertheless useful at this point.

In the balance sheet of the Cheviot Company illustrated on page 211, the assets are classified into three groups: (1) current assets, (2) plant and equipment, and (3) other assets. The liabilities are classified into two types: (1) current liabilities and (2) long-term liabilities. This classification of assets and liabilities, subject to minor variations in terminology, is

THE CHEVIOT COMPANY
Balance Sheet
December 31, 19___

Assets

Current assets:

Cash		$24,500	
U.S. government bonds		10,000	
Notes receivable		2,400	
Accounts receivable	$26,960		
Less: Allowance for bad debts	860	26,100	
Inventory		35,200	
Prepaid expenses		1,200	
Total current assets			$ 99,400

Plant and equipment:

Land		$10,000	
Building	$24,000		
Less: Accumulated depreciation	1,920	22,080	
Store equipment	$ 9,400		
Less: Accumulated depreciation	1,880	7,520	
Delivery equipment	$ 2,800		
Less: Accumulated depreciation	700	2,100	
Total plant and equipment			41,700

Other assets:

Land (future building site)		16,500
Total assets		$157,600

Liabilities and Owner's Equity

Current liabilities:

Notes payable		$11,500	
Accounts payable		19,040	
Accrued expenses payable		1,410	
Deferred revenues		1,100	
Total current liabilities			$ 33,050

Long-term liabilities:

Mortgage payable (due 1970)	25,000

Owner's equity:

George Graham, capital, Jan. 1		$89,150	
Net income for the year	$20,400		
Less: Withdrawals	10,000		
Increase in capital		10,400	
George Graham, capital, Dec. 31			99,550
Total liabilities and owner's equity			$157,600

virtually a standard one throughout American business. The inclusion of captions for the balance sheet totals is an optional step.

The purpose of balance sheet classification. The purpose underlying a standard classification of assets and liabilities is to aid management, owners, creditors, and other interested persons in understanding the financial condition of the business. The banker, for example, would have a difficult time in reading the balance sheets of all the companies which apply to him for loans, if each of these companies followed its own individual whims as to the sequence and arrangement of accounts comprising its balance sheet. Standard practices as to the order and arrangement of a balance sheet are an important means of saving the time of the reader and of giving him a fuller comprehension of the company's financial position. On the other hand, these standard practices are definitely not iron-clad rules; the form and content of a well-prepared balance sheet today are different in several respects from the balance sheet of 25 years ago. No two businesses are exactly alike and a degree of variation from the conventional type of balance sheet is appropriate for the individual business in devising the most meaningful presentation of its financial position. Standardization of the form and content of financial statements is a desirable goal; but if carried to an extreme, it might prevent the growth of new improved methods and the constructive changes necessary to reflect changes in business practices.

The analysis and interpretation of financial statements is the subject of Chapter 28; at this point our objective is merely to emphasize that classification of the items on a balance sheet aids the reader greatly in appraising the financial condition of the business. The major balance sheet classifications are discussed briefly in the following sections.

Current assets. Current assets include cash, government bonds, and other assets which will probably be converted into cash within a relatively short period. The period is usually one year, but it may be longer for those businesses having an operating cycle in excess of one year. The principal types of current assets are cash, government bonds or other marketable securities, notes and accounts receivable, inventories, and prepaid expenses. This listing also indicates the order in which current assets usually appear on the balance sheet. The amount of a company's current assets gives some indication of its short-run, debt-paying ability.

The term *operating cycle* is often used in establishing the limits of the current asset classification. Operating cycle means the average time period between the purchase of merchandise and the conversion of this merchandise back into cash. The series of transactions comprising a complete cycle often runs as follows: (1) purchase of merchandise, (2) sale of the merchandise on credit, (3) collection of the account receivable from the customer. The word cycle suggests the circular flow of capital from cash to inventory to receivables to cash again.

In a business handling fast-moving merchandise (a supermarket, for example) the operating cycle may be completed in a few weeks; for most merchandising businesses the operating cycle requires several months but less than a year. In a manufacturing business the materials purchased must be processed before they are offered for sale; consequently, the operating cycle tends to be longer. For some aircraft manufacturers the period of time from the purchase of sheet aluminum until this material is converted into cash through sale of the completed airplane is about 27 months. The inventories of aluminum are nevertheless classified as current assets, because they will be converted into cash within the operating cycle of this particular industry.

Most of the items in the current asset classification have been discussed in preceding chapters, so only a brief descriptive comment is necessary at this point.

Cash consists largely of money on deposit in banks, but it also includes currency, coin, checks, and money orders.

Notes receivable are formal written promises by debtors to pay a specified amount of money, usually with interest, at a definite time.

Accounts receivable consist principally of claims against customers arising from the sale of merchandise or services on credit. When a business sells merchandise on credit, it is inevitable that some of the accounts receivable will prove uncollectible. The illustrated balance sheet shows that the Cheviot Company has $26,960 in accounts receivable but has estimated that $860 of this amount may prove uncollectible. Consequently an *Allowance for Bad Debts*, amounting to $860, has been deducted to show a balance sheet valuation for accounts receivable of $26,100. Accounting for bad debts is discussed in Chapter 11.

Inventory consists of goods purchased or produced for the purpose of sale to customers.

Prepaid expenses include such items as rent paid in advance, insurance premiums applicable to future periods, and office supplies. Until recently, it was customary to exclude these short-term prepayments of expense from the current asset category, on the grounds that these prepayments would not be converted into cash in the same sense as accounts receivable or inventory of merchandise. In recent years, however, prepaid expenses have gained general acceptance as current assets. It is argued that a business which has just paid, say, $200 for one month's rent in advance is in just as strong a current position as if it had $200 more cash but must shortly make the rent payment.

Plant and equipment. Assets of relatively long life used in the operation of the business and not intended for sale are classified in the balance sheet as *plant and equipment,* or *fixed assets.* The most common items within this classification are land, buildings, parking lots, furniture and fixtures, office equipment, and delivery equipment. A common order of listing is to place the assets of most permanent character first. All the assets under this heading, with the exception of land, have limited useful lives and are subject to depreciation. On the balance sheet, the accumulated depreciation appears as a deduction from the original cost of these depreciable assets.

Other assets. This category includes any miscellaneous assets which do not fit in the preceding classifications. The example used in the illustrated balance sheet is a vacant lot held as a future building site.

Current liabilities. Liabilities that must be paid within the operating cycle or one year (whichever is longer) are called *current liabilities.* Current liabilities are paid out of current assets, and a comparison of the amount of current assets with the amount of current liabilities is an important step in appraising the ability of a company to pay its debts in the near future. The principal subgroups of current liabilities are as follows:

Notes payable are promissory notes given by the business to a bank when money is borrowed, or to a creditor from whom merchandise or equipment is purchased.

Accounts payable are short-term liabilities, usually arising from the purchase of merchandise or services. In contrast with a note payable, no formal written promise to pay is issued.

Accrued liabilities consist of amounts owed but not yet payable. Common examples are salaries earned by employees, interest on notes payable, and taxes owed to the government.

Deferred revenues arise when payment is received in advance from customers for services or merchandise to be delivered in the future. A magazine publisher, for example, has deferred revenue when he collects a subscription in advance. These advance collections are classified as current liabilities because current assets will be used in meeting the company's obligation.

Current ratio. Many bankers and other users of financial statements believe that for a business to qualify as a good credit risk, the total current assets should be at least twice as large as the total current liabilities. In studying a balance sheet, a banker or other creditor will compute the *current ratio* by dividing total current assets by total current liabilities. In the illustrated balance sheet of the Cheviot Company, the current assets of $99,400 are approximately three times as great as the current liabilities of $33,050; the current ratio is therefore 3 to 1, which would generally be regarded as a strong current position.

The excess of current assets over current liabilities is called *working capital;* the relative amount of working capital is another indication of short-term financial strength.

Long-term liabilities. Liabilities which do not qualify as current liabilities are called long-term liabilities, or fixed liabilities. In many cases debts with distant maturity dates are incurred to finance the purchase of plant and equipment. Mortgages payable and bonds payable are common forms of long-term liabilities.

Mortgages payable are debts secured by mortgages on specific assets of the business. Failure to pay the debt would give the creditor the legal right to force the sale of the pledged asset as a means of obtaining payment.

Bonds payable are formal long-term obligations issued by a corporation or by a government. Bonds often have a life of 40 or 50 years or more and are used principally by large corporations.

THE CHEVIOT COMPANY
Income Statement
For the Year Ended December 31, 19___

Gross sales		$310,890	
Sales returns and allowances	$ 3,820		
Sales discounts	4,830	8,650	
Net sales			$302,240
Cost of goods sold:			
Inventory, Jan. 1		$ 30,040	
Purchases	$212,400		
Transportation-in	8,300		
Delivered cost of purchases	$220,700		
Purchase returns & allow-			
ances	$2,400		
Purchase discounts	5,100	7,500	
Net purchases		213,200	
Cost of goods available for sale		$243,240	
Deduct: inventory, Dec. 31		35,200	
Cost of goods sold			208,040
Gross profit on sales			$ 94,200
Operating expenses:			
Selling expenses:			
Sales salaries	$38,410		
Advertising	10,190		
Depreciation: building	840		
Depreciation: store equipment	940		
Depreciation: delivery equipment	700		
Insurance expense	1,100		
Miscellaneous selling expense	820		
Total selling expenses		$53,000	
General expenses:			
Office salaries	$19,200		
Bad debts expense	750		
Depreciation: building	120		
Insurance expense: general	100		
Miscellaneous general expense	930		
Total general expenses		21,100	
Total operating expenses			74,100
Net income from operations			$ 20,100
Interest earned on investments			300
Net income			$ 20,400

Owner's equity. The presentation of the owners' equity in a classified balance sheet is no different from the examples in previous chapters. As explained in Chapter 1, the owners' equity section of a balance sheet for a corporation would show the two separate elements of capital stock and retained earnings rather than an owner's capital account as in the case of a single proprietorship.

Classification in the income statement. A new feature to be noted in the illustrated income statement of the Cheviot Company is the division of the operating expenses into the two categories of selling expenses and general expenses. This classification aids management in controlling expenses by emphasizing that certain expenses are the responsibility of the executive in charge of sales, and that other types of expense relate to the business as a whole. Some expenses, such as depreciation of the building, may be apportioned between the two classifications according to the portion utilized by each functional division of the business. The group caption of general and administrative expenses is an alternative title sometimes used instead of general expenses.

Another feature to note in the income statement of the Cheviot Company is that interest earned on investments is placed after the figure showing net income from operations. Other examples of such incidental, nonoperating revenues are dividends on shares of stock owned, and rent earned by leasing property not presently needed in the operation of the business. Any items of expense not related to selling or administrative functions may also be placed at the bottom of the income statement after the net income from operations. Separate group headings of nonoperating revenue and nonoperating expenses are sometimes used.

QUESTIONS

1. Suggest a control device to protect a business against the loss or nondelivery of invoices, purchase orders, and other documents which are routed from one department to another.

2. Give the accounting entry to be made, if any, for each of these events:

   a. Telephoned Apex Company and placed an order for $900 worth of merchandise.

   b. Issued a purchase order for $900 to the Apex Company in confirmation of yesterday's telephone order.

   c. Merchandise previously ordered from Apex Company was delivered today, and an invoice for $900 was received in the mail. Credit terms 2/10, n/30.

   d. Mailed check for $882 to Apex Company in full settlement of account.

3. State a general principle to be followed in assigning duties among employees if strong internal control is to be achieved.

4. Criticize the following statement: "In our company we get things done by requiring that a person who initiates a transaction follow it through in all particulars. For example, an employee who issues a purchase order is held responsible for inspecting the merchandise upon the arrival, approving the invoice, and preparing the check in payment of the purchase. If any error is made, we know definitely whom to blame."

5. What precautions should be taken in choosing the location for a cash register that will provide maximum internal control?

6. For an invoice dated October 21, what is the last day of the credit period if the credit terms are 2/10, n/30? 10 EOM?

7. Rhine Company received purchase invoices during July totaling $42,000. All these invoices carried credit terms of 2/10, n/30. It was the company's regular policy to take advantage of all available cash discounts, but because of employee vacations during July, there was confusion and delay in making payments to suppliers, and none of the July invoices was paid within the discount period.

    a. Explain briefly two alternative ways in which the amount of purchases might be presented in the July income statement.

    b. What method of recording purchase invoices can you suggest that would call to the attention of the Rhine Company management the inefficiency of operations in July?

8. Given the following data, determine the amount of the beginning inventory.

Ending inventory	*$27,600*
Purchases	*60,000*
Cost of goods sold	*41,900*
Transportation-in	*2,400*
Purchase returns and allowances	*4,600*
Purchase discounts	*1,100*

9. Explain the terms *current asset, current liability,* and *current ratio.*

10. The XYZ Company has a current ratio of 4 to 1 and working capital of $24,000. What are the amounts of current assets and current liabilities?

PROBLEMS

Group A

7A-1. The following transactions were completed by Experimentation Company during the month of April, 19___.

    Apr. 1.   Purchased merchandise from New Frontier Company, $1,000, terms 2/10, n/30.

    Apr. 4.   Purchased merchandise from Brand-Nu Corporation, $2,000, terms 2/10, n/30.

    Apr. 8.   Purchased merchandise from Jensen Company, $1,500, terms 2/10, n/60.

    Apr. 14.   Paid Brand-Nu Corporation's invoice of April 4, less cash discount.

    Apr. 15.   Merchandise having a list price of $500, purchased from Jensen Company, was found to be defective. It was returned to the seller, accompanied by debit memorandum No. 475.

    Apr. 25.   Purchased merchandise from Brand-Nu Corporation, $1,900, terms 2/10, n/30.

    Apr. 30.   Paid New Frontier Company's invoice of April 1.

    Other data. Assume the merchandise inventory on April 1, $7,244; and April 30, $6,820.

Instructions

a. Journalize above transactions, recording invoices at gross amount.

b. Journalize the above transactions, recording invoices at the net amount.

c. Prepare the cost of goods sold section of the income statement as it would appear based on journal entries in (*a*).

d. Prepare the cost of goods sold section of the income statement as it would appear based on the journal entries in (*b*).

e. What is the amount of accounts payable based on journal entries in (*a*)?

f. What is the amount of accounts payable based on journal entries in (*b*)?

7A-2. The merchandising transactions shown below for the month of October were completed by Washington Company. The terms of all sales are 2/10, n/30, and all purchase invoices are recorded at gross amount.

Oct. 1. Purchased merchandise from Pitt Company, $3,500, terms 2/10, n/30.

Oct. 1. Purchased merchandise from Sahara Company, $2,800, terms 1/10, n/30.

Oct. 1. Sold merchandise on account to Avenue A Shop, $3,250; invoice No. 145.

Oct. 3. Paid transportation charges on goods from Sahara Cómpany, $165.

Oct. 3. Sold merchandise on account to Hiller Company, $2,500; invoice No. 146.

Oct. 5. Issued credit memorandum No. 17 to Hiller Company, $450, for damaged merchandise returned.

Oct. 5. Purchased merchandise from Keystone Company, $2,500, terms 2/10, n/60. Paid the transportation charges of $92.

Oct. 6. Merchandise amounting to $300, purchased from Pitt Company, was found to be defective and was returned to the seller along with debit memorandum No. 35.

Oct. 10. Paid Pitt Company's invoice of October 1, less returns and discount.

Oct. 12. Sold merchandise on account to Clark and Company, $4,000; invoice No. 147.

Oct. 13. Received payment from Hiller Company, less cash discount.

Oct. 15. Paid Keystone Company's invoice of October 5, less discount.

Oct. 15. Issued credit memorandum No. 18 to Avenue A Shop, $150, for merchandise returned.

Oct. 22. Received payment from Clark and Company for invoice No. 147.

Oct. 30. Paid Sahara Company's invoice of October 1.

Oct. 30. Received payment from Avenue A Shop for invoice No. 145.

Instructions

a. Journalize the above transactions.

b. Prepare a partial income statement showing sales, cost of goods sold, and gross profit for the month of October. The inventory at September 30 was $16,000, and at October 31, $18,100.

c. Compute the equivalent annual interest rate indicated by the company's failure to pay the Sahara Company's invoice within the period of cash discount.

7A-3. The financial statements of Ellis Company, as prepared by the assistant bookkeeper when the bookkeeper suddenly resigned without notice, are shown below.

Other data

(1) Building was acquired 18 years ago at a cost of $80,000; esti-

mated life was 40 years. (One-quarter of building is used for sales activities.)
(2) Prepaid insurance as of December 31 amounted to $264.
(3) Office supplies on hand unused on December 31 amounted to $69.

ELLIS COMPANY
Income Statement
December 31, 19____

Income:

Sales	$196,550	
Purchase discounts	1,210	
Purchase returns and allowances	2,020	
Total		$199,780

Less: Costs and expenses:

Purchases	$145,830	
Transportation-in	6,284	
Sales returns and allowances	1,940	
Sales discounts	585	
Office salaries	3,000	
Salesmen's salaries	22,800	
Advertising expense	6,500	
Depreciation: building	2,000	
Miscellaneous selling expense	1,315	
Miscellaneous general expense	762	
Depreciation: store equipment	500	
Office supplies expense	959	
Bad debt expense	945	
Insurance expense	684	
Total		194,104
		$ 5,676
Add: Increase in inventory		4,460
Net income		$ 10,136

ELLIS COMPANY
Balance Sheet
December 31, 19____

Assets

Cash	$11,460
Accounts receivable	13,755
Notes receivable	11,000
U.S. government bonds	5,000
Land	16,000
Building	80,000
Inventory	46,110
Store equipment	12,600
Land held for future expansion	9,000
Total assets	$204,925

Liabilities

Notes payable	$ 4,100
Accounts payable	16,120
Bank loans	5,000
5% 1st mortgage bonds payable	50,000
Allowance for doubtful accounts	1,140
Accumulated depreciation: building	36,000
Accumulated depreciation: store equipment ..	5,400
Total liabilities	$117,760

Owner's Equity

Jay Ellis, capital, Jan. 1	$84,280	
Add: net increase for the year	1,285	
Jay Ellis, capital, Dec. 31	$85,565	
Deferred revenue	1,600	
Total owner's equity		87,165
		$204,925

Instructions

a. Prepare an income statement in good form for the year ended December 31.

b. Prepare a balance sheet properly classified as of December 31. Include in the owner's equity section the corrected net income and the withdrawals for the year.

Group B

7B-1. The management of Grove Company is interested in comparing for a test period the results of recording invoices at the gross amounts with results obtained by recording invoices at the net amount. Merchandising transactions for the month of May are listed below.

May 1.	Purchased merchandise from Oldham Co. The list price was $20,000 with a trade discount of 20% and terms of 2/10, n/60.
May 1.	Purchased merchandise from Ross Brothers for $8,000. Terms 1/10, n/30.
May 5.	Sold merchandise to K. R. Randall, $11,500. Terms 2/10, n/30.
May 6.	Returned to Oldham Co. damaged merchandise having a cost after trade discount of $1,000.
May 11.	Purchased merchandise from Rich Co. for $9,000. Terms 2/10, n/30.
May 11.	Paid Oldham Co. for invoice of May 1, less discount and returns.
May 15.	Received cash in full settlement of K. R. Randall account.
May 21.	Paid Rich Co. invoice of May 11, less discount.
May 22.	Sold merchandise to May Co., $38,400. Terms 2/10, n/30.
May 25.	Purchased from Able Co. merchandise with list price of $12,000, subject to trade discount of 25% and credit terms of 1/10, n/30.
May 28.	Returned for credit merchandise received from Able Co. Cost of the returned goods (after trade discount) was $200.
May 31.	Paid Ross Brothers invoice of May 1.

Instructions

a. Journalize these transactions, following the policy of recording purchase invoices at gross amount.

b. Journalize these transactions, following a policy of recording purchase invoices at the net amount.

c. Prepare partial income statements under methods (*a*) and (*b*) above, showing gross profit on sales. Assume the following inventories: April 30, $11,600; May 31, $13,300.

d. Compute the balance of accounts payable under each of the above methods.

e. Compute the effective rate of interest Grove Company would be paying if it failed to take advantage of discount terms on the Oldham Co. invoice.

7B-2. The merchandising transactions of AAA Wholesale Furniture Company for the month of March are detailed below. The company normally grants credit terms of 2/10, n/30 and records purchase invoices at the gross amount.

Mar. 2.   Purchased merchandise from Azle Manufacturing Co., $26,800. Terms 2/10, n/30.

Mar. 2.   Sold merchandise on account to Happy Furniture Co., $18,420.

Mar. 3.   Paid transportation charges on goods received from Azle Manufacturing Co., $1,120.

Mar. 3.   Sold merchandise to Roland Co. for cash, $23,410.

Mar. 5.   Issued credit memorandum No. 361 to Happy Furniture Co. for allowance on damaged goods, $620.

Mar. 6.   Purchased merchandise from Dorn Manufacturing Co., $32,600. Terms 1/10, n/30.

Mar. 8.   Returned defective goods to Dorn Manufacturing Co., $1,200, accompanied by debit memorandum No. 97.

Mar. 10.   Sold merchandise on account to Okay Furniture Stores, $26,900.

Mar. 12.   Paid Azle Manufacturing Co. account in full.

Mar. 12.   Received cash from Happy Furniture Co. in full payment of account.

Mar. 15.   Sold merchandise on account to Perch and Sons, $11,200.

Mar. 15.   Purchased merchandise from Richards Co., $13,000. Terms 2/10, n/30. Paid transportation charges on delivery, $840.

Mar. 16.   Paid Dorn Manufacturing Co. account in full.

Mar. 19.   Sold merchandise on account to Riley Furniture Co., $14,620.

Mar. 20.   Received cash from Okay Furniture Stores in full payment of account.

Mar. 25.   Paid Richards Co. account in full.

Mar. 27.   Received cash from Perch and Sons in full payment of account.

Mar. 29.   Received $2,940 cash from Riley Furniture Co. in partial payment of our invoice of March 19.

Mar. 30.   Decided to use a portion of the furniture acquired on March 6 from Dorn Manufacturing Co. to furnish a reception room. The cost of the furniture taken from stock for this purpose was $10,000.

Instructions

a. Journalize the above transactions.

b. Post the journal entries to T accounts.

c. Prepare a partial income statement showing revenue, cost of goods sold, and gross profit on sales, assuming the inventory at February 28 to be $16,200 and the inventory at March 31 to be $18,000.

7B-3. Because of the sudden illness of the full-charge bookkeeper of the National Company at the end of the year, the assistant bookkeeper, whose experience was quite limited, was asked to complete the year-end work. After considerable effort, the assistant bookkeeper presented the financial statements listed below.

NATIONAL COMPANY
Income Statement
December 31, 19___

Sales	$426,030	
Purchase returns and allowances	3,680	
Purchase discounts	7,256	
Interest earned on investments	675	
Increase in inventory	4,218	
Total		$441,859
Purchases	$313,570	
Sales returns and allowances	3,648	
Sales discounts	4,425	
Transportation-in	12,542	
Advertising expense	9,742	
Bad debts expense	1,080	
Depreciation: building	1,600	
Depreciation: store equipment	1,140	
Depreciation: delivery equipment	984	
Insurance expense	1,400	
Office salaries expense	9,462	
Executive salaries expense	16,000	
Sales salaries expense	42,638	
Miscellaneous selling expense	693	
Miscellaneous general expense	864	
		419,788
Net income		$ 22,071

NATIONAL COMPANY
Balance Sheet
December 31, 19___

Assets

Current:		
Notes receivable	$ 3,800	
Accounts receivable	22,850	
Cash	19,620	
Rent collected in advance	600	
Land	15,000	
Total		$ 61,870

Fixed:

Inventory	*$31,096*
Store equipment	*8,600*
Building	*22,000*
Delivery equipment	*3,400*
Total	*65,096*

Other assets:

Marketable securities	*$ 9,000*
Land held as future building site	*13,800*
	22,800
Total	*$149,766*

Liabilities and Owner's Equity

Liabilities:

Accounts payable	*$23,075*
Accrued salaries payable	*1,865*
Prepaid expenses	*600*
Notes payable	*8,900*
1st mortgage bonds payable	*30,000*
Allowance for bad debts	*685*
Accumulated depreciation: buildings	*3,300*
Accumulated depreciation: store equipment	*1,300*
Accumulated depreciation: delivery equipment ..	*1,700*
Total	*71,425*

Owner's equity:

Ralph Newell, capital, Jan. 1	*$70,270*
Add: increase: $22,071 — 14,000	*8,071*
Ralph Newell, capital, Dec. 31	*78,341*
Total	*$149,766*

Instructions
a. Prepare in acceptable form an income statement for the year ended December 31. (Allocate to selling expense 80% of building depreciation and $333 of insurance expense.)

b. Prepare a balance sheet as of December 31 properly classified.

8

Controlling accounts and specialized journals

In the early chapters of an introductory accounting book, basic accounting principles can most conveniently be discussed in terms of a small business with only a handful of customers and suppliers. This simplified model of a business has been used in preceding chapters to demonstrate the analysis and recording of the more common types of business transactions.

The recording procedures illustrated thus far call for recording each transaction by an entry in the journal, and then posting each debit and credit from the journal to the proper account in the ledger. We must now face the practical problem of streamlining and speeding up this recording process so that the accounting department can keep pace with the rapid flow of transactions in a modern business.

In a large business there may be hundreds or even thousands of transactions every day. It would be a physical impossibility for one bookkeeper to enter all these transactions in one journal and to post each transaction to the proper ledger accounts even though he worked 24 hours a day. If all the transactions were to be entered in one journal and posted to one ledger, it would not be possible to assign more employees to the job because only one person can work on a journal or ledger at a time.

To handle a large volume of transactions rapidly and efficiently, it is helpful to classify the transactions into like classes and to use a specialized journal for each class. This will greatly reduce the amount of detailed recording work and will also permit a division of labor, since each special-purpose journal can be handled by a different employee. The great majority of transactions (perhaps as much as 80 or 90%) usually fall into four types. These four types and the four corresponding special journals are as follows:

Type of transaction	Name of journal
Sales of merchandise on credit	Sales journal
Purchases of merchandise on credit	Purchases journal
Receipts of cash	Cash receipts journal
Payments of cash	Cash payments journal

Minor variations in the titles applied to these special journals are common; for example, the cash payments journal is sometimes called a cash disbursements journal, and a purchases journal is sometimes referred to as a purchases book or as an invoice register. However, regardless of variations in names, all types of journals are books of original entry. "Book of original entry" is a self-descriptive term, indicating the accounting record in which transactions are first entered, prior to being posted to ledger accounts.

In addition to these four special journals, a *general journal* will be used for recording transactions which do not fit into any of the above four types. The general journal is the same book of original entry illustrated in preceding chapters; the adjective general is added merely to distinguish it from the special journals.

Sales journal

Illustrated below is a sales journal containing entries for all sales on account made during November by the Seaside Company. Whenever merchandise is sold on credit, several copies of a sales invoice are prepared. The information listed on a sales invoice usually includes the date of the sale, the serial number of the invoice, the customer's name, the amount of the sale, and the credit terms. One copy of the sales invoice is used by the seller as the basis for an entry in the sales journal.

Notice that the illustrated sales journal contains special columns for recording each of these aspects of the sales transaction, except the credit terms. If it is the practice of the business to offer different credit terms to different customers, a column may be inserted in the sales book to show the terms of sale. In this illustration it is assumed that all sales are made on terms of 2/10, n/30; consequently, there is no need to write the credit terms as part of the journal entry. Only sales on credit are entered in the sales journal. When merchandise is sold for cash, the transaction is recorded in a cash receipts journal, which is illustrated later in this chapter.

		Sales Journal			(Page 1)
Date		Account debited	Invoice no.	√	Amount
19__					
Nov.	2	John Adams	301	√	450.00
	4	Harold Black	302	√	975.00
	5	Robert Cross	303	√	1,000.00
	11	H. R. Davis	304	√	620.00
	18	C. D. Early	305	√	900.00
	23	John Frost	306	√	400.00
	29	D. H. Gray	307	√	1,850.00
					6,195.00
					(5) (41)

Advantages of the sales journal. Notice that each of the above seven sales transactions is recorded on a single line. Each entry consists of a debit to a customer's account; the offsetting credit to the Sales account is understood without being written, because sales on account are the only transactions recorded in this special journal.

An entry in a sales book need not include an explanation; if more information about the transaction is desired it can be obtained by referring to the file copy of the sales invoice. The invoice number is listed in the sales journal as part of each entry. The one-line entry in the sales journal requires much less writing than would be required to record a sales transaction in the general journal. Since there may be several hundred or several thousand sales transactions each month, the time saved in recording transactions in this streamlined manner becomes quite important.

Every entry in the sales journal represents a debit to a customer's account. Charges to customers' accounts should be posted daily so that each customer's account will always be up to date and available for use in making decisions relating to collections and to the further extension of credit. Consequently, the individual amounts in the sales journal are posted as debits to customers' accounts on a day-to-day basis throughout the month. A check mark (√) is placed in the sales journal opposite each amount posted to a customer's account, to indicate that the posting has been made.

Another advantage of the special journal for sales is the great saving of time in posting credits to the Sales account. Remember that every amount entered in the sales journal represents a credit to Sales. In the illustrated sales journal above, there are seven transactions (and in practice there might be 700). Instead of posting a separate credit to the Sales account for each sales transaction, we can wait until the end of the month and make one posting to the Sales account for the total of the amounts recorded in the sales journal.

In the illustrated sales journal for November, the sales on account totaled $6,195. On November 30 this amount is posted as a credit to the Sales account, and the ledger account number for Sales (41) is entered under the total figure in the sales journal to show that the posting operation has been performed. The total sales figure is also posted as a debit to ledger account No. 5, Accounts Receivable. To make clear the reason for this posting to Accounts Receivable, an explanation of the nature of controlling accounts and subsidiary ledgers is necessary.

Controlling accounts and subsidiary ledgers

In preceding chapters all transactions involving accounts receivable from customers have been posted to a single account entitled Accounts Receivable. Under this simplified procedure, however, it is not easy to look up the amount receivable from a given customer. In practice, nearly all businesses which sell goods on credit maintain a separate account receivable with each customer. If there are 400 customers this would require a ledger with 400 accounts receivable, in addition to the accounts for other assets, and for liabilities, owner's equity, revenue, and expense. Such a ledger would be cumbersome and unwieldy. Since only one person can work on a ledger at a time, it would be difficult for the posting of all these accounts to be kept up to date. Also, the trial balance prepared from such a large ledger would be a very long one. If the trial balance showed the ledger to be out of balance, the task of locating the error or errors would be most difficult. All these factors indicate that it is not desirable to have too many accounts in one ledger. Fortunately, a simple solution is available; this solution is to divide up the ledger into several separate ledgers.

In a business which has a large number of accounts with customers and creditors, it is customary to divide the ledger into three separate ledgers. All the accounts with *customers* are placed in alphabetical order in a separate ledger, called the *accounts receivable ledger*. All the accounts with *creditors* are arranged alphabetically in another ledger called the *accounts payable ledger*. Both of these ledgers are known as *subsidiary ledgers*.

After thus segregating the accounts receivable from customers in one subsidiary ledger and placing the accounts payable to creditors in a second subsidiary ledger, we have left in the original ledger all the revenue and expense accounts and also all the balance sheet accounts except those with customers and creditors. This ledger is called the *general ledger*, to distinguish it from the subsidiary ledgers.

When the numerous individual accounts with customers are placed in a subsidiary ledger, an account entitled Accounts Receivable continues to be maintained in the general ledger. This account shows the total amount due from all customers; in other words, this single controlling account in the general ledger takes the place of the numerous customers' accounts which have been removed to form a subsidiary ledger. The general ledger is still in balance because the controlling account, Accounts Receivable, has a balance equal to the total of the customers' accounts which were removed from the general ledger. Agreement of the controlling account with the sum of the accounts receivable in the subsidiary ledger also provides assurance of accuracy in the subsidiary ledger.

A controlling account entitled Accounts Payable is also kept in the general ledger in place of the numerous accounts with creditors which have been removed to form the accounts payable subsidiary ledger. Because these two controlling accounts represent the total amounts receivable from customers and payable to creditors, a trial balance can be prepared from the general ledger alone.

Posting to subsidiary ledgers and to control accounts. To illustrate the posting of subsidiary ledgers and of control accounts, let us refer again to the sales journal illustrated on page 226. Each debit to a customer's account is posted currently during the month from the sales journal to the customer's account in the accounts receivable ledger. The accounts in this subsidiary ledger are usually kept in alphabetical order and not numbered. When a posting is made to a customer's account, a check mark (√) is placed in the sales journal as evidence that the posting has been made to the subsidiary ledger.

At month-end the sales journal is totaled. The total sales for the month, $6,195, are posted as a credit to the Sales account and also as a debit to the controlling account, Accounts Receivable, in the general ledger. The controlling account will, therefore, equal the total of all the customers' accounts in the subsidiary ledger.

The diagram on page 229 shows the day-to-day posting of individual entries from the sales journal to the subsidiary ledger. The diagram also shows the month-end posting of the total of the sales journal to the two general ledger accounts affected, Accounts Receivable and Sales. Notice that the amount of the monthly debit to the controlling account is equal to the sum of the several debits posted to the subsidiary ledger.

Purchases journal

The handling of purchase transactions when a purchases journal is used follows a pattern that is quite similar to the one described for the sales journal.

Assume that the purchases journal illustrated on page 229 contains all purchases of merchandise on credit during the month by the Seaside Company. The invoice date is shown in a separate column because the cash-discount period begins on this date.

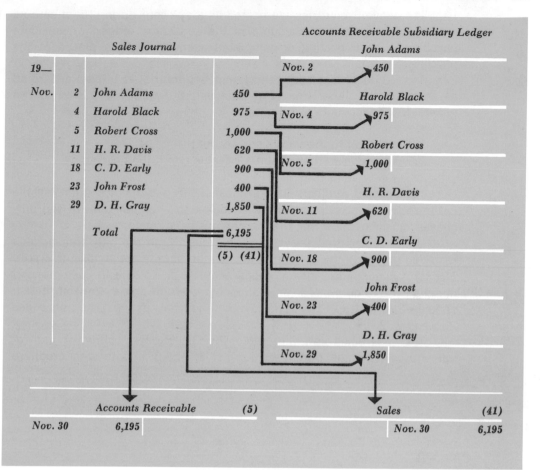

Sales Journal

19—			
Nov.	2	John Adams	450
	4	Harold Black	975
	5	Robert Cross	1,000
	11	H. R. Davis	620
	18	C. D. Early	900
	23	John Frost	400
	29	D. H. Gray	1,850
		Total	6,195
			(5) (41)

Accounts Receivable Subsidiary Ledger

John Adams — Nov. 2 450

Harold Black — Nov. 4 975

Robert Cross — Nov. 5 1,000

H. R. Davis — Nov. 11 620

C. D. Early — Nov. 18 900

John Frost — Nov. 23 400

D. H. Gray — Nov. 29 1,850

Accounts Receivable (5)

Nov. 30 6,195

Sales (41)

Nov. 30 6,195

SUBSIDIARY LEDGER POSTED DAILY; GENERAL LEDGER POSTED MONTHLY

ENTRIES FOR PURCHASES ON CREDIT DURING NOVEMBER

Purchases Journal

Date		Account credited	Invoice date		√	Amount
19—			19—			
Nov.	2	Alabama Supply Co.	Nov.	2	√	3,325.00
	4	Barker & Bright		4	√	700.00
	10	Canning & Sons		9	√	500.00
	17	Davis Co.		15	√	900.00
	27	Excelsior, Inc.		25	√	1,825.00
						7,250.00
						(50) (21)

The above five entries are posted as they occur during the month as credits to the creditors' accounts in the subsidiary ledger for accounts payable. As each posting is completed a check mark is placed in the purchases journal.

At the end of the month the purchases journal is totaled and ruled as shown in the illustration. The total figure, $7,250, is posted to two general ledger accounts as follows:

1. As a debit to the Purchases account.
2. As a credit to the Accounts Payable controlling account.

The account numbers for Purchases (50) and for Accounts Payable (21) are then placed in parentheses below the column total of the purchases journal to show that the posting has been made.

Under the particular system being described, the only transactions recorded in the purchases journal are purchases of merchandise on credit. The term *merchandise* means goods acquired for resale to customers. If **SUBSIDIARY** merchandise is purchased for cash rather than on credit, the transaction **LEDGER** should be recorded in the cash payments journal, as illustrated on pages **POSTED** **DAILY;** 236 and 237.

GENERAL The diagram below illustrates the day-to-day posting of individ- **LEDGER** **POSTED** ual entries from the purchases journal to the accounts with creditors **MONTHLY**

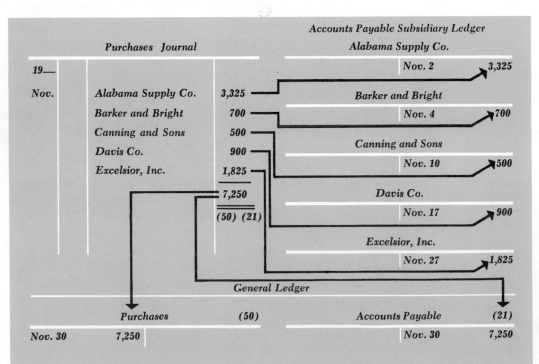

in the subsidiary ledger for accounts payable. The diagram also shows how the column total of the purchases journal is posted at the end of the month to the general ledger accounts, Purchases and Accounts Payable. One objective of this diagram is to emphasize that the amount of the monthly credit to the control account is equal to the sum of the several credits posted to the subsidiary ledger.

When assets other than merchandise are being acquired, as, for example, a delivery truck or an office desk for use in the business, the journal to be used depends upon whether a cash payment is made. If assets of this type are purchased for cash, the transaction should be entered in the cash payments journal; if the transaction is on credit, the general journal is used. The purchases journal is not used to record the acquisition of fixed assets because the total of this journal is posted to the Purchases account and this account (as explained in Chapter 6) is used in determining the cost of goods sold.

Cash receipts journal

All transactions involving the receipt of cash are recorded in the cash receipts journal. One common example is the sale of merchandise for cash. As each cash sale is made, it is rung up on a cash register. At the end of the day the total of the cash sales is computed by striking the total key on the register. This total is entered in the cash receipts journal, which therefore contains one entry for the total cash sales of the day. For other types of cash receipts, such as the collection of accounts receivable from customers, a separate journal entry may be made for each transaction. The cash receipts journal illustrated on the following two pages contains entries for selected November transactions, all of which include the receipt of cash.

Nov. 1.   R. B. Jones invested $25,000 cash to establish the Seaside Company.

Nov. 4.   Sold merchandise for cash, $300.

Nov. 5.   Sold merchandise for cash, $400.

Nov. 8.   Collected from John Adams invoice of Nov. 2, $450 less 2% cash discount.

Nov. 10.   Sold portion of land not needed in business for a total price of $7,000, consisting of cash of $1,000 and a note receivable for $6,000. The cost of the land sold was $5,000.

Nov. 12.   Collected from Harold Black invoice of Nov. 4, $975 less 2% cash discount.

Nov. 20.   Collected from C. D. Early invoice of Nov. 18, $900, less 2% cash discount.

Nov. 27.   Sold merchandise for cash, $125.

Nov. 30.   Obtained $4,000 loan from bank. Issued a note payable in that amount.

Notice that the cash receipts journal illustrated below has three debit columns and three credit columns as follows:

Debits:

1. Cash. This column is used for every entry, because only those transactions which include the receipt of cash are entered in this special journal.

2. Sales discount. This column is used to accumulate the sales discounts allowed during the month. Only one line of the cash receipts book is required to record a collection from a customer who takes advantage of a cash discount.

3. Other accounts. This third debit column is used for debits to any and all accounts other than cash and sales discounts, and space is provided for writing in the name of the account. For example, the entry of November 10 in the illustrated cash receipts journal shows that cash and a note receivable were obtained when land was sold. The amount of cash received, $1,000, is entered in the Cash debit column, the account title Notes Receivable is written in the Other Accounts debit

INCLUDES ALL TRANSACTIONS INVOLVING RECEIPT OF CASH

Cash Receipts Journal

Date		Explanation	Debits				
			Cash	Sales discounts	Other accounts		
					Name	LP	Amount
19__							
Nov.	1	Investment by owner	25,000.00				
	4	Cash sales	300.00				
	5	Cash sales	400.00				
	8	Invoice Nov. 2, less 2%	441.00	9.00			
	10	Sale of land	1,000.00		Notes Receivable	3	6,000.00
	12	Invoice Nov. 4, less 2%	955.50	19.50			
	20	Invoice Nov. 18, less 2%	882.00	18.00			
	27	Cash sales	125.00				
	30	Obtained bank loan	4,000.00				
			33,103.50	46.50			6,000.00
			(1)	(43)			(X)

column and the amount of the debit to this account, $6,000. These two debits are offset by credit entries to Land, $5,000, and to Gain on Sale of Land, $2,000, in the Other Accounts credit column.

Credits:

1. Accounts receivable. This column is used to list the credits to customers' accounts as receivables are collected. The name of the customer is written in the space entitled Account Credited to the left of the Accounts Receivable column.

2. Sales. The existence of this column will save posting by permitting the accumulation of all sales for cash during the month and the posting of the column total at the end of the month as a credit to the Sales account (41).

3. Other accounts. This column is used for credits to any and all accounts other than Accounts Receivable and Sales. In some instances, a transaction may require credits to two accounts. Such cases are handled by using two lines of the special journal, as illustrated by the transaction of November 10, which required credits to both the Land account and to Gain on Sale of Land.

| Account credited | Credits | | | | |
| | Accounts receivable | | Sales | Other accounts | |
	√	Amount		LP	Amount
R. B. Jones, Capital				30	25,000.00
			300.00		
			400.00		
John Adams	√	450.00			
Land				11	5,000.00
Gain on Sale of Land				40	2,000.00
Harold Black	√	975.00			
C. D. Early	√	900.00			
			125.00		
Notes Payable				20	4,000.00
		2,325.00	825.00		36,000.00
		(5)	(41)		(X)

Posting the cash receipts journal. It is convenient to think of the posting of a cash receipts journal as being divided into two phases. The first phase consists of the daily posting of individual amounts throughout the month; the second phase consists of the posting of column totals at the end of the month.

Posting during the month. Daily posting of the Accounts Receivable credits column is desirable. Each amount is posted to an individual customer's account in the accounts receivable subsidiary ledger. A check mark (√) is placed in the cash receipts journal alongside each item posted to a customer's account to show that the posting operation has been performed. When debits and credits to customers' accounts are posted daily, the current status of each customer's account is available for use in making decisions as to further granting of credit and as a guide to collection efforts on past-due invoices.

The debits and credits in the Other Accounts sections of the cash receipts journal may be posted daily or at convenient intervals during the month. If this portion of the posting work is done on a current basis, less detailed bookkeeping work will be left for the busy period at the end of the month. As the postings of individual items are made, the number of the ledger account debited or credited is entered in the LP column of the cash receipts journal opposite the item posted. Evidence is thus provided in the special journal as to which items have been posted.

Posting column totals at month-end. Before posting any of the column totals at the end of the month, it is first important to prove that the sum of the debit column totals is equal to the sum of the credit column totals. This proof of the equality of debits and credits is made as follows for the cash receipts journal illustrated on pages 232 and 233.

	Debits	Credits
PROVE EQUALITY OF COLUMN TOTALS BEFORE POSTING		
Debit columns:		
Cash	$33,103.50	
Sales discounts	46.50	
Other accounts	6,000.00	
Credit columns:		
Accounts receivable		$ 2,325.00
Sales		825.00
Other accounts		36,000.00
	$39,150.00	$39,150.00

After the totals of the cash receipts journal have been cross footed, the following column totals are posted:

1. Cash debit column. Posted as a debit to the Cash account.
2. Sales Discount debit column. Posted as a debit to the Sales Discount account.
3. Accounts Receivable credit column. Posted as a credit to the controlling account, Accounts Receivable.
4. Sales credit column. Posted as a credit to the Sales account.

As each column total is posted to the appropriate account in the general ledger, the ledger account number is entered in parentheses just below the column total in the special journal. This notation shows that the column total has been posted and also indicates the account to which the posting was made. The totals of the Other Accounts columns in both the debit and credit sections of the special journal are not posted, because the amounts listed in this column affect various general ledger accounts and have already been posted as individual items. The symbol X may be placed below the totals of these two columns to indicate that no posting is made.

Cash payments journal

Another widely used special journal is the cash payments journal, sometimes called the cash disbursements journal, in which all payments of cash are recorded. Among the more common of these transactions are payments of accounts payable to creditors, payment of operating expenses, and cash purchases of merchandise.

The cash payments journal illustrated on pages 236 and 237 contains entries for all November transactions of the Seaside Company which required the payment of cash.

Nov. 1.   Paid rent on store building for November, $800.
Nov. 2.   Purchased merchandise for cash, $500.
Nov. 8.   Paid Barker & Bright for invoice of November 4, $700 less 2%.
Nov. 9.   Bought land, $15,000, and building, $35,000, for future use in business. Paid cash of $20,000 and signed a promissory note for the balance of $30,000. (Land and building were acquired in a single transaction.)
Nov. 17.   Paid salesmen's salaries, $600.
Nov. 26.   Paid Davis Co. for invoice of November 17, $900 less 2%.
Nov. 27.   Purchased merchandise for cash, $400.
Nov. 28.   Purchased merchandise for cash, $650.
Nov. 29.   Paid for newspaper advertising, $50.
Nov. 29.   Paid for three-year insurance policy, $720.

Note in the illustrated cash payments journal that the three credit columns are located to the left of the three debit columns; any sequence of columns is satisfactory in a special journal as long as the column headings clearly distinguish debits from credits. The Cash column is often placed first in both the cash receipts journal and the cash payments journal because it is the column used in every transaction.

Good internal control over cash disbursements requires that all payments be made by check. The checks are serially numbered and as each transaction is entered in the cash payments journal, the check number is listed in a special column provided just to the right of the date column. An unbroken sequence of check numbers in this column gives assurance that every check issued has been recorded in the accounting records.

The use of the six money columns in the illustrated cash payments journal parallels the procedures described for the cash receipts journal.

INCLUDES ALL TRANS-ACTIONS INVOLVING PAYMENT OF CASH

Posting the cash payments journal. The posting of the cash payments journal falls into the same two phases already described for the cash receipts journal. The first phase consists of the daily posting of entries in the Accounts Payable debit column to the individual accounts of creditors in the accounts payable subsidiary ledger. Check marks (√) are en-

Cash Payments Journal

Date	Check no.	Explanation	Cash	Purchase discounts	Other accounts		
					Credits		
					Name	LP	Amount
19__							
Nov. 1	101	Paid Nov. rent	800				
2	102	Purchased merchandise	500				
8	103	Invoice Nov. 4, less 2%	686	14			
9	104	Bought land and building	20,000		Notes Payable	20	30,000
17	105	Paid salesmen	600				
26	106	Invoice of Nov. 17, less 2%	882	18			
27	107	Purchased merchandise	400				
28	108	Purchased merchandise	650				
29	109	Newspaper advertisement	50				
29	110	Three-year ins. policy	720				
			25,288	32			30,000
			(1)	(52)			(X)

tered opposite these items to show that the posting has been made. Since the accounts with creditors are posted daily, they are always up to date and available for reference. In some companies the accounts payable subsidiary ledger consists of a set of cards filed alphabetically, so that if a creditor telephones to inquire about any aspect of his account, information on all purchases and payments made to date is readily available.

The individual debit and credit entries in the Other Accounts columns of the cash payments journal may be posted daily or at convenient intervals during the month. As the postings of these individual items are made, the page number of the ledger account debited or credited is entered in the LP column of the cash payments journal opposite the item posted.

The second phase of posting the cash payments journal is performed at the end of the month. When all the transactions of the month have been journalized, the cash payments journal is ruled as shown below, and the six money columns are totaled. The equality of debits and credits is then proved as shown on page 238.

	Debits				
	Accounts payable		Purchases	Other accounts	
Account debited	√	Amount		LP	Amount
Store Rent Expense				54	800
Purchases			500		
Barker & Bright	√	700			
Land				11	15,000
Building				12	35,000
Sales Salaries Expense				53	600
Davis Co.	√	900			
Purchases			400		
Purchases			650		
Advertising Expense				55	50
Unexpired Insurance				6	720
		1,600	1,550		52,170
		(21)	(50)		(X)

PROVE
EQUALITY
OF COLUMN
TOTALS
BEFORE
POSTING

	Debits	Credits
Credit columns:		
Cash		$25,288
Purchase discounts		32
Other accounts		30,000
Debit columns:		
Accounts payable	$ 1,600	
Purchases	1,550	
Other accounts	52,170	
	$55,320	$55,320

After the totals of the cash payments journal have been proved to be in balance, the totals of the columns for Cash, Purchase Discounts, Accounts Payable, and Purchases are posted to the corresponding accounts in the general ledger. The numbers of the accounts to which these postings are made are listed in parentheses just below the respective column totals in the cash payments journal. The totals of the Other Accounts columns in both the debit and credit section of this special journal are not to be posted, and the symbol X may be placed below the totals of these two columns to indicate that no posting is required.

The general journal

When all transactions involving cash or the purchase and sale of merchandise are recorded in special journals, only a few types of transactions remain to be entered in the general journal. Examples include the purchase or sale of fixed assets on credit, the return of merchandise for credit to a supplier, and the return of merchandise by a customer for credit to his account. The general journal is also used for the recording of adjusting and closing entries at the end of the accounting period.

The following transactions of the Seaside Company during November could not conveniently be handled in any of the four special journals and were therefore entered in the general journal.

Nov. 25.   A customer, John Frost, was permitted to return for credit $50 worth of merchandise that had been sold to him on November 23.

Nov. 28.   The Seaside Company returned to a supplier, Excelsior, Inc., for credit $300 worth of the merchandise purchased on November 27.

Nov. 29.   Purchased for use in the business office equipment costing $1,225. Agreed to make payment within 30 days to XYZ Equipment Co.

		General Journal			
19__					
Nov.	25	Sales Returns and Allowances	41	50	
		Accounts Receivable, John Frost	5/√		50
		Allowed credit to customer for return of merchandise from sale of Nov. 23.			
	28	Accounts Payable, Excelsior, Inc.	21/√	300	
		Purchase Returns & Allowances	51		300
		Returned to supplier for credit a portion of merchandise purchased on Nov. 27.			
	29	Office Equipment	14	1,225	
		Accounts Payable, XYZ Equipment Co.	21/√		1,225
		Purchased office equipment on 30-day credit.			

Each of the above entries includes a debit or credit to a controlling account (Accounts Receivable or Accounts Payable); and also identifies by name a particular creditor or customer. When a controlling account is debited or credited by a general journal entry, the debit or credit must be posted twice: one posting to the controlling account in the general ledger and another posting to a customer's account or a creditor's account in a subsidiary ledger. This double posting is necessary to keep the controlling account in agreement with the subsidiary ledger.

For example, in the illustrated entry of November 25 for the return of merchandise by a customer, the credit part of the entry is posted twice:

1. To the Accounts Receivable controlling account in the general ledger; this posting is evidenced by listing the account number (5) in the LP column of the journal.

2. To the account of John Frost in the subsidiary ledger for accounts receivable; this posting is indicated by the check mark (√) placed in the LP column of the journal.

Showing the source of postings in ledger accounts

When a general journal and several special journals are in use, the ledger accounts should indicate the book of original entry from which each debit and credit was posted. An identifying symbol is placed opposite each entry in the reference column of the account. The symbols used in this text are as follows:

S1   meaning page 1 of the sales journal
P1   meaning page 1 of the purchases journal
CR1   meaning page 1 of the cash receipts journal

CP1   meaning page 1 of the cash payments journal

J1   meaning page 1 of the general journal

The running balance form of account

SUBSIDIARY
LEDGER:
ACCOUNT
RECEIVABLE

The form of account generally used in the subsidiary ledgers for accounts receivable and accounts payable has three money columns: Debit, Credit, and Balance. The following illustration shows a customer's account in a subsidiary ledger for accounts receivable.

Name of Customer			*Ref*	*Debit*	*Credit*	*Balance*
19__						
July	*1*		*S1*	*400*		*400*
	20		*S3*	*200*		*600*
Aug.	*4*		*CR7*		*400*	*200*
	15		*S6*	*120*		*320*

The advantage of this three-column form of account is that it shows at a glance the present balance receivable from the customer. The current amount of a customer's account is often needed as a guide to collection activities, or as a basis for granting additional credit. In studying the above illustration note also that the Reference column shows the source of each debit and credit.

The three-column running balance form of account is preferred by a great many companies for accounts in the general ledger as well as for subsidiary ledgers.

Accounts appearing in the accounts receivable subsidiary ledger are assumed to have debit balances. If one of these customers' accounts should acquire a credit balance by reason of overpayment or for any other reason, the word "credit" should be written after the amount in the balance column. The column headings shown in the above illustration are often omitted from printed ledger sheets.

SUBSIDIARY
LEDGER:
ACCOUNT
PAYABLE

The same three-column form of account is also generally used for creditors' accounts in an accounts payable subsidiary ledger, as indicated by the following illustration:

Name of Creditor			*Ref*	*Debit*	*Credit*	*Balance*
19__						
July	*10*		*P1*		*625*	*625*
	25		*P2*		*100*	*725*
Aug.	*8*		*CP4*	*725*		*000*
	12		*P3*		*250*	*250*

Accounts in the accounts payable subsidiary ledger normally have credit balances. If by reason of payment in advance or accidental overpayment, one of these accounts should acquire a debit balance, the word "debit" should be written after the amount in the balance column.

As previously stated, both the accounts receivable and accounts payable subsidiary ledgers are customarily arranged in alphabetical order and account numbers are not used. This arrangement permits unlimited expansion of the subsidiary ledgers, as accounts with new customers and creditors can be inserted in proper alphabetical sequence.

Ledger accounts

The general ledger. The general ledger accounts of the Seaside Company illustrated on pages 241 to 243 indicate the source of postings from the various books of original entry. The subsidiary ledger accounts appear on pages 244 to 246. To gain a clear understanding of the procedures for posting special journals, the student should trace each entry in the illustrated special journals into the general ledger accounts and also to the subsidiary ledger accounts where appropriate.

Note that the Cash account contains only one debit entry and one credit entry although there were many cash transactions during the month. The one debit, $33,103.50, represents the total cash received during the month and was posted from the cash receipts journal on November 30. Similarly, the one credit entry of $25,288.00 was posted on November 30 from the cash payments journal and represents the total of all cash payments made during the month.

GENERAL LEDGER ACCOUNTS

			Cash						*(1)*
19__ Nov.	30		CR1	33,103.50	19__ Nov.	30		CP1	25,288.00

			Notes Receivable						*(3)*
19__ Nov.	10		CR1	6,000.00					

			Accounts Receivable						*(5)*
19__ Nov.	30		S1	6,195.00	19__ Nov.	25		J1	50.00
						30		CR1	2,325.00

			Unexpired Insurance						*(6)*
19__ Nov.	29		CP1	720.00					

Land (11)

19__					19__				
Nov.	9		CP1	15,000.00	Nov.	10		CR1	5,000.00

Building (12)

19__				
Nov.	9		CP1	35,000.00

Office Equipment (14)

19__				
Nov.	29		J1	1,225.00

Notes Payable (20)

					19__				
					Nov.	9		CP1	30,000.00
						30		CR1	4,000.00

Accounts Payable (21)

19__					19__				
Nov.	28		J1	300.00	Nov.	29		J1	1,225.00
	30		CP1	1,600.00		30		P1	7,250.00

R. B. Jones, Capital (30)

					19__				
					Nov.	1		CR1	25,000.00

Gain on Sale of Land (40)

					19__				
					Nov.	10		CR1	2,000.00

Sales (41)

					19__				
					Nov.	30		CR1	825.00
						30		S1	6,195.00

Sales Returns and Allowances   (42)

19__								
Nov.	25		J1	50.00				

Sales Discounts   (43)

19__								
Nov.	30		CR1	46.50				

Purchases   (50)

19__								
Nov.	30		CP1	1,550.00				
	30		P1	7,250.00				

Purchases Returns and Allowances   (51)

				19__				
				Nov.	28		J1	300.00

Purchase Discounts   (52)

				19__				
				Nov.	30		CP1	32.00

Sales Salaries Expense   (53)

19__								
Nov.	17		CP1	600.00				

Store Rent Expense   (54)

19__								
Nov.	1		CP1	800.00				

Advertising Expense   (55)

19__								
Nov.	29		CP1	50.00				

Accounts receivable ledger. The subsidiary ledger for accounts receivable appears as follows after the posting of the various journals has been completed.

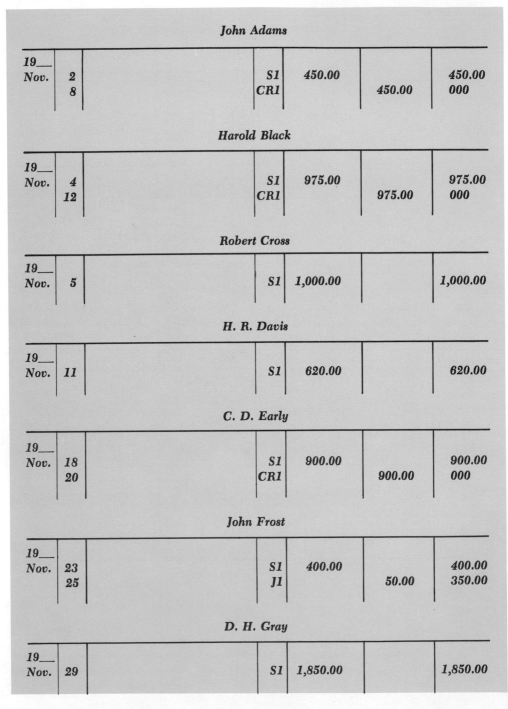

John Adams

| 19__
Nov. | 2
8 | | | S1
CR1 | 450.00 | 450.00 | 450.00
000 |

Harold Black

| 19__
Nov. | 4
12 | | | S1
CR1 | 975.00 | 975.00 | 975.00
000 |

Robert Cross

| 19__
Nov. | 5 | | | S1 | 1,000.00 | | 1,000.00 |

H. R. Davis

| 19__
Nov. | 11 | | | S1 | 620.00 | | 620.00 |

C. D. Early

| 19__
Nov. | 18
20 | | | S1
CR1 | 900.00 | 900.00 | 900.00
000 |

John Frost

| 19__
Nov. | 23
25 | | | S1
J1 | 400.00 | 50.00 | 400.00
350.00 |

D. H. Gray

| 19__
Nov. | 29 | | | S1 | 1,850.00 | | 1,850.00 |

Accounts payable ledger. The accounts with creditors in the accounts
payable subsidiary ledger are as follows:

Alabama Supply Co.

19__ Nov.	2		P1		3,325.00	3,325.00

Barker & Bright

19__ Nov.	4		P1		700.00	700.00
	8		CP1	700.00		000

Canning & Sons

19__ Nov.	10		P1		500.00	500.00

Davis Co.

19__ Nov.	17		P1		900.00	900.00
	26		CP1	900.00		000

Excelsior, Inc.

19__ Nov.	27		P1		1,825.00	1,825.00
	28		J1	300.00		1,525.00

XYZ Equipment Co.

19__ Nov.	29		J1		1,225.00	1,225.00

Proving the ledgers

At the end of each accounting period, proof of the equality of debits and
credits in the general ledger is established by preparation of a trial balance, as illustrated in preceding chapters. When controlling accounts and

subsidiary ledgers are in use, it is also necessary to prove that each subsidiary ledger is in agreement with its controlling account. This proof is accomplished by preparing a schedule of the balances of accounts in each subsidiary ledger and determining that the totals of these schedules agree with the balances of the corresponding control accounts.

<table>
<tr><td rowspan="4">GENERAL
LEDGER
TRIAL
BALANCE</td><td colspan="3" align="center">SEASIDE COMPANY
Trial Balance
November 30, 19___</td></tr>
<tr><td>Cash</td><td align="right">$ 7,815.50</td><td></td></tr>
<tr><td>Notes receivable</td><td align="right">6,000.00</td><td></td></tr>
<tr><td>Accounts receivable</td><td align="right">3,820.00</td><td></td></tr>
</table>

Cash	$ 7,815.50	
Notes receivable	6,000.00	
Accounts receivable	3,820.00	
Unexpired insurance	720.00	
Land	10,000.00	
Building	35,000.00	
Office equipment	1,225.00	
Notes payable		$34,000.00
Accounts payable		6,575.00
R. B. Jones, capital		25,000.00
Gain on sale of land		2,000.00
Sales		7,020.00
Sales returns and allowances	50.00	
Sales discounts	46.50	
Purchases	8,800.00	
Purchase returns and allowances		300.00
Purchase discounts		32.00
Sales salaries expense	600.00	
Store rent expense	800.00	
Advertising expense	50.00	
	$74,927.00	$74,927.00

SUBSIDIARY
LEDGERS IN
BALANCE
WITH
CONTROL
ACCOUNTS

Schedule of Accounts Receivable
November 30, 19___

Robert Cross	$1,000
H. R. Davis	620
John Frost	350
D. H. Gray	1,850
Total (per balance of controlling account)	$3,820

Variations in special journals

The number of columns to be included in each special journal and the number of special journals to be used will depend upon the nature of the particular business and especially upon the volume of the various kinds of transactions. For example, the desirability of including a Sales Discount column in the cash receipts journal depends upon whether a business offers discounts to its customers for prompt payment and whether the customers frequently take advantage of such discounts.

A retail store may find that customers frequently return merchandise for credit. To record efficiently this large volume of sales returns, the store may establish a sales returns and allowances journal. A purchases returns and allowances journal may also be desirable if returns of goods to suppliers occur frequently.

Special journals should be regarded as laborsaving devices which may be designed with any number of columns appropriate to the needs of the particular business. A business will usually benefit by establishing a special journal for any type of transaction that occurs quite frequently.

Direct posting from invoices

In many business concerns the efficiency of data processing is increased by posting sales invoices directly to the customers' accounts in the accounts receivable ledger rather than copying sales invoices into a sales journal and then posting to accounts in the subsidiary ledger. If the sales invoices are serially numbered, a file or binder of duplicate sales invoices arranged in numerical order may take the place of a formal sales journal. By accounting for each serial number, it is possible to be certain that all sales invoices are included. At the end of the month, the invoices are totaled on an adding machine, and a general journal entry is made debiting the Accounts Receivable controlling account and crediting Sales for the total of the month's sales invoices.

Direct posting may also be used in recording purchase invoices. As soon as purchase invoices have been verified and approved, credits to the creditors' accounts in the accounts payable ledger may be posted directly from the purchase invoices.

The trend toward direct posting from invoices to subsidiary ledgers is

---

Schedule of Accounts Payable
November 30, 19___

Alabama Supply Co.	$3,325
Canning & Sons	500
Excelsior, Inc.	1,525
XYZ Equipment Co.	1,225
Total (per balance of controlling account)	$6,575

mentioned here as further evidence that accounting records and procedures can be designed in a variety of ways to meet the individual needs
of different business concerns.

QUESTIONS

1. What advantages are offered by the use of special journals?

2. Flow Line Company uses a cash receipts journal, a cash payments journal, a
sales journal, a purchases journal, and a general journal. Indicate which journal
should be used to record each of the following transactions:

   a. Purchase of merchandise on account
   b. Purchase of delivery truck for cash
   c. Return of merchandise by a customer for credit to his account
   d. Payment of taxes
   e. Adjusting entry to record depreciation
   f. Purchase of typewriter on account
   g. Sale of merchandise on account
   h. Sale of merchandise for cash
   i. Refund to a customer who returned merchandise sold him for cash
   j. Return of merchandise to a supplier for credit

3. When accounts receivable and accounts payable are kept in subsidiary ledgers,
will the general ledger continue to be a self-balancing ledger with equal debits
and credits? Explain.

4. Explain how, why, and when the cash receipts journal and cash payments
journal are cross footed.

5. Pine Hill General Store makes about 500 sales on account each month, using
only a two-column general journal to record these transactions. What would be
the extent of the work saved by using a sales journal?

6. During November the sales on credit made by the Hardy Company actually
amounted to $41,625, but an error of $1,000 was made in totaling the amount
column of the sales journal. When and how will the error be discovered?

PROBLEMS

Group A

8A-1. All transactions of the Marshall Company for the month of September are presented below. The company has been using the following accounts in recording
transactions:

Cash	10	*Buildings*	22
Marketable securities	12	*Accumulated depreciation:*	
Notes receivable	14	*buildings*	24
Accounts receivable	16	*Equipment*	26
Supplies	17	*Accumulated depreciation:*	
Unexpired insurance	18	*equipment*	28
Land	20	*Notes payable*	30

Accounts payable	32	Purchase returns and allowances	72
Accrued salaries payable	34	Purchase discounts	74
Accrued property taxes payable	36	Transportation-in	76
Mortgage payable	40	Salaries expense	80
H. R. Redd, capital	50	Property tax expense	82
H. R. Redd, drawing	52	Supplies expense	84
Sales	60	Insurance expense	86
Sales returns and allowances	62	Depreciation expense	88
Sales discounts	64	Gain on sale of investments	90
Purchases	70	Interest expense	92

Sept. 1.   H. R. Redd invested additional capital of $8,250.

Sept. 2.   Purchased merchandise on account from Clair Company, $6,426. Invoice was dated today with terms of 2/10, n/30.

Sept. 3.   Sold merchandise to Fife Company, $4,175. Invoice No. 428; terms 2/10, n/30.

Sept. 5.   Purchased supplies for cash, $184.

Sept. 5.   Sold merchandise for cash, $680.

Sept. 7.   Paid the Clair Company invoice dated September 2.

Sept. 8.   Purchased marketable securities, $1,200.

Sept. 10.   Collected from Fife Company for invoice No. 428.

Sept. 10.   Purchased merchandise from Axle Company, $5,500. Invoice dated today with terms of 1/10, n/30.

Sept. 12.   Sold merchandise to Martin Company, $3,250. Invoice No. 429; terms 2/10, n/30.

Sept. 14.   Paid for one-year fire insurance policy, $246.

Sept. 14.   Paid freight charges of $360 on goods purchased September 10 from Axle Company.

Sept. 14.   Sold equipment for $800, receiving cash of $200 and a 30-day, 5% note receivable for the balance. (In journalizing this transaction, ignore any accumulated depreciation.)

Sept. 15.   Issued credit memorandum No. 38 in favor of Martin Company upon return of $150 of merchandise.

Sept. 15.   Employees were paid today for services during the first half of September, $1,765.

Sept. 18.   Purchased merchandise for cash, $748.

Sept. 20.   Sold merchandise on account to Evans Brothers, $2,440, invoice No. 430. Required customer to sign a 30-day, non-interest-bearing note. (Record this sale by a charge to Accounts Receivable, then transfer from Accounts Receivable to Notes Receivable by means of an entry in the general journal.)

Sept. 20.   Paid the Axle Co. invoice dated September 10.

Sept. 22.   Sold merchandise for cash, $864.

Sept. 22.   Purchased merchandise for cash, $740.

Sept. 22.   Received payment from Martin Company for invoice No. 429.

Sept. 25.   Purchased merchandise from Davis Company, $4,100. Invoice dated September 24 with terms of 2/10, n/60.

Sept. 26.   Issued debit memorandum No. 42 to Davis Company in connection with merchandise returned today amounting to $300.

Sept. 27.   Sold at a price of $1,450 the marketable securities purchased September 8.

Sept. 28.   Sold merchandise on account to Martin Company, $2,750. Invoice No. 431; terms 2/10, n/30.

Sept. 30.   Paid semimonthly salaries of $1,810 for services rendered by employees during last half of September.

Sept. 30.   Recorded accrued property taxes of $920.

Sept. 30.   Paid monthly installment on mortgage $600, $204 being interest.

Sept. 30.   Purchased equipment, paying $2,000 down and signing mortgage note for the balance of $8,000.

Instructions

a. Record the September transactions in the following journals:

General journal—2 column

Sales journal—1 column

Purchases journal—1 column

Cash receipts journal—6 column

Cash payments journal—6 column

b. Foot and rule all special journals.

c. Show how posting would be made by placing ledger account numbers and check marks in the appropriate columns of the journals.

8A-2. The cash activities of Holden Company for the month of February are presented below. The company sells and also rents heavy-duty machinery to its customers.

Feb. 1.   Received cash of $450 for machinery rented to Smith Construction Co. for month of February.

Feb. 2.   Sold merchandise to Grant Brothers for cash, $1,275.

Feb. 4.   Received check for $900 from West Company in payment of a January invoice.

Feb. 6.   Received $825 in payment of non-interest-bearing note.

Feb. 7.   Paid for repairs of $312 on company-owned automobiles.

Feb. 7.   Purchased supplies for cash, $68.

Feb. 8.   Purchased merchandise for cash, $982.

Feb. 9.   Received check from Langley Company in payment of invoice, $1,400, less 2% cash discount.

Feb. 10.   Cash sales today, $1,328.

Feb. 12.   Paid bank $1,515 in settlement of a note payable for $1,500 and interest of $15.

Feb. 14.   Paid for accumulated gas and oil purchases for company cars, $126.

Feb. 14.   Purchased office furniture at cost of $12,000, paying $4,000 cash and signing a 90-day non-interest-bearing note for balance.

Feb. 15.   Received cash from Cross & Sons, $620, as rent for machinery during remainder of February.

Feb. 15.   Paid semimonthly salaries amounting to $1,640.

Feb. 17.   Purchased merchandise for cash, $4,700.

Feb. 18.   Paid advertising for month, $518.

Feb. 20.   Received check from Baker Corporation in settlement of invoice, $1,600, less 2% cash discount.

Feb. 22.   Cash sales today, $2,120.

Feb. 22.   Paid Acker Co. invoice, $3,200, less 2% cash discount.

Feb. 24.   Paid installment on mortgage, $852, including $208 interest.

Feb. 26. Sold land, with cost of $3,000, for $3,800 cash and a 6%, two-year note receivable for $4,000.

Feb. 28. Paid utilities, $216.

Feb. 28. Paid semimonthly salaries, $1,764.

Feb. 28. Paid Royal Co. invoice, $2,200, less 2% cash discount.

Instructions

a. Record the above transactions in six-column cash receipts and cash payments journals.

b. Foot and rule the journals.

8A-3. The September 30 trial balance of Barber Company is presented below, accompanied by schedules of accounts receivable and accounts payable. Details and totals of the several journals for the month of October are also shown.

BARBER COMPANY
Trial Balance
September 30, 19___

Cash	$ 11,426	
Notes receivable	6,000	
Accounts receivable	5,718	
Marketable securities	11,500	
Inventory	17,395	
Prepaid expenses	982	
Equipment	24,600	
Accumulated depreciation: equipment		$ 5,160
Notes payable		10,000
Accounts payable		4,187
Accrued salaries payable		1,242
C. K. Barber, capital		42,317
C. K. Barber, drawing	2,080	
Sales		104,800
Sales returns and allowances	2,760	
Sales discounts	1,430	
Purchases	56,920	
Purchase returns and allowances		5,910
Purchase discounts		629
Transportation-in	6,440	
Rent expense	3,600	
Salaries expense	23,394	
	$174,245	$174,245

Schedule of Accounts Receivable

Jay Brown	$1,348.00
A. K. Mell	2,888.00
R. L. Scott	1,482.00
	$5,718.00

Schedule of Accounts Payable

Dowling Supply Co. $4,187.00

Sales Journal (page 9)

Column total $11,642.00

Details:

Oct.	3.	C. L. Steele	$1,835.00
	7.	A. K. Mell	2,751.00
	13.	Jay Brown	1,674.00
	19.	M. C. Frank	1,582.00
	24.	R. L. Scott	2,176.00
	29.	A. D. King	1,624.00

Purchases Journal (page 6)

Column total .... $ 6,642.00

Details:

Oct.	5.	Avil Wholesale Co.	$2,981.00
	13.	Dowling Supply Co.	1,764.00
	20.	Richland Company	1,102.00
	26.	Argon Trading Co.	795.00

General Journal (page 10)

Details:

Accounts Payable debits:

Oct.	6.	Dowling Supply Co.	$4,187.00
	23.	Richland Company	210.00

Other debits:

Oct.	10.	Sales Returns and Allowances	$ 196.00
	12.	Notes Receivable	1,482.00

Accounts Receivable credits:

Oct.	10.	A. K. Mell	$ 196.00
	12.	R. L. Scott	1,482.00

Other credits:

Oct.	6.	Notes Payable	$4,187.00
	23.	Purchase Returns and Allowances	210.00

Cash Receipts Journal (page 7)

Column totals:

Cash	$15,785.00
Sales Discounts	206.00
Other Accounts (debit)	400.00
Accounts Receivable	10,300.00
Sales	1,041.00
Other Accounts (credit)	5,050.00

Details:
Other Accounts (debit):

Oct. 15.	Notes Receivable	$ 400.00

Accounts Receivable:

Oct. 2.	Jay Brown	$1,348.00
5.	A. K. Mell	2,888.00
13.	C. L. Steele	1,835.00
17.	A. K. Mell	2,555.00
23.	Jay Brown	1,674.00

Other Accounts (credit):

Oct. 26.	Notes Receivable	$5,000.00
26.	Interest Earned	50.00

Cash Payments Journal (page 6)

Column totals:

Cash	$ 9,849.10
Purchase Discounts	94.90
Other Accounts (credit)	2,000.00
Accounts Payable	4,745.00
Purchases	984.00
Other Accounts (debit)	6,215.00

Details:
Other Accounts (credit):

Oct. 23.	Notes Payable	$2,000.00

Accounts Payable:

Oct. 15.	Avil Wholesale Co.	$2,981.00
23.	Dowling Supply Co.	1,764.00

Other Accounts (debit):

Oct. 2.	Rent Expense	$ 400.00
6.	Equipment	2,800.00
26.	Notes Payable	3,000.00
26.	Interest Expense	15.00

Instructions

a. Open the necessary general ledger accounts and subsidiary ledger accounts by listing the balances given as of September 30. Post to the ledger accounts the information in the journals for October transactions.

b. Prepare a trial balance and schedules of receivables and payables as of October 31.

8A-4. The two cash journals and a general journal used by Layton Company are shown on pages 254 to 256. To keep the problem fairly short, the cash journals contain only a portion of the cash transactions for the month of July; consequently, the column totals of the cash journals (which are to be posted to ledger accounts) are larger amounts than are indicated by the individual items listed in these columns.

Cash Payments Journal   (Page

Date		Explanation	Cash	Purchase discounts	Credits		
					Other accounts		
					Name	LP	Amoᵘ
19__ July	1	Paid month's rent	450.00				
	5	Invoice of June 25, less 2%	1,274.00	26.00			
	9	Purchase of equipment	200.00		Notes Payable		800
	12	Paid note and interest	3,030.00				
	18	Cash purchases	620.00				
			12,932.00	63.00			1,64(

Cash Receipts Journal   (Page

Date		Explanation	Cash	Sales discounts	Debits		
					Other accounts		
					Name	LP	Amᵉ
19__ July	2	Cash sales	546.00				
	5	Invoice No. 620, less 2%	1,144.64	23.36			
	8	Received cash dividend	210.00				
	9	Sold furniture	180.00		Loss on Sale of Furniture		ᵉ
	12	Collected note & interest	1,428.00				
			10,821.00	75.00			3ᵣ

	Debits				
Account debited	Accounts payable		Purchases	Other accounts	
	√	Amount		LP	Amount
Rent Expense					450.00
Riley Company		1,300.00			
Equipment					1,000.00
Notes Payable					3,000.00
Interest Expense					30.00
			620.00		
		5,917.00	2,116.00		6,602.00

	Credits				
Account credited	Accounts receivable		Sales	Other accounts	
	√	Amount		LP	Amount
			546.00		
A. B. Cool		1,168.00			
Dividends Earned					210.00
Furniture & Fixtures					200.00
Notes Receivable					1,400.00
Interest Earned					28.00
		7,120.00	2,090.00		2,002.00

		Journal		(page 7)
19__				
July	3	Sales Returns and Allowances	232	
		Accounts Receivable, A. B. Cool		232
		Issued credit memo No. 23 for return of merchandise.		
	10	Notes Receivable	325	
		Accounts Receivable, R. L. Moss		325
		Received 30-day non-interest-bearing note in settlement of an invoice due today.		
	16	Accounts Payable, Hammond Company	140	
		Purchase Returns and Allowances		140
		Issued debit memo No. 38 for return of goods to Hammond Company.		
	27	Accounts Payable, A. Winters Co.	375	
		Notes Payable		375
		Issued 60-day note in settlement of purchase invoice due today.		

Other data. The schedules of accounts receivable and accounts payable along with certain other account balances as of June 30 are as follows:

Accounts Receivable

A. B. Cool	$1,400
R. L. Moss	825
G. H. Pike	186
Total	$2,411

Accounts Payable

Hammond Company	$ 340
Riley Company	1,300
A. Winters Company	800
Total	$2,440

Selected General Ledger Accounts

Cash	$6,472
Notes Receivable	3,650
Equipment	7,128
Furniture and Fixtures	2,632
Allowance for Doubtful Accounts	326
Notes Payable	4,500

Instructions

a. Open general ledger and subsidiary ledger accounts by entering the balances given as of June 30. Include control accounts for accounts receivable and accounts payable.

b. Make the postings of both individual items and column totals from the illustrated journals. Cross-reference the journal entries and the postings to ledger accounts.

Group B

8B-1. The Victor Company began operations on October 1 using the chart of accounts shown.

Chart of Accounts

Cash	10	Sales	50
Marketable securities	13	Sales returns and allowances	52
Notes receivable	14	Sales discounts	54
Accounts receivable	15	Purchases	60
Merchandise inventory	17	Purchase returns and allowances	62
Prepaid rent	18	Purchase discounts	64
Unexpired insurance	19	Transportation-in	66
Land	20	Rent expense	70
Building	21	Salaries expense	72
Furniture and fixtures	23	Taxes expense	74
Notes payable	30	Supplies expense	76
Accounts payable	32	Insurance expense	78
Mortgage payable	36	Interest earned	80
H. B. Victor, capital	40	Interest expense	83
H. B. Victor, drawing	42	Loss on sale of securities	84

The transactions for the month of October are listed below.

Oct. 1. Victor deposited $20,000 in the bank under the name of the Victor Company.

Oct. 3. Paid rent for the three months ending December 31, $900.

Oct. 3. Purchased furniture for cash, $1,100.

Oct. 4. Purchased land and building on contract, paying $5,000 cash and signing a mortgage for the balance of $15,000. Estimated value of the land was $6,000.

Oct. 6. Purchased merchandise from Brill Company, $4,300. Invoice dated today; terms 2/10, n/30.

Oct. 7. Sold merchandise to J. V. Thomas, $3,100. Invoice No. 1; terms 2/10, n/60.

Oct. 7. Paid $240 for a two-year fire insurance policy.

Oct. 7. Sold merchandise for cash, $622.

Oct. 10. Paid freight charges of $205 on Brill Company purchase.

Oct. 12. Sold merchandise to Everett Company, $4,600. Invoice No. 2; terms 2/10, n/60.

Oct. 12.   Purchased merchandise for cash, $682.

Oct. 14.   Received payment in full from J. V. Thomas. Invoice No. 1, less 2% discount.

Oct. 15.   Purchased securities, $920.

Oct. 16.   Paid Brill Company invoice of October 6, less discount.

Oct. 16.   Issued credit memorandum No. 1 to Everett Company, $300, for goods returned today.

Oct. 18.   Purchased merchandise from Wyatt Corporation, $3,800. Invoice dated today; terms 2/10, n/30.

Oct. 20.   A portion of merchandise purchased from Wyatt Corporation was found to be substandard. After discussion with the vendor, a price reduction of $100 was agreed upon and debit memorandum No. 1 was issued in that amount.

Oct. 22.   Sold merchandise to E. A. Bridges, $2,800, invoice No. 3.

Oct. 22.   Received payment in full from Everett Company; invoice No. 2, less returns and discount.

Oct. 23.   Received 30-day non-interest-bearing note from E. A. Bridges in settlement of invoice No. 3.

Oct. 25.   Sold for $850 the securities purchased on October 15.

Oct. 26:   Sold merchandise for cash, $460.

Oct. 28.   Borrowed $3,000 from bank, issuing a 60-day, 5% note payable as evidence of indebtedness.

Oct. 28.   Paid Wyatt Corporation invoice dated October 18, less discount.

Oct. 30.   Paid first installment on mortgage, $500. This payment included interest of $90.

Oct. 30.   Purchased merchandise from Brill Company, $2,900. Invoice dated today; terms 2/10, n/60.

Oct. 31.   Paid monthly salaries of $1,622.

Oct. 31.   Purchased merchandise for cash, $725.

Oct. 31.   Sold merchandise to B. Frank, $2,600. Invoice No. 4; terms 2/10, n/60.

Instructions

a. Journalize the October transactions in the following journals:
   Two-column general journal
   One-column sales journal
   One-column purchases journal
   Six-column cash receipts journal
   Six-column cash payments journal

b. Indicate how postings would be made by placing ledger account numbers in the journals.

8B-2. All cash transactions of Fields and Company for the month of November are outlined below. The company uses multiple-column cash receipts and cash payments journals similar to those illustrated in Chapter 8.

Nov. 1.   The owner, P. K. Fields, invested additional cash of $6,000 in the business.

Nov. 1.   Purchased United States government bonds, $1,000.

Nov. 2.   Paid November rent, $450.

Nov. 2.   Cash sales of merchandise, $1,162.

Nov. 4.   Purchased fixtures, $1,600, making a down payment of $200 and issuing a mortgage payable for the balance.

Nov. 6.   Cash purchase of merchandise, $1,520.

Nov. 6.   Paid salesmen's commissions of $342.

Nov. 7.   Paid Wilson Company invoice, $800, less 2%.

Nov. 9.   Received $300 as partial payment of Kay Co. invoice of $900 and 60-day 5% note for the balance.

Nov. 10.   Paid gas and oil bill, $78, for automobile belonging to Mrs. P. K. Fields. (Car is not used in the business.)

Nov. 10.   Cash sales of merchandise, $956.

Nov. 12.   Received interest on investments, $54.

Nov. 12.   Paid Archer Co. invoice, $1,250, less 2%.

Nov. 13.   Sold land costing $1,500 for $1,825.

Nov. 13.   Paid garage rent on company truck, $62.

Nov. 15.   Paid semimonthly salaries, $582.

Nov. 15.   Received $588 in full settlement of Waters Company invoice after allowing 2% discount.

Nov. 17.   Cash sales of merchandise, $742.

Nov. 19.   Cash purchase of merchandise, $1,060.

Nov. 19.   Purchased store supplies, $84 (expense).

Nov. 20.   Paid note due today, $1,200 and accrued interest amounting to $24.

Nov. 21.   Sold U.S. government bonds costing $500 for $483.

Nov. 23.   Paid mortgage installment due today, $200, of which $93 represented interest expense.

Nov. 25.   Cash sales of merchandise, $1,264.

Nov. 25.   Paid Strong Company invoice, $1,600 less 2%.

Nov. 26.   Paid salesmen's commissions of $478.

Nov. 26.   Purchased three-year fire insurance policy, $186.

Nov. 28.   Cash purchase of merchandise, $944.

Nov. 28.   Paid freight charges on Grey Company invoice, $94.

Nov. 30.   Received payment in full settlement of Smith Company invoice, $1,200, less 2%.

Nov. 30.   Paid semimonthly salaries, $624.

Nov. 30.   Paid $92 for gasoline used by company truck during the month.

Nov. 30.   Received quarterly dividend of $120 on investment in Ratcliff Company stock.

Instructions

a. Journalize the above transactions in cash receipts and cash payments journals.

b. Foot and rule the journals.

8B-3. The Allen Company's trial balance and schedules of accounts receivable and accounts payable as of February 28 are presented below, followed by the details and totals of the various journals for March.

ALLEN COMPANY
Trial Balance
February 28, 19___

Cash	$11,560.20	
Marketable securities	9,000.00	
Notes receivable	3,500.00	
Accounts receivable	4,630.00	
Merchandise inventory	9,584.00	
Store supplies	716.00	
Unexpired insurance	1,046.00	
Store equipment	18,800.00	
Accumulated depreciation: store equipment		$ 3,460.00
Notes payable		5,000.00
Accounts payable		3,840.00
Commissions payable		1,630.00
J. K. Allen, capital		24,259.20
J. K. Allen, drawing	1,200.00	
Sales		44,000.00
Sales returns and allowances	1,820.00	
Sales discounts	856.00	
Purchases	19,860.00	
Purchase returns and allowances		4,310.00
Purchase discounts		624.00
Rent expense	1,350.00	
Salaries expense	2,680.00	
Interest earned		63.00
Interest expense	584.00	
	$87,186.20	$87,186.20

Schedule of Accounts Receivable

R. L. Hirschi	$2,090.00
J. E. Moss	900.00
L. K. Pett	1,640.00
	$4,630.00

Schedule of Accounts Payable

A. L. Boone Company	$1,600.00
Stevens Corporation	2,240.00
	$3,840.00

Sales Journal (page 6)

Column total $18,000.00

Details:

Mar.	1.	M. O. Arden	$2,926.00
	9.	L. K. Pett	1,800.00
	16.	V. C. Drake	2,200.00
	21.	R. L. Hirschi	3,600.00
	24.	J. E. Moss	1,952.00
	28.	M. E. Terry	2,732.00
	30.	V. C. Drake	2,790.00

Purchases Journal (page 4)

Column total $12,560.00

Details:

Mar.	5.	Reynolds Corporation	$4,800.00
	19.	A. L. Boone Company	3,000.00
	25.	Stevens Corporation	4,760.00

General Journal (page 8)

Details:

Accounts Payable debits:

Mar.	10.	A. L. Boone Company	$1,600.00
	26.	Stevens Corporation	740.00

Other debits:

Mar.	4.	Sales Returns and Allowances	$ 140.00
	7.	Notes Receivable	2,090.00

Other credits:

Mar.	10.	Notes Payable	$1,600.00
	26.	Purchase Returns and Allowances	740.00

Accounts Receivable credits:

Mar.	4.	L. K. Pett	$ 140.00
	7.	R. L. Hirschi	2,090.00

Cash Receipts Journal (page 5)

Column totals:

Cash	$20,456.00
Sales Discounts	200.00
Other Accounts (debit)	2,480.00
Accounts Receivable	12,926.00
Sales	4,180.00
Other Accounts (credit)	6,030.00

Details:
Other Accounts (debit):

Mar.	4.	Notes Receivable	$2,000.00
	12.	Loss on Sale of Store Equipment	480.00

Accounts Receivable:

Mar.	4.	M. O. Arden	$2,926.00
	6.	L. K. Pett	1,500.00
	10.	J. E. Moss	900.00
	19.	L. K. Pett	1,800.00
	26.	V. C. Drake	2,200.00
	30.	R. L. Hirschi	3,600.00

Other Accounts (credit):

Mar.	12.	Store Equipment	$4,000.00
	17.	Notes Receivable	2,000.00
	17.	Interest Earned	30.00

Cash Payments Journal (page 7)

Column totals:

Cash	$18,133.20
Purchase Discounts	200.80
Other Accounts (credit)	4,000.00
Accounts Payable	10,040.00
Purchases	3,470.00
Other Accounts (debit)	8,824.00

Details:
Other Accounts (credit):

Mar.	10.	Notes Payable	$4,000.00

Accounts Payable:

Mar.	3.	Stevens Corporation	$2,240.00
	15.	Reynolds Corporation	4,800.00
	29.	A. L. Boone Company	3,000.00

Other Accounts (debit):

Mar.	2.	Rent	$ 500.00
	10.	Store Equipment	4,600.00
	14.	Notes Payable	3,000.00
	14.	Interest Expense	54.00
	26.	Store Supplies	260.00
	30.	Unexpired Insurance	410.00

Instructions

a. Open general ledger and subsidiary ledger accounts by entering the balances given as of February 28.

b. Post to the ledger accounts the information given in the various journals for the month of March.

c. Prepare a trial balance and schedules of receivables and payables as of March 31.

8B-4. Selected portions of the cash journals and of the general journal of the Carter Corporation for the month of June are given below and on the next two pages. (The totals of the cash journals are larger than the individual items listed, as numerous transactions were omitted to avoid undue length in the problem.)

General Journal

19__					
June	8	Sales Returns and Allowances		125	
		Accounts Receivable, H. C. Brown			125
		Issued credit memorandum No. 10 for goods returned.			
	12	Notes Receivable		350	
		Accounts Receivable, O. L. Blain			350
		Received note in settlement of open account.			
	16	Accounts Payable, Eager Corp.		210	
		Purchase Returns and Allowances			210
		Issued debit memorandum No. 5 for goods returned for credit.			

Other data. A small portion of the accounts receivable from customers and accounts payable to creditors on May 31 is shown in the list below.

	Accounts receivable	Accounts payable
Customers:		
O. L. Blain	$1,350	
H. C. Brown	125	
R. K. Doan	4,000	
A. L. Hill	1,600	
Creditors:		
Beakins, Inc.		$4,400
Eager Corp.		210
C. D. Pace		(32)
Salter Company		5,000

Instructions

a. Set up subsidiary ledger accounts for the customers and creditors listed. Also open general ledger accounts as needed in posting the June transactions.

b. Do the posting from the journals; also, indicate proper posting references in journals and ledger accounts.

Cash Receipts Journal (Page 8)

Date		Explanation	Debits				
			Cash	Sales discount	Other accounts		
					Name	LP	Amount
19__ June	2	Inv. No. 431, less 2%	1,568	32			
	3	Cash sales	184				
	4	Refund from vendor	32				
	8	Inv. No. 433, less 2%	1,960	40			
	15	Cash sales	240				
	22	Sold equipment	200		Notes Receivable		800
			9,320	124			2,460

Cash Payments Journal (Page 9)

Date		Explanation	Credits				
			Cash	Purchase discounts	Other accounts		
					Name	LP	Amount
19__							
June	2	Rent for June	500				
	3	Inv. of May 24, less 2%	3,960	40			
	6	Cash purchases	390				
	9	Purchase of land	1,000		Mortgage Payable		9,000
	9	Inv. of May 31, less 1%	2,376	24			
			12,606	98			9,640

| Account credited | Credits | | | | |
| | Accounts receivable | | Sales | Other accounts | |
	√	Amount		LP	Amount
A. L. Hill		1,600			
			184		
Accounts Payable (C. D. Pace)					32
R. K. Doan		2,000			
			240		
Office Equipment					1,000
		7,260	790		3,854

| Account debited | Debits | | | | |
| | Accounts payable | | Purchases | Other accounts | |
	√	Amount		LP	Amount
Rent Expense					500
Salter Company		4,000			
			390		
Land					10,000
Beakins, Inc.		2,400			
		8,954	910		12,480

9

The control
of cash transactions

In the terminology of the accountant, the word "cash" is used in a broad sense to include coin, paper money, checks, money orders, and money on deposit with banks. However, cash does not include postage stamps, IOU's, or postdated checks, although these items are sometimes mingled with the cash funds held by a cashier.

In deciding whether a particular item comes within the classification of cash, the following rule is a useful one: any medium of exchange which a bank will accept for deposit and immediate credit to the depositor's account is included in cash. As an example, personal checks and money orders are accepted by banks for deposit and are considered as cash. Postage stamps and postdated checks are not acceptable for deposit at a bank and are not included in the accountant's definition of cash.

Balance sheet presentation

A business concern that carries checking accounts with several banks will maintain a separate ledger account for each bank account. On the balance sheet, however, the entire amount of cash on hand and cash on deposit with the several banks will be shown as a single amount. The balance sheet caption in most common use is the single word "Cash," but occasionally such titles as Cash in Bank and on Hand, or Demand Deposits in Banks and Cash on Hand are used.

The banker, credit manager, or investor who studies a balance sheet critically will always be interested in the total amount of cash as compared with other balance sheet items, such as accounts payable. These outside users of a company's financial statements are not interested, however, in such details as the number of separate bank accounts, or in the distinction between cash on hand and cash in banks. In deciding upon the amount of detailed information to be included in the balance sheet or income statement, the criterion may well be: "Will this information increase the usefulness of the financial statement?" Since short, concise financial statements are more easily read and understood than long, detailed schedules, there is good reason to avoid the inclusion of unimportant details.

Cash is a current asset. In fact, cash is the most current and most liquid of all assets. In judging whether other types of assets qualify for inclusion in the current asset section of the balance sheet, consideration is given to the length of time required for the asset to be converted into cash. Briefly stated, cash represents the ultimate degree of liquidity in assets.

Some bank accounts are restricted as to their use, so that they are not available for disbursement to meet normal operating needs of the business. An example (discussed in Chapter 21) is a bond sinking fund, consisting of cash being accumulated by a corporation for the specific purpose of paying off bonded indebtedness at a future date and not available for any other disbursement. A bank account located in a foreign country may also be restricted if monetary regulations prevent the transfer of funds between the two countries.

Any bank account which is not readily available for normal operating disbursements should be shown as a separate item and adequately described on the balance sheet. Generally, such restricted bank deposits are not regarded as current assets.

Internal control over cash

Cash is more susceptible to theft than any other asset. Furthermore, a large portion of the total transactions of a business involve the receipt or disbursement of cash. For both these reasons, internal control over cash is of great importance to the owners and also to the employees of a business.

The owner of a business is naturally interested in establishing internal controls that will prevent the theft of cash, but employees also have a direct, personal interest in internal control over cash. If a cash shortage arises in a business in which internal controls are weak or nonexistent, every employee is under suspicion. Perhaps no one employee can be proved guilty of the theft, but neither can any employee prove his innocence.

On the other hand, if internal controls over cash are adequate, theft without detection is virtually impossible except through the collusion of two or more employees. Moreover, the honest employee can always prove exactly what amounts of cash he has handled. Good internal control over cash transactions is, therefore, important not only in avoiding monetary losses but also in maintaining good employee relations.

How can adequate internal control over cash be achieved? One important step toward this goal is indicated by the following simple rule which is applicable to nearly every type of business. *Deposit each day's cash receipts, intact, in the bank, and make all disbursements by check.* The word "intact" in this statement means that no withdrawal or substitution of checks or currency shall be made; in other words, every cash item received shall be promptly deposited.

When each day's cash receipts are deposited intact and all payments are made by check, the bank's record of deposits made and checks issued by the company should match exactly the company's own record of cash received and paid. A double record of cash transactions is, therefore, available: one record maintained by the business firm, and the other record kept by the bank. At the end of each month a comparison should be made between the internal record of cash and the external (bank) record. This comparison of the two independently prepared records is most valuable in proving the accuracy of the cash balance.

Cash receipts. The general principles to be followed in establishing internal control over cash receipts are:

1. The function of receiving cash should be completely separated from that of disbursing cash. The same person should not handle cash receipts and also make cash disbursements.

2. A record of cash received should be made promptly at the time of receipt. For cash sales this means ringing up the sale on a cash register in the presence of the customer. For cash received through the mail, a list of cash receipts should be compiled when the mail is opened, by an employee other than the cashier or bookkeeper. Operating procedures should be designed to ensure that all cash received is recorded. Once a record has been made of the receipt, any misuse of cash is likely to be disclosed through normal control procedures.

3. The function of cash handling should be completely separated from the maintenance of accounting records. The cashier should not maintain the accounting records and should not have access to the records. The bookkeeper should not have access to the cash receipts.

4. Each day's cash receipts should be deposited, intact, in the bank.

Use of cash registers. Cash received over the counter at the time of a sale should be rung up on a cash register, so located that the customer will see the amount recorded. If store operations can be so arranged that two employees must participate in each sales transaction, stronger internal control will be achieved than when one employee is permitted to handle a transaction in its entirety. In some stores this objective is accomplished by employing a central cashier who rings on a cash register the sales made by all clerks.

At the end of the day, the store manager or other supervisor should remove the cash register tape showing the total sales for the day, compare the total recorded sales with the cash turned in by the cashier, and transmit this total to the bookkeeper, who will make an entry in the cash receipts journal. The cash receipts for the day should be deposited in the bank by an employee other than the bookkeeper.

Use of prenumbered sales tickets. Internal control may be further strengthened by writing out a prenumbered sales ticket in duplicate at the time of each sale. The original is given to the customer and the carbon copy retained. At the end of the day an employee computes a total sales figure from these duplicate tickets, and also makes sure that no tickets are missing from the series. The total amount of sales as computed from the duplicate sales tickets is then compared with the total sales recorded on the cash register.

If collections of accounts receivable are received in cash over the counter, a separate series of prenumbered tickets should be used. These tickets should be prepared in three or more copies. The original is given to the customer as a receipt; a duplicate is sent to the accounting department for posting to the customer's account in the subsidiary ledger for accounts receivable; and a third copy is used in summarizing and recording the day's cash collections of accounts receivable.

Cash received through the mail. The procedures for handling checks and currency received through the mail are also based on the internal control principle that two or more employees should participate in every transaction.

The employee who opens the mail should prepare a list of the amounts received. In order that this list shall represent the total receipts of the day, the totals recorded on the cash registers may be included in the list. One copy of the list is forwarded with the cash to the cashier, who will deposit the funds in the bank. Another copy of the list is sent with the customers' remittance letters to the bookkeeper, who will record the cash collections.

The total cash receipts recorded each day by the bookkeeper should agree with the amount of the cashier's deposit, and also with the list prepared by the employee assigned to open the mail and to read the cash registers. When these procedures are followed consistently, any irregularities in the handling of cash receipts should be quickly disclosed.

Cash over and short. In handling over-the-counter cash receipts, errors in change making will inevitably occur. These errors will cause a cash shortage or overage at the end of the day, when the cash is counted and compared with the reading on the cash register.

For example, assume that the total cash sales for the day as recorded by the cash register amount to $500, but that the cash in the drawer when counted amounts to only $499. The following entry would be made to record the day's sales and the cash shortage of $1.

ENTRY FOR CASH SHORTAGE

Cash	499	
Cash Over and Short	1	
Sales		500

The preceding entry illustrates a cash shortage. To illustrate a cash overage, assume that the cash register reading shows sales for the day of $650, but that the cash, when counted, amounts to $652. The entry for the day's cash transactions would be as follows:

Cash 652		
Sales		*650*
Cash Over and Short		*2*

Notice that the Cash Over and Short account is debited with shortages and credited with overages. If the cash shortages during an entire accounting period are in excess of the cash overages, the Cash Over and Short account will have a debit balance and will be shown as a miscellaneous expense in the income statement. On the other hand, if the overages exceed the shortages, the Cash Over and Short account will show a credit balance at the end of the period and should be treated as an item of miscellaneous revenue.

Cash disbursements. The basic principles to be followed in establishing internal control over cash disbursements are:

1. All disbursements should be made by check. Since an adequate system of internal control over cash receipts requires that each day's cash receipts be deposited intact in the bank, payments cannot be made out of cash receipts. Making payments by check provides a permanent record of the transaction, and requires joint action of two or more employees. The danger of fraudulent payments is thereby reduced.

2. Checks should be prenumbered. Any spoiled checks should be marked "Void" and filed in proper numerical sequence so that all checks in the series can be accounted for. This procedure guards against the possibility of a check being issued without any record of its issuance being made.

3. Checks should be signed only when supported by approved invoices or vouchers. The procedure for verification of invoices was described in Chapter 6. When a check is presented to an official for signature, it should be accompanied by the approved invoice and voucher showing that the transaction has been fully verified and deserves to be paid. The official who signs checks should not be the same one who approves invoices for payment.

4. Checks should be signed by one person and countersigned by another. This procedure illustrates again the principle of subdividing the work so that fraud is impossible without the collusion of two or more persons.

5. When a check is signed, the supporting invoices and vouchers should be perforated or stamped "Paid" to eliminate any possibility of their later being presented in support of another check.

BANK CHECKING ACCOUNTS

Opening a bank account

The use of checks for making nearly all payments of consequence is an accepted business practice. Consequently, every business concern maintains one or more bank accounts. When a bank account is first opened, the depositor must sign his name on a signature card, exactly as he will sign checks. The signature card is kept on file by the bank, so that any check bearing a signature not familiar to bank employees may be compared with the depositor's signature card.

Making deposits

A deposit ticket supplied by the bank is filled out by the depositor for each deposit. The deposit ticket illustrated on page 272 contains separate spaces for listing each check deposited, and also space for listing the amounts of coin and currency. Each check deposited is identified on the deposit ticket by the printed code number of the bank on which it is drawn.

Banks give the depositor a duplicate deposit ticket, or similar written evidence of each deposit, which is helpful in proving that all cash receipts have been deposited. If each day's cash receipts are deposited intact, there will be a duplicate deposit ticket corresponding exactly to each day's cash receipts as recorded in the cash receipts journal. Since the duplicate deposit ticket shows separately each check deposited, it is possible to compare the items listed in the cash receipts journal with the items deposited in the bank. The currency and coin received each day will also appear as separate items on the duplicate deposit ticket. If a dishonest employee should attempt to substitute worthless checks for cash receipts, his fraudulent act could be discovered by comparison of the duplicate deposit ticket with the individual entries in the cash receipts journal.

Bank columns in cash journals. If all cash receipts are deposited daily, the cash debit column of the cash receipts journal becomes, in effect, a record of bank deposits. For companies which maintain two bank accounts, the cash receipts journal may be expanded to include a debit column for each bank. Similarly, the cash payments journal may be expanded by creating a separate cash credit column for each bank. A separate ledger account should be maintained for each bank account, rather than a single ledger account for Cash.

Writing checks

A check is a written order prepared by the depositor (drawer) directing the bank to pay a specific amount of money to the person designated, or to his order. Checks are available in bound books and in a variety of loose-leaf forms. A form commonly used by individuals and small business concerns is illustrated on page 273.

EACH CHECK
DEPOSITED
IS LISTED
SEPARATELY

Checking Account

Bank of America
Los Angeles, California

Deposit for credit of:

Bradbury Company

3100 Main Street, Davis, California

Date January 12, 1961

	Dollars	Cents
Currency	110	00
Coin		
Checks (list each check by bank number)		
1 16-368	325	00
2 16-302	700	00
3 16-316	65	00
4		
5		
6		
7		
8		
9		
10		
Total	1,200	00

When this form of check and attached stub is used, the record of each check issued is maintained on the stub. The bank balance may be computed on each stub by adding to the old balance any deposits made since the previous check was issued, and deducting the amount of the present check.

For a small fee the bank will provide prenumbered checks with the depositor's name and address printed on each check. If the checks and stubs are not prenumbered, it is advisable to enter consecutive numbers on all checks and stubs before the checkbook is used. In writing each check it is also advisable to fill out the stub before writing the check to ensure that the recording of the data on the stub will not be forgotten.

The bank statement

Each month the bank will provide the depositor with a statement of his account, accompanied by the checks paid and charged to the account during the month. The paid checks returned with the statement are sometimes called canceled checks: they have been marked "Paid" with a perforating stamp, and also bear the date of payment by the bank.

The bank statement, illustrated on page 274, is a duplicate copy of the ledger account which the bank maintains with the depositor, The Parkview Company. The statement shows the balance on deposit at the beginning of the month, the deposits made during the month, the checks paid and other charges, and the new balance at the end of the month.

The same transactions are, of course, recorded on the depositor's books and on the bank's books, but from opposite points of view. From the depositor's point of view, his bank account is an asset, which is increased by debits and decreased by credits. From the bank's point of view the account with the depositor is a liability, which is increased by credits and decreased by debits. A debit entry on the monthly statement obtained from the bank should, therefore, be regarded as the equivalent of a credit on the depositor's accounting records; a credit on the bank statement corresponds to a debit on the depositor's books.

CHECK AND
CHECK STUB

No. 901 $ 125.00		
June 1 19--		
To Western Supply Co.		
For Merchandise		
	DOLLARS	CENTS
Balance brought forward	3,987	50
Amount deposited	500	00
Total	4,487	50
Amount this check	125	00
Balance carried forward	4,362	50
NOTICE: Make no alteration or change on any check. If error is made, write new check.		

WESTWOOD VILLAGE BRANCH   No. 901

Bank of America
NATIONAL TRUST AND SAVINGS ASSOCIATION
16-318
1223

LOS ANGELES, CALIFORNIA____June 1____19--

PAY TO THE
ORDER OF:____Western Supply Co.____ $ 125.00

One hundred twenty-five and no/100 -------------------- DOLLARS

James W. Bennett

NSF checks. On the illustrated statement the symbol "NSF" appears opposite the check for $50.25, which was charged against the account on July 18. The letters NSF mean "not sufficient funds." This check was

Bank of America
Los Angeles

The Parkview Company
19101 Parkview Road
Los Angeles, California

Customer's Statement

Date	Checks			Deposits	Balance
19__					
June 30	Balance brought forward				5,029.30
July 1				300.00	5,329.30
2	100.00			250.00	5,479.30
3	415.20	10.00			5,054.10
4	25.00	90.00	36.50	185.10	5,087.70
7				60.00	5,147.70
10	96.00	400.00			4,651.70
12	500.00			147.20	4,298.90
15	425.00				3,873.90
18	50.25 NSF			200.00	4,023.65
21	85.00			101.19	4,039.84
24	150.27			83.25	3,972.82
28	95.75			500.00 CM	4,377.07
31	2.00 SC			625.10	5,000.17

Please examine at once. If no errors are reported within ten days the account will be considered correct.

The last amount in this column is your balance.

received by The Parkview Company from J. B. Ball on July 12 and was included in that day's deposit. When the bank learned that Ball did not have a sufficient amount on deposit to cover this check, it charged the check back against the account of The Parkview Company.

After being informed by the bank that Ball's check is not good, The Parkview Company will make a journal entry debiting an account receivable from J. B. Ball and crediting Cash. The NSF check is in the possession of The Parkview Company, but it is no longer regarded as cash. An effort will be made to collect directly from Ball the amount of this NSF check.

Bank service charges. Under the date of July 31 on the illustrated bank statement is a debit for $2 accompanied by the symbol SC. This symbol means "service charge," a charge made by the bank to cover the expense of handling the account. The amount of the service charge is based upon such considerations as the average balance of the account and the number of checks and deposits. Small accounts with a great deal of activity are unprofitable for the bank, and service charges are, therefore, set at relatively high amounts on such accounts.

Reconciling the bank account

The balance shown on the monthly statement received from the bank will usually not agree with the balance of cash shown by the depositor's books. The reason why these two related records do not agree is that certain transactions recorded by the depositor will not yet have been recorded by the bank. Also, some transactions recorded by the bank may not yet have been recorded by the depositor.

The term *reconciliation* means determining those items which make up the difference between the balance appearing on the bank statement and the balance of cash according to the depositor's records. By listing and studying these discrepancies, it is possible to determine the correct figure for cash to appear on the balance sheet.

Transactions which may appear on the depositor's books but which have not yet been recorded by the bank include:

1. Outstanding checks. A check issued by the depositor but not yet presented to the bank for payment is called an outstanding check. Most checks are presented for payment within a few days, but some may remain outstanding for several weeks.

2. Deposits in transit. When a depositor mails a deposit to the bank, the entry on the bank's books will normally be made a day or two later than the entry on the depositor's records. A deposit mailed to the bank just before the monthly bank statement is issued will probably not appear on that statement.

Transactions which may appear on the bank statement but which have not yet been recorded by the depositor include:

1. Service charges. The depositor's first knowledge of a service charge is usually the appearance of the item on the bank statement.

2. Charges for NSF checks. The bank will notify the depositor immediately when a check he has deposited proves to be uncollectible and must be charged against his account. The depositor, however, may postpone making any entry until he receives the monthly bank statement.

3. Charges for collection. The bank may make a charge for collecting notes receivable left by the depositor for collection. These charges are quite similar to service charges.

In some cases the bank reconciliation will be complete after taking into account such items as outstanding checks, deposits in transit, and miscellaneous bank charges. Other cases may require the correction of errors by the bank or by the depositor to complete the reconciliation. Errors by the bank, such as charging one customer with a check drawn by another customer with a similar name, will cause the bank statement to differ from the depositor's records. Similarly, errors in the depositor's records must be corrected to complete a bank reconciliation.

Procedures for preparing a bank reconciliation. Specific steps to be taken in preparing a bank reconciliation are:

1. Compare the deposits listed on the bank statement with the deposits listed on the check stubs. (In business concerns which deposit each day's cash receipts intact, each deposit listed on the bank statement should also correspond with a daily total in the cash receipts journal.) Any deposits not recorded by the bank must be added to the balance shown on the bank statement.

2. Arrange the paid checks in numerical order and compare each check with the corresponding entry in the cash payments journal. In the case of personal bank accounts for which the only record maintained is the checkbook, compare each paid check with the check stub. Place a check mark on each stub for which the related check has been returned by the bank. The unchecked stubs should then represent outstanding checks, which must be deducted from the balance shown on the bank statement.

3. Deduct from the checkbook balance any debit memoranda issued by the bank which have not been recorded by the depositor. A debit memorandum for a service charge is an example.

4. Add to the checkbook balance any credit memoranda issued by the bank which have not been recorded by the depositor. An example would be collection of a note receivable left with the bank by the depositor for the purpose of collection.

5. Determine whether the checks listed as outstanding in the bank reconciliation for the preceding month have been returned by the bank this month. If not, such checks should again be listed as outstanding in the current reconciliation.

6. Determine that any deposits in transit on the preceding reconciliation have been properly credited on the current month's bank statement.

7. Prepare a bank reconciliation statement, reflecting the preceding steps, similar to the illustration on page 278.

8. Make journal entries for any debits or credits on the bank statement which have not yet been recorded in the accounts.

Illustration. The July bank statement prepared by the bank for The Parkview Company was illustrated on page 278. This statement shows a balance of cash on deposit at July 31 of $5,000.17. We shall assume that The Parkview Company's records at July 31 show a bank balance of $4,172.57. The difference between the balances shown by the two sets of records is the rather substantial amount of $827.60. The purpose of preparing the bank reconciliation is to find out what items make up this discrepancy. Perhaps the bank has made an error of this amount; perhaps The Parkview Company's records are wrong. The more probable explanation is that certain transactions (such as the issuance of checks) have been recorded on one set of records but not on the other.

Let us assume that the specific steps to be taken in preparing a bank reconciliation have been carried out with respect to the July bank statement of The Parkview Company and that the following reconciling items have been discovered:

1. A deposit of $310.90 mailed to the bank on July 31 does not appear on the bank statement.

2. A credit memorandum issued by the bank on July 28 in the amount of $500 was returned with the July bank statement and appears in the deposits column of that statement. This credit represents the collection of a note receivable left with the bank by The Parkview Company for collection purposes. The collection of the note has not yet been recorded by The Parkview Company.

3. Four checks issued in July or prior months have not yet been paid by the bank. These checks are:

Check no.	Date	Amount
801	June 15	$100.00
888	July 24	10.25
890	July 27	402.50
891	July 30	205.00

4. A debit memorandum issued by the bank on July 31 in the amount of $2 was enclosed with the July bank statement. This item was listed on the bank statement among the checks but was identified by the symbol SC, denoting a service charge by the bank. No entry has yet been made on the records of The Parkview Company to record this expense.

5. Check No. 875 was issued July 20 in the amount of $85 but was erroneously listed on the check stub and in the cash payments journal as $58. The check, in payment of telephone service, was paid by the bank, returned with the July bank statement, and correctly listed on the bank statement as an $85 charge to the account.

6. No entry has as yet been made in The Parkview Company's accounts to reflect the bank's action on July 18 of charging against the account the NSF check for $50.25 drawn by J. B. Ball.

The July 31 bank reconciliation for The Parkview Company follows:

BANK
STATEMENT
AND
DEPOSITOR'S
RECORDS
MUST BE
RECONCILED

THE PARKVIEW COMPANY
Bank Reconciliation
July 31, 19___

Balance per books, July 31		$4,172.57
Add: Note receivable collected for us by bank		500.00
		$4,672.57
Deduct: Service charge	$ 2.00	
NSF check of J. B. Ball	50.25	
error on check stub No. 875	27.00	79.25
Adjusted book balance		$4,593.32
Balance per bank statement, July 31		$5,000.17
Add: deposit of July 31 not recorded by bank		310.90
		$5,311.07
Deduct: outstanding checks No. 801	$100.00	
No. 888	10.25	
No. 890	402.50	
No. 891	205.00	717.75
Adjusted balance (as above)		$4,593.32

The corrected balance of $4,593.32 is the amount of cash owned by The Parkview Company and is, therefore, the amount which should appear as cash on the July 31 balance sheet.

Notice that the corrected balance of cash differs from both the bank statement and the depositor's records. This difference is explained by the fact that neither set of records is up to date as of July 31, and also by the existence of an error on The Parkview Company's records.

Adjusting the records after the reconciliation. To make The Parkview Company's records up to date and accurate, entries are necessary for

1. The note receivable collected by the bank. Debit Cash $500; credit Notes Receivable $500.

2. The service charge by the bank. Debit Miscellaneous Expense $2; credit Cash $2.

3. The N.S.F. check of J. B. Ball. Debit Accounts Receivable—J. B. Ball for $50.25 and credit Cash $50.25.

4. The error in recording the $85 check for telephone service as a $58 item. If the bank reconciliation is completed and the error discovered before the cash payments journal is footed and posted, the correction can be made by drawing a line through the incorrect amount and inserting the correct figure. If the cash payments journal has been posted before the

error is discovered, the correction can be made in the general journal by an entry debiting Telephone Expense and crediting Cash for $27. A complete explanation should be included in the entry.

Certified checks

An element of doubt often exists as to the collectibility of a personal check. To eliminate any question about the worth of a check, the drawer may present it to his bank to be certified. After referring to the drawer's account to make certain that the balance is sufficient to cover the check, the bank cashier stamps the word "Certified" on the check along with the date and the name of the bank. The bank deducts the check from the drawer's account at this time, and the certified check immediately becomes a direct liability of the bank. Consequently, anyone receiving a certified check need have no doubt as to its value.

In preparing a bank reconciliation, certified checks should not be included in the list of outstanding checks, because a certified check is deducted from the drawer's account at the time of certification. Certified checks, when paid, are usually retained by the bank rather than being returned to the drawer.

Cashier's check

A cashier's check is a check drawn by a bank on itself and signed by the cashier of the bank. A cashier's check may be purchased by anyone and used to pay an obligation. Some state agencies refuse to accept personal checks and insist upon cashier's or certified checks. This policy eliminates any possibility of loss from worthless checks.

Payroll bank accounts

A business which pays a large number of employees by check will usually find it convenient to establish a separate payroll bank account. At the end of each pay period, a check is drawn on the general bank account for the entire amount of the payroll. This check is deposited in the payroll bank account. Pay checks for individual employees are then issued on the payroll bank account, which is thereby immediately exhausted. Some concerns keep an extra fixed amount, such as $100 or $500, in the payroll bank account so that funds will be available for making salary advances to employees and for issuing termination pay checks to employees who leave the company between regular pay dates.

Among the advantages to be gained by establishing a separate payroll bank account are the following:

1. The executives who sign regular checks are relieved of the considerable work of signing a large number of pay checks. Mechanical means of signing pay checks are often utilized.

2. Internal control is improved because of the convenience of comparing the total payroll with a single disbursement from the general bank account. The use of a separate payroll bank account also permits greater subdivision of duties, which is conducive to stronger internal control.

3. The bank reconciliation work can be spread among more employees. Reconciliation of the general bank account will be much simpler without the need to list large numbers of outstanding payroll checks.

The use of a separate payroll bank account may be regarded as one more step in establishing strong internal control over cash transactions. Such control is a characteristic of a well-managed business.

Petty cash

As previously emphasized, adequate internal control over cash requires that all receipts be deposited in the bank and all disbursements be made by check. However, every business finds it convenient to have a small amount of cash on hand with which to make some very small expenditures. Examples include payments for postage stamps, collect telegrams, and taxi fares.

Internal control over these small cash payments can best be achieved through the establishment of a petty cash fund. To create a petty cash fund, also called an *imprest fund*, a check is written for a round amount such as $50 or $100, which will cover the small expenditures to be paid in cash for a period of two or three weeks. This check is cashed and the money kept on hand in a petty cash box or drawer in the office.

The entry in the cash payments journal for the issuance of the check would be:

ENTRY TO CREATE PETTY CASH FUND

Petty Cash 100		
Cash	100	

This entry records a decrease of $100 in the cash on deposit, and creates a debit balance of $100 in the new ledger account called Petty Cash.

As cash payments are made out of the petty cash box, the custodian of the fund is required to fill out a petty cash voucher for each expenditure. A petty cash voucher, as illustrated on page 283, shows the amount paid, the purpose of the expenditure, the date, and the signature of the person receiving the money. If an invoice can be obtained from the person receiving the payment, it is attached to the voucher. A petty cash voucher should be prepared for every payment made from the fund. The petty cash box should, therefore, always contain cash and/or vouchers totaling the exact amount of the fund.

The petty cash custodian should be informed that occasional surprise counts of the fund will be made and that he is personally responsible for the fund being intact at all times. Careless handling of petty cash has often been a first step toward large defalcations; consequently, misuse of petty cash funds should not be tolerated. The significant internal control feature of an imprest fund is that, under proper operation, the full amount of the fund will always be on hand in the form of cash and/or petty cash vouchers.

Replenishing the petty cash fund. Assume that a petty cash fund of

$100 was established on June 1 and that the following payments were made from the fund:

<table>
<tr><td rowspan="8">SUM OF
VOUCHERS
AND CASH
EQUALS
AMOUNT
OF FUND</td><td>June</td><td>2.</td><td>Postage</td><td>$ 1.60</td></tr>
<tr><td></td><td>3.</td><td>Taxi fare</td><td>3.10</td></tr>
<tr><td></td><td>5.</td><td>Collect telegram</td><td>2.80</td></tr>
<tr><td></td><td>6.</td><td>Express charges on merchandise purchased</td><td>6.00</td></tr>
<tr><td></td><td>8.</td><td>Postage</td><td>59.00</td></tr>
<tr><td></td><td>12.</td><td>Gasoline: business use of employee's car</td><td>5.25</td></tr>
<tr><td></td><td>12.</td><td>Collect telegram</td><td>2.00</td></tr>
<tr><td></td><td>13.</td><td>Washing windows</td><td>10.00</td></tr>
<tr><td></td><td></td><td></td><td>$89.75</td></tr>
</table>

Since the $100 originally placed in the fund is nearly exhausted, it is necessary that the fund be replenished. The procedures for replenishing the fund may follow this pattern:

1. The fund is counted by a representative of the accounting department. The petty cash vouchers, plus the remaining cash, should equal $100, the amount of the fund.
2. The vouchers are reviewed to determine that all expenditures were for legitimate purposes.
3. The vouchers are perforated or otherwise canceled to prevent their being submitted again at a later date.
4. The vouchers are classified by expense accounts.
5. A check is drawn payable to petty cash for the exact amount of the expenditures, $89.75. This check is cashed and the money placed in the petty cash box. The fund once again contains $100 in cash.
6. The entry to record the issuance of the check replenishing the fund is:

<table>
<tr><td rowspan="6">JOURNAL
ENTRY FOR
REPLENISH-
MENT OF
FUND</td><td>Postage Expense</td><td>60.60</td><td></td></tr>
<tr><td>Telephone & Telegraph Expense</td><td>4.80</td><td></td></tr>
<tr><td>Freight-in</td><td>6.00</td><td></td></tr>
<tr><td>Gasoline Expense</td><td>5.25</td><td></td></tr>
<tr><td>Miscellaneous Expense</td><td>13.10</td><td></td></tr>
<tr><td>Cash</td><td></td><td>89.75</td></tr>
</table>

7. The petty cash vouchers are filed as supporting evidence for the replenishment check.

Petty cash book. Some companies record each payment from the petty cash fund in a *petty cash book* similar to that illustrated on page 282. The petty cash book is a memorandum record and is not an essential part of a petty cash system. It is a convenient device, however, for listing and classifying the payments from the fund.

When the petty cash fund is replenished, the columns of the petty cash book are totaled, and the amount shown as the balance on hand is verified by a count of the remaining cash. The totals of the distribution columns of the petty cash book show the amounts to be charged to the various expense accounts and thus provide in convenient form the information needed for the entry to record replenishment of the fund.

A USEFUL RECORD FOR PETTY CASH TRANSACTIONS

Petty Cash Book

Date 196___		Voucher or check number	Re-ceipts	Pay-ments	Distribution of payments			
					Postage	Tele-phone & Tele-graph	Other	
							Account	Amount
June	1	Ck 67	100.00					
	2							
	2	Vou 331		1.60	1.60			
	3	332		3.10			Misc. Expense	3.10
	5	333		2.80		2.80		
	6	334		6.00			Freight-in	6.00
	8	335		59.00	59.00			
	12	336		5.25			Gasoline Exp.	5.25
	12	337		2.00		2.00		
	13	338		10.00			Misc. Expense	10.00
		Total	100.00	89.75	60.60	4.80		24.35
		Balance		10.25				
			100.00	100.00				
		Balance	10.25					
	13	Ck 98	89.75					
	13	Balance	100.00					

In studying the procedures for operation of a petty cash fund, emphasis should be placed on the fact that the Petty Cash account is debited only when the fund is first established. Expense accounts will be debited each time the fund is replenished. There will be no further entries in the petty cash fund after it is established, unless the fund is discontinued or a decision is made to change the size of the fund from the original $100 amount.

Concisely stated, the bookkeeping entries relating to a petty cash fund are:

1. For establishment of the fund: Debit Petty Cash; credit Cash.

To keep the business from insolvency, Wilson agreed to sell at a bargain price a half interest in the company. The sale was made to Brown, who had had considerable experience in the industry. One condition for the sale was that Brown should become the general manager of the business. The cash investment by Brown for his half interest was sufficient for the company to meet the demands on it and continue operations.

Immediately after Brown entered the business, he launched an investigation of Green's activities. During the course of this investigation the following irregularities were disclosed.

(1) When checks were received from customers in payment of their accounts, Green had frequently recorded the transaction by debiting an expense account and crediting accounts receivable. In such cases Green had removed from the cash receipts an equivalent amount of currency, thus substituting the check for the currency and causing the bank deposit to agree with the recorded cash receipts.

(2) Numerous legitimate sales of merchandise on account had been charged to fictitious customers. When the actual customer later made payment for the goods, Green abstracted the check or cash and made no entry. The account receivable with the fictitious customer remained on the books.

(3) During the last few months of Green's employment with the company, bank deposits were much smaller than the cash receipts. Green had abstracted most of the receipts and substituted for them a number of worthless checks bearing fictitious signatures. These checks had been accumulated in an envelope marked "Cash Receipts—For Deposit Only."

(4) For many sales made over the counter Green had recorded lesser amounts on the cash register or had not rung up any amount. He had abstracted the funds received but not recorded.

(5) More than $1,000 a month had been stolen from petty cash. Fraudulent petty cash vouchers, mostly charged to the Purchases account, had been created to conceal these thefts and to support the checks cashed to replenish the petty cash fund.

(6) To produce income statements that showed profitable operations, Green had recorded many fictitious sales. The recorded accounts receivable included many from nonexistent customers.

(7) In preparing bank reconciliations, Green had omitted many outstanding checks, thus concealing the fact that the cash in the bank was less than the amount shown by the ledger.

Instructions

a. For each of the numbered paragraphs, describe one or more internal control procedures you would recommend to prevent the occurrence of such fraud.

b. Apart from specific internal controls over cash and other accounts, what general precaution could Wilson have taken to assure himself that the accounting records were properly maintained and the company's financial statements complete and dependable? Explain fully.

9A-2. Collegeville Sporting Goods Company received the bank statement for the month of September shown below.

COLLEGEVILLE SPORTING GOODS CO.
Collegeville, Calif.

In Account with
THE FIRST NATIONAL BANK
OF COLLEGEVILLE

Vouchers returned   24

Checks			Deposits	Date		Balance
				Sept.	1	1,538.76
25.87	34.25	128.00	66.32	Sept.	2	1,416.96
55.00			256.77	Sept.	5	1,618.73
68.35	485.00		225.45	Sept.	7	1,290.83
75.00				Sept.	8	1,215.83
12.00	75.05		420.10	Sept.	9	1,548.88
26.00			128.15	Sept.	12	1,651.03
675.00			176.48	Sept.	14	1,152.51
			188.00	Sept.	16	1,340.51
86.00			275.40	Sept.	19	1,529.91
25.24	122.65			Sept.	20	1,382.02
41.62	67.30		65.00	Sept.	21	1,338.10
165.54			355.06	Sept.	23	1,527.62
10.60			586.73	Sept.	26	2,103.75
300.00	250.00	200.00	63.42	Sept.	28	1,417.17
50.00	11.25	2.20 SC	128.00	Sept.	30	1,481.72

Other data. The entries in the cash books for the month of September were as follows:

Cash Receipts

Date			Cash dr
Sept.	1		66.32
	3		256.77
	6		225.45
	8		420.10
	10		128.15
	13		176.48
	15		188.00
	17		275.40
	20		65.00
	22		355.06
	24		586.73
	27		63.42
	29		128.00
	30		148.25
			3,083.13

Cash Disbursements

Date			Ck no.	Cash cr
Sept.	1		65	128.00
	1		66	75.00
	1		67	34.25
	2		68	25.87
	4		69	55.00
	4		70	68.35
	5		71	485.00
	9		72	75.05
	10		73	12.00
	10		74	26.00
	13		75	675.00
	19		76	122.65
	19		77	41.62
	19		78	86.00
	20		79	25.24
	21		80	35.26

Sept.	22		81	67.30
	22		82	165.54
	23		83	148.76
	26		84	10.60
	28		85	250.00
	28		86	100.00
	28		87	200.00
	28		88	300.00
	30		89	11.25
	30		90	42.50
	30		91	50.00
				3,316.24

Of the 24 vouchers returned by the bank, 23 were canceled checks, the other being a debit memorandum for service charges.

The cash balance as of August 31 per books agreed with the balance per bank statement.

Instructions

a. Prepare a bank reconciliation statement as of September 30.

b. Prepare necessary journal entries to adjust the cash account as of September 30.

9A-3. *Instructions*

a. Prepare a bank reconciliation for the firm of R. J. Baldwin & Company as of December 31, based on the information given below.

b. After completing the bank reconciliation, prepare journal entries (in general journal form) to correct the cash account at December 31. Assume that the books have not been closed.

Data

(1) The ledger account for Cash showed a balance on November 30 of $7,321.36.

(2) The cash receipts journal for December showed total cash received of $22,640.50.

(3) The credit to the Cash account posted from the cash disbursement journal at December 31 was $19,369.20.

(4) The cash received on December 31 amounted to $975.60. It was left at the bank in the night depository chute after banking hours on December 31 and was therefore not recorded by the bank on the December statement.

(5) The December bank statement showed a closing balance of $12,019.02.

(6) Among the canceled checks returned by the bank with the December bank statement was a check issued by J. R. Bellwin for $169.00. The bank had erroneously charged this check to the account of R. J. Baldwin & Company.

(7) Also included with the December bank statement was a debit memorandum from the bank for $3.50 representing service charges for December.

(8) A credit memorandum enclosed with the December bank statement indicated that a non-interest-bearing note receivable for $2,020 from T. R. Bell, left with the bank for collection, had been collected and the proceeds credited to R. J. Baldwin & Company's account.

(9) Comparison of the paid checks returned by the bank with the entries in the cash payments journal revealed that check No. 821 for $463.90 issued on December 15 in payment for office equipment had been erroneously entered in the cash payments journal as $436.90.

(10) Examination of the paid checks also revealed that these checks, all issued in December, had not yet been paid by the bank: No. 811 for $421.96; No. 814 for $93.00; No. 823 for $116.50; and a certified check, No. 825 for $104.50.

(11) Included with the December bank statement was a $50.00 check drawn by William Davis, a customer of R. J. Baldwin & Company. This check was marked NSF. It had been included in the deposit of December 27 but had been charged back against the company's account on December 31.

9A-4. *Instructions.* From the information listed below, prepare

    a. A bank reconciliation for the Glenbar Company at September 30

    b. Journal entries in general journal form for the purpose of stating the Cash account correctly

Data

(1) The ledger account for Cash showed a balance at September 30 of $5,932.64. The bank statement at September 30 indicated a balance of $6,214.50.

(2) The September 30 cash receipts of $1,896.20 had been mailed to the bank on that date and did not appear among the deposits on the September bank statement.

(3) Included with the September bank statement was an NSF check for $210 signed by a customer, James Carlson. This amount had been charged against the account on September 30.

(4) The following checks had been outstanding at the time of the previous reconciliation, August 31.

Check no.	Amount	Check no.	Amount
721	$ 100.00	784	$310.50
728	2.00	785	96.20
765	36.25	786	3.65
782	1,250.00	787	40.00

All of these checks were returned with the September bank statement except for No. 728 and No. 765.

(5) Of the checks issued in September, the following were not included among the paid checks returned by the bank:

Check no.	Amount	Check no.	Amount
824	$ 65.00	843	$817.00
840	122.10	844	90.00
841	3.00	845	862.71

(6) The paid checks returned by the bank included one drawn by Glen Barr for $100, which had been charged in error by the bank against the Glenbar Company's account.

(7) A non-interest-bearing note receivable for $500 owned by the Glenbar Company had been left with the bank for collection. On September 30 the Company received a memorandum from the bank indicating that the note had been collected and credited to the company's account after deduction of a $2.50 collection charge. No entry has been made by the company to record collection of the note.

(8) A debit memorandum for $7.50 was enclosed with the paid checks at September 30. This charge covered the printing of checkbooks bearing the Glenbar Company's name and address.

9A-5. A petty cash fund of $75 was established by the Seaward Company on September 1. During September the transactions relating to petty cash were as follows:

Sept. 1.	Drew check No. 754 for $75 to establish a petty cash fund.
Sept. 3.	Purchased stamps, $2.45.
Sept. 4.	Purchased stationery for office use, $5.45.
Sept. 4.	Collect telegram, $2.
Sept. 5.	Purchased stamps, $15.
Sept. 6.	Repairs to lock on office door, $13.
Sept. 6.	Gasoline for employee's car used on company business, $5.
Sept. 6.	Paid $5 for boys to distribute advertising handbills.
Sept. 7.	Collect telegram, $3.
Sept. 10.	Paid Railway Express $2.40 for transportation-in.
Sept. 10.	Purchased stamps, $20.
Sept. 11.	Replenished petty cash fund for expenditures to date. Check No. 772 was drawn for this purpose.

Instructions

a. Enter the above transactions in a petty cash book similar to the one illustrated in this chapter. Number petty cash vouchers consecutively.

b. Prepare entries (in general journal form) to record the establishment of the fund and its replenishment.

Group B

9B-1. *Instructions.* From the information given below, prepare

a. A bank reconciliation for Webster Drugstore as of September 30

b. The necessary adjusting entries in general journal form

Data

(1) Cash balance per bank statement, as of September 30, was $4,325.76.

(2) Two debit memoranda accompanied the bank statement: one for $2.00 was for service charges for the month; the other for $25.00 was attached to an NSF check of P. J. Green.

(3) The paid checks returned with the September bank statement disclosed two errors in the cash records. Check No. 615 for $123.50 had been erroneously recorded as $132.50 in the cash disbursements journal, and Check No. 632 for $55.44 had been recorded as $44.55. Check No. 615 was issued in payment for a store display counter; Check No. 632 was for telephone expense.

(4) A check drawn by Western Drugstore for $75.00 was included among the paid checks returned by the bank.

(5) Cash receipts of September 30 amounting to $386.77 were mailed to the bank too late to be included in the September bank statement.

(6) Checks outstanding as of September 30 were as follows: No. 652 for $125.00, No. 655 for $137.75, and No. 657 for $45.00.

(7) The Cash account showed the following entries:

				Cash				*(111)*
Sept.	*1*	*Balance*		*4,177.75*	*Sept. 30*		*CD5*	*8,665.64*
	30		*CR4*	*8,996.56*				

9B-2. *Instructions.* Prepare

    a. A bank reconciliation for Kaye and Company on March 31, based on the information given below

    b. Necessary journal entries

Data

(1) The balance per books of Kaye and Company is $3,895.82.

(2) The bank statement shows a balance of $5,738.73 as of March 31.

(3) Accompanying the bank statement was a check of W. W. Ward for $77.32, which was marked NSF by the bank.

(4) Checks outstanding as of March 31 were as follows: No. C57 for $902.68 and No. C62 for $1,005.

(5) Also accompanying the bank statement was a paid check for $57.62 of King Company; the bank had charged this check to the account of Kaye and Company erroneously.

(6) On March 29, the bank collected a non-interest-bearing note for Kaye and Company. The note was for $152.50; the bank charged a fee of $2.50.

(7) A deposit of $157.63 was in transit; it had been mailed to the bank on March 31.

(8) In recording a $90 check received on account from a customer, Barton Company, the bookkeeper for Kaye and Company erroneously listed the collection in the cash receipts journal as $9. The check appeared correctly among the deposits on the March bank statement.

(9) The service charges on the account for March amount to $3.20; a debit memo in this amount was returned with the bank statement.

9B-3. *Instructions.* From information for George Gayley and Company below, prepare

    a. A bank reconciliation statement as of September 30

    b. The journal entries necessary to correct the Cash account

Data

(1) As of September 30, cash per books was $1,418.73; per bank statement, $1,676.62.

(2) Cash receipts of $248.25 on September 30 were not deposited until October 1.

(3) Among the paid checks returned by the bank was one for $150.00 drawn by a George Garland, and charged in error to George Gayley and Company.

    (4) The following memoranda accompanied the bank statement:

    (*a*) A debit memo for service charges for the month of September, $2.50.

    (*b*) A debit memo attached to a check of H. Hastings, marked "NSF," for $45.76.

(c) A credit memo for $498, representing the proceeds of a non-interest-bearing note collected by the bank for George Gayley and Company. The note was for $500; the bank deducted a collection fee of $2.

(5) The following checks had been issued but were not included in the canceled checks returned by the bank: No. 225 for $106.00, No. 227 for $82.35, and No. 228 for $18.05.

9B-4. The internal control procedures over cash transactions in the Maynard Company were not adequate. Howard Ward, the cashier-bookkeeper, handled cash receipts, made small disbursements from the cash receipts, maintained accounting records, and prepared the monthly reconciliations of the bank account. At November 30, the statement received from the bank showed a balance of $15,550. The outstanding checks were as follows: No. 62 for $116.25; No. 183 for $150; No. 284 for $253.25; No. 8621 for $190.71; No. 8623 for $206.80; and No. 8632 for $145.28. The balance of cash as shown by the Maynard Company records was $18,901.62, which included the cash on hand. The bank statement for November showed a credit of $100 arising from the collection of a note left with the bank; the company's books did not include an entry to record this collection.

Recognizing the weakness existing in internal control over cash transactions, Ward removed all of the cash on hand in excess of $3,794.41, and then prepared the following reconciliation in an attempt to conceal his theft.

Balance per books, Nov. 30		$18,901.62
Add: outstanding checks:		
No. 8621	$190.71	
No. 8623	206.80	
No. 8632	145.28	442.79
		$19,344.41
Deduct: cash on hand		3,794.41
Balance per bank statement, Nov. 30		$15,550.00
Deduct: unrecorded credit		100.00
True cash, Nov. 30		$15,450.00

Instructions

a. Determine how much the cashier took and explain how he attempted to conceal his theft. Prepare a correct bank reconciliation.

b. Suggest some specific control devices for the Maynard Company.

9B-5. The transactions relating to petty cash given below were completed by Cambridge Company.

Sept. 16. Established a petty cash fund for $100.

Sept. 17. Paid Great Southern Railroad $24.25 for freight on merchandise purchased. (Number petty cash vouchers consecutively, starting with No. 1.)

Sept. 17. Postage expense, $8.

Sept. 18. Donated $15 to Community Chest.

Sept. 18. Reimbursed employee $3 for company telephone calls.

Sept. 19. Purchased stamps, $20.

Sept. 20. Telegrams, $4.

Sept. 23. Paid Quality Motor $11 for repairs on delivery truck.

Sept. 23. Collect telegram, $5.

Sept. 24. Cash in the petty cash fund amounted to $9.50. In addition to re-plenishing the expenditures and cash over and short, it was decided to increase the fund to $200. Voucher No. 1185 was issued for that purpose, and check No. 1017 was drawn.

Sept. 27. Purchased office supplies, $17.50.

Sept. 28. Paid Great Southern Railroad $35.40 for freight on merchandise purchased.

Sept. 29. Purchased stamps, $20.

Sept. 30. Paid newspaper boy $2.20 for monthly paper subscription.

Sept. 30. Cash in the petty cash fund amounted to $124.90. Since it was the end of a fiscal year, the fund was replenished by the issuance of voucher No. 1201. Check No. 1030 was drawn.

Instructions

a. Enter the above transactions in a petty cash book similar to the one illustrated in Chapter 9.

b. Prepare entries (in general journal form) to record the establishment of the fund, its replenishment, and the change in amount of the fund.

10

Notes and interest

Definition of promissory notes

A promissory note is an unconditional promise in writing to pay on demand or at a future date a definite sum of money.[1]

The person who signs the note and thereby promises to pay is called the *maker* of the note. The person to whom payment is to be made is called the *payee* of the note. In the illustration on page 294 G. L. Smith is the maker of the note and A. B. Davis is the payee.

From the viewpoint of the maker, G. L. Smith, the illustrated note is a liability and is recorded by crediting the Notes Payable account. However, from the viewpoint of the payee, A. B. Davis, this same note is an asset and is recorded by debiting the Notes Receivable account. The maker of a note expects to pay cash at the maturity date; the payee expects to receive cash at that date.

Maturity dates

The date when payment of a note is required may be indicated in several different ways, as for example:

1. The maturity date may be named in the note: "I promise to pay $1,000 on September 30."
2. The note may be payable after the expiration of a stated period of time. The time period may be stated in years, months, or days, as follows:

[1] A more precise definition, taken from the Uniform Negotiable Instruments Act, is as follows: "A negotiable promissory note within the meaning of this act is an unconditional promise in writing made by one person to another, signed by the maker, engaging to pay on demand or at a fixed or determinable future time a sum certain in money to order, or to bearer."

$1,000   Los Angeles, California   July 10, 19__

........One month................after date..........I..........promise to pay

to the order of.................A. B. Davis...

...............-----One thousand and no/100-------..............dollars

payable at.....First National Bank of Los Angeles.............

for value received, with interest at.........6 per cent.............

H. L. Smith

a. Time period stated in years: "Five years after date I promise to pay $1,000." If this note were dated September 30, 1960, the maturity date would be September 30, 1965.

b. Time period stated in months: "Six months after date I promise to pay $1,000." If this note were dated January 15 it would mature on July 15, regardless of the fact that some of the intervening months had more or less than 30 days. In other words, it is not necessary to count days to determine the maturity date of a note drawn in terms of months or years.

c. Time period stated in days: "Ninety days after date I promise to pay $1,000." If this note were dated March 15, the maturity date would be June 13, computed as follows:

> *Days remaining in March (31 − 15)* **16**
> *Days in April* **30**
> *Days in May* **31**
> —————
> **77**
> *Days in June* **13**
> —————
> **90**

Note that the day on which the note is issued is not counted as part of the 90-day period but that the date on which payment must be made (June 13) is included as one of the 90 days.

3. The note may mature in installments. For example, a note dated June 10, 1961, in the amount of $1,000, might provide for a

series of payments by the following wording of the maturity clause. "I promise to pay the principal sum of $1,000 in ten equal successive installments of $100 each, commencing on July 10, 1961, and continuing on the same date of each month thereafter until fully paid."

Nature of interest

Interest is a charge made for the use of money. To the borrower (maker of a note) interest is an expense; to the lender (payee of a note) interest is revenue. The heavy borrowings of the Federal government through the issuance of savings bonds, United States Treasury notes, and long-term bonds have been much publicized in recent years. As a result of these borrowings the government incurs several billion dollars of interest expense each year. The business concerns and individuals who own these government notes and bonds have a corresponding amount of interest revenue each year.

Computing interest. A formula used in computing interest is as follows:

$$\text{Principal} \times \text{rate of interest} \times \text{time} = \text{interest}$$

Interest rates are usually stated on an annual basis. For example, the interest on a $1,000, one-year, 6% note is computed as follows:

$$\$1,000 \times 0.06 \times 1 = \$60$$

If the term of the note were only four months instead of a year, the interest charge would be $20, computed as follows:

$$\$1,000 \times 0.06 \times 4/12 = \$20$$

If the term of the note is expressed in days, the exact number of days must be used in computing the interest. As a matter of convenience, however, it is customary to assume that a year contains 360 days. Suppose, for example, that a 75-day, 6% note for $1,000 is drawn on June 10. The interest charge would be computed as follows:

$$\$1,000 \times 0.06 \times 75/360 = \$12.50$$

The principal of the note ($1,000) plus the interest ($12.50) equals $1,012.50, and this amount (the maturity value) will be payable on August 24. The computation of days to maturity is as follows:

Days remaining in June $(30 - 10)$	*20*
Days in July	*31*
Days in August to maturity date	*24*
Total days called for by note	*75*

Sixty-day, 6% method. A considerable saving of time is often possible by using the 60-day, 6% method of computing interest. If the interest rate is 6% a year, the interest for 60 days on any amount of money may be determined merely by moving the decimal point two places to the left. For example,

> *The interest at 6% for 60 days on $1,111.00 is $11.11*
> *The interest at 6% for 60 days on $9,876.43 is $98.76*

The reasoning underlying the 60-day, 6% short cut may be summarized as follows:

> *Since interest on $1.00 for one year is $0.06*
> *And 60 days is 1/6 of a year*
> *Interest on $1.00 for 60 days is $0.01 (1/6 of $0.06)*

If the interest on $1.00 at 6% for 60 days can be computed by moving the decimal point two places to the left, then the interest on any amount at 6% for 60 days can be computed in the same manner.

The 60-day, 6% method can be used for time periods other than 60 days. The time of the note can be stated as a fraction or a multiple of 60 days and the interest quickly computed. For example, assuming an annual interest rate of 6%, what is the interest on $8,844 for 15 days?

> *Interest for 60 days on $8,844 is $88.44*
> *Interest for 15 days on $8,844 is 1/4 of $88.44, or $22.11*

What is the interest on $9,312 for 70 days?

> *Interest for 60 days on $9,312 is $ 93.12*
> *Interest for 10 days on $9,312 is   15.52   (1/6 of $93.12)*
> *Interest for 70 days on $9,312 is $108.64*

The 60-day, 6% method can also be applied when the interest rate is higher or lower than 6%. If the interest rate is something other than 6%, the interest is first computed at 6%, and an adjustment is then made for the difference between 6% and the actual rate. For example, what is the interest at 8% on $963 for 60 days?

Interest at 6% on $963 for 60 days is $ 9.63
Interest at 2% on $963 for 60 days is   3.21 (1/3 × $9.63)

Interest at 8% for 60 days is $12.84

What is the interest at 5% on $1,368 for 30 days?

Interest at 6% on $1,368 for 60 days is $13.68

Interest at 6% on $1,368 for 30 days is $ 6.84 (1/2 × $13.68)
Deduct 1/6 of $6.84   1.14

Interest at 5% on $1,368 for 30 days $ 5.70

Although this short-cut method of computing interest can be used for almost any rate and any time period, not much time is saved by using it in cases in which elaborate adjustments are required.

Notes payable

Notes payable are issued whenever bank loans are obtained. Other transactions giving rise to notes payable include the purchase of real estate or costly equipment, the purchase of merchandise, and the substitution of a note for a past-due open account. The use of notes payable in each of these situations is illustrated below.

ALL NOTES PAYABLE ENTERED IN ONE ACCOUNT

Recording notes payable. All notes payable may be recorded in a single Notes Payable account in the general ledger, as illustrated below:

				Notes Payable			
19__				*19__*			
July	*1*	*J. A. Doyle*	*6,000*	*May*	*2*	*J. Doyle, 60 days*	*6,000*
				Aug.	*5*	*B. R. Lee, 90 days*	*1,500*
				Oct.	*9*	*D. E. Ray, 60 days*	*1,200*
					11	*W. J. Cook, 90 days*	*1,000*

Each credit entry in this liability account represents the issuance of a note payable and includes a notation showing the name of the payee and the life of the note. The debit entry in the Notes Payable account indicates that payment of a note has been made. The debit entry includes a listing of the name of the payee, thereby making it possible to tell from inspection of the ledger account which notes have been paid and which have not.

When a note payable is issued, a carbon copy should be prepared and retained in the files of the maker. If a need should arise for detailed information concerning the terms of an outstanding note, reference can be made to the duplicate note. The carbon copies of notes payable may be kept in a tickler file, that is, filed according to the dates due. When the holder of a note receives payment, he should perforate the note or stamp it "Paid" and return it to the maker. The maker can then destroy the carbon copy but should keep the original paid note on file as evidence that the liability has been discharged. The existence of the file of carbon copies of outstanding notes and of the file of original copies of paid notes makes it unnecessary to establish a subsidiary ledger for notes payable, although such ledgers are maintained by some companies.

Uses of notes payable. *For purchase of assets.* The following journal entry illustrates the recording of a non-interest-bearing, 60-day note payable given in connection with the purchase of office equipment from ABC Office Supply Co.

<table>
<tr><td>NOTE
ISSUED
AND . . .</td><td>

Office Equipment 4,800
  Notes Payable 4,800
Issued a 60-day, non-interest-bearing note for office equipment purchased from ABC Office Supply Co.
</td></tr>
</table>

The entry 60 days later to record payment of the note would be:

<table>
<tr><td>. . . NOTE
PAID</td><td>

Notes Payable 4,800
  Cash 4,800
Paid 60-day, non-interest-bearing note to ABC Office Supply Co. at maturity date.
</td></tr>
</table>

Regardless of whether a note is interest-bearing or non-interest-bearing, the credit to the Notes Payable account is always for the face amount of the note. Referring again to the purchase of office equipment, let us assume that the ABC Office Supply Co. insisted upon a note bearing interest at 6%. The only change in the entry recording issuance of the note would be in the explanation, as shown below.

<table>
<tr><td>INTEREST-
BEARING
NOTE
ISSUED
AND . . .</td><td>

Office Equipment 4,800
  Notes Payable 4,800
Issued a 60-day, 6% note for purchase of office equipment from ABC Office Supply Co.
</td></tr>
</table>

At the maturity date of this interest-bearing note, the journal entry to record payment of the principal and interest would be as follows:

... NOTE
AND
INTEREST
PAID

> *Notes Payable* 4,800
> *Interest Expense* 48
>   *Cash* 4,848
> *Paid 60-day, 6% note to ABC Office Supply Co.*
> *at maturity date.*

For settlement of past-due accounts. If an account payable owed by a retail business to a wholesaler becomes past due, it is not uncommon for the retailer to be asked to issue a promissory note to replace the open account. From the standpoint of the creditor, a note is preferable to the open account for which it was received because the debtor by signing the note acknowledges the validity of the debt and promises to make payment at a definite future date. Furthermore, if the note is of the interest-bearing type, the creditor will obtain some compensation in the form of interest revenue for the delay in collection of the receivable.

Although a note in theory may be no more binding or collectible than an open account, businessmen generally have a strong aversion to failure to pay a note on the due date. To default on a note payable does much more damage to the credit standing of a firm than permitting open accounts to become past due. The substitution of a note for a past-due open account may, therefore, strengthen the position of a creditor in an intangible but significant manner.

As an example of a note given to replace an open account payable, assume that the Pacific Company is unable to pay its $1,800 open account with the Eastern Corporation on the due date. The parties agree that a 90-day, 4% note shall replace the open account. Pacific Company will record the issuance of the note by the following entry:

NOTE
ISSUED TO
REPLACE
OPEN
ACCOUNT

> *Accounts Payable, Eastern Corporation* 1,800
>   *Notes Payable* 1,800
> *Issued a 90-day, 4% note in settlement of*
> *open account.*

At the maturity date of this 90-day, 4% note, the entry to record payment would be:

NOTE AND
INTEREST
PAID

> *Notes Payable* 1,800
> *Interest Expense* 18
>   *Cash* 1,818
> *Paid 90-day, 4% note to Eastern Corporation*
> *on maturity date.*

For purchase of merchandise. Assume that a 60-day, non-interest-bearing note is issued by the Southern Company in connection with a purchase of merchandise on credit from National Supply Co. at an invoice price of $2,000. The transaction could be recorded by debiting Purchases and crediting Notes Payable. However, a better record of the business done with National Supply Co. will be available if the purchase is run through the account payable maintained for National Supply Co. in the subsidiary ledger. The following pair of entries should be made at the time of the purchase. (In practice, the first of these two entries would be made in the purchases journal.)

PURCHASE
MAY BE
RUN
THROUGH
ACCOUNTS
PAYABLE
WHEN
NOTE IS
ISSUED TO
SUPPLIER

Purchases	*2,000*	
Accounts Payable, National Supply Co.		*2,000*
To record purchase of merchandise.		
Accounts Payable, National Supply Co.	*2,000*	
Notes Payable		*2,000*
Issued a 60-day, non-interest-bearing note to		
National Supply Co. for merchandise.		

Whenever information is needed for managerial purposes concerning the volume of business done with a particular supplier or customer, it is desirable to have a ledger card or page available which will show at a glance the complete picture of all transactions with the firm in question, regardless of whether the transactions were handled on open account or by use of promissory notes.

For borrowing from banks. When a business concern borrows money from a bank, the form of the note will depend upon whether payment is to be made in installments or at a single future date. The language used in the note will also depend upon whether specific assets are pledged to secure payment of the loan or the note is unsecured. One of the most common forms of commercial loans (loans to business concerns) is the single-payment, unsecured loan.

Assume that John Caldwell, the sole proprietor of a retail business, applies to his bank for a 90-day, unsecured loan of $5,000. In support of the loan application Caldwell submits a balance sheet and income statement. The business has recently been audited by a certified public accountant, whose audit report is attached to the financial statements. This report indicates that the balance sheet and income statement have been prepared in accordance with generally accepted accounting principles and present fairly the financial condition of the business and the results of operations.

After studying the financial statements, reading the auditor's report, and making inquiries about Caldwell's credit rating, the bank indicates its willingness to lend the $5,000 requested, at an interest rate of 6%. Interest on $5,000 for 90 days amounts to $75, and this interest charge is included in the face of the note. The note which Caldwell signs will read as shown below, if we omit some of the minor details.

The journal entry on Caldwell's books to record this borrowing from the bank is:

NOTES PAYABLE CREDITED FOR FACE AMOUNT OF NOTE

> *Cash* *5,000*
> *Discount on Notes Payable* *75*
>   *Notes Payable* *5,075*
> *Borrowed $5,000 for 90 days at 6%.*

Notice that the amount of money borrowed ($5,000) was less than the face amount of the note ($5,075). However, as in all previous illustrations, the amount of the credit to the Notes Payable account was the face amount of the note.

On September 13, the maturity date of the note, Caldwell will hand the bank a check for $5,075 in payment of the note and will make the following journal entries:

ENTRIES FOR PAYMENT OF NOTE AND FOR INTEREST EXPENSE

> *Notes Payable* *5,075*
>   *Cash* *5,075*
> *Paid bank at maturity date of loan.*
>
>
> *Interest Expense* *75*
>   *Discount on Notes Payable* *75*
> *To record expiration of interest.*

Alternative forms of notes for bank loans. Instead of including the interest in the face of the note as described above, Caldwell might have issued a note drawn as shown on page 302.

This loan is essentially the same as the one previously described; in both cases the borrower receives $5,000 on June 15 and repays $5,075

INTEREST INCLUDED IN FACE AMOUNT OF NOTE

> Los Angeles, California   June 15, 19__
>
> On September 13, 19__ the undersigned promises to pay to Security National Bank or order the sum of $5,075 .
>
>   *John Caldwell*

Los Angeles, California   June 15, 19__

Ninety days after date I promise to pay to Security National
Bank the sum of $.5,000   with interest at the rate of 6 per cent per
annum.

John Caldwell

on September 13. The cost of the loan is, therefore, $75, regardless of
whether the interest is included in the face amount or stated separately.
However, the entries on the borrower's books will vary as between the
two forms of the note, because the credit to Notes Payable should agree
with the face amount of the note in each case. For the note in which the
interest is stated separately and not included in the face amount, the entry
to be made on Caldwell's books is as follows:

Cash	*5,000*	
Notes Payable		*5,000*
Borrowed $5,000 for 90 days at 6%.		

When the note is paid on September 13, the entry to be made is:

Notes Payable	*5,000*	
Interest Expense	*75*	
Cash		*5,075*
Paid bank at maturity date of loan.		

The form of note described in this latter illustration is sometimes
called an interest-bearing note, in contrast to the one presented in the
preceding illustration, which may be called a non-interest-bearing note.
These terms are somewhat misleading, however, because as shown in
these two illustrations the interest charge is always present on a bank
loan, even though interest is not separately listed in the note. By drawing
a non-interest-bearing note for an amount greater than the cash received
by the borrower, the objective of charging interest for the use of money
is easily attained.

Discounting a note payable. If the borrower receives less cash than
the face amount of the note he issues to the lender, he is said to be discounting a note payable. Referring again to the illustration in which Caldwell borrowed $5,000 from his bank and signed a non-interest-bearing

note for $5,075, this transaction could be termed discounting a note payable.

A somewhat different meaning for the term discount is found in a practice formerly common among banks, in which the interest charge was based on the face of the note and deducted in advance. For example, William Smith requested a 90-day, 6% loan for $5,000 from his bank. Suppose that the bank computes the interest charge as $75, gives Smith $4,925, and has him sign a note for $5,000. This procedure is no longer followed by most banks because of two specific objections to this form of "discounting." In the first place, the borrower applied for a loan of $5,000 and received only $4,925. If his credit rating warrants a $5,000 loan and he needs that amount to carry out his plans, there is no reason for the bank to reduce the loan to $4,925. In the second place, if the borrower receives only $4,925 but pays an interest charge of $75 for the use of this sum for 90 days, he is paying an interest rate somewhat higher than the 6% rate mentioned in the negotiations leading to the loan. The amount borrowed is logically the basis for the interest charge, and 6% interest on $4,925 for 90 days amounts to $73.88, not to $75.

In recognition of these points it is now common practice for banks to base the interest charge on the cash made available to the borrower and to include the interest charge in the face of the note. Consequently, a businessman who applies for a 90-day, 6% $5,000 loan should expect to receive a full $5,000 in cash and to sign a non-interest-bearing note in the face amount of $5,075. At the maturity date of the loan he will repay $5,075. The cost of borrowing is then $75, which is the interest expense computed at 6% for a period of 90 days.

Adjustments for interest at end of period. Interest expense is incurred continuously throughout the life of a note payable. When the note is issued in one accounting period and matures in a later period, the interest expense must be apportioned. At the end of an accounting period, the interest to date on interest-bearing notes payable is accrued by an adjusting entry debiting Interest Expense and crediting Accrued Interest Payable. The purpose of this adjustment is to have the accounts reflect all interest expense incurred during the period before these accounts are used to prepare the financial statements. When the note matures and the interest is paid in the following period, the entry for payment will include a debit to Accrued Interest Payable for the amount of the accrual and a debit to Interest Expense for the remainder of the interest payment.

Assume that a 6%, 60-day note payable for $10,000 is issued on December 1 in payment for machinery, and the following entry is made:

ENTRY FOR ISSUANCE OF INTEREST-BEARING NOTE AND . . .

Machinery	*10,000*	
Notes Payable		*10,000*
To record issuance of 6%, 60-day note for fixed asset.		

At December 31, the following adjusting entry would be made to accrue the interest expense to date.

Interest Expense 50
     Accrued Interest Payable 50
To record interest expense for December
($10,000 × 6% × 30/360).

When the note is paid on January 30 of the following year, the entry is:

Notes Payable 10,000
Accrued Interest Payable 50
Interest Expense 50
    Cash 10,100
To record payment of 6%, 60-day note dated
Dec. 1.

A different type of adjustment is necessary at the end of the period for notes payable to banks in which the interest has been included in the face amount of the note. For example, assume that Baker Company borrows $10,000 from its bank on November 1 on a 6%, six-month note with interest of $300 included in the face of the note. The entry for the borrowing on November 1 would be:

Cash 10,000
Discount on Notes Payable 300
    Notes Payable 10,300
Issued to bank a 6%, six-month note payable with
interest included in face amount.

At December 31, the adjusting entry required is:

Interest Expense 100
    Discount on Notes Payable 100
To record interest expense incurred to end of year
on 6%, six-month note dated Nov. 1.

On May 1, when the six-month note matures and the Baker Company pays the bank, the entry is:

Notes Payable	*10,300*	
Interest Expense	*200*	
Cash		*10,300*
Discount on Notes Payable		*200*
To record payment to bank of 6%, six-month note		
dated Nov. 1, with interest included in face of note.		

Discount on notes payable should be classified as a contra-liability account and deducted from the face value of notes payable in the current liability section of the balance sheet. This treatment results in showing as a liability at statement date the principal of the debt plus the accrued interest payable at that time. Discount on notes payable is sometimes called "prepaid interest" and classified as a current asset, a practice which has no theoretical justification. It is literally impossible to "prepay" interest because any attempt to do so simply reduces the amount of money borrowed and increases the effective rate of interest.

Notes receivable

In some lines of business, notes receivable are seldom encountered; in other fields they occur frequently and may constitute an important part of total assets. Business concerns that sell high-priced durable goods such as automobiles and farm machinery often accept notes receivable from their customers. As previously explained, many companies obtain notes receivable in settlement of past-due accounts. Notes receivable may also arise as a result of loans made to officers and employees for their personal convenience. In banks and finance companies, notes receivable usually represent the largest asset group and produce the bulk of the revenue earned.

Good accounting records are perhaps even more important for notes receivable than for notes payable. In the case of notes payable, the payee may be depended upon to demand prompt payment, so there is little danger of overlooking the maturity date. However, in the case of notes receivable the holder must be alert to act promptly at the maturity date if payment is not received. A company owning notes receivable may therefore elect to file these notes chronologically by the maturity dates as a convenient means of facilitating collection.

All notes receivable are usually recorded in a single account in the general ledger. A subsidiary ledger is not essential because the notes themselves, when filed by due dates, are the equivalent of a subsidiary ledger and provide any necessary information as to maturity, interest rates, collateral pledged, and other details.

ALL NOTES RECEIVABLE ENTERED IN ONE ACCOUNT	Notes Receivable							
	19__				19__			
	Oct.	9	J. Ryan, 90 days	2,000	Dec.	4	D. Ball	1,000
	Nov.	4	D. Ball, 30 days	1,000				
		20	R. Blue, 60 days	3,500				
	Dec.	6	T. James, 30 days	6,000				

Each debit entry in the illustrated general ledger account indicates that an asset in the form of a note receivable has been acquired, and also shows the name of the maker and the life of the note. The amount debited to Notes Receivable is always the face amount of the note, regardless of whether or not the note bears interest. When an interest-bearing note is collected, the amount of cash received will be larger than the face amount of the note. The interest collected is credited to an Interest Earned account, and only the face amount of the note is credited to the Notes Receivable account.

Illustrative entries. Assume that a 6%, 90-day note receivable is acquired from a customer, Marvin White, in settlement of an existing account receivable of $2,000. The entry for acquisition of the note is as follows:

NOTE RECEIVED TO REPLACE ACCOUNT RECEIVABLE	Notes Receivable 2,000	
	Accounts Receivable, Marvin White	2,000
	Accepted 6%, 90-day note in settlement of account receivable.	

The entry 90 days later to record collection of the note will be:

COLLECTION OF PRINCIPAL AND INTEREST	Cash 2,030	
	Notes Receivable	2,000
	Interest Earned	30
	Collected 6%, 90-day note from Marvin White.	

When a note is received from a customer at the time of making a sale of merchandise, two entries should be made as follows:

SALE MAY
BE RUN
THROUGH
ACCOUNTS
RECEIVABLE
WHEN NOTE
RECEIVED
FROM
CUSTOMER

Accounts Receivable, F. H. Russ *1,500*		
Sales		*1,500*
To record sale of merchandise.		
Notes Receivable *1,500*		
Accounts Receivable, F. H. Russ		*1,500*
To record acquisition of note from customer.		

When this procedure is employed, the customer's account in the subsidiary ledger for accounts receivable provides a complete record of all transactions with him, regardless of the fact that some sales may have been made on open account and others may have involved a note receivable. Having a complete history of all transactions with a customer on a single ledger card may be helpful in reaching decisions as to collection efforts or further extensions of credit.

For business concerns which obtain notes receivable for a large portion of their sales transactions, a special notes receivable journal may be desirable. Another alternative practice when many notes are being received from customers is to create a separate debit column for notes in the general journal. Numerous other variations in the form of the journals may be employed to achieve maximum efficiency in the recording of large numbers of notes receivable. These variations are based on the principle that a special journal may be created or a special column added to an existing journal whenever a sufficient number of like transactions occurs to justify such modification of the accounting records. In this chapter, however, we are concerned with the basic principles to be used in accounting for notes, rather than the design of special records to handle a large volume of transactions.

When the maker of a note defaults. A note receivable which cannot be collected at maturity is said to have been dishonored by the maker. Failure by the maker to pay interest or principal of a note at the due date is also known as defaulting on the note. Immediately after the dishonor or default of a note, an entry should be made by the holder to transfer the amount due from the Notes Receivable account to an account receivable from the debtor.

Assuming that a 60-day, 6% note receivable from Robert Jones is not collected at maturity, the following entry would be made:

ENTRY FOR
DEFAULT
OF NOTE
RECEIVABLE

Accounts Receivable, Robert Jones *1,010*		
Notes Receivable		*1,000*
Interest Earned		*10*
To record dishonor by Robert Jones of a 6%, 60-day note.		

Note that the interest earned on the note is recorded as a credit to Interest Earned and is also included in the account receivable from the maker. The interest receivable on a defaulted note is just as valid a claim against the maker as is the principal of the note; if the principal is collectible, then presumably the interest too can be collected.

By transferring past-due notes receivable into accounts receivable, two things are accomplished. First, the Notes Receivable account is limited to current notes not yet matured and is, therefore, regarded as a highly liquid type of asset. Secondly, the account receivable ledger card will show that a note has been dishonored and will present a complete picture of all transactions with the customer.

Renewal of a note receivable. Sometimes the two parties to a note agree that the note shall be renewed rather than paid at the maturity date. If the note does not bear interest, the entry could be made as follows:

RENEWAL OF NOTE SHOULD BE RECORDED

Notes Receivable	*1,000*	
Notes Receivable		*1,000*
A 60-day, non-interest-bearing note from Ray Bell renewed today with new 60-day, 6% note.		

Since the above entry causes no change in the balance of the Notes Receivable account, a question may arise as to whether the entry is necessary. The renewal of a note is an important transaction requiring managerial attention; a general journal entry is needed to record the action taken by management and to provide a permanent record of the transaction. If journal entries were not made to record the renewal of notes, confusion might arise as to whether some of the notes included in the balance of the Notes Receivable account were current or past due. A past-due note is generally regarded as an asset of somewhat doubtful value.

In some cases agreement to renew a note is reached prior to the maturity date, and no default is involved. In other cases a default of the original note occurs, and this is followed by an agreement between the maker and the payee for the issuance of a renewal note. In the latter situation, the defaulted note and interest would first be charged to an account receivable, and then later transferred to the Notes Receivable account. A complete history of credit transactions with the debtor is thus provided.

At the time of renewal, the holder of a note will often attempt to collect the interest earned on the original note. Payment of the interest on a defaulted note is regarded as an indication of good faith on the part of the maker.

Sometimes a portion of the principal of a note is collected at the maturity date along with the interest earned. The uncollected portion should be debited to an account receivable with the maker and then transferred into the Notes Receivable account to record the receipt of the renewal note.

Adjustments for interest at end of period. Notes receivable acquired in one accounting period often do not mature until a following period. Interest is being earned throughout the life of the note, and this revenue should be apportioned between the two accounting periods on a time basis. At the end of the accounting period, interest earned to date on notes receivable should be accrued by an adjusting entry debiting the asset account, Accrued Interest Receivable, and crediting the revenue account, Interest Earned. When the note matures and the interest is received in the following period, the entry to be made consists of a credit to Accrued Interest Receivable for the amount of the accrual, and a credit to Interest Earned for the remainder of the interest collected.

For example, assume that a 6%, three-month note is acquired on November 1 in settlement of an existing account receivable of $3,000 from James Brothers. The following entry records acquisition of the note.

ACQUIRED INTEREST-BEARING NOTE RECEIVABLE	*Notes Receivable* *3,000*	
	Accounts Receivable, James Brothers	*3,000*
	Received a 6%, three-month note.	

At the end of the accounting period on December 31, the following adjusting entry would be made:

ADJUSTMENT FOR INTEREST EARNED TO END OF YEAR	*Accrued Interest Receivable* *30*	
	Interest Earned	*30*
	To record interest earned during November and December on 6%, three-month note from James Brothers, dated Nov. 1.	

When the note was collected on February 1, the entry would be:

ONE-THIRD OF INTEREST EARNED IN SECOND YEAR	*Cash* *3,045*	
	Notes Receivable	*3,000*
	Accrued Interest Receivable	*30*
	Interest Earned	*15*
	Collected principal and interest on 6%, three-month note from James Brothers.	

The note was outstanding for two months in the first accounting period and for one month in the second period. Consequently, two-thirds of the interest revenue, amounting to $30, was allocated to the first period, and the remaining one-third, or $15, was allocated to the second period.

Installment contracts receivable

The terms of sale for high-priced, durable goods such as automobiles or farm machinery often provide for a series of payments by the purchaser over a period of months. Title to the property may be conveyed at the time of the sale, subject to a mortgage held by the seller, or title may not be conveyed until the series of monthly payments has been completed. A down payment is commonly required and a "service charge" or interest charge is usually added to the sales price. When the seller retains title during the payment period or holds a mortgage on the property, he has the right to repossess the goods in the event of any default by the customer. The note signed by the purchaser under these terms is often referred to as an *installment contract* rather than a promissory note.

Entries for installment contracts receivable. Assume that the Hillside Machinery Company, a dealer in farm machinery, sells to Roger Smith a machine priced at $7,000. The terms of sale provide for a down payment of $1,000, with the balance plus interest to be paid in 12 equal monthly installments. The interest charge is set at $360 (computed at 6% of $6,000 for one year). The total amount of the installment contract is, therefore, $6,360, and each monthly payment is to be 1/12 of this amount, or $530.

Although an interest rate of 6% was used in computing the interest charge of $360, the effective rate of interest is actually much higher than 6%. The amount of borrowed money during the first month is $6,000, but the principal amount is decreased by each monthly payment. During the twelfth month, the unpaid balance of the contract principal is only $500. Because the principal amount of the loan is reduced steadily by the series of payments, the effective rate of interest on installment contracts is often much higher than the rate mentioned in describing this type of financing. On some installment contracts, however, especially in the field of real estate financing, the interest is computed on the unpaid balance of the loan rather than on the original amount. In these cases the quoted rate of interest is also the effective rate.

The installment contract used for the sale of machinery to Roger Smith by the Hillside Machinery Company might be drawn as shown on page 311.

The entry on the books of the Hillside Machinery Company to record this sale is as follows:

ENTRY FOR INSTALLMENT CONTRACT RECEIVABLE

Cash	1,000	
Installment Contracts Receivable	6,360	
Sales		7,000
Unearned Interest		360
Received installment note from Roger Smith for machinery sold today, collectible in 12 equal monthly installments.		

Unearned interest should be classified as a contra-asset account and deducted from installment contracts receivable in the current asset section of the balance sheet. The installment contract is thus reported as an asset at its principal amount plus accrued interest receivable to date. Unearned interest is sometimes erroneously classified as a deferred revenue account and shown among the current liabilities. We have noted that interest cannot be paid in advance; similarly, interest cannot be received in advance. Unearned interest is therefore not comparable to such deferred revenue accounts as rent collected in advance. The gradual transfer from unearned interest to interest revenue simply reflects the accruing of interest on the installment contract.

As each payment of $530 is received, it will be recorded as follows:

INTEREST CHARGE BASED ON ORIGINAL AMOUNT OF DEBT

Cash	*530*	
Unearned Interest	*30*	
Installment Contracts Receivable		*530*
Interest Earned		*30*
Collected monthly payment on Roger Smith contract.		

MONTHLY PAYMENT RECEIVED ON INSTALLMENT CONTRACT

Under this method of accounting for an installment contract, the interest is considered to be earned at a uniform rate of $30 a month throughout the life of the contract. Therefore, at the time of each monthly collection, the amount of $30 is transferred from the contra-asset account, Unearned Interest, to the revenue account, Interest Earned. There are a number of alternative methods of accounting for the interest earned on installment contracts, and also some rather involved accounting problems to be considered when customers default on installment contracts and the merchandise is repossessed by the seller. Because of the com-

July 15, 1962 $6,360

For value received the undersigned promises to pay to Hillside Machinery Company or order the sum of $6,360 in installments as follows: $530 on the same day of each successive month beginning August 15, 1962, and so continuing until paid.

Roger Smith

plexity of these issues, further consideration of installment contracts is reserved for advanced courses in accounting.

Discounting notes receivable. Many business concerns which obtain notes receivable from their customers prefer to sell the notes to a bank for cash rather than to hold the notes until maturity. One of the advantages of a note over an account receivable is the ease with which a note can be converted into cash by sale to a bank or finance company. Selling a note receivable to a bank or finance company is often called "discounting a note receivable." The holder of the note signs his name on the back of the note (as in endorsing a check) and delivers the note to the bank. The bank expects to collect from the maker of the note at the maturity date, but if the maker fails to pay, the bank can demand payment from the endorser.

When a businessman endorses a note and turns it over to a bank for cash, he is promising to pay the note if the maker fails to do so. The endorser is therefore contingently liable to the bank. A *contingent liability* may be regarded as a potential liability which either will develop into a full-fledged liability or will be eliminated entirely by a subsequent event. The subsequent event in the case of a discounted note receivable is the payment (or dishonoring) of the note by the maker. If the maker pays, the contingent liability of the endorser is thereby ended. If the maker fails to pay, the contingent liability of the endorser becomes a real liability. In either case the period of contingent liability ends at the maturity date of the note.

Contingent liabilities should be reflected in the balance sheet, because they have a considerable bearing on the credit rating of the person or firm contingently liable. A business concern with large contingent liabilities may encounter greater difficulties in obtaining bank loans than would otherwise be the case.

The discounting of notes receivable with a bank may be regarded by the businessman as an alternative to borrowing by issuing his own note payable. To issue his own note payable to the bank, would, of course, mean the creation of a liability; to obtain cash by discounting a note receivable creates only a contingent liability. In some situations it may be possible for a businessman to discount notes receivable without guaranteeing payment in the event of default by the maker. To make clear that no contingent liability for payment was being assumed, the businessman would endorse the note by writing the words "Without recourse" and signing his name just below them. This type of qualified endorsement is usually not acceptable to banks and finance companies and is not widely used.

Computing the proceeds. The amount of cash obtained by discounting a note receivable is called the *proceeds* of the note. The following procedure is used to compute the proceeds:

1. Determine the maturity value of the note. The maturity value is the amount (including interest) which the holder of the note will be en-

titled to collect when the note matures. For a non-interest-bearing note the maturity value is the face amount. For an interest-bearing note, the maturity value is the face amount plus the interest.

2. Determine the length of the discount period by counting the exact number of days from the date of discount to the date of maturity. In counting the number of days, exclude the date of discount but include the maturity date. The discount period is usually shorter than the life of the note; occasionally it equals the life of the note, but obviously it can never exceed the life of the note.

3. Compute the discount by applying the discount rate (interest rate) charged by the bank to the maturity value of the note for the discount period.

4. Deduct the discount from the maturity value. The resulting amount represents the cash received from the bank, or the proceeds of the note.

To illustrate the application of the above steps, assume that on July 1 Roger Barnes receives a 75-day, non-interest-bearing note for $8,000 from William Dailey. The note will mature on September 14 (30 days in July, 31 days in August, and 14 days in September). On July 16, Roger Barnes discounts this note receivable with his bank, which charges a discount rate of 6% a year. How much cash does Barnes receive? The computation is as follows:

Face of the note	*$8,000*
Add: interest from date of note to maturity	*000*
Maturity value	*$8,000*
Deduct: bank discount at 6% for the discount period of 60 days (July 16 to Sept. 14)	*80*
Proceeds (cash received from bank)	*$7,920*

Let us now go through the same steps for the discounting of an interest-bearing note. Assume that Roger Barnes also received on July 1 a 75-day, 6% note for $8,000 from Raymond Kelly. On July 16 he discounts the Kelly note at the bank, which again charges a 6% discount rate. How much cash does Barnes receive for the Kelly note?

FACE
AMOUNTS
OF NOTES
RECORDED

Face of the note	*$8,000*
Add: interest from date of note to maturity	*100*
Maturity value	*$8,100*
Deduct: bank discount at 6% for the discount period of 60 days (July 16 to Sept. 14)	*81*
Proceeds (cash received from bank)	*$8,019*

An additional point to observe in the two preceding examples is that the cash received from discounting a note receivable may be either more or less than the face amount of the note.

Entries for discounting notes receivable. To continue the example in which Roger Barnes is the holder of notes receivable from William Dailey and Raymond Kelly, the Notes Receivable account in the ledger of Roger Barnes would appear as follows:

Notes Receivable							
19__							
July	*1*	*W. Dailey, 75 days*	8,000				
	1	*R. Kelly, 75 days*	8,000				

When Barnes discounts these two notes receivable at the bank on July 16, he is giving up ownership of two assets. It might therefore appear that the asset account, Notes Receivable, should be credited. To credit Notes Receivable, however, would not provide a record showing that Barnes is contingently liable to the bank for payment of the notes. In order to show the contingent liability in the accounts, the credit is made to an account entitled Notes Receivable Discounted.

The entry to record the discounting of the William Dailey note is as follows:

PROCEEDS
MAY BE
LESS THAN
FACE OF
NOTE

Cash 7,920
Interest Expense 80
    Notes Receivable Discounted 8,000
Discounted William Dailey note at bank at 6%.

When Barnes discounted the Kelly note he received cash in an amount greater than the face of the note, because the interest earned to the date of maturity was greater than the amount of the discount charged by the bank. The transaction, therefore, involved interest revenue rather than interest expense, as shown by the following entry:

PROCEEDS
MAY BE
GREATER
THAN FACE
OF NOTE

Cash 8,019
    Notes Receivable Discounted 8,000
    Interest Earned 19
Discounted Raymond Kelly note at bank for 6%.

The ledger of Barnes now contains two accounts dealing with notes receivable: one with a debit balance of $16,000, the other with a credit

CONTINGENT
LIABILITY
ACCOUNT
OFFSETS
ASSET
ACCOUNT

balance of $16,000. Since the two accounts offset each other, they show that the investment in notes receivable is down to zero, but they also show that a contingent liability of $16,000 exists. The two accounts now appear as follows:

Notes Receivable										
19__										
July	1	W. Dailey, 75 days	8,000							
	1	R. Kelly, 75 days	8,000							

Notes Receivable Discounted										
					19__					
					July	16	W. Dailey		8,000	
						16	R. Kelly		8,000	

Discounted note receivable paid by maker. Before the maturity date of the discounted notes, the bank will notify the makers (William Dailey and Raymond Kelly) that it is holding the notes. Assuming that both Dailey and Kelly pay their respective notes at the bank on the maturity date, the contingent liability of Roger Barnes to the bank is thereby ended, and he will make the following entries:

CONTINGENT
LIABILITY
ENDS WHEN
MAKER PAYS
BANK

Notes Receivable Discounted 8,000
　　　Notes Receivable 8,000
To remove from the accounts the discounted William Dailey note and the contingent liability to the bank.

Notes Receivable Discounted 8,000
　　　Notes Receivable 8,000
To remove from the accounts the discounted Raymond Kelly note and the contingent liability to the bank.

ACCOUNTS
SHOW CON-
TINGENT
LIABILITY
ELIMINATED

After these entries have been posted, the Notes Receivable account and the Notes Receivable Discounted account in the ledger of Roger Barnes will appear as follows:

Notes Receivable										
19__					19__					
July	1	W. Dailey, 75 days	8,000		Sept.	14	W. Dailey		8,000	
	1	R. Kelly, 75 days	8,000			14	R. Kelly		8,000	

		Notes Receivable Discounted						
19__				19__				
Sept.	14	W. Dailey	8,000	July	16	W. Dailey	8,000	
	14	R. Kelly	8,000		16	R. Kelly	8,000	

Discounted notes receivable dishonored by maker. When a note receivable is discounted, the new holder (endorsee) is obligated to present the note to the maker at maturity and demand payment. If the maker does not pay the note, the holder must give proper notice of dishonor to the endorser. Unless this procedure of demanding payment and giving notice of dishonor is followed promptly by the holder, the endorser cannot be held liable for payment.

In some cases the holder of the note may notify the endorser in an informal manner of the default by the maker. In other instances, the holder may retain the services of a notary public to prepare a formal written *notice of protest,* which is sent to the maker and to the endorser. The endorser is obligated to pay the holder for the fee of the notary public as well as the principal and interest of the note.

To illustrate the entries to be made when a discounted note receivable is dishonored by the maker, let us assume that William Dailey and Raymond Kelly both fail to pay their notes on the maturity date, and the bank gives notice of dishonor to the endorser, Roger Barnes. Barnes immediately becomes obligated to pay and will make the following entries:

ENTRIES WHEN MAKER OF DISCOUNTED NOTE RECEIVABLE FAILS TO PAY

Accounts Receivable, William Dailey	*8,000*	
Cash		*8,000*
To record payment to the bank of the discounted Dailey note, dishonored by maker.		
Notes Receivable Discounted	*8,000*	
Notes Receivable		*8,000*
To remove from the accounts the dishonored note receivable from William Dailey and the contingent liability to the bank.		

Similar entries are required for the dishonored note of Raymond Kelly; however, in this case the payment to the bank must include interest as well as principal.

Accounts Receivable, Raymond Kelly	*8,100*	
Cash		*8,100*
To record payment to the bank of the discounted Kelly note, dishonored by maker.		

> Notes Receivable Discounted 8,000
>   Notes Receivable   8,000
> *To remove from the accounts the dishonored note*
> *receivable from Raymond Kelly and the contingent*
> *liability to the bank.*

The above entries show that Barnes's contingent liability to the bank has become a real liability and has been discharged by a cash payment. These entries also show that Barnes now has accounts receivable from the makers of the dishonored notes for the amounts which he was compelled to pay to the bank.

Note that the entry debiting Notes Receivable Discounted and crediting Notes Receivable is made at the maturity of the note regardless of whether the maker pays the note or fails to pay it. In either event the endorser has no contingent liability after the discounted note has matured. He is either completely freed of liability as a result of the maker paying the note, or his contingent liability becomes a real liability because the maker defaults on the note.

The contingent liability of the endorser of an interest-bearing note is actually equal in amount to the principal plus the interest, but as a matter of convenience it is customary to enter in the Notes Receivable Discounted account only the face amount of the discounted note.

Balance sheet presentation of notes receivable and notes receivable discounted. The contingent liability arising from the discounting of notes receivable is usually disclosed in the balance sheet by a footnote. The amount listed for Notes Receivable on the asset side of the balance sheet is equal to the debit balance in the Notes Receivable ledger account minus the credit balance in the Notes Receivable Discounted account.

WHICH NOTES HAVE BEEN COLLECTED? WHICH DISCOUNTED?

To illustrate this procedure, let us assume that the ledger of the Jamestown Company contains the following accounts, among others, at December 31.

					Notes Receivable					
19__						19__				
Sept.	10	B. L. Dent, 30 days	J3	1,000		Oct.	10	B. L. Dent	CR1	1,000
Nov.	15	R. M. Lee, 30 days	J5	5,000		Dec.	15	R. M. Lee	J8	5,000
Dec.	5	H. D. Blue, 60 days	J6	9,000						
	19	A. B. Weeks, 90 days	J8	9,500						
	19	T. R. James, 30 days	J8	2,000						

				Notes Receivable Discounted					
19___					*19___*				
Dec.	*15*	*R. M. Lee*	*J8*	*5,000*	*Nov.*	*25*	*R. M. Lee*	*J6*	*5,000*
					Dec.	*10*	*H. D. Blue*	*J7*	*9,000*

These two accounts tell the following story of the five notes receivable handled by the Jamestown Company:

1. B. L. Dent note. This 30-day note receivable for $1,000 was acquired on September 10 and collected on October 10.

2. R. M. Lee note. This 30-day note receivable for $5,000 was acquired on November 15 and discounted at the bank on November 25. The contingent liability of the Jamestown Company as endorser ended on December 15, the maturing date.

3. H. D. Blue note. This 60-day note receivable for $9,000 was acquired on December 5 and discounted at the bank on December 10. A contingent liability exists at December 31, the date of the balance sheet.

4. A. B. Weeks note. This 90-day note receivable for $9,500 was acquired on December 19 and should appear as an asset on the December 31 balance sheet.

5. T. R. James note. This 30-day note receivable for $2,000 was acquired on December 19 and should appear as an asset on the December 31 balance sheet.

OBSERVE TREATMENT OF NOTES, INTEREST, AND CONTINGENT LIABILITY

The balance sheet should show among the assets the item of Notes Receivable in the amount of $11,500, representing the notes of A. B. Weeks and T. R. James which are still owned by the Jamestown Company at December 31. A footnote to the balance sheet should indicate the existence of the contingent liability of $9,000 resulting from discounting the H. D. Blue note, which has not yet matured. A balance sheet for the Jamestown Company might appear as follows:

JAMESTOWN COMPANY
Balance Sheet
December 31, 19___
Assets

Current assets:		
Cash	$10,000	
Notes receivable	11,500	
Accrued interest receivable	23	
Accounts receivable	31,000	
Inventory	40,000	$ 92,523

Fixed assets:			
Land		*$15,000*	
Building	*$30,000*		
Less: accumulated depreciation	*6,000*	*24,000*	*39,000*
			$131,523

Liabilities and Owner's Equity

Current liabilities:		
Notes payable	*$20,000*	
Accounts payable	*28,600*	
Accrued wages, interest, and taxes payable	*1,000*	*$ 49,600*
Owner's equity:		
Edward James, capital		*81,923*
		$131,523

Note: At December 31, 19___, the company was contingently liable for notes receivable discounted in the amount of $9,000.

Note that the accrued interest receivable at December 31 is listed among the current assets. This item was created by an adjusting entry debiting Accrued Interest Receivable and crediting Interest Earned. Accrued interest on notes payable has been combined with other expense accruals (wages and taxes payable) in the current liability section. Each of these accruals would be represented by a separate account in the ledger, but combination of like items of modest amount is desirable in the balance sheet to achieve a concise financial statement.

QUESTIONS

1. Determine the maturity dates of the following notes:
   a. A three-month note dated February 3
   b. A 30-day note dated October 29
   c. A 90-day note dated July 5

2. Use the 60-day, 6% method to compute interest on the following notes:
   a. $2,167 at 6% for 60 days
   b. $3,946 at 6% for 90 days
   c. $7,124 at 6% for 30 days
   d. $8,415 at 4% for 60 days
   e. $12,636 at 7% for 120 days
   f. $4,626 at 5% for 90 days

3. James Barker applied to his bank for a loan of $12,000 for a period of three months. The loan was granted at an interest rate of 6%. Indicate how the note would be drawn if (*a*) interest is included in the face amount and (*b*) interest is not included in the face of the note.

4. Referring to question 3, give the journal entry required on the books of James Barker for issuance of each of the two types of notes.

5. Among the assets of the Barnes Company at December 31, 1961, was a 60-day, 6% note receivable for $8,000 dated November 16, 1961. (*a*) Give the adjusting entry to record the interest accrued to December 31. (*b*) Give the entry to record collection of the note at maturity.

6. Three notes, each in the amount of $5,000, were discounted by a businessman at his bank on May 10. The bank charged a discount rate of 6%. From the following data compute the proceeds of each note.

Date of note	Interest rate, %	Life of note
Apr. 10	6	3 months
Mar. 31	5	60 days
Mar. 11	8	90 days

PROBLEMS

Group A

10A-1. In the fiscal year ended June 30 the Stanley Corporation engaged in the following transactions involving promissory notes.

Feb. 6.   Received a 45-day, 6% note from a long-time employee, E. J. Glade, as evidence of a loan in the amount of $1,500.

Mar. 12.   Purchased office equipment from Daily Company. The invoice amount was $2,400 and the Daily Company agreed to accept as full payment a 6% three-month note for the invoiced amount.

Mar. 17.   Discounted the Glade note at Security Bank. The discount rate charged by the bank was 6%.

May 1.   Borrowed $30,000 from Security Bank at an interest rate of 6% per annum; signed a 90-day note with interest included in the face amount of the note.

June 8.   Sold merchandise in the amount of $1,300 to A. B. Kay. Accepted in settlement a 90-day note bearing interest at 4%.

June 12.   The $2,400 note payable to Daily Company matured today. Paid the interest accrued and issued a new 30-day, 6% note to replace the maturing one.

Instructions

a. Prepare journal entries (in general journal form) to record the above transactions.

b. Prepare the adjusting entries needed at June 30, prior to closing the books.

10A-2. The transactions relating to notes receivable and notes payable shown below were carried out by the Edgewood Company during the three months ended June 30:

Mar. 6.   Sold merchandise to E. D. Hughes on open account, $840.

Apr. 8.   E. D. Hughes reported that he was unable to make payment as agreed for his purchase of March 6. Accepted in settlement of this account a 5%, 60-day note signed by Hughes.

Apr. 20. Borrowed $2,000 from First National Bank today and signed a 30-day, 6% note as evidence of indebtedness. The interest was included in the face amount of the note.

May 10. Discounted the Hughes note at the First National Bank. The bank charged a discount rate of 6%.

May 20. Paid note due today at First National Bank.

June 7. Received notification from the bank that Hughes had failed to pay note at maturity. Bank also charged a protest fee of $2.

Instructions. Prepare all necessary journal entries (in general journal form) to record the above transactions (*a*) on the Edgewood Company's books, and (*b*) on Hughes's books. Show all supporting computations.

10A-3. Among the receivables of the Randy Company on January 1, 1962, were the following items:

Accounts receivable:

A. B. Cole	$ 420
M. E. White	700
I. J. Wall	1,600
Total	$2,720

Notes receivable:

R. K. Rogers, 6%, 45-day note, due Jan. 20, 1962	$ 875
P. J. King, 4 1/2%, 60-day note, due Mar. 2, 1962	396
Total	$1,271

Installment contracts receivable:

L. D. Harris (monthly payment $159)	$ 954

Other data. The installment contract receivable represents the unpaid balance of a 6%, one-year contract dated July 1, 1961. During the month of January, 1962, the following additional transactions took place.

Jan. 3. Received a 30-day, 5% note from A. B. Cole in full settlement of his account.

Jan. 10. Purchased merchandise in the amount of $1,800 from P. L. Larsen, giving a 30-day, 5% note dated today in payment thereof.

Jan. 14. M. E. White paid $300 on his account and gave a 60-day, 4% note to cover the balance.

Jan. 20. R. K. Rogers wrote that he would be unable to pay his note due today. He included a check to cover the interest due and a new 30-day, 6% note renewing the old note.

Jan. 27. Discounted the A. B. Cole note at the bank. The discount rate charged by the bank was 7%.

Jan. 30. Received the monthly payment on the L. D. Harris contract.

Instructions

a. Prepare journal entries (in general journal form) for January, including any adjusting entries relating to accrued interest at January 31.

b. Show how the accounts relating to notes receivable, accounts receivable, installment contracts receivable, and interest would appear on the balance sheet as of January 31. Show the actual balances.

10A-4. On February 1 Thurgood Chemical Company adopted a policy of requesting customers whose accounts become past due to substitute interest-bearing notes for
the open accounts. In many cases the company discounts with its bank the notes
receivable obtained from customers. The bank charges a 6% discount on such
transactions.

   The ledger accounts shown below reflect the note transactions, interest
expense, and interest earned during February and March. The company maintains
its accounts on the basis of a fiscal year ending March 31.

Notes Receivable

Feb.	6	C. K. Vern, 30-day	J2	600.00		Mar.	8	C. K. Vern	J4	600.00
	24	R. V. John, 60-day	CD1	1,400.00						
Mar.	12	A. M. Karl, 90-day	J6	3,000.00						
	18	B. E. Rule, 30-day, 5%	J7	900.00						

Interest Earned

						Mar.	8	C. K. Vern	J4	3.00
							8	R. V. John	CR1	2.69
							31		J10	9.50

Notes Receivable Discounted

						Mar.	8	R. V. John	CR1	1,400.00
							20	B. E. Rule	CR1	900.00

Notes Payable

						Feb.	18	G. L. Luke, 90-day, 5% (settle open account)	J3	2,100.00

Interest Expense

Mar.	20	B. E. Rule	CR1	.47						
	31		J10	11.96						

Instructions

a. Prepare (in general journal form) all entries made by the company in recording the information contained in the above ledger accounts. Assume that all notes bear interest at the rate of 6% unless otherwise indicated. Also assume that the accounts include the necessary adjustments for interest at March 31, the end of the company's fiscal year.

b. Show how the facts regarding all notes disclosed in your journal entries should be shown in the balance sheet.

c. With respect to the two notes receivable discounted, make the computations necessary to determine whether the bank has in fact charged interest at the agreed annual rate of 6%.

Group B

10B-1. The Fabian Company makes most of its sales on 30-day open account but requires customers who fail to pay invoices as agreed to substitute 6% promissory notes for their past-due accounts. Notes payable are also used by the Fabian Company in transactions with its suppliers and in obtaining bank credit. A partial list of recent transactions relating to notes receivable and payable is as follows:

Apr. 16.   Sold merchandise to G. H. Blair on account, $1,500. Terms 2/10, n/30.

Apr. 22.   Purchased merchandise on account from Conklin and Sons, $1,200. Issued a 45-day, 5% note in the amount of the purchase invoice.

May 16.   Received a 30-day, 6% note from G. H. Blair in settlement of his open account.

May 31.   Discounted the Blair note. The bank discount rate was 7%.

June 6.   Paid the Conklin note due today.

June 15.   Received notice from the bank that the Blair note was dishonored at maturity.

June 18.   Loaned $6,000 to J. D. Black on a 60-day, 6% note.

Instructions

a. Prepare in general journal form the entries necessary to record the above transactions.

b. Prepare any adjusting journal entries needed at June 30, the end of the company's fiscal year.

10B-2. The Phillips Company sells a large part of its total output to the Range Company and often accepts promissory notes in payment for merchandise. Listed below are a few of the transactions between the two companies relating to notes and interest.

Aug. 7.   Phillips Co. sold merchandise to the Range Company amounting to $24,000. The terms stated on the invoice were net cash.

Aug. 9.   Phillips Company accepted from the Range Company on a 6% discount basis a 60-day, 6% note dated August 3 in the amount of $18,000, which had been issued to the Range Company by one of its customers, A. Blaine. The balance of the receivable from the August 7 sale was collected in cash.

Oct. 2. A. Blaine dishonored his note and Phillips Company collected from the endorser, Range Company.

Nov. 15. Range Company collected $12,000 from Blaine; the balance of the receivable was written off as worthless.

Instructions. Prepare the necessary journal entries (in general journal form) to record the above transactions on the books of (*a*) the Phillips Company, and (*b*) the Range Company.

10B-3. The transactions listed below represent a small portion of the business transacted by the firm of Gage and Bunker, a partnership, during the three months ended December 31.

Oct. 7. Sale of merchandise to J. V. Bills on a one-year, 6%, installment contract for $1,800. Received a cash down payment of $300. Balance is payable in 12 equal monthly installments of $132.50 each. First installment due November 1.

Oct. 9. Received $500 cash and a 30-day, 5% note from E. D. Lynn in settlement of open account due today in the amount of $1,100.

Oct. 17. Purchased factory machinery from Edwards Company for $1,200, giving a 45-day, 4 1/2% note in settlement thereof.

Oct. 24. Discounted the Lynn note. The bank charge was 6%.

Nov. 1. Received first installment due on the Bills contract.

Nov. 15. Purchased merchandise from Horace Agee, $9,000.

Nov. 16. Issued 60-day note bearing interest at 6% in settlement of Agee account.

Nov. 25. Borrowed $18,000 from First Security Bank, giving a 60-day, 6% note as evidence of indebtedness. Interest was included in face of note.

Dec. 1. Paid the 45-day, 4 1/2% note due to Edwards Co. Received second installment payment on Bills contract.

Instructions

a. Prepare journal entries (in general journal form) to record the listed transactions for the three months ended December 31.

b. Prepare adjusting entries for interest at December 31.

c. Prepare a partial balance sheet reflecting the results of the above note transactions as of December 31.

10B-4. Merchant Company is short of working capital and attempts to minimize the funds tied up in receivables by discounting at the bank notes receivable obtained from customers. The bank charges a discount rate of 6% on these transactions. The company makes sales on 30-day open account, but any customer who does not pay in full within 30 days is asked to substitute an interest-bearing note for the past-due account. Despite the shortage of working capital, Merchant Company attempts to take advantage of all cash discounts offered by its suppliers.

A partial list of transactions of Merchant Company for the six months ended December 31 is given below.

July 3. Sale of merchandise to E. Edwards on account, $848, FOB destination. It was agreed that Edwards would submit a 60-day, 6% note upon receipt of the merchandise.

July 5. Received from Edwards a letter stating that he had paid $20 freight on the shipment of July 3. He enclosed a 60-day, 6% note dated July 5 for the net amount owed.

July 20. Purchased merchandise on account, $960, from Arvin Company, terms 2/10, n/30.

July 29. Discounted Edwards note at bank in order to take advantage of discount on Arvin Company purchase.

July 30. Paid Arvin Company account in full.

Aug. 8. Sold merchandise to D. E. Baker on account, $1,200, terms 2/10, n/30.

Aug. 24. Purchased merchandise on account, $1,500 from Smithers Company, terms 2/10, n/30.

Sept. 3. Received notice from the bank that Edwards had dishonored his note due today. Made payment to bank.

Sept. 7. Received a 30-day, 5% note from D. E. Baker in settlement of open account.

Sept. 23. Issued a 60-day, 5% note in settlement of account with Smithers Company.

Oct. 7. D. E. Baker was unable to pay his note due today. Received a new 60-day, 6% note in settlement of old note and interest.

Oct. 24. Received cash from E. Edwards in full settlement of his account due today, including interest at 6% from maturity date of note.

Nov. 10. Purchased equipment from Ace Equipment Co., $1,800. Issued 60-day, 6% note in settlement.

Nov. 22. Paid Smithers Co. note and accrued interest.

Dec. 6. Collected D. E. Baker note due today.

Dec. 16. Borrowed $10,000 from bank, giving a 45-day, 6% note as evidence of indebtedness. Interest was included in the face amount of the note.

Instructions

a. Prepare journal entries (in general journal form) to record the above listed transactions.

b. Prepare any necessary adjusting entries for interest at December 31.

c. Prepare a partial balance sheet at December 31 showing the notes and interest resulting from the above transactions.

11

Accounts receivable

One of the key factors underlying the tremendous expansion of the American economy has been the trend toward selling all types of goods and services on credit. The automobile industry has long been the classic example of the use of retail credit to achieve the efficiencies of large-scale output. Today, however, in nearly every field of retail trade it appears that sales and profits can be increased by granting customers the privilege of making payment a month or more after the date of sale. The sales of manufacturers and wholesalers are made on credit to an even greater extent than in retail trade.

The credit department

No business concern wants to sell on credit to a customer who will prove unable or unwilling to pay his account. Consequently, most business organizations include a credit department which must reach a decision on the credit worthiness of each prospective customer. The credit department investigates the debt-paying ability and credit record of each new customer and determines the maximum amount of credit to be extended.

If the prospective customer is a business concern as, for example, a retail store, the financial statements of the store will be obtained and analyzed to determine its financial condition and the trend of operating results. The credit department will always prefer to rely upon financial statements which have been audited by independent public accountants.

Regardless of whether the prospective customer is a business concern or an individual consumer, the investigation by the credit department will probably include the obtaining of a credit report from a local credit agency or from a national credit-rating institution such as Dun and Bradstreet. A credit agency compiles credit data on individuals and business concerns, and distributes this information to its clients. Most business concerns that make numerous sales on credit find it worthwhile to subscribe to the services of one or more credit agencies.

Losses from uncollectible accounts

A business that sells its goods or services on credit will inevitably find that some of its accounts receivable are uncollectible. Regardless of how thoroughly the credit department investigates prospective customers, some credit losses will arise as a result of errors in judgment or because of unanticipated developments. As a matter of fact, a limited amount of credit losses is evidence of a sound credit policy. If the credit department should become too cautious and conservative in rating customers, it might avoid all credit losses but, in so doing, lose profitable business by rejecting many acceptable accounts.

Reflecting credit losses in the financial statements

Assume that the Arlington Company began business on January 1, 1962, and made most of its sales on credit throughout the year. At December 31, the company prepared the following financial statements without giving any consideration to probable credit losses.

INCOME STATEMENT: NET INCOME OVERSTATED

THE ARLINGTON COMPANY
Income Statement
For the Year Ended December 31, 1962

Sales		$1,000,000
Cost of goods sold:		
Purchases	$800,000	
Less: inventory, Dec. 31	100,000	700,000
Gross profit on sales		$ 300,000
Expenses (other than credit losses)		250,000
Net income		$ 50,000

BALANCE SHEET: WHICH ITEMS ARE OVERSTATED?

THE ARLINGTON COMPANY
Balance Sheet
December 31, 1962

Assets

Cash	$ 75,000
Accounts receivable	200,000
Inventory	100,000
Other assets	175,000
	$550,000

Liabilities and Owner's Equity

Liabilities:	
Accounts payable	$250,000
Owner's equity:	
John Arlington, capital	300,000
	$550,000

Both of the financial statements are incomplete and misleading because of the failure to give consideration to the probable losses from uncollectible accounts. If a balance sheet is to reflect fairly the financial condition of a business, it should show for accounts receivable the net amount which will probably be collected. The amount which the Arlington Company will ultimately collect from the total receivables of $200,000 is almost certainly something less than $200,000.

Accountants often use the expression "realizable value" to describe the amount of cash expected to be produced through collection of receivables. Since the accounts receivable of the Arlington Company appear in the balance sheet at their face amount rather than at their realizable value, the balance sheet contains an overstatement of assets and a corresponding overstatement of the owner's equity.

The net income figure shown in the income statement is also in error, because one of the expenses of operating the business, bad debts expense, was omitted.

One of the most fundamental principles of accounting is that *revenue must be matched with the expenses incurred in securing that revenue.* The income statement of the Arlington Company lists as revenue all the credit sales made in 1962. It follows that *all* the expenses incurred in 1962 must also be included in that year's income statement.

Bad debt losses are caused by selling goods on credit to customers who fail to pay their bills; such losses, therefore, are incurred in the year in which the sales are made, even though the accounts are not determined to be uncollectible until the following year. An account receivable which originates from a sale on credit in the year 1962 and is determined to be uncollectible sometime during 1963 represents an expense of the year 1962. Unless each year's bad debt expense is estimated and reflected in the year-end balance sheet and income statement, both of these financial statements will be seriously deficient.

To illustrate the proper presentation of the Arlington Company's financial statements, let us assume that the management reviewed the status of its accounts receivable at December 31, 1962, giving particular study to accounts which were past due. This review indicated that the collectible portion of the $200,000 of accounts receivable amounted to approximately $190,000. In other words, management estimated that bad debt expense for the first year of operations amounted to $10,000. The following adjusting entry should be made at December 31, 1962:

PROVISION FOR BAD DEBTS

Bad Debts Expense 10,000
     Allowance for Bad Debts   10,000
To record the estimated bad debt expense for the year 1962

The Bad Debts Expense account created by the debit part of this entry is closed into the Income Summary account in the same manner as any other expense account. The Allowance for Bad Debts account which was credited in the above entry will appear in the balance sheet as a deduction from the face amount of the accounts receivable. It serves to reduce the accounts receivable to their realizable value in the balance sheet.

Revised statements for the Arlington Company, after giving effect to the estimate of bad debt losses, are as follows:

REVISED INCOME STATEMENT

THE ARLINGTON COMPANY
Income Statement
For the Year Ended December 31, 1962

Sales		$1,000,000
Cost of goods sold:		
Purchases	$800,000	
Less: inventory, Dec. 31	100,000	700,000
Gross profit on sales		$ 300,000
Expenses (other than credit losses)	$250,000	
Bad debts expense	10,000	260,000
Net income		$ 40,000

REVISED BALANCE SHEET

THE ARLINGTON COMPANY
Balance Sheet
December 31, 1962

Assets

Cash		$ 75,000
Accounts receivable	$200,000	
Less: allowance for bad debts	10,000	190,000
Inventory		100,000
Other assets		175,000
		$540,000

Liabilities and Owner's Equity

Liabilities:	
Accounts payable	$250,000
Owner's equity:	
John Arlington, capital	290,000
	$540,000

In comparing these corrected statements with those presented earlier on page 327, note that the recognition of bad debts expense has caused a decrease in the reported net income by $10,000, and a corresponding reduction in assets and in the owner's equity.

The allowance for bad debts account

Since every year's operations produce credit losses, it is often possible to estimate future bad debt losses rather closely on the basis of past experience. For example, if the bad debt losses of a particular company have been equal to approximately 1% of sales for each of the last 10 years, we may reasonably predict that credit losses will amount to about 1% of sales in the current year. Remember, however, that each individual account receivable is believed to be collectible at the time of making the sale to the customer. It is only when we consider the accounts receivable ledger in its entirety and in the light of past experience that we recognize that some accounts in the group will inevitably prove to be worthless.

There is no way of telling in advance which accounts will be collected and which ones will prove to be worthless. It is therefore not possible to credit the account of any particular customer to reflect our over-all estimate of the year's credit losses. Neither is it possible to credit the accounts receivable control account in the general ledger. If the accounts receivable controlling account were to be credited with the estimated amount of bad debts, this account would no longer be in balance with the total of the numerous customers' accounts in the subsidiary ledger. The only practicable alternative, therefore, is to credit a separate account called Allowance for Bad Debts with the amount estimated to be uncollectible. The credit balance of the Allowance for Bad Debts account is shown on the balance sheet as a deduction from the total amount of accounts receivable. The resulting net figure is the estimated realizable value of the accounts receivable.

In the preceding chapters accounts have repeatedly been classified into five groups: (1) assets, (2) liabilities, (3) owner's equity, (4) revenue, and (5) expense. In which of these five groups of accounts does the Allowance for Bad Debts account belong? The answer is indicated by the position of the Allowance for Bad Debts on the balance sheet. It appears among the assets and is used to reduce an asset (Accounts Receivable) from a gross value to a net realizable value. From the standpoint of account classification, the Allowance for Bad Debts is, therefore, included in the asset category.

The Allowance for Bad Debts account is sometimes described as a *contra* account, an *offset* account, an *asset reduction* account, a *negative asset* account, and most frequently of all, a *valuation* account. All of these terms are derived from the fact that the Allowance for Bad Debts is an account with a credit balance, which is offset against an asset account to produce the proper balance sheet value for an asset.

An alternative title for the Allowance for Bad Debts account is Reserve for Bad Debts. Other variations in terminology include Allowance for Uncollectible Accounts and Allowance for Collection Losses.

The term *reserve* has been greatly overworked by accountants. It has been used not only to describe deductions from assets but also to indicate liabilities of estimated amount, and to segregate certain categories of the owner's equity in balance sheets of corporations. In recognition of the confusion surrounding this term, the American Institute of Certified Public Accountants has recommended discontinuance of the use of *reserve* to describe deductions from asset accounts. Although Allowance for Bad Debts is being used more and more, the title of Reserve for Bad Debts is still frequently encountered.

Other valuation accounts

The Allowance for Bad Debts account has a good deal in common with the Allowance for Depreciation account, which appears on the balance sheet as a deduction from fixed asset accounts such as buildings or office equipment. Both the Allowance for Bad Debts and the Allowance for Depreciation are created by adjusting entries and are based on estimates rather than on precisely determined amounts. In each case the debit side of the adjusting entry affects an expense account (Bad Debts Expense or Depreciation Expense).

In some respects, however, these two valuation accounts perform quite different functions. The Allowance for Bad Debts serves to reduce the accounts receivable to net realizable value. The Allowance for Depreciation is *not* intended to reduce a fixed asset to realizable value but merely to show what portion of the original cost of the fixed asset has expired and has been recorded as expense. Realizable value is not a significant concept in accounting for fixed assets, since these properties are not intended to be sold but are to be used in the operation of the business.

Entries for bad debts

Writing off an uncollectible account receivable. Whenever an account receivable from a customer is determined to be uncollectible, it no longer qualifies as an asset and should immediately be written off the books. To write off an account receivable is to reduce the balance of the customer's account to zero. The journal entry to accomplish this consists of a credit to the accounts receivable control account in the general ledger and to the customer's account in the subsidiary ledger, and an offsetting debit to the Allowance for Bad Debts.

Referring again to the example of the Arlington Company as shown on page 327, the ledger accounts were as follows after the adjusting entry for estimated bad debts had been made on December 31, 1962.

Accounts receivable	**$200,000**
Less: allowance for bad debts	**10,000**

Next let us assume that on January 27, 1963, a customer by the name of William Benton became bankrupt and the account receivable from him in the amount of $1,000 was determined to be worthless. The following entry should be made by the Arlington Company:

> *Allowance for Bad Debts* *1,000*
>   *Accounts Receivable, William Benton* *1,000*
> *To write off the receivable as uncollectible.*

The important thing to notice in this entry is that the debit is made to the Allowance for Bad Debts and *not* to the Bad Debts Expense account. Estimated losses are charged to the Bad Debts Expense account at the end of each accounting period. When a particular account receivable is later ascertained to be worthless and is written off, this action does not represent an additional loss but merely confirms our previous estimate of the loss. If the Bad Debts Expense account were first charged with estimated credit losses and then later charged with proved credit losses, we would be guilty of double-counting of bad debt expense.

After the entry writing off William Benton's account has been posted, the Accounts Receivable control account and the Allowance for Bad Debts account appear as follows:

Accounts Receivable			
1962 *Dec. 31*	*200,000*	*1963* *Jan. 27*	*1,000*

Allowance for Bad Debts			
1963 *Jan. 27*	*1,000*	*1962* *Dec. 31*	*10,000*

Note that the *net* amount of the accounts receivable was unchanged by writing off William Benton's account against the allowance for bad debts.

Before the Write-off		*After the Write-off*	
Accounts receivable	*$200,000*	*Accounts receivable*	*$199,000*
Less: allowance for bad		*Less: allowance for bad*	
debts	*10,000*	*debts*	*9,000*
Net value of receivables	*$190,000*	*Net value of receivables*	*$190,000*

The fact that writing off an uncollectible account against the allowance for bad debts does not change the net carrying value of accounts receivable shows that no loss is entered in the books when an account is written off. The loss had already been entered in the Bad Debts Expense account on the basis of an estimate made at the close of the preceding accounting period. This example bears out the point stressed earlier in the chapter: credit losses belong in the period in which the sale is made, not in a later period in which the account is discovered to be uncollectible.

Write-offs seldom agree with previous estimates. The total amount of accounts receivable written off in a given year will seldom, if ever, be exactly equal to the estimated amount previously credited to the Allowance for Bad Debts account.

If the amounts written off as uncollectible turn out to be less than the estimated amount, the Allowance for Bad Debts account will continue to show a credit balance. If the amounts written off as uncollectible are greater than the estimated amount, the Allowance for Bad Debts account will acquire a debit balance.

Continuing the illustration of the Arlington Company, let us assume that the accounts receivable written off as uncollectible during 1963 (including the William Benton account) totaled $10,600. Since the Allowance for Bad Debts account had a credit balance of only $10,000 at the beginning of the year, it would have acquired a debit balance of $600 by the end of 1963.

On December 31, 1963, the management of the Arlington Company would again review its accounts receivable and make an estimate of the uncollectible portion. Let us assume that at December 31, 1963, the accounts receivable total $300,000 and management estimates that there are $15,000 of probable collection losses contained therein. Since the Allowance for Bad Debts presently has a debit balance of $600, it will be necessary to make the adjusting entry in the amount of $15,600 in order to establish the desired credit balance of $15,000 in the valuation account.

Recovery of an account previously written off. The write-off of an account receivable is made whenever management decides that a given account is uncollectible. Sometimes there is dramatic evidence of noncollectibility, such as bankruptcy of the customer, but usually an account is written off because it is long past due and collection is unlikely.

Occasionally an account which has been written off as worthless will later be collected in full or in part. Such collections are often referred to as *recoveries* of bad debts. Collection of an account previously written off is evidence that the write-off was an error; the write-off entry should therefore be reversed. Reversing the write-off of a customer's account will also make the subsidiary ledger card a complete and more useful record. When a customer pays an account previously considered uncollectible, he reestablishes his credit standing to some extent. If, at a later date, the customer again seeks to buy goods on credit, a complete history of past dealings with him, including the write-off and subsequent recovery, will be available by referring to the subsidiary ledger card.

Let us assume, for example, that a past-due account receivable in the amount of $400 from J. B. Barker was written off by the following entry:

BARKER
ACCOUNT
CONSIDERED
UNCOL-
LECTIBLE

> *Allowance for Bad Debts* *400*
>   *Accounts Receivable, J. B. Barker* *400*
> *To write off the receivable as uncollectible.*

At some later date the customer, J. B. Barker, pays his account in full. The reversing entry to restore Barker's account will be:

BARKER
ACCOUNT
REINSTATED

> *Accounts Receivable, J. B. Barker* *400*
>   *Allowance for Bad Debts* *400*
> *To reverse the entry writing off Barker's account.*

A separate entry will be made in the cash receipts book to record the collection from Barker. This entry will debit Cash and credit Accounts Receivable.

If only a partial collection is made of an account previously written off, a reversing entry should generally be made for the amount recovered. If eventual collection of the remaining amount is considered likely, the entire receivable may be restored to the books in the same manner as when a full recovery is made.

Estimating bad debts expense

Before the books are closed and financial statements are prepared at the end of the accounting period, an estimate of bad debts expense must be made. This estimate will usually be based upon past experience, perhaps modified in accordance with current business conditions. In a period of increasing business activity and high employment, there is obviously less risk of collection losses than in a period of declining activity and spreading unemployment.

Since the allowance for bad debts is necessarily an estimate and not a precise calculation, the factor of personal judgment may play a considerable part in determining the size of this valuation account. There is a fairly wide range of reasonableness within which the amount may be set. Most businessmen intend that the allowance shall be adequate to cover probable losses. The term *adequate,* when used in this context, suggests an amount somewhat larger than the minimum probable loss.

Conservatism as a factor in valuing accounts receivable. The larger the allowance established for bad debts, the lower the net valuation of accounts receivable will be. Some accountants and some businessmen always favor the most conservative valuation of assets that logically can be supported. Conservatism in the preparation of a balance sheet implies a tendency to state assets at their minimum values rather than to establish values in a purely objective manner. From a theoretical point of view, the doctrine of balance sheet conservatism is difficult to support, but from the viewpoint of bankers and others who use financial statements as a basis for granting loans, conservatism in valuing assets has long been regarded as a desirable policy.

Assume that the balance sheet of Company A presents optimistic, exaggerated values for the assets owned. Assume also that this "unconservative" balance sheet is submitted to a banker in support of an application for a loan. The banker studies the balance sheet and makes a loan to Company A in reliance upon the values listed. Later the banker finds it impossible to collect the loan and also finds that the assets upon which he had based the loan were greatly overstated in the balance sheet. The banker will undoubtedly consider the overly optimistic character of the balance sheet as partially responsible for his loss. Experiences of this type have led bankers as a group to stress the desirability of conservatism in the valuation of assets.

In considering the merits of balance sheet conservatism, it is important to recognize that the income statement is also affected by the estimates made of probable bad debt losses. The act of providing a relatively large allowance for bad debts involves a correspondingly heavy charge to bad debts expense. Setting asset values at a minimum in the balance sheet has the related effect of stating the current year's net income at a minimum amount. Further consideration will be given to the doctrine of balance sheet conservatism in the chapters dealing with the valuation of inventories and the depreciation of fixed assets.

Two methods of estimating bad debts expense

The provision for bad debts is an estimate of losses to be sustained. Two alternative approaches are widely used in making the annual estimate for bad debts. One method consists of adjusting the valuation account to a new balance equal to the estimated uncollectible portion of the existing accounts receivable. This method is referred to as the *balance sheet approach* and rests on an aging of the accounts receivable. The adjusting entry takes into consideration the existing balance in the Allowance for Bad Debts account.

The alternative method requires an adjusting entry computed as a percentage of the year's net sales. This *percentage of sales method* emphasizes the expense side of the adjustment and leaves out of consideration any existing balance in the valuation account. If any substantial balance should accumulate in the allowance account, however, a change in the percentage figure being applied to sales might be appropriate. These two methods are explained below.

Aging the accounts receivable. One of the most common approaches to estimating bad debt losses is to analyze the individual accounts receivable on hand at the balance sheet date. In making this analysis, the age of each account is a key factor. A past-due account is always viewed with some suspicion. The fact that an account is past due suggests that the customer is either unable or unwilling to pay. The analysis of accounts by age is known as aging the accounts, as illustrated by the schedule given below.

IF YOU WERE CREDIT MAN- AGER . . . ?

			1–30 days past due	*31–60 days past due*	*61–90 days past due*	*Over 90 days past due*
Customer	*Total*	*Not yet due*				
A. B. Adams ..	$ 500	$ 500				
B. L. Baker ...	150			$ 150		
R. D. Carl	800	800				
H. V. Davis ...	900				$ 800	$ 100
R. M. Evans ..	400	400				
Others	32,250	16,300	$10,000	4,200	200	1,550
	$35,000	$18,000	$10,000	$4,350	$1,000	$1,650
Per cent	100	51	29	12	3	5

Analysis of Accounts Receivable by Age, December 31, 19___

This analysis of accounts receivable gives management a useful picture of the status of collections and the probabilities of credit losses. Almost half of the total accounts receivable are past due. The question "How long past due?" is pertinent, and is answered by the bottom line of the aging analysis. About 29% of the total receivables are past due from 1 to 30 days; another 12% are past due from 31 to 60 days; about 3% are past due from 61 to 90 days; and 5% of the total receivables consist of accounts past due more than three months. If an analysis of this type is prepared at the end of each month, management will be continuously informed of the trend of collections and can take appropriate action to ease or tighten credit policy. Moreover, a yardstick is available to measure the effectiveness of the persons responsible for collection activities.

The further past due an account receivable becomes, the greater the likelihood that it will not be collected in full. In recognition of this principle, the analysis of receivables by age groups can be used as a stepping-stone in determining the proper amount to add to the Allowance for Bad Debts. To make this determination it is desirable to estimate the percentage of probable loss for each age group of accounts receivable. This percentage, when applied to the dollar amount in each age group, gives a probable bad debt loss for each group. By adding together the probable bad debt losses for all the age groups, the required balance in the Allowance for Bad Debts is determined. The following schedule lists the group totals from the preceding illustration and shows how the total probable bad debt loss is computed.

ESTIMATE OF
PROBABLE
BAD DEBT
LOSS

Accounts Receivable by Age Groups			
	Amount	Per cent considered uncollectible	Allowance for bad debts
Not yet due	$18,000	1	$ 180
1–30 days past due	10,000	3	300
31–60 days past due	4,350	10	435
61–90 days past due	1,000	20	200
Over 90 days past due	1,650	50	825
	$35,000		$1,940

This summary indicates that an allowance for bad debts of $1,940 is required. Before making the adjusting entry, it is necessary to consider the existing balance in the allowance account. If the allowance for bad debts presently has a credit balance of, say, $500, the adjusting entry should be for $1,440 in order to bring the account up to the estimated probable loss of $1,940.

ENTRY TO
INCREASE
ALLOWANCE
FOR BAD
DEBTS

Bad Debts Expense	1,440	
Allowance for Bad Debts		1,440
To increase the valuation account to the estimated probable loss of $1,940, computed as follows:		
Present credit balance of account	500	
Current provision for bad debts	1,440	
New balance in valuation account	1,940	

On the other hand, if the Allowance for Bad Debts account contained a debit balance of $500 before adjustment, the adjusting entry would be made in the amount of $2,440 ($1,940 + $500) in order to create the desired credit balance of $1,940.

Estimating bad debts as a percentage of net sales. An alternative approach of providing for bad debts preferred by some companies consists of computing the charge to bad debts expense as a percentage of the net sales for the year. This method may be regarded as the *income statement approach* to estimating bad debts. The question to be answered is not "How large a valuation allowance is needed to show our receivables at realizable value?" Instead, the question is stated as "How much bad debt expense is associated with this year's volume of sales?"

As an example, assume that during the last several years bad debt losses have consistently averaged 1% of net sales (sales minus returns and allowances and sales discounts). At the end of the current year, before adjusting entries are made, the following account balances appear in the ledger:

Sales		$1,060,000
Sales Returns and Allowances	$40,000	
Discount on Sales	20,000	
Allowance for Bad Debts		1,500

The net sales of the current year amount to $1,000,000; 1% of this amount is $10,000. The existing balance in the Allowance for Bad Debts account should be ignored because the percentage of net sales method stresses the relationship between bad debts expense and net sales rather than the current valuation of receivables at the balance sheet date. The entry is:

BAD DEBT
PROVISION
BASED ON
PERCENTAGE
OF NET
SALES

Bad Debts Expense	10,000	
Allowance for Bad Debts		10,000
To record bad debt expense of 1% of the year's		
sales (0.01 × $1,000,000).		

If a concern makes both cash sales and credit sales, it may be desirable to exclude the cash sales from consideration and to compute the percentage relationship of bad debts expense to credit sales only.

Direct charge-off method of recognizing credit losses. Instead of making adjusting entries to record bad debts expense on the basis of estimates, some concerns merely charge uncollectible accounts to bad debt expense at the time the accounts are determind to be uncollectible. This method makes no attempt to match revenue and related expenses. Bad debt expense is recorded in the period in which accounts are deter-mined to be worthless rather than in the period in which the sales were made.

To illustrate the direct charge-off (or direct write-off) method, assume that a long-past-due account receivable for $100 from Andrew Scott is determined to be worthless. The following entry would be made:

DIRECT
CHARGE-OFF
ENTRY

Bad Debt Expense	100	
Accounts Receivable, Andrew Scott		100
To write off an uncollectible account.		

When the direct charge-off method is in use, the accounts receivable will be listed in the balance sheet at their gross amount, and no valuation allowance account will be used. The accounts are, therefore, not stated at their probable realizable value.

If an account which has been written off to Bad Debt Expense is subsequently collected, the entry to record the recovery consists of a debit to Accounts Receivable and a credit to a revenue account, Bad Debts Recovered. Assume, for example, that Andrew Scott, whose account was written off as worthless, should later pay in full. His account would be reinstated by the following entry:

REINSTATE-
MENT
UNDER
DIRECT
CHARGE-OFF
METHOD

> *Accounts Receivable, Andrew Scott* *100*
>   *Bad Debts Recovered* *100*
> *Recovered an account previously charged off.*

An entry would then be made in the cash receipts journal debiting Cash for $100 and crediting Accounts Receivable, Andrew Scott.

It is sometimes argued in behalf of the direct charge-off method that considerable time is saved by not aging the accounts receivable and not preparing estimates of bad debt expense. However, many business concerns find it worthwhile to age the accounts receivable as frequently as once a month in order to be currently informed of the trend of collections. If management is immediately aware of any deterioration in the receivables through a slowing down of collections, it may be able to take aggressive action which will prevent large credit losses.

In the determination of taxable income under Federal income tax regulations, both the direct charge-off method and the allowance method of estimating bad debt expense are acceptable. Whichever method is used must be followed consistently from year to year.

Valuation allowances for sales returns and for cash discounts

In certain lines of business, such as the department store field, customers are prone to return for credit a considerable portion of their purchases. The accounts receivable at the balance sheet date might, therefore, be regarded as consisting of three portions: (1) the portion that will be collected; (2) the portion that will prove to be uncollectible; and (3) the portion that will be wiped out when customers return merchandise for credit to their accounts. To achieve the objective of showing accounts receivable in the balance sheet at their realizable value, it might be desirable to create a valuation allowance for sales returns as well as an allowance for bad debts.

In manufacturing and wholesaling concerns which offer cash discounts to their customers for payment within a specified time period, another type of valuation allowance theoretically may be desirable in reducing accounts receivable to their realizable value. This valuation account, sometimes called Allowance for Cash Discounts, is based on the premise that cash collections will amount to less than the recorded amount of accounts receivable because many customers will make payment in time to qualify for the cash discount.

Allowances for sales returns and allowances for cash discounts, although theoretically valid, are very seldom encountered in practice. Among the reasons why such valuation accounts have not been widely used are the difficulty of making accurate estimates, the relatively small amounts involved, and the nonacceptance of such adjustments for income tax purposes.

Classification of accounts receivable in the balance sheet

Accounts receivable from customers will ordinarily be collected within a few months from the date of sale; they are therefore listed among the current assets on the balance sheet. Receivables may also arise from miscellaneous transactions other than the sale of goods and services. These miscellaneous receivables, such as advances to officers and employees, and claims against insurance companies for losses sustained, should be listed separately on the balance sheet and should not be merged with trade accounts receivable. If an account receivable from an officer or employee originates as a favor to the officer or employee, efforts at collection may await the convenience of the debtor. Consequently, it is customary to exclude receivables of this type from the current asset category. An exception to this rule is found in the case of retail stores, which may sell merchandise to employees in accordance with regular credit policy and may enforce collection of employee accounts on the same basis as for other customers. Under these circumstances the receivables from employees may properly be intermingled with customers' accounts.

When miscellaneous receivables arising from advances to officers and employees, claims against insurance companies, and other transactions apart from the sale of goods or services are excluded from the current asset section of the balance, they are usually placed under the caption of Other Assets.

Credit balances in accounts receivable

Customers' accounts in the accounts receivable subsidiary ledger normally have debit balances, but occasionally a customer's account will acquire a credit balance. This may occur because of overpayment, payment in advance, or the return of merchandise. Any credit balances in the accounts receivable subsidiary ledger should be written in red or be accompanied by the notation "Cr" to distinguish them from accounts with normal debit balances. Such credit balances are sometimes referred to as "opposite balances" or "red balances."

Suppose that the Accounts Receivable controlling account in the general ledger has a debit balance of $9,000, representing the following individual accounts with customers in the subsidiary ledger:

49 accounts with debit balance	*$10,000*
1 account with a credit balance	*1,000*
Net debit balance of 50 customers' accounts	*$ 9,000*

The amount which should appear as accounts receivable in the balance sheet is not the $9,000 balance of the controlling account, but the $10,000 total of the accounts with debit balances. The account with the $1,000 credit balance is a liability and should be shown as such rather than being concealed as an offset against asset accounts. The balance sheet presentation should be as follows:

Current assets:
  Accounts receivable *10,000*

Current liabilities:
  Credit balances in customers'
    accounts *1,000*

Similar treatment is required if the accounts payable subsidiary ledger is found to contain any accounts with debit balances. The amount to appear as a liability in the balance sheet will not be the balance of the Accounts Payable controlling account. Instead, the balance sheet should show as a liability the total of the accounts payable accounts having credit balances, and as an asset the total of the accounts payable having debit balances. For example:

Current assets:
  Debit balances in vendors'
    accounts *500*

Current liabilities:
  Accounts payable *22,000*

One of the basic rules in preparing financial statements is that assets and liabilities should be shown in their gross amounts rather than being netted against each other.

QUESTIONS

1. At the end of its first year in business the Globe Company had accounts receivable totaling $72,600. After careful analysis of the individual accounts, the credit manager estimated that $70,500 would ultimately be collected. Give the journal entry indicated by this estimate.

2. In February of its second year of operations, the Globe Company learned of the bankruptcy of a customer, Raybar Company, which owed Globe $900. Nothing could be collected. Give the journal entry to recognize the uncollectibility of the receivable from Raybar.

3. Suggest a procedure by which management could be informed each month of the status of collections and the over-all quality of the accounts receivable on hand.

4. In making the annual adjusting entry for bad debts, a company may utilize a *balance sheet approach* to making the estimate or may use an *income statement approach.* Explain these two alternative approaches.

5. What is the *charge-off method* of handling credit losses? What is its principal shortcoming?

6. Rogers Manufacturing Company has accounts receivable from 100 customers; the controlling account shows a debit balance of $200,000. The subsidiary ledger shows that 99 customers' accounts have debit balances and 1 has a credit balance of $10,000. How should these facts be shown in the balance sheet? Give the reason for the treatment you recommend.

7. The Hale Company, which has accounts receivable of $142,000 and an allowance for bad debts of $3,300, decides to write off as worthless a past-due account receivable for $1,200 from J. B. Lund. What effect will the write-off have upon total current assets? Upon net income for the period? Explain.

PROBLEMS

Group A

11A-1. For the past three years, the Fox Company, owned by George Fox, has been engaged in selling paper novelty goods to retail stores. During this entire period the company has followed the policy of providing for bad debt expense at the rate of 1/2 of 1% of net sales. However, it appears that this provision has been inadequate, because the Allowance for Bad Debts account has a debit balance of $1,172.55 at December 31 prior to making the annual provision for any bad debts. Fox has therefore decided to change the method of estimating bad debt expense and to rely upon an analysis of the age and character of the accounts receivable on the books at the end of each accounting period.

At December 31, the accounts receivable totaled $74,360; this total amount included past-due accounts in the amount of $14,270. None of these past-due accounts was considered hopeless; all accounts regarded as worthless had been written off the books as rapidly as they were determined to be uncollectible. These write-offs had totaled $2,172.55 during the year. After careful investigation of the past-due accounts at December 31, George Fox decided that the probable loss contained therein was 10%, and that in addition he should anticipate a loss of 1% of the current accounts receivable.

Instructions
a. Compute the probable bad debt loss contained in the accounts receivable on the books at December 31, based on the analysis by the owner.

b. Prepare the journal entry necessary to carry out the change in company policy with respect to providing for bad debts expense.

11A-2. The Philip Porter Co. sells novelty goods to customers in 11 states. The terms of sale call for immediate payment upon receipt of invoice.

The company determines its allowance for bad debts at December 31 by aging the accounts receivable and applying the percentages listed in the table below. (Receivables arising from sales billed in December are to be included in the 1–30 days bracket.)

Days	Probable loss, %
1–30	0.5
31–60	5
61–90	10
91–120	25
121–180	50
Over 180	75

Other data. At December 31, the accounts receivable ledger included the nine accounts given below which had been slow in making payments. In addition to these nine slow accounts, there were accounts with other customers totaling $96,450 arising from sales in December.

Accounts Receivable Subsidiary Ledger

Date			Posting reference	Debit	Credit	Balance
		John Anderson				
Jan.	6		S 10	890		890
Feb.	4		S 12	180		1,070
	16		CR 14		890	180
Mar.	8		CR 17		180	000
July	6		S 24	643		643
Aug.	2		CR 30		243	400
Sept.	1		S 29	100		500
	10		CR 32		200	300
		Richard Edwards				
Apr.	6		S 17	362		362
	8		S 17	194		556
May	10		CR 22		200	356
	12	Return on Apr. 6 sale	J 8		26	330
June	3		S 22	218		548
July	6		CR 27		330	218
Aug.	4		S 27	464		682
Nov.	18		CR 37		218	464

Accounts Receivable Subsidiary Ledger

Date			Posting reference	Debit	Credit	Balance
		John Moreland				
Nov.	24		S 37	1,014		1,014
	26		S 37	1,086		2,100
	29		S 37	943		3,043
Dec.	6		CR 40		1,086	1,957
	11		S 38	646		2,603
	14		S 38	1,326		3,929
	21		CR 40		943	2,986
	29		S 38	418		3,404

Date			Posting reference	Debit	Credit	Balance
		Richard Post				
July	5		S 24	984		984
	27		CR 27		400	584
Aug.	6		S 27	318		902
	18		CR 30		300	602
Sept.	8		S 29	287		889
	15		CR 32		184	705
Oct.	8		S 32	1,064		1,769
	14		CR 34		100	1,669
Nov.	18		S 34	464		2,133
Dec.	1		CR 40		318	1,815
	10		S 38	1,114		2,929
	14		S 38	412		3,341
	15		CR 40		1,064	2,277
	26		S 38	894		3,171
	31		CR 40		412	2,759

Date			Posting reference	Debit	Credit	Balance
		William Thompson				
Oct.	8		S 32	843		843
	11		S 32	194		1,037
	17	Return on sale of Oct. 8	J 12		31	1,006
Nov.	1		CR 37		812	194
	13		S 34	263		457
Dec.	8		S 38	715		1,172

Accounts Receivable Subsidiary Ledger

Date			Posting reference	Debit	Credit	Balance
		Gregory Tyler				
Feb.	3		S 12	812		812
Mar.	1		CR 17		812	000
July	7		S 24	421		421
	16	Note	J 6		321	100
Sept.	1		S 27	634		734
	10		CR 30		100	634
		Max Vaughn				
Aug.	11		S 27	362		362
	26		CR 30		362	000
Oct.	26		S 32	726		726
Nov.	8		S 34	463		1,189
Dec.	6		CR 40		400	789
	23		S 38	218		1,007
		Phillip Walker				
Dec.	8		S 38	171		171
	16		S 38	374		545
	21		CR 40		171	374
		John Warner				
Apr.	10		S 17	646		646
	26	Return	J 3		141	505
	30		S 17	286		791
May	3		CR 22		500	291
	3	Adjustment	J 3		5	286
June	6		S 22	861		1,147
	10		CR 25		286	861
July	8		S 24	431		1,292
	10		S 26	462		1,754
	17		CR 27		861	893

Accounts Receivable Subsidiary Ledger

Date		Posting reference	Debit	Credit	Balance
Aug.	2	CR 30		462	431
Sept.	8	S 29	261		692
Oct.	4	S 32	841		1,533
Nov.	2	S 34	118		1,651
	10	CR 37		841	810
Dec.	3	CR 40		118	692
	26	S 38	206		898

Instructions

a. Prepare an aging schedule of accounts receivable at December 31.

b. Compute the allowance for bad debts.

c. Prepare journal entries to provide for bad debts, assuming:

(1) A zero balance in the Allowance for Bad Debts account.

(2) A credit balance of $460 in the Allowance for Bad Debts account.

11A-3. Michael Brick, owner of the Brick Building Co., estimates that his company has expense resulting from bad debts of 1/2 of 1% of net sales.

At December 31, 1962, the Allowance for Bad Debts account had a balance before adjustments of $41,218. Net sales for 1962 had been $4,316,800.

During 1963 the following transactions took place:

Jan. 11. Notice was received that John White Co. was in bankruptcy and no payment could be expected. Invoice No. 13800 was due from White for $13,872.

Mar. 6. James & London Co. remitted $1,970. This account had been considered worthless and written off in a prior year.

Apr. 7. The Amazon Co. paid $41,400, applicable to its account totaling $44,000. The Amazon Company had gone out of business and no further collection was considered possible.

June 4. John Barry, a customer, notified Brick Building Co. that his partner had absconded with all the company funds. Barry stated that he had been forced to quit business and would not be able to pay the $1,768 owed. Investigation confirmed these statements.

Aug. 8. Wrote off as uncollectible the account of H. O. Troll for $2,627.

Nov. 11. Received $326 from John Barry as a proportionate share of money recovered from Barry's partner.

Dec. 31. Wrote off as uncollectible various accounts in the amount of $26,871.

Dec. 31. Net sales for the year were $3,841,000.

Instructions

a. Prepare the journal entry to record the provision for bad debt expense at December 31, 1962; the closing entry at December 31, 1962; the transaction entries for the year 1963; the adjusting entry for bad debt expense at December

31, 1963; and the closing entry at this date. All journal entries are to be made in general journal form.

b. Open general ledger accounts for Bad Debts Expense and for the Allowance for Bad Debts. Post the entries called for in (*a*) to these accounts.

c. State the amount of bad debts expense which should appear in the 1963 income statement.

11A-4. During January and early February, the Mason Sales Company had the transactions shown below relating to accounts receivable. All sales were on account and carried terms of 2/10, n/30.

Jan. 2.   Sold goods to Fred Powers for $287, invoice No. 2610.

Jan. 3.   Sold goods to Jones & Walker for $2,781, invoice No. 2611.

Jan. 4.   Sold goods to Warner Co. for $3,640, invoice No. 2612.

Jan. 6.   Issued credit memorandum No. 364 for $180 to Jones & Walker for goods returned.

Jan. 8.   Received check for $281.26 from Fred Powers in payment of invoice No. 2610.

Jan. 10.   Sold goods to Moore Trading Co. for $1,000, invoice No. 2613.

Jan. 12.   Received $200 from Moore Trading Co., as partial payment for invoice No. 2613.

Jan. 13.   Received from Jones & Walker the balance due on account.

Jan. 14.   Sold goods to Warner Co. for $2,848, invoice No. 2614.

Jan. 16.   Received $3,600 from the Warner Co. The check was marked "in full payment of invoice 2612." A note attached to the check stated "A little late with this payment, so we're not claiming the full discount." Since the Warner Company had been a good customer, Mason decided to allow the discount indicated by the remittance.

Jan. 17.   Sold goods to Roger Midland for $1,431, invoice No. 2615.

Jan. 22.   Sold goods to Carl Booth for $98, invoice No. 2616.

Jan. 23.   Received $1,000 from the Moore Trading Co. in payment of invoice No. 2613. The Moore Trading Co. was notified of the overpayment and decided to let it apply to their order for February.

Jan. 24.   Sold goods to the Warner Co. for $6,469, invoice No. 2617.

Jan. 25.   Sold goods to Jack Paris for $896, invoice No. 2618.

Jan. 27.   Received check for $878.08 from Jack Paris.

Jan. 29.   Received payment from Warner Co., invoice No. 2614.

Jan. 29.   Sold goods to Roy Anderson for $1,666, invoice No. 2619.

Jan. 31.   John Mason estimated that 2% of all charge sales (less sales returns and sales discounts) will prove uncollectible.

Feb. 4.   The Mason Sales Company received notice that Carl Booth had become bankrupt. Invoice No. 2616 is therefore regarded as uncollectible.

Instructions

a. Prepare entries in general journal form to record the above transactions.

b. Post all entries to the accounts receivable subsidiary ledger accounts. Posting to general ledger accounts is not required.

c. Prepare a schedule of accounts receivable at January 31.

d. Prepare a partial balance sheet at January 31 showing proper presentation of customers' accounts.

Group B

11B-1. At December 31, 1961, the balance sheet of the Dixie Company included accounts receivable of $265,300 and an allowance for bad debts of $7,600. The company's sales volume in 1962 reached a new high of $2,105,000, and cash collections from customers amounted to $2,025,640. Among these collections was the recovery in full of a $3,600 receivable from James Walburn, a customer whose account had been written off as worthless late in 1961. During 1962 it was necessary to write off as uncollectible customers' accounts totaling $8,325.

On December 1, 1962, the Dixie Company sold for $150,000 a tract of land acquired as a building site several years earlier at a cost of $120,000. The land was now considered unsuitable as a building site. Terms of sale were $50,000 cash and a 6%, six-month note for $100,000. The buyer was a large corporation and the note was regarded as fully collectible.

At December 31, 1962, the accounts receivable included $46,210 of past-due accounts. After careful study of all past-due accounts, the management estimated that the probable loss contained therein was 20%, and that in addition, 2% of the current accounts receivable might prove uncollectible.

Instructions

a. Prepare journal entries, in general journal form, for all 1962 transactions relating to accounts and notes receivable.

b. Prepare the necessary adjusting entries at December 31, 1962.

c. What amount should appear in the income statement for 1962 as bad debt expense?

d. Prepare a partial balance sheet at December 31, 1962, showing the accounts indicated above.

11B-2. At December 31, Donald Anthony, the president of the Anthony Company, noticed that the heavy write-offs of accounts receivable had created a debit balance in the Allowance for Bad Debts account. In past years the provision for bad debts had been made in a rather arbitrary manner. Anthony decided to have his accountant analyze the company's credit losses over the preceding five years and to prepare a schedule of probable losses based on an aging of the accounts receivable. The following schedule was prepared.

Age of receivables	Estimated loss, %
Not yet due	1
1–30 days past due	5
31–60 days past due	10
61–90 days past due	25
91–180 days past due	40
Over 180 days past due	60

Other data. The credit policy of the Anthony Company provides that all sales invoices are due on the first of the month following the invoice date, except that sales made on or after the twenty-fifth of each month are not due until the first day of the second month from the invoice date. For example, a sales invoice dated September 24 would be due October 1, but a sales invoice dated September 25 would not be considered due until November 1.

The accounts receivable subsidiary ledger is shown below:

Accounts Receivable Subsidiary Ledger

Date			Debit	Credit	Balance
		Baker Sales Co.			
Jan.	6		871		871
	18			871	000
Feb.	11		1,213		1,213
Mar.	7		461		1,674
Apr.	9			1,213	461
May	7			461	000
Aug.	11		931		931
Nov.	6			500	431
Dec.	8		346		777
		Cooper Company			
Aug.	14		1,114		1,114
Sept.	6		724		1,838
Oct.	17		126		1,964
	21	*Return on sale of Sept. 6*		124	1,840
Nov.	11		371		2,211
	26			1,714	497
Dec.	9		463		960
		Donald & Moore			
Feb.	7		1,243		1,243
	11		128		1,371
Aug.	6	*On account*		400	971
		Front Sales Co.			
Nov.	6		1,412		1,412
	18		3,614		5,026
	21		2,641		7,667
	26			1,000	6,667
Dec.	1		2,786		9,453
	3			4,026	5,427
	11		1,871		7,298
	27			2,000	5,298

Accounts Receivable Subsidiary Ledger

Date		Debit	Credit	Balance
	Longshore Co.			
Oct. 6		2,171		2,171
11		141		2,312
16	Return, Oct. 6 sale		312	2,000
Nov. 6		2,643		4,643
11			141	4,502
Dec. 8		1,111		5,613
16			2,643	2,970
	Monroe & Adams			
July 27		843		843
Aug. 7			246	597
16		1,202		1,799
17			597	1,202
Sept. 8		1,000		2,202
16			2,000	202
Nov. 9		966		1,168
25		841		2,009
Dec. 1			202	1,807
18		3,100		4,907
	Parker Co.			
Nov. 11		1,819		1,819
14	Return		900	919
Dec. 14		2,386		3,305
17			1,100	2,205
	Small & Walker			
Sept. 8		864		864
Oct. 16			864	000
Nov. 16		1,874		1,874
Dec. 1			874	1,000
16		3,617		4,617
28		2,861		7,478

Accounts Receivable Subsidiary Ledger

Date		Debit	Credit	Balance
	Vaughn Company			
Dec. 16		461		461
26		1,107		1,568
31			1,658	(90)

	Warner Sales Co.			
July 7		814		814
11			400	414
Aug. 6		100		514
11			200	314
Sept. 26		1,487		1,801
Oct. 9			801	1,000
Nov. 6		2,173		3,173
14		4,618		7,791
26			5,591	2,200
Dec. 8		1,364		3,564
19		864		4,428
26		8,461		12,889

Instructions

a. Prepare an aging schedule at December 31.

b. Compute the total amount of indicated loss from uncollectible accounts.

c. Prepare the necessary journal entry or entries to provide for bad debts, assuming the Allowance for Bad Debts account has a debit balance of $641 prior to adjustment at December 31.

d. Prepare the necessary journal entry to provide for bad debts, assuming that the Allowance for Bad Debts account has a credit balance of $409 prior to adjustment at December 31.

11B-3. The Hall Desk Co., owned by John Hall, has been engaged in the manufacture of desks for the last 15 years. Sales are made to furniture wholesalers and also to retail dealers. Although most sales are made on credit, there have been few bad debt losses of consequence. The company's experience has shown that an annual provision for bad debts expense of 1/4 of 1% of net sales is adequate.

In April, 1962, the Hall Desk Co. decided to develop a new sales territory in the Pacific Northwest. Sales of $116,000 were achieved in this new territory during 1962, but some of the sales were made to customers of questionable credit standing. Hall estimated that during the period of development of the new territory the bad debt provision for sales made in this area should be 3% of net sales.

During the latter part of 1962, the anticipated credit losses became apparent. The Redwood Furniture Company, which owed $1,100, notified Hall Desk Co. that it had been forced to suspend operations and was unable to pay any of its existing debts. Further collection efforts proved futile, and on September 12 the account was written off as worthless.

Another new customer, Elm Furniture House, entered receivership. On October 10, the receiver sent Hall Desk Co. a check for $590 and stated that nothing further could be paid. The balance of the account prior to this compromise settlement had been $1,475. The uncollected balance of the account was written off as worthless.

On October 15, receivables of $663 from the Maple Furniture Co. and $1,124 from the Oak Furniture Company were written off as uncollectible, after extensive collection efforts had failed. On November 2, however, both of these accounts were collected in full.

Total sales during 1962 by the Hall Desk Co. amounted to $867,500, including sales in the new territory. At the beginning of the year, the credit balance in the Allowance for Bad Debts account had amounted to $7,320. In addition to the credit losses in the new sales territory, accounts receivable aggregating $1,762.75 had been written off as worthless during 1962 in the company's old territory.

Instructions

a. Prepare journal entries (in general journal form) for all the indicated 1962 transactions including the sales, all of which were credit transactions.

b. Open general ledger accounts for Bad Debts Expense and for the Allowance for Bad Debts. Post the entries called for in (*a*) to these accounts.

c. Compute the bad debt expense for 1962, make the adjusting entry and closing entry needed at December 31, 1962, and post these entries to the ledger accounts required in (*b*).

11B-4. The Williams Wholesale Co., owned by Frank Williams, sells paint and supplies to retail stores. Sales are made on credit and an accounts receivable subsidiary ledger is maintained. Credit terms to all customers are 1/10, n/30.

During March, you are employed by Williams to substitute for the accounts receivable bookkeeper who is on vacation. You are to record the following transactions affecting accounts receivable.

Sales

Date		Customer	Amount	Invoice no.
Mar.	8	Acme Paint Stores	826.00	9184
	9	Cooper Hardware Co.	724.00	9185
	18	Maxon Paint Co.	725.00	9186
	21	Lyon Hardware & Paint	2,186.00	9187
	24	Porter Paint Shop	361.00	9188
	30	Willard Paint Co.	3,640.00	9189
	31	Other sales transactions	41,138.00	9190–9760

Cash Receipts

Date		Customer	Amount	Invoice no.
Mar.	11	Cooper Hardware Co.	716.76	9185
	19	Acme Paint Stores	817.74	9184
	25	Porter Paint Shop	361.00	9188
	31	Other collections (all within		
		discount period)	36,630.00	

Sales Returns

Date		Customer	Amount	Invoice no.
Mar.	25	Porter Paint Co. (credit		
		memo No. 184)	111.00	9188

Other data. On March 30, notice is received that the Maxon Paint Co. has become bankrupt. Invoice No. 9186 for $725 is therefore recorded as uncollectible. The Allowance for Bad Debts account had a credit balance of $845 on March 1. On March 31, Williams instructs you to make the necessary entry to carry out the company's established policy of providing for bad debts at a rate of 1% of net sales.

Instructions

a. Prepare individual entries in general journal form for March.

b. Post the entries to the customers' accounts in the accounts receivable subsidiary ledger, omitting posting references. General ledger posting is not required.

c. Draft the relevant sections of the balance sheet at March 31.

12

Inventories

Some basic questions relating to inventory

In earlier sections of this book the procedures for recording inventory at the end of the accounting period have been illustrated. The use of the inventory figure in both the balance sheet and the income statement has been demonstrated, and particular emphasis has been placed on the procedure for computing the cost of goods sold by deducting the ending inventory from the cost of goods available for sale during the period.

In all the previous illustrations, the dollar amount of the ending inventory has been given with only a brief explanation as to how this amount was determined. The valuation of inventory, as for most other types of assets, has been stated to be at cost, but the concept of cost as applied to inventories of merchandise has not been explored or defined.

In this chapter we shall consider some of the fundamental questions involved in accounting for inventories. Among the questions to be considered are these:

1. What goods are to be included in inventory?
2. How is the amount of the ending inventory determined?
3. What are the arguments for and against each of several alternative methods of inventory valuation?

Inventory valuation and the measurement of income

In measuring the gross profit earned during an accounting period, we subtract the cost of goods sold from the total sales of the period. The figure for sales is easily accumulated from the daily record of sales transactions, but no day-to-day record is maintained showing the cost of merchandise sold.[1] The figure representing the cost of goods sold during an entire accounting period is computed at the end of the period by separating the cost of goods available for sale into two elements:

1. The cost of the goods sold
2. The cost of the goods not sold, which therefore comprise the ending inventory

This idea, with which you are already quite familiar, may be concisely stated in the form of an equation as follows:

FINDING COST OF GOODS SOLD

$$\text{Cost of goods available for sale} - \text{ending inventory} = \text{cost of goods sold}$$

Determining the amount of the ending inventory is the key step in establishing the cost of goods sold. In separating the *cost of goods available for sale* into its components of *goods sold* and *goods not sold,* we are just as much interested in establishing the proper amount for cost of goods sold as in determining a proper figure for inventory. Throughout this chapter you should bear in mind that the procedures for determining the amount of the ending inventory are also the means for determining the cost of goods sold. The valuation of inventory and the determination of the cost of goods sold are in effect the two sides of a single coin.

The American Institute of Certified Public Accountants has summarized this relationship between inventory valuation and the measurement of income in the following words: "A major objective of accounting for inventories is the proper determination of income through the process of matching appropriate costs against revenues."[2] The expression "matching costs against revenues" means determining what portion of the cost of goods available for sale should be deducted from the revenues of the current period and what portion should be carried forward (as inventory) to be matched against the revenues of the following period.

Inventory defined

One of the largest and most valuable assets of a retail store or of a wholesale business is the inventory of merchandise. Since the principal function of both retail and wholesale businesses is the purchase and sale of merchandise, these businesses are often referred to as merchandising concerns. The inventory of a merchandising concern consists of all goods

---

[1] As explained in Chap. 6, a company that maintains perpetual inventory records will have a day-to-day record of the cost of goods sold and of goods in inventory. Our present discussion, however, is based on the assumption that the periodic method of inventory is being used.

[2] American Institute of Certified Public Accountants, *Restatement and Revision of Accounting Research Bulletin 43* (New York: 1953), p. 28.

owned and held for sale in the regular course of business. Merchandise held for sale will normally be converted into cash within less than a year's time and is therefore regarded as a current asset. In the balance sheet, inventory is listed immediately after accounts receivable, because it is just one step further removed from conversion into cash than are the accounts receivable.

In manufacturing businesses there are three major types of inventories: raw materials, goods in process of manufacture, and finished goods. All three classes of inventories are included in the current asset section of the balance sheet.

The term *inventory* has been defined by the American Institute of Certified Public Accountants to mean "the aggregate of those items of tangible personal property which (1) are held for sale in the ordinary course of business, (2) are in process of production for such sale, or (3) are to be currently consumed in the production of goods or services to be available for sale." [3]

Importance of an accurate valuation of inventory

The most important current assets in the balance sheets of most companies are cash, accounts receivable, and inventory. Of these three, the inventory of merchandise is usually much the largest. Because of the relatively large size of this asset, an error in the valuation of inventory may cause a material misstatement of financial condition. An error of 20% in valuing the inventory may have as much effect on the financial statements as would the complete omission of the asset cash.

An error in inventory will of course lead to other erroneous figures in the balance sheet, such as the total current assets, total assets, owner's equity, and the total of liabilities and owner's equity. The error will also affect key figures in the income statement, such as the cost of goods sold, the gross profit on sales, and the net income for the period. Finally, it is important to recognize that the final inventory of one year is also the beginning inventory of the following year. Consequently, the income statement of the second year will also be in error by the full amount of the original error in inventory valuation.

Illustration of the effects of an error in valuing inventory. Assume that on December 31, 1961, the inventory of the Hillside Company is actually $100,000 but, through an accidental error, is recorded as $90,000. The effects of this $10,000 error on the income statement for the year 1961 are indicated in the following illustration, which shows two income statements side by side. The left-hand set of figures shows the inventory of December 31, 1961, at the proper value of $100,000 and represents a correct income statement for the year 1961. The right-hand set of figures represents an incorrect income statement, because the ending inventory is erroneously listed as $90,000. Note the differences between the two statements with respect to net income, gross profit on sales, and cost of goods sold.

[3] *Ibid.*

HILLSIDE COMPANY
Income Statement
For the Year Ended December 31, 1961

	Statement with correct ending inventory		Statement with incorrect ending inventory	
Sales		$240,000		$240,000
Cost of goods sold:				
Beginning inventory,				
Dec. 31, 1960	$ 75,000		$ 75,000	
Purchases	210,000		210,000	
Cost of goods available for sale .	$285,000		$285,000	
Deduct: ending inventory,				
Dec. 31, 1961	100,000	185,000	90,000	195,000
Gross profit		$ 55,000		$ 45,000
Operating expenses		30,000		30,000
Net income		$ 25,000		$ 15,000

This illustration shows that an understatement of $10,000 in the ending inventory for the year 1961 caused an understatement of $10,000 in the net income for 1961. Next, consider the effect of this error on the net income of the following year. The ending inventory of 1961 is, of course, the beginning inventory of 1962. The preceding illustration is now continued to show side by side a correct statement and an incorrect statement for 1962. The ending inventory for the year 1962 is the same in both statements and is to be considered correct. Note that the $10,000 error **EFFECT ON** in the beginning inventory of the right-hand statement causes an error in **SUCCEEDING** the cost of goods sold, in gross profit, and in net income for the year 1962. **YEAR**

HILLSIDE COMPANY
Income Statement
For the Year Ended December 31, 1962

	With correct beginning inventory	With incorrect beginning inventory
Sales	$265,000	$265,000
Cost of goods sold:		
Beginning inventory,		
Dec. 31, 1961	$100,000	$ 90,000
Purchases	230,000	230,000
Cost of goods available for sale .	$330,000	$320,000

Deduct: ending inventory, Dec. 31, 1962	$120,000	$210,000	$120,000	$200,000
Gross profit		$ 55,000		$ 65,000
Operating expenses		33,000		33,000
Net income		$ 22,000		$ 32,000

Counterbalancing errors. The illustrated income statements for the years 1961 and 1962 show that an understatement of the ending inventory in 1961 caused an understatement of net income in that year and an offsetting overstatement of net income for 1962. Over a period of two years the effects of an inventory error on net income will counterbalance, and the total income for the two years taken together is the same as if the error had not occurred. Since the error in reported profits for the first year

COUNTER-
BALANCING
EFFECT
ON NET
INCOME

	With inventory correctly stated	With inventory at Dec. 31, 1961 understated	
		Reported income will be	Reported income will be overstated (understated)
Income for 1961	$25,000	$15,000	($10,000)
Income for 1962	22,000	32,000	10,000
Total income for two years	$47,000	$47,000	000

is exactly offset by the error in reported profits for the second year, it might be argued that an inventory error has no serious consequences. Such an argument is not sound, for it disregards the fact that accurate yearly figures for net profit are a primary objective of the accounting process. Moreover, many actions by management and many decisions by creditors and owners are based directly on the annual financial statements. To produce dependable annual statements, inventory must be accurately determined at the end of each accounting period.

Relation of inventory errors to cost of goods sold and to net income. The effects of errors in inventory upon the cost of goods sold and upon the net income may be summarized as follows:

1. When the *ending* inventory is understated, the cost of goods sold will be overstated and the net income for the period will be understated.

2. When the *ending* inventory is overstated, the cost of goods sold will be understated and the net income for the period will be overstated.

3. When the *beginning* inventory is understated, the cost of goods sold will be understated and the net income for the period overstated.

4. When the *beginning* inventory is overstated, the cost of goods sold will be overstated and the net income for the period will be understated.

Taking a physical inventory

At the end of each accounting period the values for most of the assets will be shown by the balances in the ledger accounts. For inventory, however, the balance in the ledger account represents the beginning inventory, because no entry has been made in the inventory account since the end of, the preceding year. All purchases of merchandise during the present year have been recorded in the purchases account. The ending inventory, or stock of goods on hand, does not appear anywhere in the ledger accounts; it must be determined by a physical count of merchandise.

Establishing a balance sheet valuation for the ending inventory requires two steps: (1) determining the quantity of each kind of merchandise on hand, and (2) multiplying the quantity by the cost per unit. The first step is called *taking the inventory;* the second is called *pricing the inventory.* Taking inventory, or more precisely, taking a physical inventory, means making a systematic count of all merchandise on hand.

In most merchandising businesses the taking of a physical inventory is a year-end event. In some lines of business an inventory may be taken at the close of each month. It is common practice to take inventory after regular business hours or on Sunday so that all employees can be utilized for the counting process. By taking the inventory while business operations are suspended, it is possible to make a more accurate count than would be possible if goods were being sold or received while the count was in process.

There are various methods of counting merchandise. One of the simplest procedures is carried out by the use of two-man teams. One member of the team counts and calls the description and quantity of each item. The other person lists the descriptions and quantities on an inventory sheet. When all goods have been counted and listed, the items on the inventory sheet are priced at cost, and the unit prices are multiplied by the quantities to determine the valuation of the inventory.

Planning the physical inventory. Unless the taking of a physical inventory is carefully planned and supervised, serious errors are apt to occur which will invalidate the results of the count. To prevent the double counting of items, the omission of goods from the count, and other quantitative errors, it is desirable to plan the inventory so that the work of one person serves as a check on the accuracy of another.

Prenumbered inventory tags, as shown in the illustration on page 360, are helpful in securing an accurate count. Each tag bears a serial number and provides space for listing the description of the item, the identification number, location, quantity, and signatures of the persons counting and verifying the inventory.

A sufficient number of tags is issued to each inventory team to provide a separate tag for each kind of merchandise on hand. As the count is made, the quantity of each item is listed on a tag, along with the de-

Tag No. 102

Item...

Identification No..

Department..

Quantity..

Counted by...

Verified by...

Date..

scription of the item, its identification number, and location. The tag is signed by the person preparing it and is attached to the merchandise. When the counting of goods has been completed, every lot of merchandise in the store should have a tag attached.

At this point supervisors should inspect all areas to make sure that every lot of merchandise has been counted and bears a tag. To ensure the accuracy of the recorded counts, a representative number of items should be recounted by supervisors. Some businesses make a practice of counting all merchandise a second time and comparing the quantities established by the different teams. The initials of the person making the second count should also be placed on the inventory tag. Once it is known that all merchandise has been tagged and that the counts are accurate, the tags are gathered and sent to the accounting office for completion of the inventory.

The tags are next assembled in numerical sequence, including any unused tags. By accounting for all numbers of the series, assurance is gained that no tags have been lost or left attached to merchandise. After determining that all tags have been accounted for, the accounting department will transfer information on the tags to inventory summary sheets.

Inventory Summary Sheet
Dec. 31, 19___
Sheet No. _____

Item	*Tag no.*	*Quantity*	*Cost price*	*Amount*
Golf bags	*201*	*30*	*$20*	*$600*
Golf clubs	*202*	*22*	*10*	*220*
Sweaters	*203*	*60*	*12*	*720*

The inventory summary sheets are completed by entering the unit cost of the products and multiplying the cost price by the quantity on hand. Totals are computed for individual inventory sheets, for each department of the business, and for the entire inventory.

Including all goods owned. All goods to which the company has title should be included in the inventory, regardless of their location. Title to merchandise ordinarily passes from seller to buyer at the time the goods are delivered. No question arises as to the ownership of merchandise on the shelves, in stock rooms, or in warehouses. A question of ownership does arise, however, for merchandise which has been ordered from suppliers but not yet received on the last day of the period. A similar question of ownership concerns goods in the process of shipment to customers at year-end.

Do goods in transit belong in the inventory of the seller or of the buyer? If the seller makes delivery of the merchandise in his own trucks, the merchandise remains his property while in transit. If the goods are shipped by rail, air, or other public carrier, the question of ownership of the goods while in transit depends upon whether the public carrier is acting as the agent of the seller or of the buyer. If the terms of the shipment are FOB (free on board) shipping point, title passes at the point of shipment and the goods are the property of the buyer while in transit. If the terms of the shipment are FOB destination, title does not pass until the shipment reaches the destination, and the goods belong to the seller while in transit. In deciding whether goods in transit at year-end should be included in inventory, it is therefore necessary to refer to the terms of the agreements with vendors and customers.

At the end of the year a company may have received numerous orders from customers, for which goods have been segregated and packed but not yet shipped. These goods should generally be included in inventory. An exception to this rule is found occasionally when the goods have been prepared for shipment but are being held for later delivery at the request of the customer.

The debit to the customer's account and the offsetting credit to the sales account should be made when title to the goods passes to the customer. It would obviously be improper to set up an account receivable and at the same time to include the goods in question in inventory. Great care is necessary at year-end to ensure that all last-minute shipments to customers are recorded as sales of the current year and, on the other hand, that no customer's order is recorded as a sale until the date when the goods are shipped. Sometimes, in an effort to meet sales quotas, companies have recorded sales on the last day of the accounting period, when in fact the merchandise was not shipped until early in the next period. Such practices lead to an overstatement of the year's earnings and are not in accordance with generally accepted principles of accounting.

Merchandise in inventory is valued at cost, whereas accounts receivable are stated at the sales price of the merchandise sold. Consequently, the recording of a sale prior to delivery of the goods results in an unjustified increase in the total assets of the company. The increase will equal the difference between the cost and the selling price of the goods in question. The amount of the increase will also be reflected in the income statement, where it will show up as additional earnings. An unscrupulous company, which wanted to make its financial statements present a more favorable picture than actually existed, might do so by treating year-end orders from customers as sales even though the goods were not yet shipped.

Pricing the inventory

One of the most interesting and widely discussed problems in accounting is the pricing of inventory. Even those businessmen who have little knowledge of accounting are usually interested in the various methods of pricing inventory, because inventory valuation has a direct effect upon reported profits. Federal income taxes are based on profits, and the choice of inventory method may have a considerable effect upon the amount of taxes which a business is required to pay. Federal income tax authorities are therefore much interested in the problem of inventory valuation and have taken a definite position on the acceptability of various alternative methods of pricing inventory.

In approaching our study of inventory valuation, however, it is important that we do not overemphasize the income tax aspects of the problem. It is true that in selected cases one method of inventory valuation may lead to a substantially lower income tax liability than would another method, but there are other important considerations in pricing inventory apart from the objective of minimizing the current tax burden. Since inventory is one of the largest current assets and is also a major factor in determining the net income for the period, it is desirable that the method to be used in pricing the inventory should produce valid and realistic figures in both the balance sheet and the income statement. Proper valuation of inventory is one part of a larger undertaking, that is, to measure income accurately and to provide all those persons interested in the financial condition and operating results of a business with accounting data which are dependable and of maximum usefulness as a basis for business decisions.

Although there are several acceptable methods used in pricing the inventory, the most significant basis of accounting for inventories is cost. Another important method, which is acceptable for income tax purposes and is widely used, is known as the "lower of cost or market." First we shall consider the cost basis of accounting for inventories, for an understanding of the meaning of the term *cost* as applied to inventories is a first essential in appreciating the complexity of the over-all problem of inventory valuation.

Cost basis of inventory valuation

"The primary basis of accounting for inventory is cost, which has been defined generally as the price paid or consideration given to acquire an asset. As applied to inventories, cost means in principle the sum of the applicable expenditures and charges directly or indirectly incurred in bringing an article to its existing condition and location." [4]

Since accounting is based primarily on cost, the valuation of inventories at cost is consistent with the treatment of several other important groups of accounts. To acquire a clear understanding of the meaning of cost as applied to an inventory of merchandise, we need to focus our attention upon the incidental expenditures relating to the acquisition of goods, such as transportation-in, insurance of goods in transit, the salary of the purchasing agent and of the employees responsible for receiving and inspecting the merchandise.

Transportation-in as an element of cost. The starting point in determining the cost of an article of merchandise is the price paid, as shown by the vendor's invoice. To this acquisition cost should be added the cost of transportation incurred in bringing the merchandise to the location where it is to be offered for sale.

The logic of treating transportation-in as part of the cost of goods purchased is indicated by the following example. A Los Angeles appliance dealer orders 10 refrigerators from a Chicago manufacturer. The manufacturer pays the cost of shipping the refrigerators to Los Angeles and submits an invoice in the amount of $2,000. This is the total amount to be paid by the Los Angeles merchant, so the cost of the goods is clearly $2,000. Now assume that the appliance dealer places a second order for another 10 identical refrigerators. On this second order the invoice from the Chicago manufacturer is for only $1,800; under the terms of this purchase, however, the Los Angeles merchant is required to pay the railroad for the freight charges of $200 applicable to the shipment. On both of these identical shipments the total cash paid by the Los Angeles merchant was $2,000, so clearly the charge for transportation is part of the cost of merchandise purchased.

At the end of the year when a physical inventory is taken, the cost of each kind of merchandise is multiplied by the quantity on hand to determine the dollar amount of the ending inventory. The price paid for an article may readily be found by referring to the invoice from the supplier, but often there is no convenient method of determining how much transportation cost may have been incurred on specific types of merchandise. This is particularly true when certain shipments have included various kinds of merchandise and the freight charge was for the shipment as a whole. For reasons of convenience and economy, therefore, a merchandising business may choose to determine inventory cost at year-end by listing each item in stock at the purchase invoice price, and then adding to the inventory as a whole a reasonable proportion of the transportation charges incurred on inbound shipments during the year.

In many lines of business it is customary to price the year-end inventory without giving any consideration to transportation charges. This practice may be justified by the factors of convenience and economy, even though it is not theoretically sound. If freight charges are not material in

[4] *Ibid.*, p. 28.

amount, it is advisable in terms of operating convenience to treat the entire amount as part of the cost of goods sold during the year. Accounting textbooks stress theoretical concepts of cost and of income determination; the student of accounting should be aware, however, that in many business situations an approximation of cost will serve the purpose at hand. In other words, the extra work involved in computing more precise cost data must be weighed against the benefits to be obtained.

Other charges relating to acquisition of merchandise. If transportation-in is part of the cost of merchandise purchased, what about the other incidental charges relating to the acquisition of merchandise, such as the salary of the purchasing agent, insurance of goods in transit, cost of receiving and inspecting the merchandise, etc.? Although in theory these incidental charges should be identified and apportioned among the various items of merchandise purchased, the expense of computing cost on such a precise basis would usually outweigh the benefit to be derived. The costs of operating the purchasing department and the receiving department are customarily treated as expense of the period in which incurred, rather than being carried forward to another period by inclusion in the balance sheet amount for inventory.

Purchase discounts and the concept of cost. When a merchant purchases goods he often has the opportunity of saving 1 or 2% of the invoiced amount by making payment within a specified period, usually 10 days. For example, an invoice for $1,000 bearing terms of 2/10, n/30 may be satisfied by a payment of $980 within 10 days. If the invoice is, in fact, paid within the discount period by issuance of a check for $980, then our definition of cost as "the price paid or consideration given to acquire an asset" would indicate that the cost of the merchandise is $980 and not the invoiced amount of $1,000. This reasoning was illustrated earlier in Chapter 7, when purchase discounts were shown in the income statement as a deduction from purchases in determining the cost of goods available for sale.

Referring again to the above example of an invoice for $1,000 bearing terms of 2/10, n/30, let us assume that the purchaser waits the full 30 days before making payment and then issues a check for $1,000. Should the merchandise then be regarded as having a cost of $1,000? Let us make the reasonable assumption that it is the policy of the purchasing company to take all discounts available and that failure to pay the invoice in question within the discount period was the result of negligence. Is it not more sensible to recognize the consequences of this act of negligence as an expense of the period than to conceal the "loss" by raising the cost of the merchandise from the net cash price of $980 to the invoiced amount of $1,000?

Some accountants might defend a cost of $1,000 under these circumstances on the ground that this was the amount actually paid. If the accounting records are to be of maximum usefulness to management, however, the preferable treatment is to consider the cost of the goods as the net cash price of $980 which was available to the purchaser, and to show cash discounts *not taken* as an expense of the period.

Determining cost when purchase prices vary

The prices of many kinds of merchandise are subject to frequent change. When identical lots of merchandise are purchased at various dates during the year, each lot may be acquired at a different cost price. In some lines of business each article of merchandise may bear an identifying serial number or other distinctive mark, which makes it possible to tell from which of several purchases the article came. In many other types of business, however, the items purchased in various lots are identical and interchangeable. When identical lots of merchandise have been purchased at varying prices, how may the accountant determine at the end of the year which purchase prices apply to the units sold and which prices apply to the units remaining in stock?

To illustrate the several alternative methods in common use for determining which purchase prices apply to the units remaining in inventory at the end of the period, assume the data shown below.

SPECIFIC-IDENTIFICATION METHOD AND . . .

	Number of units	*Cost per unit*	*Total cost*
Beginning inventory	10	$ 8	$ 80
First purchase (Mar. 1)	5	9	45
Second purchase (July 1)	5	10	50
Third purchase (Oct. 1)	5	12	60
Fourth purchase (Dec. 1)	5	13	65
Available for sale	30		$300
Units sold	18		
Units in ending inventory	12		

This schedule shows that 18 units were sold during the year and that 12 units are on hand at year-end to make up the ending inventory. In order to establish a dollar amount for cost of goods sold and for the ending inventory, we must make an assumption as to which units were sold and which units remain on hand at the end of the year. There are several acceptable assumptions on this point; four of the most common will be considered. Each assumption made as to the identity of the units in the ending inventory leads to a different method of pricing inventory and to different amounts in the financial statements. The four assumptions (and inventory valuation methods) to be considered are known as: (1) specific identification, (2) average cost, (3) first-in, first-out, and (4) last-in, first-out.

Although each of these four methods will produce a different answer as to the cost of goods sold and the cost of the ending inventory, the valuation of inventory in each case is said to be at "cost." In other words, these methods represent alternative definitions of cost. The American Institute of Certified Public Accountants has stated: "Cost for inventory purposes may be determined under any one of several assumptions as to the flow of cost factors (such as first-in, first-out, average, and last-in, first-out); the major objective in selecting a method should be to choose the one which, under the circumstances, most clearly reflects periodic income." [5]

Specific identification method. If the units in the ending inventory can be identified as coming from specific purchases, they may be priced at the amounts listed on the purchase invoices. Continuing the example already presented, if the ending inventory of 12 units can be identified as, say, five units from the purchase of March 1, four units from the purchase of July 1, and three units from the purchase of December 1, the cost of the ending inventory may be computed as follows:

Five units from the purchase of Mar. 1 @ $9	*$ 45*
Four units from the purchase of July 1 @ $10	*40*
Three units from the purchase of Dec. 1 @ $13	*39*
Ending inventory (specific identification)	*$124*

The cost of goods sold during the period is determined by subtracting the ending inventory from the cost of goods available for sale.

. . . COST OF GOODS SOLD COMPUTATION

Cost of goods available for sale	*$300*
Deduct: ending inventory	*124*
Cost of goods sold	*$176*

Average-cost method. If the units purchased at various times and prices during the year are identical and interchangeable, it may not be possible (or desirable) to identify the units in the ending inventory according to a specific purchase. As an alternative, the ending inventory may be valued at a weighted average cost. Average cost is computed by dividing the total cost of goods available for sale by the number of units available for sale. This computation gives a weighted average unit cost, which is then applied to the units in the ending inventory.

AVERAGE-COST METHOD AND . . .

Cost of goods available for sale	*$300*
Number of units available for sale	*30*
Average unit cost	*$ 10*
Ending inventory (12 units @ $10)	*$120*

[5] *Ibid.*

Note that this method, when compared with the actual invoice price method, leads to a different amount for cost of goods sold as well as a different amount for the ending inventory.

. . . COST
OF GOODS
SOLD COM-
PUTATION

Cost of goods available for sale	$300
Deduct: ending inventory	120
Cost of goods sold	$180

When the average-cost method is used, the cost figure determined for the ending inventory is influenced by all the various prices paid during the year. The price paid early in the year may carry as much weight in pricing the ending inventory as a price paid at the end of the year. If prices have been rising during the year, as in this example, the average unit cost will be less than the current cost prevailing at the balance sheet date. Conversely, if prices have been declining throughout the year, the average unit cost would be higher than the current cost at the year-end. A common criticism of the average-cost method of pricing inventory is that it attaches no more significance to current prices than to prices which prevailed several months earlier.

First-in, first-out method. The first-in, first-out method, which is often referred to as *fifo,* is based on the assumption that the first merchandise acquired is the first merchandise sold. In other words, each sale is made out of the oldest goods in stock; the ending inventory therefore consists of the most recently acquired goods. The fifo method of determining inventory cost may be adopted by any business regardless of whether or not the physical flow of merchandise actually corresponds to this assumption of selling the oldest units in stock. Using the same data as in the preceding illustrations, the 12 units in the ending inventory would be regarded as consisting of the most recently acquired goods, as follows:

**FIRST-IN,
FIRST-OUT
METHOD
AND . . .**

Five units from the Dec. 1 purchase @ $13	$ 65
Five units from the Oct. 1 purchase @ $12	60
Two units from the July 1 purchase @ $10	20
Ending inventory (at fifo cost)	$145

During a period of rising prices the first-in, first-out method will result in a larger amount being assigned as the cost of the ending inventory than would be assigned under the average-cost method. When a relatively large amount is allocated as cost of the ending inventory, a relatively small amount will remain as cost of goods sold, as indicated by the following calculation:

Cost of goods available for sale	*$300*
Deduct: ending inventory	*145*
Cost of goods sold	*$155*

It may be argued in support of the first-in, first-out method that the inventory valuation reflects recent costs and is therefore a realistic value in the light of conditions prevailing at the balance sheet date.

Last-in, first-out method. The title of this method of pricing suggests that the most recently acquired goods are sold first, and that the ending inventory consists of "old" merchandise acquired in the earliest purchases. Such an assumption is, of course, not in accord with the actual physical movement of goods in most businesses, but there is nevertheless a strong logical argument to support this method. As merchandise is sold, more goods must be purchased to replenish the stock on hand. Since the making of a sale necessitates a replacement purchase of goods, the cost of replacement should be offset against the sales price to determine the income realized. The supporters of last-in, first-out, or *lifo*, as it is commonly known, contend that the accurate determination of income requires that primary emphasis be placed on the matching of current costs of merchandise against current sales prices, regardless of which physical units of merchandise are being delivered to customers. Keeping in mind the point that the flow of costs is more significant than the physical movement of merchandise, we can say that, under the lifo method, the cost of goods sold consists of the cost of the most recently acquired goods and the ending inventory consists of the cost of the oldest goods which were available for sale during the period. The American Institute of Certified Public Accountants Committee on Accounting Procedure has expressed this idea as follows:

"In accounting for the goods in the inventory at any point of time, the major objective is the matching of appropriate costs against revenues in order that there may be a proper determination of the realized income. Thus, the inventory at any given date is the balance of costs applicable to goods on hand remaining after the matching of absorbed costs with concurrent revenues." [6]

Using the same data as in the preceding illustrations, the 12 units in the ending inventory would be priced as if they were the oldest goods available for sale during the period, as follows:

Ten units from the beginning inventory @ $8	*$80*
Two units from the purchase of Mar. 1 @ $9	*18*
Ending inventory (at lifo cost)	*$98*

[6] *Ibid.*

Notice that the lifo cost of the ending inventory ($98) is very much lower than the fifo cost ($145) of ending inventory in the preceding example. Since a relatively small part of the cost of goods available for sale is assigned to ending inventory, it follows that a relatively large portion must have been assigned to cost of goods sold, as shown by the following computation:

. . . COST
OF GOODS
SOLD COM-
PUTATION

Cost of goods available for sale	$300
Deduct: ending inventory	98
Cost of goods sold	$202

Comparison of the alternative methods of pricing inventory. We have now illustrated four common methods of pricing inventory at cost; the specific identification method, the average-cost method, the first-in, first-out method, and the last-in, first-out method. There are a number of other alternative methods, but these can more appropriately be considered in advanced accounting courses. By way of contrasting the results obtained from the four methods illustrated, especially during a period of rapid price changes, let us summarize the amounts computed for ending inventory, cost of goods sold, and gross profit on sales under each of the four methods. Assume that sales for the period amounted to $275.

FOUR
METHODS
OF DETER-
MINING
COST
COMPARED

	Specific identification	Average cost	First-in, first-out	Last-in, first-out
Sales	$275	$275	$275	$275
Cost of goods sold:				
Beginning inventory	$ 80	$ 80	$ 80	$ 80
Purchases	220	220	220	220
Cost of goods available for sale	$300	$300	$300	$300
Deduct: ending inventory	124	120	145	98
Cost of goods sold	$176	$180	$155	$202
Gross profit on sales	$ 99	$ 95	$120	$ 73

This comparison of the four methods makes it apparent that during periods of *rising prices,* the use of lifo will result in lower profits being reported than would be the case under the other methods of inventory valuation. Perhaps for this reason many businesses have adopted lifo in recent years. Current income tax regulations permit virtually any business to use the last-in, first-out method in reporting taxable income.

During a period of *declining prices,* the use of lifo will cause the reporting of relatively large profits as compared with fifo, which will hold reported profits to a minimum. Obviously, the choice of inventory method becomes of greatest significance during prolonged periods of drastic changes in price levels.

Some accountants have suggested that each of the inventory methods will lead to the same total profit over a complete business cycle. Such statements appear to be valid only when based upon the rather unrealistic assumption that each complete business cycle sees the price level return to its starting point. An assumption of more or less continual rise in prices is, in the opinion of many businessmen and economists, more nearly in accord with the economic trends of this century.

Which method of inventory valuation is best? All four of the inventory methods described are regarded as acceptable accounting practice and all four are acceptable in the determination of taxable income. No one method of inventory valuation can be considered as the "correct" or the "best" method. In the selection of a method, consideration should be given to the probable effect upon the balance sheet, upon the income statement, upon the amount of taxable income, and upon such business decisions as the establishment of selling prices.

In a period of changing prices, decisions must be made by every business as to the advisability of raising or lowering the prices of the goods it sells. If the basis for such decisions consists of information taken from the accounting records concerning current profits, the apparent need for a change in selling prices will depend largely upon which method of inventory valuation is in use. When prices are changing drastically, the most significant cost data to use as a guide to sales policies are probably the current replacement costs of the goods being sold. The lifo method of inventory valuation comes closer than any of the other methods described to measuring profits in the light of current selling prices and current replacement costs.

On the other hand, the use of lifo during a period of rising prices is apt to produce a balance sheet figure for inventory which is far below the current replacement cost of the goods on hand. The fifo method of inventory valuation will lead to a balance sheet valuation of inventory more in line with present replacement costs.

Some business concerns which adopted lifo 20 years ago now show a balance sheet figure for inventory which is less than half the present replacement cost of the goods in stock. An inventory valuation method which gives significant figures for the income statement may thus produce misleading amounts for the balance sheet, whereas a method which produces a realistic figure for inventory on the balance sheet may provide less realistic data for the income statement.

The search for the "best" method of inventory valuation is rendered difficult because the inventory figure is used in both the balance sheet and the income statement, and these two statements are intended for different purposes. In the income statement the function of the inventory figure is to permit a matching of costs and revenues. In the balance sheet the inventory and the other current assets are regarded as a measure of the company's ability to meet its current debts. For this purpose a valuation of inventory in line with current replacement cost would appear to be most significant.

The high rates of income tax in recent years have stimulated the interest of businessmen in the choice of inventory methods. No one can predict with certainty the course of future prices or tax rates. Increasing numbers of businesses, however, have reacted to the experience of rising prices, large profits, and high income taxes by adopting lifo as a means of minimizing reported profits and required income tax payments. Many accountants believe that the use of average cost or of fifo during a period of rising prices results in the reporting of fictitious profits and consequently in the payment of an unreasonable amount of income taxes.

The lower-of-cost-or-market rule

Although cost is the primary basis for valuation of inventories, circumstances may arise under which inventory may properly be valued at less than its cost. If the utility of the inventory has fallen below cost by reason of physical deterioration, obsolescence, or decline in the price level, a loss has occurred. This loss may appropriately be recognized as a loss of the current period by reducing the accounting value of the inventory from cost to a lower level designated as *market*. The word "market" as used in this context means current replacement cost. For a merchandising concern, market is the amount which the concern would have to pay at the present time for the goods in question, purchased in the customary quantities through the usual sources of supply and including transportation-in. To avoid misunderstanding, the rule might better read "lower of cost or replacement cost."

In the early days of accounting when the principal users of financial statements were creditors and attention was concentrated upon the balance sheet, conservatism was a dominant consideration in asset valuation. The lower-of-cost-or-market rule was then considered justifiable because it tended to produce a "safe" or minimum value for inventory. The rule was widely applied for a time without regard for the possibility that although replacement costs had declined, there might be no corresponding and immediate decline in selling prices.

As the significance of the income statement has increased, considerable dissatisfaction with the lower-of-cost-or-market rule has developed. If ending inventory is written down from cost to a lower market figure but the merchandise is sold during the next period at the usual selling prices, the effect of the write-down will have been to reflect a fictitious loss in the first period and an exaggerated profit in the second period. Arbitrary application of the lower-of-cost-or-market rule ignores the historical fact that selling prices do not always drop when replacement prices decline. Even if selling prices do follow replacement prices downward, they may not decline by a proportionate amount.

Because of these objections, the lower-of-cost-or-market rule has undergone some modification and is now qualified in the following respects. If the inventory can probably be sold at prices which will yield a normal profit, the inventory should be carried at cost even though current replacement cost is lower. Assume, for example, that merchandise is purchased for $1,000 with the intention of reselling it to customers for $1,500. The replacement cost then declines from $1,000 to $800, but it is believed that the merchandise can still be sold to customers for $1,450. The carrying value of the inventory could then be written down from $1,000 to $950. There is no justification for reducing the inventory to the replacement cost of $800 under these circumstances.

Another qualification of the lower-of-cost-or-market rule is that inventory should never be carried at an amount greater than *net realizable value*, which may be defined as prospective selling price minus anticipated selling expenses. Assume, for example, that because of disturbed market conditions, it is believed that goods acquired at a cost of $500 and having a current replacement cost of $450 will probably have to be sold for no more than $520 and that the selling expenses involved will amount to $120. The inventory should then be reduced to a carrying value of $400, which is less than current replacement cost.

Application of the lower-of-cost-or-market rule. The lower of cost or market for an inventory is most commonly computed by determining the cost and the market figures for each item in inventory and using the lower of the two amounts in every case. If, for example, item A cost $100 and market is $90, the item should be priced at $90. If item B cost $200 and market is $225, this item should be priced at $200. The total cost of the two items is $300 and total market is $315, but the total inventory value determined by applying the lower-of-cost-or-market rule to each item in inventory is only $290. This application of the lower-of-cost-or-market rule is illustrated by the tabulation shown below.

PRICING
INVENTORY
AT LOWER
OF COST OR
MARKET

Application of Lower-of-cost-or-market Rule, Item by Item Method

| *Item* | *Quantity* | *Unit price* | | *Lower of cost or market* |
		Cost	*Market*	
A	10	$100	$ 90	$ 900
B	8	200	225	1,600
C	50	50	60	2,500
D	80	90	70	5,600
Totals	148			$10,600

If the lower-of-cost-or-market rule is applied item by item, the carrying value of the above inventory would be $10,600. However, in some circumstances the lower-of-cost-or-market rule may be applied to the total of the entire inventory rather than to the individual items. If the above inventory is to be valued by applying the lower-of-cost-or-market rule to the total of the inventory, the balance sheet amount for inventory is determined merely by comparing the total cost of $12,300 with the total replacement cost of $11,300 and using the lower of the two figures. This application of the lower-of-cost-or-market rule is appropriate when no loss of income is anticipated, because the decline in cost prices of certain goods is fully offset by higher replacement costs for other items.

Gross profit method of estimating inventories

The taking of a physical inventory is a time-consuming and costly job in many lines of business; consequently, a physical inventory may be taken only once a year. Monthly financial statements are needed, however, for intelligent administration of the business, and the preparation of monthly statements requires a determination of the amount of inventory at the end of each month. This dilemma may be solved satisfactorily by estimating the inventory each month by using the gross profit method.

The gross profit method of estimating the inventory is based on the assumption that the rate of gross profit remains approximately the same from year to year. This assumption is a realistic one in many fields of business. The first step in using the gross profit method is to obtain from the ledger the figures for beginning inventory, purchases, and sales. Cost of goods sold is then computed by reducing the sales figure by the usual gross profit rate. The difference between the cost of goods sold and the cost of goods available for sale represents the ending inventory.

To illustrate, let us assume that the beginning inventory is $25,000, the purchases of the period $70,000, and the net sales $100,000. The gross profit rate is assumed to have approximated 40% of net sales for the past several years. This information is now assembled in the customary form of an income statement as follows:

GROSS-
PROFIT
METHOD

Net sales		*$100,000 (100%)*
Beginning inventory	*$25,000*	
Purchases	*70,000*	
Cost of goods available for sale	*$95,000*	
Deduct: ending inventory	*?*	
Cost of goods sold		*60,000 (60%)*
Gross profit (40% × $100,000)		*$ 40,000 (40%)*

Customarily, in preparing an income statement, the ending inventory is deducted from the cost of goods available for sale to determine the cost of goods sold. In this case our calculation to determine the ending inventory consists of deducting the estimated cost of goods sold from the cost of goods available for sale.

Cost of goods available for sale	*$95,000*
Deduct: cost of goods sold (60% of $100,000)	*60,000*
Ending inventory (estimate)	*$35,000*

The gross profit method of estimating inventory has several uses apart from the preparation of monthly financial statements. This calculation may be used after the taking of a physical inventory to confirm the over-all reasonableness of the amount determined by the counting and pricing process. In the event of a fire which destroys the inventory, the approximate amount of goods on hand at the date of the fire may also be computed by the gross profit method.

The retail method of inventory valuation

The retail method of estimating an ending inventory is somewhat similar to the gross profit method. It is widely used by chain stores, department stores, and other types of retail business. Goods on sale in retail stores are marked at the retail prices; it is therefore more convenient to take inventory at current retail prices than to look up invoices to find the unit cost of each item in stock. After first determining the value of the inventory at retail price, the next step is to convert the inventory to cost price by applying the ratio prevailing between cost and selling price during the current period. This method of approximating an inventory may also be carried out by using data from the accounts without taking any physical count of the goods on hand. The underlying basis for the retail method of inventory valuation is the percentage of markup for the current period, whereas the gross profit method of estimating inventory rests on the rate of gross profit experienced in preceding periods.

When the retail method of inventory is to be used, it is necessary to maintain records of the beginning inventory and of all purchases during the period in terms of selling price as well as at cost. Goods available for sale during the period can then be stated both at cost and at selling price. By deducting the sales for the period from the sales value of the goods available for sale, the ending inventory at retail may be determined without the need for a physical count. The ending inventory at retail is then converted to a cost basis by using the percentage of cost to selling price for the current period.

In practice, the application of this method may be complicated because the originally established sales prices are modified by frequent markups and markdowns. These frequent changes in retail price present some difficulties in determining the correct rate to use in reducing the inventory from selling price to cost. The following illustration shows the calculation of inventory by the retail method, without going into the complications which would arise from markups and markdowns in the original retail price.

	Cost price	Selling price
Beginning inventory	$20,000	$30,000
Net purchases during the month	11,950	15,000
Merchandise available for sale	$31,950	$45,000
Deduct: net sales for the month		20,000
Ending inventory at selling price		$25,000
Percentage relationship between cost and selling price of merchandise available for sale ($31,950 ÷ $45,000)		71%
Ending inventory at cost (71% × $25,000)	$17,750	

Consistency in the valuation of inventory

A business has considerable latitude in selecting a method of inventory valuation best suited to its needs; once a method has been selected, however, that method should be followed consistently from year to year. A change from one inventory method to another will ordinarily cause reported income to vary considerably in the year in which the change occurs. Frequent switching of methods would therefore make the income statements quite undependable as a means of portraying operating results.

The need for consistency in the valuation of inventory does not mean that a business should *never* make a change in inventory method. However, when a change is made, the approval of tax authorities must be obtained, and full disclosure of the nature of the change and of its effect upon the year's net income should be included in the financial statements or in a footnote to the statements. Even when the same method of inventory pricing is being followed consistently, the financial statements should include a disclosure of the pricing method in use.

QUESTIONS

1. Is the establishment of an appropriate valuation for the merchandise inventory at the end of the year important in producing a dependable income statement, or in producing a dependable balance sheet?

2. Explain the meaning of the term *physical inventory*.

3. Through an accidental error in counting of merchandise at December 31, 1961, the Trophy Company overstated the amount of goods on hand by $8,000. Assuming that the error was not discovered, what was the effect upon net income for 1961? Upon the owners' equity at December 31, 1961? Upon the net income for 1962? Upon the owners' equity at December 31, 1962?

4. Near the end of December, Hadley Company received a large order from a major customer. The work of packing the goods for shipment was begun at once but could not be completed before the close of business on December 31. Since a written order from the customer was on hand and the goods were nearly all packed and ready for shipment, Hadley felt that this merchandise should not be included in the physical inventory taken on December 31. Do you agree? What is probably the reason behind Hadley's opinion?

5. During a prolonged period of rising prices, will the fifo or lifo method of inventory valuation result in higher reported profits?

6. Throughout several years of strongly rising prices, Company A used the lifo method of inventory valuation and Company B used the fifo method. In which company would the balance sheet figure for inventory be closer to current replacement cost of the merchandise on hand? Why?

7. Explain the usefulness of the gross profit method of estimating inventories.

8. Estimate the inventory by the gross profit method, given the following data: beginning inventory $40,000; purchases $100,000; net sales $106,667; average gross profit rate 25%.

PROBLEMS

Group A

12A-1. In taking the physical inventory on December 31, 1961, the Apex Office Supply Company used the type of work sheet shown below to price the inventory on a basis of the lower of cost or market.

Item	Quantity	Unit value		Total value	
		Cost	Market	Cost	Market

As each item was listed, it was extended into the total value columns at both cost and market price. The total of the cost column was $173,200 and the total of the market column was $172,400. The company used the latter figure to reflect the value of the inventory in the balance sheet.

Instructions

a. Did the company follow acceptable procedures in determining the balance sheet amount for inventory?

b. What alternative procedures might have been followed? Would the alternative procedures have led to a higher or lower inventory valuation? Would net income be affected?

c. If the lower-of-cost-or-market rule is applied consistently in both 1961 and 1962, will the balance sheet and the income statement both reflect "conservative" figures in 1962? Explain.

12A-2. Bleak, controller for the Madden Company, prepared the income statement shown below from the accounting records at December 31, 1961. This statement indicated a significant improvement over the preceding year; the net income had been $207,000 for the year ended December 31, 1960.

MADDEN COMPANY
Income Statement
For the Year Ended December 31, 1961

Sales			$3,640,000
Less: Sales returns and allowances		$ 28,000	
Sales discounts		71,000	99,000
Net sales			$3,541,000
Cost of goods sold:			
Inventory, Jan. 1		$ 840,000	
Purchases	$2,022,000		
Deduct: Purchases returns &			
allowances	$ 8,000		
Purchase discounts	12,000	20,000	
		$2,002,000	
Transportation-in		18,000	2,020,000
Cost of goods available for sale		$2,860,000	
Deduct: Inventory, Dec. 31		143,000	
Cost of goods sold			2,717,000
Gross profit on sales			$ 824,000
Selling and administrative expenses			588,000
Net income			$ 236,000

Other data. On June 3, 1962, while reviewing inventory records, Bleak noted that incoming shipments of merchandise received near the annual closing dates had been handled as follows:

(1) Purchases in transit amounting to $16,000 on December 31, 1960, had not been included in the closing inventory of that year, although the invoice had been entered in the purchases journal on December 29, 1960, and the goods had been shipped FOB shipping point on December 28.

(2) Goods on hand on December 31, 1961, in the amount of $9,600 were not included in the inventory as of that date. The reason for this omission was that the purchase invoice for this $9,600 shipment had not yet been received and the employee supervising the physical count was of the opinion that the goods were not the property of the company until the purchase invoice was recorded. The purchase invoice in question arrived in the afternoon mail on December 31, 1961, but no entry was made for it before closing the books for 1961. The invoice was recorded on January 6, 1962, in the purchases journal as a January transaction.

Instructions

a. Compute the corrected net income for the years 1960 and 1961. State the effect of the errors on the net income for the year 1962.

b. Indicate which items, if any, were incorrectly stated in the income statement for 1961, and in the balance sheet prepared at December 31, 1961. Consider particularly whether the figures for total assets, total liabilities, and owners' equity were correctly stated. For any items you list as incorrect indicate whether the item was understated or overstated, and the dollar amount of the error.

c. Prepare any correcting journal entries you consider necessary as of June 3, 1962, the date of discovery of the errors.

12A-3. The management of the Deakin Company has been considering for some time the desirability of changing the method of pricing the year-end inventory in order to take full advantage of any tax savings which might be available. The company is presently using a weighted average cost method of pricing the inventory and has requested your recommendation as to the method to be used. The inventory on December 31, 1961, consisted of 80,000 units at a cost of 60 cents per unit. During the year 1962, sales amounted to 277,000 units @ $1 per unit, and the following purchases took place.

Date	Units	Cost
Mar. 24	44,000	$26,840
May 11	60,000	37,200
July 14	50,000	32,500
Nov. 8	96,000	63,360
Dec. 20	72,000	48,240

Instructions

a. Compute the amount of the inventory at December 31, 1962, under the weighted-average-cost method; under the first-in, first-out method; and under the last-in, first-out method.

b. Prepare comparative income statements showing the effects of the three alternative inventory valuation methods on net income. Assume that selling and administrative expenses totaled $40,000 and that the income tax rate is 50%.

c. Prepare a brief memorandum recommending one of the three methods and explaining the reasons for your choice.

12A-4. You have been employed by an insurance adjuster to examine the records of the Eddy Company, which suffered the loss by fire of its entire inventory on April 10, 1962. Your investigation has produced the income statement shown below for the year ended December 31, 1961.

THE EDDY COMPANY
Income Statement
For the Year Ended December 31, 1961

Net sales		$300,000
Cost of goods sold:		
Inventory, Jan. 1	$ 80,000	
Purchases	340,000	
Cost of goods available for sale	$420,000	
Less: Inventory, Dec. 31	180,000	240,000
Gross profit on sales		$ 60,000
Expenses		20,000
Net income		$ 40,000

Other data. Included in the purchases figure shown in the income statement was $11,250 of office equipment which the Eddy Company had acquired late in

December for its own use from a competing concern which was quitting business. The bookkeeper of the Eddy Company had not understood the nature of this transaction and had recorded it by debiting the Purchases account. The sales figure of $300,000 did not include $5,000 of merchandise packaged and ready for shipment to a customer, Miller Company, on December 31, 1961. The Miller Company had originally ordered this merchandise for delivery on December 10; just prior to that date they had requested, because of overcrowded warehouses, that the goods be held by the Eddy Company until January 10. It was agreed that the regular 30-day credit terms should run from December 10 per the original agreement. This merchandise had not been included in the Eddy Company's year-end inventory; the goods were shipped on January 10 and payment was received the same day.

Records salvaged from the fire revealed the merchandise transactions from December 31, 1961, to the date of the fire to be: Sales, $110,000; sales returns and allowances, $1,200; transportation-in, $800; purchases, $76,000; purchases returns and allowances, $1,000.

Instructions

a. Prepare a report directed to the insurance adjuster summarizing your findings. Include an estimate of the inventory value as of the date of the fire and a computation of the applicable gross profit rate.

b. Explain how the gross profit method of estimating inventories may be used other than in case of a fire loss.

c. Is the rate of gross profit customarily computed as a percentage of the cost of merchandise or as a percentage of sales? Show how the gross profit rate in this problem would vary if based on cost of goods sold rather than on sales.

12A-5. Excello, Incorporated, a retail store, carries a wide range of merchandise consisting mostly of articles of low unit price. The selling price of each item is plainly marked on the merchandise. At each year-end, the company has taken a physical count of goods on hand and has priced these goods at cost by looking up individual purchase invoices to determine the unit cost of each item in stock. Barnes, the store manager, is anxious to find a more economical method of assigning dollar values to the year-end inventory. He explains that it takes much more time to price the inventory than to count the merchandise on hand.

By reference to the accounting records, you determine that the sales of the year 1962 amounted to $650,000. During the year, net purchases of merchandise aggregated $500,000; the retail selling price of this merchandise was $700,000. At the end of 1962, a physical inventory showed goods on hand priced to sell at $150,000. This represented a considerable increase over the inventory of a year earlier. At December 31, 1961, the inventory on hand had appeared in the balance sheet at cost of $60,000, although it had a retail value of $100,000.

Instructions

a. Outline a plan whereby the inventory can be computed without the necessity of looking up individual purchase invoices. List step by step the procedures to be followed. Ignoré the possibility of markups and markdowns in the original retail price of merchandise.

b. Compute the cost of the inventory at December 31, 1962, using the method described in (a).

c. Explain how the adoption of the inventory method you have described would facilitate the preparation of monthly financial statements.

Group B

12B-1. The Level Company makes most of its sales to an agency of the Federal government and holds long-term contracts specifying the quantities to be delivered and the prices to be received. On December 31 of each year, the company takes a complete physical inventory. Included in the inventory on December 31, 1961, was a slightly damaged item which had cost $4,200. The current replacement cost (market value) was $3,750 and the sales price to be realized under the company's contract with the government agency was $4,300. The estimated cost of making the necessary repairs to place the damaged article in perfect condition and thus to permit its delivery under the sales contract was $300.

Instructions

a. At what price should the company record this item for inventory purposes?

b. Is the value you selected in conformity with the lower-of-cost-or-market rule? If not, how do you explain the acceptability of your choice?

c. In what ways would your answers to (*a*) and (*b*) differ if the net realizable value was $3,500? Explain.

d. Describe the various alternative procedures which may be followed in determining the amount of the inventory for balance sheet purposes in conformity with the lower-of-cost-or-market rule. Which procedure will produce the most conservative inventory value?

12B-2. The income statements of Baker Company for the years ended December 31, 1961 and 1962, may be summarized as follows:

	1961	*1962*
Net sales	$330,000	$350,000
Cost of goods sold:		
Beginning inventory	$120,000	$126,520
Net purchases	204,663	213,480
Cost of goods available for sale	$324,663	$340,000
Ending inventory	126,520	130,000
Cost of goods sold	$198,143	$210,000
Gross profit on sales	$131,857	$140,000
Expenses	45,000	50,000
Net income	$ 86,857	$ 90,000

The balance sheets of the company showed retained earnings as follows: December 31, 1960, $100,000; December 31, 1961, $186,857; and December 31, 1962, $276,857.

Other data. In May, 1962, John Wyman, chief accountant for the Baker Company, decided to make a careful review of the documents and procedures which had been used in taking the physical inventory at December 31, 1961. Wyman felt that this review might disclose errors which still required correction or, at least, should be given consideration to assure maximum accuracy in the taking of the next annual physical inventory. Wyman's investigation disclosed the following items:

(1) Merchandise costing $3,420, which had been received on December 31, 1961, had been included in the inventory taken on that date, although the purchase was not recorded until January 8, when the vendor's invoice arrived. The invoice was then recorded in the purchases journal as a January transaction.

(2) Merchandise shipped to a customer on December 31, 1961, FOB shipping point, was included in the physical inventory taken that day. The cost of the merchandise was $1,450 and the sales price was $1,800. Because of the press of year-end work, the sales invoice was not prepared until January 10, 1962. On that date the sale was recorded as a January transaction by entry in the sales journal, and the sales invoice was mailed to the customer.

(3) An error of $250 had been made in footing one of the inventory sheets at December 31, 1961. This clerical error had caused the inventory total to be overstated.

Instructions

a. Prepare corrected income statements for the years ended December 31, 1961 and 1962. It may be helpful to set up T accounts for Sales 1961 and Sales 1962; Purchases 1961 and Purchases 1962; and Inventory Dec. 31, 1961. Corrections may then be entered in these accounts.

b. Compute corrected amounts for retained earnings at December 31, 1961 and 1962.

c. Prepare any correcting journal entries you consider necessary at May 12, 1962, the date that these items came to Wyman's attention.

d. Assume that the $3,420 worth of merchandise described in item (1) had not been included in inventory on December 31, 1961. Would this handling of the transaction have caused an error in the cost of goods sold for 1961?

12B-3. The Heart Corporation deals in a single product of relatively low cost. The volume of sales in 1962 was $280,000, at a unit price of $4. The inventory at January 1, 1962, amounted to 12,000 units valued at cost of $24,000; purchases for the year were as follows: 21,000 units @ $2.05; 33,000 units @ $2.15; 23,000 units @ $2.20; and 9,600 units @ $2.30.

Instructions

a. Compute the December 31, 1962, inventory using (1) the first-in, first-out method; (2) the last-in, first-out method; and (3) the weighted-average method. Compute average unit cost to the nearest cent.

b. Prepare an income statement for each of the above three methods of pricing inventory. The income statements are to be carried only to the determination of gross profit on sales.

c. Which of the three methods of pricing inventory would be most advantageous from an income tax standpoint during a period of rising prices? Comment on the significance of the inventory figure under the method you recommend with respect to current replacement cost.

12B-4. Bailey Corporation stresses a rapid turnover of merchandise at a relatively low margin of profit. Emphasis is placed on holding expenses to a minimum. The company has regularly taken a physical inventory of merchandise each December 31, as a preliminary step toward preparing annual financial statements. Recently management has decided that monthly financial statements are needed as an aid to more efficient administration. But the company is reluctant to interrupt operations and incur the expense of a physical inventory at the end of each month.

You are called upon to make an investigation of the company's records and to suggest a means by which monthly financial statements can be developed without the taking of a monthly physical inventory.

You find that the company has in recent years consistently priced its goods to sell at approximately 125% of cost. Management indicates that this pricing policy will continue unchanged during 1963.

At December 31, 1962, the physical inventory indicated goods on hand with a cost of $380,000. Purchases and sales during the first three months of 1963 were as follows:

	Purchases (cost)	Sales (selling price)
January	$160,000	$180,000
February	180,000	190,000
March	240,000	280,000

Instructions

a. Compute the estimated inventories at cost at the end of each of the three months of 1963. State the rate of gross profit on sales.

b. Show how your computations in (*a*) would vary if the gross profit experiences in the past had been 25% of sales. Show how you arrive at cost of goods sold.

c. If the gross profit rate computed above had resulted from sales of a variety of products, would this have required any special consideration? Explain.

12B-5. The Halstrom Company, a retail sporting goods store, specializes in marine equipment and is divided into three departments as follows: (1) boats, (2) outboard motors, and (3) boat accessories. The principal item offered in the accessories department is boat trailers, which virtually control the average rate of mark-on in that department. The income statement for the year 1962 has just been prepared by the company accountant and the reported net income is $15,720.

The store manager is concerned about the practice of using the average-cost ratio for the year in computing the inventory and has enlisted your aid in an attempt to determine whether this method is misstating the inventory valuation under the retail inventory method. Sales for all departments totaled $486,000, whereas purchases (net) amounted to $385,000 at cost and were marked to sell at $510,000. The physical count of goods at December 31, 1962, at selling prices amounted to $94,000; the balance sheet figure as of December 31, 1961, reflected an inventory costing $50,000 and priced to sell at $70,000.

You have been able to determine the rates of mark-on for each of the departments as follows: boats, 40%; motors, 65%; and accessories, 80%.

Instructions

a. Compute the cost ratio, for the store as a unit, which was used to determine the inventory valuation on December 31, 1962. Also, compute the cost value of the inventory at December 31, 1962.

b. Would the valuation of the inventory differ if consideration was given to the departmental rates instead of the over-all cost ratio actually used?

13

Fixed assets and depreciation

Nature of fixed assets

Fixed assets are long-lived assets acquired for use in the operation of the business and not intended for resale to customers. Among the more common examples are land, buildings, machinery, furniture and fixtures, office equipment, and automobiles. A delivery truck in the showroom of an automobile dealer is inventory; when this same truck is sold to a drugstore for use in making deliveries to customers, it becomes a fixed asset.

With the exception of land, fixed assets have limited useful lives. It may even be argued that the usefulness of land as a business site is often of limited duration, because of the tendency of certain business districts to deteriorate. In accounting practice, however, it is customary to treat land as a nondepreciable asset and therefore to carry it on the books permanently at cost.

Although land used in a business is classified as a fixed asset, a tract of land acquired as a future building site and not presently used in the business is not a fixed asset. Land held as a potential building site may be classified under the balance sheet caption of Investments or under Other Assets. Similar reasoning indicates that a building formerly used in the business, but now idle and not required for operation purposes, should be excluded from the fixed asset category.

Fixed assets represent "bundles of services" to be received

It is convenient to think of a fixed asset as a bundle of services to be received by the owner over a period of years. Ownership of a delivery truck, for example, may provide about 100,000 miles of transportation. The cost of the delivery truck is customarily entered in a fixed asset account entitled Delivery Truck, which in essence represents payment in advance for several years of transportation service. Similarly, a building may be regarded as several years' supply of housing services. As the years go by, these services are utilized by the business and the cost of the fixed asset is gradually transferred into depreciation expense.

Suppose that a business is considering the construction of a building to cost $20,000 and estimated to have a useful life of 20 years. As an alternative the business has an opportunity to lease an identical building for a period of 20 years by making an advance payment of $20,000, representing 20 years' prepaid rent expense. Both the purchase and the lease transactions require a payment of $20,000, and both provide 20 years of housing for the business. An awareness of the similarity between fixed assets and prepaid expenses is essential to an understanding of the accounting process by which the cost of fixed assets is allocated to the years in which the benefits of ownership are received.

Classification of fixed assets

Fixed assets are customarily classified into one of the following groups:

I. Tangible fixed assets. The term *tangible* denotes bodily substance, as exemplified by land, a building, or a machine. Tangible fixed assets may be subdivided into two main groups:
   A. Plant property. This group includes physical property used in the operation of the business such as land, buildings, and equipment. This category of fixed assets may be subdivided again into two distinct classifications:
      1. Plant property subject to depreciation. Included in this group are plant assets of limited useful life, such as buildings and office equipment.
      2. Land. The only plant asset not subject to depreciation is land, which has an unlimited term of existence.
   B. Natural resources subject to depletion. Examples are mines, oil and gas wells, and tracts of timber. The term *depletion* means the exhaustion of a natural resource through mining, pumping, cutting, or otherwise using up the deposit or growth.
II. Intangible fixed assets. Examples are patents, copyrights, trademarks, franchises, organizations costs, leaseholds, leasehold improvements, and goodwill. Intangible assets are sometimes classified into two subgroups as follows:
   A. Intangibles having a limited term of existence and therefore subject to amortization. Patents and copyrights, for example, have a term of existence limited by law. The term *amortization* means the accounting process of gradually writing off (transferring to expense) the cost of an intangible asset during the years of its useful life. This is another example of matching costs and revenues as a means of measuring periodic income. The cost of the intangible asset is

allocated as expense of periods in which this intangible asset contributes to the revenues of the business.

B. Intangibles not having a limited term of existence, and therefore not subject to amortization. Trademarks and perpetual franchises are among the few intangible assets considered to have virtually unlimited life. Although goodwill is sometimes included in this group, the trend of current thinking is to regard goodwill as an asset of limited life and therefore subject to amortization.

Accounting problems relating to fixed assets

Some major accounting problems relating to fixed assets are indicated by the following questions:

1. How is the "cost" of a fixed asset determined?

2. How should the costs of fixed assets be allocated against revenues?

3. How should charges for repairs, maintenance, and replacements be treated?

We are presently concerned with answering the first of these questions; an understanding of how the cost of a fixed asset is determined will be helpful in subsequent study of the problem of depreciation.

Determining the cost of fixed assets. The cost of a fixed asset includes all expenditures reasonable and necessary in acquiring the asset and placing it in a position and condition for use in the operations of the business. Only *reasonable* and *necessary* expenditures should be included. For example, if the company's truck driver receives a traffic ticket while hauling a new machine to the plant, the traffic fine is *not* part of the cost of the new machine. If the machine is dropped and damaged while being unloaded, the expense of repairing the damage should not be added to the cost of the asset.

Cost is most easily determined when an asset is purchased for cash. The cost of the asset is then equal to the cash outlay necessary in acquiring the asset plus any expenditures for freight, insurance while in transit, installation, and any other miscellaneous charges necessary to make the asset ready for use. If fixed assets are purchased on the installment plan or by issuance of notes payable, the interest element or carrying charge should be recorded as interest expense and not as part of the cost of the fixed assets.

This principle of including in the cost of a fixed asset all the incidental charges necessary to put the asset in use is illustrated by the following example. A factory in Los Angeles orders a machine from a San Francisco tool manufacturer at a list price of $2,000, with terms of 2/10, n/30. A sales tax of 3% must be paid, also freight charges of $200. Drayage from the railroad station to the factory costs $25 and installation labor amounts to $100. The cost of the fixed asset and the amount to be entered in the Machinery account are computed as follows:

List price of machine	$2,000.00
Deduct: cash discount (2% × $2,000)	40.00
Net cash price	$1,960.00
Sales tax (3% × $1,960)	58.80
Freight	200.00
Drayage	25.00
Installation labor	100.00
Cost of machine	$2,343.80

Why should all the incidental charges relating to the acquisition of a fixed asset be included in its cost? Why not treat these incidental charges as expenses of the period in which the fixed asset is acquired?

The answer is to be found in the basic accounting principle of matching costs and revenues. The benefits of owning the machine will be received over a span of years, 10 years, for example. During those 10 years the operation of the machine will contribute to the revenues of the factory. Consequently, the total costs of acquiring the machine should be recorded in the fixed asset account and then allocated equitably against the revenues of the 10 years by the process of depreciation. All costs incurred in acquiring the machine are costs of the services to be received from using the machine.

If the freight charge or the sales tax applicable to the machine were charged to an expense account at the time of payment, the operations of the year of acquisition would be unfairly penalized. There is no more reason for treating such outlays as expense of the year in which the fixed asset is acquired than there would be in assigning them to any other single year during which services are obtained from the machine.

Land. When land is purchased, various incidental charges are generally incurred, in addition to the purchase price. These additional costs may include commissions to real estate brokers, escrow fees, legal fees for examining and insuring the title, accrued taxes paid by the purchaser, and fees for surveying, draining, clearing, grading, and landscaping the property. All these expenditures are part of the cost of the land and should be recorded in the fixed asset account entitled Land. Assessments for local improvements such as the paving of a street or the installation of sewers may also be charged to the Land account, for the reason that a more or less permanent value is being added to the property.

Separate ledger accounts are necessary for land and buildings, because buildings are subject to depreciation and land is not. The treatment of land as a nondepreciable fixed asset is based on the premise that land used as a building site has an unlimited life. When land and building are purchased for a lump sum, the purchase price must be apportioned between the land and the building. An appraisal may be necessary for this purpose. Assume, for example, that land and a building are purchased for a total price of $100,000. The apportionment of this cost on the basis of an appraisal may be made as follows:

	Value per appraisal	Per cent of total	Apportionment of cost
Land	$ 40,000	33 1/3%	$ 33,333
Building	80,000	66 2/3%	66,667
Total	$120,000	100%	$100,000

Sometimes a tract of land purchased as a building site has on it an old building which is not suitable for the buyer's use. The Land account should be charged with the entire purchase price plus any costs incurred in tearing down or removing the building. Salvage proceeds received from sale of the building are recorded as a credit in the Land account.

Land improvements. Improvements to real estate such as driveways, fences, parking lots, and sprinkler systems have a limited life and are therefore subject to depreciation. For this reason they should be recorded not in the Land account but in a separate fixed asset account entitled Land Improvements. On the other hand, any improvements which will last indefinitely and are not to be depreciated are entered in the Land account. The cost of landscaping, for example, may be regarded as not subject to depreciation and therefore charged to Land.

Buildings. Old buildings are sometimes purchased with the intention of repairing them prior to placing them in use. Repairs made under these circumstances are charged to the Building account. After the building has been placed in use, ordinary repairs are considered as maintenance expense when incurred.

When a building or other fixed asset is constructed by the business itself, rather than being purchased, cost includes the materials and labor used plus an equitable portion of overhead or indirect expenses, such as executive salaries. Any other expenses specifically relating to the construction such as architectural fees, insurance during the construction period, liability insurance, and building permits should also be included in the cost of the building. If money is borrowed to finance the construction of the building, the interest charges during the construction period may also be treated as part of the cost of the building. This treatment of interest charges is based on the fact that the flow of services to be derived from the building will not begin until the construction is finished and the building placed in use. All outlays including interest may therefore be included in the total cost figure which will be allocated as an expense over the years of useful life.

A building, machine, or other fixed asset constructed by a company for its own use should be recorded in the accounts at cost, not at the price which might have been paid to outsiders if the building had been acquired through purchase.

Determining cost of fixed assets when payment is made in property other than cash. An interesting theoretical question arises when fixed assets are paid for by transfer of noncash assets. Assume, for example, that the Broadacres Company owns a tract of land acquired 20 years ago as a future building site at a cost of $25,000. In the intervening years the land has risen greatly in value and a year ago a cash offer of $100,000 for the property was received and refused. The company now has an opportunity to exchange the land for a modern factory building, appropriate to its operations. The estimated value of the factory building at present prices is $150,000, but a trade is arranged in which the land is exchanged on an even basis for the factory.

At what amount should the factory property be recorded on the books of the Broadacres Company? The alternatives which deserve consideration are (1) $25,000, the original cost of the land exchanged for the factory; (2) $100,000, the indicated cash value of the land, as substantiated by a recent offer which was declined; and (3) $150,000, the estimated market value of the factory at the time of acquisition.

If the land had been sold for $100,000 in cash and the factory purchased for a price of $150,000, there would be no question as to the proper way to record the transaction. A gain of $75,000 would be recognized on the sale of the land, and the cost of the factory would be the price actually paid of $150,000. The journal entries would appear as follows:

<table>
<tr><td>ASSUMING
SEPARATE
CASH
TRANSAC-
TIONS</td><td>(a) Cash 100,000
        Land   25,000
        Gain on Sale of Land   75,000
   Sold land at a profit.

(b) Factory Building 150,000
        Cash   150,000
   Purchased factory building for cash.</td></tr>
</table>

If the land is traded for the factory, however, without any cash changing hands, traditional accounting practice would hold that no gain had been realized, and that the factory should be recorded at a cost of $25,000, the book value of the asset given in exchange. Supporters of this accounting treatment of an exchange might argue that accounting is basically the process of compiling a historical record of financial transactions that actually occur, and therefore is not concerned with prices that might have been paid or received. This argument could be reinforced with the contention that estimated prices for land and factory buildings are likely to vary widely from one appraiser to the next, and that "asking prices" are often based on nothing more tangible than wishful thinking on the part of the prospective seller. The "cash offer" which was received and declined by the Broadacres Company might be dismissed as mere talk unsubstantiated by a bona fide transaction.

Not all accountants would agree with the above arguments. One opposing view holds that the book value (undepreciated cost) of the asset given in exchange should be treated as the cost of the new asset only if there is no more meaningful basis available. To bring out this side of the argument more forcefully, let us change our assumptions slightly and assume that the Broadacres Company traded not land but marketable securities, which it had acquired many years ago at a cost of $25,000. Assume also that the securities are listed on a stock exchange and that the quoted price at the date of exchanging the securities for the factory was $100,000. This dollar valuation is not merely an estimate; it is the present market value of the securities, readily available to anyone who wishes to sell securities for cash. The exchange of securities for a factory building can logically be regarded as the equivalent of selling the securities for cash and using the cash to purchase the factory. A gain of $75,000 should be recognized on the exchange, and the factory building should be recorded at a cost of $100,000, as shown by the following entry:

RECOGNITION OF GAIN ON EXCHANGE

Factory Building 100,000		
Marketable Securities	25,000	
Gain on Disposal of Securities	75,000	

To recognize gain on exchange of marketable securities for factory building; prevailing market price of securities used as basis for recognition of gain.

The majority view in present-day accounting practice would probably favor recording the exchange of land for a factory building at an amount equal to the cost of the land, but would utilize current market price in recording the exchange of marketable securities for a fixed asset. From the standpoint of Federal income taxes, too, a distinction between the two transactions would probably be made, with a taxable gain recognized on the exchange of the securities, but no gain recognized on the exchange of land for a building. The circumstances surrounding the particular exchange transaction must always be given consideration, however, in determining whether income tax regulations require recognition of taxable income on the exchange.

The somewhat dubious logic underlying this majority viewpoint is indicative of the fact that many problems faced by the accountant have no one "correct" answer. Accounting practice is in a state of gradual but continuous change. The student of accounting should be concerned with the reasoning underlying prevailing accounting concepts, rather than accepting "current practice" as a final answer.

Depreciation

Allocating the cost of fixed assets. Fixed assets, with the exception of land, are of use to a company over a limited number of years, and the cost of each fixed asset is allocated as an expense of the years in which it is used. Accountants use the term *depreciation* to describe this gradual conversion of the cost of a fixed asset into expense.

Depreciation, as the term is used in accounting, does not mean the physical deterioration of an asset. Neither does depreciation mean the decrease in market value of a fixed asset over a period of time. Depreciation *does* mean the allocation of the cost of a fixed asset to the periods in which services are received from the asset.

When a delivery truck is purchased, its cost is first recorded as an asset. This cost becomes expense over a period of years through the accounting process of depreciation. When gasoline is purchased for the truck, the price paid for each tankful is immediately recorded as expense. In theory, both outlays (for the truck and for a tank of gas) lead to the acquisition of assets, but since it is reasonable to assume that a tankful of gasoline will be consumed in the accounting period in which it is purchased, we record the outlay for gasoline as an expense immediately. To record the cost of 10 gallons of gas as an asset and then almost immediately to transfer the cost to an expense account would require excessive bookkeeping effort and would serve no useful purpose. It is important to recognize, however, that both the outlay for the truck and the payment for the gasoline become expense in the period or periods in which each is assumed to render services.

Depreciation is described by the American Institute of Certified Public Accountants Committee on Accounting Procedure in these words:

"The cost of a productive facility is one of the costs of the services it renders during its useful economic life. Generally accepted accounting principles require that this cost be spread over the expected useful life of the facility in such a way as to allocate it as equitably as possible to the periods during which services are obtained from the use of the facility. This procedure is known as depreciation accounting, a system of accounting which aims to distribute the cost or other basic value of tangible capital assets, less salvage (if any), over the estimated useful life of the unit . . . in a systematic and rational manner. It is a process of allocation, not of valuation."[1]

Depreciation not a process of valuation. Accounting records and financial statements do not purport to show the constantly fluctuating market values associated with fixed assets. Occasionally the market value of a building may rise substantially over a period of years because of a change in the price level, or for other reasons. Depreciation is continued, however, regardless of the increase in market value. The accountant recognizes that the building will render useful services for only a limited

---

[1] *Accounting Research Bulletin 43* (New York: 1953), p. 76.

number of years, and that its full cost must be allocated as expense of those years regardless of temporary fluctuations in market value.

Causes of depreciation. There are two major causes of depreciation, physical deterioration and obsolescence.

Physical deterioration. Physical deterioration of a fixed asset results from use, and also from exposure to sun, wind, and other climatic factors. When a fixed asset has been carefully maintained, it is not uncommon for the owner to claim that the asset is as "good as new." Such statements are not literally true. Although a good repair policy may greatly lengthen the useful life of a machine, every machine eventually reaches the point at which it must be discarded. In brief, the making of repairs does not lessen the need for recognition of depreciation.

Obsolescence. The term *obsolescence* means the process of becoming out of date or obsolete. An airplane, for example, may become obsolete even though it is in excellent physical condition; it becomes obsolete because better planes of superior design and performance have become available. Obsolescence relates to the capacity of a fixed asset to render services to a particular company for a particular purpose. An airplane which has become obsolete for the purpose of oceanic flights because of the development of larger, faster planes may still be satisfactory for use in short domestic flights. Used airplanes are frequently sold by one airline to another for this reason.

Expiration of the usefulness of a fixed asset may also arise because of the growth of a company to such an extent that the present equipment is inadequate. Inadequacy of a fixed asset may necessitate replacement with a larger unit even though the asset is in good physical condition and is not obsolete. Obsolescence and inadequacy are often closely associated; both relate to the opportunity for economical and efficient use of an asset rather than to its physical condition.

Obsolescence is probably a more significant factor than physical deterioration in putting an end to the usefulness of most fixed assets. Current accounting practice, however, does not usually attempt to separate the effects of physical deterioration and obsolescence. Depreciation accounting is intended to allocate the cost of the asset among the periods in which services are received, regardless of whether obsolescence or physical deterioration is the key factor in bringing an end to the useful life of the asset.[2]

Methods of computing depreciation

Straight-line method. The simplest and most widely used method of computing depreciation is the straight-line method. This method was described in Chapter 3 and has been used repeatedly in problems through-

---

[2] Bulletin F, published by the Internal Revenue Service, provides comprehensive tables of "average useful lives" of various kinds of buildings and equipment. It is obtainable from the Superintendent of Documents, Washington.

out the book. Under the straight-line method, an equal portion of the cost of the asset is allocated to each period of use; consequently, this method is most appropriate when usage of an asset is fairly uniform from year to year.

In theory, the computation of the periodic charge for depreciation is made by deducting the estimated residual or salvage value from the cost of the asset and dividing the remaining depreciable cost by the years of estimated useful life, as shown in the following example:

COMPUTING DEPRECIA- TION BY STRAIGHT- LINE METHOD

Cost of the fixed asset	*$5,200*
Deduct: estimated salvage value (amount to be realized by sale of asset when it is retired from use)	*400*
Total amount to be depreciated	*$4,800*
Estimated useful life	*4 years*
Depreciation expense each year ($4,800 ÷ 4)	*$1,200*

CONSTANT ANNUAL CHARGE

The following schedule summarizes the accumulation of depreciation over the useful life of the asset. The amount to be depreciated is $4,800 (cost of $5,200 minus scrap value of $400).

Depreciation Schedule: Straight-line Method

Year	*Computation*	*Depreciation expense*	*Accumulated depreciation*	*Book value*
				$5,200
First	*(1/4 × $4,800)*	*$1,200*	*$1,200*	*4,000*
Second	*(1/4 × $4,800)*	*1,200*	*2,400*	*2,800*
Third	*(1/4 × $4,800)*	*1,200*	*3,600*	*1,600*
Fourth	*(1/4 × $4,800)*	*1,200*	*4,800*	*400*
		$4,800		

In practice, the possibility of salvage value is often ignored and the annual depreciation charge computed merely by dividing the total cost of the asset by the number of years of estimated useful life. This practice is justified in many cases in which salvage value is not material and is diffi- cult to estimate accurately. Under this approach the yearly depreciation charge in the above example would be $5,200 ÷ 4, or $1,300.

Units-of-output method. A more equitable distribution of the cost of some fixed assets can be obtained by dividing the original cost by the estimated units of output rather than by the estimated years of useful life. A truck line or bus company, for example, might compute depreciation on its vehicles by a mileage basis. If a truck costs $10,000 and is estimated to have a useful life of 200,000 miles, the depreciation charge per mile of operation is 5 cents ($10,000 ÷ 200,000). At the end of each year, the amount of depreciation to be recorded would be determined by multiplying the 5-cent rate by the number of miles the truck had operated during the year. This method is not widely used, perhaps because it is not very suitable to situations in which obsolescence is an important factor.

Declining-amount methods. Some accountants have long believed that depreciation is greatest in the early years of an asset's life and correspondingly less in the later years. This belief is based in part upon an awareness that plant and equipment are most efficient when new, and therefore contribute more and better services in the early years of useful life.

The current trend toward adoption of declining-amount methods of depreciation may also be explained on the grounds that the increasingly rapid pace of invention of new products is making obsolescence a factor of much greater significance than physical deterioration. When an industry is in a period of rapid technological change, fixed assets may have to be replaced within much shorter periods than would be necessary in a less dynamic economy. Businessmen may, therefore, reason that the acquisition of a new plant facility is justified only if most of the cost can be recovered within a comparatively short period of years. Also significant is the pleasing prospect of reducing the current year's income tax burden by recognizing a relatively large amount of depreciation expense.

Another argument for allocating a relatively large share of the cost of a fixed asset to the early years of use is that repair expenses tend to increase as assets grow older. A method of depreciation which provides heavy depreciation charges in the first year and lesser depreciation charges in each succeeding year will tend to offset the rising trend of repair expenses. The combined expense of depreciation and repairs may be more uniform from year to year under a declining-amount method of depreciation than when straight-line depreciation is followed.

Fixed-percentage-on-declining-balance method. For income tax purposes, one of the acceptable methods of "rapid write-off" of fixed assets consists of doubling the normal rate of depreciation and applying this doubled rate each year to the undepreciated cost (book value) of the asset.

Assume, for example, that an automobile is acquired for business use at a cost of $4,000. Estimated useful life is four years; therefore, the normal depreciation rate under the straight-line method would be 25%. To depreciate the automobile by the fixed-percentage-on-declining-balance method, we double the normal rate of 25% and apply the doubled rate of 50% to the cost. Depreciation expense in the first year would then amount to $2,000. In the second year the depreciation expense would drop to $1,000, computed at 50% of the remaining book value of $2,000. In the third year depreciation would be $500, and in the fourth year only $250. The following table shows the allocation of cost under this method of depreciation.

RAPID
WRITE-OFF:
FIXED-PER-
CENTAGE-ON-
DECLINING-
BALANCE

Depreciation Schedule: Fixed-percentage-on-declining-balance Method

Year	Computation	Depreciation expense	Accumulated depreciation	Book value
				$4,000
First	(50% × $4,000)	$2,000	$2,000	2,000
Second....	(50% × $2,000)	1,000	3,000	1,000
Third	(50% × $1,000)	500	3,500	500
Fourth	(50% × $500)	250	3,750	250

Assuming that the asset is retired from use at the end of the fourth year the undepreciated cost of $250 will be written off the books at the time of disposal. Any excess of the proceeds from sale over book value will be recognized as a gain; if the proceeds from disposal are less than the book value of $250 the difference will be recorded as a loss on the disposal of the asset.

If the automobile is continued in use beyond the estimated life of four years, depreciation will be continued at the 50% rate on the undepreciated cost. In the fifth year, for example, the depreciation expense will be $125, and in the sixth year $62.50. When the fixed-percentage-on-declining-balance method is used, the cost of a fixed asset will never be entirely written off as long as the asset continues in use. Perhaps because of the existence of this undepreciated balance of original cost, the tax regulations do not require any deduction from original cost for salvage value when this method of depreciation is used.

Sum-of-the-years'-digits method. This is another method of allocating a large portion of the cost of an asset to the early years of its use. The depreciation rate to be used is a fraction, of which the numerator is the remaining years of useful life and the denominator is the sum of the years of useful life. Consider again the example of an automobile costing $4,000 and having an estimated life of four years, but in this instance assume an estimated salvage value of $400. (Present income tax regulations require that salvage value be taken into account when either the straight-line method or the sum-of-the-years'-digits method of depreciation is used.) Since the automobile has an estimated life of four years, the denominator of the fraction will be 10, computed as follows (1 + 2 + 3 + 4 = 10). For the first year, the depreciation will be 4/10 × $3,600, or $1,440. For the second year, the depreciation will be 3/10 × $3,600, or $1,080; in the third year 2/10 × $3,600, or $720; and in the fourth year, 1/10 × $3,600, or $360. In tabular form this depreciation program will appear as follows:

Depreciation Schedule: Sum-of-the-years'-digits Method				
Year	*Computation*	*Depreciation expense*	*Accumulated depreciation*	*Book value*
				$4,000
First	*(4/10 × $3,600)*	*$1,440*	*$1,440*	*2,560*
Second . . .	*(3/10 × $3,600)*	*1,080*	*2,520*	*1,480*
Third	*(2/10 × $3,600)*	*720*	*3,240*	*760*
Fourth	*(1/10 × $3,600)*	*360*	*3,600*	*400*

Special considerations of depreciation

Depreciation and income taxes. In recent years declining-amount methods of depreciation have received increased attention because the Federal government has permitted their use for income tax purposes. By offering businessmen the opportunity of writing off as depreciation expense a large portion of the cost of a new asset during its first year of use, the government has provided a powerful incentive for investment in new productive facilities. Since an increased charge for depreciation expense will reduce taxable income, the businessman may feel that by purchasing new assets and writing off a large part of the cost in the early years of use, he is in effect paying for the new assets with dollars that otherwise would have been used to pay income taxes.

Some countries have gone further than the United States in liberalizing the treatment of depreciation for income tax purposes, even permitting the entire cost of a new fixed asset to be treated as an expense of the year of acquisition. However, with such immediate write-off, there can be no depreciation expense in the remaining years of use of the property. Furthermore, if income tax rates are raised during the life of the asset, the taxpayer may derive less tax benefit from early depreciation of the asset than he would from the alternative policy of spreading depreciation expense uniformly over its useful life.

In theory, the ideal depreciation policy is one that allocates the cost of a fixed asset to the several periods of its use in proportion to the services received each period. Declining-amount methods of depreciation sometimes fail to allocate the cost of an asset in proportion to the flow of services from the property and therefore prevent the determination of annual net income on a realistic basis. If annual net income figures are misleading, stockholders, creditors, management, and others who use financial statements as a basis for business decisions may be seriously injured. For income tax purposes, however, declining-amount methods of depreciation may be effective in encouraging businessmen to invest in new productive facilities and thereby to raise the level of business activity.

Accelerated depreciation of emergency facilities. During World War II the government encouraged businessmen to construct additional plant facilities needed for military production by permitting depreciation of these "emergency facilities" for tax purposes on the basis of a 60-month life. This type of accelerated depreciation gives a greater degree of assurance to the businessman that the cost of the plant can be recovered during the period of emergency production. This program has been continued in the postwar period, and much of our present industrial plant has been depreciated for income tax purposes on a 60-month basis, although the useful economic life of the property may actually cover a much longer period.

Emergency facilities which are being written off in 60 months for tax purposes may be depreciated according to expected useful life for general accounting purposes. For example, a new building classified as an emergency facility might be written off on a 60-month basis for tax purposes, but depreciated over a period of 20 or 30 years for financial reporting purposes. Net income for accounting purposes may differ significantly from taxable income computed under existing tax laws.

Depreciation and inflation. The valuation of fixed assets on a cost basis and the computation of depreciation in terms of cost works very well during periods of stable price levels. In the preceding discussion of depreciation as a major factor in the determination of net income, there has been an implicit assumption of unchanging price levels. However, the great rise in the price level in recent years has led many businessmen to suggest that a more realistic measurement of net income could be achieved by basing depreciation on the estimated replacement cost of fixed assets rather than on the original cost of the assets presently in use. An alternative proposal is to adjust each year's depreciation charge by a price index measuring changes in the purchasing power of the dollar. This price-level adjustment would cause depreciation expense to be stated in *current dollars,* as are such expenses as wages and taxes.

As a specific illustration, assume that a manufacturing company purchased machinery in 1945 at a cost of $100,000. Estimated useful life was 15 years and straight-line depreciation was used. Throughout this 15-year period the price level rose sharply. By 1960 the machinery purchased in 1945 was fully depreciated; it was scrapped and replaced by new machinery in 1960. Although the new machines were not significantly different from the old, they cost $300,000, or three times as much as the depreciation expense which had been recorded during the life of the old machinery. Many businessmen would argue that the depreciation expense for the 15 years was in reality $300,000, because this was the outlay required for new machinery if the company was merely to "stay even" in its productive facilities. It is also argued that reported profits will be overstated during a period of rising prices if depreciation is based on the lower plant costs of some years ago. An overstatement of profits causes higher income taxes and perhaps larger demands for wage increases than are justified by the company's financial position and earnings.

As yet there has been no general acceptance of the suggestion for basing depreciation on replacement cost. Replacement cost is difficult to determine on any objective basis; who can say how much it will cost to buy a new machine 15 years from now? The proposal to use a general price index to adjust each year's depreciation expense appears more promising. The American Institute of Certified Public Accountants in its Accounting Research Bulletin 43 has recognized that business management faces a serious problem in replacing fixed assets at costs far higher than those of assets now in use. The desirability of making price-level adjustments in computing depreciation for price studies and other managerial uses is recognized. For annual reports to stockholders, creditors, and government, however, the AICPA holds that "no basic change in the accounting treatment of depreciation of plant and equipment is practicable or desirable under present conditions to meet the problem created by the decline in the purchasing power of the dollar." [3]

Depreciation and the problem of replacement. Many readers of financial statements who have not studied accounting mistakenly believe that accumulated depreciation accounts (depreciation reserves) represent funds accumulated for the purpose of buying new fixed assets when the present facilities wear out. Perhaps the best way to combat such mistaken notions is to emphasize that the credit balance in an accumulated depreciation account represents the expired cost of assets acquired in the past. The amounts credited to the accumulated depreciation account could, as an alternative, have been credited directly to the fixed asset account. An accumulated depreciation account has a *credit* balance, it does not represent an asset, and it cannot be used in any way to pay for new equipment. To buy a new fixed asset requires cash; the total amount of cash owned by a company is shown by the asset account for cash.

Recording depreciation

The adjusting entry to record depreciation has been repeatedly illustrated in previous chapters. It consists of a debit to a depreciation expense account and a credit to an accumulated depreciation account. The accumulated depreciation account appears in the balance sheet as a deduction from the related asset.

A separate depreciation expense account and a separate accumulated depreciation account are maintained for each group of depreciable fixed assets such as buildings, office equipment, and automobiles. Depreciation is recorded at least once a year and may be recorded more frequently. Most businesses prepare monthly financial statements, and for this purpose depreciation entries may be made on the work sheet only. It is common practice to enter depreciation in the books on an annual basis, even though the computation is made on work sheets each month.

Depreciation for fractional periods. In the case of fixed assets acquired sometime during the year, it is customary to figure depreciation to the nearest month. For example, if a building is acquired on July 5 at

[3] *Ibid.,* p. 68.

a cost of $48,000 and is estimated to have a useful life of 20 years, the depreciation to be recorded at December 31 would cover the six-month period from July 1 to December 31 and would amount to $1,200. It is often convenient to express the useful life of a fixed asset in months rather than years. The building in our example has an estimated life of 20 years, or 240 months. The monthly depreciation charge is $48,000 ÷ 240, or $200. Since the building has been in use only six months during the first year, the depreciation to be recorded at December 31 is $1,200 (6 × $200). If the building had been acquired on July 18 (or any other date in the latter half of July), only five months' depreciation would have been recorded at the end of the year.

Some businesses prefer to begin depreciation on the first of the month following the acquisition of a fixed asset. This method, or any one of many similar variations, is acceptable so long as it is followed consistently by the business.

Capital expenditures and revenue expenditures

The term *expenditure* means making a payment or incurring an obligation to make a future payment for an asset or service received. The acquisition of an asset (such as an automobile) or of a service (such as repairs to the automobile) may be for cash or on credit. In either situation the transaction is properly referred to as an expenditure.

Expenditures for the purchase of land, buildings, and other semi-permanent properties are called capital expenditures and are recorded in asset accounts. Expenditures for repairs, maintenance, fuel, and other items necessary to the ownership and use of a fixed asset are called revenue expenditures and are charged to expense accounts.

The purchase of a delivery truck is an example of a capital expenditure. The outlay for the delivery truck results in a flow of benefits or services over a period of years. It is recorded by debiting the asset account, Delivery Truck, and crediting either Cash or a liability account. The purchase of gasoline for the truck (or of repair parts such as new spark plugs) is an example of a revenue expenditure. The benefits from this type of expenditure will generally be limited to the present accounting period, and the transaction will be recorded by a debit to an expense account, such as Gasoline Expense, or Repair Expense. The charge to an expense account is based on the assumption that the benefits from the expenditure will be used up in the current period, and the payment should therefore be deducted from the revenues of the current period in determining the net income.

Examples. Consistency in distinguishing between capital expenditures and revenue expenditures is essential to a proper determination of net income and to an accurate accounting for fixed assets. Many companies have developed formal policy statements defining capital and revenue expenditures as a means of achieving consistency in making this distinction in their various branches and divisions, and from year to year.

Often these policy statements include a provision that no expenditure below a specified amount (such as $50 or $100) shall be capitalized. Charging small expenditures to expense at the time of acquisition requires less time and paper work than entering them in fixed asset accounts and making depreciation entries over a period of years. For example, the acquisition of a pencil sharpener at a cost of, say, $3 is reasonably charged to expense, despite the fact that it will probably have a useful life extending beyond the current accounting period.

Among the more common types of capital expenditures are the following:

1. Acquisition cost of a fixed asset, including freight, sales tax, and installation charges. When secondhand property is purchased, the cost of any repairs made to put the property in good operating condition before placing it in use are also considered as capital expenditures and are charged to the asset account.

2. Additions. If a building is enlarged by adding a new wing or a mezzanine floor, the benefits from the expenditure will be received over a period of several years, and the outlay should be debited to the asset account.

3. Betterments. The replacement of a stairway with an escalator is an example of an expenditure for a betterment or improvement which will yield benefits over a period of years and should therefore be charged to the asset account.

The leading example of revenue expenditures is ordinary repairs. The term *ordinary repairs* is used to include all types of repair, maintenance, lubrication, cleaning, and inspection necessary to keep an asset in good operating condition. The cost of replacing small component parts of an asset (such as window panes in a building or tires and battery in an automobile) are also included in ordinary repairs.

Any expenditure made for the purpose of maintaining a fixed asset in normally efficient working condition is an expense, and will appear on the income statement as a deduction from the revenues of the current period. The treatment of an expenditure as a deduction from the revenues of the current period is the reason for the term revenue expenditure.

Effect of errors in distinguishing between capital and revenue expenditures. Because a capital expenditure is recorded by debiting an asset account, the transaction has no immediate effect upon net income. However, the depreciation of the amount entered in the asset account will be reflected as an expense in future periods. A revenue expenditure, on the other hand, is recorded by debiting an expense account and therefore represents an immediate deduction from earnings in the current period.

If a capital expenditure is erroneously recorded as a revenue expenditure, as, for example, charging the cost of a new typewriter to the Office Expense account, the result will be an understatement of the current year's net income. If the error is not corrected, the net income of subsequent years will be overstated because no depreciation expense will be recognized during the years in which the typewriter is used.

If a revenue expenditure is erroneously treated as a capital expenditure, as, for example, charging the outlay for truck repairs to the asset account, Delivery Truck, the result will be an overstatement of the current year's net income. If the error is not corrected, the net income of future years will be understated because of excessive depreciation charges based on the inflated amount of the Delivery Truck account.

These examples indicate that a careful distinction between capital and revenue expenditures is essential to attainment of one of the most fundamental objectives of accounting—the determination of net income for each year of operation of the business.

Extraordinary repairs

The term *extraordinary repairs* has a specific meaning in accounting terminology; it means a repair that will extend the useful life of a fixed asset beyond the original estimate. For example, a new automobile may be depreciated on the basis of an estimated useful life of four years. Assume that after three years of use, a decision is made to install a new engine in the automobile and thereby to extend its over-all useful life from the original estimate of four years to a total of six years.

An extraordinary repair of this type may be recorded by debiting the accumulated depreciation account. This entry is sometimes explained by the argument that the extraordinary repair cancels out some of the depreciation previously recorded. The effect of this reduction (debit entry) in the accumulated depreciation account is to *increase* the book value of the asset by the cost of the extraordinary repair. Since an extraordinary repair causes an increase in the book value of the asset and has no immediate direct effect upon income, it may be regarded as a form of capital expenditure.

To expand the above example of an extraordinary repair to an automobile, assume the following data: on January 1, 1960, a new automobile was acquired at a cost of $4,000, estimated useful life, four years; salvage value, zero; annual depreciation expense, $1,000. Three years later on December 31, 1962, extraordinary repairs (a new engine) were made at a cost of $1,100. Estimated useful life of the automobile beyond this date was thereby increased from the original estimate of one year to a revised estimate of three more years. The ledger accounts will appear as follows after recording these events.

EXTRAORDI-
NARY
REPAIR
CHARGED TO
ACCUMU-
LATED DE-
PRECIATION

	Automobile		Accumulated Depreciation		
Jan. 1, 1960	*4,000*		*Dec. 31, 1962* *1,100*	*Dec. 31, 1960*	*1,000*
				Dec. 31, 1961	*1,000*
				Dec. 31, 1962	*1,000*

The book value of the automobile is now $2,100, and the balance sheet presentation will be as follows on December 31, 1962.

INCREASED
NET FIGURE
FOR FIXED
ASSETS

Fixed assets:
    Automobile $4,000
      Less: accumulated depreciation 1,900   2,100

In the remaining three years of estimated life for the automobile, the annual depreciation provision will be $700 (book value $2,100 ÷ 3). Three years later at the end of 1965, the automobile will be fully depreciated, and the Accumulated Depreciation account will show a credit balance of $4,000 (credits of $5,100 and debits of $1,100). The valuation account now exactly offsets the asset account and no more depreciation can be taken. Observe that the total depreciation recorded during the six years the automobile was in use amounts to $5,100; this agrees exactly with the total expended for the automobile and for the extraordinary repair. In other words, these two capital expenditures have been transformed into expense over a period of six years, during which the business was receiving the benefits from the expenditures.

TOTA' DE-
PRECIATION
EQUALS
TOTAL
COST
INCURRED

Accumulated Depreciation			
Dec. 31, 1962	1,100	Dec. 31, 1960	1,000
		Dec. 31, 1961	1,000
		Dec. 31, 1962	1,000
		Dec. 31, 1963	700
		Dec. 31, 1964	700
		Dec. 31, 1965	700

Charging extraordinary repairs that arrest depreciation and appreciably prolong the life of the property to accumulated depreciation is an approved procedure for income tax purposes.

QUESTIONS

1. The Manning Company purchased machinery with a list price of $24,000 and credit terms of 2/10, n/30. Payment was made immediately. Freight charges on the machinery amounted to $1,200 and the labor cost of installing the machines in the plant was $2,000. During the unloading and installation work a part of the machinery fell off the loading platform and was damaged. Replacement of the damaged parts cost $1,800. After the machinery had been in use for three months it was thoroughly cleaned and lubricated at a cost of

$400. State the total amount which should be capitalized by charge to the Machinery account.

2. Factory machinery owned by the Dodge Company is considered physically capable of being used for 15 years, but management believes that the development of new, more efficient types of machines will make it necessary to replace the present equipment within 10 years. After using the machines for two years, the company changed from its customary one shift per day to operating three shifts per day. The new three-shift operation was considered necessary for about a year to meet a temporary increase in demand resulting from a strike affecting competing plants.

Assuming that the company employs straight-line depreciation, what period of useful life should be used? Should the company increase its depreciation charges proportionately during the year when operations were increased from one to three shifts daily?

3. A factory machine acquired at a cost of $93,600 was to be depreciated by the sum-of-the-years'-digits method over an estimated life of eight years. Residual salvage value was estimated to be $1,600. State the amount of depreciation during the first year and during the eighth year.

4. Identify the following expenditures as capital expenditures or revenue expenditures:

a. Purchased new spark plugs at a cost of $6.40 for two-year-old delivery truck.

b. Installed an escalator at a cost of $3,800 in a three-story building which had previously been used for some years without elevators or escalators.

c. Purchased a pencil sharpener at a cost of $1.25.

d. Immediately after acquiring new delivery truck at a cost of $3,800, paid $75 to have the name of the store and other advertising material painted on the truck.

e. Painted delivery truck at a cost of $75 after two years of use.

5. Criticize the following quotation:

"We shall have no difficulty in paying for new fixed assets needed during the coming year because our estimated outlays for new equipment amount to only $20,000, and we have more than twice that amount in our depreciation reserves at present."

PROBLEMS

Group A

13A-1. The White Company is engaged in manufacturing in a highly competitive industry, in which products and methods of producing them change very rapidly. Because of the significance of the obsolescence factor, the company is interested in depreciating some newly acquired equipment by allocating most of the cost to the early years of estimated useful life. The president of the White Company has asked that comparative figures be developed showing the annual depreciation charges under (*a*) the straight-line method and (*b*) the sum-of-the-years'-digits method.

The equipment was acquired on January 1, 1960, at a cost of $104,000. Estimated useful life is five years, and scrap value is estimated as $4,000.

Instructions. Prepare separate five-year depreciation schedules for (*a*) the straight-line method and (*b*) the sum-of-the-years'-digits method, with column heads as shown below.

Year ending Dec. 31	Cost of equip- ment	Scrap value	Amount to be depre- ciated	Annual depre- ciation expense	Accumu- lated depre- ciation	Book value

13A-2. On July 1, 1960, Jameson Company purchased a new machine at the advertised price of $8,000. The terms of payment were 2/10, n/30 and payment was made immediately, including a 4% state sales tax. On July 3, the machine was de-livered; Jameson Company paid freight charges of $181.40 and assigned its own employees to the task of installation. The labor costs for installing the machine amounted to $665. During the process of installation, carelessness by a workman caused damage to an adjacent machine, with resulting repairs of $90.

On October 15, after more than three months of satisfactory operation, the machine was thoroughly inspected, cleaned, and oiled at a cost of $85.

The useful life of the machine was estimated to be 10 years and the scrap value to be zero. The policy of the Jameson Company is to use straight-line de-preciation and to begin depreciation as of the first of the month in which a fixed asset is acquired. During 1960 and 1961, however, numerous changes in the company's accounting personnel were responsible for a number of errors and deviations from policy.

At December 31, 1961, the unaudited financial statements of the Jameson Company showed the machine to be carried at a cost of $7,840 and the accumu-lated depreciation as $1,176. Net income reported for 1960 was $21,250 and for 1961 $23,800.

Instructions

a. Prepare entries in general journal form for all the above transactions from July 1 to December 31, 1960. Include the year-end entry for depreciation and the related closing entry.

b. Compute the correct balances for the Machinery account and for ac-cumulated depreciation at December 31, 1961.

c. Compute revised figures for net income for 1960 and 1961.

13A-3. The Carson company, owned by John K. Carson, is a manufacturer of electrical equipment. At December 31, 1961, the fixed assets of the company were as follows:

	Date acquired	Cost	Salvage value	Useful life, years	Accumu- lated depre- ciation
Building A	July 1, 1957	$126,000	$6,000	20	$27,000
Machinery	Jan. 1, 1958	29,000	1,000	7	16,000
Office equipment	July 1, 1957	14,000	1,500	5	11,250
Delivery equipment ..	Apr. 1, 1958	20,000	2,000	4	16,875
Land	July 1, 1957	34,000			

During 1962 and early 1963, the following transactions took place:

1962

Jan. 1. Purchased for $80,000 a tract of land and three buildings. An independent appraiser's report on this property showed a total valuation of $100,000 broken down as follows: land, $50,000; building B, $20,000; building C, $25,000; and building D, $5,000. The appraisal indicated a useful life of 20 years for buildings B and C and 5 years for building D with no salvage value for any of the three.

Jan. 2. Building D was demolished to make room for construction of a new storage building. The necessity of this move had been taken into consideration by management in purchasing the property. The expense was nominal.

Apr. 1. Purchased new delivery equipment with a list price of $24,000. Paid nothing down, but signed a note for $25,440 payable in 12 equal monthly installments of $2,120 each. Useful life of this equipment was estimated as four years, scrap value as $1,600. The old delivery equipment was retained for emergency use. (Entries for payments on the note are not required.)

July 1. Construction of a new storage building, building E, was completed at a contract price of $28,000. The building was erected by the Carson Construction Company owned by William Carson, a brother of John K. Carson. John K. Carson stated that other contractors had bid $50,000 or more to do the job. Made payment by delivery of marketable securities acquired five years previously at cost of $20,000. Stock market quotations indicated a present value of $28,000. Life was estimated as 20 years, with no salvage value.

Oct. 1. Purchased additional office equipment for $5,600 cash. Estimated useful life, five years; salvage value, $600.

1963

Jan. 6. Extraordinary repairs costing $4,000 were made to the machinery. It was estimated that these repairs would extend the useful life of the machinery by four years.

Instructions

a. Prepare journal entries in general journal form to record the 1962 transactions. Use a separate asset account for each building (buildings A, B, etc.).

b. Prepare a depreciation schedule to compute the 1962 depreciation expense. Use the following column headings for this schedule:

Type of asset	Date of acquisition	Cost	Salvage value	Amount to be depreciated	Useful life	Accumulated depreciation, Dec. 31, 1961	Depreciation expense, 1962

In this schedule use a separate line for each of the four depreciable items owned at December 31, 1961, and a separate line for each unit of plant and equipment acquired during 1962. For assets acquired during the year, compute depreciation for an appropriate fraction of the year, including the month in which the acquisition occurred.

c. Prepare a compound journal entry to record depreciation expense for 1962. Combine the depreciation on all buildings into a single amount. Also make the necessary combinations with respect to items of office equipment and delivery equipment.

d. Prepare a partial balance sheet showing plant and equipment and accumulated depreciation at December 31, 1962.

e. Prepare the journal entry for the extraordinary repairs to machinery on January 6, 1963.

f. Prepare the adjusting entry at December 31, 1963, to record the depreciation expense for machinery. Include in the explanation the computations necessary to determine the depreciation to be taken.

13A-4. The Burnside Company on January 1, 1961, was able to buy from a bankrupt competitor some nearly new machinery at a bargain price. The machinery had originally been purchased new on January 1, 1960, by a competing company, Farside Corporation, for $50,000 and had been depreciated by the straight-line method on the basis of a 10-year useful life with no scrap value. Because of financial difficulties which interrupted operations of the Farside Corporation early in 1960, the machines had been used for only a few weeks, but a full year's depreciation had been recorded at December 31, 1960.

Burnside Company acquired the slightly used machinery on January 1, 1961, by making a cash payment of $5,000 and agreeing to assume full responsibility for a note payable and past-due interest thereon to the manufacturer of the machinery. The note had been issued to the machinery manufacturer on January 1, 1960, by the Farside Corporation in the amount of $20,000 with interest at 6% per annum payable semiannually (July 1 and January 1). The principal amount was due on January 1, 1963. The Farside Corporation had failed to make the semiannual interest payments during 1960; immediately upon acquisition of the machinery on January 1, 1961, Burnside Company, in accordance with the terms of the purchase agreement, sent a check for the delinquent interest payments to the machinery manufacturer along with a letter stating that prompt payment of interest and principal could be expected in the future.

Immediately after acquisition by Burnside Company, the machinery was overhauled on January 2 at a cost of $500. Freight and installation costs amounting to $750 were paid on January 3. Mr. Burns, owner of the Burnside Company, decided that the original estimate of a 10-year life made when the machinery was new had been a valid estimate, and that straight-line depreciation should be employed with no provision for scrap value. Other machinery of similar nature purchased new by the Burnside Company was being depreciated at 10% a year.

Although new improved models of machinery had come on the market in recent months, Mr. Burns felt that the used machinery he had acquired was in perfect physical condition and worth the full original price of $50,000. He therefore instructed the bookkeeper to debit the Machinery account for $50,000, to credit Cash for $5,000, Notes Payable for $20,000, and Miscellaneous Revenue for $25,000. All other outlays relating to the acquisition of the machinery were charged to expense accounts.

At December 31, 1962, the balance sheet of the Burnside Company gave the following information on the machinery acquired from the Farside Corporation:

Machinery	*$50,000*	
Less: accumulated depreciation	*10,000*	*$40,000*

Net income reported by Burnside Company since acquisition of the machinery was as follows: 1961, $42,000; 1962, $35,000. Interest payments on the note had been made as agreed, and a check for the principal and final interest payment was mailed on December 31, 1962.

Instructions

a. Prepare journal entries in accordance with generally accepted accounting principles to record all matters pertaining to the machinery, including depreciation and the transactions relating to the note payable. It is not necessary to correct the erroneous entries now on the books.

b. Compute the correct balance of the machinery and accumulated depreciation at December 31, 1962.

c. Compute corrected net income figures for 1961 and 1962, assuming that proper accounting principles had been followed.

Group B

13B-1. Adam Brewster, an investor and retired executive, was considering the purchase of Stream Company, a single proprietorship engaged in manufacturing. The net earnings of Stream Company for the last four years were stated by the management to have been as follows: 1958, $26,000; 1959, $19,000; 1960, $18,000; and 1961, $20,000. To satisfy himself that the reported earnings figures were dependable, Brewster retained James Wade, a certified public accountant, to review the accounting records of Stream Company for the last four years. In his investigation, Wade noted these transactions relating to fixed assets.

(1) Machinery acquired on January 2, 1953, at a cost of $40,000 had been retired from use at the end of 1958 when new improved types of machinery were acquired on a lease basis by Stream at an annual fee of $5,000. The old machinery had been depreciated on the straight-line basis on the assumption of a 10-year life. When it was retired from use and placed in storage on December 31, 1958, the Stream Company had reduced the depreciation rate for subsequent years to 3%, on the grounds that since the machinery was not in use it would last considerably longer than the original estimated life of 10 years. The company had charged $2,000 per year of the rental cost of the new machines to the Machinery account, the remainder being recorded as Machine Rental Expense. The bookkeeper defended the annual debits to the asset account on the grounds that by leasing the machines rather than purchasing them, the company achieved a net annual saving of $2,000 in taxes, repairs, and depreciation.

(2) In June, 1958, the parking lot of the Stream Company had been covered with asphalt at a cost of $8,000, which had been charged to the Land account. The constant movement of heavy trucks across this area had caused the paving to deteriorate rapidly and in June, 1960, the old pavement was torn up and replaced with concrete at a cost of $14,000. The only entry made to record this improvement of the parking lot was to charge the $14,000 to the Land account. Wade was informed by the construction firm which installed the concrete pavement that it should have a useful life of about 10 years under prevailing use.

Instructions. Compute revised amounts of annual earnings of Stream Company for the years 1958 through 1961 based upon Wade's findings. Income taxes need not be considered.

13B-2. The London Company has acquired four costly machines in recent years, but management has given little consideration to depreciation policies. At the time of acquisition of each machine, a different bookkeeper was employed; consequently, various methods of depreciation have been adopted for the several machines. Information concerning the four machines may be summarized as follows:

Machine	Date acquired	Cost	Estimated useful life, years	Estimated scrap value	Method of depreciation
A	Jan. 1, 1960	45,000	6	None	Fixed-percentage-on-declining-balance
B	June 30, 1960	72,000	8	10%	Straight-line
C	Jan. 1, 1961	56,000	10	$1,000	Sum-of-the-years'-digits
D	Jan. 1, 1962	33,000	12	None	Fixed-percentage-on-declining-balance

Instructions

a. Compute the amount of accumulated depreciation, if any, on each machine at December 31, 1961. For machines A and D, assume that the depreciation rate was double the rate which would be applicable under the straight-line method.

b. Prepare a depreciation schedule for use in the computation of the 1962 depreciation expense. Use the following column headings:

Machine	Method of depreciation	Date of acquisition	Cost	Salvage value	Amount to be depreciated	Useful life	Accumulated depreciation, Dec. 31, 1961	Depreciation expense, 1962

c. Prepare journal entries to record the 1962 depreciation expense.

13B-3. After occupying rented quarters for several years, Rogers Manufacturing Co. decided to construct its own plant. On January 1, 1962, the company purchased a tract of land on which two old buildings were located. The old buildings were torn down and construction of the new plant was begun at once. All expenditures relating to the new plant were charged to a single account entitled Land and Buildings.

Construction of the new plant was completed on November 30 and regular production operations were begun in the new facilities on December 1, 1962. The balance in the Land and Buildings account at the end of the year was $842,500. Information for use in computing depreciation was as follows:

Asset	Useful life, years	Salvage value, %
Building	20	10
Land Improvements	20	
Machinery and Equipment	15	10
Office Equipment	10	10

Other data. Entries in the Land and Buildings account during 1962 were as follows:

Debits:

Cost of land and old buildings purchased as site for construction of new plant (appraised value of old buildings, $10,000)	$125,000
Legal fees involved in securing title to property	300
Cost of demolishing old buildings	12,700
Surveying and grading costs	12,000
Contract price of new building, $445,000, paid for by delivery to contractor of $450,000 par value of United States government bonds, which had cost the Rogers Manufacturing Co. $490,000 and had a market value at date of delivery to contractor of $445,000	490,000
Salary paid R. Brown, plant engineer, assigned to supervise construction of new plant (Jan. 1 to Nov. 30)	14,000
Paving of plant parking lot	4,000
Cost of machinery badly damaged by fire while awaiting installation in new building. Sold as scrap. Not insured	40,000
Machinery for new plant, including units to replace those damaged by fire	94,000
Cost of installing machinery in new plant	6,000
Landscaping of grounds	4,000
Office equipment	18,000
Rent for December on old plant. Vacated on Nov. 30; lease expired Dec. 12	2,000
Retaining walls and fences	14,000
Payment to architect for design of plant, and services during construction	19,000
Insurance on building during construction	2,000
Paneling and special finishing work on executive offices	4,000
Repairs to building damaged by earthquake on Dec. 20	1,500
Total debits	$862,500

Credits:

Proceeds from sale of materials from old buildings demolished	$ 4,000
Proceeds from sale of machinery damaged by fire	16,000
Total credits	$ 20,000
Balance, Dec. 31, 1962	$842,500

Instructions

a. Reclassify the items in the Land and Buildings account to the proper ledger accounts. This reclassification may conveniently be made on an analytical work sheet.

b. Prepare a depreciation schedule showing the fractional-year depreciation for 1962 (straight-line method) for each type of depreciable asset.

13B-4. Among the plant assets used by Drive Company is a large machine which was acquired new on March 31, 1959, at a cost of $66,000. Depreciation has been computed by the straight-line method based on an estimated life of five years and residual scrap value of $6,000.

In early January of 1962, extraordinary repairs (which were almost equivalent to a rebuilding of the machine) were performed at a cost of $11,000. Because of the thoroughgoing nature of these extraordinary repairs, the normal life of the machine was extended materially. The revised estimate of useful life was four years from January 1, 1962.

Instructions

a. Prepare journal entries to record original purchase of the machine; the provision for depreciation on December 31, 1959, 1960, and 1961; the expenditure for the extraordinary repairs in January, 1962; and the provision for depreciation on December 31, 1962.

b. Reconstruct the ledger accounts for machinery and accumulated depreciation, showing all entries from date of purchase through December 31, 1962.

14

Fixed assets, natural resources, and intangibles

Disposal of fixed assets

When fixed assets wear out or become obsolete, they must be discarded, sold, or traded in on new equipment. Upon the disposal or retirement of a depreciable fixed asset, the cost of the property is removed from the fixed asset account, and the accumulated depreciation is removed from the related valuation account. Assume, for example, that office equipment purchased 10 years ago at a cost of $500 has been fully depreciated and is no longer useful. The entry to record the discarding of the worthless equipment is as follows:

SCRAPPING FULLY DE- PRECIATED ASSET

Accumulated Depreciation: Office Equipment *500*
     Office Equipment *500*
To remove from the accounts the cost and the accumu- lated depreciation on fully depreciated office equipment now being discarded. No salvage value.

Some fixed assets last much longer than the original estimate of useful life; others may be discarded earlier than indicated by the estimate of useful life. When an asset has been fully depreciated, no more depreciation should be recorded on it, even though the property is in good condition and is continued in use. The objective of depreciation is to spread the *cost* of an asset over the periods of its usefulness; in no case can depreciation expense be greater than the amount paid for the asset. When a fully depreciated asset is continued in use beyond the original estimate of useful life, the asset account and the accumulated depreciation account may be permitted to remain on the books without further entries until the date of discarding the asset.

Gains and losses on disposal of fixed assets. The book value of a fixed asset is its cost minus the total recorded depreciation, as shown by the accumulated depreciation account. For a fully depreciated asset, the book value is zero, since the credit balance in the accumulated depreciation account exactly offsets the debit balance in the asset account. If a fixed asset is discarded before it is fully depreciated, a loss results in an amount equal to the book value of the asset. If a fixed asset is sold before or after being fully depreciated, the loss or gain on the disposal is computed by comparing the book value with the amount received from the sale. A sales price in excess of the book value produces a gain; a sales price below the book value produces a loss. The occurrence of such gains and losses suggests that depreciation taken in prior years may have been too great or too small. From this standpoint, these "gains and losses" may be regarded as corrections of prior year's earnings.

Gains and losses from the retirement of fixed assets may be presented in the income statement under a caption such as Other Revenue and Expense, or Nonoperating Gains and Losses. This type of gain or loss is listed near the bottom of the income statement after the income from operations has been shown. Other alternative methods of separating nonoperating or extraordinary gains and losses from operating results will be considered in Chapter 20.

Sale at a price above book value. The following data illustrate the realization of a gain on the retirement of a fixed asset.

GAIN ON ASSET DISPOSED OF

Machinery (cost)	*$10,000*
Accumulated depreciation	*8,000*
Book value	*$ 2,000*
Proceeds from sale	*3,000*
Gain on disposal	*$ 1,000*

The journal entry to record this sale at a profit is as follows:

Cash	*3,000*	
Accumulated Depreciation: Machinery	*8,000*	
Machinery		*10,000*
Gain and Loss on Disposal of Fixed Assets		*1,000*
To record sale of machinery at price above book value.		

Sale at a price below book value. The following data illustrate the retirement of a fixed asset at a loss.

Machinery (cost)	$10,000
Accumulated depreciation	8,000
Book value	$ 2,000
Proceeds from sale	500
Loss on disposal	$ 1,500

The journal entry to record this retirement at a loss is as follows:

LOSS ON ASSET DISPOSED OF

Cash	500	
Accumulated Depreciation: Machinery	8,000	
Gain and Loss on Disposal of Fixed Assets	1,500	
Machinery		10,000
To record sale of machinery below book value.		

Sale at a price equal to book value. Generally the disposal of fixed assets will result in a gain or loss, but occasionally the disposal proceeds may be exactly equal to the book value. Assume the following facts as to the retirement of the asset.

Machinery	$10,000
Accumulated depreciation	8,000
Book value	$ 2,000
Proceeds from sale	2,000

The journal entry to record this sale at book value is:

NO GAIN OR LOSS

Cash	2,000	
Accumulated Depreciation: Machinery	8,000	
Machinery		10,000
To record sale of machinery at book value.		

Depreciation for fractional period preceding disposal. When fixed assets are disposed of at any date other than the end of the year, it is customary to record depreciation for the fraction of the year ending with the date of disposal. Assume that the accounts showed the following balances as of December 31.

Office Equipment	$2,000
Accumulated Depreciation: Office Equipment	1,600

The balance of $1,600 in the accumulated depreciation account was the result of eight annual credits of $200 each. On the following March 31, the office equipment was sold for $100. No depreciation had been recorded since the books were adjusted and closed on December 31. Two entries are necessary at the time of disposing of the fixed asset: one to record depreciation for the three months ending with the date of disposal, and a second to record the sale of the equipment.

<table>
<tr><td>RECORD DE-
PRECIATION
TO DATE OF
DISPOSAL</td><td>Depreciation Expense: Office Equipment . . . .
      Accumulated Depreciation: Office Equipment
To record depreciation for the three months prior to
disposal of office equipment ($200 × 1/4).</td><td>50</td><td>
50</td></tr>
<tr><td></td><td>Cash . . . .
Accumulated Depreciation: Office Equipment . . . . . .
Gain and Loss on Disposal of Fixed Assets . . . .
      Office Equipment . . . .
To record sale of office equipment at less than book
value.</td><td>100
1,650
250</td><td>

2,000</td></tr>
</table>

Trading in used assets on new

Certain types of fixed assets, such as automobiles and office equipment, are customarily traded in on new assets of the same kind. The trade-in allowance granted by the dealer may differ materially from the book value of the old asset. If the dealer grants a trade-in allowance in excess of the book value of the asset being traded in, there is the suggestion of a profit being realized on the exchange. The evidence of a gain is not conclusive, however, because the list price of the new asset may purposely have been set higher than a realistic cash price to permit the offering of inflated trade in allowances.

For the purpose of determining taxable income, no gain or loss is recognized when a fixed asset is traded in on another similar asset. The tax regulations provide that the cost of the new asset shall be the sum of the book value of the old asset traded in plus the additional amount paid or to be paid in acquiring the new equipment.

To illustrate the handling of an exchange transaction in the manner required for tax purposes (and followed for general accounting purposes by most companies), assume that a delivery truck is acquired at a cost of $3,200. The truck is depreciated on the straight-line basis with the assumption of a four-year life. After three years of use, the truck is traded in on a new model having a list price of $4,000. The truck dealer grants a trade-in allowance of $1,200 for the old truck; the additional amount to be paid to acquire the new truck is, therefore, $2,800 ($4,000 list price minus $1,200 trade-in allowance). The cost basis of the new truck is computed as follows:

**TRADE-IN:
COST OF
NEW
EQUIPMENT**

Cost of old truck	*$3,200*
Deduct: accumulated depreciation	*2,400*
Book value of old truck	*$ 800*
Add: cash payment for new truck (list price, $4,000 — $1,200	
* trade-in allowance)*	*2,800*
Cost basis of new truck	*$3,600*

The trade-in allowance and the list price of the new truck are not recorded in the accounts; their only function lies in determining the amount which the purchaser must pay in addition to turning in the old truck. The journal entry for this exchange transaction is as follows:

**ENTRY FOR
TRADE-IN**

Delivery Truck (new)	*3,600*	
Accumulated Depreciation: Delivery Truck	*2,400*	
* Delivery Truck (old)*		*3,200*
* Cash*		*2,800*

To remove from the accounts the cost of old truck and accumulated depreciation thereon, and to record new truck at cost equal to book value of old truck traded in plus cash paid.

An alternative method of recording trade-ins (not acceptable for tax purposes but having theoretical support) calls for recognizing a gain or loss on the exchange in an amount equal to the difference between the book value of the old asset and its estimated fair market value at the time of the trade-in. The validity of this alternative method rests upon the assumption that the cash value of the old truck can be estimated with reasonable accuracy. Some of the principal theoretical arguments concerning the use of estimated cash values in recording gains and losses on trade transactions were discussed in Chapter 13.

Revision of depreciation rates

Depreciation rates are based on estimates of the useful life of a fixed asset. Estimates of useful life are seldom precisely correct and sometimes are grossly in error. Consequently, the annual depreciation expense based on the estimated useful life may be either excessive or inadequate. What action should be taken when, after a few years of using a fixed asset, it is decided that the asset is actually going to last for a considerably longer or shorter period than was originally estimated? When either of these situations arises, a revised estimate of useful life should be made and the periodic depreciation charge decreased or increased accordingly.

The procedure for correcting the depreciation program may be stated in very few words; *spread the undepreciated cost of the asset over the years of remaining useful life.* The annual depreciation charge is increased or decreased sufficiently so that the depreciation program will be completed in accordance with the revised estimate of remaining useful life. The following data illustrate a revision which increases the estimate of useful life and thereby decreases the annual depreciation charge.

DATA
PRIOR TO
REVISION
OF DEPRE-
CIATION
RATE

Cost of asset	$10,000
Estimated scrap value	000
Estimated useful life	10 years
Annual depreciation charge	$ 1,000
Accumulated depreciation at end of six years ($1,000 × 6) . .	$ 6,000

At the beginning of the seventh year, it is decided that the asset will last for eight more years. The revised estimate of useful life is, therefore, a total of 14 years (six years of use to date plus eight years of expected future use). The depreciation expense to be recognized during the seventh year and in each of the remaining years of useful life is $500, computed as follows:

REVISION
OF DEPRE-
CIATION
PROGRAM

Undepreciated cost at end of sixth year ($10,000 − $6,000) . .	$4,000
Revised estimate of remaining years of useful life	8 years
Revised amount of annual depreciation expense ($4,000 ÷ 8) .	$ 500

At the end of the seventh year (and in each subsequent year), the entry to record depreciation will be as follows:

ENTRY
USING
REVISED
RATE

Depreciation Expense	500	
Accumulated Depreciation		500
To record depreciation for seventh year in accordance with revised estimate of useful life ($4,000 ÷ 8).		

Alternative method of revising depreciation program. The method described above for changing depreciation charges to conform to revised estimates of useful life is generally used and is acceptable in the determination of taxable income. In theory, however, it is more logical to recognize a material revision of useful life by adjusting the Accumulated Depreciation account to the amount it would have contained if the past depreciation charges had been based on the revised estimate of useful life. This alternative method involves some interesting theoretical issues concerning the reinstating of costs previously absorbed in operating expense. Discussion of these issues is deferred to advanced courses in accounting.

Maintaining control over fixed assets. Subsidiary ledgers

Unless internal controls over fixed assets are carefully designed, many units of equipment are likely to be broken, discarded, or stolen without any entry being made in the accounting records for their disposal. The asset accounts will then be overstated, and depreciation programs for such missing units of equipment will presumably continue. Consequently, net income will be misstated because of the omission of losses on retirement of fixed assets and because of erroneous depreciation charges.

One important control device which guards against failure to record the retirement of assets is the use of control accounts and subsidiary ledgers for plant and equipment. The general ledger ordinarily contains a separate asset account and related depreciation accounts for each major classification of fixed assets, such as land, buildings, office equipment, and delivery equipment. For example, the general ledger will contain the account Office Equipment, and also, the related accounts Depreciation Expense: Office Equipment, and Accumulated Depreciation: Office Equipment. The general ledger account for office equipment contains entries for a variety of items: typewriters, filing cabinets, dictaphones, desks, etc. It is not possible in this one general ledger account to maintain adequate information concerning the cost of each item, its estimated useful life, book value, insured value, and other data which may be needed by management as a basis for decisions on such issues as replacement, insurance, and taxation.

A subsidiary ledger should therefore be established for office equipment, and for each of the other general ledger accounts which represents many separate units of plant property. The subsidiary ledger usually consists of a card file, with a separate card for each unit of property, such as a typewriter or desk. Each card shows the name of the asset, identification number, and such details as date of acquisition, cost, useful life, depreciation, accumulated depreciation, insurance coverage, repairs, and gain or loss on disposal. The general ledger account, Office Equipment, serves as a control; the balance of this control account is equal to the total cost of the items in the subsidiary ledger for office equipment. The general ledger account, Accumulated Depreciation: Office Equipment, is also a control account; its balance is equal to the total of the accumulated depreciation shown on all the cards in the office equipment ledger. Every acquisition of office equipment is entered in the control account and also on a card in the subsidiary ledger. Similarly, every disposal of an item of office equipment is entered in both the control account and the subsidiary ledger.

Each card in a subsidiary ledger for fixed assets shows an identification number which should also appear in the form of a metal tag attached to the asset itself. Consequently, a physical inventory of fixed assets is easily taken and will prove whether all units of equipment shown by the records are actually on hand and being used in operations.

Other advantages afforded by a plant and equipment ledger are the ready availability of information for the periodic computation of depreciation, and for entries to record the disposal of individual items of property. A better basis is also available for supporting the data in tax returns, for obtaining proper insurance coverage, and for supporting claims for losses sustained on insured property. In well-managed companies, it is standard practice to control expenditures for fixed assets by preparing a budget of all planned acquisitions for at least a year in advance. A first essential to the preparation of such a budget is a detailed record showing the assets presently owned, their cost, age, and remaining useful life.

NATURAL RESOURCES

Accounting for natural resources

Mining properties, oil and gas wells, and tracts of standing timber are leading examples of natural resources or "wasting assets." The distinguishing characteristics of these assets, in contrast to such fixed assets as buildings and machinery, is that they are physically consumed and converted into inventory. In a theoretical sense, a coal mine might even be regarded as an "underground inventory of coal"; however, such an inventory is certainly not a current asset. In the balance sheet, mining property and other natural resources are usually listed as a separate subgroup under the major heading of fixed assets.

Natural resources should be recorded in the accounts at cost. As the resource is consumed through the process of mining, cutting, or drilling, the asset account must be proportionately reduced. The carrying value (book value) of a coal mine, for example, is reduced by a small amount for each ton of coal mined. The original cost of the mine is thus gradually transferred out of the asset account and becomes part of the cost of the coal mined and sold.

Depletion. The term *depletion* is used to describe the pro rata allocation of cost of a wasting asset to the units removed and is computed by dividing the cost of the natural resource by the estimated available number of units, such as barrels of oil or tons of coal. The depletion charge per unit is then multiplied by the number of units actually produced during the year to determine the total depletion charge for that period.

To illustrate the computation of depletion expense, assume that the sum of $500,000 is paid for a coal mine believed to contain 1 million tons of coal. The depletion charge per unit is $500,000 ÷ 1,000,000, or 50 cents a ton. Assuming that 200,000 tons of coal were mined and sold during the first year of operation, the depletion charge for the year would be 50 cents × 200,000, or $100,000. The journal entry necessary at the end of the year to record depletion of the mine would be as follows:

ENTRY FOR
DEPLETION

Depletion Expense *100,000*
    Accumulated Depletion *100,000*
To record depletion expense for the year;
200,000 tons mined @ 50 cents per ton.

The book value of an asset subject to depletion is determined by deducting the accumulated depletion from the cost of the property. The balance sheet presentation is similar to that for a depreciable fixed asset.

ACCUMU-
LATED
DEPLETION
IN BALANCE
SHEET

Mining Property *$500,000*
    Less: accumulated depletion *100,000*   *400,000*

Depletion expense in a mining business might be compared with the purchases account in the ledger of a retail store. The purchases account represents the cost to the store of the goods available for sale; the depletion expense account in a mining company represents a part of the cost of the coal or other product available for sale. To the extent that coal produced during the year is not sold but is carried forward as inventory for sale in the following year, the depletion charge will also be carried forward as part of the inventory value. In other words, depletion is recorded in the year in which extraction of the product occurs but becomes a deduction from revenue in the period in which the product is sold. Of course, the cost of the inventory of coal or other extracted product on hand at the end of the year includes not only the depletion charge but also the labor cost and other expenditures necessarily incurred in bringing the coal to the surface.

Development costs. The cost of a natural resource may include not only the purchase price of the property, but also expenditures for recording fees, surveying, and a variety of exploratory and developmental charges.

Some exploratory and developmental expenditures will prove to be unproductive; these expenditures should be recognized as losses or expenses of the current period and not carried forward as assets. The dividing line between productive and nonproductive expenditures for exploration and development is not always easy to draw. The drilling of a dry hole in a new oil field might be regarded as a net loss, or, on the other hand, as an integral step in an over-all successful development of the area.

There is a noticeable trend for companies engaged in the extraction of natural resources to plan for continuity of existence, rather than to end their operations with the exhaustion of a single property. These companies maintain their productive capacity by carrying on a continuous program of exploration and development of new areas. Since outlays for exploration and development thus become normal and continuous, these expenditures are commonly charged to expense in the year in which the exploration or development is performed. Such practices have been condoned by accountants more on the grounds of expediency than on theoretical considerations.

Depreciation of fixed assets closely related to natural resources. Assume that a building costing $20,500 and having a normal useful life of 20 years is erected at the site of a mine estimated to contain 100,000 tons of ore. Once the mine is exhausted, the building will have only scrap value, say, $500. Production of ore is being carried on at a rate which will probably exhaust the mine within four to six years. During the first year after construction of the building, ore is mined in the amount of 25,000 tons. How much depreciation should be recognized on the building?

In this situation, depreciation of the building should be based on the life of the mine, and computed in the same manner as depletion. Cost, $20,500, minus scrap value, $500, times 25,000/100,000 equals $5,000 depreciation for the first year. The formula may be concisely stated as

$$Depreciation \ per \ year = (cost - scrap) \times \frac{units \ produced}{estimated \ total \ units}$$

INTANGIBLE ASSETS

Characteristics

As the word "intangible" suggests, assets in this classification have no physical substance. Leading examples are goodwill, leaseholds, copyrights, franchises, licenses, and trademarks. Intangible assets are classified on the balance sheet as a subgroup of fixed assets. However, not all assets which lack physical substance are regarded as intangible assets; an account receivable, for example, or a prepaid expense, is of nonphysical nature but is classified as a current asset and is never regarded as an intangible. In brief, intangible assets are noncurrent and nonphysical.

The basis of valuation for intangible assets is cost. In some companies, certain intangible assets such as trademarks may be of great importance but may have been acquired without the incurring of any cost. An intangible asset should appear on the balance sheet *only* if a cost of acquisition or development has been incurred.

Since a variety of items is included in the intangible asset category, it will be helpful to emphasize some of the characteristics common to most intangible assets. Many types of intangible assets are not transferable, and therefore have no liquidation value or realizable value. Goodwill, for example, is so closely related to the business as a whole that it cannot be sold without disrupting operations. Because of this lack of realizable value, many companies choose to carry their intangible assets on the balance sheet at a nominal valuation of $1. Such treatment of intangible assets may be in part a carry-over from the days when financial statements were produced largely for use by bankers and creditors. Persons extending credit to a company were naturally concerned over the possibility of being able to make collection in the event that the company encountered financial difficulties. Since intangible assets of a company in financial trouble would usually produce nothing in an enforced sale, creditors preferred that such assets not be listed on the balance sheet.

There is little doubt, however, that in some companies the intangible assets, such as goodwill or trademarks, may be vitally important to profitable operations. The carrying of intangible assets on the balance sheet is justified only when there is good evidence that future earnings will be derived from these assets. The value of an intangible asset rests solely upon its capacity to produce future earnings. If the earning power of a company is not adequate in relation to the amount of its tangible assets, there is good reason to be skeptical of any accounting valuation placed on intangible assets.

To summarize the characteristics common to many (but not all) intangible assets, we can point to lack of physical substance, lack of realizable value, difficulty of transfer, close relationship to the business as a whole, and dependence upon future earnings as a justification for being listed on the balance sheet.

Classification

In accounting literature, intangible assets have traditionally been classified for discussion purposes into two broad groups as follows:

1. Those with limited useful lives
2. Those with an unlimited term of existence

This classification emphasizes that the cost of an intangible asset with a limited useful life must be written off to expense during its years of usefulness, whereas a "permanent" intangible asset such as a perpetual franchise granted to a public utility company need not be written off. Even though an intangible asset may have an unlimited legal life, the probability of an unending economic usefulness may well be open to question.

Amortization

The term *amortization* is used to describe the systematic write-off to expense of the cost of an intangible asset over the periods of its economic usefulness. The accounting entry for amortization consists of a debit to an expense account and a credit to accumulated amortization, or a direct credit to the intangible asset account. The amortization of an intangible asset is a process parallel to the depreciation of a fixed tangible asset and to the depletion of a natural resource.

Although it is difficult to estimate the useful life of such intangibles as goodwill, it is highly probable that such assets will not contribute to future earnings on a permanent basis. The cost of the intangible asset should, therefore, be deducted from revenues during the years in which it may be expected to aid in producing revenues.

Arbitrary write-off of intangibles. Arbitrary, lump-sum write-off of intangibles (leaving a nominal balance of $1 in the accounts) is a practice sometimes found in companies which have not adopted a systematic amortization program. Arguments for this practice emphasize the factors of conservatism, the practical difficulty of estimating an appropriate period for amortization, and the absence of any realizable value for intangibles. Accountants generally agree that whenever any event occurs which indicates that an intangible has lost all value, immediate write-off of the entire cost is warranted regardless of whether an amortization program has previously been followed.

On the other hand, arbitrary write-offs of valuable, revenue-producing intangible assets are no more in accordance with accounting theory than would be the arbitrary write-off of land or buildings. Systematic amortization of assets over their estimated useful lives is an appropriate theoretical objective for both tangible and intangible fixed assets. Accounting measurements are based on the assumption of a going concern: the absence of a liquidation value is therefore no justification for arbitrary write-off of any fixed asset.

Amortization for income tax purposes. Present income tax regulations permit deductions from revenue for the amortization of those intangibles having a definite limitation of usefulness, such as a patent, a license, or a franchise. In refusing to permit amortization of such intangibles as goodwill, the tax authorities are probably guided by considerations of administrative convenience rather than accounting theory. It is the responsibility of professional accountants to build a logical and integrated body of accounting theory regardless of the provisions of current regulations governing taxation.

Goodwill

Businessmen and lawyers used the term "goodwill" in a variety of meanings before it became a part of accounting terminology. One of the more common meanings of goodwill in a nonaccounting sense concerns the benefits derived from a favorable reputation among customers. To accountants, however, goodwill has a very specific meaning not necessarily limited to customer relationships. It means the *present value of expected future earnings over and above the earnings normally realized in the industry.* Above-average earnings may arise, not only from favorable customer relations, but also from such factors as location, monopoly, manufacturing efficiency, and superior management.

The existence of the intangible asset of goodwill is indicated when an entire business is sold for a price in excess of the fair market value of the other assets. The willingness of the purchaser of a going business to pay a price greater than the sum of the values of the tangible assets indicates that he is paying for intangible assets as well. If the business does not include such specific intangibles as patents or franchises, the extra amount paid is presumably for goodwill. Goodwill exists when the rate of average net income earned by a particular enterprise is above normal for the industry. Excess profits in past years are of significance to a prospective purchaser of an enterprise only to the extent that he believes such excess earnings may continue after he acquires the business. If the prospective purchaser believes that by purchasing a particular company with a record of superior earnings in the past, he will receive these above-average earnings in the future, he may reasonably be expected to pay a premium price for the business. The premium which he pays represents the cost of purchased goodwill and may properly be recorded in the accounting records of the new owner in a Goodwill account.

MEASURING SUPERIOR EARNING POWER

Assume that two businesses in the same line of trade are for sale and that the normal rate of earnings on capital invested in this industry is 10% a year. The relative earning power of the two companies during the past five years is indicated by the following schedule.

	Company X	Company Y
Net assets other than goodwill	$1,000,000	$1,000,000
Normal rate of earnings on invested capital	10%	10%
Average net income	$ 100,000	$ 140,000
Net income computed at normal rate (10%) on net assets other than goodwill	100,000	100,000
Earnings above average	000	$ 40,000

A prospective investor would be willing to pay more for Company Y than for Company X because Y has a record of superior earnings which will presumably continue for some time in the future. Company Y has goodwill; Company X does not. A businessman interested in entering this industry might just as well start from scratch by creating a new enterprise as to buy out Company X, because the rate of return on the capital invested in a new concern would presumably approximate the 10% rate assumed to prevail in this industry. The maximum price which anyone would pay for Company X is, therefore, $1 million, the valuation of the various tangible assets making up this enterprise.

How much would a prospective purchaser be willing to pay for Company Y with its record of superior earning power? The answer depends largely on how long the additional or excess annual earnings of $40,000 are expected to continue. Very few concerns are able to maintain above-average earnings for more than a few years. Consequently, the purchaser of a business will usually limit his payment for goodwill to not more than four or five times the excess annual earnings.

Estimating the amount of goodwill. Goodwill is to be recorded in the accounts only when paid for; this situation usually occurs only when a going business is purchased in its entirety. When ownership of a business changes hands, any amount paid for goodwill rests on the assumption that earnings in excess of normal will continue under the new ownership. The following are methods of reaching agreement on a value for goodwill:

1. Arbitrary agreement between buyer and seller of the business may be reached on the amount of goodwill. For example, it might be agreed that the fair market value of the net tangible assets is $95,000 and that the total purchase price for the business will be $100,000, thus providing a $5,000 payment for goodwill.

2. Goodwill may be determined as a multiple of the average profits of past years. For example, assume that a business has earned an average annual net profit of $25,000 during the past five years. The business is sold for the book value of the net tangible assets, plus two years' average net income. The payment for goodwill is, therefore, $50,000. This method may be criticized because it ignores completely the concept of *excess* earnings as a basis for estimating goodwill.

3. Goodwill may be determined as a multiple of the amount by which the average annual earnings exceed normal earnings. To illustrate, assume the following data:

GOODWILL AS MULTIPLE OF EXCESS EARNINGS

Average investment in the business	*$100,000*
Average annual earnings (rate of 14%)	*$ 14,000*
Normal earnings for this industry (rate of 10%)	*10,000*
Average earnings in excess of normal	*$ 4,000*
Multiple of excess annual earnings	*4*
Goodwill	*$ 16,000*

This method is more in accord with the concept of goodwill as earning power in *excess* of normal, whereas method 2 relates goodwill to the *total* profits.

4. Goodwill may be determined as the capitalized value of excess earning power, using a capitalization rate considered normal in the industry. Assume that the normal rate of earnings in a given line of business is 10% and that a particular company presents the following picture:

GOODWILL BASED ON CAPITALIZATION OF EXCESS EARNINGS

Average investment in the business	*$100,000*
Average annual earnings (rate of 14%)	*$ 14,000*
Normal earnings for this industry (rate of 10%)	*10,000*
Average earnings in excess of normal	*$ 4,000*
Goodwill, computed by capitalizing excess earnings at 10% ($4,000 ÷ 0.10)	*$ 40,000*

The high valuation for goodwill resulting from this last method is caused by the assumption that the above normal earnings of $4,000 a year will continue permanently. The valuation of $40,000 for goodwill represents the present value of a permanent annuity of $4,000 a year. By paying an additional amount of $40,000, the purchaser is acquiring the right to an additional profit of $4,000 a year; this is a return on the investment in goodwill of 10%. Since we have assumed a normal return of 10% in the industry, it appears reasonable that a business which would produce a *permanent* excess income of $4,000 a year should sell for an additional $40,000. The purchaser of the business would then receive the standard rate of 10% on his entire cost, including the amount paid for goodwill.

The questionable part of this approach is of course the assumption that the excess earning power can be maintained indefinitely. There is also the difficulty of determining a rate of normal return for the industry. Generally speaking, buyers of businesses are unwilling to assume that excess earnings will continue for more than four or five years.

Of the four methods described for the computation of goodwill, the first and second have little to recommend them, because they give no recognition to the fact that goodwill is based on *excess* earnings. The third and fourth methods do rest on an evaluation of excess or above-average earning power, but they should not be regarded as representing anything more than an approach to the problem. These calculations may be useful in setting certain boundaries within which the buyer and seller may bargain to fix a price for goodwill.

Amortization of goodwill. As previously explained, the cost of goodwill usually represents the price paid to obtain extra profits for four or five years from the date of purchase, and the goodwill account should be written off against earnings in those same years. This treatment is consistent with the general principle of matching costs and revenues.

For the purpose of computing taxable income, no expense deduction may be made for the amortization of goodwill. Perhaps partially for this reason, some companies have kept goodwill on the books permanently at cost. Other companies with a bent for conservatism in their financial statements have chosen to write goodwill down arbitrarily to a value of $1 without regard to the likelihood of future benefits to be received. The current trend of accounting thinking is to make the treatment of goodwill consistent with that accorded other tangible and intangible fixed assets; that is, to write off the cost over the years that benefits are expected. In the event that a company which has purchased goodwill should encounter a period of operating losses, the goodwill may justifiably be written off the books at once. The carrying of intangible assets on the balance sheet is justified only when there is good reason for believing that benefits will definitely be derived from such assets in future periods. The existence of goodwill is predicated on expected superior earnings; failure of such earnings to materialize indicates that goodwill is no longer present.

Leaseholds and leasehold improvements

In discussing the leasing of business property, it is convenient to refer to the owner as the "lessor" and to the tenant as the "lessee." The signing of a long-term lease of business property does not necessarily call for the use of a leasehold account. A leasehold account is needed only when the lease requires a substantial advance payment applicable to future years. Some leases merely provide for regular monthly payments of rent; in these cases the lease is not recorded in the accounts. The monthly payments to the lessor are recorded as rent expense by the lessee when paid.

To illustrate the use of the Leasehold account, assume that the lease covers a period of five years and that the lessee pays the entire rent of $15,000 in advance at the time of signing the lease. The lessee would charge the $15,000 advance payment to the intangible asset account, Leasehold. Since the advance payment is merely prepaid rent, why not record it among the prepaid expense accounts? The answer is that the prepaid expense classification is part of the current assets, which must be limited to short-term prepayments of operating expenses applicable to the next operating cycle. The Leasehold account will be written off to Rent Expense each year as shown by the following entry.

LEASEHOLD
ACCOUNT
CONVERTED
INTO RENT
EXPENSE

Rent Expense	*3,000*	
Leasehold		*3,000*
To write off as expense 1/5 of the cost of a five-year leasehold.		

Amortization of a leasehold in this manner serves to allocate the total cost of the lease as deductions from revenues in the years in which the business has the use of the leased premises. Sometimes a lease is so drawn as to require the payment in advance of only the final year's rent. Rent payments for all but the final year may be made on a month-to-month basis. In this case the Leasehold account will be debited with the advance payment of the final year's rent at the time the lease is signed, and this amount will remain in the account until the final year of the lease, at which time the advance payment will be transferred to the Rent Expense account.

During periods of rising property values, a long-term lease may become extremely valuable because the agreed rental is much less than would be charged under current market conditions. Such a development is particularly likely for leases that run for 20 or 30 years or more. No entry is usually made in the accounts to reflect the increased value of the lease attributable to rising property values, because assets are accounted for on the basis of cost, not on the basis of estimated market values.

When buildings or other improvements are constructed on leased property by the lessee, the costs should be recorded in a Leasehold Improvements account, and written off as expense during the remaining life of the lease or of the estimated useful life of the building, whichever is shorter. This procedure is usually followed even though the lessee has an option to renew the lease, because there is no assurance in advance that conditions will warrant the exercise of the renewal clause.

Patents

A patent is an exclusive right granted by the Federal government for manufacture, use, and sale of a particular product. Patents, like other intangible assets, should be recorded in the accounts at cost. Since patents may be acquired by purchase, or may be obtained directly from the government by the inventor, the cost may consist of the purchase price or of the expenditures for research and development leading to the application for the patent. In addition, cost may include legal fees for obtaining the patent and for infringement suits. Companies which carry on extensive research and development programs on a permanent basis often treat the costs of such work as expense when incurred, on the grounds that constant research is necessary merely to maintain a competitive position in the industry. Often it is difficult to determine what portion of research expenditures are related to a given patent, and what earnings may be derived from the patented device. For these reasons, it is common to find that patents developed within the organization are carried on the books at a nominal valuation.

Patents are granted for a period of 17 years, and the period of amortization must not exceed that period. However, if the patent is likely to lose its usefulness in less than 17 years, amortization should be based on the shorter period of estimated useful life. Assume that a patent is purchased from the inventor at a cost of $30,000, after five years of the legal life have expired. The remaining *legal* life is, therefore, 12 years, but if the estimated *useful* life is only five years, amortization should be based on this shorter period. The entry to be made to record the annual amortization expense would be:

ENTRY FOR AMORTIZA- TION OF PATENT	*Amortization Expense: Patents* 6,000	
	Accumulated Amortization: Patents	6,000
	To amortize cost of patent on a straight-line basis and estimated life of five years.	

In the amortization of patents and other intangible assets, the credit entry is sometimes made directly to the asset account, but the use of a valuation account, as illustrated above, is recommended for the same reasons explained with respect to depreciation of tangible assets.

Copyrights

A copyright is an exclusive right granted to protect the production and sale of literary or artistic materials for a period of 28 years. The cost of obtaining a copyright is minor and therefore chargeable to expense when paid. Only when a copyright is purchased will the expenditure be material enough to warrant capitalization and spreading over the useful life. The revenues from copyrights are usually limited to only a few years, and the purchase cost should, of course, be amortized over the years in which the revenues are expected.

Trademarks

A permanent exclusive right to the use of a trademark, brand name, or commercial symbol may be obtained by registering it. Because of the unlimited legal life, a trademark may be carried without amortization at the original cost. If the use of the trademark is abandoned or if its contribution to earnings becomes doubtful, immediate write-off of the cost is called for. The outlay for securing a trademark is often not consequential, and it is common practice to treat such outlays as expense when incurred.

QUESTIONS

1. Describe briefly three situations in which debit entries may properly be made in accumulated depreciation accounts.

2. Under what circumstances does good accounting call for a mining company to depreciate a fixed asset over a period shorter than the normal useful life?

3. A tractor which cost $4,800 had an estimated useful life of five years and an estimated salvage value of $800. Straight-line depreciation was used. Give the entry required by each of the following alternative assumptions:

    a. The tractor was sold for cash of $3,000 after two years' use.

    b. The tractor was traded in after three years on another tractor with a list price of $6,000. Trade-in allowance was $2,700. The trade-in was recorded in a manner acceptable for income tax purposes.

    c. The tractor was scrapped after four years' use. Since scrap dealers were unwilling to pay anything for the tractor, it was given to a scrap dealer for his services in removing it.

4. The Williams Show Store obtained its store building under a 10-year lease at $400 a month. The lease agreement required payment of rent for the tenth year at the time of signing the lease. All other payments were on a monthly basis. Give the journal entry required at the date of signing the lease when Williams wrote a check for $5,200, representing payment of the current month's rent and the $4,800 applicable to the tenth year of the lease. What entries, if any, are indicated for the tenth year of the lease?

5. Growth Company paid $40,000 cash to acquire the entire business of Young Company, a strong competitor. In negotiating this lump-sum price for the business, a valuation of $8,000 was assigned to goodwill, representing four times the amount by which Young Company's annual earnings had exceeded normal earnings in the industry. Assuming that the goodwill is recorded on the books of Growth Company, should it remain there permanently or be amortized? What basis of amortization might be used?

PROBLEMS

Group A

14A-1. Jackson's Bakery was organized by Samuel Jackson on January 1, 1956, at which time four identical new delivery trucks were purchased at a total cost of $12,000 cash. Estimated useful life of the delivery trucks was four years, and the sum-of-the-years'-digits method of depreciation was adopted. However, despite the normal life period of four years for this equipment, Jackson preferred to trade in his delivery trucks on new models every two years so that the truck fleet would always appear clean and modern. In all such acquisitions he acquired a group of identical trucks. During the first six years of operation of the business, transactions relating to delivery equipment as shown below were completed, in addition to the original purchase described above.

1958
Jan. 1.　　Purchased four new delivery trucks at a cost of $3,500 each. A total trade-in allowance of $6,600 was received for trucks Nos. 1, 2, 3, and 4. The new trucks were designated as Nos. 5, 6, 7, and 8.

1960
Jan. 1.　　Sold truck No. 7 for $1,000 cash, and traded in Nos. 5, 6, and 8 on trucks Nos. 9, 10, 11, 12, and 13. A trade-in allowance of $5,475 was granted against the total purchase price of $25,000.

1962
Jan. 1.　　Traded in trucks Nos. 9, 10, 11, and 12 for trucks Nos. 14, 15, 16, and 17. The truck dealer granted a trade-in allowance of $8,280 against the $24,000 total price of the four new trucks.

Dec. 31.　Sold truck No. 13 for $750 cash.

Instructions. Prepare general journal entries to record all the transactions and related depreciation expense from January 1, 1956, to December 31, 1962.

14A-2. The Bishop Mining Company acquired a coal mine on January 1, 1959, at a cost of $280,000. The purchase agreement provided for an immediate cash payment of $180,000, with the balance covered by a three-year note payable. Interest for the entire three years at 6% per year was included in the face amount of the note. No payment on either interest or principal was required until the maturity of the note.

　　Estimates by the company's engineers indicated that the mine contained 1,400,000 tons of coal. The equipment required to extract the coal from the mine was purchased January 2, 1959, for $98,000 cash. The useful life of this equipment was estimated to be five years, with a residual scrap value of $8,000. The straight-line method of depreciation was used by the company on this equipment and on all its depreciable assets.

　　On July 1, 1959, three trucks intended for use around the mine were purchased for $26,000 cash. Depreciation was to be computed on the basis of an estimated useful life of four years, with a residual scrap value of $2,000.

　　Construction of a frame building to be used as a mine office was completed on July 1, 1959, at a cost of $18,000 cash. Estimated life of this building was 10 years; the residual scrap value was estimated as no more than enough to cover the cost of demolition.

　　An assortment of secondhand office equipment approximately five years old was purchased on July 1, 1959, for $2,500 cash. The remaining useful life of this used equipment was estimated at five years, and the residual scrap value was estimated at $500.

During 1959, a total of 110,000 tons of coal was mined and sold. In 1960, production increased to 190,000 tons, and again the entire output was sold. On March 31, 1961, after 50,000 tons of coal had been extracted and sold, the mine and all related property were sold for $346,000 cash. The Bishop Mining Company planned to invest this cash in other property and therefore did not choose to pay the note payable issued at time of acquiring the mine until the maturity date of the note. The contract covering the sale of the mine specified the following prices for the various assets being transferred: mine, $270,000; equipment, $50,000; trucks, $10,000; building, $15,000; and office equipment, $1,000.

Instructions

a. Prepare general journal entries to **record** all transactions and necessary adjustments from January, 1959, through **January**, 1962. Include depreciation entries using the straight-line method. Record depreciation for the fraction of 1961 prior to the sale.

b. Prepare a schedule showing the gain **or** loss on the disposal of each of the fixed assets.

14A-3. After several years of managerial experience in the retailing of sporting goods, James French decided to buy an established business in this field. He is now attempting to make a choice among three similar concerns which are available for purchase. All three **companies** have been in business for five years. The balance sheets presented **by** the three companies may be summarized as follows:

Assets	*Company A*	*Company B*	*Company C*
Cash	*$ 10,000*	*$ 10,000*	*$ 20,000*
Accounts receivable	*112,000*	*114,000*	*126,000*
Inventory	*200,000*	*160,000*	*180,000*
Fixed assets (net)	*60,000*	*80,000*	*50,000*
Goodwill		*2,000*	
	$382,000	*$366,000*	*$376,000*

Liabilities & Owner's Equity			
Current liabilities	*$162,000*	*$160,000*	*$200,000*
Owner's equity	*220,000*	*206,000*	*176,000*
	$382,000	*$366,000*	*$376,000*

The average net earnings of the three businesses during the past five years had been as follows: Company A, $36,000; Company B, $30,000; and Company C, $28,000.

With the permission of the owners of the three businesses, French arranged for a certified public accountant to examine the accounting records of the companies. This investigation disclosed the following information:

Accounts Receivable. In Company A, no provision for bad debts had been made at any time, and no accounts receivable had been written off. Numerous past-due receivables were on the books, and the estimated uncollectible items which had accumulated during the past five years amounted to $10,000. In both Company B and Company C, the receivables appeared to be carried at net realizable value.

Inventories. Company B had adopted the first-in, first-out method of inventory valuation when first organized but had changed to the last-in, first-out method after one year. As a result of the change in method of accounting for inventories, the present balance sheet figure for inventories was approximately $15,000 less than replacement cost. The other two companies had used the first-in, first-out method continuously, and their present inventories were approximately equal to replacement cost.

Fixed Assets. In each of the three companies, the fixed assets included a building which had cost $50,000 and had an estimated useful life of 25 years with no residual scrap value. Company A had taken no depreciation on its building; Company B had used straight-line depreciation at 4% annually; and Company C had depreciated its building by applying a constant rate of 4% to the undepreciated balance. All fixed assets other than buildings had been depreciated on a straight-line basis in all companies. French believed that the book value of the fixed assets of all three companies would approximate fair market value if depreciation were uniformly computed on a straight-line basis.

Goodwill. The item of goodwill, $2,000, on the balance sheet of Company B, represented the cost of a nonrecurring advertising campaign conducted during the first year of operation.

French is willing to pay for net tangible assets (except cash) at book value, plus an amount for goodwill equal to three times the average annual net earnings in excess of 10% on the net tangible assets. Cash will not be included in the transfer of assets.

Instructions

a. Prepare a revised summary of balance sheet data after correcting all errors made by the companies. In addition to correcting errors, make the necessary changes to apply straight-line depreciation and first-in, first-out inventory methods in all three companies.

b. Determine revised amounts for average net **earnings** of the three companies after taking into consideration the correction **of** errors and changes of method called for in (*a*) above.

c. Determine the price which French should offer for each of the businesses.

14A-4. Mason Company on January 1 decided to acquire certain new factory machinery manufactured by the Decker Company. The machinery was priced at $120,000 and had an estimated useful life of 10 years. Charles Mason, owner of the Mason Company, had heard from some business acquaintances that leasing machinery was often more advantageous than buying, especially if the lease contained an option clause permitting the lessee to acquire title to the machinery at the expiration of the lease. He therefore asked the Decker Company if it would be possible to lease the machinery with an option to buy it later. After some negotiation, Decker Company offered the Mason Company a choice of three plans:

Plan A. The machinery would be sold to Mason Company for cash at a price of $120,000 plus 4% sales tax.

Plan B. The machinery would be sold to Mason Company at a price of $120,000, plus sales tax of 4%, with payments deferred. The sum of $4,800 must be paid in cash upon delivery of the machinery, and notes receivable bearing interest at 6% per annum would be accepted for the remaining $120,000. The notes would be in denominations of $30,000; the first note would mature on March 31 and the others at intervals of three months. Payment would therefore be spread over a period of 12 months. Interest on each note would be payable at the maturity date. Mason Company would have the privilege of paying all or any part of the outstanding notes any time, thus cutting off further interest expense.

Plan C. The machinery would be leased to Mason Company for a period of 12 months in consideration of an initial cash payment of $4,500 plus a monthly charge of $10,000. As a matter of convenience, it was agreed that the payments (other than the initial $4,500) should be on a quarterly basis: $30,000 on March 31, and a like amount on June 30, September 30, and December 31. Any necessary repairs were to be borne by Mason Company. At the end of the 12-month period of the contract, Mason Company would have the right to acquire title to the machinery by payment of an additional $4,800.

Instructions

a. Assuming that plan A is followed, give the journal entries (in general journal form) to record acquisition of the machinery. Also give the entry for depreciation at the end of the year.

b. Assuming that plan B is followed, give journal entries for acquisition of the machinery, payment of the notes at the scheduled maturity dates, and depreciation at the end of the year.

c. Assuming that plan C is followed and that the Mason Company intends to exercise the option to acquire title upon completion of the rental period, give the journal entries required throughout the year, including the exercise of the option on December 31 and depreciation, if any. Emphasize the substance of the plan rather than its outward form.

d. Evaluate the three plans. Indicate how the financial statements would differ, if at all, according to the choice of plan. Make a recommendation for action by Mason and give the reasons underlying your recommendation.

Group B

14B-1. Crowley Company purchased equipment on July 1, 1958, at a cost of $34,300. Useful life was estimated to be 10 years and scrap value $1,300. Crowley Company depreciates its fixed assets by the straight-line method and closes its books annually on June 30.

In June, 1961, after considerable experience with the equipment, the company decided that the estimated total life should be revised from 10 years to 6 years and the residual scrap value lowered from $1,300 to $700. This revised estimate was made prior to recording depreciation for the fiscal year ended June 30, 1961.

On December 31, 1962, the equipment was sold for $3,050 cash.

Instructions. Prepare journal entries to record all the above transactions and the depreciation expense from July 1, 1958, to December 31, 1962.

14B-2. The Fast Fleet Cab Company purchased two taxicabs at a cost of $2,600 each on June 30, 1961. Three additional cabs were purchased on September 30, 1961, at a cost of $2,800 each. The company depreciates its cabs on a mileage basis of 50,000 miles of useful life with an expected residual value of $600. Cab No. 1

was wrecked on January 1, 1962, after being driven 26,000 miles and was considered a total loss.

As of June 30, 1962, the close of the fiscal year, cab No. 2 had been driven 42,600 miles; cab No. 3, 29,800 miles; cab No. 4, 26,000 miles; and cab No. 5, 27,200 miles. On July 1, 1962, cabs Nos. 2 and 3 were traded in on cabs Nos. 6 and 7. The dealer allowed $2,000 on the total purchase price of $6,000 for the two new cabs.

Because of an increased demand for service, cabs Nos. 8, 9, 10, 11, and 12 were purchased on November 1, 1962. The list price for the new cabs totaled $16,000, but the dealer allowed $600 trade-in on cab No. 4, which had been driven 40,000 miles. Cab No. 5 had been driven 49,000 miles on December 1, 1962, at which time it was sold to a private party for $700 cash.

Instructions. Prepare entries in general journal form to record all the transactions, including depreciation, from June 30, 1961, to December 1, 1962.

14B-3. On January 1, 1961, Ryan Oil Company, an established concern, borrowed $1,500,000 from the National City Bank, issuing a note payable in five years with interest at 6% payable annually, on December 31. Also on January 1, the company purchased for $600,000 an undeveloped oil field estimated to contain at least 1,500,000 barrels of oil. Movable equipment having an estimated useful life of five years and no scrap value was also acquired at a cost of $22,500.

During January the company spent $100,000 in developing the field and several shallow wells were brought into production. The established accounting policy of the company was to treat drilling and development charges of this type as expense of the period in which the work was done.

Construction of a pipeline was completed on May 1, 1961, at a cost of $180,000. Although this pipeline was physically capable of being used for 10 years or more, its economic usefulness was limited to the productive life of the wells; therefore, the depreciation method employed was based on the estimated number of barrels of oil to be produced.

Operating costs incurred during 1961 (other than depreciation and depletion) amounted to $150,000, and 180,000 barrels of oil were produced and sold.

In January, 1962, further drilling expense was incurred in the amount of $80,000, and the estimated total capacity of the field was raised from the original 1,500,000 barrels to 1,940,000 barrels, including oil produced to date.

Cash operating costs for 1962 amounted to $240,000. Oil production totaled 600,000 barrels, of which all but 60,000 barrels were sold during the year.

Instructions. Prepare journal entries to record the transactions of 1961 and 1962, including the setting up of the inventory at December 31, 1962. The inventory valuation should include an appropriate portion of the operating costs of the year, including depletion and depreciation.

14B-4. The Warfield Company is considering purchase of the assets of Strand Company, exclusive of cash, on January 2, 1963. The Strand Company has been in business for six years and had average net earnings of $12,800 during this period.

The purchase plan calls for a cash payment of $50,000 and a 6% note payable, due January 2, 1965, with interest payable annually, as payment for the net assets including goodwill after any necessary adjustments have been made.

The goodwill is to be determined as four times the average excess earnings over a normal rate of return of 8% on the present net tangible assets.

The balance sheet of Strand Company on December 31, 1962, follows:

STRAND COMPANY
Balance Sheet
December 31, 1962

Assets

Cash			$ 10,000
Other current assets			30,000
Plant and equipment:			
Land		$20,000	
Buildings	$81,000		
Less: accumulated depreciation	20,500	60,500	
Machinery	$66,000		
Less: accumulated depreciation	45,500	20,500	
Equipment	$40,000		
Less: accumulated depreciation	22,500	17,500	118,500
Patents			11,025
Goodwill			3,000
			$172,525

Liabilities and Owner's Equity

Current liabilities	$ 24,000
Long-term liabilities:	
Mortgage note payable, 5%	74,500
Walter Strand, capital	74,025
	$172,525

Other data

(1) Goodwill was written on the books three years ago when Strand decided that the increasing profitability of the company should be recognized.

(2) The patent appears at original cost. It was acquired by purchase six years ago from a competitor who had recorded amortization for two years on a basis of its legal life. The patent is highly useful to the business.

Instructions

a. Prepare any adjusting entries needed on the books of Strand Company as a preliminary step toward carrying out the sale agreement.

b. Determine the amount to be paid by Warfield Company for goodwill after considering the effects of the entries in (a).

c. Prepare the entries on Strand Company books to record the sale to Warfield Company.

d. Prepare the entries on Warfield Company books to record the purchase of assets and the goodwill determined in (b).

e. Prepare a revised balance sheet for the Strand Company as of January 2, 1963, after the journal entries in (c) are posted.

15

Partnerships

Three types of business organization are common to American industry; the single proprietorship, the partnership, and the corporation. All these forms of organization have been discussed and illustrated in preceding chapters, although emphasis has been placed on the single proprietorship. In this chapter and the next, we shall concentrate our attention on the accounting problems peculiar to a partnership. The Uniform Partnership Act, which has been adopted by many states to govern the formation and operation of partnerships, defines a partnership as "an association of two or more persons to carry on, as co-owners, a business for profit."

Reasons for formation of partnerships

In the professions and in businesses which stress the factor of personal service, the partnership form of organization is widely used. The laws of the state may even deny the incorporation privilege to persons engaged in such professions as medicine, law, and public accounting, because the personal responsibility of the professional practitioner to his client might be lost behind the impersonal legal entity of the corporation. In the fields of manufacturing, wholesaling, and retail trade, partnerships are also popular, because they afford a means of combining the capital and abilities of two or more persons. Perhaps the most common factor which impels a businessman to seek a partner is the lack of sufficient capital of his own to carry on a business. A partnership is customarily referred to as a firm; the name of the firm often includes the word "company" as, for example, "Adams, Barnes, and Company."

Significant features of a partnership

Before taking up the accounting problems peculiar to partnerships, it will be helpful to consider briefly some of the distinctive characteristics of the partnership form of organization. These characteristics (such as limited life and unlimited liability) all stem from the basic point that a partnership is not a separate entity in itself but merely a voluntary association of individuals.

Ease of formation. A partnership can be created without any legal formalities. When two persons agree to become partners, a partnership is automatically created. A partnership is based upon a voluntary contract, but the contract does not have to be in writing. It may be written, oral, or implied from the conduct of the parties. However, it is always desirable that a partnership contract be in writing, in order to reduce the possibilities of misunderstanding and later disputes.

The voluntary aspect of a partnership agreement means that no one can be forced into a partnership or forced to continue as a partner. Since each member of a partnership is bound by the acts of his partners and is personally liable for all debts of the partnership, it is reasonable that he should have a right to choose the persons with whom he is associated in partnership.

Suppose that A and B form a partnership and that some time later A wants to bring his son, C, into the business as a third partner. This would be possible only with the consent of B. The addition of a third partner may be regarded as a termination of the old two-man firm and the creation of a new three-man partnership. The new firm is based on the voluntary agreement of A, B, and C to become associated as partners.

Limited life. A partnership may be ended at any time by the death or withdrawal of any member of the firm. Other factors which may bring an end to a partnership include the bankruptcy or incapacity of a partner, the expiration of the period specified in the partnership contract, or the completion of the project for which the partnership was formed. The admission of a new partner, or the retirement of an existing member, means an end to the old partnership, although the business may be continued by the formation of a new partnership. For these reasons, many partnerships are short-lived, although the long-continued existence of a few large partnerships in the fields of public accounting and of stock brokerage indicates that these uncertainties of the partnership form are sometimes successfully handled.

Mutual agency. Each partner acts as an agent of the partnership, with authority to form contracts for the purchase and sale of goods and services. The partnership is bound by the acts of any partner as long as these acts are within the scope of normal operations.

The factor of mutual agency suggests the need for exercising great caution in the selection of a partner. To be in partnership with an irresponsible person or one lacking in integrity is an intolerable situation.

Unlimited liability. Each partner is personally responsible for all the debts of the firm. The lack of any ceiling on the liability of a partner may deter a wealthy person from entering a partnership. Assume, for example, that Ames, Baker, and Carroll form a partnership, each investing $10,000.

They agree to share profits and losses equally. Ames is a wealthy individual, but Baker and Carroll have no resources other than their investments in the firm. Assume that the business fails, owing creditors $50,000 more than the assets of the partnership. Creditors of the firm can collect the entire $50,000 from Ames; they need not be concerned with the fact that Ames had only a one-third equity in the business. After Ames pays off the partnership creditors from his personal funds, he has a legal right to reimbursement from the other two partners, but this legal right may be of no economic value.

When a new member joins an existing partnership, he may or may not assume liability for debts incurred by the firm prior to his admission. When a partner withdraws from membership, he must give adequate public notice of his withdrawal, or he may be held liable for partnership debts incurred subsequent to his withdrawal. The retiring partner remains liable for partnership debts existing at the time of his withdrawal unless the creditors agree to release him.

Co-ownership of partnership property. When a partner invests a building, inventory, or other property in a partnership, he does not retain any personal right to the assets contributed. The property becomes jointly owned by all partners.

Assume that Rogers, Smith, and Trent form a partnership and agree to share profits and losses equally. Rogers and Smith each invest $25,000 in cash, and Trent invests a building valued at $25,000. Some years later the partnership receives an offer of $40,000 cash for the building and accepts the offer. The $15,000 profit on the sale of the building belongs to the partnership, not to Trent personally. After a partner has contributed property to the firm he has no claim on the particular asset contributed but merely an equity in the total assets of the partnership.

Co-ownership of profits. The profits earned by the partnership may be divided among the partners in any ratio which they agree upon. Every member of a partnership has an ownership right in the profits; one of the tests of existence of a partnership is the intention of co-ownership of profits and losses.

Sometimes a store manager or other supervisory employee is allowed a certain percentage of the profits as a bonus, or in lieu of a fixed salary. This arrangement is merely a device for computing the bonus or salary; it does *not* give the employee an ownership right in the profits and does not make him a partner. Some retail stores rent their buildings under an agreement calling for a yearly rental computed as a percentage of profits. This type of rental agreement does not make the landlord a partner. To be a partner one must have an ownership right in the profits.

Advantages and disadvantages of a partnership

Perhaps the most important advantage and the principal reason for the formation of most partnerships is the opportunity to bring together sufficient capital to carry on a business. The opportunity to combine special skills, as, for example, the specialized talents of an engineer and an accountant, may also induce individuals to join forces in a partnership. The formation of a partnership is much easier and less expensive than the organization of a corporation. Operating as a partnership may produce income tax advantages. The partnership itself is not a legal entity and does not have to pay income taxes as does a corporation, although the individual partners pay taxes on their respective shares of the firm's income. Members of a partnership enjoy more freedom and flexibility of action than do the owners of a corporation; the partners may withdraw funds and make business decisions of all types without the necessity of formal meetings or legalistic procedures.

Offsetting these advantages of a partnership are such serious disadvantages as limited life, unlimited liability, and mutual agency. Furthermore, if a business is to require a large amount of capital, the partnership is a less effective device for raising funds than is a corporation.

The partnership contract

Although a partnership can be formed without any written agreement, it is highly desirable that a written contract of partnership be prepared by an attorney, setting forth the understanding between the partners on such points as the following:

1. The name, location, and nature of the business.
2. Names of the partners, and the duties and rights of each.
3. Amount to be invested by each partner. Procedure for valuing any noncash assets invested.
4. Procedure for sharing profits and losses.
5. Withdrawals to be allowed each partner.
6. Provision for insurance on the lives of partners, with the partnership or the surviving partners named as beneficiaries.
7. The accounting period to be used.
8. Provision for periodic audit by certified public accountants.
9. Provision for arbitration of disputes.
10. Provision for dissolution. This part of the agreement may specify a method for computing the equity of a retiring or deceased partner and a method of settlement which will not disrupt the business.

Many profitable partnership enterprises are forced out of existence because of misunderstandings and disputes among the partners. A written partnership agreement can help in avoiding these difficulties; it is far easier to reconcile conflicting viewpoints and to secure agreement on troublesome points at the beginning of the venture than it is after operations have begun. One of the advantages of a complete written contract of partnership is that in the process of developing such a detailed document many issues will be discussed and clarified in advance before the opportunity for misunderstanding and resentment has arisen.

Partnership accounting

An adequate accounting system and an accurate measurement of income are needed by every business, but they are especially important in a partnership because the net profit is divided among two or more owners. Each partner needs current, accurate information on profits so that he can make intelligent decisions on such questions as additional investments, expansion of the business, or sale of his interest.

To illustrate the significance to partners of accurate accounting data, consider the following case. Allen and Baker became partners, each investing $50,000. Allen maintained the accounting records and fraudulently contrived to make the financial statements show operating losses although the business was in fact quite profitable. Discouraged by these misleading financial statements, Baker sold his share of the business to Allen for $20,000, when in fact his equity was worth considerably more than his original investment of $50,000.

Partnership accounting requires the maintenance of a separate capital account for each partner; a separate drawing account for each partner is also desirable. The other distinctive feature of partnership accounting is the division of each year's net profit or loss among the partners in the proportions specified by the partnership agreement. In the study of partnership accounting, the new concepts lie almost entirely in the owners' equity section; accounting for partnership assets and liabilities follows the same principles as for other forms of business organization.

Opening the books

When a partner contributes assets other than cash, a question always arises as to the value of such assets; the valuations assigned to noncash assets should be their *fair market values* at the date of transfer to the partnership. The valuations assigned must be agreed to by all the partners.

To illustrate the opening entries for a newly formed partnership, assume that John Blair and Richard Cross, who operate competing retail stores, decide to form a partnership by consolidating their two businesses. A capital account will be opened for each partner and credited with the agreed valuation of the *net assets* he contributes. The journal entries to open the books of the partnership of Blair and Cross are as follows:

ENTRIES
FOR
FORMATION
OF PART-
NERSHIP

Cash	*20,000*	
Accounts Receivable	*30,000*	
Inventory of Merchandise	*45,000*	
Accounts Payable		*15,000*
John Blair, Capital		*80,000*
To record the investment by John Blair in the		
partnership of Blair and Cross.		

Cash	5,000	
Land	30,000	
Building	50,000	
Inventory of Merchandise	30,000	
Accounts Payable		35,000
Richard Cross, Capital		80,000
To record the investment by Richard Cross in the partnership of Blair and Cross.		

The values assigned to assets on the books of the new partnership may be quite different from the amounts at which these assets were carried on the books of their previous owners. For example, the land contributed by Cross and valued at $30,000 might have appeared on his books at a cost of $10,000. The building which he contributed was valued at $50,000 by the partnership, but it might have cost Cross only $40,000 some years ago and might have been depreciated on his records to a book value of $30,000. Assuming that market values of land and buildings had risen sharply while Cross owned this property, it is no more than fair to recognize the present market value of these assets at the time he transfers them to the partnership and to credit his capital account accordingly. Depreciation of the building will begin anew on the partnership books and will be based on the assigned value of $50,000 at date of acquisition by the partnership.

As another example, assume that an individual contributes to a partnership land and a building carried on his own books at $100,000 but having a fair market value of only $60,000. The property should be recorded on the partnership books at $60,000. Regardless of whether market values have risen or fallen, the partnership represents a new business relationship to which partners contribute economic resources. The value of these resources at the time the partnership is formed is clearly the only basis for establishing the capital contributions of partners on a comparable basis.

Additional investments

Assume that after six months of operation the firm is in need of more cash, and the partners make an additional investment of $5,000 each on July 1. These additional investments are credited to the capital accounts as shown by the following journal entry:

ENTRY FOR ADDITIONAL INVESTMENT

Cash	10,000	
John Blair, Capital		5,000
Richard Cross, Capital		5,000
To record additional investments.		

The capital accounts of the partners at the end of the year, before the books are closed will appear as follows:

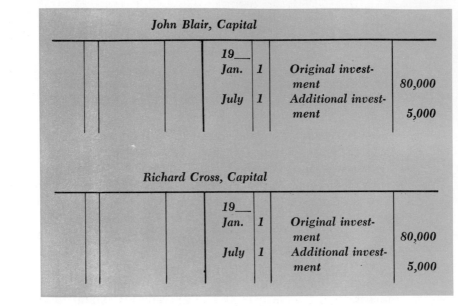

John Blair, Capital

		19__			
		Jan.	1	Original investment	80,000
		July	1	Additional investment	5,000

Richard Cross, Capital

		19__			
		Jan.	1	Original investment	80,000
		July	1	Additional investment	5,000

Drawing accounts

The drawing account maintained for each partner serves the same purpose as the drawing account of the owner of a single proprietorship. The transactions calling for debits to the drawing accounts of partners may be summarized as follows:

1. Cash or other assets withdrawn by a partner
2. Payments from partnership funds of the personal debts of a partner
3. Partnership cash collected in behalf of the firm by a partner but retained by him personally

When merchandise is withdrawn by a partner for his personal use, his drawing account should be debited for the cost of the merchandise; the offsetting credit is to the Purchases account. Since the transaction is not a sale in the usual sense of the word and does not produce any element of profit, it is preferably recorded in the general journal as a withdrawal.

A member of a partnership may sometimes find it convenient to have his personal debts (such as bills from department stores) paid from the funds of the business. Such disbursements of business cash should be recorded by debiting his drawing account. When this practice of having the business pay the personal expenses of the partner is in use, the danger always exists that the payments may erroneously be debited to expense accounts. Such an error will penalize the other partners as well as invalidate the accounting data showing the results of operating the business. One of the continuing problems in accounting for either a single proprietorship or a partnership is to maintain a clear distinction between business transactions and the personal affairs of the owners. A dishonest businessman seeking to evade personal income taxes may deliberately try to include some of his personal living expenditures as expenses of the business. Business expenditures are deductible in arriving at taxable income; personal expenditures are not, but it is sometimes quite difficult to draw the line between business and personal expense.

When a partner makes a collection from a customer of the business or collects cash in behalf of the firm for any reason, such collections should be promptly deposited in the partnership bank account just as all other cash receipts are. Only in this way can adequate internal control over cash transactions be maintained. However, a partner is an owner, and if he chooses to withdraw assets from the business by retaining cash collected in behalf of the firm, he has a right to do so, provided he discloses the transaction fully. The appropriate journal entry would be a debit to the partner's drawing account and a credit to Accounts Receivable—assuming that the cash came from collection of a receivable.

Credits to the drawing accounts are seldom encountered; one rather unusual transaction requiring such an entry consists of the payment of a partnership liability by a partner out of his personal funds.

Withdrawals by a partner could be recorded as debits in his capital account, thus eliminating the need for using a drawing account. A more useful record is created, however, when separate accounts are employed to show the permanent capital investment and the current drawings of each partner. The debit balance in a partner's drawing account at the end of the accounting period is customarily transferred to his capital account so that his total equity in the business will appear in one place. This amount is of particular significance if the partnership agreement provides that a certain minimum capital investment must be maintained by each partner.

Loans from partners

Ordinarily any funds furnished to the firm by a partner are recorded by crediting his capital account. Occasionally, however, a partnership may be in need of funds but the partners do not wish to increase their permanent investment in the business, or perhaps one partner is willing to advance funds when the others are not. Under these circumstances, the advance of funds may be designated as a loan from the partner and credited to a partner's loan account. Liabilities to outsiders always take precedence over any claims of partners.

Closing the books of a partnership

At the end of the accounting period, adjusting entries are made, and the revenue and expense accounts of a partnership are closed to the Income Summary account in exactly the same manner as in a single proprietorship or corporation. The balance in the Income Summary account is then closed to the partners' capital accounts, in accordance with the profit-sharing provisions of the partnership contract. If there is no agreement to the contrary, the law assumes that the intention of the partners was for an equal division of profits and losses. If the partnership agreement specifies a method of dividing profits but does not mention the possibility of losses, any losses are divided in the proportions provided for sharing profits.

In the previous illustration of the firm of Blair and Cross, an equal sharing of profits was agreed upon. Assuming that a profit of $30,000 was realized during the first year of operations, the entry to close the Income Summary account would be as follows:

CLOSING INCOME SUMMARY: PROFITS SHARED EQUALLY

Income Summary 30,000		
John Blair, Capital		*15,000*
Richard Cross, Capital		*15,000*
To divide net income for 1961 in accordance with		
partnership agreement to share profits equally.		

The next step in closing the books is to transfer the balance of each partner's drawing account to his capital account. Assuming that withdrawals during the year amounted to $6,000 for Blair and $4,000 for Cross, the entry at December 31 to close the drawing accounts is as follows:

CLOSING THE DRAWING ACCOUNTS

John Blair, Capital 6,000		
Richard Cross, Capital 4,000		
John Blair, Drawing		*6,000*
Richard Cross, Drawing		*4,000*
To transfer debit balances in partners' drawing		
accounts to their respective capital accounts.		

The nature of partnership profits

The profit earned by a partnership, like that of a single proprietorship, may be regarded as consisting of three distinct elements: (1) compensation for the personal services rendered by the partners, (2) compensation (interest) for the use of invested capital, and (3) a "pure" profit or reward for the entrepreneurial functions of risk taking and policy making. Recognition of these three elements of partnership profits will be helpful in formulating an equitable plan for the division of profits. If one partner devotes full time to the business while another does not participate actively, the profit-sharing plan should give weight to this disparity in contributions of services. Any salaries authorized for partners *are regarded as a preliminary step in the division of profits, not as an expense of the business.*

The partner is considered an owner, not an employee. The services which he renders to the firm are, therefore, considered to be rendered in anticipation of a share in profits, not in contemplation of a salary. Another reason for not treating salaries of partners as an expense of the business is that the amounts are often set arbitrarily without the arm's-length bargaining typical of employer-employee contracts. Consequently, the salary of a partner may not be closely related to the fair market value of the personal services he renders to the business. The net profit reported by a partnership cannot readily be compared with the profit earned by a corporation of similar size, because the corporation treats as expense any payments to owner-managers for personal services rendered.

In the solution of problems in this book, the student should record all withdrawals of assets by partners as debits to the partners' drawing accounts, regardless of whether or not the withdrawals are described as salaries. Some alternative treatments of salaries of partners can be more effectively explored in advanced accounting courses.

Working papers. The working papers for a partnership include a pair of columns for each partner. In order to shorten the illustration of working papers on pages 444 and 445, the work sheet is begun with the adjusted trial balance. Columns for a trial balance and columns for adjustments would be the same as for a single proprietorship or a corporation.

Income statement for a partnership. The income statement for a partnership differs from that of a single proprietorship in only one respect: a final section may be added to show the division of the net income between the partners, as illustrated on this page for the firm of Blair and Cross.

NOTE DISTRIBUTION OF NET INCOME

BLAIR AND CROSS
Income Statement
For the Year Ended December 31, 19___

Sales		$300,000
Less: cost of goods sold:		
Inventory, Jan. 1	$ 75,000	
Purchases	155,000	
Cost of goods available for sale	$230,000	
Less: ending inventory	100,000	
Cost of goods sold		130,000
Gross profit on sales		$170,000
Less: operating expenses:		
Selling expenses	$100,000	
General & administrative expenses	40,000	140,000
Net income		$ 30,000
Distribution of net income:		
To John Blair (50%)	$ 15,000	
To Richard Cross (50%)	15,000	$ 30,000

BLAIR AND CROSS
Working Papers
For the Year Ended December 31, 19__

	Adjusted trial balance		Income statement	
Cash	30,000			
Accounts receivable	60,000			
Inventory, Jan. 1	75,000		75,000	
Land	30,000			
Building	50,000			
Accumulated depr.: bldg.		2,000		
Accounts payable		78,000		
John Blair, capital		85,000		
John Blair, drawing	6,000			
Richard Cross, capital		85,000		
Richard Cross, drawing	4,000			
Sales		300,000		300,000
Purchases	155,000		155,000	
Selling expenses	100,000		100,000	
General & adm. expenses	40,000		40,000	
	550,000	550,000		
Inventory, Dec. 31				100,000
			370,000	400,000
Net income, divided equally			30,000	
			400,000	400,000
Capitals at end of year:				
Blair, capital				
Cross, capital				

John Blair, capital		Richard Cross, capital		Balance sheet	
				30,000	
				60,000	
				30,000	
				50,000	
					2,000
					78,000
	85,000				
6,000					
			85,000		
		4,000			
				100,000	
	15,000		15,000		
6,000	100,000	4,000	100,000		
94,000					94,000
		96,000			96,000
100,000	100,000	100,000	100,000	270,000	270,000

Balance sheet for a partnership. A balance sheet for a partnership differs from a balance sheet for a single proprietorship in one respect: instead of a single capital account, there is one for each partner. These accounts should be totaled to show the entire owners' equity in the business.

NOTE
PARTNERS'
EQUITY
SECTION

BLAIR AND CROSS
Balance Sheet
December 31, 19___

Assets

Current assets:

Cash		$ 30,000
Accounts receivable		60,000
Inventory of merchandise		100,000
Total current assets		$190,000

Fixed assets:

Land		$ 30,000
Building	$50,000	
Less: allowance for depreciation	2,000	48,000
Total fixed assets		$ 78,000
Total assets		$268,000

Liabilities and Partners' Equity

Current liabilities:

Accounts payable		$ 78,000
Partners' equity:		
John Blair, Capital	$94,000	
Richard Cross, Capital	96,000	190,000
Total liabilities and partners' equity		$268,000

The partners will usually want an explanation of the change in their capital accounts from one year-end to the next. A supplementary schedule called a *statement of partners' capitals* is prepared to show this information.

CHANGES IN
CAPITAL
ACCOUNTS
DURING THE
YEAR

BLAIR AND CROSS
Statement of Partners' Capitals
For the Year Ended December 31, 19___

	Blair	Cross	Total
Investment, Jan. 1, 19___	$ 80,000	$ 80,000	$160,000
Add: additional investment ...	5,000	5,000	10,000
Net income for the year	15,000	15,000	30,000
Totals	$100,000	$100,000	$200,000
Deduct: withdrawals	6,000	4,000	10,000
Balances, Dec. 31, 19___	$ 94,000	$ 96,000	$190,000

This detailed picture of the changes in the capital accounts of the partners could be inserted in the proprietorship section of the balance sheet, but in practice a separate statement of partners' capital is usually preferable. By using the separate statement to show changes in the capital accounts, the balance sheet is held to a more convenient length. Moreover, the partners can avoid unnecessary publicity as to their personal withdrawals, since the statement of partners' capitals is generally not distributed to creditors or others outside the business.

Partnership profits and income taxes

Partnerships are not required to pay income taxes. However, a partnership is required to file an information tax return showing the amount of the partnership net income and the share of each partner in the net income. Each partner must include his share of the partnership profit on his individual income tax return. Partnership net income is thus taxable to the partners individually in the year in which it is earned. In the partnership of Blair and Cross illustrated above, each would report and pay tax on $15,000 of partnership net income.

Notice that partners report and pay tax on their respective shares of the profits earned by the partnership during the year and not on the amount which they have drawn out of the business during the year. The entire net income of the partnership is taxable to the partners each year, even though there may have been no withdrawals. This treatment is consistent with that accorded a single proprietorship.

Factors influencing the profit-sharing plan

The profits of a partnership have been stated to consist of three elements: (1) compensation to partners for personal services; (2) compensation for the use of invested capital; and (3) a residual "pure" profit. If all members of a partnership contribute the same amount of capital and render the same amount of personal services, then an equal division of the profits seems fair and reasonable. An equality of capital invested and services rendered were assumed in the preceding illustrations, and profits were divided equally between the partners. We are now ready to consider cases in which the partners invest unequal amounts of capital and services.

Assume that Partner A contributes 75% of the capital of the firm of A and B and works full time in managing the business, while B contributes only 25% of the required capital and devotes no time to the business. What would be an equitable plan for dividing the partnership profits? Or suppose the business operated at a loss: how should the loss be divided between A and B?

The partners may make any agreement they choose for the division of profits and losses. In most cases they will prefer a plan which gives consideration to the differences in capital invested and personal services contributed. The personal services of one partner may be much more valuable than those of another even though equal amounts of time are devoted to the business. Other factors which vary between partners and which may require consideration in devising the profit-sharing plan include business contacts and reputation, seniority, and personal credit standing. A partner who possesses extensive property outside the partnership may add considerably to the credit standing of the firm because partnership creditors know they can call on him personally for payment.

Alternative methods of dividing profits and losses

The following alternative methods of dividing profits and losses place varying degrees of emphasis on the three elements (interest, salaries, and "pure" profit) comprising partnership profits.

1. A fixed ratio
2. A capital ratio
3. Interest on capital, salaries to partners, and remaining profits in a fixed ratio

Many combinations and variations of the above three basic devices for profit sharing may be devised. Some of these variations will be considered in the following sections of this chapter.

Fixed ratio. The fixed-ratio method has already been fully illustrated in the example of the Blair and Cross partnership in which profits were divided equally. A fixed ratio can also be used in cases in which one partner contributes more to the business than do his copartners. For example, a fixed ratio might call for a two-thirds share of profits to Partner A and a one-third share to Partner B. In firms consisting of several partners, a fixed ratio of profit sharing is conveniently expressed in percentages; for example, 40% to A, 30% to B, 20% to C, and 10% to D. The percentage specified for each partner is applied to the net income for the year to determine the amount to be transferred from the Income Summary account to his capital account.

CAPITAL
ACCOUNTS
USED IN
ILLUSTRA-
TION

In demonstrating the various methods of profit sharing, the following capital accounts will be used:

A. B. Adams, Capital			B. C. Barnes, Capital		
	19__			19__	
	Jan. 1	40,000		Jan. 1	10,000
	July 1	5,000		July 1	5,000

During the first year of operations, Adams withdrew a total of $6,000 in cash and merchandise; Barnes made withdrawals of $4,000. These withdrawals were recorded by debits in the partners' drawing accounts. At year-end, the Income Summary account showed a credit balance of $24,000, representing the net income for the year, before any salaries or interest to partners.

Capital ratio. The division of profits on the basis of relative capital investments may be appropriate in a merchandising or manufacturing business if invested capital is regarded as the most important factor in the production of income. The capital ratio would generally not be a satisfactory basis for sharing profits in a partnership of professional men, such as a law firm or public accounting firm. The technical skill and professional reputations of attorneys and accountants are usually much more significant in achieving profitable operations than is the small amount of capital required to establish a professional firm. When partners agree to base their profit-sharing plan on the factor of capital invested, the question of whether to use beginning capital balances or average capital must be decided.

Ratio of beginning capitals. The beginning capitals for the firm of Adams and Barnes were as follows: A. B. Adams, $40,000, and B. C. Barnes, $10,000. If the partners agreed to share profits in the ratio of their beginning capitals, the division of the first year's net income of $24,000 would be computed as follows:

PROFIT SHARING; BEGINNING CAPITALS AS BASIS

	Beginning capitals	*Percentage of total*
A. B. Adams	$40,000	80
B. C. Barnes	10,000	20
	$50,000	100

	Division of profit
A. B. Adams ($24,000 × .80)	$19,200
B. C. Barnes ($24,000 × .20)	4,800
Total	$24,000

The entry to close the Income Summary account is as follows:

Income Summary	24,000	
A. B. Adams, Capital		19,200
B. C. Barnes, Capital		4,800

To close the Income Summary account by dividing the year's profit in the ratio of the beginning capitals.

The capital accounts of Adams and Barnes in this illustration will not remain in the original 80:20 proportion for two reasons: neither the additional investments made by the partners on July 1 nor the withdrawals of cash and merchandise during the year were in the proportion of the original investments. When profits are to be divided in the ratio of "beginning capitals," the partnership agreement may provide that the ratio will be set at the first of each year on the basis of the *new capital balances,* or the agreement may provide for the original ratio to remain in force regardless of subsequent changes in capital accounts.

Ratio of average capital investments. If the balances in the capital accounts change significantly during the course of a year, the partners may prefer to use the average capitals rather than the beginning balances as the basis for dividing profits. To compute the average capital for a partner during the year, the first step is to multiply the capital balance at the beginning of the year by the number of months until the date of a change in the capital account. Multiply the new balance in the capital account by the number of months until the next change in the account. After carrying out this procedure for the entire year, add together the amounts thus obtained. The total represents the dollar-months of capital invested. Each partner's share of profits is equal to the ratio of his dollar-months to the total dollar-months for all the capital accounts.

In the partnership of Adams and Barnes the beginning capitals were $40,000 and $10,000, respectively. The only change in the capital accounts occurred on July 1 when each partner invested an additional $5,000. The division of the year's profit of $24,000 would be computed as follows:

	Dollar-months
A. B. Adams:	
January 1 to June 30 ($40,000 × 6 months)	$240,000
July 1 to December 31 ($45,000 × 6 months)	270,000
Total	$510,000
B. C. Barnes:	
January 1 to June 30 ($10,000 × 6 months)	$ 60,000
July 1 to December 31 ($15,000 × 6 months)	90,000
Total	$150,000
Total dollar-months for both partners	$660,000

	Division of profit
A. B. Adams $\left(\dfrac{510,000}{660,000} \times \$24,000 \text{ } profit\right)$	$ 18,545
B. C. Barnes $\left(\dfrac{150,000}{660,000} \times \$24,000 \text{ } profit\right)$	5,455
Total profit divided	$ 24,000

The entry to close the Income Summary account is:

Income Summary 24,000		
A. B. Adams, Capital		*18,545*
B. C. Barnes, Capital		*5,455*
To divide the year's net income between the part-		
ners in the ratio of average capital investments.		

Salaries, interest, and remainder in a fixed ratio. Since partners often contribute varying amounts of personal services as well as different amounts of capital, partnership agreements often provide for partners' salaries as a factor in the division of profits.

As a first example, assume that Adams and Barnes agree that Adams will be allowed an annual salary of $6,000 and Barnes an annual salary of $12,000. Any remaining profits will be divided equally. It is agreed that the salaries will be withdrawn in cash each month and recorded by debits to the drawing accounts.[1] The authorized salaries total $18,000 a year; this amount represents a first step in the division of the year's profit and is therefore subtracted from the net income of $24,000. The remaining profit of $6,000 will be divided equally.

Net income to be divided		*$24,000*
Salaries to partners:		
To A. B. Adams	$ 6,000	
To B. C. Barnes	12,000	18,000
Remaining profit, to be divided equally		$ 6,000
To A. B. Adams	$ 3,000	
To B. C. Barnes	3,000	6,000

The entries to close the Income Summary account at December 31 are:

Income Summary 18,000		
A. B. Adams, Capital		6,000
B. C. Barnes, Capital		12,000
To credit each partner with his authorized salary		
as a first step in closing the Income Summary		
account.		

[1] Salaries may be used as a device for dividing partnership net income, even though the partners do not wish to make any withdrawals of cash whatsoever. In this illustration, however, it is assumed that cash is withdrawn by each partner in an amount equal to his authorized salary.

```
Income Summary  ..........................  6,000
        A. B. Adams, Capital  .................:...          3,000
        B. C. Barnes, Capital  ..................          3,000
To divide equally between the partners the credit
balance remaining in the Income Summary account
after crediting each partner with his authorized
salary.
```

The preceding example took into consideration the difference in the value of personal services contributed by Adams and Barnes but ignored the disparity in capital contributions. In the next example, we shall assume that the partners agree to a profit-sharing plan providing for interest on beginning capitals as well as salaries. Salaries, as before, are authorized at $6,000 for Adams and $12,000 for Barnes. Each partner is to be allowed interest at 6% on his beginning capital balance, and any remaining profit is to be divided equally.

Distribution of Net Profit

Net profit to be divided			$24,000
Salaries to partners:			
A. B. Adams	$ 6,000		
B. C. Barnes	12,000	$18,000	
Interest on invested capital:			
A. B. Adams ($40,000 × 0.06)	$ 2,400		
B. C. Barnes ($10,000 × 0.06)	600	3,000	21,000
Remaining profit to be divided equally			$ 3,000
To A. B. Adams		$ 1,500	
To B. C. Barnes		1,500	3,000

This three-step division of the year's profit of $24,000 has resulted in giving Adams a total of $9,900 and Barnes a total of $14,100. The amounts credited to each partner may be summarized as follows:

	Adams	Barnes	Together
Salaries	$6,000	$12,000	$18,000
Interest on beginning capitals ...	2,400	600	3,000
Remaining profit divided equally ..	1,500	1,500	3,000
Totals	$9,900	$14,100	$24,000

The entries to close the Income Summary account will be:

PROFIT
SHARING;
SALARIES,
INTEREST,
AND FIXED
RATIO AS
BASIS

Income Summary	18,000	
A. B. Adams, Capital		6,000
B. C. Barnes, Capital		12,000

To credit each partner with his authorized salary as a first step in closing the Income Summary account.

Income Summary	3,000	
A. B. Adams, Capital		2,400
B. C. Barnes, Capital		600

To credit each partner with interest on his beginning capital at 6% as provided in partnership contract.

Income Summary	3,000	
A. B. Adams, Capital		1,500
B. C. Barnes, Capital		1,500

To divide equally between the partners the credit balance remaining in the Income Summary account after crediting each partner with authorized salary and interest.

Authorized salaries and interest in excess of net income. In the preceding example the total of the authorized salaries and interest was $21,000 and the net income to be divided was $24,000. Suppose that the net income had been only $15,000; how should the division have been made?

If the partnership contract provides for salaries and interest on invested capital, these provisions are to be followed even though the net profit for the year is less than the total of the authorized salaries and interest. If the net income of the firm of Adams and Barnes amounted to only $15,000, this amount would be distributed as follows:

Distribution of Net Income

Net income to be divided			$15,000
Salaries to partners:			
To A. B. Adams	$ 6,000		
To B. C. Barnes	12,000	$18,000	
Interest on invested capital:			
A. B. Adams ($40,000 × 0.06)	$ 2,400		
B. C. Barnes ($10,000 × 0.06)	600	3,000	21,000
Residual loss to be divided equally			$ 6,000
A. B. Adams		$ 3,000	
B. C. Barnes		3,000	6,000

The result of this distribution of the net income of $15,000 has been to give Adams a total of $5,400 and Barnes a total of $9,600. The entries to close the Income Summary account will be as follows:

AUTHORIZED
SALARIES
AND
INTEREST
MAY EXCEED
NET INCOME

Income Summary	18,000	
A. B. Adams, Capital		6,000
B. C. Barnes, Capital		12,000
To credit each partner with his authorized salary as a first step in closing the Income Summary account.		
Income Summary	3,000	
A. B. Adams, Capital		2,400
B. C. Barnes, Capital		600
To credit each partner with interest on his beginning capital as provided in partnership contract.		
A. B. Adams, Capital	3,000	
B. C. Barnes, Capital	3,000	
Income Summary		6,000
To close the Income Summary account by dividing equally between the partners the remaining debit balance.		

The first two entries in this series transferred a total of $21,000 from the Income Summary account to the partners' capital accounts, and caused the Income Summary account to acquire a debit balance of $6,000. The debit balance, or residual loss, must be divided equally because the partnership contract states that profits and losses are to be divided equally after providing for salaries and interest.

It would be possible for the partnership agreement to make the credit for a partner's salary conditional upon the business achieving a certain amount of net profit, but this is seldom done. To illustrate the issue as sharply as possible, assume that one partner spends his full time in the management of the business and that the other partner devotes no time to the enterprise. If the business breaks even for the year or shows a small loss, it seems equitable that the managing partner should still be compensated for the managerial services rendered. If he had not served as manager, the services of an employee-manager would have been necessary and would have represented an additional expense to the business. If the salaries authorized for partners are realistic in terms of the value of the personal services rendered, there is every reason for utilizing the salary provisions in the division of profits and losses regardless of the degree of profitability of the business.

Other methods of dividing profits

It should be apparent that the preceding illustrations of profit sharing by partners do not represent a complete list of the possible variations. In evaluating any particular profit-sharing plan, it is helpful to keep in mind the statement made earlier in this chapter: Partnership profits generally include three distinct elements: (1) compensation for personal services rendered by partners, (2) compensation for the use of invested capital, and (3) a "pure" profit or reward for the functions of risk taking and policy making. An equitable plan for dividing net income should take into account the relative contribution of each partner in each of these three areas.

QUESTIONS

1. List and describe briefly five distinctive characteristics of a partnership.

2. Awalers is the proprietor of a small manufacturing business. He is considering the possibility of joining in partnership with Bracken, whom he considers to be thoroughly competent and congenial. Prepare a brief statement outlining the advantages and disadvantages of the potential partnership to Awalers.

3. A partnership agreement may cover any matter the partners desire. Of the provisions you would expect to find in a typical well-drawn partnership agreement, which have the greatest accounting significance?

4. Avery has land having a book value of $5,000 and a fair market value of $8,000, and a building having a book value of $50,000 and a fair market value of $40,000. The land and building become Avery's sole capital contribution to a partnership. What is Avery's capital balance in the new partnership? Why?

5. State the effect of each of the transactions given below on a partner's capital and drawing accounts:

   a. Partner borrows funds from the business.
   b. Partner collects a partnership account receivable while on vacation and uses the funds for personal purposes.
   c. Partner receives in cash the salary allowance provided in the partnership agreement.
   d. Partner takes home merchandise (cost $40; selling price $65) for his personal use.
   e. Partner has loaned money to the partnership. The principal together with interest at 6% is now repaid in cash.

6. Explain how you would expect the balance sheet and income statement of a partnership to differ from those of a proprietorship.

7. Partner X withdraws $25,000 from a partnership during the year. When the statements are made at the end of the year, X's share of the partnership income is $15,000. Which amount must he report on his income tax return?

8. What factors should be considered in drawing up an agreement as to the way in which income shall be shared by two or more partners?

9. Partner A has a salary allowance, as provided in the partnership agreement, of $600 per month. He actually withdraws from the company only $400 per month. Will this have any effect on his share of the partnership income?

10. Partner X has a choice to make. He has been offered by his partners a choice between no salary allowance and a one-third share in the partnership income or a salary of $6,000 per year and a one-quarter share of residual profits. Write a brief memorandum explaining the factors he should consider in reaching a decision.

PROBLEMS

Group A

15A-1. The information appearing on the trial balance of Ankers-Shippe at the end of the current year is given below.

Accounts payable	$ 20,000
Accounts receivable	38,480
Accrued liabilities	13,400
Administrative expenses	84,790
Allowance for depreciation: equipment	9,000
Allowance for bad debts	2,420
Ankers, capital	52,000
Ankers, drawing	5,600
Cash	25,400
Equipment	55,000
Inventory	23,200
Merchandise purchases	274,300
Prepaid expenses	6,300
Sales	465,800
Selling expenses	75,350
Shippe, capital	42,400
Shippe, drawing	4,200
Transportation-in	12,400

Other data. There were no changes in partners' capital accounts during the year.

The inventory at the end of the year was $17,380. The partnership agreement provides that partners are to be allowed 10% interest on invested capital as of the beginning of the year and are to divide residual profits in the ratio of Ankers 60%, Shippe 40%.

Instructions
a. Prepare an income statement for the year.
b. Prepare a statement of partners' capital accounts.
c. Prepare a balance sheet as of the end of the year.

15A-2. L, M, and N are partners of the Lemen Company. During the current year their average capital balances were as follows: L, $50,000; M, $30,000; and N, $20,000. The partnership agreement provides that partners shall receive an annual allowance of 6% of their average capital balance and a salary allowance as follows: L, none; M, $10,000; and N, $8,000. Partner M, who manages the business, is to receive a bonus of 25% of the income in excess of $12,000 after partners' interest and salary allowances. Residual profits are to be divided: L, 1/2; M, 1/3; and N, 1/6.

Instructions. Prepare separate schedules showing how income will be divided among the three partners in each of the following cases. The figure given is the annual income available for distribution among the partners.

    a. Loss of $9,000
    b. Income of $15,000
    c. Income of $31,200
    d. Income of $60,000

15A-3. The following account balances appear on the records of the J-D Company as of December 31, the close of the current year, after all revenue and expense accounts have been closed to Income Summary:

	December 31 Balance	
	Debit	*Credit*
Partner J, capital		$48,320
Partner J, drawing	$10,490	
Partner D, capital		37,250
Partner D, drawing	7,460	
Income summary		9,510

Other data

(1) During the year Partner D took out of stock for his personal use merchandise which cost the company $540 and had a retail value of $900. The bookkeeper credited Sales and charged Miscellaneous Expense for the retail value of all merchandise taken by D.

(2) Partner J paid $500 from his personal funds on November 18 to an attorney for legal services. Of this amount $180, which was for services relating to partnership business, should be treated as an additional investment by J.

(3) Partner D borrowed $4,800 from the partnership on September 1 of the current year, giving a six-month note with interest at 5%. The only record made of this transaction was a charge to D's drawing account for $4,800 at the time of the loan. D intends to repay the loan with interest at maturity.

(4) Partner J had the full-time use of a company-owned car. All operating expenses were paid by the partnership. It was agreed that J's drawing account would be charged 5 cents per mile for all miles driven for personal use. At the end of the year J reported that he had driven 6,000 miles for personal reasons, but the bookkeeper filed this information and made no entry.

(5) On March 31 Partner J invested an additional $8,000 in the business. Other than this no changes in partners' capital accounts have been recorded during the year.

Instructions

a. Make any adjusting entries that are necessary on the basis of the above information, as of December 31. The portion of any entry affecting revenue or expense accounts may be charged or credited directly to Income Summary.

b. Prepare a schedule showing how the adjusted partnership income would be divided between the partners. The partnership agreement calls for salary allowances of $400 per month to J and $600 per month to D. The balance of profits are to be shared in a 3:2 ratio.

c. What effect did the adjustments disclosed by the audit have on J's share of the partnership income for the year? Determine the amount and explain briefly.

d. Prepare a statement of changes in partners' capital accounts for the year.

15A-4. The partners of the Ipswich Company had the following capital balances at the beginning of the current calendar year: Ambic, $36,000; Pentam, $62,000.

Each of the partners had originally invested $50,000 in the business. It had been agreed at the outset that a partner should be *credited* with 6% interest (1/2% per month) on the amount by which his capital exceeded $50,000 during the year, and should be *charged* with 6% interest on the amount by which his capital was less than $50,000 during the year. (For example, if a partner had a capital balance of $51,000 during the first six months of the year and $50,000 during the last six months he would receive credit for $30, that is, 6% interest on the $1,000 excess for one-half year.) It was also agreed that Pentam would be allowed a salary of $7,200 and that residual profits were to be divided 70% to Ambic and 30% to Pentam.

The partnership contract provided that each partner might withdraw up to $5,000 per year in anticipation of profits, and that any drawings up to this amount would not be charged against capital until the books were closed at the end of the year. Each partner withdrew the full $5,000 during the year. On August 1 of the current year Ambic made an additional investment in the firm of $10,000. On October 1 Pentam withdrew from capital $6,000.

The net income of the partnership before any consideration of division among the partners was $13,000.

Instructions

a. Prepare a schedule showing how the partnership income of $13,000 should be divided between the two partners.

b. Make the journal entries necessary to close the accounts at the end of the year.

c. Prepare a statement of changes in partners' capital accounts during the year.

d. After reading this statement of changes in partners' capital accounts, Ambic wants to know what effect his deficiency in capital had on his share of partnership income. He asks, "If I had had a capital of $50,000 throughout the year, how much larger would my share of the $13,000 income have been?" Write a brief statement answering his query.

Group B

15B-1. James Hall is the sole owner of the Campus Bookshop. Because he needs additional working capital in the business and has an immediate personal need for $5,000 in cash, Hall agreed on October 31, 1962, to join in partnership with Nancy Reynolds. It is agreed that Hall will contribute all noncash assets of his bookstore to the partnership and will withdraw (from funds supplied by Reynolds) $5,000 in cash. Nancy Reynolds will invest $15,000 in the business. The partnership contract provides that income shall be divided 60% to Hall and 40% to Reynolds.

Information as to the assets and liabilities of the Campus Bookshop at October 31, 1962, and their agreed valuation is as follows:

	Per Hall's books	*Agreed valuation*
Accounts receivable	*$12,000*	*$9,600*
Allowance for uncollectibles	*1,000*	
Merchandise on hand	*20,800*	*15,000*
Store equipment	*3,800*	*2,500*
Allowance for depreciation	*1,600*	
5% notes payable (dated May, 1962;		
due Apr. 30, 1963)	*8,000*	*8,200*
Accounts payable	*4,000*	*4,000*

It is agreed that the new partnership (to be called the Hall-Reynolds Company) will assume the present debts of the Campus Bookshop.

Instructions

a. Make the necessary journal entries to record the formation of the Hall-Reynolds partnership at October 31, 1962.

b. At the end of November, after all adjusting entries, the Income Summary account of the Hall-Reynolds Company shows a credit balance of $1,200. The partners' drawing accounts have debit balances as follows: Hall, $840; Reynolds, $650. Make the journal entries necessary to complete the closing of the partnership books at the end of November.

c. Prepare a statement of partners' capital for the month of November.

15B-2. Changes in the capital accounts of the XYZ Partnership during the current year were as follows:

	Partner X	*Partner Y*	*Partner Z*
Balance at Jan. 1	*$52,000*	*$30,000*	*$20,000*
Added investment on Apr. 1			*8,000*
Withdrawal on Sept. 1	*(12,000)*		
Balance at Dec. 31	*$40,000*	*$30,000*	*$28,000*

Instructions. For each of the situations described below, prepare a schedule showing how the partnership income would be divided among X, Y, and Z.

a. Net income $20,800. Income to be divided on the basis of average invested capital.

b. Net income $25,620. Salary allowances of $6,000 to X, $8,000 to Y, and $10,000 to Z. Profits divided in ratio of 5:3:2, respectively.

c. Net income $12,510. Interest to be allowed partners at rate of 6% on capital as of beginning of the year. Residual profits to be shared in ratio of 4:3:2, respectively.

d. Net loss $800. Partners to be allowed 5% on the average amount of capital invested during the year, and monthly salaries as follows: X, $500; Y, $400; Z, $600. Residual profits to be shared among X, Y, and Z on a 1/2:1/6:1/3 basis, respectively.

15B-3. The accounts shown below appear on the books of the Seebee Company after all revenue and expense accounts have been closed at the end of the first year of operations:

Partner C, Capital

			Jan. 1	Bal.	48,000
			Nov. 1	Invest	24,000

Partner C, Drawing

Dec. 31	Bal.	6,000	

Partner B, Capital

			Jan. 1	Bal.	48,000
July 31	Excess withdrawal	9,000			

Partner B, Drawing

Dec. 31	Bal.	7,200	

Income Summary

		Dec. 31	Bal.	32,000

The partnership agreement (drawn up by C's uncle) contains the following provision relative to the division of income: "Partner C shall be allowed a salary of $500 per month; Partner B shall be allowed a salary of $600 per month. Each partner shall be allowed 20% per annum on his invested capital. Any excess or deficiency shall be divided equally. Withdrawals in excess of above salary allowances in any month shall be charged against capital."

At the end of the year, the partners find they cannot agree on the division of income. Partner B maintains that 20% interest on capital as of the *beginning* of the year should be credited to each partner. Partner C maintains that the 20% should be applied to capital as of the *end* of the year and that he should be credited with $14,400 and B with $7,800. When it is apparent that agreement is impossible, the partners consent to submit their controversy to arbitration.

Instructions

a. As an arbitrator, how would you settle this disagreement? How might the partnership agreement be amended to avoid this difficulty in future years?

b. Assuming that your decision in (*a*) is adopted, make the journal entries necessary to complete the closing of the partnership books as of December 31.

15B-4. Guil and Lory are considering the formation of a partnership to engage in the business of aerial photography. Guil is a licensed pilot, is currently employed at a salary of $10,000 a year, and has $25,000 to invest. Lory is a recent college graduate who has been earning $5,000 a year working in a photographic shop; he has just inherited $75,000 which he plans to put into the business. The partners, after a careful study of their requirements, conclude that $50,000 additional funds will be required, and they have been assured by a local investor, J. R. Roberts, that he will lend them this amount on a five-year, 6% note. Both partners will devote full time to the business. They have prepared a careful estimate of their prospects and expect that revenues during the first year will just cover expenses, with the exception of the interest expense on the $50,000 loan from Roberts. During the second year the estimates indicate that revenues should exceed expenses (other than the interest expense on the loan) by $15,000. For the third year it is believed that revenues will exceed expenses (other than the interest expense on the loan) by $30,000.

Instructions

a. On the basis of the above information, draw up a brief statement of the income-sharing agreement you would recommend that the partners adopt, explaining the basis for your proposal.

b. Assuming that the income expectations of the partners are reasonable, draw up a schedule for each of the three years showing how the partners will share in income under the arrangement you have proposed in (*a*). Write a brief statement defending the results.

16

Partnerships (continued)

As indicated in Chapter 15, a partnership is a somewhat unstable form of organization; its existence may end at any time by reason of the death or retirement of a member or by the addition of a new partner. The termination of a partnership, however, does not necessarily mean putting an end to the business or even interrupting the continuity of operations. Every successful partnership business anticipates changes in the personnel of the firm through the admission of new younger partners and the retirement of older partners.

Admission of a new partner

The admission of a new partner requires the consent of all members of the firm and a new partnership agreement, or at least some revision of the existing contract. A partner may gain admission to the firm in either of two ways: (1) by buying an interest from one or more of the present partners, or (2) by making an investment in the partnership. When an incoming partner purchases his equity from a present member of the firm, his payment goes personally to the old partner, and there is no change in the assets or liabilities of the partnership. On the other hand, if the incoming partner acquires his equity by making an investment in the partnership, the assets of the firm are increased by the amount paid in by the new partner.

By purchase of an interest. When a new partner buys an interest from a present member of a partnership, the transaction is between the two individuals. The partnership is neither paying nor receiving anything. Consequently, the only change in the accounts will be a transfer from the capital account of the selling partner to the capital account of the incoming partner.

Assume, for example, that L has a $25,000 equity in the partnership of L, M, and N. Partner L arranges to sell his entire interest to X for $40,000 cash. Partners M and N agree to the admission of X, and the transaction is recorded on the partnership books by the following entry:

L, Capital	25,000	
· X, Capital		25,000
To record the transfer of L's equity to the incoming partner, X.		

Note that the entry on the partnership books was for $25,000, the recorded amount of Partner L's equity. The amount of this entry was not influenced by the price paid the retiring partner by the new member. The payment of $40,000 from X to L was a personal transaction between the two men; it did not affect the assets or liabilities of the partnership and is therefore not entered on the partnership books.

As a separate but related example, assume that X is to gain admission to the firm of L, M, and N by purchasing one-fourth of the equity of each partner. The present capital accounts are as follows: Partner L, $40,000; Partner M, $40,000; and Partner N, $40,000. The payments by the incoming partner X are to go to the old partners personally and not to the partnership. Therefore, regardless of the amounts paid by X, the only entry required on the partnership books is the following:

L, Capital	10,000	
M, Capital	10,000	
N, Capital	10,000	
X, Capital		30,000
To record the admission of X to a one-fourth interest in the firm by purchase of one-fourth of the equity of each of the three old partners.		

By an investment in the firm. When an incoming partner acquires his equity by making an investment in the firm, his payment increases the partnership assets and also the total proprietorship of the firm. As an example, assume that D. E. Phillips and J. K. Ryan are partners, each having a capital account of $50,000. They agree to admit B. C. Smith to a one-half interest in the business upon his investment of $100,000 in cash. The entry to record the admission of Smith would be as follows:

Cash	100,000	
B. C. Smith, Capital		100,000
To record the admission of B. C. Smith to a one-half interest in the firm.		

Although Smith has a one-half equity in the net assets of the new firm of Phillips, Ryan, and Smith, he is not necessarily entitled to receive one-half of the profits. Profit sharing is a matter for agreement among the partners; if the new partnership contract contains no mention of profit sharing, the assumption is that the three partners intended to share profits and losses equally.

Allowance of a bonus to former partners. If an existing partnership has exceptionally high earnings year after year, the total value of the business as a going concern may exceed the sum of the values of the land, building, inventory, and other individual assets comprising the business. This excess value arises from the unusually large profits being realized; or more precisely, the excess value arises from the expectation that the unusually large profits will continue and thus benefit a new member of the firm. Under these circumstances, many people may be interested in joining the firm, and the present partners may demand a bonus as a condition for admission of a new partner. In other words, to acquire an interest of, say, $40,000, the incoming partner may be required to invest $60,000 in the partnership. The excess investment of $20,000 may be regarded as a bonus to the old partners and credited to their capital accounts in the established ratio for profit sharing. Some alternative ways of handling a premium paid to gain admission to a successful partnership will be discussed later in this chapter.

To illustrate the recording of a bonus to the old partners, let us assume that James Rogers and Richard Steel are members of a highly successful partnership. As a result of profitable operations, the partners' capital accounts have doubled within a few years and presently stand at $50,000 each. David Taylor desires to join the firm and offers to invest $50,000 for a one-third interest. Rogers and Steel refuse this offer but extend a counteroffer to Taylor of $60,000 for a one-fourth interest in the capital of the firm and a one-fourth interest in profits. Taylor accepts these terms because of his desire to share in the unusually large profits of the business. The recording of Taylor's admission to partnership is based on the following calculations:

CALCULA-	*Total net assets (owners' equity) of old firm* $100,000
TION OF	*Cash investment by Taylor* 60,000
BONUS	
TO OLD	*Total net assets (owners' equity) of new partnership* $160,000
PARTNERS	
	Taylor's one-fourth interest . . . . $ 40,000

To acquire an interest of $40,000 in the net assets of $160,000, Taylor has invested $60,000. His excess investment or bonus of $20,000 will be divided equally between Rogers and Steel, since their partnership agreement called for equal sharing of profits and losses. A bonus allowed to the old partners under the agreement for admission of a new member is always divided between the old partners according to their established ratio for sharing profits and losses.

The entry to record Taylor's admission to partnership is as follows:

Cash	*60,000*	
David Taylor, Capital		*40,000*
James Rogers, Capital		*10,000*
Richard Steel, Capital		*10,000*
To record admission of David Taylor as a partner		
with a one-fourth interest in capital and profits.		

Recording goodwill of the old partnership. In the preceding section, a part of Taylor's investment for a one-fourth interest in the firm was treated as a bonus to the old partners, Rogers and Steel. An alternative method of handling this transaction is to say that the old partnership possesses goodwill and to record goodwill in the accounts at a value based on the investment by Taylor of $60,000 for a one-fourth interest in the business.

As explained in the discussion of goodwill in Chapter 14, the willingness of the purchaser of a going business to pay a price greater than the value of the tangible assets indicates that he is paying for intangible assets. An incoming partner is buying a portion of a going business. If his investment is greater than his share of the tangible assets, the excess may be regarded as evidence of the existence of goodwill, which should be recorded on the books. This treatment is an alternative to the previously described method of recording the excess payment by the new partner as a bonus to the old partners.

To illustrate the recording of goodwill upon the admission of a partner, let us restate the Rogers and Steel partnership example previously used. Rogers and Steel are partners each having a capital of $50,000. They agree to admit Taylor as a partner with a one-fourth interest in capital and profits upon his investing $60,000. If a one-fourth interest in the business is worth $60,000, the entire business must be worth four times as much, or $240,000. The amount of goodwill to be recognized may be computed as follows:

Investment by Taylor for a one-fourth interest in capital		*$ 60,000*
Indicated value of the business ($60,000 × 4)		*$240,000*
Book value of the business before recording goodwill:		
Capital of old partners ($50,000 each)	*$100,000*	
Investment by new partner	*60,000*	*160,000*
Goodwill		*$ 80,000*

The sale of a one-fourth interest to Taylor for $60,000 indicated that the entire business was worth $240,000. Since the tangible net assets (including Taylor's cash investment of $60,000) total only $160,000, the difference of $80,000 must be the intangible asset of goodwill. The journal entries to record Taylor's admission with goodwill being recognized are as follows:

<table>
<tr><td>ENTRIES
FOR
INVESTMENT
AND
INDICATED
GOODWILL</td><td>*Cash* 60,000
    David Taylor, Capital ....
Investment by new partner for a one-fourth interest
in the firm.

Goodwill 80,000
    James Rogers, Capital ....
    Richard Steel, Capital ....
To bring on the books the goodwill indicated to
exist by new partner's investment of $60,000 for
a one-fourth interest.</td><td>
60,000

40,000
40,000</td></tr>
</table>

The goodwill method of handling the excess investment by the new partner causes the capital accounts of all three partners to be larger than if the bonus method had been used. The capital accounts are larger because the recorded assets have been increased by entering goodwill on the books. The price that Taylor was willing to pay is evidence that unrecorded goodwill existed in the business at that time. Until Taylor made his investment, objective evidence was lacking as to the existence and amount of goodwill. The arm's-length transaction between Taylor and the existing partners, however, provided objective evidence that constitutes the basis for entering the amount of goodwill on the balance sheet.

The making of a journal entry to bring goodwill on the books as an asset does not make the business any more valuable. It is the existence of goodwill, and not the act of recording it on the books, that gives value to a business. The new partner, David Taylor, has made a cash investment of $60,000, and he may prefer to see a balance of $60,000 in his capital account rather than $40,000. Under either method the significant facts are that he now owns one-fourth of the business and that the value of the business has not been increased by the act of listing goodwill among the assets.

Probably many businessmen would prefer to use the bonus method, because the presence of a large amount of goodwill on the balance sheet may create a skeptical attitude on the part of some readers of the financial statements. Bankers, financial analysts, and other informed users of financial statements know that many highly successful companies possess goodwill even though it is not listed on their balance sheets. Consequently, the company that does include a large amount of goodwill among the assets on its balance sheet may arouse an unfavorable reaction; readers of the statement may feel that the company is trying to exaggerate its size and financial strength. Many businessmen feel that the best evidence that goodwill exists consists of an income statement showing above-average earnings, and not the mere listing of goodwill on the balance sheet. In the preceding example, the existence of $80,000 of goodwill would also be evidenced by average earnings on the larger amount of invested capital after recording goodwill as an asset. To summarize, the question of whether goodwill should or should not be recognized rests squarely on the quality of the evidence as to its existence.

BONUS METHOD VERSUS GOODWILL METHOD

The following schedule affords a comparison of the results from the two alternative methods of recording a new partner's investment when he pays a premium to gain admission to the firm:

	Bonus method		Goodwill method	
	Amount	Fractional interest	Amount	Fractional interest
James Roger, Capital	$ 60,000	3/8	$ 90,000	3/8
Richard Steel, Capital	60,000	3/8	90,000	3/8
David Taylor, Capital	40,000	2/8	60,000	2/8
Totals	$160,000	8/8	$240,000	8/8

Allowing goodwill to new partner. A new partner may be the owner of a profitable business of his own which he contributes to the partnership rather than investing cash. Assume, for example, that William Jones and Robert Brown are partners, each having a capital account of $40,000. In order to induce Henry Smith, the owner of a very profitable competing business, to enter partnership with them, they agree to allow Smith goodwill of $10,000. The tangible assets of Smith's business which will be brought into the partnership are valued at $30,000. This amount represents the present fair market value of Smith's assets, not necessarily the carrying value on his books. All three partners in the new firm of Jones, Brown, and Smith are to have equal interests in the business. The entry to record Smith's admission to the firm would be as follows:

NEW PARTNER MAY CONTRIBUTE GOODWILL

Goodwill	10,000	
Various Tangible Assets	30,000	
Henry Smith, Capital		40,000

To record admission of Smith to a one-third interest upon contribution of various tangible assets and goodwill.

Allowing a bonus to a new partner. An existing partnership may sometimes be very anxious to bring in a new partner who can bring needed
cash to the firm. In other instances the new partner may be a man of
extraordinary ability or possessed of advantageous business contacts that
will presumably add to the profitability of the partnership. Under either of
these sets of circumstances, the old partners may offer the new member
a bonus in the form of a capital account larger than the amount of his
investment.

Assume, for example, that A. M. Bryan and R. G. Davis are equal
partners, each having a capital account of $18,000. Since the firm is in
desperate need of cash, they offer to admit K. L. Grant to a one-third
interest in the firm upon his investment of only $12,000 in cash. The
amounts of the capital accounts for the three members of the new firm
are computed as follows:

Total capital of old partnership:		
A. M. Bryan, Capital	*$18,000*	
R. G. Davis, Capital	*18,000*	*$36,000*
Cash invested by K. L. Grant		*12,000*
Total capital of new three-man partnership		*$48,000*
Capital of each partner in the new firm:		
A. M. Bryan ($48,000 × 1/3)	*$16,000*	
R. G. Davis ($48,000 × 1/3)	*16,000*	
K. L. Grant ($48,000 × 1/3)	*16,000*	*48,000*

The following journal entry records the admission of Grant to a one-
third interest in the business and also adjusts each capital account to the
required level of $16,000.

Cash	*12,000*	
A. M. Bryan, Capital	*2,000*	
R. G. Davis, Capital	*2,000*	
K. L. Grant, Capital		*16,000*
To record admission of Grant to a one-third inter-		
est, and the allowance of a bonus to him.		

The bonus of $4,000 to the new partner represents a loss to the old
partners; this loss is divided equally between Bryan and Davis because
of their original agreement to share profits and losses equally. Would it
be appropriate, as an alternative method of recording Grant's admission
to partnership, to bring $6,000 of goodwill on the books along with the

$12,000 of cash invested by the new partner? If this were done, it would avoid the necessity of reducing the capital accounts of the two old partners. Both Bryan and Davis had capital accounts of $18,000; when they agreed to admit Grant to a one-third interest upon investment of $12,000 in cash, why not enter $6,000 of goodwill on the books and credit Grant with a contribution of $18,000? This would make the total capital $54,000 and give each partner a capital account of $18,000. The answer must be in the negative. To enter goodwill on the books under these circumstances is not appropriate because there is no evidence that any superior earning power exists. In fact, the firm's desperate need of cash and the willingness of the old partners to sell a one-third interest in the business at less than book value suggests that the total value of the old partnership may be less than indicated on the books. Goodwill is not to be placed in the accounts merely as a balancing figure or as a matter of convenience. Goodwill should be recorded only when objective evidence (usually a transaction involving the payment of money) indicates that it exists. In the example just presented, the incoming partner did not pay a premium that indicated the existence of asset values in excess of those recorded on the books. There was nothing in the terms of admission of Grant to partnership to indicate the existence of goodwill.

Revaluation of assets

As repeatedly stated in earlier chapters, cost is ordinarily the proper basis for valuation of assets in a going concern. (The term *cost basis* is understood to mean cost less depreciation in the case of assets with limited lives.) Whenever a change in the personnel of a partnership occurs, however, such as the death of a partner or the admission of a new partner, the ownership of assets is changing hands, and the current market value of the assets should be recognized in order to achieve a fair transfer price.

As an example, assume that the retirement of a partner (or the admission of a new partner) is about to occur in the firm of Miller, Neves, and Paulson. The partnership agreement calls for an equal division of profits and losses. The book values of the assets are compared with their present market values or cash realizable values. This comparison indicates that the land is presently worth about $30,000 more than its cost as shown in the Land account. The accounts receivable of $100,000 are estimated to contain uncollectible accounts of $5,000, but the present balance of the Allowance for Bad Debts is only $2,000. To make the books reflect current values of the assets, the partners, therefore, agree to increase the Land account by $30,000 and increase the Allowance for Bad Debts account by $3,000.

The journal entry to carry out these adjustments divides the resulting net gain of $27,000 equally among the three partners in the following way.

Land *30,000*		
Allowance for Bad Debts		*3,000*
Miller, Capital		*9,000*
Neves, Capital		*9,000*
Paulson, Capital		*9,000*

To adjust the carrying values of assets to current realizable value in connection with a change in personnel of partnership. Resulting gain is divided in agreed ratio of sharing profits and losses.

At times what appears to be goodwill is actually a reflection of the failure to recognize the value of specific assets. If a thorough job of adjusting asset valuations is carried out at the time of a change in partnership personnel, it may be discovered that little or no goodwill exists. Goodwill is essentially the difference between the value of the business as a whole and the sum of the values assigned to the net assets that constitute the resources of the business. It should not be brought on the books merely to compensate for an undervaluation of individual identifiable assets.

Retirement of a partner

A partner interested in retirement may, with the consent of his partners, sell his interest to an outsider. In this case the payment by the incoming partner goes directly to the retiring partner, and there is no change in the assets or liabilities of the partnership. The only entry required is to transfer the capital account of the retiring partner to an account with the new partner. This transaction is virtually the same as the one described on page 463 for the admission of a partner by purchase of an interest.

As an example, assume that A, B, and C are partners and that each has a capital account of $50,000. With the consent of his partners, C sells his interest to D for a price of $60,000. This is a payment from D to C personally, with no effect on the partnership assets or liabilities. The entry required is for the amount of C's capital account and not for the amount of money paid by D to C.

C, Capital *50,000*		
D, Capital		*50,000*

To record sale by C of his interest to D, with consent of other partners.

A transaction of this type does not ordinarily lead to any revaluation of the partnership assets. Next, let us change our assumptions slightly and say that C, the retiring partner, sells his interest to his fellow partners, A and B, in equal amounts. A and B make the agreed payment to C from their personal funds, so again the partnership assets and liabilities are not changed. Regardless of the price agreed to for C's interest, the transaction can be handled on the partnership books merely by transferring the $50,000 balance in C's capital account to the capital accounts of the other two partners.

NO CHANGE IN TOTAL CAPITAL

C, Capital *50,000*
    A, Capital *25,000*
    B, Capital *25,000*
To record the sale of C's interest in equal portions to A and B.

There are other acceptable methods of handling this transaction. For example, if A and B agree to pay C an amount greater than the balance of his capital account, the reason for the excess payment may be that the present market values of the partnership assets are greater than the amounts shown by the books. Under these circumstances a revaluation of the assets may be decided upon. This situation will be more fully explored in the following section.

Payment to retiring partner from partnership assets. In both of the preceding illustrations the retiring partner received payment from the personal funds of the person or persons buying his interest. Now we shall consider the case of a retiring partner who is paid for his interest out of partnership funds. He may be paid an amount equal to his capital account, or an amount larger or smaller than his capital account, depending upon the outcome of the negotiations between the retiring partner and the continuing members.

Why should the settlement with a retiring partner be set at an amount greater or smaller than the balance in his capital account? Two reasons are immediately apparent: (1) the present market values of the partnership assets may be above or below the book figures; and (2) the partnership may have developed goodwill of significant value which is not carried on the books.

One solution to the problem of a discrepancy between book values and market values at the time of a partner's retirement is to adjust the asset accounts to current appraised values and to place goodwill on the books. The resulting net increase or decrease in the assets is offset by a corresponding increase or decrease in the partners' capital accounts, divided according to the agreed ratio for sharing profits and losses. Each partner's capital account will now represent his interest in the business on the basis of current market values; an equitable settlement with the retiring partner can, therefore, be made by paying him the exact amount of his capital account.

A retiring partner may, however, be paid more than the balance of his capital account after the revaluation of assets, merely because his fellow partners are anxious to get rid of him. On the other hand, a partner anxious to escape from an unsatisfactory relationship may be willing to surrender his interest for less than book value.

In many cases when a partner retires, the continuing partners prefer not to revalue the assets. As an alternative, any increase or decrease in asset values is merely taken into consideration in negotiating a settlement amount to be paid the retiring partner. Any excess payment to the retiring partner is then treated as a bonus. This situation may be illustrated by using again the example of A, B, and C, equal partners with capital accounts of $50,000 each. At the time of C's retirement, it is agreed that in consideration of some increase in the market values of assets and the probable existence of goodwill, C will be paid $70,000 for his interest. This negotiated settlement includes a $20,000 bonus to C, which must be charged against the capital accounts of the continuing partners in the agreed ratio for sharing profits and losses.

BONUS PAID TO RETIRING PARTNER	*C, Capital* *50,000*	
	A, Capital *10,000*	
	B, Capital *10,000*	
	Cash	*70,000*
	To record the retirement of partner C, and payment of his capital account plus a bonus of $20,000.	

As a separate example, assume that C is to receive a settlement smaller than his capital account balance, because certain assets are believed to be worth less than book value or because he agrees to take a loss in order to expedite the settlement. If C surrenders his $50,000 interest for $40,000, the entry will be:

PAYMENT TO RETIRING PARTNER OF LESS THAN BOOK EQUITY	*C, Capital* *50,000*	
	Cash	*40,000*
	A, Capital	*5,000*
	B, Capital	*5,000*
	To record the retirement of C, and settlement in full for $10,000 less than the balance of his capital account.	

Death of a partner

A partnership is dissolved by the death of any member. To determine the amount owing to the estate of the deceased partner, it is usually necessary to close the books and prepare financial statements. This serves to credit each partner with his share of the net income earned during the fractional accounting period ending with the date of dissolution.

The partnership contract should desirably include a section outlining the procedures to be employed in making settlement with the estate of a deceased partner. Such provisions may prescribe an audit by independent certified public accountants, a formula for computing goodwill and adjusting asset values, and a schedule for payments on the installment plan to the estate of the former partner. If there is some delay in making payment to the estate, the amount owed should be carried in a liability account replacing the deceased partner's capital account.

Insurance on lives of partners. The partnership contract may provide for insurance on the lives of partners with the firm being named as beneficiary. Upon the death of a partner, the firm will collect from the insurance company and can use the funds received to pay the estate of the deceased partner. An alternative plan is to have each partner named as the beneficiary of an insurance policy covering the life of his partner. In the absence of insurance on the lives of partners, there might be insufficient cash available to pay the deceased partner's estate without disrupting the operation of the business.

Liquidation of a partnership

A partnership is terminated or dissolved whenever a new partner is added or an old partner withdraws. The termination or dissolution of a partnership, however, does not necessarily indicate that the business is to be discontinued. Often the business continues with scarcely any outward evidence of the change in membership of the firm. Termination of a partnership indicates a change in the membership of the firm, which may or may not be followed by liquidation.

The process of breaking up and discontinuing a partnership business is called *liquidation.* Liquidation of a partnership spells an end to the business. If the business is to be discontinued, the assets will be sold, the liabilities paid, and the remaining cash distributed to the partners.

PARTNER-
SHIP AT
TIME OF
SALE
    Sale of the business. The partnership of X, Y, and Z sells its business to the Nationwide Corporation. The balance sheet appears as follows:

X, Y, AND Z
Balance Sheet
December 31, 19___

Cash	$ 25,000	Accounts payable	$ 50,000
Inventory	100,000	X, Capital	70,000
Other assets	75,000	Y, Capital	60,000
		Z, Capital	20,000
	$200,000		$200,000

The terms of sale provide that the partnership will retain the cash of $25,000 and will pay the liabilities of $50,000. The inventory and other assets will be sold to the Nationwide Corporation for a consideration of $115,000. The entry to record the sale of the inventory and other assets is as follows:

Nationwide Corporation, Account Receivable .. *115,000*
Loss on Sale of Business *60,000*
          Inventory *100,000*
          Other Assets *75,000*
*To record the sale of all assets other than cash
to Nationwide Corporation.*

Cash *115,000*
          Nationwide Corporation, Account Receiv-
          able *115,000*
Collected the receivable from sale of assets.

Division of the gain or loss from sale of the business. The gain or loss from the sale of the business must be divided among the partners in the agreed profit- and loss-sharing ratio *before* any cash is distributed to them. The amount of cash to which each partner is entitled in liquidation cannot be determined until his capital account has been increased or decreased by his share of the gain or loss on disposal of the assets. Assuming that X, Y, and Z share profits and losses equally, the entry to allocate the $60,000 loss on the sale of the business will be as follows:

X, Capital *20,000*
Y, Capital *20,000*
Z, Capital *20,000*
          Loss on Sale of Business *60,000*
*To divide the loss on the sale of the business among
the partners in the established ratio for sharing
profits and losses.*

Distribution of cash. The balance sheet of X, Y, and Z appears as follows after the loss on the sale of the assets has been entered in the partners' capital accounts:

X, Y, AND Z
Balance Sheet
(After the sale of all assets except cash)

Assets		Liabilities & Partners' Equity	
Cash	$140,000	Accounts Payable	$ 50,000
		X, Capital	50,000
		Y, Capital	40,000
		Z, Capital	000
	$140,000		$140,000

The creditors must be paid in full before cash is distributed to the partners. The sequence of entries is, therefore, as follows:

---

1. Pay creditors:

Accounts Payable	*50,000*	
Cash		*50,000*
To pay the creditors in full.		

2. Pay partners:

X, Capital	*50,000*	
Y, Capital	*40,000*	
Cash		*90,000*
To complete liquidation of the business by distributing the remaining cash to the partners according to the balances in their capital accounts.		

Note that the equal division of the $60,000 loss on the sale of the business reduced the capital account of Partner Z to zero; therefore, he received nothing when the cash was distributed to the partners. This action is consistent with the original agreement of the partners to share profits and losses equally. In working partnership liquidation problems, accounting students sometimes make the error of dividing the cash among the partners in the profit- and loss-sharing ratio. A profit- and loss-sharing ratio means just what the name indicates; it is a ratio for sharing profits and losses, not a ratio for sharing cash or any other asset. The amount of cash which a partner should receive in liquidation will be indicated by the balance in his capital account after the gain or loss from the disposal of assets has been divided among the partners in the agreed ratio for sharing profits and losses.

Treatment of debit balance in a capital account. In the preceding illustration of the liquidation of a partnership business, the loss incurred on the sale of the assets caused Partner Z's capital account to be reduced to zero and he received nothing from the sale of the business. If the loss on the sale of the assets had been any greater, Z's capital account would have acquired a debit balance, and he would have been called on to pay in sufficient cash to the firm to make good the debit balance in his account.

To illustrate this situation, let us change our assumptions slightly concerning the sale of the assets by the firm of X, Y, and Z, and say that the loss incurred on the sale of assets was $72,000 rather than the $60,-000 previously illustrated. Z's one-third share of a $72,000 loss would be $24,000, which would wipe out the $20,000 credit balance in his capital account and create a $4,000 debit balance. After the liabilities had been paid, a balance sheet for the partnership would appear as follows:

X, Y, AND Z
Balance Sheet
(After the sale of all assets except cash)

Cash	$78,000	X, Capital	$46,000
Z, Capital	4,000	Y, Capital	36,000
	$82,000		$82,000

To eliminate the debit balance in his capital account, Z should pay in $4,000 cash. If he does so, his capital balance will become zero, and the cash on hand will be increased to $82,000, which is just enough to pay X and Y the balances shown by their capital accounts.

If Z is unable to pay the $4,000 due to the firm, how should the $78,000 of cash on hand be divided between X and Y, whose capital accounts stand at $46,000 and $36,000, respectively? Failure of Z to pay in his debit balance means an additional loss to X and Y; according to the original partnership agreement, X and Y are to share profits and losses equally. Therefore, each must absorb $2,000 of the $4,000 additional loss thrown on them by Z's inability to meet his obligations. The $78,000 of cash on hand should be divided between X and Y in such a manner that the capital account of each will be paid down to $2,000, his share of the additional loss. The journal entry to record this distribution of cash to X and Y is as follows:

X, Capital	44,000	
Y, Capital	34,000	
Cash		78,000

To divide the remaining cash by paying down the capital accounts of X and Y to a balance of $2,000 each, representing the division of Z's loss between them.

After this entry has been posted the only accounts still open in the partnership books will be the capital accounts of the three partners. A trial balance of the ledger will appear as follows:

X, Y, AND Z
Trial Balance
(After distribution of cash)

X, Capital		$2,000
Y, Capital		2,000
Z, Capital	$4,000	
	$4,000	$4,000

These accounts could be closed by debiting the capital accounts of X and Y for $2,000 each and crediting Z for $4,000. This entry should not be made, however, for by leaving the accounts open, the partnership books will show that X and Y each have a claim of $2,000 against Z. Perhaps at some future time they may be able to collect this claim.

When a partner's capital account acquires a debit balance during the process of winding up a partnership business, it is sometimes not known immediately whether this debit balance is collectible. If the other partners want the cash on hand to be distributed immediately, the only safe procedure is to follow the distribution pattern already illustrated; that is, pay down the capital accounts of X and Y to $2,000 each. If Z is able later to pay in his $4,000 debit balance, X and Y will then receive the additional $2,000 each indicated by the credit balances in their accounts. If Z is not able to make good his debit balance, the distribution of cash to X and Y will have been equitable under the circumstances.

QUESTIONS

1. Explain the difference between being admitted to a partnership by buying an interest from an existing partner and by making an investment in the partnership.

2. An interest in a partnership is composed of two primary elements. What are they and what is their significance?

3. Why does the admission of a new partner to a partnership in return for an investment by him constitute objective evidence of the existence of a previously unrecorded amount of goodwill?

4. Distinguish between the dissolution and the liquidation of a partnership.

5. X and Y are partners having capital balances of $20,000 and $10,000, respectively, and sharing profits equally. They agree to admit Z to a one-third interest in the partnership for an investment of $18,000. Describe two different approaches that might be used in recording the admission of Z.

6. The capital accounts of the CDE partnership are as follows: C, $24,000; D, $12,000; E, $18,000. Profits are shared equally. Partner D is withdrawing from the partnership and it is agreed that he shall be paid $15,000 for his interest because the business is worth more than the book value of its net assets. Assuming that the increase in asset value indicated by D's withdrawal is to be recorded as goodwill, give the entries to record D's retirement.

7. U and V are partners, sharing net income in a 60:40 ratio. They admit W to the partnership, agreeing that he is to have a one-quarter interest in income and that U and V are to retain their former relationship. What is the profit-sharing relationship in the new partnership?

8. The LMN partnership is being liquidated. After all liabilities have been paid and all assets sold, the balances of the partners' capital accounts are as follows: L, $6,000 credit balance; M, $4,000 debit balance; N, $9,000 credit balance. The partners share profits equally. How should the available cash be distributed if it is impossible to determine at this date whether M is able to pay the $4,000 he owes the firm?

PROBLEMS

Group A

16A-1. The capital accounts and profit- and loss-sharing ratios of the partners of the Bohemia Company at the close of the current year are given below. At this date it is agreed that a new partner, Peter Olds, is to be admitted to the firm.

	Capital	*Profit-sharing ratio*
Bill Stewart	*$32,000*	*5/8*
Fred Chapman	*24,000*	*1/4*
Jack Pitts	*16,000*	*1/8*

Instructions. For each situation involving the admission of Olds to the partnership, give the necessary journal entry to record his admission.

a. Olds purchases one-half of Chapman's interest in the firm, paying Chapman $15,000.

b. Olds buys a one-quarter interest in the firm for $20,000 by purchasing one-fourth of the present interest of each of the three partners.

c. Olds invests $42,000 and receives a one-quarter interest in the capital and profits of the business. Give the necessary journal entries to record Olds's admission under two alternative interpretations, and write a brief paragraph explaining the circumstances under which each method of recording his admission would be appropriate.

16A-2. The statement given below shows the position of a partnership on June 30, on which date it was agreed to admit a new partner, Charlie. Able and Baker share income in a ratio of 3:2 and will continue this relationship after Charlie's admission.

ABLE-BAKER COMPANY
Balance Sheet, June 30

Current assets	*$ 30,000*	*Liabilities*	*$ 20,000*
Fixed assets (*net*)	*70,000*	*Able, capital*	*50,000*
		Baker, capital	*30,000*
	$100,000		*$100,000*

Instructions. Below are described five different situations under which Charlie might be admitted to partnership. Considering each independently, prepare the journal entries necessary to record the admission of Charlie to the firm.

a. Charlie purchases a one-half interest in the partnership from Able for $43,000.

b. Charlie purchases one-half of Able's interest and one-half of Baker's interest, paying Able $30,000 and Baker $18,000.

c. Charlie invests $50,000 in the partnership and receives a one-half interest in capital and income. It is agreed that there will be no change in the valuation of the present net assets.

d. Charlie invests $90,000 in the partnership and receives a one-half interest in capital and income. It is agreed that the allowance for bad debts is currently overstated by $3,000. Assets are carried at amounts approximating current fair value; therefore, any further revaluation necessary to record Charlie's investment is to be identified as goodwill.

e. Charlie invests $34,000 for a one-third interest in capital and income. The amount of his investment was agreed upon after a review of partnership assets indicated that all were carried at approximately current fair value except the June 30 inventory, which was stated in excess of the amount that can be realized from its sale. The inventory should therefore be revalued by an amount necessary to record Charlie's investment in the partnership properly.

16A-3. The following is the balance sheet of the NOP Company at the end of the current year:

NORRIS-OLSON-PETERSON COMPANY
Balance Sheet
Close of Current Year

Cash	*$ 40,000*	*Liabilities*	*$ 28,000*
Receivables	*20,000*	*Norris, capital*	*34,000*
Inventory	*15,000*	*Olson, capital*	*20,000*
Equipment (net)	*25,000*	*Peterson, capital*	*18,000*
	$100,000		*$100,000*

The partners share profits on a 5:3:2 ratio, respectively. It is agreed that Peterson is to withdraw from the partnership on this date.

Instructions. Below are listed a number of different situations involving the retirement of Peterson from the firm. Give the general journal entry necessary to record Peterson's withdrawal in each case.

a. An analysis of the assets indicates that $2,000 of the receivables will probably prove uncollectible, and that inventories are understated by $5,000 and equipment is understated by $7,000. It is agreed to pay Peterson an amount equal to the book value of his adjusted interest.

b. Olson buys one-fourth of Peterson's interest for $5,000, and Norris buys three-fourths for $15,000.

c. Peterson, with the permission of the other partners, gives his interest to his brother-in-law, Potts.

d. Peterson is paid $20,000 from partnership funds for his interest. The remaining partners agree to recognize in full the goodwill indicated by this payment.

e. The partnership agrees to give Peterson $22,000 for his interest in view of the fact that equipment is undervalued on the books. Peterson is given $10,000 in cash and a two-year, 5% note for $12,000.

f. Peterson is given $15,000 in cash and equipment having a book value of $15,000. The remaining partners agree that no revaluation of assets will be made.

16A-4. The balance sheet of Jay and Company at the end of the current year is as follows:

JAY AND COMPANY
Balance Sheet
End of Current Year

Cash	$10,000	Liabilities	$30,000
Other assets	65,000	Jay, capital	20,000
		Kay, capital	15,000
		Ell, capital	10,000
	$75,000		$75,000

Jay, Kay, and Ell share profits in a ratio of 3:2:1, respectively. At the date of the above balance sheet the partners decide to liquidate the business.

Instructions. Prepare schedules showing how the liquidation of the partnership would affect the various balance sheet items and how the cash would be distributed under each of the following circumstances. Use six money columns in your schedules, as follows:

Cash	Other assets	Lia- bilities	Jay, capital	Kay, capital	Ell, capital

a. Other assets are sold for $56,000.

b. Other assets are sold for $23,000. All partners have personal assets and will contribute any necessary amounts to the partnership.

c. Other assets are sold for $20,600. Kay has personal assets and will contribute any necessary amounts; Jay and Ell are both personally bankrupt.

d. Other assets are sold for $17,000. Ell is personally solvent and will contribute any amount for which he is liable. Jay and Kay both have personal debts in excess of their personal assets.

Group B

16B-1. Bush, Crandal, and Davis are partners who share profits as follows: Bush, 40%; Crandal, 50%; and Davis, 10%. At the end of the current year the partners' capital accounts are as follows: Bush, $50,000; Crandal, $32,000; and Davis, $10,000. At this time Bush desires to retire from the firm.

Instructions. Below are described a number of independent situations involving the retirement of Bush. In each case prepare the journal entries necessary to reflect the withdrawal of Bush from the firm.

a. Davis buys three-fourths of Bush's interest for $48,000 and Crandal buys one-fourth for $15,000, paying Bush out of their personal funds.

b. The partners agree that certain assets are carried at amounts which do not represent their current value. Land is undervalued by $8,000; a building purchased five years ago for $70,000 and depreciated on a 20-year basis should have been depreciated on a 40-year basis. A patent having a book value of $15,000 is currently worth at least $45,000. It is agreed that these adjustments will be made on the books and that Bush will receive in cash from the partnership an amount equal to the adjusted book value of his interest.

c. Bush accepts $15,000 in cash and all rights in a patent having a book value of $15,000 in full payment for his interest. The remaining partners agree that a revaluation of remaining assets is not warranted.

d. Bush receives $20,000 in cash and a 10-year, 4% note for $46,000 in payment for his interest. The partners agree that goodwill in the amount of $40,000 should be recorded on the partnership books.

16B-2. Jones and Smith are partners. They share profits in a 60:40 relationship and at the end of the current year their capital balances are as follows: Jones, $32,000; Smith, $24,000. At this time the partners agree to admit Brown to the partnership and to give him a one-fourth interest in net assets and in income.

Instructions. Below are listed a number of possible situations involving the admission of Brown. For each of these, give the general journal entry to record Brown's admission to the partnership:

a. Brown buys his interest from Jones for $18,000.

b. Brown buys his interest from Smith for $10,000.

c. Brown invests $20,000 for his interest. The partners agree that no revaluation of assets is necessary.

d. Brown invests $20,000 for his interest. The partners agree that the goodwill indicated by Brown's investment should be recorded on the books.

e. Brown invests $12,000 for his interest. It is agreed that no asset revaluation is to be made.

f. Brown contributes certain tangible assets having a fair market value of $12,000 for his interest, and it is agreed that he is to be allowed goodwill of $6,667. (Use the account title Various Tangible Assets.)

g. Brown invests $12,000 for his interest. Partners agree that Brown's capital will be $12,000 and that one of the assets, Patents, is overstated on the books of the partnership.

16B-3. On December 31, 1961, the capital accounts on the books of the Frank-Goode-Hart Company show the following credit balances: Frank, $48,000; Goode, $36,000; and Hart, $27,600. On this date it was agreed that Goode would retire from the firm, receiving a cash payment of $30,000 in settlement of his interest. It was understood that inventories would be written down by $9,000 and that goodwill of $15,000 now on the books would be written off. Any difference between the adjusted capital of Goode and the amount paid for his interest is to be treated as a bonus. The profit sharing arrangement of the firm was: Frank, 1/2; Goode, 1/3; Hart, 1/6.

Frank and Hart agreed that they would share profits in the new firm in the same ratio as in the old, but that a salary allowance of $6,000 per year was to be credited to Hart in recognition of the greater amount of time spent by him in managing the firm. During 1962 the new partnership earned $22,400 before any remuneration to the partners. Frank withdrew $12,000 from the firm and Hart withdrew $6,000 during 1962. On December 31, 1962, the partners decided to admit Elwood to the firm and to give him a one-third interest in profits and capital upon his investment of $37,000.

Instructions

a. Prepare the journal entries necessary to record Goode's retirement from the partnership.

b. Prepare a statement of changes in partners' capital accounts for the firm of Frank and Hart during 1962.

c. Prepare the necessary journal entry to record the admission of Elwood to the firm on December 31, 1962, assuming that no revaluation of net assets is to be made at that time.

16B-4. Rice, Stans, and Trowe decided some time ago to liquidate their partnership. All the assets have been sold, but the accounts receivable remain uncollected. The balances in the general ledger at the present time are:

Cash		*$12,000*
Accounts receivable		*66,000*
Allowance for uncollectibles		*$ 3,000*
Liabilities		*21,000*
Rice, capital (profit share 30%)		*24,000*
Stans, capital (profit share 50%)		*18,000*
Trowe, capital (profit share 20%)		*12,000*

Instructions. Present in general journal form the entries necessary to record the liquidation of the partnership and the distribution of all cash under each of the circumstances shown below. Support all entries with adequate explanations showing how amounts were determined.

a. Collections of $40,000 are made on receivables, and the remainder are deemed uncollectible.

b. Receivables are sold to a collection agency; the partnership receives in cash as a final settlement one-third of the gross amount of its receivables. The personal financial status of the partners is uncertain, but all available cash is to be distributed at this time.

c. Assume the same conditions as in (*b*). After all available cash had been distributed, it was discovered that partners Rice and Trowe were solvent and could make good any capital deficiencies, and that partner Stans could pay in any amount up to $1,200 to make good any capital deficiencies. [Do not repeat entries that are the same as those in (*b*); make only those additional entries required by the changed conditions.]

17

Corporations: organization and operation

The corporation has become the dominant form of business organization on the American economic scene, probably because it gathers together large amounts of capital more readily than single proprietorships or partnerships. Because of its efficiency as a device for pooling the savings of many individuals, the corporation is an ideal means of obtaining the capital necessary for large-scale production and its inherent economies. Virtually all large businesses are corporations. As our economy utilizes more fully the advantages of large-scale production, an ever-increasing proportion of the national output of goods and services is produced by corporations.

There are still many more single proprietorships and partnerships than corporations, but in terms of dollar volume of output, the corporations hold an impressive lead. In the field of manufacturing, more than three-quarters of the total value of goods produced comes from corporations. In such industries as public utilities, banking, transportation, and mining, corporations account for the major portion of the goods and services supplied. The rise of the corporation to this commanding position has been inseparably linked with the trend toward larger factories and stores, organized research and development of new products, nationwide marketing areas, and the professionalization of business management.

Definition

The corporation was defined by Chief Justice Marshall in these words: "A corporation is an artificial being, invisible, intangible, and existing only in contemplation of the law." This definition indicates that one of the most significant characteristics of the corporation is its separate legal entity. The corporation is regarded as a legal person, having a continuous existence apart from that of its owners. By way of contrast, a partnership is a relatively unstable type of organization which is dissolved by the death or retirement of any one of its members, whereas the continuous existence of a corporation is in no way threatened by the death of a stockholder.

Ownership in a corporation is evidenced by transferable shares of stock, and the owners are called stockholders or shareholders. To administer the affairs of the corporation, the stockholders elect a board of directors. The directors in turn select a president and other corporate officers to carry on active management of the business. The stockholders do not own the assets of the corporation nor do they owe the debts of the corporation. Because the corporation is a separate legal entity, apart from its owners, it is capable of owning property in its own name, of borrowing money and making contracts in its own right, of hiring and firing employees, and of performing all other acts necessary to the operation of the business.

Advantages of the corporation

The corporation offers a number of advantages not available in other forms of organization. Among these advantages are the following:

1. Greater amounts of capital can be gathered together. Some corporations have a half million or more stockholders. The sale of stock is a means of obtaining funds from the general public; both small and large investors find stock ownership a convenient means of participating in ownership of business enterprise.

2. Limited liability. Creditors of a corporation have a claim against the assets of the corporation only, not against the personal property of the owners of the corporation. Since a stockholder has no personal liability for the debts of the corporation, he can never lose more than the amount of his investment. This feature of limited liability is one reason why corporations find it easy to gather funds from people in all economic levels.

3. Shares of stock in a corporation (stock certificates) are readily transferable. The ease of disposing of all or part of one's stockholdings in a corporation makes this form of investment particularly attractive. A member of a partnership or a single proprietor who finds himself in need of funds cannot readily sell a fraction of his business, but a person who owns, say, 100 shares in a well-known corporation can sell 5 shares, 10 shares, or any other fraction of his investment merely by making a telephone call to a stockbroker.

4. Continuous existence. A corporation is a separate legal entity with a perpetual existence. The continuous life of the corporation despite changes in ownership is made possible by the issuance of transferable shares of stock.

5. Centralized authority. The power to make all kinds of operating

decisions is lodged in the president of a corporation. He may delegate to others limited authority for various phases of operations, but he retains final authority over the entire business. This clear-cut centralization of authority permits rapid decisive action and avoids the arguments and conflicts characteristic of a partnership, which has two or more active "bosses."

6. Owners need not participate in management. The person who owns a few shares of stock in a large corporation usually has neither the time nor the detailed knowledge of the business necessary for intelligent participation in operating problems. One of the attractive features of stock ownership is the opportunity it affords to share in the benefits of owner-ship without assuming the responsibilities of management. Many investors own stocks in a number of corporations, thus achieving a diversification of investments which offers greater safety than putting "all one's eggs in one basket." This type of diversified investment program would be im-practicable if ownership of stock were accompanied by the responsibility to participate in management.

7. Professional management. Since the functions of management and of ownership are sharply separated in the corporate form of organi-zation, the corporation is free to employ as executives the best managerial talent available.

Disadvantages of the corporation

1. Heavy taxation. A corporation must pay a high rate of taxation on its net income. If part of this income is distributed to the owners in the form of dividends, the dividends are considered to be personal income to the stockholders and are subject to personal income tax. This practice of taxing income twice (first when earned by the corporation and again when distributed to the stockholders) is sometimes referred to as "double taxation of corporate income." "Double taxation" does not occur if a business is organized as a partnership or single proprietorship because these forms of business organization are not considered to be separate entities from their owners. The fact that a corporation is a legal entity, with an existence separate and apart from that of its owners, provides a theoretical basis for taxing the income of the business entity in addition to taxing the income distributed by the business to its owners.

2. Greater regulation. Corporations come into existence under the terms of state laws and these same laws may provide for considerable regulation of the corporation's activities. For example, the withdrawal of funds from a corporation is subject to certain limits set by law rather than being left entirely to the judgment of the owners. Large corporations, especially those with securities listed on stock exchanges and owned by large numbers of the public, have gradually come to accept the necessity for full public disclosure of their affairs.

3. Separation of ownership and control. The separation of the func-tions of ownership and management may be an advantage in some cases but a disadvantage in others. On the whole, the excellent record of growth

and earnings in most large corporations indicates that the separation of ownership and control has benefited rather than injured stockholders. In a few instances, however, a management group has chosen to operate a corporation for the benefit of insiders (for example, paying excessive executive salaries and bonuses). The stockholders may find it difficult in such cases to take the concerted action necessary to oust the officers. The existing management is difficult to dislodge, because the management group has the privilege of using company funds to solicit proxies from stockholders. Most stockholders who become dissatisfied with existing management policies are inclined to sell their stock rather than to try to influence management policies.

Formation of a corporation

To form a corporation an application signed by at least three incorporators is submitted to the corporation commissioner (or other designated official) of the state in which the company is to be incorporated. This application contains such information as the following:

1. Name and address of the corporation
2. Names and addresses of the incorporators
3. Nature of the business to be conducted
4. Description of the capital stock to be issued
5. Names of subscribers to the company's capital stock and the number of shares subscribed to by each
6. Names of directors who will serve until the first meeting of stockholders is held

The application for a charter is often referred to as the articles of incorporation. After payment of an incorporation fee to the state and approval of the articles of incorporation by the designated state official, the corporation comes into existence. A charter, which may be merely the approved application, is issued as evidence of the company's corporate status. The incorporators (who have subscribed for capital stock and therefore are now stockholders) hold a meeting to elect directors and to pass bylaws as a guide to the conduct of the company's affairs. The directors in turn hold a meeting at which officers of the corporation are appointed to serve as active managers of the business; capital stock certificates are issued to the subscribers; and the formation of the corporation is complete.

Organization costs. The formation of a corporation is a much more costly step than the organization of a partnership. The necessary costs include the payment of an incorporation fee to the state, the payment of fees to attorneys for their services in drawing up the articles of incorporation, payments to promoters, travel expenses, and a variety of other outlays necessary to bring the corporation into existence.

The result of these expenditures is the existence of the corporate entity; consequently, the benefits derived from these expenditures may be regarded as extending over the entire life of the corporation. To treat organization costs as an expense of the year in which the corporation was formed would unreasonably reduce the net earnings from operations during the first year. The benefits from organization costs are no more applicable to the first year of corporate existence than to the second, third, or final year; consequently, these expenditures are recorded by debiting an intangible asset account entitled "Organization Costs." Once the corporation has begun operations, there should be no further charges to this account. In the balance sheet, organization costs appear under the group heading of Intangible Assets, along with such items as goodwill, patents, and trademarks.

Since organization costs are applicable to the entire life span of the company and since this is indefinite, carrying the asset organization cost at its full amount until dissolution is in prospect is in accord with accounting theory. Because present income tax law permits organization costs to be written off over a period of five years or more, however, most companies amortize organization costs in order to reduce their income taxes. Accountants have been willing to condone this practice, despite the lack of theoretical support, on the grounds that such costs are relatively immaterial in relation to other assets. Unnecessary detail on the balance sheet is always to be avoided, and there seems to be little reason for carrying indefinitely organization costs of modest amount.

The role of the stockholder. The ownership of stock in a corporation usually carries the following basic rights:

1. To vote for directors, and thereby to be represented in the management of the business. The approval of a majority of stockholders may also be required for such important corporate actions as the incurring of long-term debts.

2. To share in profits by receiving dividends declared by the board of directors.

3. To share in the distribution of assets if the corporation is liquidated. When a corporation ends its existence, the creditors of the corporation must first be paid in full; any remaining assets are divided among stockholders in proportion to the number of shares owned.

4. To subscribe for additional shares in the event that the corporation decides to increase the amount of stock outstanding. This pre-emptive right entitles each stockholder to maintain his original percentage of ownership in the company by subscribing, in proportion to his present stockholdings, to any additional shares issued.

The ownership of stock does not give a person the right to intervene in the management of a corporation or to transact business in its behalf. Although the stockholders as a group own the corporation, they do not personally own the assets of the corporation. Neither do they personally owe the debts of the corporation. The stockholders have no direct claim on profits earned; income earned by a corporation does not become income to the stockholders unless the board of directors orders the distribution of earnings to stockholders in the form of a dividend.

Stockholders' meetings are usually held once a year, and such questions as the election of directors, the appointment of auditors, the granting of stock options to officers, and increases in the amount of capital stock are presented for approval. Each share of stock is entitled to one vote. In large corporations with stock owned by great numbers of people, these annual meetings are usually attended by relatively few persons, often by less than 1% of the stockholders. Prior to the meeting, the management group will request stockholders who do not plan to attend in person to send in proxy statements assigning their votes to the existing management. Through this use of the proxy system, management may secure the right to vote as much as, perhaps, 75% or more of the total outstanding shares. The meetings are then generally routine affairs since a favorable vote is assured on all proposals sponsored by the management. However, the discussions of operating results and other issues raised during the meeting are widely publicized in the press; consequently, the stockholders' meetings are in effect public forums in which management reports on its stewardship of the company's resources.

The lack of any direct active participation in management by most stockholders seems inevitable when stock ownership is widely dispersed among the public. The owner of a few shares of stock can hardly afford to travel to annual meetings or to devote sufficient time to the company's problems to have an informed opinion on many involved issues. Most stockholders are happy to leave the management function in the hands of professional managers, as long as profits earned and dividends paid reach satisfactory levels. If earnings and dividends do not seem satisfactory to the stockholder, his usual reaction is to sell his stock. The tremendous growth of many leading corporations indicates that the separation of ownership and control has been conducive to profitable operation and expansion.

The role of the board of directors. The board of directors is elected by the stockholders; the primary functions of the board are to manage the enterprise and to protect the interests of the stockholders. At this level, management may consist principally of formulating policies and reviewing acts of the officers. Specific duties of the directors include declaring dividends, setting the salaries of officers, authorizing officers to arrange loans from banks, and authorizing important contracts of various kinds.

The extent of active participation in management by the board of directors varies widely from one company to another. In some corporations the officers also serve as directors and a meeting of directors may differ only in form from a conference of operating executives. In other corporations the board may consist of outsiders who devote little time to the corporation's affairs and merely meet occasionally to review and approve policies which have been formed and administered by the officers.

The official actions of the board are recorded in minutes of their meetings. The minute book is the source of many of the accounting entries affecting the owners' equity accounts.

The role of the officers. Corporate officers usually include a president, one or more vice-presidents, a treasurer, a controller, and a secretary. A vice-president is often made responsible for the sales function; other vice-presidents may be given responsibility for such important functions as manufacturing, engineering, and industrial relations.

The work of the controller, treasurer, and secretary is most directly related to the accounting phase of business operation. The treasurer has custody of the company's funds and must forecast the company's cash position well in advance. A cash forecast requires scheduling in advance the estimated cash receipts and disbursements month by month for a period of perhaps one year. Advance planning of this type makes it possible for a company to arrange for bank loans and for the issuance of additional stock on more advantageous terms than would otherwise be possible. The preparation of cash forecasts and of forecasts of sales, expenses, and other phases of operations is called *budgeting*; it represents one of the newest but most important specialized fields of accounting.

The controller is the chief accounting officer. He is responsible for the maintenance of adequate internal control,[1] and for the preparation of accounting records and financial statements. Such specialized activities as budgeting and taxes are also usually under the jurisdiction of the controller. The work of the treasurer and the controller are closely related. A budget or forecast, for example, may be prepared by the controller and his staff from information in the accounting records, and transmitted to the treasurer for his use in planning financial transactions.

The secretary of the corporation is the officer who maintains minutes of the meetings of directors and stockholders and who acts as the official agent of the corporation in many contractual and legalistic matters. In small corporations one officer sometimes acts as both secretary and treasurer. The organization chart on page 490 indicates lines of authority extending from the stockholders to the directors to the president and other officers.

Contributed capital and retained earnings. The sections of a balance sheet showing assets and liabilities will be much the same for a corporation as for a single proprietorship or partnership. The owners' equity section is the principal point of contrast. In a corporation the term stockholders' equity is synonymous with owners' equity. The capital of a corporation, as for other types of business organizations, is equal to the excess of the assets over the liabilities. However, the capital of a corporation may be divided into several segments. In succeeding chapters, these various classifications of corporate capital will be considered in some detail, but at this point we are concerned with a simplified model in which the capital

[1] A system of internal control includes the plan of organization and all other measures used by a business for the purposes of (1) safeguarding assets against waste or fraud; (2) developing accuracy and reliability in accounting data; (3) encouraging compliance with company policy; and (4) measuring the efficiency of operations.

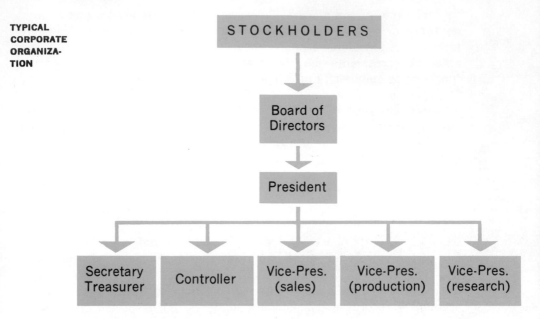

of a corporation is carried in only two ledger accounts and shown on the balance sheet in two separate portions. These two classifications are (1) the capital contributed by the stockholders, and (2) the capital accumulated through profitable operations.

The capital contributed by stockholders is regarded as permanent capital not ordinarily subject to withdrawal.[2] The unit of corporate ownership is a share of stock, and the balance of the Capital Stock account is always equal to the total number of shares of stock issued, multiplied by a stipulated amount (par value or stated value) per share.

The second major type of corporate capital is retained earnings. At the end of each accounting period, the balance of the Income Summary account is closed into the Retained Earnings account. Any dividends distributed to stockholders serve to reduce the Retained Earnings account. Consequently, the balance of the Retained Earnings account at any balance sheet date represents the accumulated earnings of the company since the date of incorporation, minus any losses and minus all dividends distributed to stockholders. (Various types of dividends are discussed in Chapter 19.) An alternative name for the Retained Earnings account is Earned Surplus. This is an older term which is gradually being replaced by Retained Earnings.

Stockholders' equity on the balance sheet. For a corporation with $100,000 of capital stock and $40,000 of retained earnings, the stockholders' equity section of the balance sheet will appear as follows:

[2] For legal reasons, the contributed capital may be divided into two portions: (1) legal capital, equal to par or stated value times the number of shares issued, and (2) excess of contributed capital over and above legal capital.

CON-
TRIBUTED
CAPITAL
AND
EARNED
CAPITAL

> *Stockholders' Equity*
>
> *Capital stock* $100,000
> *Retained earnings* 40,000   *140,000*

If this same company had been unprofitable and had incurred losses aggregating $30,000 since its organization, the capital section of the balance sheet would be as follows:

CON-
TRIBUTED
CAPITAL
REDUCED
BY LOSSES
INCURRED

> *Stockholders' Equity*
>
> *Capital stock* $100,000
> *Less: deficit* 30,000   *70,000*

This second illustration tells us that $30,000 of the original $100,-000 invested by stockholders has been lost. Notice that the capital stock in both illustrations remains at the fixed amount of $100,000, the stockholders' original investment. The accumulated profits or losses since the organization of the corporation are shown as retained earnings or as a deficit and are not intermingled with the contributed capital.

Income taxes on corporate financial statements. A corporation is a legal entity subject to corporation income tax; consequently, the ledger of a corporation should include accounts for recording income taxes. No such accounts are needed for a business organized as a single proprietorship or partnership.

Income taxes are based on a corporation's earnings. At year-end, before preparing financial statements, income taxes are recorded by an adjusting entry such as the following:

CORPORATE
INCOME TAX

> *Income Taxes* 14,104
>   *Income Taxes Payable*   14,104
> *To record the estimated income taxes payable for*
> *the year ended December 31, 19___*

The account debited in this entry, Income Taxes, is an expense account and usually appears as the very last deduction in the income statement as follows:

FINAL STEP
IN INCOME
STATEMENT

> *Net income before income taxes* $37,700
> *Income taxes* 14,104
> *Net income* $23,596

The liability account, Income Taxes Payable, will ordinarily be paid within a few months and should, therefore, appear in the current liability section of the balance sheet. More detailed discussion of corporation taxes is presented in Chapter 27.

AUTHORIZED CAPITAL STOCK

The articles of incorporation specify the number of shares of capital stock which a corporation is authorized to issue and the par value, if any, per share. The corporation may choose not to issue immediately all of the authorized shares; in fact, it is customary to secure authorization for a larger number of shares than presently needed. In future years if more capital is needed, the previously authorized shares will be readily available for issue; otherwise the corporation would be forced to apply to the state for permission to alter its charter by increasing the number of authorized shares.

Capital stock outstanding

The unit of stock ownership is the share, but the corporation may issue stock certificates in denominations of 10 shares, 100 shares, or any other number. The total capital stock outstanding at any given time represents 100% ownership of the corporation. Outstanding shares are those in the hands of stockholders. Assume for example, that the Midwest Corporation is organized with authorization to issue 5,000 shares of stock. However, only 1,000 shares are issued, because this amount of stock provides all the capital presently needed. The holders of the 1,000 shares of stock own the corporation in its entirety.

If we assume further that Richard Jones acquires 100 shares of the 1,000 shares outstanding, we may say that Jones has a 10% interest in the corporation. Suppose that Jones now sells 50 shares to Smith. The total number of shares outstanding remains unchanged at 1,000, although Jones's percentage of ownership has declined and a new stockholder, Smith, has acquired an interest. The sale of 50 shares from Jones to Smith had no effect upon the corporation's assets, liabilities, or amount of stock outstanding. The only way in which this transfer of stock affects the corporation is that the list of stockholders must be revised to show the number of shares presently held by each owner.

Preferred and common stock

In order to appeal to as many investors as possible, a corporation may issue more than one kind of stock, just as an automobile manufacturer may make sedans, convertibles, and station wagons in order to appeal to various groups of car buyers. When only one type of stock is issued, it is called common stock. Common stock has the four basic rights previously mentioned. Whenever these rights are modified, the term *preferred stock* (or sometimes class B common) is used to describe this second type of stock. A few corporations issue two or three classes of preferred stock, each class having certain distinctive features designed to interest a particular type of investor. In summary, we may say that every business corporation has common stock, a good many corporations also issue preferred stock, and a few companies have two or more types of preferred stock.

Common stock may be regarded as the basic, residual element of ownership. It carries voting rights and, therefore, is the means of exercising control over the business. Common stock has unlimited possibilities of increase in value; during the decade of the 1950s the market prices of common stocks of many leading corporations rose to three or four times their former values. On the other hand, common stocks lose value more rapidly than other types of securities when corporations encounter periods of unprofitable business.

The following stockholders' equity section illustrates the balance sheet presentation for a corporation having both preferred and common stock; note that the item of retained earnings is not apportioned between the two groups of stockholders.

BALANCE SHEET PRESENTATION

Stockholders' Equity:
Preferred Stock, 5% cumulative, $100 par value, authorized and issued 100,000 shares $10,000,000
Common Stock, $5 par value, authorized and issued 1 million shares 5,000,000
Retained Earnings 3,500,000

Total $18,500,000

Characteristics of preferred stock. Most preferred stocks have the following distinctive features:

1. Preferred as to dividends
2. Preferred as to assets in event of the liquidation of the company
3. Callable at the option of the corporation
4. No voting power

Another very important but less common feature is a clause permitting the conversion of preferred stock into common at the option of the holder. Preferred stocks vary widely with respect to the special rights and privileges granted. Careful study of the terms of the individual preferred stock contract is a necessary step in the evaluation of any preferred stock.

Stock preferred as to dividends. Stock preferred as to dividends is entitled to receive each year a dividend of specified amount before any dividend is paid on the common stock. The dividend is usually stated as

DIVIDEND
STATED AS
DOLLAR
AMOUNT

a dollar amount per share. For example, the balance sheet of General Motors Corporation shows two types of preferred stock outstanding, one paying $5.00 a year and the other $3.75 a year, as shown below:

> *Capital stock:*
>   *Preferred, without par value (authorized 6 million shares)*
>   *$5.00 series; stated value $100 per share (issued 1,875,366 shares;*
>   *less in treasury 39,722 shares; outstanding 1,835,644 shares)* .. *$183,564,400*
>   *$3.75 series; stated value $100 per share (issued and outstand-*
>   *ing 1 million shares)* *100,000,000*

Some preferred stocks state the dividend preference as a percentage of par value. For example, a 5% preferred stock with a par value of $100 per share would mean that $5 must be paid yearly on each share of preferred stock before any dividends are paid to the common. An example of the percentage method of stating the dividend on a preferred stock is found in the balance sheet of The American Tobacco Company:

DIVIDEND
STATED AS
PERCENTAGE

> *Capital stock:*
>   *Preferred, 6% cumulative, par value $100 per share* .. *$52,783,100*

The holder of a preferred stock has no assurance that he will always receive the indicated dividend. A corporation is obligated to pay dividends to stockholders only when the board of directors declares a dividend. Dividends must be paid on preferred stock before anything is paid to the common stockholders, but if the corporation is not prospering, it may decide not to pay dividends on either preferred or common stock. For a corporation to pay dividends, profits must be earned and cash must be available. However, preferred stocks in general offer more assurance of regular dividend payments than do common stocks.

The dividend preference carried by most preferred stocks is a cumulative one. If all or any part of the regular dividend on the preferred stock is omitted in a given year, the amount in arrears must be paid in a subsequent year before any dividend can be paid on the common stock.

Dividend payments during periods of prosperity. If a corporation earns very large profits, its common stock may become much more valuable than the preferred. As an example, let us assume that the Baker Corporation has 10,000 shares of common stock and 1,000 shares of $5 preferred stock outstanding. Baker Corporation adopts the policy of distributing 70% of its earnings as dividends. In three successive years

NO CEILING ON COMMON STOCK DIVIDENDS the company's earnings are $40,000, $100,000, and $200,000. The dividends to be paid on preferred and common stock during the three years are indicated by the following schedule:

	First year	Second year	Third year
Net income	$40,000	$100,000	$200,000
Per cent of net income to be distributed	70%	70%	70%
Dividends paid	$28,000	$ 70,000	$140,000
Dividends on preferred ($5 × 1,000)	5,000	5,000	5,000
Dividends on common	$23,000	$ 65,000	$135,000
Dividends per share of common	$ 2.30	$ 6.50	$ 13.50

Note that the preferred stockholders received the same dividend of $5 a share throughout this period. The dividend on the common stock, however, was increased in accordance with the company's earnings.

Dividends in arrears. Assume that a corporation was organized January 1, 1960, with 1,000 shares of $4 cumulative preferred stock and 1,000 shares of common stock. Dividends paid in 1960 were at the rate of $4 per share of preferred stock and $3 per share of common. In 1961, earnings declined sharply and the only dividend paid was $1 per share on the preferred stock. No dividends were paid in 1962. What is the status of the preferred stock as of December 31, 1962? Dividends are in arrears in the amount of $7 a share ($3 omitted during 1961 and $4 omitted in 1962). On the entire issue of 1,000 shares of preferred stock, the dividends in arrears amount to $7,000.

In 1963, we shall assume that the company earned large profits and wished to pay dividends on both the preferred and common stocks. Before paying a dividend on the common, the corporation must pay the $7,000 in arrears on the cumulative preferred stock plus the regular $4 a share applicable to the current year. The preferred stockholders would, therefore, receive a total of $11,000 in dividends in 1963; the board of directors would then be free to declare dividends on the common stock.

Dividends in arrears are never listed among the liabilities of a corporation, because no liability exists until a dividend is declared by the board of directors. Nevertheless, the amount of any dividends in arrears on preferred stock is an important factor to investors and other users of the company's financial statements and should always be disclosed. This disclosure is usually made by a footnote to the balance sheet such as the following:

"As of December 31, 1962, dividends on the $5 cumulative preferred stock were in arrears to the extent of $18 per share, and amounted in total to $180,000."

For a noncumulative preferred stock, any unpaid or omitted dividend is lost forever. Because of this factor, investors view the noncumulative feature as an unfavorable element, and very few noncumulative preferred stocks are issued.

Participating clauses in preferred stock. Since participating preferred stocks are very seldom issued, discussion of them will be brief. A fully participating preferred stock is one which, in addition to the regular speci- fied dividend, is entitled to participate equally with the common in any additional dividends paid. For example, a $5 participating preferred stock would be entitled to receive $5 a share before the common stock received anything. After $5 a share had been paid to the preferred stockholders, a $5 dividend could be paid on the common stock. If the company desired to pay an additional dividend to the common, say, an extra $3 per share, the preferred stock would also be entitled to receive an extra $3 dividend. In brief, a fully participating preferred stock participates dollar for dollar with the common stock in any dividends paid in excess of the stated rate on the preferred.

A partially participating preferred stock is one which participates with the common in additional dividends up to a stated maximum, such as $10 per share. Corporations generally are unwilling to issue any form of participating preferred stock, because it offers too generous terms to a particular group of shareholders. Since preferred stockholders incur less risk than the common stockholders, there is little reason for allowing them the same opportunity to share in large profits.

Stock preferred as to assets. Most preferred stocks carry a preference as to assets in the event of liquidation of the corporation. If the business is terminated, the preferred stock is entitled to payment in full of a stated liquidation value (or par value) before any payment is made on the com- mon stock.

For example, assume that a corporation in the process of liquidation has converted all its assets into cash, which amounts to $300,000. There are $50,000 of liabilities, $200,000 par value of preferred stock, and $200,000 par value of common stock. Since the assets amount to less than the total of the liabilities and the capital stocks, it is apparent that **WHO TAKES** the corporation has incurred losses and now has a substantial deficit:
THE LOSS?

Balance Sheet

Assets		*Liabilities & Stockholders' Equity*	
Cash	*$300,000*	*Liabilities*	*$ 50,000*
		Preferred stock	*200,000*
		Common stock	*200,000*
		Deficit	*(150,000)*
	$300,000		*$300,000*

Assume that the preferred stock consists of 2,000 shares of $100 par value; liquidation value is stated as $105 per share plus any dividends in arrears. Also assume that dividends in arrears amount to $10 per share. How should the $300,000 of cash be divided?

The first step in distributing cash would be to pay in full the $50,000 due to creditors, which will reduce the cash balance to $250,000. Next, each preferred share will receive $115 (liquidation value of $105 plus $10 dividends in arrears), making a total payment of $230,000 and leaving only $20,000 for distribution to the common stockholders.

Some issues of preferred stock are entitled to receive only the par value of their shares in the event of liquidation. Other issues may carry no preference over the common stock. An investor in preferred stock must refer to the terms printed on the stock certificate or to detailed descriptions of the issue to ascertain just what his rights would be if the corporation were dissolved.

Callable preferred stock. Most preferred stocks are callable at the option of the corporation at a stipulated price, usually slightly above the issuance price. The call price or redemption price for a $100 par value preferred stock is often $103 or $104 per share.

In the financing of a new or expanding corporation, the organizers usually hold common stock which assures them control of the company. However, it is often necessary to obtain outside capital. One way of doing this without the loss of control or any serious reduction in possible future earnings on the common stock, is to issue a callable preferred stock. The capital paid in for the preferred stock will be available as long as needed and can be paid off when the corporation has earned and retained sufficient profits to finance the business.

The existence of a call provision means that preferred stockholders may very possibly be eliminated from the company if the business proves to be highly successful. This prospect is not as much of a deterrent to investment in preferred stock as might be thought at first glance, because preferred stock is ordinarily limited to a fixed amount of dividends and therefore does not share in the benefits of growth and expanding profits in any event. The call provision does tend to establish a ceiling for the market price of a preferred stock unless the stock is convertible into common.

It may be argued that the position of the holder of a callable preferred stock is more like that of a creditor than that of an owner. He supplies capital to the company for an agreed rate of return, has no voice in management, and may find his relationship with the company terminated at any time through the calling in of his certificate. If a company is so fortunate as to enter upon a period of unusually high earnings, it will probably increase the dividend payments on its common stock, but it will not even consider increasing the return of the preferred stockholder. On the contrary, the corporation may decide that this era of prosperity is a good time to eliminate the preferred stock through exercise of the call provision.

Regardless of the fact that preferred stock lacks many of the traditional aspects of ownership, it is universal practice to include all types of preferred stock in the owners' equity section of the balance sheet.

Convertible preferred stock. In order to add to the attractiveness of preferred stock as an investment, corporations sometimes offer a conversion privilege which entitles the preferred stockholder to exchange his shares for common stock in a stipulated ratio. If the corporation prospers, its common stock will probably rise in market value, and dividends on the common stock will probably be increased. The investor who buys a convertible preferred stock rather than common stock has greater assurance of regular dividends. In addition, through the conversion privilege, he is assured of sharing in any substantial increase in value of the company's common stock.

As an example, assume that the Remington Corporation issued a 5% convertible preferred stock on January 1, 1962, at a price of $100 a share. Each share was convertible into five shares of the company's common stock at any time. The common stock had a market price of $20 a share on January 1, 1962, and an annual dividend of $1.00 a share was being paid. The yield on the preferred stock was 5% ($5 ÷ $100); the yield on the common stock was also 5% ($1 ÷ $20).

During the next few years, the Remington Corporation's earnings increased, the dividend on the common stock was raised to an annual rate of $1.50, and the market price of the common stock rose to $30 a share. At this point the preferred stock would have a market value of $150, since it could be converted at any time into five shares of common stock with a market value of $30 each. In other words, the market value of a convertible preferred stock will tend to move in accordance with the price of the common. When the dividend rate is increased on the common stock, many holders of the preferred stock will convert their holdings into common stock in order to obtain a higher return on their investments.

The preceding illustration was based on the assumption that the Remington Corporation enjoyed larger earnings after the issuance of its convertible preferred. Let us now take a contrary assumption and say that shortly after issuance of the convertible preferred stock, the company's profits declined and the directors deemed it necessary to cut the annual dividend on the common stock from $1.00 a share to 20 cents a share. A stockholder who acquired common stock at a cost of $20 a share now finds that his dividend income has dropped to a rate of 1% ($0.20 dividend ÷ $20 cost). The dividend on the preferred stock remains at $5 a share, however, for this amount must be paid each year before any dividend is paid on the common stock.

These two illustrations indicate that the convertible preferred stock has two important advantages from the viewpoint of the investor: it increases in value along with the common stock when the company prospers, and it offers greater assurance of steady dividend income during a period of poor earnings.

QUESTIONS

1. Distinguish between corporations and partnerships in terms of the following characteristics: (*a*) owners' liability, (*b*) transferability of ownership interest, (*c*) continuity of existence, and (*d*) Federal taxation on net income.

2. The corporate form of organization is usually considered advantageous for large enterprises. Why do you suppose large firms of certified public accountants, attorneys, or architects do not incorporate?

3. Describe three kinds of expenses that may be incurred in the process of organizing a corporation. How are such expenditures treated for accounting purposes? Why?

4. What are the basic rights of the owner of a share of corporate stock? In what way are these basic rights commonly modified with respect to the owner of a share of preferred stock?

5. Describe the usual nature of the following features as they apply to a share of preferred stock: (*a*) cumulative, (*b*) participating, (*c*) convertible, and (*d*) callable.

6. Why is noncumulative preferred stock considered a very unattractive form of investment opportunity?

7. Smith owns 200 of the 8,000 shares of common stock issued and outstanding in X Company. The company issued 2,000 additional shares of stock. What is Smith's position with respect to the new issue if he is entitled to pre-emptive rights?

8. Atlas Corporation has outstanding two classes of $100 par value stock: 1,000 shares of 6% cumulative preferred and 5,000 shares of common. The company has a $10,000 deficit at the beginning of the current year, and preferred dividends have not been paid for two years. During the current year the firm earns $50,000. What will be the balance in retained earnings at the end of the year if the company pays a dividend of $2 per share on common stock?

PROBLEMS

Group A

17A-1. Ingils Corporation was organized on July 1, 1963, with authorized stock of 10,000 shares of $30 par value common and 5,000 shares of $100 par value, 6% preferred stock. Mr. Ingils was given 100 shares of preferred and 100 shares of common for his work and expenses in organizing and promoting the corporation. Attorneys' fees of $800 in connection with the formation of the corporation have been billed but not paid. Near the end of July, 8,000 shares of common were sold at par for cash, $30,000 of which was used to buy land and $170,000 applied to the price of a building. The building cost $470,000; the balance was represented by a 6% mortgage due in 10 years. Mr. Ingils transferred assets from a previous business in exchange for 2,000 shares of preferred. The current fair value of these assets was as follows: notes receivable, $120,000; inventories, $20,000; equipment, $60,000. The business did not begin operation until after July 31, but interest of $500 accrued on the notes receivable between the time they were turned over to the corporation and July 31.

Instructions. Prepare in good form the balance sheet of the Ingils Corporation as of July 31, 1963.

17A-2. At the end of 1961, the balance sheet of the Hazard Company appears in condensed form as follows:

HAZARD COMPANY
Balance Sheet
December 31, 1961

Assets	$400,000	*Liabilities*	$110,000
		Stockholders' equity:	
		Common stock $50 par;	
		authorized 10,000 shares;	
		issued 5,000 shares	250,000
		Retained earnings	40,000
	$400,000		$400,000

Other data. During 1962 the Hazard Company's net income after operating expenses but before income taxes was $80,000, equal to 20% of net sales. Gross margin on sales was 35%. Income taxes were 40% of net income and none have been paid as of December 31, 1962.

The company's 1962 net income before income taxes was represented by an increase in assets of $65,000 and a decrease in liabilities (other than income taxes payable) of $15,000.

The company is authorized to issue 12,000 shares of 7% preferred stock, $25 par value. On January 1, 1962, 10,000 shares of preferred were sold at par, and the proceeds were used to buy plant and equipment. Regular dividends were paid on preferred at the end of 1962 and a dividend of $2.50 per share was paid on common stock outstanding.

Instructions
a. Prepare a condensed income statement for the corporation for 1962.
b. Prepare in summary form the balance sheet of the corporation at the end of 1962. Show assets and liabilities (other than income taxes payable) as single amounts, but show details of the stockholders' equity section. In a separate schedule, show how you determined the balance of retained earnings at December 31, 1962.

17A-3. *Instructions.* For each of the independent situations described below, prepare in good form the stockholders' equity section of the balance sheet as of December 31, 1962. Include a supporting schedule for each case showing your determination of the balance of retained earnings that should appear in the balance sheet.

Data
(1) Corporation A was organized in 1960 and was authorized to issue 10,000 shares of $10 par value common. The stock was issued at par, and the

corporation reported a net loss of $4,000 for 1960 and a net loss of $13,000 in 1961. In 1962 net income was $3.20 per share.

(2) Corporation B was organized in 1958. The company was authorized to issue 5,000 shares of $50 par value common and 1,000 shares of preferred stock. All of the preferred and 4,000 shares of common were issued at par. The preferred stock was callable at 103% of its $100 par value, and was entitled to dividends of 6% before any dividends were paid to common. During the first five years of its existence, the corporation earned a total of $120,000 and paid dividends of 50 cents per share each year on common stock.

(3) Corporation C was organized in 1959, issuing at par one-half of the 40,000 shares of $25 par common stock authorized. On January 1, 1960, the company sold at par the entire 2,000 authorized shares of $100 par value, 5%, cumulative preferred. On January 1, 1961, the company issued 1,000 shares of an authorized 3,000 shares of $6 no-par preferred, for $100,000. The $6 preferred carried a provision that after common stockholders had received $3 per share, it participated in all additional dividends on a share-for-share basis up to $6 per share. The company suffered losses in 1959 and 1960, reporting a deficit of $12,000 at the end of 1960. Dividends of $1 per share of common were paid in 1961. In 1962 the $6 preferred stock participated to the extent of $1.50 per share with common stockholders in dividends. The company earned a total of $225,000 during 1961 and 1962.

17A-4. Wattles Corporation was organized at the beginning of 1960. The company issued 6,000 of 8,000 authorized shares of $100 par value common stock, and 10,000 shares, the entire authorization of $50 par value, cumulative, 6% preferred stock, receiving a total of $1,100,000, out of which $48,000 in organization costs was paid. The preferred stock is entitled to dividend preference and to preference on liquidation to the extent of 110% of par plus any dividends in arrears.

The corporation earned $100,000 during 1960 and paid a full year's dividends on the preferred and $6 per share on common stock. During 1961 the company earned $40,000 and paid preferred but no common dividends. During 1962 the company lost $35,000 and paid no dividends. The stockholders agreed to liquidate the corporation. On January 3, 1963, all assets other than organization costs were sold for 70% of their valuation on the corporation books. Organization costs were written off and liabilities of $250,000 paid in full.

Instructions

a. Prepare a schedule showing the determination of the balance of retained earnings at December 31, 1962. Use the following five columnar headings:

Year	*Net income*	*Preferred dividends*	*Common dividends*	*Balance of retained earnings*

b. Prepare in good form the stockholders' equity section of the Wattles Corporation balance sheet as it would appear on December 31, 1962.

c. Prepare a schedule showing the amount of cash available to stockholders on January 3, 1963.

d. Determine the amount per share that would be distributed to preferred and common stockholders on January 3, 1963.

Group B

17B-1. On December 31, 1961, the three partners of the Prosser Company agreed to incorporate. The balance sheet is given below.

PROSSER COMPANY
Balance Sheet
As of December 31, 1961

Assets	$120,000	Liabilities	$ 20,000
		Prosser, capital	50,000
		Jules, capital	30,000
		Dant, capital	20,000
	$120,000		$120,000

Other data. The partners applied for and received a charter authorizing 1,000 shares of $100 par value common stock and 1,000 shares of $100 par value, 6% cumulative preferred stock. Organization costs were $2,400. On January 1, 1962, the corporation was formed, and each partner was issued, at par, common stock for one-half of his capital interest and preferred stock for the remaining half. Organization costs were not amortized.

During 1962 the corporation earned $25,000 before income taxes, represented by an increase in assets of $40,000 and an increase in liabilities of $15,000. The provision for income taxes was 30%. Dividends were paid on preferred stock, and dividends of $4 per share were paid on common stock.

Instructions. Prepare the balance sheet of the Prosser Corporation as of December 31, 1962. Show in a separate schedule how you arrived at the balance of retained earnings at that date.

17B-2. Buffen Corporation has net assets of $1,000,000, represented $400,000 by 6% cumulative preferred stock and $600,000 by common shares. A prospective investor, Yates, is interested in comparing the return that will accrue to preferred and common stockholders under five different assumptions as to the corporation's earnings before income taxes:

Case	Assumed rate of earnings (before taxes) on net assets, per cent	Amount of earnings
1	1.0	$ 10,000
2	2.4	24,000
3	5.0	50,000
4	10.0	100,000
5	20.0	200,000

The corporation is subject to income taxes at the rate of 30% on the first $25,000 of earnings and 50% on all earnings over $25,000.

Instructions

a. Prepare a schedule for Yates, showing the relative amounts that would be received by preferred and common stockholders in each of these five cases, assuming that assets equal to 100% of net income after taxes are distributed to stockholders as dividends. Use the following headings:

			Applicable to			
Net income before taxes	*Income taxes*	*Net income after taxes*	*Preferred stock*		*Common stock*	
			Amount	*Per cent ****	*Amount*	*Per cent ****

* *"Per cent" in this column refers to the return accruing to preferred and common stockholders as a percentage of their respective investment in net assets.*

b. From this schedule it may be shown that in case 5 the net income applicable to common stockholders is a larger percentage of their investment than the percentage of corporate net income after taxes to the total net assets of the corporation. Write a statement explaining the reason for this result.

17B-3. *Instructions.* For each of the situations described below, prepare in good form the stockholders' equity section of the corporate balance sheet as of the end of 1962, together with a schedule showing how you arrived at the amount of retained earnings shown on your statement. Each case is independent of the others.

Data

(1) Corporation X was authorized to issue 20,000 shares of $20 par value common stock. In 1960, 18,000 shares were issued at par and the corporation reported a net income of $36,000 and paid dividends of $1.20 per share. A net loss of $2.60 per share was reported in 1961, and in 1962 the company's net loss was $21,000.

(2) Corporation Y, organized in 1959, was authorized to issue 10,000 shares of $25 par common stock and 2,000 shares of $100 par value, 6%, cumulative preferred stock. On July 1, 1959, one-half of the authorized common and three-fourths of the authorized preferred shares were issued at par, and the company began operations. The board of directors followed a policy of distributing as dividends 90% of all amounts available for common stock and 100% of all amounts assignable to preferred stock during any calendar year. Net income was $32,000 in 1959; $4,100 in 1960; and $25,150 in 1962. A loss of $3,000 was sustained in 1961.

(3) Corporation Z on January 1, 1960, issued at par all its authorized 10,000 shares of $50 par value common stock and its authorized 5,000 shares of 5%, cumulative preferred stock, par value $100. The preferred stock may be called at $106 per share at any time. On January 1, 1962, the corporation called and retired 2,000 shares of the preferred, charging the call premium of $6 per share against retained earnings. Z Corporation earned $80,000 in 1960, $100,000 in 1961, and $120,000 in 1962; it paid dividends on common of $5 per share in all three years.

17B-4. Each of the cases described below is independent of the others.

Case A. On May 31, 1962, Dina Corporation has outstanding 32,000 of 50,000 authorized shares of $20 par value common stock, and 3,000 of 10,000 shares of $7 preferred stock, cumulative, par value $100. The preferred is entitled to liquidation preference of par plus dividends in arrears. The company has been in existence for three years and has lost money in each year, accumulating a deficit of $24,000 as of May 31, 1962. On that date all assets, other than cash on hand of $40,000, were sold for one-half of their book value, and liabilities of $200,000 were paid in full.

Instructions. Prepare a schedule showing the amount of assets available for distribution to stockholders, and the amount per share that would be received in liquidation on each of the two kinds of stock as of May 31, 1962.

Case B. Elba Corporation was organized on January 1, 1961, and authorized to issue 50,000 shares of $10 par value common stock and 20,000 shares of $2 cumulative preferred stock, par value $40 per share. Promoters and attorneys were given 5,000 shares of common stock for their services in organizing the corporation, and 30,000 shares were sold at par for cash. During 1961 the company lost $40,000. At the beginning of 1962 the company needed funds, and in order to sell its preferred at par, the contract was altered to make the preferred fully participating with the common stock. On this basis, 10,000 shares of preferred were sold at par. During 1962 Elba Corporation earned $215,000 and declared a dividend of $3 per share on common stock.

Instructions. Prepare in good form the stockholders' equity section of the balance sheet as of December 31, 1962. Show in a separate schedule how you arrived at the balance of retained earnings at that date.

Case C. Folt Corporation had net assets of $800,000 as of January 1, 1962, represented by 4,000 shares of $100 par value common and 1,200 shares of 6%, $100 par value, cumulative preferred stock. All shares had been issued at par. The preferred stock is convertible into common at any time on the basis of three shares of preferred for two shares of common. Net operating income before income taxes is expected to be 20% of net assets during 1962. The company is subject to income taxes at an average rate of 45%.

Instructions. Assuming that earnings are as forecast

a. Compute the amount of net income in 1962 that is allocable to common stock, assuming that none of the preferred shares is converted during the year.

b. Compute the 1962 net income available per share of common stock, assuming that all preferred shares are converted at the beginning of 1962.

c. Determine the maximum legal dividend per share of common that could be paid at the end of 1962, assuming that all shares of preferred were converted at the beginning of 1962.

18

Corporations: capital stock transactions

Par value

In an earlier period of the history of American corporations, all capital stock had par value, but in more recent years state laws have permitted corporations to choose between par value stock and no-par value stock. The corporate charter always states the par value, if any, of the shares to be issued.

Par value may be $1 per share, $5, $100, or any other amount decided upon by the corporation. The par value of the stock is no indication of its market value; the par value merely indicates the amount per share to be entered in the Capital Stock account. Most corporations issuing par value stock today choose a relatively low par value per share, perhaps $10 or less, as a means of minimizing the Federal stock transfer tax, which is based in part upon the par value of shares transferred from one investor to another. A generation ago, it was customary for stock to have a par value of $100 a share.

Many people attach an unwarranted significance to par value and are inclined to believe, for example, that a $100 par value share has an intrinsic worth of $100. The fallacy of such thinking will become apparent as our study of corporation accounting progresses; at present the objective is to emphasize that par value indicates the amount per share to be entered in the Capital Stock account and does not mean market value.

The chief significance of par value is that it represents the legal capital per share; that is, the amount below which stockholders' equity cannot be reduced except by (1) losses from business operations, or (2) legal action taken by a majority vote of stockholders. A dividend cannot be declared by a corporation if such action would cause the stockholders' equity to fall below the par value of the outstanding shares. Par value, therefore, may be regarded as a minimum cushion of capital existing for the protection of creditors.

Authorization of a stock issue

In the series of illustrations which follows, it is assumed that a corporation has been authorized to issue 10,000 shares of $10 par value stock. Mere authorization of a stock issue does not bring an asset into existence, nor does it give the corporation any capital. The obtaining of authorization from the state for a stock issue merely affords a legal opportunity to obtain assets by sale of stock. No journal entry is required to record the receipt of authorization for a stock issue, but a notation should be made in the ledger as follows:

NOTATION
IN LEDGER
OF SHARES
AUTHORIZED

Capital Stock

(Authorized for issuance 10,000 shares of $10 par value)

When par value stock is issued, the Capital Stock account is always credited with the par value of the shares issued, regardless of whether the issuance price is more or less than par.

Stock issued at par for cash. The simplest situation to illustrate is one in which capital stock is issued at par for cash. Assuming that 6,000 of the authorized 10,000 shares are issued at a price of $10 each, the entry is as follows:

SHARES
ISSUED

Cash *60,000*
     Capital Stock *60,000*
Issued 6,000 shares at par of $10.

After this entry has been posted the Capital Stock account appears as follows:

PERMANENT
CAPITAL

Capital Stock

(Authorized for issuance 10,000 shares of $10 par value)

1961
Jan. 2 (Issued 6,000 shares) 60,000

Stock issued at a price above par. This illustration differs from the preceding one in only one respect; the issuance price of the 6,000 shares of stock is assumed to be $15 per share. When stock is sold for more than par value, the Capital Stock account is credited with the par value of the shares issued, and a separate account, Paid-in Capital in Excess of Par Value, is credited for the excess of selling price over par. The entry is as follows:

CAPITAL
CONTRIB-
UTED IN
EXCESS OF
PAR VALUE

Cash	90,000	
Capital Stock		60,000
Paid-in Capital in Excess of Par Value		30,000
Issued 6,000 shares of $10 par value stock at a price of $15 a share.		

An alternative title for the account Paid-in Capital in Excess of Par Value is Premium on Capital Stock. The premium or amount received in excess of par value does not represent a profit to the corporation. It is part of the invested capital and it will be added to the capital stock on the balance sheet to show the total amount of contributed capital. The capital section of the balance sheet would be as follows (the existence of $10,000 in retained earnings is assumed in order to have a complete illustration):

CAPITAL
CLASSIFIED
BY SOURCE

Stockholders' Equity

Capital stock, $10 par value, authorized 10,000 shares, issued and outstanding 6,000 shares	$ 60,000
Paid-in capital in excess of par value	30,000
Total contributed capital	$ 90,000
Retained earnings	10,000
Total capital	$100,000

Stock issued at a price below par. In this illustration the issuance price of the $10 par value shares is assumed to be $8 a share. The issuance of stock at a discount rarely occurs in present-day corporate finance, and the transaction is illustrated here merely to bring out the theoretical implications. The entry for the issuance of 6,000 shares at $8 is as follows:

SHARES
ISSUED AT
DISCOUNT

Cash	48,000	
Discount on Capital Stock	12,000	
Capital Stock		60,000
Issued 6,000 shares of $10 par value stock at a price of $8 a share.		

In the balance sheet the discount account would appear as a deduction from the capital stock, as follows:

NOTE
DISTINCTION
BETWEEN
CON-
TRIBUTED
CAPITAL
AND
EARNED
CAPITAL

Stockholders' Equity

Capital stock, $10 par value, authorized 10,000 shares, issued and outstanding 6,000 shares	$60,000
Less: discount on stock	12,000
Total contributed capital	$48,000
Retained earnings	10,000
Total capital	$58,000

Notice that the balance sheet presentation shows all the essential facts about the stock issue, including the par value per share, the number of shares authorized, and the number of shares issued and outstanding.

Nature of discount on capital stock. Many states now prohibit the issuance of stock at less than par. Moreover, such a transaction would be undesirable from the viewpoint of the investor. Under the laws of some states, if a corporation becomes unable to pay its debts, the holders of stock issued at less than par value may be held personally liable to the creditors of the corporation for an amount equal to the discount on the stock held. Consequently, most investors are unwilling to purchase capital stock unless it bears the inscription "Fully paid and nonassessable."

In planning the issuance of capital stock, the corporation is free to set the par value of the shares as low as it pleases, and a par value of $1 a share is not uncommon. Since par value is usually set at an amount considerably below the offering price, the question of discount on capital stock is of little practical importance. In the past a par value of $100 per share was customary; under those circumstances, the issuance of stock at a discount was not unusual. Once stock has been issued, it may be sold by one investor to another at more or less than par without any effect on the corporation's accounts. In other words, discount on stock refers only to the original issuance of shares by a corporation at a price below par.

The underwriting of stock issues

When a large amount of stock is to be issued by a corporation, it is customary to utilize the services of an investment banking firm or *underwriter.* The underwriter guarantees the issuing corporation a specific price for the stock and makes a profit by selling the stock to the investing public at a higher price. For example, an issue of 100,000 shares of $10 par value common stock might be sold to the public at a price of $52 a share, of which $2 a share might be retained by the underwriter and $50 transmitted to the corporation. The corporation, in recording the issuance of the stock, would enter on its books only the net amount received from the underwriter, $50 for each share issued, or a total of $5 million. The use of an underwriter assures the corporation that the entire stock issue will be sold without delay, and the entire amount of funds to be raised will be available on a specific date.

Market price of common stock

The preceding sections concerning the issuance of stock at prices above and below par raise a question as to how the market price of stock is determined. The price which the corporation sets on a new issue of stock is based on several factors including (1) an appraisal of the company's expected future earnings, (2) the probable dividend rate per share, (3) the present financial condition of the company, and (4) the current state of the investment market.

After the stock has been issued, the price at which it will be traded among investors will tend to reflect the progress of the company, with primary emphasis being placed on earnings and dividends per share. At this point in our discussion, the significant fact to emphasize is that market price is not related to par value, and tends to reflect expected future earnings and dividends.

Stock issued for assets other than cash

Corporations generally sell their capital stock for cash and use the cash obtained in this way to buy the various types of assets needed in the business. Sometimes, however, a corporation may issue shares of its capital stock in a direct exchange for land, buildings, or other assets. Stock may also be issued in payment for services rendered by accountants, attorneys, and promoters.

When a corporation issues capital stock in exchange for services or for assets other than cash, a question arises as to the proper valuation of the property or services received. For example, assume that a corporation issues 1,000 shares of its $1 par value stock in exchange for a tract of land. A problem may exist in determining the fair market value of the land, and consequently in determining the amount of capital contributed. If there is no direct evidence of the value of the land, we may value it by using indirect evidence as to the alternative amount of cash for which the shares might have been sold. Assume that the company's stock is listed on a stock exchange and is presently selling at $90 a share. The 1,000 shares which the corporation exchanged for the land could have been sold for $90,000 cash, and the cash could have been used to pay for the land. The direct exchange of stock for land may be considered as the equivalent of selling the stock for cash and using the cash to buy the land. It is therefore logical to say that the cost of the land to the company was $90,000, the market value of the stock given in exchange for the land. Notice that the par value of the stock is not any indication of the fair value of the stock or of the land.

Once the valuation question has been decided, the entry to record the issuance of stock in exchange for noncash assets can be made, following the pattern previously illustrated for recording the issuance of capital stock.

Land 90,000		
Capital Stock		*1,000*
Paid-in Capital in Excess of Par Value		*89,000*

To record the issuance of 1,000 shares of $1 par value stock in exchange for land. Current market value of stock ($90 a share) used as basis for valuing the land.

Par value and no-par value stock

An understanding of no-par stock can best be gained by reviewing the reasons why par value was originally required in an earlier period of American corporate history. The use of the par value concept in state laws was intended for the protection of creditors and of public stockholders. In some states stock could not be issued at less than par value; in most states if stock *was* issued at less than par value the purchaser was contingently liable for the discount below par. A corporation was thus discouraged from selling its stock to the public at, say, $100 a share and concurrently to insiders or promoters at, say, $10 a share.

Protection was also afforded to creditors by laws prohibiting a corporation from paying any dividend which would "impair its capital" (reduce its capital to an amount less than the par value of the outstanding shares). Because of these statutes concerning par value, a creditor of a corporation could tell by inspection of the balance sheet the amount which owners had invested permanently in the corporation. This permanent investment of ownership capital (par value times number of outstanding shares) represented a buffer which protected the corporation creditor from the impact of any losses sustained by the corporation. Such protection for creditors was considered necessary because stockholders have no personal liability for the debts of the corporation.

The par value device proved rather ineffective in achieving its avowed objective of protecting creditors and public stockholders. Although corporations were prohibited from selling their shares at less than par, the law could easily be circumvented by issuing shares in exchange for property other than cash. In some cases large amounts of stock were issued for worthless mining claims, patents, and other assets of unproved value. The assets acquired in this manner were recorded at the par value of the stock issued in payment, resulting in a serious overstatement of asset values and invested capital on the balance sheet. Such abuses of the par value concept paved the way for legislation permitting the issuance of stock with no-par value.

Advantages of no-par stock. In 1912 New York State enacted legislation permitting corporations to issue stock without par value. Other states passed similar laws. The proponents of no-par stock offered the following arguments:

1. The printing of a par value figure, such as $100, on a stock certificate had led many naïve investors to believe that the stock was worth $100. Especially for corporations which had been operating unsuccessfully for some time, a fair market value of the stock might be far less than par value. Omission of a par value figure, it was hoped, would force the investor to consider more fundamental factors such as earnings and dividends before purchasing a stock.

2. No-par stock would avoid any discount liability. If a stock with $100 par value is issued at, say, $80, the purchaser is contingently liable for the discount of $20 and may be required to pay in that amount if the corporation is unable to meet its debts. A no-par share can be sold at any amount without imposing a contingent liability on the holder.

3. No-par stock would reduce the incentive for corporations to overvalue property received in exchange for capital stock. Deliberate overvaluation of noncash assets received for par value stock was attributed to the fact that the company could not find buyers for its stock at par value and was thus forced into the subterfuge of inflating the book values of property received in exchange for stock. Since no-par stock could be sold at any price, it was hoped that property acquired through issuance of no-par stock would be recorded at realistic values.

4. No-par stock would eliminate the distinction between legal capital and contributed capital. Proponents of no-par stock apparently assumed that whatever amount was received for no-par shares would be credited to the capital stock account as contributed capital. This result was not achieved, however, because the states found it necessary to establish a "stated value" for no-par shares, a feature very similar to par value.

Transfer tax on no-par stock. Laws pertaining to the transfer of shares of stock and to fees for incorporation provide that no-par shares shall be assumed, for tax purposes, to have a par value of $100. If the no-par share is actually low in price, perhaps $5 to $10, such tax treatment is very burdensome.

"Low-par" stock. Most of the advantages claimed for no-par stock can be attained by using capital stock of very low par value. It is increasingly common to establish a par value of $1 or perhaps $5, even though the stock is issued at a much higher rate. A low-par stock may also avoid the tax disadvantage previously mentioned in connection with no-par shares.

Stated capital and no-par value stock. Creditors of a corporation can look only to the corporation for payment of their claims and not to the stockholders personally. Consequently, creditors want assurance that the capital invested in a corporation by stockholders will not be withdrawn in the event the corporation encounters financial difficulties.

When all stock was of the par value type, the par value of the shares issued represented the stated capital or legal capital not available for dividends or withdrawal by stockholders. With the advent of no-par stock, state legislatures attempted to continue the protection of corporate creditors by designating all or part of the amount received by the corporation for its no-par shares as stated capital not subject to withdrawal.

Recording the issuance of no-par shares. Assume that a share of no-par stock is issued at a price of $25. How much of the $25 of contributed capital is stated capital to be recorded by a credit to the Capital Stock account? In some states the law requires that the entire amount received from issuance of no-par stock be credited to the Capital Stock account. Other states permit the board of directors of the issuing corporation to decide upon the stated value per share. Once the stated value has been established, it applies to all shares issued. A few states require that a specified minimum amount, such as $1 or $5 per share, be considered stated capital and credited to the Capital Stock account for each no-par share issued. The remaining portion of the amount received from the stockholders is credited to an account called Paid-in Capital in Excess of Stated Value. (An alternative title formerly in wide use and still frequently encountered is "Paid-in Surplus.")

Illustrative entries for issuance of no-par stock. Assume that a corporation is organized in a state which requires the entire proceeds from issuance of no-par shares to be treated as stated capital. The corporation obtains authorization to issue 10,000 shares of no-par stock, and makes a memorandum notation in the Capital Stock account to record this authorization. Six thousand shares are issued at a price of $12 each. The entry is as follows:

NOTE PRECEDING ASSUMPTION AS TO STATE LAW	*Cash* .... 72,000 *Capital Stock* .... *Issued 6,000 shares of no-par value stock at $12 each.*	72,000

After this entry has been posted, the ledger account for Capital Stock will appear as follows:

ENTIRE PROCEEDS IN CAPITAL STOCK ACCOUNT	*Capital Stock* ———————————————————— *(Authorized for issuance 10,000 shares of no-par value stock)* *Date* *(Issued 6,000 shares)* 72,000

As a second illustration, assume that the corporation was organized in a state which did not require all the proceeds from issuance of stock to be credited to the Capital Stock account. The board of directors passed a resolution setting the stated value per share at $5, and, as in the first illustration, a total of 6,000 shares was issued at $12 each. The journal entry to record the issuance is as follows:

<table>
<tr><td>NOTE
STATED
VALUE PER
SHARE</td><td>Cash .... 72,000</td><td></td></tr>
</table>

Cash *72,000*
    Capital Stock *30,000*
    Paid-in Capital in Excess of Stated Value ..   *42,000*
Issued 6,000 shares of no-par value stock at $12
each. Stated value set by directors at $5 per share.

The owners' equity section of the balance sheet will be as follows:

ONLY
PART OF
PROCEEDS
IN CAPITAL
STOCK
ACCOUNT

Stockholders' Equity

Capital stock, no par value, stated value $5 per share,
   authorized 10,000 shares, issued and outstanding 6,000
   shares *$30,000*
Paid-in capital in excess of stated value *42,000*

   Total contributed capital *$72,000*
Retained earnings *10,000*

   Total capital *$82,000*

Subscriptions to capital stock

The preceding illustrations were based on the assumption that a corporation issued its stock in exchange for cash or other property. In many cases, however, stock is sold by subscription contracts. The investor signs a contract promising to pay at a later date for a specified number of shares at an agreed price. In return, the corporation agrees to issue the shares when payment is received.

From the corporation's viewpoint, a subscription contract is an asset, a special type of account receivable. The asset is recorded by debiting an account called Subscriptions Receivable. This receivable will ordinarily be collected within a short time, so it is classified on the balance sheet as a current asset.

When a corporation receives a subscription contract it is acquiring an asset, and the increase in assets is matched by an increase in owners' equity. The credit side of the entry consists of a credit to Capital Stock Subscribed for the par value or stated value of the shares to be issued at a later date, and a credit to Paid-in Capital in Excess of Par Value or to Paid-in Capital in Excess of Stated Value if the subscription price is in excess of the par or stated value of the shares.

Both Subscriptions Receivable and Capital Stock Subscribed are temporary accounts. Subscriptions Receivable will be converted into cash when payment is received from the subscriber. At the time payment is received, the corporation will issue the shares of stock and will record this action by debiting Capital Stock Subscribed and crediting Capital Stock. If financial statements are prepared between the date of obtaining subscriptions and the date of issuing the stock, the Capital Stock Subscribed account will appear in the owners' equity section of the balance sheet.

In most states a person who signs a subscription contract immediately acquires the legal rights and privileges of a stockholder even though he does not receive a stock certificate until he makes payment. It is appropriate, therefore, that the stockholders' equity section of the balance sheet show the amount of stock which has been subscribed but not yet issued as of the balance sheet date.

If a corporation obtains subscriptions to both common stock and preferred stock, separate accounts should be used for each issue. For the issue of common stock the titles would be Subscriptions Receivable: Common Stock and Common Stock Subscribed. For the preferred stock the account titles would be Subscriptions Receivable: Preferred Stock and Preferred Stock Subscribed. If there are a large number of subscribers, the subscriptions receivable accounts may become control accounts supported by subscribers' ledgers containing an individual account with each subscriber.

Illustration of subscription transactions: par value stock. In the following illustrations of the sale of par value stock by subscription, it is assumed that a corporation has been authorized to issue 100,000 shares of $10 par value common stock.

Stock subscribed at par and subscriptions collected in full. In this first illustration, 10,000 shares are subscribed at par. The subscriptions are collected on the due date and the stock certificates are delivered at that time.

INVESTORS SUBSCRIBE

Subscriptions Receivable *100,000*
    Common Stock Subscribed *100,000*
Received subscriptions for 10,000 shares at par
of $10 a share.

When the subscriptions are collected and the certificates delivered, the following two entries will be made:

Cash 100,000
        Subscriptions Receivable 100,000
Collected subscriptions in full for 10,000 shares.

Common Stock Subscribed 100,000
        Common Stock 100,000
Issued certificates for 10,000 fully paid $10 par
value shares.

Stock subscribed at a premium. Some subscriptions collected in full, other subscriptions only partly collected. In this example, 10,000 shares of $10 par value stock are subscribed at a price of $15. Subscriptions for 6,000 shares are collected in full. A partial payment is received on the other 4,000 shares.

Subscriptions Receivable 150,000
        Common Stock Subscribed 100,000
        Paid-in Capital in Excess of Par 50,000
Received subscriptions for 10,000 shares of $10
par value stock at price of $15 a share.

When the subscriptions for 6,000 shares are collected in full, certificates for 6,000 shares will be issued. The following entries are made:

Cash 90,000
        Subscriptions Receivable 90,000
Collected subscriptions in full for 6,000 shares at
$15 each.

Common Stock Subscribed 60,000
        Common Stock 60,000
Issued certificates for 6,000 fully paid $10 par
value shares.

The subscriber to the remaining 4,000 shares paid only half of the amount of his subscription but promised to pay the remainder within a few days. Stock certificates will not be issued to him until his subscription is collected in full, but the partial collection is recorded by the following entry:

<table>
<tr><td>PARTIAL
COLLECTION
OF SUB-
SCRIPTION</td><td>

Cash *30,000*
    Subscriptions Receivable *30,000*
Collected partial payment on subscription for
4,000 shares.

</td></tr>
</table>

Illustration of subscription transactions: no-par value stock. The entries to record subscription transactions for no-par stock differ only slightly from those illustrated for par value stock. In the following two illustrations, it is assumed that the corporation has been authorized to issue 100,000 shares of no-par value common stock.

No stated value; entire proceeds treated as legal capital. In this illustration subscriptions are received for 10,000 shares of no-par stock at $20 a share.

<table>
<tr><td>SUBSCRIP-
TION
RECEIVED;
NO STATED
VALUE</td><td>

Subscriptions Receivable *200,000*
    Common Stock Subscribed *200,000*
Received subscriptions for 10,000 no-par shares
at $20 per share.

</td></tr>
</table>

When the subscriptions are collected, the stock certificates will be issued and the following entries made:

<table>
<tr><td>SUBSCRIP-
TIONS
COLLECTED;
NO-PAR
SHARES
ISSUED</td><td>

Cash *200,000*
    Subscriptions Receivable *200,000*
Collected in full subscriptions to 10,000 no-par
value shares at $20 each.

Common Stock Subscribed *200,000*
    Common Stock *200,000*
Issued certificates for 10,000 fully paid, no-par
value shares.

</td></tr>
</table>

Stated value $5 per share; subscriptions collected in full. Most corporations which intend to issue no-par stock choose to incorporate in a state which permits the establishment of stated value at considerably less than the issuance price. The entry to record the subscription of no-par shares then includes a credit to Paid-in Capital in Excess of Stated Value for the excess of the subscription price over the stated value. In the following illustration, it is assumed that the board of directors has established a stated value of $5 a share and that 10,000 shares are subscribed at a price of $20 each. The entry for the subscription is as follows:

<table>
<tr><td>SUBSCRIP-
TIONS
RECEIVED
FOR STATED-
VALUE
SHARES</td><td>Subscriptions Receivable 200,000
     Common Stock Subscribed   50,000
     Paid-in Capital in Excess of Stated Value   150,000
Received subscriptions for 10,000 shares of no-
par stock, stated value $5 a share, subscription
price $20 a share.</td></tr>
</table>

When the subscriptions are collected, the stock certificates will be issued and the following two entries will be made:

<table>
<tr><td>SUBSCRIP-
TIONS
COLLECTED;
STATED-
VALUE
SHARES
ISSUED</td><td>Cash 200,000
     Subscriptions Receivable   200,000
Collected in full subscriptions for 10,000 no-par
shares.

Common Stock Subscribed 50,000
     Common Stock   50,000
Issued certificates for 10,000 fully paid, no-par
value shares. Stated value $5 a share.</td></tr>
</table>

Defaults by subscribers to capital stock. When corporations sell stock by subscription the possibility of default by subscribers cannot be ignored. The terms of the subscription contract sometimes call for an immediate cash down payment, with the balance due at a later date, possibly in installments. If the subscriber fails to make the required payments, the disposition of the contract and of the amount paid in by the subscriber will depend upon the laws of the state and upon the policy of the corporation. In some cases the amount paid in by the subscriber is refunded (perhaps after deducting any expenses or losses in reselling the shares); in other cases the subscription contract may be amended to call for a reduced number of shares corresponding to the cash paid in before default; still another alternative under some state laws calls for a forfeiture by the subscriber of the amount paid in prior to the default.

If the corporation retains permanently any amounts paid in on defaulted subscriptions, this increment in capital should be credited to a separate owners' equity account with a descriptive title such as Capital from Defaulted Stock Subscriptions. The objective in recording all elements of corporate capital is a classification by source.

Special records of corporations

The financial page of today's newspaper reports that the most actively traded stocks on the New York Stock Exchange today were the following:

	Number of shares sold	*Closing price*
United States Steel	*92,100*	*$106*
General Electric	*62,500*	*99 1/4*
General Motors	*40,800*	*53 1/2*

Several significant facts concerning capital stock transactions are implicit in this brief news item. In the first place the three corporations listed did not buy or sell any shares of their stock today. The quantities of shares listed above were sold by existing stockholders to other investors. When a corporation first issues its stock, the transaction is between the corporation and the investor; once the stock is outstanding, any further stock transactions are between individuals and do not affect the corporation which issued the stock.[1] However, the corporation must be informed of each such stock transaction so that it can correct its records of stock ownership by crossing off the name of the former owner and adding the name of the new owner.

A second observation which might be drawn from the above news item is that a great volume of trading occurs each business day in the stocks of large corporations listed on the nation's stock exchanges. The availability of a ready market which permits the individual investor to convert his stockholdings into cash at any time is one of the principal reasons that corporations have become the dominant form of business organization.

Stock certificates. Ownership of a corporation is evidenced by stock certificates. A large corporation with stock listed on an organized stock exchange usually has many millions of shares outstanding and may have several hundred thousand stockholders. The number of shares changing hands on a typical business day may be as much as 50,000 to 100,000 shares, most of which is traded in 100-share lots. Standard Oil Company of New Jersey, for example, has about 200 million shares of stock outstanding. These shares are owned by approximately 400,000 investors. (The term *investor* as used in this discussion is meant to include investment groups or entities such as pension funds, investment clubs, and similar organizations, as well as individual investors.)

Even a small corporation is apt to have a considerable number of stock certificates to account for. It is essential, therefore, that detailed records be maintained showing exactly how many shares are outstanding and the names and addresses of the shareholders. These capital stock

---

[1] Occasionally a corporation may reacquire some of its own shares by purchase in the open market, but such transactions are relatively rare. Shares reacquired by a corporation are called *treasury stock* (see chap. 20).

records are in a process of continual change to reflect the purchase and sale of shares among the army of public investors.

A small corporation may order blank stock certificates from a printer, usually in a bound book with stubs similar to a checkbook. The certificates and the stubs are serially numbered by the printer, which aids the corporation in maintaining control over both the outstanding and the unissued certificates. At the time of issuance, a certificate is signed by the president and the secretary of the corporation, the number of shares represented by the certificate is filled in, and the certificate is delivered to a stockholder.

A stock certificate and the related stub are shown below on this page. This certificate is ready to be detached from the stub and delivered to the shareholder, Richard Warren. Notice that the certificate has been signed by the officers of the company and that the following information is listed on both the certificate and the stub:

1. Certificate number 901
2. Name of shareholder . . . . Richard Warren
3. Number of shares 100
4. Date issued . . . . January 10, 1962

The certificate is now detached from the stub and delivered to Richard Warren. The open stubs in the certificate book (stubs without any certificates attached) represent outstanding certificates. If a stockholder sells his shares, his certificate is returned to the company, canceled, and at-

Certificate No. 901

For -100- Shares
Of the Common Stock of
The Gold Cup Corporation

ISSUED TO:

Richard Warren

Date January 10, 1962

FROM WHOM TRANSFERRED:

--Original issue--

No. of Original Certificate	No. of Original Shares	No. of Shares Transferred

Certificate No. 901 -100- Shares

THE GOLD CUP CORPORATION

Par Value $5 per Share Common Stock
Incorporated under the Laws of the State of California

THIS IS TO CERTIFY that Richard Warren is the owner of -one hundred- fully paid and non-assessable shares of the common capital stock of The Gold Cup Corporation, transferable only on the books of this corporation by the said owner hereof in person or by attorney, upon surrender of this certificate properly endorsed. Witness the seal of the corporation and the signatures of its duly authorized officers on this -10th- day of -January- , 1962.

THE GOLD CUP CORPORATION INCORPORATED 1961

Murray Whitehall
President

Byron Bancroft
Secretary

tached to the corresponding stub in the stock certificate book. The total number of shares of stock outstanding at any time can be determined by adding up the number of shares listed on all the open stubs.

Stockholders' ledger. For a company with a large number of stockholders, it is not practicable to include in the general ledger an account with each stockholder. Instead a single controlling account entitled Common Stock is carried in the general ledger and a subsidiary stockholders' ledger with individual stockholders is maintained. (A ledger is usually in the form of a file of cards rather than a book when a great many separate accounts must be maintained.) In this stockholders' ledger, each stockholder's account shows the number of shares which he owns, the certificate numbers, and the dates of acquisition and sale. Entries are not made in dollars but in number of shares. Since these accounts relate to owners' equity, credit entries are used for shares acquired and debit entries represent shares sold.

The stockholders' ledger contains essentially the same information as the stock certificate book, but the arrangement of the information is in an alphabetical listing of stockholders rather than in the sequence of stock

SAMPLE
ACCOUNT
FROM
STOCK-
HOLDERS'
LEDGER

certificate numbers. One stockholder may own a number of certificates, acquired at various dates. His entire holdings would be summarized in his account in the stockholders' ledger. The account with Richard Warren (showing stock certificate No. 901 previously described) is as follows:

<table>
<tr><td colspan="9" align="center">**RICHARD WARREN**
304 Cheviot Drive
Los Angeles 64, California</td></tr>
<tr><td colspan="4" align="center">*Certificates canceled*</td><td colspan="4" align="center">*Certificates issued*</td><td rowspan="2" align="center">*Shares held*</td></tr>
<tr><td>*Date*</td><td>*Ref*</td><td>*Certificate no.*</td><td>*No. of shares*</td><td>*Date*</td><td>*Ref*</td><td>*Certificate no.*</td><td>*No. of shares*</td></tr>
<tr><td></td><td></td><td></td><td></td><td>*1962*
Jan. 10</td><td></td><td>*901*</td><td>*100*</td><td>*100*</td></tr>
</table>

Transfer of shares between investors. Assume that Richard Warren calls his stockbroker and orders him to sell at the going market price 50 of the 100 shares acquired on January 10. If the stock is that of a listed corporation, the sale will be completed within a few minutes, even though the buyer may be thousands of miles away. The seller will not even know the name of the buyer, as the transaction will be executed through the medium of a stock exchange with seller and buyer represented by different brokers. For the purpose of this illustration, assume that the purchaser of the 50 shares was James Weber of Chicago. To transfer the 50 shares sold, Warren will endorse his certificate for 100 shares on the reverse side, in the same manner that one endorses a check, and turn the certificate over to his broker, who will forward it to the issuing corporation.

When certificate No. 901 for 100 shares, endorsed by the seller, is presented to the corporation (or to its authorized transfer agent), this certificate will be canceled and attached to stub No. 901. Two new certificates for 50 shares each will then be prepared and issued, one certificate being returned to Warren to show that he still owns 50 shares and the other certificate being sent to James Weber, the stockholder who purchased the 50 shares sold by Warren. The ledger accounts for Richard Warren and James Weber in the stockholders' ledger will appear as follows after this transfer of 50 shares has been completed.

RICHARD WARREN
304 Cheviot Drive
Los Angeles 64, California

Certificates canceled				Certificates issued				Shares held
Date	Ref	Certificate no.	No. of shares	Date	Ref	Certificate no.	No. of shares	
1962 Aug. 1	TJ-1	901	100	1962 Jan. 10		901	100	100 000
				Aug. 1	TJ-1	1227	50	50

JAMES WEBER
9457 Elm Street
Chicago 16, Illinois

Certificates canceled				Certificates issued				Shares held
Date	Ref	Certificate no.	No. of shares	Date	Ref	Certificate no.	No. of shares	
				1962 Aug. 1	TJ-1	1228	50	50

The notations in the posting reference columns refer to the Stock Transfer Journal, which will be discussed in the following section.

Stock transfer journal. A stock transfer journal is used by some companies to provide a chronological record of capital stock transfers between shareholders. The following illustration indicates the form of a stock transfer journal or register.

Stock Transfer Journal									
Transferred from					Transferred to				
Date	Name	Certificate no.	No. of shares	Ref	Date	Name	Certificate no.	No. of shares

The transactions entered in this journal are posted to the accounts with individual stockholders in the stockholders' ledger. Transfers of stock from one person to another do not change the total amount of stock outstanding; consequently, no posting is made from the stock transfer journal to the control account for capital stock in the general ledger. Small corporations with very few capital stock transactions may consider a stock transfer journal unnecessary. As an alternative procedure, the stockholders' ledger can be posted directly from the stubs of the stock certificate book.

Stock transfer agent and stock registrar. The large corporation with thousands of stockholders and a steady flow of stock transfers usually turns over the function of maintaining capital stock records to an independent stock transfer agent and a stock registrar. A bank or trust company serves as stock transfer agent and another bank acts as the stock registrar. When certificates are to be transferred from one owner to another, the certificates are sent to the transfer agent, who cancels them, makes the necessary entries in the stockholders' ledger, and signs new certificates which are forwarded to the stock registrar. The function of the registrar is to prevent any improper issuance of stock certificates. To accomplish this objective, the bank acting as registrar maintains records showing the total number of shares outstanding at all times. The use of an independent stock transfer agent and a stock registrar is an excellent control device, which eliminates the possibility that a dishonest officer or employee of a corporation might issue stock certificates for cash without making any entry in the records.

Minute book. A corporate minute book consists of a narrative record of all actions taken at official meetings of the corporation's board of directors and of its stockholders. Typical of the actions described in the minute book are the declaration of dividends by the board of directors, the authorization of important transactions such as the obtaining of bank loans or the purchase of plant and equipment, the setting of officers' salaries, and the adoption of retirement plans or pension agreements.

The company's accountant is interested in the minute book because it provides information which must be recorded in the accounting records. Audits of a corporation by certified public accountants will always include a careful reading of the minute book to acquaint the independent auditor with company policies, and as a means of verifying that accounting entries for such transactions as dividend declarations were properly authorized.

The minutes of stockholders' meetings are often kept in a separate section of the same book used for minutes of directors' meetings. At the annual meeting of stockholders, approval may be obtained by majority vote for such important corporate actions as the issuance of additional securities or the adoption of an incentive-type program of management compensation.

QUESTIONS

1. In theory, a corporation may sell its stock for an amount greater or less than par value; in practice, stock is seldom if ever issued for less than par. Explain the significance of par value and why it is impractical to issue shares for less than par.

2. What are the advantages and disadvantages of the use of no-par capital stock?

3. When stock is issued by a corporation in exchange for assets other than cash, the accountant faces the problem of determining the dollar amount at which to record the transaction. Discuss the factors he should consider and explain their significance.

4. What is the nature of amounts on a corporate balance sheet labeled "paid-in capital in excess of par value"? Why is this title preferable to the older "capital surplus" or "paid-in surplus"?

5. What is the classification (asset, liability, stockholders' equity, or expense) of each of the following accounts:

a. Subscriptions receivable: common
b. Organization costs
c. Capital stock, common
d. Retained earnings

e. Capital stock subscribed: preferred
f. Premium on common stock
g. Discount on preferred stock
h. Federal and state income taxes

6. Explain the following terms:

a. Stock transfer agent
b. Stockholders' ledger
c. Underwriter

d. Stock transfer journal
e. Minute book
f. Stock registrar

PROBLEMS

Group A

18A-1. The stockholders' equity section of the Bartlett Corporation's balance sheet at the close of the current year is given below.

BARTLETT CORPORATION
Stockholders' Equity
December 31, Current Year

$2.75 preferred stock, $50 par value, authorized 10,000 shares:

Issued	$160,000	
Subscribed	120,000	$280,000

Common stock, no par, $20 stated value, authorized 20,000 shares:

Issued	$166,000	
Subscribed	36,000	202,000

Paid-in capital in excess of par or stated value:

On preferred	$28,000	
On common	20,200	48,200
Retained earnings		(80,000)
Total stockholders' equity		$450,200

Among the assets of the corporation appear the following items: subscriptions receivable, preferred: $55,200; subscriptions receivable, common: $24,120.

Instructions. On the basis of this information, write a brief answer to the following questions, showing any necessary supporting computations.

a. How many shares of preferred and common have been issued?

b. How many shares of preferred and common have been subscribed?

c. What was the average price per share received by the corporation on its preferred stock?

d. What was the average price per share received by the corporation on its common stock?

e. What is the average amount per share that subscribers of preferred stock have yet to pay on their subscriptions?

f. What is the total contributed capital of the Bartlett Corporation?

g. What is the total legal or stated value of its capital stock?

h. What is the average amount per share that common stock subscribers have already paid on their subscriptions? (Assume common subscribed at $22.)

18A-2. Janes Corporation was organized on August 1 of the current year, with the following capital structure: authorized 1,000 shares of 6%, cumulative, $100 par, preferred stock and 20,000 shares of $30 par value common stock. A summary of the transactions during August appears below.

Aug. 1.   Subscriptions were received for 500 shares of preferred at 103 1/2, and one-half the subscription price was received in cash.

Aug. 5.   Received subscriptions for 4,000 shares of common at $48; one-fourth of the subscription price received immediately in cash.

Aug. 10.   Paid legal fees in connection with drawing up articles of incorporation and filing of corporate charter. Attorneys agreed to accept $800 in cash and 25 shares of common stock.

Aug. 18.   Persons who had subscribed to 3,000 shares of common stock on August 5 paid the balance of their subscription in cash, and the shares were issued.

Aug. 22. Persons who had subscribed to 240 shares of preferred on August 1 paid their subscriptions in full, in cash, and the shares were issued.

Instructions

a. Record the above transactions in general journal form.

b. Post to T accounts.

c. Prepare a balance sheet for Janes Corporation as of August 31.

18A-3. The Kennedy Manufacturing Company was organized on September 1 of the current year. On September 30 its capital structure was as follows:

5% preferred stock, $100 par, cumulative, authorized 15,000 shares .....　**—0—**

$2 convertible preferred stock, no par, stated value $50, authorized

　20,000 shares ....　**—0—**

Common stock, no par, authorized 50,000 shares, issued 15,000 ....　**$300,000**

During the next three months the corporation completed the following transactions:

Oct. 5. Issued 2,000 shares of common stock to Kennedy, one of the promoters. Of this, 200 shares were in payment for his services and expenses incurred by him in organizing the company. The remaining 1,800 shares were in payment for an inventory of materials reasonably valued at $30,000, and for patent rights which the board of directors agrees are worth $6,000.

Oct. 10. Sold 4,000 shares of 5% preferred stock at 101 1/2.

Oct. 13. Received subscriptions to 7,000 shares of convertible preferred stock. Subscribers paid $13 per share (one-fourth of the subscription price) in cash and agreed to pay the balance before December 31.

Nov. 8. The company offered a combination of two shares of convertible preferred and one share of common stock at $120 for the three-share package. A total of $240,000 was received from the sale of shares in this manner.

Dec. 10. Subscribers to 6,500 shares of convertible preferred paid the balance of their subscriptions, and the shares were issued.

Dec. 20. Sold 7,200 shares of common stock at 19 1/2.

Dec. 28. Sold 1,000 shares of 5% preferred stock at 98.

Dec. 31. Subscribers to 500 shares of convertible preferred stock defaulted on their subscription contract. Under the laws of the state, any amount paid in is forfeited to the corporation.

Instructions. Prepare in general journal form the entries necessary to record these transactions.

18A-4. The following accounts appear on the ledger of the Maynard Corporation on January 1, 1962:

6% preferred stock, $100 par, authorized 10,000 shares ....　**—0—**

5% convertible preferred stock, $100 par, authorized 10,000 shares .....　**$600,000**

Common stock, no par, stated value $10 per share, authorized 80,000 shares　**400,000**

Paid-in capital in excess of par or stated value ....　**85,000**

Retained earnings, January 1, 1962 ....　**687,400**

Events relating to the stockholders' equity occurred during 1962 as given below.

(1) The company's 1962 net income after taxes was $154,000.

(2) On July 1, the holders of 4,000 shares of convertible preferred stock exercised the option to convert their shares into common stock at the ratio of six shares of common for each share of preferred. Common stock had a market value of $30 per share on June 30.

(3) On March 1 the company received subscriptions for 1,000 shares of its 6% preferred at $102 per share; one-half of the subscription price was received immediately in cash and the other half was to be paid on September 30, 1962.

(4) On September 30, subscribers to 900 shares of preferred paid the balance of their subscriptions and the shares were issued. Subscribers to 100 shares defaulted. The subscription contract states that upon default the shares not fully paid will be sold for the best price possible; the difference between the proceeds of the sale and the amount originally subscribed will be deducted from amounts paid in on the shares; and the balance will be refunded to the original subscribers.

(5) On November 30 the 100 shares of preferred in default were sold for $98 per share. A liability should be set up for the amount due the original subscribers, but no payment had been made by December 31, 1962.

(6) The following dividend payments were made during the year:

July 1. One-half year's dividend on convertible preferred.

Dec. 31. One-half year's dividend on convertible preferred.

$0.50 per share on 100 shares of preferred sold on November 30

$1.50 per share on 900 shares of preferred fully paid by September 30

$2.00 per share on all common stock issued at December 31

Instructions

a. Prepare in general journal form the entries necessary to record the events described in (2), (3), (4), and (5).

b. Prepare a schedule showing the determination of the balance of retained earnings at December 31, 1962.

c. Prepare in good form the stockholders' equity section of the balance sheet as of December 31, 1962.

Group B

18B-1. *Case A.* The Raymar Corporation has agreed to issue 20,000 shares of common stock in exchange for a manufacturing plant having an agreed valuation of $500,000.

Instructions. Give the journal entry that should be made to record this transaction under each of the following assumptions:

a. The stock has a $25 par value.

b. The stock has a $1 par value.

c. The stock has a $40 par value.

d. The stock is no par, with a stated value of $10.

e. The stock is no par, having no stated value.

Case B. Several years later the Raymar Corporation issued 1,000 shares of its $25 par value common in exchange for certain patent rights. The patent rights were entered on the books at $25,000. At the time Raymar common stock was quoted on the over-the-counter market at "35 bid and 37 asked," that is, sellers were offering a given quantity of the stock at $37 per share, and buyers were offering to buy certain quantities at $35 per share.

Instructions. Comment on the company's accounting treatment of this transaction. Write a brief statement explaining whether you agree or disagree, and why. What is the essential difference between the evidence available to the accountant as a basis for his record in case *A* and the evidence available in case *B*?

18B-2. The Simpson Corporation was organized on March 1 of the current year. The company is legally authorized to issue 10,000 shares of $3 preferred stock, no par, stated value $50 per share, and 35,000 shares of no-par common, having no stated value. The transactions given below took place during March and April:

Mar. 1.   Issued 2,000 shares of preferred for $52 per share.

Mar. 10.   Received subscriptions for 4,000 shares of preferred at $54 per share, and one-half the subscription price in cash.

Mar. 12.   Issued 3,000 shares of common stock at $28 per share.

Mar. 15.   Received subscriptions for 10,000 shares of common at $30 per share.

Apr. 10.   Subscribers to 2,400 shares of preferred paid the balance of their subscriptions in cash and shares were issued.

Apr. 18.   Received from attorneys a bill for $3,200 covering legal services in connection with the organization of the corporation. In lieu of payment, they agreed to accept 100 shares of common stock.

Apr. 19.   Issued 12,000 shares of common in full payment for land and building appraised at $375,000, of which 10% applies to the land.

Apr. 25.   Received 25% of the subscription price from March 15 subscribers.

Instructions
a. Record the above transactions in general journal form.
b. Post entries to T accounts.
c. Prepare a balance sheet for the Simpson Corporation as of April 30.

18B-3. Metal Products Company received its charter on April 1 of the current year, and was authorized to issue 10,000 shares of $50 par value common stock.

On April 3, subscriptions were received for 3,000 shares at 55.

On April 10, the company issued 1,300 shares in exchange for land worth $15,000 and a building valued at $87,000. The building was subject to a $30,000, 5% mortgage due in 15 years.

On April 20, subscribers for 1,700 shares paid their subscription contracts in full, and subscribers for 1,200 shares paid 40% of the subscription price.

On April 30, the company acquired an important patent in order to protect its manufacturing process. The inventor, Kovars, was given 1,500 shares of stock for his patent rights, and it was agreed that he would be employed by Metal Products Company at a salary of $960 per month. In lieu of his salary for the month of May, Kovars agreed to accept an additional 16 shares of stock. The company also agreed to issue to Kovars 3,600 shares of its common stock in exchange for 1,800 shares of Amalgamated Titanium Corporation stock owned by him. The current market value of the Titanium stock is $120 per share.

By May 15 it was clear that, as of April 3, subscribers to 100 shares of stock had defaulted on their subscription contract. Since nothing had been paid on this subscription, the company decided to cancel the agreement.

Instructions. Prepare in general journal form the entries necessary to record the above transactions on the books of the Metal Products Company.

18B-4. At the end of the current year, the bookkeeper has prepared the following state-ment of stockholders' equity for the Jayde Products Corporation:

JAYDE PRODUCTS CORPORATION
Capital
December 31, Current Year

Preferred stock, 5,000 shares	$317,300
Preferred stock, no par, issued 2,400 shares	180,000
Common stock, par value $25	300,000
Surplus	161,500
Total capital	$958,800

The company has two classes of preferred stock. It is authorized to issue 5,000 shares of 5 1/2%, $100 par value, preferred, and 8,000 shares of $4, no par, preferred, stated value $75. To date 2,000 shares of the 5 1/2% preferred have been sold for cash at 102 per share, and 2,200 shares have been subscribed at 103 per share. One-half of the subscription price has thus far been received by the company. The $4 preferred was issued in exchange for property. At the date of acquisition the board of directors, after careful investigation, estimated that the fair market value of the property was $200,000.

Common stock authorization is 20,000 shares, of which 12,000 shares were sold for cash and 400 shares were given to promoters in settlement of a charge for $10,000 covering legal costs and services in organizing the company. The bookkeeper states that the corporation realized a gain by issuing 4,000 shares of its common stock at a price that was $6 per share in excess of par value, and that this gain is included in the surplus balance. The company has had a net income during its lifetime of $225,000 and has paid $87,500 in dividends.

Instructions
a. Prepare in good form a revised version of the stockholders' equity sec-tion of the balance sheet.
b. Some of the changes you should make in the bookkeeper's figures will increase or decrease the net assets reported by this company. Prepare a schedule showing the amount of the increase or decrease resulting from your corrections and the source of the change, that is, the asset or liability accounts and amounts involved.

19

Corporations: retained earnings, dividends, and reserves

Retained earnings (earned surplus)

In preceding chapters the term *retained earnings* has been used to describe that portion of stockholders' equity derived from profitable operation of a corporation. *Earned surplus,* however, is the traditional term for this element of owners' equity. Because of the misleading connotations of the word "surplus," the American Institute of Certified Public Accountants has recommended that use of the term be discontinued. In accordance with this recommendation, a strong trend has developed to use the phrase retained earnings in place of earned surplus in corporate balance sheets. However, earned surplus is a well-entrenched term and no doubt will continue in use for many years. In this chapter, it is convenient to make considerable use of the word surplus (coupled with various modifiers) in order to trace the changes in accounting practice leading up to today's form of corporate balance sheet.

Early usage of the term surplus. The balance sheets prepared by many corporations in earlier days of corporate accounting listed only two items in the owners' equity section, capital stock and surplus. The capital stock was properly shown at par value, but the item of surplus often included capital derived from a variety of sources. Among these sources were premium on capital stock, "gains" from treasury stock transactions,[1] donated capital, increases in capital from arbitrary write-up of assets, and retained earnings. A surplus account of $1 million on one balance sheet might represent earnings of that amount; on another balance sheet a surplus account of $1 million might be the net balance resulting from

---

[1] Treasury stock consists of shares of a corporation's own stock which have been issued, fully paid, and reacquired but not canceled. Treasury shares may be held indefinitely or may be reissued again at any time. Problems relating to treasury stock are discussed in chap. 20.

combining $2 million in paid-in capital with $1 million of an operating deficit. In recognition of the confusion caused by such practices, accountants began to separate surplus into several items classified by source.

Capital surplus and earned surplus. When accountants first began to classify surplus by source, it was common for a balance sheet to contain the two separate items of capital surplus and earned surplus. The term *capital surplus* was used by some companies in a narrow sense to mean contributed capital in excess of par or stated value; other companies, however, included in capital surplus any nonoperating gains and losses and also any increases in capital arising from arbitrary write-up of asset values. Earned surplus designated retained earnings in their entirety, or in other cases retained earnings from operating transactions only. Capital surplus still appears on a few published financial statements, but the term is no longer in good standing.

Paid-in surplus. In an effort to eliminate the confusion and uncertainty as to the meaning of capital surplus, accountants introduced the term *paid-in surplus,* meaning surplus arising from transactions with stockholders. Among the several sources of paid-in surplus are: (1) premiums on par value stock, (2) excess of issuance price over stated value of no-par stock, (3) excess of proceeds from reissuance of treasury stock over the cost of these shares, (4) purchase and retirement of shares at a cost less than the issuance price, and (5) donations of property to the corporation.

A separate ledger account should be used for each specific type of paid-in surplus. Examples of the appropriate ledger titles are Premium on Capital Stock, Additional Paid-in Capital in Excess of Stated Value, Paid-in Capital from Treasury Stock Transactions, Paid-in Capital from Retirement of Stock, and Surplus from Donated Property. This last account usually arises when a city or a civic organization donates land or other property as a means of persuading corporations to locate in the area.

Is paid-in capital available for dividends? Although the laws of many states make it legally possible to declare dividends from paid-in capital, this is rarely done. Whenever a corporation does declare a dividend from any source other than retained earnings, it is obligated to disclose to stockholders that the dividend is of a liquidating nature, representing a return of paid-in capital rather than a distribution of earnings.

Unrealized appreciation of assets. A generation ago it was not unusual during periods of rising prices for corporations to write up the carrying value of plant and equipment from cost to a higher appraised value. The purpose of this departure from the cost basis of asset valuation was usually to present a more impressive balance sheet and thereby aid in making sales of additional capital stock or in obtaining credit. The write-ups were sometimes recorded by increasing earned surplus by the amount of the increase in asset values. Accountants generally opposed this maneuver and urged that if a write-up were to be made, it should be recorded in a manner that would disclose what had happened. An entry such as the following would make clear that the increment in owners' equity was based on an appraisal rather than on profitable operations.

Land	*100,000*	
Buildings and Equipment	*200,000*	
Surplus from Appraisal: Buildings		*300,000*
To increase the carrying value of fixed assets in accordance with an appraisal of current replacement cost.		

Other account titles suggested for the increment in owners' equity resulting from asset write-ups were Revaluation Surplus and Unrealized Appreciation from Revaluation of Assets. The objective of accountants in devising these titles was to prevent the inclusion of such unrealized increments in capital from being disguised as earned surplus. The term *unrealized,* as applied to appreciation of fixed assets, means that no sale of the property has occurred with cash, receivables, or other assets being received as objective evidence of the increment in value.

Many of the companies which made these arbitrary write-ups during the 1920s also made arbitrary write-downs during the deflation of the 1930s. Since 1940 there has been little or no writing-up of assets, as accountants have given general support to the use of cost as a basis for valuation of plant and equipment.

Retained earnings and deficits. Retained earnings is a historical concept, representing the accumulated net earnings minus dividends paid or declared from the date of incorporation to the present. Each year the Income Summary account is closed by transferring the net income or net loss into the Retained Earnings account. If we assume that all types of gain and loss are cleared through the Income Summary account, the only entries in the Retained Earnings account will be the periodic transfer from the Income Summary account and the debit entries for dividends.

In successful corporations the Retained Earnings account normally has a credit balance, but if total losses should exceed total profits the Retained Earnings account will acquire a debit balance. This debit amount will be listed in the balance sheet under the title Deficit and will be deducted from the total of the capital stock and paid-in surplus, as shown in the accompanying illustration:

Stockholders' Equity	
Capital stock, $10 par value, authorized and issued	
100,000 shares	*$1,000,000*
Paid-in surplus	*1,000,000*
Total contributed capital	*$2,000,000*
Deduct: deficit	*600,000*
Total capital	*$1,400,000*

Dividends

The term *dividend,* when used by itself, is generally understood to mean a distribution of cash by a corporation to its stockholders. The dividend is stated as a specific amount per share as, for example, a dividend of $1 per share. It follows that the amount received by each stockholder is in proportion to the number of shares owned.

Dividends are occasionally paid in assets other than cash. In times of war, for example, when various types of merchandise were very scarce, some distilleries distributed merchandise dividends to their stockholders. When a corporation goes out of existence (particularly a small corporation with only a few stockholders), it may choose to distribute noncash assets to its owners rather than to convert all assets into cash. In theory, a corporation which is short of cash might pay a dividend by issuing promissory notes to its stockholders calling for payment at some future date. In practice, however, such dividends almost never occur, because corporations which are short of cash are usually careful not to incur any unnecessary liabilities.

A dividend may also be paid in the form of additional shares of a company's own stock. This type of distribution is called a *stock dividend.* Stock dividends are of great practical importance and also of much theoretical interest. They will be discussed at length later in this chapter.

A *liquidating* dividend occurs when a corporation returns to stockholders all or part of their paid-in capital investment. Liquidating dividends are usually paid only when a corporation is going out of existence or is making a permanent reduction in the size of its operations. Normally dividends are paid from the profits of a corporation, and the recipient of a dividend is entitled to assume that the dividend represents a distribution of profits unless he is specifically notified that the dividend is a return of invested capital.

Dividends are paid only through action by the board of directors. The board has full discretion to declare a dividend or to refrain from doing so. Once the declaration of a dividend has been announced, the obligation to pay the dividend is a current liability of the corporation and cannot be rescinded.

Cash dividends. The prospect of receiving cash dividends is a principal reason for investing in the stocks of corporations. An increase or decrease in the amount of dividends will usually cause an immediate rise or fall in the market price of the company's stock. Stockholders are keenly interested in prospects for future dividends and as a group are generally strongly in favor of more generous dividend payments by the corporations in which they hold stock. The board of directors, on the other hand, is apt to be primarily concerned with the long-run growth and financial strength of the corporation; it may prefer to restrict dividends to a minimum in order to conserve cash for purchase of plant and equipment or for other needs of the company. The so-called "growth companies" generally plow back into the business most of their earnings and pay very little in cash dividends.

The preceding discussion of dividends has indicated the requirements for the payment of an ordinary cash dividend. These requirements are:

1. Retained earnings. Since dividends represent a distribution of earnings to stockholders, the theoretical maximum for dividends is the total net profit (after income taxes) of the company. As a practical matter, most corporations limit dividends to somewhere near 50% of earnings, in the belief that a major portion of the profits must be retained in the business if the company is to grow and to keep pace with its competitors.

2. An adequate cash position. The fact that the company has earned large profits does not mean that it will have a large amount of cash in the bank. Earnings may have been invested in new plant and equipment, or in paying off debts, or in stocking a larger inventory. There is no necessary relationship between the balance in the Retained Earnings account and the balance in the Cash account. The traditional expression of "paying dividends out of surplus (or retained earnings)" is misleading. Cash dividends can be paid only "out of" cash. Before the board of directors declares a dividend it must decide whether the cash position is sufficiently strong to permit a distribution to stockholders and also to meet the company's payroll and its obligations to creditors.

3. Dividend action by the board of directors. Even though the company's profits are substantial and its cash position seemingly satisfactory, dividends are not paid automatically. A positive action by the directors is necessary to declare a dividend. There are some legal restraints to prevent a board of directors from unreasonably refusing to declare dividends, but by and large, dividends are paid only when the board of directors considers it advisable to do so.

Dividend dates. Four significant dates are involved in the distribution of a dividend. These dates are:

1. Date of declaration. On the day on which the dividend is declared by the board of directors, a liability to make the payment comes into existence. The Retained Earnings account is reduced and a liability account, Dividends Payable, is created.

2. Date of record. The date of record always follows the date of declaration, usually by a period of three or four weeks, and is always stated in the dividend declaration. In order to be eligible to receive the dividend, a person must be listed as a stockholder in the company's capital stock records on the date of record.

3. Ex-dividend date. The ex-dividend date is significant for investors in companies with stocks traded on the stock exchanges. To permit the compilation of the list of stockholders as of the record date, it is customary for the stock to go "ex-dividend" three business days before the date of

record. A stock is said to be selling ex-dividend on the day that it loses the right to receive the latest declared dividend. A person who buys the stock before the ex-dividend date is entitled to receive the dividend; conversely, a stockholder who sells his shares in the period between the date of declaration and the ex-dividend date is selling his right to receive the dividend as well as the stock itself.

4. Date of payment. The declaration of a dividend always includes announcement of the date of payment as well as the date of record. Usually the date of payment comes from two to four weeks after the date of record. The act of payment cancels the liability created by the prior declaration of the dividend.

Entries for declaration and payment of a dividend. As an illustration of the entries required for the declaration and later payment of a cash dividend, let us assume that on April 1 the board of directors of the Exposition Corporation declares the regular quarterly dividend of $1 per share on the 40,000 shares of $100 par, 4% preferred stock outstanding and also a dividend of 50 cents per share on the 100,000 shares of outstanding common stock. Separate accounts are used for the preferred and common dividends, as shown by the following entries:

DIVIDENDS DECLARED AND . . .

Apr.	*1*	*Dividends on Preferred Stock*	*40,000*	
		Dividends on Common Stock	*50,000*	
		Dividends Payable on Preferred Stock		*40,000*
		Dividends Payable on Common Stock		*50,000*
		Declared dividend of $1 on preferred stock and 50 cents on common stock, payable May 15 to stockholders of record as of May 1.		

. . . DIVIDENDS PAID

May	*15*	*Dividends Payable on Preferred Stock*	*40,000*	
		Dividends Payable on Common Stock	*50,000*	
		Cash		*90,000*
		Paid the dividends declared on April 1.		

The Dividends on Preferred Stock account and the Dividends on Common Stock account will be closed into Retained Earnings at the end of the year. These dividend accounts are not expense accounts and, consequently, are *not* closed into the Income Summary account. The declaration of a dividend creates a liability, Dividends Payable, and reduces the owners' equity by an equal amount. The decrease in owners' equity could be recorded by debiting the Retained Earnings account directly at the time of the dividend declaration, but it is convenient to use a Dividends account to summarize the regular quarterly dividends and any special dividends for the year. In terms of account classification, the Dividends on Preferred Stock account and the Dividends on Common Stock account are regarded as "negative" owners' equity accounts, similar to a drawing account in the ledger of a single proprietorship or partnership.

Regular and special dividends. Many corporations establish a regular quarterly or annual dividend rate and pay this same amount for a period of years regardless of the year-to-year changes in earnings. Such a policy gives a higher investment quality to a company's stock. A strong cash position is necessary if a company is to be prepared to make regular dividend payments regardless of current changes in the level of business. Such a dividend policy also indicates that a company is distributing only a portion of its earnings; the portion retained permits continued growth and also provides a cushion for dividend payments in less profitable years.

If profits increase but the increase is regarded as a temporary condition, the corporation may decide to pay a "special dividend" in addition to the regular dividend. The implication of a special dividend is that the company is making no commitments as to a permanent increase in the amount of dividends to be paid. Of course, even a "regular" dividend may be reduced or discontinued at any time, but well-financed companies which have long-established regular dividend rates are not likely to omit or reduce dividend payments except in extreme emergencies.

Dividends on preferred stock. As indicated in Chapter 17, a preferred stock carries a stated annual dividend rate, such as $5 per share, or 5% of par value. Under no circumstances does a corporation pay more than the required dividend on preferred stock. This policy of not permitting the preferred stockholder to share in any unusually large profits suggests that the corporation views the preferred stockholder only as a supplier of capital rather than as a full-fledged owner in the traditional sense of the word.

Dividends on preferred stocks are not paid unless declared by the board of directors. Since most preferred stocks are of the cumulative variety, any omitted dividend must be made up before any payment can be made to the common. Dividends in arrears on preferred stock do not constitute a liability of the corporation but should be disclosed by a footnote to the balance sheet.

Stock dividends. *Stock dividend* is an important but confusing term which requires close attention. It is confusing because all dividends are distributions to stockholders and the word "stock dividend" may suggest to some people merely a dividend on capital stock. A stock dividend is a prorata distribution of additional shares to a company's stockholders; in brief, the dividend consists of shares of stock rather than cash. Perhaps a better term for a stock dividend would be a "dividend payable in capital stock," but the expression "stock dividend" is too firmly entrenched to be easily replaced. Most stock dividends consist of common stock distributed to holders of common stock, and this discussion will be limited to this type of stock dividend.

What is the effect of a stock dividend on the company's financial position? Why does a corporation choose to pay a dividend in shares of stock rather than in cash? Would you as an investor prefer to receive a stock dividend or a cash dividend? These questions are closely related, and a careful analysis of the nature of a stock dividend should provide a basis for answering them.

A cash dividend reduces the assets of a corporation and reduces the owners' equity by the same amount. A stock dividend, on the other hand, causes no change in assets and no change in the total amount of the owners' equity. The only effect of a stock dividend on the accounts is to transfer a portion of the retained earnings into the Capital Stock and Paid-in Surplus accounts. In other words, a stock dividend merely "reshuffles" the owners' equity accounts, increasing the permanent capital accounts and decreasing the Retained Earnings account without any change being made in the total amount of capital.

A corporation does not reduce its assets or its total capital by paying a stock dividend. A stockholder who receives a stock dividend will possess an increased number of shares, but his equity in the company will be no larger than before. Consequently, a stock dividend is not considered as income to the stockholder.

An example may make this fundamental point clear. Assume that a corporation with 800 shares of stock is owned equally by James Adams and Frank Barnes, each owning 400 shares of stock. The corporation pays a stock dividend of 25% and distributes 200 additional shares (25% of 800 shares), with 100 shares going to each of the two stockholders. Adams and Barnes now hold 500 shares apiece, but each still owns one-half of the business. The corporation has not changed; its assets and liabilities and its total capital are exactly the same as before the dividend. From the stockholder's viewpoint, the ownership of 500 shares out of a total of 1,000 outstanding shares represents no more than did the ownership of 400 shares out of a total of 800 shares previously outstanding.

Assume that the market value of this stock was $10 per share prior to the stock dividend. Total market value of all the outstanding shares was, therefore, 800 times $10, or $8,000. What would be the market value per share and in total after the additional 200 dividend shares were issued? The 1,000 shares now outstanding should have the same total market value as the previously outstanding 800 shares, because the "pie" has merely been divided into more but smaller pieces. The price per share should have dropped from $10 to $8, and the aggregate market value of outstanding shares would consequently be computed as 1,000 shares times $8, or $8,000. Whether the market price per share will, in actuality, decrease in proportion to the change in number of outstanding shares is another matter, for market prices are subject to many conflicting influences, some as unpredictable as the state of mind of investors.

Reasons for paying stock dividends. Many reasons have been given for the increasing popularity of stock dividends. Some of them seem to be valid arguments; others appear rather feeble. The following reasons have been frequently advanced:

1. To conserve cash. When the trend of profits is favorable but cash is needed for expansion, a stock dividend may be an appropriate device for "passing along the profits" to stockholders without weakening the corporation's cash position.

2. To reduce the market price of a corporation's stock to a more convenient trading range by increasing the number of shares outstanding. This objective is usually present in large stock dividends (25 to 100% or more). A stock dividend which doubles the number of outstanding shares is much the same as a stock split, which will be discussed later in this chapter.

3. To avoid income tax on stockholders. Stock dividends are not considered as income to the recipients; therefore, no income tax is levied.

4. To increase the total amount of cash dividends to be paid without increasing the rate per share.

5. To mollify stockholders when poor operating results do not permit the payment of cash dividends. Since many stockholders do not understand the nature of stock dividends, they may be content to accept additional shares in lieu of cash.

6. To avoid giving the impression of excessive profits, which might result if the cash dividends and the market price per share reached very high levels.

Some critics of stock dividends argue that a stock dividend is not really a dividend at all. These critics say that a company which cannot afford to pay a cash dividend should pay no dividends, rather than trying to deceive stockholders by increasing the number of outstanding shares. The popularity of stock dividends, according to such critics, is based largely upon irrational behavior by stockholders.

Regardless of the merit of the arguments for and against stock dividends, most stockholders welcome these distributions. In many cases a small stock dividend has not caused the market price per share to decline appreciably; consequently, the increase in the number of shares in the hands of each stockholder has, regardless of logic, resulted in an increase in the total market value of his holdings.

Entries to record stock dividends. Assume that a corporation had the following stockholders' equity accounts on December 15, 1962, just prior to declaring a 10% stock dividend:

STOCK-
HOLDERS'
EQUITY
BEFORE
STOCK
DIVIDEND

Stockholders' Equity	
Common stock, $10 par value, authorized 30,000 shares,	
issued and outstanding 10,000 shares	*$100,000*
Paid-in capital in excess of par	*50,000*
Retained earnings	*200,000*
Total capital	*$350,000*

STOCK
DIVIDEND
DECLARED;
NOTE USE
OF MARKET
PRICE
Assume also that the closing market price of the stock on December 15, 1962, was $30 a share. The company declares and issues a 10% stock dividend, consisting of 1,000 shares (10% × 10,000 = 1,000). The entry to record the declaration of the dividend is as follows:

```
1962
Dec. 15    Retained Earnings .......................... 30,000
                Stock Dividends Payable ...............         10,000
                Paid-in Capital from Stock Dividends .....       20,000
           To record declaration of a 10% stock dividend con-
           sisting of 1,000 shares of $10 par value. To be dis-
           tributed on February 9, 1963, to stockholders of
           record on January 15, 1963. Amount of retained
           earnings capitalized was based on market price of
           $30 a share on December 15, 1962.
```

The entry to record distribution of the dividend shares is as follows:

```
1963
Feb.  9    Stock Dividends Payable ..................... 10,000
                Capital Stock .........................         10,000
           To record payment of stock dividend by distribu-
           tion of 1,000 shares.
```

Notice that the amount of retained earnings transferred to permanent capital accounts by the above entries is not the par value of the new shares, but the *fair market value* as indicated by the market price prevailing at the date of record. The Committee on Accounting Procedure of the American Institute of Certified Public Accountants has recommended that the amount of retained earnings to be capitalized for small stock dividends be equal to the fair market value of the shares previously outstanding. The Securities and Exchange Commission has also approved this method. The reasoning behind these recommendations can more conveniently be explored in advanced accounting courses. The amount of retained earnings to be capitalized is transferred to the Capital Stock and Paid-in Capital from Stock Dividends accounts.

The procedure for recording a stock dividend is essentially the same for both par value shares and no-par value stock. For both types of stock the fair market value of the stock is used to determine the amount of retained earnings to be capitalized. In cases involving no-par stock, the Capital Stock account is credited with the stated value of the dividend shares and the Paid-in Capital from Stock Dividends account is credited with the remainder of the amount transferred from the Retained Earnings account.

The Stock Dividends Payable account is not a liability, because there is no obligation to distribute cash or any other asset. If a balance sheet is **STOCK DIVIDEND DECLARED BUT NOT YET DISTRIBUTED** prepared between the date of declaration of a stock dividend and the date of distribution of the shares, the facts concerning the dividend should be presented in the stockholders' equity section of the balance sheet, as indicated in the following illustration:

Stockholders' Equity

Contributed capital:		
Common stock, $10 par value, authorized 30,000 shares		
Issued and outstanding 10,000 shares	*$100,000*	
To be issued Feb. 9, 1963, as a stock dividend:		
1,000 shares	*10,000*	*$110,000*
Paid-in capital in excess of par value	*$ 50,000*	
Paid-in capital from stock dividends	*20,000*	*70,000*
Total contributed capital		*$180,000*
Retained earnings		*170,000*
Total stockholders' equity		*$350,000*

Effect of stock dividends upon retained earnings and contributed capital. Stock dividends are a popular means of increasing the number of outstanding shares by transferring from retained earnings to capital stock and paid-in surplus an amount equal to the market value of the shares issued as a dividend. Because so many companies have used stock dividends to transfer retained earnings into the permanent capital accounts, the capital stock account as it appears in many of today's corporate balance sheets is considerably larger than the total cash actually paid in by stockholders over the life of the business. The amounts transferred from retained earnings into the permanent capital accounts may, however, be regarded as a special type of contribution by stockholders since these transfers are approved by the directors acting as representatives of the stockholders.

Stock splits. Most large corporations are interested in as wide as possible a distribution of their stock among the investing public. If the market price reaches very high levels as, for example, $150 per share, the corporation may feel that by splitting the stock 5 for 1 and thereby reducing the price to $30 per share, the number of shareholders may be increased. The bulk of trading in securities occurs in 100-share lots and an extra commission is charged on smaller transactions. Many investors with limited funds prefer to make their investments in 100-share lots of lower-priced stocks. The majority of leading American corporations have split their stock; some have done so several times. Generally the number of shareholders has increased noticeably after splitting the stock.

A stock split consists of increasing the number of outstanding shares and reducing the par or stated value per share in proportion. For example, assume that a corporation has outstanding 1 million shares of $10 par value stock. The market value is $90 per share. The corporation now reduces the par value from $10 to $5 per share and increases the number of shares from 1 million to 2 million. This action would be called a 2 for 1 stock split. A stockholder who formerly owned 100 shares of the $10 par old stock would now own 200 shares of the $5 par new stock. Since the number of outstanding shares has been doubled without any change in the affairs of the corporation, the market price will probably drop from $90 to approximately $45 a share.

A stock split does not change the balance of any ledger account; consequently, the transaction may be recorded merely by a memorandum notation in the general journal and in the Capital Stock account. Another alternative is to indicate the change in par value by an entry such as the following:

ENTRY FOR
STOCK
SPLIT

Capital Stock, $10 par	10,000,000	
Capital Stock, $5 par		10,000,000

To record stock split with increase of out-
standing shares from 1 million to 2 mil-
lion, and a reduction in par value from
$10 to $5 per share.

Distinction between stock splits and large stock dividends. What is the difference between a 2 for 1 stock split and a 100% stock dividend? Both will double the number of outstanding shares without making any change in the total capital, and both will serve to cut the market price of the stock in half. The stock dividend, however, will cause a transfer from the Retained Earnings account to the permanent capital accounts, whereas the stock split does not affect retained earnings and does not change the balance of any account.

After a stock split or a stock dividend each stockholder will own more shares, but his holdings will represent the same percentage of the outstanding stock as before the split or dividend. Since the net assets of the corporation remain unchanged, it follows that the equity of each stockholder in those net assets is also unchanged. The amount of net assets represented by each share of stock is decreased, but this change is exactly compensated by the increased number of shares.

Reserves created from retained earnings

In our discussion up to this point only two kinds of entries affecting the Retained Earnings account have been considered: the Retained Earnings account is credited each year with the profit transferred from the Income Summary account and debited for the amount of any dividends declared. The balance of the Retained Earnings account, therefore, represents the accumulated net profits of the business minus any dividends to stockholders.

Some corporations prefer to subdivide their retained earnings into two or more accounts. This subdivision is accomplished by journal entries which transfer a portion of the accumulated profits from the Retained Earnings account into various reserve accounts. A reserve account created in this manner is referred to as an *appropriation of retained earnings* or as an *appropriated surplus reserve*.

Assume, for example, that a corporation is engaged in a highly speculative business in which operations may result in either large profits or large losses from one year to the next. The corporation has accumulated a balance of $1 million in the Retained Earnings account after a period of favorable operating conditions. The board of directors decides to make half of this amount unavailable for dividends by transferring $500,000 from the Retained Earnings account to a Reserve for Contingencies. The journal entry to carry out the decision of the directors is as follows:

<table>
<tr><td>ENTRY
CREATING
RESERVE
FOR CON-
TINGENCIES</td><td>*Retained Earnings* 500,000
     Reserve for Contingencies   500,000
To record the establishment of a reserve for con-
tingencies by order of the board of directors.</td></tr>
</table>

The point of this action is to make clear to stockholders and other readers of the financial statements that $500,000 of the retained earnings is to be held more or less permanently in the business and is therefore not available for dividends. The Reserve for Contingencies appears in the stockholders' equity section of the balance sheet. The corporation still has a total of $1 million of retained earnings, but it has chosen to carry this $1 million divided into two separate items on the balance sheet, as follows:

<table>
<tr><td>NO CHANGE
IN TOTAL
CAPITAL</td><td>*Stockholders' Equity*
Capital Stock .... $ _____
Retained earnings:
  Free and available for dividends $500,000
  Reserve for contingencies   500,000   1,000,000</td></tr>
</table>

The total capital of the corporation is unchanged by this subdivision of retained earnings, and the net assets represented by each share of stock are unchanged in amount.

Contractual and voluntary surplus reserves. The reserve for contingencies described in the preceding section was created voluntarily by the board of directors. The board may bring an end to the existence of the reserve at any time merely by ordering it to be transferred back into the Retained Earnings account. The entry to dispose of the reserve would be as follows:

Reserve for Contingencies *500,000*		
Retained Earnings		*500,000*

To eliminate the reserve for contingencies by transferring it back to Retained Earnings, in accordance with a resolution by the board of directors.

Another example of a voluntary surplus reserve is a Reserve for Plant Expansion. A company which plans to retain a considerable part of its profits as a means of financing the construction of additional plant facilities may wish to inform its stockholders of this plan by transferring a portion of the retained earnings into a separate owners' equity account with the descriptive title of Reserve for Plant Expansion. Once the plant expansion program is complete, the board of directors may decide to order the Reserve for Plant Expansion to be closed by transferring its balance back to the Retained Income account. However, the company is presumably in no stronger cash position after completion of the building program than it was before; there is, therefore, no logical reason for elimination of the surplus reserve at this point.

Not all appropriations of retained earnings are voluntary. When a corporation borrows money through the issuance of long-term notes or bonds, the borrowing contract may place a limit on the dividends which the corporation can pay during the life of the indebtedness. One means of limiting dividends is to transfer a portion of the retained earnings into a reserve account with a title such as Reserve for Retirement of Long-term Debt, or Reserve for Bond Sinking Fund.

Another example of a contractual or obligatory surplus reserve is found occasionally when a corporation agrees with its preferred stockholders that a specified number of preferred shares shall be redeemed each year out of the profits from operations. A reserve created under the terms of such an agreement is usually called Reserve for Retirement of Preferred Stock.

Regardless of whether a reserve created out of retained earnings is voluntary or is required by law or contract, the amount in the reserve account is still part of retained earnings. The only possible disposition of such reserves when no longer desired is to restore them to the Retained Earnings account.

Reserves do not consist of assets. Many readers of financial statements erroneously assume that a Reserve for Plant Expansion consists of cash set aside to pay for a new building. This is completely untrue. A Reserve for Plant Expansion has a credit balance; it does not consist of cash or any other assets; it is an owners' equity account, and merely a subdivision of retained earnings.

These comments apply not only to Reserve for Plant Expansion but to all reserves created from retained earnings. If management wishes to set aside a fund of cash for a specific future use, this is done by transferring cash out of the general bank account and into a special bank account. The special account would be a fund and not a reserve. It would have a debit balance and would appear on the asset side of the balance sheet. The use of funds will be more fully discussed in Chapter 21; at this point our objective is merely to emphasize that a reserve created from retained earnings does not consist of cash or any other assets.

Are surplus reserves necessary or desirable? The only function of a voluntary surplus reserve is to inform readers of the financial statements that the board of directors considers a portion of the retained earnings to be required for a specific purpose and not available for dividends. This information could be conveyed more directly with less danger of misunderstanding by a footnote to the balance sheet.

Only the board of directors has authority to declare dividends. If the board wishes to retain the earnings in the business for plant expansion or other purposes, it is free to do so without going through the procedure of dividing the Retained Earnings account into two or more portions. A reserve voluntarily created by the board of directors may be eliminated by the board at any time. Furthermore, the only possible means of disposing of an appropriated surplus reserve is to restore it to the Retained Earnings account.

The case for contractual reserves is hardly any stronger. Certainly long-term creditors of a corporation will want the corporation to conserve its resources as a means of paying the long-term debts at maturity. One important factor in conserving resources is to limit dividends and retain profits in the business. Such a policy may be imposed by creditors through a requirement that dividend payments shall not exceed a specified percentage of net profits during the period of indebtedness. Such a direct limitation is much more effective than a contractual reserve created from retained earnings.

In the interest of achieving more understandable financial statements, it is encouraging to see that many corporations are discontinuing the use of appropriated surplus reserves. If the total retained earnings of a corporation are presented as a single figure in the balance sheet and labeled as Retained Earnings or Earnings Reinvested in the Business, there is less opportunity for misunderstanding than when the retained earnings have been divided up into various "reserve accounts."

QUESTIONS

1. Why is the distinction between contributed capital and retained earnings of interest to the reader of a corporate balance sheet?

2. What are the arguments for using the term *retained earning* in place of the older term *earned surplus?*

3. Explain the significance of the following dates relating to dividends: date of declaration, date of record, date of payment, ex-dividend date.

4. Rolland purchased 10 shares of stock in X Corporation at the time it was organized. At the end of the first year's operations the corporation reported earnings (after taxes) of $5 per share, and declared a dividend of $2.50 per share. Rolland complains that he is entitled to the full distribution of the amount earned on his investment. Is there any reason why a corporation that earns $5 per share may not be able to pay a dividend of this amount? Are there any advantages to Rolland in the retention by the company of one-half of its earnings?

5. Distinguish between a stock split and a stock dividend. Is there any reason for the difference in accounting treatment of these two events?

6. Bock owns 1,000 of the total outstanding 10,000 shares of common stock in the Precision Corporation. The net assets of the Precision Corporation at the end of the current year are $200,000, and the market value of the stock is $24 per share. At year-end the company declares a stock dividend of one share for each five shares held. If all parties concerned clearly recognized the nature of the stock dividend, what would you expect the market value of Precision's common stock to be at the ex-dividend date?

7. What is the purpose of an appropriation of retained earnings? What are the arguments for and against the use of such appropriations?

8. Explain the nature of the following items appearing on a corporate balance sheet: reserve for depreciation, reserve for income taxes payable, and reserve for future plant expansion.

PROBLEMS

Group A

19A-1. The stockholders' equity of the Signode Corporation on January 1 of the current year is as follows:

> *Stockholders' Equity:*
> | | |
> |---|---:|
> | 5% preferred stock, $100 par (5,000 shares authorized) . | $ 250,000 |
> | Common stock, $10 par value (100,000 shares authorized) .... | 400,000 |
> | *Paid-in capital in excess of par value:* | |
> | Premium on common stock .... | 160,000 |
> | Premium on preferred stock .... | 12,500 |
> | *Retained earnings:* | |
> | Reserve for plant expansion .... | 125,000 |
> | Unappropriated .... | 450,000 |
> | Total stockholders' equity .... | $1,397,500 |

The transactions relating to capital accounts during the current year are shown below.

Jan. 16. Paid regular semiannual dividend on preferred stock, and $1.50 per share cash dividend on common. Both these dividends were declared in December of the past year and properly recorded at that time.

July 1. Declared semiannual dividend on preferred stock, to stockholders of record on July 15, payable on July 28.

Sept. 30. Declared a 10% stock dividend on common to stockholders of record of October 14, payable on November 1. Market value $24 a share.

Nov. 10. Sold 2,500 shares of common stock for $24 per share.

Dec. 15. The board of directors authorized the addition of $10,000 to the reserve for plant expansion.

Dec. 28. Declared regular semiannual dividend on preferred stock and a dividend of $1.40 per share on common shares of record at January 8, payable on January 14.

Instructions

a. Prepare in general journal form the entries necessary to record these transactions on the books of the Signode Corporation during the current year.

b. Did Signode Corporation increase or decrease the total amount of cash dividends declared on common shares this year in comparison with the dividends declared last year? Explain.

19A-2. The information given below is related to the stockholders' equity of the Ivano Corporation:

(1) The company has received a total of $128,000 in exchange for the 2,000 shares of 6% preferred stock, par value $50, that are currently outstanding (authorized: 6,000 shares).

(2) The company has received from stockholders $262,000 in exchange for 10,000 outstanding shares of no-par value common stock having a stated value of $25 per share (authorized: 35,000 shares).

(3) Total net income since the date of organization has been $174,000.

(4) Cash dividends paid since date of organization, $78,000.

(5) Stock dividend declared (but not yet distributed to stockholders) amounts to 1,000 shares of common. The market value of the common at the date of record was $40 per share.

(6) Certain land having an assessed valuation of $6,000, was donated to the corporation by the city as a site for a manufacturing plant. The fair market value of the land at the time of the gift was $16,000.

(7) The amount of $20,000 was recently authorized by the board of directors as a reserve for contingencies.

(8) Patents which cost $20,000 to develop were appraised at $150,000, and the board of directors authorized that the asset be written up to this amount as of the end of the current year.

Instructions. On the basis of this information, prepare in good form the stockholders' equity section of the Ivano Corporation balance sheet.

19A-3. The capital accounts of the Gulf Company at the beginning of the current year were as shown below.

Stockholders' equity:

6% preferred stock, $100 par, authorized 12,000 shares		
Common stock, $50 par value, authorized 40,000 shares, issued		
10,000 shares		$ 500,000
Paid-in capital in excess of par value:		
On common shares		50,000
Total contributed capital		$ 550,000
Unrealized appreciation of investment in Randolph Co. stock		132,000
Retained earnings:		
Appropriated for contingencies	$ 80,000	
Unappropriated	330,000	410,000
Total stockholders' equity		$1,092,000

During the year these transactions relating to stockholders' equity occurred:

Jan. 5. Sold 4,000 shares of preferred stock at 101 1/2.

Jan. 18. Paid dividend of $2 per share on common stock declared during December of past year. Declaration was properly recorded in December.

Mar. 1. Paid damages awarded in a lawsuit against the Gulf Company of $75,000. In anticipation of this, the board of directors had authorized the appropriation for contingencies last year. The board now directs that the appropriation be discontinued. The damages will be treated as a loss on the income statement.

June 10. The board of directors declared semiannual dividend on preferred stock to stockholders of record on July 1, payable on July 10.

July 1. The board of directors declared a dividend of 20% on common stock, payable in shares of common stock. Common is currently selling for $45 per share. Date of record is July 15; dividend is payable on July 20.

Sept. 30. Stockholders voted to reduce the par value of common shares from $50 to $25 per share, and to issue additional shares so that stated capital remains unchanged.

Dec. 15. The board of directors declared a dividend of 80 cents per share on common stock and the regular semiannual dividend on preferred, to stockholders of record on December 26, payable on December 31.

Dec. 31. The Income Summary account, after closing all revenue and expense accounts, has a debit balance of $28,000. The board of directors directs that a reserve for bond retirement be established in the amount of $125,000, and that the investment in Randolph stock should be written up by an additional $12,000, representing appreciation during the current year.

Instructions

a. Prepare in general journal form the entries necessary to record these transactions.

b. Prepare in good form the stockholders' equity section of the Gulf Company balance sheet as of the end of the current year. (It may be advisable to set up T accounts on scratch paper to summarize the entries in (*a*), but these need not be presented as part of the solution.)

19A-4. Near the end of the current year, the board of directors of the Beseler Company is presented with the following statement of the company's capital position:

Common stock (10,000 shares issued)	*$200,000*
Paid-in capital in excess of par value	*120,000*
Retained earnings	*160,000*
Total stockholders' equity	*$480,000*

Beseler Company has paid dividends of $3.60 per share in each of the last five years. After careful consideration of the company's cash needs, the board of directors declared a stock dividend of 2,000 shares of common stock. Shortly after the stock dividend had been distributed, and before the end of the year, the company declared a cash dividend of $3 per share.

James Pratt owned 2,400 shares of Beseler common stock which he acquired several years ago. The market price of this stock before any dividend action was $60 per share.

Instructions. On the basis of the above information, answer each of the following questions, showing computations where pertinent.

a. What is Pratt's share (in dollars) of the net assets as reported in the financial statement of the Beseler Company before the stock dividend action? What is his share after the stock dividend action? Explain why there is or is not any change as a result of the stock dividend.

b. What are the probable reasons why the market value of Pratt's stock differs from the amount of net assets per share shown on the books.

c. Compare the amount of cash dividends that Pratt receives this year with dividends received in prior years.

d. On the day the common stock went ex-dividend (with respect to the stock dividend), its quoted market value fell from $60 to $50 per share. Did this represent a loss to Pratt? Explain.

e. If the Beseler Company had announced that it would continue its regular cash dividend of $3.60 per share for the current year, would you expect the market value of the common stock to react in any way different from the change described in (*d*)? Why?

Group B

19B-1. The Jerrod Corporation was organized early in 1961 and was authorized to issue 70,000 shares of $10 par value common stock and 18,000 shares of $50 par value 7% preferred stock. During 1961 the company sold 30,000 shares of common, at an average price of $31 per share, and issued 10,000 shares in exchange for certain patents worth $300,000. The company earned a net income of $87,000 and paid dividends of 75 cents per share during 1961.

On January 1, 1962, the company issued 12,000 shares of preferred stock in exchange for timber property valued at $625,000. Quarterly dividends were declared and paid on preferred shares in April, July, and October of 1962. On December 28, 1962, the company declared the fourth quarterly dividend on preferred stock and a 10% stock dividend payable to common stockholders. Net income for 1962 was $114,000. The market value of common stock at the end of 1962 was 30 3/4 per share.

Instructions. Prepare the stockholders' equity section of the Jerrod Corporation balance sheet at:

a. December 31, 1961   **b.** December 31, 1962

19B-2. The net assets of the McNair Corporation were represented at a given date by the following capital elements:

Legal capital: 10,000 shares of $40 par common stock $400,000
Paid-in capital in excess of legal capital 128,000
Retained earnings 169,000

Total stockholders' equity $697,000

The items listed below describe certain subsequent events relating to the McNair Corporation capital.

(1) The board of directors authorized an appropriation of $100,000 of retained earnings for retirement of the mortgage on certain plant property.

(2) The directors declared a cash dividend of $3 per share.

(3) The company made an advance payment on its mortgage involving a total expenditure of $107,500. Paid on principal, $100,000; accrued interest, $6,000; penalty for payment before due date, $1,500.

(4) The company sold 1,000 shares of stock for 43 1/2 per share.

(5) The board of directors distributed a stock dividend of one share for each five shares held. The market value of the shares just prior to the date of the stock dividend was $42 per share. The company treasurer objected that there was not a sufficient balance in retained earnings to make this a legal dividend; to remove this objection, the directors ordered that the reserve for mortgage payment be discontinued.

(6) Stockholders approved a proposal by the board of directors to split the company's stock 2 for 1, and to decrease the par value from $40 to $15 per share.

Instructions

a. Prepare in general journal form the entries necessary to record on the books of McNair Corporation each of the above events.

b. Assuming no transactions other than those listed, compute the dollar amount of the net assets of the company after all these events have been reflected in the accounts.

19B-3. The stockholders' equity of the Nardack Corporation on January 1 of the current year was as follows:

5% convertible preferred stock, par value $100, authorized 25,000
shares, issued 3,000 shares $300,000
Common stock, no par, stated value $5 per share, authorized 200,000
shares, issued and outstanding, 72,600 shares 363,000
Paid-in capital in excess of stated value on common shares 85,000
Retained earnings:
Reserve for retirement of preferred stock $125,000
Unappropriated 83,000   208,000

$956,000

The company's preferred stock may be called at any time by the company at 105, or it may be converted into 15 shares of common per share of preferred stock at any time, at the option of the holder. The transactions given below relating to the capital accounts of the Nardack Corporation occurred during the current year:

Feb. 10. 160 shares of preferred were presented for conversion into common shares under the terms of the preferred contract.

June 30. The company called 1,000 shares of preferred stock, paying 105 plus a dividend for one-half year. Semiannual dividend was also declared on the remaining preferred stock outstanding, payable on July 12.

Aug. 31. The board of directors authorized that $105,000 of the reserve for retirement of preferred be discontinued, and that a stock dividend of 15,000 shares of common be declared and distributed. (Record declaration and distribution in a single entry.) Common shares had a current market value of $7 per share.

Nov. 1. A new board of directors elected on November 1 authorized a change in common shares from $5 stated value to $10 par value, with a corresponding decrease in the number of shares outstanding. Old shares were called in and new shares issued in their place.

Dec. 31. Net income for the year was $118,000. The board of directors declared regular semiannual dividend on preferred stock, and $1.10 per share on the newly reissued common shares. The board authorized an appropriation of $30,000 to the reserve for retirement of preferred stock.

Instructions

a. Prepare in general journal form the entries necessary to record the above events on the books of the Nardack Corporation.

b. Prepare the stockholders' equity section of the balance sheet at the end of the year.

c. Prepare a schedule listing the source and dollar amount of the changes in the net assets of Nardack Corporation between the beginning and the end of the current year.

19B-4. In the late 1950s, the management of the Magnum Corporation began to give serious consideration to a program of expansion and diversification of their business. On January 1, 1960, the corporation had retained earnings of $535,000, of which $400,000 had been appropriated in a reserve for plant expansion. Outstanding were 60,000 shares of no-par common stock, at a stated value of $15 per share, which had been issued at an average price of $42.50 per share. The events relating to the company's capital accounts over the next few years are:

Dec. 31, 1960. Net income for the year $180,000; cash dividends declared $60,000; added to reserve for plant expansion $100,000.

May 15, 1961. Issued 20,000 shares of Magnum Corporation common stock in exchange for all the outstanding common stock (par value $500,000) of the Rehan Corporation. The current market value of the Rehan common was $800,000.

Dec. 31, 1961. Net income for the year $165,000; cash dividends declared 50 cents per share; added to reserve for plant expansion $120,000.

Dec. 31, 1962. Net income for the year $200,000; cash dividends declared 40 cents per share; added to reserve for plant expansion $150,000.

Apr. 10, 1963. Completed construction of additional plant facilities costing $750,000. Board of directors directed that reserve for plant expansion be discontinued.

Apr. 30, 1963. Board authorized distribution of a stock dividend of 3 shares of common stock for each 16 shares now held. Current market value of the Magnum common is $48 per share.

Instructions

a. Prepare in good form the stockholders' equity section of the Magnum Corporation balance sheet on December 31, 1962. In a separate schedule show how you determined the amount of retained earnings on this date.

b. Give the general journal entries necessary to record the events that took place on April 10, 1963, and on April 30, 1963.

c. Is there any relationship between the reserve for plant expansion and the purchase of the Rehan Corporation shares on May 15, 1961? Is there any relationship between the stock dividend on April 30, 1963, and the reserve for plant expansion? Explain your answers.

20

Corporations: extraordinary gains and losses; treasury stock; book value

The preceding chapters on corporations have emphasized the differences between corporate financial statements and those of single proprietorships and partnerships. Basic concepts, such as the separate entity of the corporation, the nature of capital stock, and the meaning of retained earnings and dividends, have received careful attention. Accountants are fairly well in agreement on these basic concepts, but for certain other issues, such as the proper treatment of extraordinary gains and losses, considerable difference of opinion exists. In this chapter we shall round out our study of the corporation by consideration of alternative methods of accounting for extraordinary gains and losses; methods of accounting for treasury stock; and the computation and significance of *book value* for a share of capital stock.

Extraordinary gains and losses

From time to time most businesses will realize unusual gains and incur unusual losses of relatively large amount apart from their regular operations. Examples include: (1) gains and losses on the sale of land, buildings, or other fixed assets, (2) losses from fires, floods, and earthquakes, (3) gains and losses from the sale of marketable securities held as an investment, (4) damages awarded in a lawsuit, (5) losses from defalcations not covered by fidelity bonds, and (6) "starting-up costs" in the opening of new plants. Gains and losses of these types are shown separately in financial statements, usually under a caption such as Extraordinary Gains and Losses, or Nonrecurring Gains and Losses, or Nonoperating Gains and Losses. To warrant recognition in this manner, the item must be relatively important in amount as well as being unusual and apart from regular operations of the business.

Two opposing views exist as to the proper presentation of these non-operating gains and losses in the financial statements. One group of accountants believes that these gains and losses should be included in the income statement of the year in which they occur, but listed as separate items and clearly described. The extraordinary gain or loss would then be reflected in the amount of net income reported for the year. Other accountants favor charging or crediting large nonrecurring losses and gains directly to the Retained Earnings account and thus excluding them from the determination of the current year's income. Under this approach, the extraordinary gain or loss would appear in the statement of retained earnings which accompanies the balance sheet and income statement. Both methods provide for full disclosure, but the key figure of net income, to which many investors attach great significance, may differ materially under these two alternative approaches.

Current operating performance income statement. An income statement which includes only revenue and expense items regarded as normal and recurring is sometimes referred to as a *current operating performance* income statement. The argument for this approach is that the income statement should reflect earning power which can be expected to continue in the future, and that nonrecurring gains and losses should therefore be excluded from the statement.

If only normal recurring items of revenue and expense are included in the income statement, comparisons of reported earnings from year to year may give a better picture of the trend of earning power than would be available if extraordinary, nonoperating gains and losses were included in the net income figures of the years in which these items happened to occur. The discussion concerns material items only; all accountants agree that small items, even though unusual in nature, should be included in computing the current year's income.

The following income statement and statement of retained earnings illustrate the current operating performance concept of net income.

STRESSES
CURRENT
OPERATING
PERFORM-
ANCE

BUTTERFIELD CORPORATION
Income Statement
For the Year Ended December 31, 1963

Net sales	$1,000,000
Cost of goods sold	600,000
Gross profit on sales	$ 400,000
Deduct: operating expenses	250,000
Net income before income taxes	$ 150,000
Deduct: income taxes	60,000
Net income	$ 90,000

BUTTERFIELD CORPORATION
Statement of Retained Earnings
For the Year Ended December 31, 1963

Retained earnings, Dec. 31, 1962		$300,000
Add:		
Net income	$90,000	
Gain on sale of old plant	32,000	122,000
Total		$422,000
Deduct:		
Loss from flood damage	$20,000	
Dividends	52,000	72,000
Retained earnings, Dec. 31, 1963		$350,000

These statements, prepared in accordance with the current operating performance concept of net income, should be compared with the statements below and on page 554, which contain the same data presented in accordance with the clean surplus theory. Note the variation in the reported net income under these two alternative approaches.

All-inclusive income statement (clean surplus theory). An income statement which includes all extraordinary, nonrecurring gains and losses as well as normal operating revenue and expense is called an *all-inclusive income* statement. This type of statement results from following the *clean surplus theory*. The financial statements of the Butterfield Corporation, presented above and on page 552, are now shown rearranged to illustrate the all-inclusive income statement:

CLEAN
SURPLUS
THEORY

BUTTERFIELD CORPORATION
Income Statement
For the Year Ended December 31, 1963

Net sales		$1,000,000
Cost of goods sold		600,000
Gross profits on sales		$ 400,000
Deduct: operating expenses		250,000
Net income from operations		$ 150,000
Nonrecurring gains and losses:		
Gain on sale of old plant	$32,000	
Loss from flood damage	20,000	12,000
Net income before income taxes		$ 162,000
Deduct: income taxes		60,000
Net income		$ 102,000

BUTTERFIELD CORPORATION
Statement of Retained Earnings
For the Year Ended December 31, 1963

Retained earnings, Dec. 31, 1962	$300,000
Add: net income for the year	102,000
Total	$402,000
Deduct dividends	52,000
Retained earnings, Dec. 31, 1963	$350,000

Under this approach the only items which appear in the statement of retained earnings are the net income and dividends declared.

In these statements the net income is reported as $102,000. In the current operating performance income statement on pages 552 and 553 (top), the net income for this same data was reported as $90,000. If we assume that in the preceding year (1962) the Butterfield Corporation earned a net profit of $100,000, the choice of reporting methods in 1963 will determine whether the company reports a $2,000 increase in net income over the preceding year or a $10,000 decrease. Which method of reporting will be more useful to investors and other users of the financial statements? Opinion on this question is divided, but the clean surplus theory leading to the all-inclusive income statement is currently being followed by an increasing majority of companies. The following arguments appear to have been instrumental in the trend toward the all-inclusive concept of net income.

1. Many readers of the financial statements concentrate their attention on the figure for net income and may not be aware that this figure does not include important gains and losses, if these items have been "buried" in the statement of retained earnings.

2. Who is to decide which gains and losses are sufficiently unusual to warrant exclusion from the income statement? There are no universally accepted standards for distinguishing between *usual* and *unusual* gains and losses, and the distinction cannot be made consistently from company to company or even from year to year within a particular company.

3. A management that is deliberately trying to understate reported earnings can do so by labeling a variety of forms of revenue as nonoperating and crediting them directly to retained earnings. Similarly, a company that wished to exaggerate its earnings could omit various loss transactions from the income statements by charging them directly to retained earnings. Although so-called extraordinary gains and losses are often described as nonrecurring, experience shows that such items do recur year after year. Consequently, they are part of the whole picture of earnings and should be included in the income statement.

4. Another argument in support of the all-inclusive income statement is that many so-called extraordinary gains and losses arise because of inaccuracies in measuring operating income in prior years. Assume, for example, that an airline depreciates an airplane which cost $1 million over a period of seven years. At the end of the seventh year, the fully depreciated airplane is still in sound condition and is sold to a smaller airline at a price of $250,000. This "extraordinary gain" of $250,000 may be regarded as a compensating correction of excessive depreciation charges recorded as operating expense in the previous seven years. It is, therefore, illogical to consider the gain as nonoperating in nature. If all gains and losses are included in the income statement, the total net income reported over a series of years will tend to be correct, and an average net income figure computed from the series of income statements will be a dependable one.

Correction of errors made in current period. Occasional errors in the recording of transactions will inevitably occur even in the best-run business. For example, assume that a new machine purchased by a manufacturing company at a cost of $10,000 on January 2, 1962, was erroneously charged to Repairs Expense rather than to the asset account, Machinery. The machine was estimated to have a 10-year useful life and was therefore subject to depreciation at the rate of 10% a year. Assume that the error in recording the acquisition of the machine was discovered on December 31, after the year-end entries for depreciation and other adjustments had been made but before the revenue and expense accounts had been closed into the Income Summary account. The adjustment for depreciation of the various machines was based on the incorrect balance in the Machinery account. How should the error be corrected? Efforts to correct errors in the accounts sometimes result in the making of additional erroneous entries. To assure that the correction is properly carried out, the following analytical procedure is recommended:

1. Write out the entry as it was erroneously made in the books.
2. Write the entry as it should have been made originally.
3. After comparing the above two entries, prepare a correcting entry which will produce the desired balances in all accounts involved.

CORRECTING ENTRIES REQUIRE CAREFUL ANALYSIS

Applying this procedure to the example of the $10,000 machine, the analysis would appear as follows:

Erroneous entry as originally made		*Entry that should have been made originally*	
Repairs Expense .. 10,000		Machinery 10,000	
Cash	10,000	Cash	10,000

Correcting entries

1962
(a) Dec. 31.   Machinery 10,000
                    Repairs Expense   10,000
                To correct erroneous entry of Jan. 2, 1962, in
                which cost of new machine purchased was im-
                properly charged to Repairs Expense.

(b) Dec. 31.   Depreciation Expense 1,000
                    Accumulated Depreciation: Machinery.   1,000
                To record depreciation at 10% per annum on
                machinery, which had been improperly re-
                corded in Repairs Expense at time of purchase,
                Jan. 2, 1962.

If this error had not been discovered and corrected before the books
were closed December 31, 1962, both the income statement and the balance sheet would have been in error as follows:

HOW
ERRORS
DISTORT
STATEMENTS

Income statement:
    Repairs expense overstated $10,000
    Depreciation expense understated   1,000
    Net income understated .... $ 9,000

Balance Sheet:
    Machinery account understated $10,000
    Accumulated Depreciation: Machinery understated   1,000
    Retained Earnings understated .... $ 9,000

Correction of errors made in previous periods. Next, assume that the
above-described error of $10,000 made in 1962 was not discovered until
the beginning of the following year. In the meantime the erroneous balances in the Repairs Expense and Depreciation Expense accounts for 1962
had been closed into the Income Summary account and this account in
turn had been closed to Retained Earnings. How should the error be corrected when discovered in 1963? There are two alternative answers to
this question, one representing the clean surplus theory and the other
based on the current operating concept of net income. Under the clean
surplus theory, errors of prior years are corrected through the income
statement; under the current operating concept of net income, corrections of errors of prior years are made directly to the Retained Earnings
account.

As previously stated, majority practice favors the clean surplus theory (all-inclusive income statement). Under this approach the correction entry in 1963 would be as follows:

CORRECTION OF PRIOR YEARS' ERRORS: CLEAN SURPLUS THEORY

Machinery *10,000*		
Accumulated Depreciation: Machinery		*1,000*
Correction of Prior Years' Income		*9,000*
To correct (1) the entry of Jan. 2, 1962, in which		
the cost of a new machine was erroneously charged		
to Repairs Expense; and (2) the related inadequacy		
in providing for depreciation in 1962.		

The Correction of Prior Years' Income account would appear in the bottom section of the income section along with any extraordinary gains and losses as shown by the following illustration:

CORRECTION AFFECTS NET INCOME

McCONNELL CORPORATION
Income Statement
For the Year Ended December 31, 1963

Net sales		*$1,500,000*
Cost of goods sold		*1,000,000*
Gross profit on sales		*$ 500,000*
Operating expenses		*350,000*
Net income from operations		*$ 150,000*
Nonoperating credits:		
Correction of prior years' income	*$ 9,000*	
Gain on sale of investments	*31,000*	*40,000*
Net income		*$ 190,000*

If, on the other hand, the company followed the current operating performance concept of net income, the correction entry would include a direct credit to the Retained Earnings account as follows:

CORRECTION OF PRIOR YEARS' EARNINGS; NO EFFECT ON CURRENT EARNINGS

Machinery *10,000*		
Accumulated Depreciation: Machinery		*1,000*
Retained Earnings		*9,000*
To correct (1) the entry of Jan. 2, 1962, in which the		
cost of a new machine was erroneously charged to		
Repairs Expense, and (2) the related inadequacy in		
providing for depreciation in 1962.		

When the correcting entry is made in this manner, the correction will not affect the net income for the year 1963; the statement of retained earnings will be used to show the $9,000 adjustment. The arguments for these two alternative methods of correcting errors of prior years are the same as the arguments presented on pages 551 to 555 relating to extraordinary gains and losses.

The preceding discussion of the correction of errors of prior years is applicable only to errors of material amount, that is, material in relation to the net income of the company. Prior years' errors of minor amount are customarily corrected through the operating expense accounts of the year in which the error comes to light. For example, assume that a delivery truck was sent out for repairs in November, 1962, but that through oversight the invoice for $25 was not received from the garage until the following February, 1963. Because of the smallness of the amount, the invoice would be charged to repair expense in 1963, without regard to the fact that the expenditure was, strictly speaking, part of 1962 operating expenses. Simplicity and convenience dictate the method of correcting errors which are not material in amount.

Treasury stock

Corporations occasionally reacquire shares of their own capital stock by purchase in the open market. The effect of reacquiring shares is to reduce the assets of the corporation and to reduce the stockholders' equity by the same amount. One reason for such purchases is to have stock available to reissue to officers and employees under some type of bonus plan. Treasury stock may be defined as a corporation's own stock which has been issued, fully paid, and reacquired but not canceled. Treasury shares may be held indefinitely or may be issued again at any time. Treasury stock is not entitled to share in dividends. It has no voting rights, no pre-emptive right to share in new issues, and no right to share in assets in the event of dissolution of the company. The only significant difference between treasury stock and unissued stock is that treasury stock may be issued at less than par without giving rise to a discount liability. It is also possible to distinguish treasury stock from unissued stock by saying that treasury shares were at some time in the past issued and outstanding, whereas unissued stock was never outstanding.

Recording purchases and sales of treasury stock. The procedures for recording treasury stock transactions are the same for both par value and no-par value stocks. Purchases of treasury stock should be recorded by debiting the Treasury Stock account with the cost of the stock.

For example, if a corporation reacquires 10 shares of its own $100 par stock at a price of $150 per share, the entry is as follows:

TREASURY STOCK RECORDED AT COST

Treasury Stock	*1,500*	
Cash		*1,500*
Purchased 10 shares of $100 par treasury stock at $150 per share.		

Treasury stock is customarily recorded at cost regardless of whether it is par value stock or no-par stock, and regardless of the price paid or of the price at which the shares were originally issued. In short, it is current practice to record all treasury stock at cost. When and if the treasury shares are reissued, the Treasury Stock account is credited for the cost of the shares sold.

To demonstrate fully the procedures for recording sales of treasury stock, three separate situations need to be presented: (1) the reissuance of the shares at cost; (2) reissuance at a price above cost; and (3) reissuance at a price below cost.

For the first illustration, assume that the 10 shares acquired at a cost of $1,500 are reissued for the same price of $1,500. The entry is as follows:

REISSUED AT COST

Cash *1,500*
          Treasury Stock *1,500*
Sold 10 shares of treasury stock at cost of $150 per share.

To illustrate the reissuance of treasury stock at a price above cost, assume that the 10 shares acquired at a cost of $1,500 are reissued for a higher price, $1,800. The entry is:

REISSUED ABOVE COST

Cash *1,800*
          Treasury Stock *1,500*
          Paid-in Capital from Treasury Stock Trans-
             actions *300*
Sold 10 shares of treasury stock, which cost $1,500, at a price of $180 each.

The third illustration concerns the sale of the 10 treasury shares at a price below cost and requires a reduction in an owners' equity account. If a paid-in capital account exists as a result of previous treasury stock transactions, this account may be debited. For example, if the 10 shares are reissued for a total price of $1,300, the entry is as follows:

REISSUED BELOW COST

Cash *1,300*
Paid-in Capital from Treasury Stock Transactions ... *200*
          Treasury Stock *1,500*
Issued 10 shares of treasury stock at a price below cost.

If there were no paid-in capital as a result of previous treasury stock transactions, the $200 excess of cost over reissuance price could be charged against any other paid-in capital account, as, for example, capital arising from the original issuance of stock at a price in excess of par or stated value. If there is no paid-in capital other than the Capital Stock account, the $200 difference between selling price and cost of the treasury stock should be charged against retained earnings, as shown in the following entry: [1]

REISSUED BELOW COST: ALTERNA- TIVE ENTRY	*Cash* 1,300	
	Retained Earnings 200	
	Treasury Stock	*1,500*
	Reissued 10 shares of treasury stock at a price below cost.	

Donated treasury stock. Occasionally a major stockholder in a company which needs cash desperately may decide to donate a portion of his shares to the company so that these shares may be resold to provide cash. When treasury shares are acquired by donation, there is no reduction in total assets and no change in owners' equity; consequently, no entry is necessary other than a memorandum of the number of shares received. NO CHANGE If 1,000 shares of treasury stock were donated to a corporation on July 1, IN OWNERS' the following notation could be made in the Treasury Stock account: EQUITY

Treasury Stock	
July 1 *(1,000 shares donated)*	

Assume that the 1,000 donated shares were reissued at a price of $10 per share. The entire proceeds from the reissuance of the donated shares represent an increase in contributed capital and should be credited to Paid-in Capital from Treasury Stock Transactions, as shown by the following entry:

STOCK- HOLDERS' EQUITY INCREASED	*Cash* 10,000	
	Paid-in Capital from Treasury Stock Trans-	
	actions	*10,000*
	Reissued 1,000 donated treasury shares for cash.	

[1] Conflicting views as to whether the sale of treasury stock at less than cost affects paid-in capital or retained earnings, or both, are more appropriately considered in advanced accounting courses.

Treasury stock not an asset. Treasury shares are much the same as unissued shares, and an unissued share of stock is definitely not an asset. A share of stock represents an interest in the net assets (assets minus liabilities) of the corporation. A fractional interest in the net assets cannot itself be regarded as a part of the assets; to do so would be the equivalent of counting some portion of the assets twice.

When treasury stock is purchased, the corporation is eliminating a part of the stockholders' equity by paying off one or more stockholders. If the program of acquiring its own stock were carried far enough, the corporation would hand out all its assets and eliminate all the stockholders' equity. It is, therefore, reasonable to think of the purchase of treasury stock not as the acquisition of an asset, but as the returning or refunding of capital to stockholders.

Conversely, if the treasury shares are later reissued, this is a separate transaction in which the corporation is securing additional invested capital. Assume, for example, that a corporation pays $10 to acquire a share of treasury stock and later reissues this share for $15. Has the corporation made a $5 profit on this transaction with its owners? Definitely not; there is no profit or loss on treasury stock transactions. When the treasury share was reissued for $15, the corporation was merely receiving a larger amount of invested capital than was previously withdrawn when a stockholder surrendered the share to the company. A corporation earns profits by selling goods and services to outsiders at a price above cost, not by issuing or reissuing shares of its own stock.

Restriction of retained earnings by cost of treasury stock purchased. If a corporation is to maintain its contributed capital intact, it must not pay out to its stockholders any more than it earns. As previously stated in the section dealing with dividends, the amount of dividends to be paid must not exceed the corporation's earnings or the corporation will be returning the stockholders' original investment to them.

The payment of cash dividends and the acquisition of treasury stock have a good deal in common. In both transactions, the corporation is handing out cash to its stockholders. Of course, the dividend payment is spread out among all the stockholders, whereas the payment to purchase treasury stock may go to only a few stockholders, but this does not alter the fact that the corporation is turning over its assets to its owners. The total amount which a corporation may pay to its stockholders without impairing its permanent capital is shown by the balance in the Retained Earnings account. Consequently, it is important that a corporation keep track of the total amount disbursed in payment for treasury stock and make sure that this amount plus any dividends paid does not exceed the company's earnings. This objective is conveniently accomplished by restricting the availability of retained earnings for dividends to the extent of the cost of treasury stock purchased.

As an illustration, assume that a corporation with a Retained Earnings account of $100,000 is considering the purchase of 1,000 shares of its own stock at a cost of $25,000. If this transaction is carried out, what would be the maximum which the corporation could then pay in cash dividends? The answer is $75,000. The Retained Earnings account will still show a balance of $100,000 after the purchase of the treasury stock, but $25,000 of this amount will be restricted and unavailable for dividends. This restriction must be disclosed in the balance sheet. One method of disclosure is merely to divide the retained earnings into two balance sheet items. One portion ($25,000 in our example) could be labeled Reserve for Treasury Stock, or Retained Earnings, Unavailable for Dividends; the other portion ($75,000 in our example) could be entitled Retained Earnings, Available for Dividends. A more popular and equally satisfactory method of making disclosure of the restriction in the balance sheet is to insert an explanatory note opposite the item of Retained Earnings. This procedure is used in the illustration in the following section.

Balance sheet presentation of treasury stock. Treasury stock is customarily carried on the books at cost and shown in the balance sheet at cost as a deduction from the combined total of the contributed capital and retained earnings. The following example of the stockholders' equity section of a balance sheet illustrates two main points concerning treasury stock: (1) the restriction of retained earnings by the cost of the treasury shares, and (2) the treatment of treasury stock as a deduction (at cost) from the combined total of capital stock and other equity accounts.

RETAINED EARNINGS RESTRICTED; TREASURY STOCK DEDUCTED

Stockholders' Equity

Common stock, $10 par value; authorized and issued 10,000 shares, of which 1,000 shares are held in the treasury	$100,000
Paid-in capital in excess of par	10,000
Retained earnings (of which $25,000, an amount equal to the cost of treasury stock purchased, is unavailable for dividends)	100,000
Total	$210,000
Deduct: cost of treasury stock (1,000 shares)	25,000
Total stockholders' equity	$185,000

Book value per share of capital stock

The word "value" is applied with various meanings to a share of stock. Par value, stated value, and market value per share have previously been discussed. Since there are several other types of value for a share of stock, to avoid confusion the term "value" should be used only with a qualifying adjective, as for example, book value, liquidation value, and redemption value.

The *book value* of a share of stock, as the name suggests, is determined by referring to the books of account, or more specifically to a balance sheet prepared from the books. If a corporation has issued common stock only, the book value per share is computed by dividing the stockholders' equity by the number of shares outstanding.

For example, assume that a corporation has 4,000 shares of common stock outstanding and the stockholders' equity section of the balance sheet is as follows:

HOW MUCH
IS BOOK
VALUE PER
SHARE?

Common stock	*$10,000*
Paid-in capital in excess of par value	*40,000*
Retained earnings	*50,000*
Total capital	*$100,000*

The book value per share is $25; it is computed by dividing the stockholders' equity of $100,000 by the 4,000 shares of outstanding stock. In computing book value, we are not concerned with the number of authorized shares but merely with the outstanding shares, because the total of the outstanding shares represents 100% of the stockholders' equity. In determining the number of outstanding shares, treasury shares are not to be included.

What is the significance of book value per share of stock? The stockholders' equity in total is equal to the book value of the assets minus the liabilities. Therefore, the stockholders' equity is equal to the *net assets* (assets minus liabilities), and the book value of each share of stock may be thought of as the net assets represented by a single share. In a business which is operating at a profit and retaining a portion of the profits each year, the book value per share can be expected to increase steadily.

Book value does *not* indicate the amount which the holder of a share of stock would receive if the corporation were to be dissolved. In liquidation the assets would probably be sold at prices quite different from their carrying values on the books, and the stockholders' equity would go up or down accordingly.

Book value is of some significance in judging the reasonableness of the market price of a stock. However, it must be used with great caution; the fact that a stock is selling at less than its book value does not necessarily indicate a bargain. Earnings per share and dividends per share are usually more important factors affecting market price than is book value. Nevertheless, book value is of significance, and most thoughtful investors give some weight to the relationship existing between book value and market value.

The concept of book value is of vital importance in many contracts. For example, a majority stockholder might obtain an option to purchase the shares of the minority stockholders at book value at a specified future date. Many court cases have hinged on definitions of book value.

Book value when company has both preferred and common stock. When a company has two or more issues of stock outstanding, the book value for each class of stock may be computed by dividing the paid-in capital and retained income applicable to that class of stock by the number of shares outstanding. Book value is generally computed for common stock only, so the practical aspect of the question may be stated as follows: How is book value per common share computed when a company has both preferred and common stock?

Assuming that there are no dividends in arrears on the preferred stock, book value per common share is equal to the total stockholders' equity (exclusive of the par value of the preferred stock) divided by the number of common shares outstanding. More concisely stated, net assets reduced by the amount of preferred stock and divided by the number of common shares equals book value per share of common stock.

To illustrate, assume that the stockholders' equity is as follows:

**TWO
CLASSES
OF STOCK**

5% preferred stock, $100 par	$1,000,000
Common stock, no-par; $5 stated value; authorized 100,000 shares	
Issued and outstanding 80,000 shares	400,000
Paid-in capital in excess of par value	800,000
Retained earnings	800,000
Total capital	$3,000,000

All the capital belongs to the common stockholders, except the $1 million par value applicable to the preferred (and any dividends in arrears on the preferred stock). This reasoning is supported by the general practice of making the preferred stock callable at or near its issuance price, so that the eventual elimination of the preferred stock is not at all improbable. The calculation of book value per share of common stock can therefore be made as follows:

**COMPUTE
BOOK VALUE
PER SHARE
OF COMMON**

Total capital	$3,000,000
Deduct: preferred stock (at call price)	1,000,000
Equity of common stockholders	$2,000,000
Number of shares of common stock outstanding	80,000
Book value per share $\dfrac{2,000,000}{80,000}$	$25

The computation of book value is made in the same way for par value and no-par value stock. The basic concept is the net assets per share.

Other values for capital stock. A brief recapitulation of the various types of stock values may be useful at this point.

Par value. Par is the nominal value or face value of a stock, the amount printed on the stock certificate. It has no relationship to market value or book value. It may also be defined as the legal capital per share, the amount that must be paid in to make the stock "fully paid." The capital stock account is credited with the par value of all shares issued.

Stated value. When a corporation issues no-par stock, it may assign a stated value per share. This stated value is the amount to be credited to the Capital Stock account; any excess of the issuance price over the stated value is credited to Paid-in Capital in Excess of Stated Value. The treatment of stated value in the accounts parallels the treatment of par value. Stated value is not related to market value or book value.

Redemption value or call price. Most preferred stocks are subject to call or redemption by the issuing corporation at a price slightly above par. Common stock is not callable.

Book value. This is equal to the net assets per share of stock. It is computed by dividing the paid-in capital and retained earnings applicable to a class of stock by the number of outstanding shares of that class.

Liquidation value. Liquidation value per share is an estimate of the amount which each share would be entitled to receive if the corporation were to be dissolved by converting all its assets into cash, paying all liabilities, and distributing the remaining cash to the shareholders. Liquidation value differs from book value in that the former is based on estimated amounts which would be realized from forced sales of assets, and the latter reflects the values at which assets are carried on the books.

Market value. Market value is the price at which the stock can currently be sold. For securities listed on the stock exchanges, the market price is reported in each day's newspapers. It is based primarily on the prospects for future earnings and dividends. The amount and trend of past earnings is a principal guide in forecasting these future prospects.

COMPARE
WITH
PUBLISHED
FINANCIAL
STATEMENTS

Illustration of stockholders' equity section. The following illustration of a stockholders' equity section of a balance sheet shows a fairly detailed classification by source of the various elements of capital:

Stockholders' Equity

Capital stock:			
6% preferred stock, $100 par value, authorized and issued			
1,000 shares	$100,000		
Common Stock, no-par, stated value $5 a share, authorized			
100,000 shares, issued 60,000 shares, of which 1,000 are			
held in the treasury	300,000		
Common stock subscribed, 6,000 shares	30,000		$430,000
Additional paid-in capital:			
Premium on preferred stock	$ 10,000		
Paid-in capital in excess of stated value: common stock	330,000		
Paid-in capital from treasury stock transactions	5,000		345,000
Retained earnings (of which $12,000, an amount equal to the cost of			
treasury stock purchased, is unavailable for dividends)			162,000
			$937,000
Deduct: cost of treasury stock			12,000
Stockholders' equity			$925,000

The published financial statements of leading corporations indicate that there is no one standard arrangement for the various items making up the stockholders' equity section. Variations occur in the selection of titles, in the sequence of items, and in the extent of detailed classification. Some companies, in an effort to avoid excessive detail in the balance sheet, will combine several related ledger accounts into a single balance sheet item with a title such as Additional Paid-in Capital.

QUESTIONS

1. Nillo Company has completed its accounting records for the current year. The controller of the company has prepared an income statement under the current operating approach showing a net income of $84,000. The assistant controller has prepared an income statement under the all-inclusive approach showing an income of $24,000. Explain why two statements prepared for the same company reflect different amounts of net income, and suggest the possible sources of the difference.

2. The accountant of J Company discovers during the current year that the merchandise inventory at the end of the prior year was understated by $24,000. Compare the effect of this discovery on the reported net income for the current year under the current operating performance concept and under the all-inclusive concept of net income.

3. What is treasury stock? How is it reported on a corporate financial statement?

4. Z Corporation has purchased 1,000 shares of its own common stock in the market at $30 per share. The company intends to reissue these shares at some future date and therefore the president favors reporting the shares as an asset. Explain why you would approve or disapprove of this treatment.

5. In many states the corporation law requires that retained earnings be restricted for dividend purposes to the extent of the cost of treasury shares. What is the reason for this legal rule?

6. Differentiate the following terms relating to shares of stock: book value, stated value, call price, liquidation value, market value.

7. K owns 1,000 out of a total of 20,000 outstanding common shares of Javo Corporation. The Javo Corporation reports total assets of $340,000 and total liabilities of $120,000 at the end of the current year, and at that time the board declared a stock dividend of 1 share for each 10 shares held. Compute the book value *per share* of K's stock and the total book value of K's investment in the corporation: (*a*) before the stock dividend; (*b*) after the stock dividend.

PROBLEMS

Group A

20A-1. *Instructions.* Prepare general journal entries (omitting explanations) to reflect the events given below on the records of the Rhoda Company, which has outstanding 1,000 shares of $50 par value, 6% preferred stock and 20,000 shares of no-par common stock having a stated value of $5 per share. (It may be assumed that the events are described in chronological order.)

Data

(1) Purchased 100 shares of preferred stock to be held in the treasury, paying $45 per share.

(2) Common stockholders agreed to donate 20% of their shares to the company, which shares are to be used in an employee stock option program.

(3) Employees purchased 800 shares of treasury stock (common) at $22 per share. The fair market value of the stock at time of purchase was $27 per share. (Charge Salary Expense for the "bargain" element in the purchase.)

(4) Sold 75 shares of preferred treasury stock for $50 per share.

(5) At the end of the current year it was discovered that a portion of the inventory at the end of the previous year had been counted twice. The cost of the goods double-counted was $23,700. (The company follows the current operating performance approach in reporting net income.)

(6) The company filed a claim for a refund of income taxes for last year, as a result of the error in (5). The refund is expected to amount to 52% of the misstatement of income resulting from the inventory error.

(7) The board of directors authorized an appropriation of retained earnings equal to the cost of treasury shares on hand, as required by state law.

(8) The board of directors declared the required annual dividend on preferred stock and a dividend of $2 per share on common stock.

20A-2. The secretary of the Analere Company prepared the following income statement for the current year:

Net sales		$600,000
Gain on sale of treasury stock		24,000
		$624,000
Less:		
Cost of goods sold	$325,000	
Operating expenses	180,000	
Loss on disposal of obsolete equipment	36,000	
Understatement of depreciation in prior years	17,000	
Dividends declared on common stock	25,000	
Addition to reserve for contingencies	20,000	
Provision for income taxes	27,000	
		630,000
Net loss for the year		$ (6,000)

At the beginning of the current year the audited financial statements of the company show unappropriated retained earnings of $190,000.

Instructions

a. Prepare a revised income statement and a statement of retained earnings, assuming that the current operating performance concept of income is to be used.

b. Prepare a revised income statement and a statement of retained earnings, assuming that the all-inclusive concept of income is to be used.

20A-3. The stockholders' equity of the Mason Corporation at December 1 of the current year was as follows:

> *Common stock, $50 par value, authorized 10,000 shares,*
>   *issued and outstanding 8,000 shares* *$400,000*
> *Paid-in capital in excess of par value* *60,000*
> *Retained earnings* *174,000*
>   *$634,000*

The following events relating to equity accounts took place prior to December 25: The company repurchased 400 shares of its common stock for $38,000. Stockholders donated back to the company 10% of their shares, which were immediately issued in exchange for certain patent rights valued at $75,000. Of the shares repurchased for cash, 100 were sold for $98 per share.

The company's retained earnings on January 1 of the current year were $150,000; the company had declared and paid a cash dividend of $2 per share on July 31. December net income was $15,000, and on December 30 the board of directors declared a cash dividend of $2.50 per share.

Instructions

a. Prepare the stockholders' equity section of the balance sheet as of December 31.

b. Prepare a statement of retained earnings for the year.

c. Compute the book value per share of common stock as of December 1 and December 31 of the current year.

20A-4. A comparative statement of the stockholders' equity of the Multnomah Corporation, together with certain additional information, is given below:

MULTNOMAH CORPORATION
Stockholders' Equity

	June 30, 1962	June 30, 1963	
Common stock, par value $40, authorized 5,000 shares; issued:			
1962, 3,000 shares	*$120,000*		
1963, 4,400 shares (600 held in treasury)		*$176,000*	
Stock dividend payable (380 shares) .		*15,200*	*$191,200*
Additional paid-in capital:			
On common stock, in excess of par value	*32,000*	*$ 62,000*	
Earnings capitalized in stock dividend		*14,800*	
On sale of treasury shares		*7,600*	*84,400*
Total contributed capital	*$152,000*		*$275,600*

Retained earnings:
  Appropriated:
    Reserve for plant expansion $30,000
    Reserve for treasury stock ...... $ 36,600
    Unappropriated 42,100   72,100   21,900   58,500

Total contributed capital and retained
  earnings $334,100
Less: cost of treasury stock   36,600
Total stockholders' equity $224,100 $297,500

Late in 1962, the company repurchased 1,000 shares of its own common stock at $61 per share. In May of 1963, 400 shares of treasury stock were sold at $80 per share. Cash dividends of $3 per share were declared on June 15, 1963, and a stock dividend was declared on June 30, 1963.

Instructions
a. Prepare general journal entries to record transactions relating to stockholders' equity that apparently took place during the year ended June 30, 1963.
b. Prepare a statement of retained earnings for the year ended June 30, 1963. Use three columnar headings: Unappropriated, Reserve for plant expansion, Reserve for treasury stock.

Group B

20B-1. The treasurer of the Lindholm Corporation has prepared a statement of the stockholders' equity at the end of the current year, as given below.

Stockholders' equity:
  6% cumulative preferred stock, 3,000 shares $300,000
  Common stock, 20,000 shares   292,000
  Surplus   363,000
    Total $955,000

The company is authorized to issue 10,000 shares of $100 par value preferred and 50,000 shares of $15 par value common. Of the 3,000 shares of preferred issued, 2,000 were issued at par and 1,000 were issued at 106 per share. A total of 22,000 shares of common have been issued at an average price of $22 per share. Of this total, 2,000 shares have been reacquired by the company at a cost of $38,000, which amount the treasurer has deducted from the capital stock account.

The preferred stock is callable at 107 per share. The company plans to call 1,000 shares of preferred in the future, and the board of directors has authorized that retained income be earmarked as not available for dividends to this extent. The company is organized in a state whose corporation law provides that the repurchase of treasury shares shall not impair stated capital.

Instructions. Restate the stockholders' equity section of the Lindholm Corporation in acceptable form.

20B-2. The stockholders' equity of the Marble Corporation at December 31, 1963, is shown below.

$6 preferred stock, no par, stated value $100; authorized 4,000 shares, issued and outstanding 3,000 shares	*$300,000*
Common stock, no par, stated value $20 per share; authorized 10,000 shares, issued and outstanding 7,500 shares	*150,000*
Additional capital paid in: common stock	*50,000*
Retained earnings, January 1, 1963	*15,000*
Net loss for 1963	*(12,000)*
	$503,000

The company paid no dividends on common stock during 1963, since dividends of $12 per share were in arrears on the preferred stock at January 1, 1963.

An audit at the end of 1963 disclosed the following: On July 1, 1962, the company had purchased equipment for $24,000, which was charged to an expense account by mistake. The equipment has an estimated service life of 10 years and an estimated salvage value of 10% of cost. On March 1, 1963, the company paid a three-year insurance premium in the amount of $1,800, which the bookkeeper charged in full to operating expense. Included in the computation of the net loss for the year was an item of $15,000 labeled "loss on resale of treasury stock (common)," which should be charged against Paid-in Capital in Excess of Stated Value.

Instructions

a. Prepare the necessary journal entries to correct the errors discovered in the audit. Any adjustments of revenue or expense for the current year may be made through the Income Summary account. Assume that the company follows the current operating performance concept of net income.

b. Prepare a statement of retained earnings for 1963.

c. Compute the book value per share of the common stock as of December 31, 1963.

20B-3. The accounts listed alphabetically below appear in the general ledger of the Brombach Corporation at December 31, 1963, after the books have been closed.

Accounts payable	*$ 34,720*
Accounts receivable	*96,510*
Accrued liabilities	*23,590*
Accumulated depreciation on buildings	*170,000*
Accumulated depreciation on equipment	*149,600*
Allowance for uncollectibles	*7,000*
Buildings	*490,000*
Capital from treasury stock transactions	*12,200*
Capital in excess of stated value: common	*30,000*
Cash	*30,490*
Common stock, no par	*300,000*
Dividends payable	*12,000*

Equipment	*$453,800*
Income taxes payable	*32,000*
Inventories (fifo cost)	*140,000*
Land	*50,000*
Long-term notes payable, due July 1, 1970	*200,000*
Notes receivable	*28,400*
Organization costs	*25,000*
Preferred stock, 6%	*200,000*
Premium on preferred stock	*10,000*
Prepaid expenses	*5,300*
Reserve for future plant expansion	*80,000*
Reserve for treasury stock	*58,700*
Retained earnings, as of Dec. 31	*58,390*
Treasury stock (at cost), (2,000 shares)	*58,700*

The company is authorized to issue 10,000 shares of 6%, $100 par value, preferred stock and 40,000 shares of no-par common, stated value $25.

Instructions. Prepare the December 31, 1963, balance sheet for the Brombach Corporation in a form suitable for publication.

20B-4. The stockholders' equity of the Mystic-Pak Corporation on December 31, 1963, appears below.

Common stock, 11,500 shares outstanding, par value $30	*$360,000*
Additional paid-in capital	*67,000*
Retained earnings	*120,000*
	$547,000
Less: treasury stock (at cost: 500 shares)	*18,000*
Total stockholders' equity	*$529,000*

On the basis of the number of shares outstanding at the end of each year, the book value of the common stock was $85 per share on December 31, 1962, and $100 per share on December 31, 1961. Early in 1963, the company split its shares 2 for 1 and repurchased 500 shares of stock shortly after the stock split had been made. A 20% stock dividend was declared in 1962, at a time when the market value of the stock was $77 per share.

The balance of retained earnings on January 1, 1961, was $140,000, and the changes in retained earnings throughout the three-year period result solely from net income and dividends.

Jacobs, a stockholder of Mystic-Pak, owned 100 shares of stock on December 31, 1961, and has neither sold any shares nor purchased additional shares. He received cash dividends at the end of each year as follows: 1961, $140; 1962, $180; 1963, $240.

Instructions. On the basis of the above information:
a. Prepare a statement of stockholders' equity at December 31, 1962.
b. Prepare a statement of stockholders' equity at December 31, 1961.
c. Determine the net income of the Mystic-Pak Corporation for each of the three years 1961, 1962, and 1963.

21

Bonds payable and sinking funds

Alternative methods of obtaining capital

One of the most interesting questions facing corporate management is the choice of methods of raising capital. Short-term capital needed for seasonal peaks of activity is often obtained through borrowing from banks; long-term funds for such purposes as new plant and equipment may be provided through long-term borrowing. Good financial management requires that short-term notes be used only to provide working capital. For example, a six-month bank loan might be arranged in order to buy merchandise for the peak selling season. The sale of the merchandise would provide cash with which to repay the bank loan. If funds are needed for a long-term purpose such as to pay for construction of a new building, the borrowing should be on a long-term basis. This will allow time for the increased earnings arising from the new plant to be used in retiring the loan.

Mortgage notes and corporation bonds. A small business in need of funds that will not be repaid for many years will often issue a long-term mortgage note, secured by a mortgage on land, buildings, and other fixed assets. The note is a promise to repay with interest the money borrowed; the accompanying mortgage gives the lender the right to take possession of the mortgaged property in the event of default by the borrower. The borrower (or mortgagor) promises not only to make regular interest payments and to repay the principal amount at the maturity of the note, but also to keep the mortgaged property adequately insured and to pay the taxes on the property as they become due.

A large corporation may also obtain funds through a mortgage note, but usually the amount of money needed is greater than any single lender can supply. In this case the corporation may sell bonds to the investing public, thus splitting the loan into a great many units, usually of $1,000 each. An example of corporation bonds is the 4% General Mortgage Bonds of The Atchison, Topeka and Santa Fe Railway Company due October 1, 1995, by which the Santa Fe borrowed approximately $156 million. These bonds are listed on the New York Stock Exchange and are bought and sold by investors daily.

The typical corporation bond is a formal promise to pay $1,000 at a fixed future date, with interest payments being made semiannually. The entire series of bonds is covered by a mortgage or deed of trust, which mortgages the corporation's fixed assets to a trustee for the benefit and protection of all the bondholders. It is the responsibility of the trustee to see that the corporation lives up to all the requirements of the mortgage contract or deed of trust. If the corporation fails to meet these requirements, the trustee may foreclose the mortgage, take possession of the pledged assets, and sell them to satisfy the claims of the bondholders. Foreclosure of a bond issue has been rare in recent years. In appraising the safety of an investment in corporate bonds, investors are inclined to place more importance upon the general financial strength and the earnings prospects of the company than upon the amount of pledged assets.

Characteristics of a bond

A bondholder is a creditor of the corporation; a stockholder is an owner. From the viewpoint of the issuing corporation, bonds payable constitute a long-term liability. Throughout the life of this liability the corporation makes semiannual payments of interest to the bondholder for the use of his money. These interest payments constitute an expense to the corporation and are deducted from each year's revenues in arriving at net income for the year.

Formal approval of the board of directors and of the stockholders is usually required before bonds can be issued. The contract between the corporation and the trustee representing the bondholders may place some limitation on the payment of dividends to stockholders during the life of the bonds and may require that cash or total current assets not be permitted to fall below specified levels. These restrictions are intended for the protection of the bondholders. Since the life of a bond may be for 50 years or more, the prospects for payment at maturity depend largely upon sound and profitable management of the business.

Funds to repay a long-term bond issue will presumably come from the retention of earnings. If earnings are not sufficient, the company may be unable to pay the bonds at maturity. In such cases the corporation may attempt to sell new bonds or stock to raise the necessary money, but these steps are difficult to carry out unless the earnings record is satisfactory. Consequently, the most essential element in repaying long-term debts is adequate earnings.

Of course, in the event that the corporation encounters financial difficulties and is unable to make the required payments of interest or principal, the bondholders may foreclose on the pledged assets, but this is a slow and complicated procedure which bondholders look upon only as a last-ditch alternative. When investing in a bond, the bondholder hopes and expects to receive all payments promptly without the need for taking any legal action. Inclusion in the bond indenture of restrictions upon dividend payments represents one precautionary step by the bondholder intended to increase the likelihood that the company will have cash available to make the required payments on the bonds.

Not all bonds are secured by the pledge of specific assets. An unsecured bond is called a debenture bond; its value rests upon the general credit of the corporation. A debenture bond issued by a very large and strong corporation may have a higher investment rating than a secured bond issued by a corporation in less satisfactory financial condition.

Some bonds have a single fixed maturity date for the entire issue. Other bond issues, called serial bonds, provide for varying maturity dates to lessen the problem of accumulating cash for payment. For example, serial bonds in the amount of $10 million issued in 1960 might call for $1 million of bonds to mature in 1975, and an additional $1 million to become due in each of the succeeding nine years. A bond issue is *callable* if the corporation reserves the right to pay off the bonds in advance of the scheduled maturity date. The call price is usually somewhat higher than the face value of the bonds.

As an additional attraction to investors, corporations sometimes include a conversion privilege in the bond indenture. A convertible bond is one which may be exchanged for common stock at the option of the bondholder. The advantages to the investor of the conversion feature in the event of increased earnings for the company have already been described in Chapter 17 with regard to convertible preferred stock.

Registered bonds and coupon bonds. Registered bonds derive their name from the fact that the name of the owner of the bond is registered with the issuing corporation, and payments of interest are made by checks mailed to the bondholder. The bondholder is thus protected against loss or theft of the bond. When the owner of a registered bond wishes to sell it, he endorses the bond just as in the case of a stock certificate.

Some bonds are registered *as to principal only,* and have coupons attached for the semiannual interest payments. Each six months during the life of the bond, one of these coupons becomes due. The bondholder detaches the coupon and deposits it with a bank for collection. This procedure is economical for the issuing corporation because it eliminates the need for issuing large numbers of interest checks. The bondholder is still protected against loss or theft of the principal amount of his investment by the fact that his ownership is registered with the issuing corporation.

Unregistered bonds also have interest coupons attached, but they are not registered in the name of the owner as to either interest or principal. Since unregistered bonds do not bear the name of the owner, ownership is transferred merely by delivery, and the risk of loss or theft is much greater.

Transferability of bonds. Corporation bonds, like capital stocks, are traded daily on organized security exchanges. The holder of a 50-year bond need not wait 50 years to convert his investment into cash. By placing a telephone call to a broker, he may sell his bond within a matter of minutes at the going market price. This quality of liquidity is one of the most attractive features of an investment in corporation bonds. When the investor sells a bond he receives payment from the person purchasing it. The transaction does not affect the issuing corporation, which continues to have the use of the borrowed funds until the maturity date of the bonds regardless of how many times the bonds may change hands.

Quotations for bonds. Corporate bond prices are quoted at a given amount per $100 of face value. For example, assume that a bond of $1,000 face amount (par value) is quoted at 106. The total price for the bond is 10 times 106, or $1,060. Market quotations for corporate bonds use an eighth of a dollar as the minimum variation. The following line from the financial page of a daily newspaper summarizes the day's trading in the bonds of Radio Corporation of America.

Bonds	*Sales*	*High*	*Low*	*Close*	*Net change*
RCA 3 1/2 80	49	94 1/2	93 7/8	94	+1/4

This line of condensed information indicates that 49 of Radio Corporations of America's 3 1/2 per cent $1,000 bonds maturing in 1980 were traded today. The highest price paid is reported as 94 1/2, or $945 for a bond of $1,000 face value. The lowest price was 93 7/8, or $938.75 for a $1,000 bond. The closing price (last sale of the day) was 94, or $940. This was one-quarter of a dollar above the closing price of the previous day, an increase of $2.50 in the price of a $1,000 bond.

Comparison of stocks and bonds

Interest payments on bonds payable are deductible as an expense in determining net income subject to corporation income tax, but dividends paid on common and preferred stock are not. Since corporations pay out more than half of their net income as Federal income tax, the use of bonds to obtain long-term capital offers a considerable tax saving as compared with the issuance of additional capital stock.

The interest rate on bonds is often lower than the dividend rate which would be necessary to raise a similar amount of capital through the sale of preferred stock. The borrowing costs arising from a bond issue also may have less impact upon the earnings of the common stockholders than would the dilution of the stock equity through issuance of additional shares of common stock.

Bonds do not carry voting rights and consequently do not pose a threat to the existing control of the corporation as long as interest payments are met promptly. If the corporation finds itself able to repay the borrowed funds before the scheduled maturity date, it may purchase the bonds from their holders and thus curtail the interest expense. Offsetting these advantages of bonds as a means of securing long-term funds is the fact that bond interest payments are a fixed charge which *must* be paid on schedule or the corporation may be forced to suspend business.

Effect of long-term borrowing upon common stock earnings. Assume that a growing and profitable corporation with common stock of $5 million is in need of $10 million cash to finance new buildings. The management is considering whether to issue 6% preferred stock or 5% bonds. Assume also that after acquisition of the new plant the net annual earnings of the corporation before deducting interest expense or income taxes will amount to $2 million. From the viewpoint of the common stockholders, which financing plan is preferable: 6% preferred stock or 5% bonds payable? The following schedule shows the net earnings available to the common stockholder under the two alternative methods of financing.

WHICH FINANCING PLAN IS BETTER?

	If 6% preferred stock is issued	If 5% bonds are issued
Annual net earnings before bond interest or income taxes	$2,000,000	$2,000,000
Deduct: interest on bonds		500,000
Net earnings before income taxes	$2,000,000	$1,500,000
Deduct: income taxes (assume 50% rate)	1,000,000	750,000
Net income	$1,000,000	$ 750,000
Deduct: preferred stock dividends	600,000	
Net income available for common stock dividends	$ 400,000	$ 750,000
Net earnings per share of common stock (50,000 shares outstanding)	$8	$15

The use of 5% bonds rather than 6% preferred stock under these circumstances offers a yearly saving to common stockholders of $350,000, or $7 per share of common stock. The saving arises from two factors: a $250,000 tax savings because of the deductibility of bond interest and a $100,000 saving because the bonds can be marketed at an interest rate lower than the dividend rate necessary on the preferred stock.

The principal argument for the 6% preferred stock as opposed to the 5% bond issue is that if the company's earnings should fall drastically, the operation of the business might be disrupted by inability to meet the fixed expense of bond interest payments, whereas a preferred dividend could be postponed for a year or two without serious repercussions.

Management planning of the bond issue

A corporation wishing to borrow money by issuing bonds faces months of preliminary work. Decisions must be made on such points as the amount to be borrowed, the interest rate to be offered, the maturity date, and the property to be pledged, if any. Answers must be found for such questions as the following: How much debt can the company safely handle in the event of adverse business conditions? What volume of sales will be necessary for the company to "break even" in the future after the fixed expenses have been increased by agreeing to make regular interest payments?

In forecasting the company's cash position for future periods, consideration must be given to the new requirement of semiannual bond interest payments as well as to the long-range problem of accumulating the cash required to pay the bonds at maturity. If the borrowed funds are to be invested in new plant facilities, will this expansion produce an increase in the cash inflow sufficient to meet the interest payments? If the bond issue includes a call provision, the company may plan to call in bonds in small amounts each year as cash becomes available. Perhaps the bond issue should be of the convertible variety; this feature might attract investors even though the interest rate were set at a relatively low level. In addition, if the bonds are convertible, the company may not have to accumulate cash for repayment of the entire issue. Effective long-range planning of the company's financial needs will greatly reduce the cost of securing capital and will leave the door open to issuing additional securities in the future on advantageous terms. More than one expanding corporation has discovered shortly after marketing a bond issue that additional funds would soon be necessary but that the first issue had involved pledging all the company's choice properties.

Report to directors on the proposed financing. The treasurer and the controller must work together, and in collaboration with investment bankers and other outside financial consultants, in finding the answers to the questions a bond issue raises. These officers will probably prepare a written report for the board of directors summarizing the proposed financing. This report may explain the company's need for the funds and the probable effects of the borrowing upon future earnings and financial condition. Various alternative types of bond issues may be described and the advantages and disadvantages of each explained. A report of this type can be most useful to the board of directors in reaching a decision.

Authorization of a bond issue. After the board of directors has decided upon the details of a bond issue, the proposal is presented to stockholders for their approval. Once this approval has been gained, the deed of trust is drawn and the bonds are printed. The trust deed describes the property to be mortgaged and states the maximum amount of bonds authorized. If the company's present financial requirements are for less than the amount of bonds authorized, only a portion of the bonds may be issued at this time. As each bond is issued it must be signed or "authenticated" by the trustee. Any authorized bonds not immediately issued are readily available for later issuance whenever additional capital is needed by the company.

No formal entry in the accounts is required for the act of authorization; however, a memorandum notation may be made in the Bonds Payable ledger account indicating the total amount of bonds authorized. The total authorized amount of a bond issue should always be disclosed in the balance sheet presentation of bonds payable.

Recording the issuance of bonds. To illustrate the entries for issuance of bonds, assume that a corporation was authorized on June 1, 1961, to issue $1 million of 20-year 5% bonds. All the bonds in the issue bear the June 1, 1961, date, and interest is computed from this date. Half were issued on June 1 at face value, and the following entry was made:

**ISSUANCE
OF BONDS**

Cash *500,000*
    Bonds Payable *500,000*
    To record sale of 500 5%, 20-year bonds at par.

If a balance sheet were prepared after this transaction, the information to be shown concerning bonds payable would be as follows:

**BONDS
PAYABLE
IN THE
BALANCE
SHEET**

Long-term liabilities:
    5% first mortgage bonds payable due June 1, 1981;
        authorized $1,000,000; issued *$500,000*

Information concerning the authorized amount of bonds as well as the amount issued is important to persons analyzing the company's statements. The possibility that additional bonds may be issued is significant in comparing the amount of bonds outstanding with the amount of property pledged as security, or in comparing the bond interest expense with the company's earnings.

Recording the issuance of bonds between interest dates. Bonds are frequently issued some time after the date printed on the bond. The investor is then required to pay the interest accrued to date of issuance in addition to the stated price of the bond. This practice enables the corporation to pay a full six months' interest on all bonds outstanding at the semiannual interest payment date. The accrued interest collected from an investor purchasing a bond between interest payment dates is thus returned to him on the next interest payment date. For example, assume that $100,000 face value of 6% bonds are issued at par and accrued interest, two months after the interest date printed on the bonds. The entry will be:

**BONDS
ISSUED
BETWEEN
INTEREST
DATES**

Cash *101,000*
    Bonds Payable *100,000*
    Bond Interest Expense *1,000*
    Issued $100,000 face value of 6%, 20-year bonds
    at 100 plus accrued interest.

Four months later on the regular semiannual interest payment date, a full six months' interest ($30 per bond) will be paid to all bondholders regardless of when they purchased their bonds. The entry for the semiannual interest payment is as follows:

**HOW MUCH
NET
INTEREST
EXPENSE?**

Bond Interest Expense *3,000*
        Cash *3,000*
*Paid semiannual interest on $100,000 face value of
6% bonds.*

The combination of this $3,000 debit to Bond Interest Expense and the $1,000 credit made at the time of selling the bonds leaves a $2,000 debit balance in Bond Interest Expense, representing the cost of the borrowed money for the four months that the bonds were outstanding. Now, consider these interest transactions from the standpoint of the investor. He paid for two months' accrued interest at the time of purchasing the bonds, and he received a check for six months' interest after holding the bonds for only four months. He has, therefore, been reimbursed properly for the use of his money for four months.

Setting the contract rate of interest. A corporation wishing to borrow money by issuing bonds must pay the going market rate of interest for loans of this category. The market rate of interest fluctuates from day to day in response to changes in the demand for and supply of funds. On any given date the going market rate of interest is in reality a whole schedule of rates corresponding to the financial strength of different borrowers. The stronger the financial standing of a corporation, the lower the interest rate at which it will be able to borrow. United States government bonds are considered the safest of all types of bonds and carry the lowest interest rates. However, the rate of interest on government bonds may change considerably over a period of time. If the prevailing rate of interest on 20-year government bonds on a given date is 4%, the market rate might be 5% for the highest grade bonds of leading industrial corporations, and for companies of lesser financial standing the market rate might be 5 1/2 or 6%.

The preparation of a corporate bond issue requires several months' work, during which time the bond indenture is drawn, authorizations secured, and the bonds printed. The rate of interest to be printed on the bonds must be decided upon months before the bonds are offered for sale. In setting this rate, the corporation estimates what the prevailing market rate of interest for bonds of this type will be on the planned date of sale. Since market rates of interest are constantly fluctuating, it must be expected that the contract rate of interest printed on the bonds will seldom agree with the market rate of interest at the date the bonds are issued.

Bond discount

In contrast with capital stock, bonds may be sold at less than par value or face value without creating any contingent liability on the part of the investor. The bondholder is not an owner; he is merely lending money to the corporation, and under no circumstances does he have any obligation to the corporation or to its other creditors.

If the interest rate carried by an issue of bonds is lower than the market rate for bonds of this grade, the bonds can be sold only at a discount. For example, assume that a corporation issues $1 million face value of 5%, 10-year bonds. Each bond will pay the holder $50 interest (5% $\times$ $1,000) each year, consisting of two semiannual payments of $25 each. If the market rate of interest were exactly 5%, the bonds would sell at par, but if the market rate of interest is higher than 5%, no one will be willing to pay $1,000 for a bond which will return only $50 a year. The price at which the bonds can be sold will, therefore, be less than par. Assume that the best price obtainable is 98 ($980 for each $1,000 bond). The issuance of the bonds will be recorded by the following entry:

ISSUING BONDS AT DISCOUNT	*Cash* .... 980,000 *Discount on Bonds Payable* .... 20,000 *Bonds Payable* .... 1,000,000 *Issued $1,000,000 face value of 5%, 10-year bonds at 98.*

Bond discount as part of the cost of borrowing. In the preceding illustration the corporation received $980 for each $1,000 bond issued; 10 years later when the bond matures, the corporation must repay the bondholder $1,000. If there were no semiannual interest payments, the cost of borrowing would be $20 per bond, the difference between the amount borrowed and the amount repaid. In addition to this $20 interest cost, however, the corporation must pay $50 interest a year ($25 every six months) during the 10 years the bond is outstanding, or a total of $500 in regular cash interest payments. The total cost of borrowing is, therefore, $520 for each bond, or $52 on a yearly basis. To state this principle in more general terms, we may say that whenever bonds are issued at a discount, *the total interest cost over the life of the issue is equal to the amount of the discount plus the regular cash interest payments.*

For the $1 million bond issue in our example, the total interest cost is $520,000, of which $500,000 represents 20 semiannual cash payments of interest and $20,000 represents the discount on the issue. On a yearly basis, total interest expense is $52,000, consisting of $50,000 paid in cash and $2,000 of the bond discount. This picture of the cost of borrowing can be made more vivid by the following tabulation of the total amounts of cash received and paid out by the corporation in connection with the bond issue.

Cash to be paid:		
Face value of bonds at maturity	$1,000,000	
Interest ($50,000 a year for 10 years)	500,000	
Total cash to be paid		$1,500,000
Cash received:		
From issuance of bonds at a discount		980,000
Excess of cash to be paid over cash received (total interest expense) .		$ 520,000
Yearly interest expense ($520,000 ÷ 10)		$ 52,000

In our example the Bond Discount account has an initial debit balance of $20,000; each year one-tenth of this amount, or $2,000, will be amortized or written off to Bond Interest Expense. Amortizing bond discount means transferring a portion of the discount to bond interest expense each accounting period during the life of the bonds. As indicated by the above schedule, the annual interest expense is $52,000. This balance is produced in the Bond Interest Expense account each year as a result of debits for $50,000 in cash interest payments and debits for $2,000 transferred from the Bond Discount account. Assuming that the interest payment dates are June 30 and December 31, the entries to be made each six months to record bond interest expenses are as follows:

PAYMENT
OF BOND
INTEREST
AND AMOR-
TIZATION
OF BOND
DISCOUNT

Bond Interest Expense	25,000	
Cash		25,000
Paid semiannual interest on $1,000,000 of 5% 10-year bonds.		
Bond Interest Expense	1,000	
Discount on Bonds Payable		1,000
Amortized 1/20 of discount on 10-year bond issue.		

The above entries serve to charge Bond Interest Expense with $26,000 each six months, or a total of $52,000 a year. Bond interest expense will be uniform throughout the 10-year life of the bond issue, and the Discount on Bonds Payable account will be completely written off by the end of the tenth year.

Bond premium

Let us now change our basic illustration by assuming that the $1 million issue of 5%, 10-year bonds is sold at a premium rather than a discount. Bonds will sell above par if the contract rate of interest specified on the bonds is higher than the current market rate for bonds of this grade. Assume that the bonds are sold at a price of 102 ($1,020 for each $1,000 bond); the entry will be as follows:

```
Cash ...................................  1,020,000
        Bonds Payable .................            1,000,000
        Premium on Bonds Payable ........            20,000
Issued $1,000,000 face value of 5%, 10-year
bonds at price of 102.
```

The amount received from issuance of the bonds is $20,000 greater than the amount which must be repaid at maturity. This $20,000 premium is not a gain but is to be offset against the regular cash interest payments in determining the net cost of borrowing. Whenever bonds are issued at a premium, *the total interest cost over the life of the issue is equal to the regular cash interest payments minus the amount of the premium.* In our example the total interest cost over the life of the bonds will be $480,000, as shown by the following tabulation:

```
Cash to be paid by the borrowing corporation:
    At maturity: face amount of the bonds ............  $1,000,000
    In interest: payable in 20 semiannual payments of
        $25,000 each ................................     500,000    $1,500,000

Cash received by the borrowing corporation:
    From issuance of bonds at a premium .............                 1,020,000

Total interest expense over 10-year life of the bonds ....            $  480,000

Interest expense each year ..........................                $   48,000
```

Each year's interest expense of $48,000 consists of two elements: (1) the $50,000 paid in cash to the bondholders, and (2) an offsetting $2,000 transferred from the Premium on Bonds Payable account to the credit side of the Interest Expense account. The semiannual entries on June 30 and December 31 to record payment of bond interest and amortization of bond premium are as follows:

PAYMENT
OF BOND
INTEREST
AND AMOR-
TIZATION
OF BOND
PREMIUM

```
Bond Interest Expense ....................  25,000
        Cash ...............................            25,000
Paid semiannual bond interest on $1,000,000 of
5%, 10-year bonds.

Premium on Bonds Payable ..................   1,000
        Bond Interest Expense ...............             1,000
Amortized 1/20 of premium on 10-year bond issue.
```

Year-end adjustments for bond interest expense

In the preceding illustration, it was assumed that one of the semiannual dates for payment of bond interest coincided with the end of the company's accounting year. In most cases, however, the semiannual interest payment dates will fall during an accounting period rather than on the last day of the year.

For purposes of illustration, assume that $1 million of 5%, 10-year bonds are issued at a price of 98 on October 1, 1962. Interest payment dates are April 1 and October 1. The total discount to be amortized amounts to $20,000, or $1,000 in each six-month interest period. The company keeps its accounts on a calendar-year basis; consequently, adjusting entries will be necessary as of December 31 for the accrued interest and the amortization of discount applicable to the three-month period since the last interest payment date.

ADJUSTING
ENTRIES
FOR BOND
INTEREST

Bond Interest Expense	*12,500*	
Accrued Bond Interest Payable		*12,500*
To record bond interest accrued for three-month period from October 1 to December 31.		
Bond Interest Expense	*500*	
Discount on Bonds Payable		*500*
To record amortization of bond discount for three-month period from October 1 to end of year.		

The effect of these year-end adjusting entries is to make the Bond Interest Expense account show the proper interest expense ($13,000) for the three months that the bonds were outstanding (October 1 to December 31) during 1962. The Bond Interest Expense account will be closed to the Income Summary account; the Accrued Bond Interest Payable account will remain on the books as a liability until the next regular interest payment date.

Bond discount and bond premium in the balance sheet

In the preceding example in which a 5%, 10-year bond issue of $1 million was issued for $980,000, a balance sheet prepared immediately after the issuance of the bonds should show the facts as follows:

BOND
DISCOUNT
ON BALANCE
SHEET . . .

Long-term liabilities:		
5% bonds payable	*$1,000,000*	
Less: bond discount	*20,000*	*$980,000*

One year later, the bond discount would have been amortized to the extent of $2,000 and the liability would have risen accordingly in the balance sheet.

Long-term liabilities:
5% bonds payable *$1,000,000*
Less: bond discount *18,000*   *$982,000*

At the maturity of the bond issue ten years after issuance, the corporation must pay $1,000,000, but at the time of issuing the bonds, the "present value" of this debt is $980,000. As the bond discount is amortized, the net amount of the liability shown on each succeeding balance sheet will be $2,000 greater than for the preceding year. At the maturity date of the bonds the valuation account, Discount on Bonds Payable, will have been reduced to zero and the liability will have risen to $1 million.

Parallel reasoning applies to bond premium, which is logically shown on the balance sheet as an addition to bonds payable. As the premium is amortized, the net amount of the liability is reduced year by year, until, at the maturity date of the bonds, the premium will have been completely written off and the liability will stand at the face amount of the bond issue.

Although the above-described treatment of bond discount and bond premium is regarded as theoretically sound by most accountants, some corporation balance sheets continue the older practice of showing bond discount among the assets, under the group caption of Deferred Charges. Under this method of balance sheet presentation, bond discount is regarded as deferred interest that will become interest expense over the life of the bonds. Similarly, premium on bonds may be listed under the heading of Deferred Credits on the liability side of the balance sheet.

The role of the underwriter in marketing a bond issue

An investment banker or underwriter is usually employed to market a bond issue, just as in the case of capital stock. The corporation turns the entire bond issue over to the underwriter at a specified price (say, $104); the underwriter sells the bonds to the public at a slightly higher price (say, $105). By this arrangement the corporation is assured of receiving the entire amount of funds on a specified date. The calculation of the bond discount or bond premium is based on the net amount which the issuing corporation receives from the underwriter, not on the price paid by the public for the bonds.

As an illustration, assume that an issue of $10 million of 5% bonds is sold to the public through an underwriter at a price of $1,050 per bond, or a total of $10,500,000. The underwriting agreement provides that the underwriter is to retain $10 for each bond sold and to transmit the remaining $1,040 to the issuing corporation. The corporation would receive a total of $10,400,000 and would consider the bonds to have been sold at a premium of $400,000.

Bond sinking fund

To make a bond issue attractive to investors, the corporation may agree in the bond indenture to create a sinking fund, exclusively for use in paying the bonds at maturity. A bond sinking fund is created by setting aside a specified amount of cash at regular intervals. The cash is usually deposited with a trustee, who invests it in conservative securities and adds the interest earned on these securities to the amount of the sinking fund. The periodic deposits of cash plus the interest earned on the sinking fund securities should cause the fund to equal the amount of the bond issue by the maturity date. When the bond issue approaches maturity, the trustee sells all the securities in the fund and uses the cash proceeds to pay the holders of the bonds. Any excess cash remaining in the fund will be returned to the corporation.

The amount of cash that must be deposited in the fund each year to build a fund sufficient to pay the bonds at maturity depends upon the rate of compound interest earned on the sinking fund securities. Referring again to the example of a 5%, 10-year bond issue of $1 million, assume that the sinking fund trustee will be able to keep the entire sinking fund invested and will earn exactly 3% a year. The amount of interest earned will increase from year to year because of the increasing size of the fund. According to compound interest tables, a deposit of $87,230 each year and investment of the fund to earn 3% annually will produce a fund of approximately $1 million in 10 years. The accumulation of such a fund is illustrated in the following schedule:

Fund Accumulation Schedule			
End of year	Interest earned	Amount deposited	Amount of fund
1		$87,230	$ 87,230
2	$ 2,617	87,230	177,077
3	5,312	87,230	269,619
4	8,089	87,230	364,938
5	10,948	87,230	463,116
6	13,894	87,230	564,240
7	16,928	87,230	668,398
8	20,052	87,230	775,680
9	23,270	87,230	886,180
10	26,586	87,234 *	1,000,000

* The deposit in the tenth year was increased by $4 to compensate for the omission of odd cents from the deposits of preceding years.

Entries illustrating operation of a sinking fund. The key steps in the operation of a sinking fund are as follows: (1) annual deposits of cash in the fund; (2) investment of the sinking fund cash so that interest will be earned; (3) collection of interest by the trustee; (4) sale of sinking fund securities; and (5) use of the sinking fund cash to pay the bonds.

1. Annual deposits in the fund. A check is drawn on the general bank account and turned over to the trustee. The cash segregated by this action is still owned by the corporation but is no longer classified as a current asset, because it is not available for payment of current liabilities. The journal entry to record a deposit of cash with the sinking fund trustee is:

DEPOSIT
OF CASH IN
SINKING
FUND

Sinking Fund Cash	87,230	
Cash		87,230
To record annual deposit of cash with trustee.		

2. Investment of sinking fund cash in securities. If the fund is to grow as planned, all cash received by the trustee must be invested promptly. As a practical matter, however, it is not always possible to invest odd amounts or to purchase securities immediately upon receipt of funds. For these reasons the earnings on the fund may vary from the scheduled amounts. Purchase of securities by the trustee is recorded as follows:

SINKING
FUND CASH
INVESTED

Sinking Fund Securities	87,230	
Sinking Fund Cash		87,230
Purchase of investments by trustee of sinking fund.		

3. Collection of income earned on sinking fund securities. Interest earned on sinking fund securities will be received at various dates during the year. The following entry represents a year's interest earnings on securities acquired with the first annual deposit:

EARNINGS
ON SINKING
FUND

Sinking Fund Cash	2,617	
Sinking Fund Income		2,617
Interest collected on sinking fund investments.		

4. Sale of sinking fund securities. At the end of the tenth year, the trustee will convert the sinking fund securities into cash so that he can pay off the bondholders. Some gain or loss will ordinarily be realized when the securities are sold, and as a result the fund will either exceed or be somewhat short of the amount required to pay the bondholders. In the following entry, it is assumed that a gain of $8,000 was realized on the sale of the sinking fund securities:

SINKING
FUND
SECURITIES
SOLD

Sinking Fund Cash *894,180*
    Sinking Fund Securities *886,180*
    Gain on Sale of Sinking Fund Securities .   *8,000*
To record sale by trustee of sinking fund securi-
ties at a profit.

5. *Payment of the bonds.* After sale of the sinking fund securities, the fund consists solely of cash in the amount of $1,008,000, derived from the following sources:

Cash from tenth annual deposit .... $ 87,234
Interest collected during tenth year   26,586
Cash from sale of sinking fund securities   894,180
    Total cash in fund $1,008,000

Of this fund, $1 million is used by the trustee to pay the bondholders and the excess cash of $8,000 remaining in the fund is returned to the corporation's general bank account. The entries for these two final steps are as follows:

UTILIZATION
OF FUND

Bonds Payable *1,000,000*
    Sinking Fund Cash *1,000,000*
Paid bonds at maturity.

Cash *8,000*
    Sinking Fund Cash *8,000*
To restore to general bank account the excess
cash remaining in sinking fund after payment
of bonds.

If the sale of the sinking fund securities by the trustee at the end of the tenth year had resulted in a loss, it would have been necessary for the corporation to make a cash contribution to the fund to enable the trustee to pay the bonds.

Bond sinking fund and sinking fund income in the financial statements. The cash and securities comprising a bond sinking fund usually appear as a single amount in the Other Assets section of the balance sheet. Under no conditions should the fund be included in current assets because it is not available for payment of current liabilities. Some companies prefer to show the bond sinking fund and any other noncurrent investments in a separate group entitled Investments, placed just below the current asset section.

Interest earned on sinking fund securities constitutes earnings of the corporation, and the Sinking Fund Income account is closed each year into the Income Summary account. In the income statement, the sinking fund earnings are usually shown at the bottom of the statement under the heading of Other Income.

Reserve for sinking fund

The nature of appropriated surplus reserves (or reserves created from retained earnings) was discussed at length in Chapter 19. Since a reserve for sinking fund is an example of this type of reserve, the following section is merely an extension of the previous discussion of reserves.

It was formerly the custom for a bond indenture to require not only a sinking fund for the protection of bondholders, but also a reserve for sinking fund. The reserve was merely a subdivision of retained earnings transferred to a separate account to indicate unavailability for dividends. The only function of a sinking fund reserve was to place a restriction on dividend payments during the life of a bond issue. However, the creation of a reserve proved to be an ineffective means of restricting dividends, and the use of sinking fund reserves has been virtually abandoned in present-day corporation finance. It is now the custom to protect bondholders by including in the bond indenture a requirement that dividends shall not exceed a specified percentage of earnings as long as the bonds are outstanding. Another effective form of restriction is a provision that during the life of the bond issue no dividends shall be paid which would have the effect of reducing the working capital (current assets minus current liabilities) below a specified amount. In short, direct restrictions on dividend payments have now largely replaced sinking fund reserves as a device for protection of bondholders. The sinking fund itself is a useful device; the reserve for sinking fund is of little use.

To illustrate the purpose (and also the ineffectiveness of a reserve for sinking fund), assume that a corporation issues 10-year bonds payable and that the bond indenture requires a sinking fund to be accumulated at the rate of $100,000 a year. Assume also that the annual earnings of the corporation are $150,000. Since most of the cash inflow from earnings will be used to make the annual deposits in the sinking fund, the corporation will need to restrict its dividends to a relatively small portion of the earnings. Otherwise the combined outflow of cash for sinking fund deposits and dividends might reduce the company's working capital to the point of endangering continued operation.

To prevent such impairment of working capital during the life of the bonds, the bond indenture might require that each year the company must transfer from the Retained Earnings account to a Reserve for Sinking Fund account an amount of $100,000. The credit balance in the reserve account, although still part of the stockholders' equity, would not be available for dividends. The annual entry to comply with a sinking fund reserve requirement would be as follows:

"RESERVE"
IS NOT
CASH

> Retained Earnings 100,000
>   Reserve for Sinking Fund   100,000
> *To transfer part of retained earnings to a reserve*
> *account.*

Ten years later after the bonds have matured and been paid, the reserve is restored to the Retained Earnings account by the following entry:

ELIMINATION
OF THE
RESERVE

> Reserve for Sinking Fund 1,000,000
>   Retained Earnings   1,000,000
> *To eliminate the reserve by transfer to Re-*
> *tained Earnings.*

Since the reserve for sinking fund is merely retained earnings under another name, it would appear as follows in a balance sheet prepared three years after issuance of the bonds:

RESERVE
IS PART OF
RETAINED
EARNINGS

> *Stockholders' equity*
>   *Capital stock* $5,000,000
>   *Retained earnings:*
>   *Reserve for sinking fund* $300,000
>   *Free and available for dividends* 900,000
>   *Total retained earnings*   1,200,000
>   *Total stockholders' equity* $6,200,000

The weakness in the use of a reserve for sinking fund as a device for restricting dividends is that a corporation with a relatively large Retained Earnings account at the date of the bond issue could make the required annual transfers to the sinking fund reserve, yet still be able, if it chose, to pay dividends equal to the full amount of its earnings, thereby draining working capital out of the corporation to a dangerous extent.

Another objection to reserves for sinking funds is the misunderstanding and confusion which they cause many readers of the corporation's financial statements. The title Reserve for Sinking Fund suggests to many people that this item represents cash or other assets held "in reserve" for payment of the bonds. Such interpretations are completely in error. The Reserve for Sinking Fund is not an asset account; it has a credit balance and is created by transfer from Retained Earnings. To divide the company's Retained Earnings account into two accounts and call one of them a Reserve for Sinking Fund causes no basic change in the company's financial condition. To understand the nature of a sinking fund reserve, it is helpful to emphasize that the only possible disposition of the reserve is to return it to the Retained Earnings account.

Retirement of bond issues from general funds

The payment of bonds at maturity out of a sinking fund accumulated through regular deposits with a trustee has been described. However, not all bond issues require the creation of a sinking fund. If a sinking fund is not used, the bonds are paid at maturity out of the general bank account of the corporation. One year before the maturity date, the bonds should be reclassified as current liabilities on the balance sheet, because they are to be paid from current assets. When a sinking fund is used to pay bonds at maturity, there should be no reclassification of the Bonds Payable account from a fixed liability to a current liability. However, when a sinking fund does not exist, failure to reclassify the bonds payable to the status of a current liability as the maturity date approaches will result in a misstatement of working capital. The entry to record the retirement of bonds from the general cash fund of the company will be as follows:

RETIRING
BONDS
WITHOUT
SINKING
FUND

Bonds payable .... *xxx*
    Cash .... *xxx*
Paid bonds at maturity.

A serial bond issue, as explained earlier in this chapter, is one that provides a series of maturity dates for various portions of the issue. Sinking funds are generally considered unnecessary for serial bonds. One year before the maturity date of each series, that portion of the issue should be reclassified from the status of a long-term liability to that of a current liability.

Retirement of bonds before maturity

Bonds are sometimes retired before the scheduled maturity date. Most bond issues contain a call provision, permitting the corporation to redeem the bonds by paying a specified price, usually a few points above par. Even without a call provision, the corporation may retire its bonds before maturity by purchasing them in the open market. If the bonds can be purchased by the issuing corporation at less than their book value, a gain is realized on the retirement of the debt. By *book value* is meant the face value of the bonds plus any unamortized premium or minus any unamortized discount.

For example, assume that the Pico Corporation has outstanding a $1 million bond issue and there is unamortized premium on the books in the amount of $20,000. The bonds are callable at 105 and the company exercises the call provision on 100 of the bonds, or 10% of the issue. The entry would be as follows:

BONDS CALLED AT PRICE ABOVE BOOK VALUE

Bonds Payable	100,000	
Premium on Bonds Payable	2,000	
Loss on Retirement of Bonds	3,000	
Cash		105,000
To record retirement of $100,000 face value of bonds called at 105.		

The book value of each of the 100 called bonds was $1,020, whereas the call price was $1,050. For each bond called the company incurred a loss of $30, a total loss of $3,000 on the bonds retired. Notice that when 10% of the total issue was called, 10% of the unamortized premium was written off.

To illustrate a gain on the retirement of bonds, assume that Rodeo Corporation has outstanding a bond issue of $1 million face value, and has on its books unamortized discount of $50,000. Rodeo Corporation buys 100 of its bonds on the open market at a price of 88. The retirement of the bonds results in a gain because the purchase price is less than the book value of the liability being eliminated, as shown by the following entry:

BONDS REACQUIRED AT PRICE BELOW BOOK VALUE

Bonds Payable	100,000	
Cash		88,000
Discount on Bonds Payable		5,000
Gain on Retirement of Bonds		7,000
Purchased 100 bonds for retirement at price of 88.		

Each of the Rodeo Corporation bonds had a book value of $950 (face value $1,000 minus unamortized discount of $50). To dispose of a liability carried at this amount, the corporation handed out assets of only $880, thereby effecting a gain of $70 on each bond retired.

Illustration of corporation balance sheet

In this chapter and the preceding chapters on corporations, sections of balance sheets have been shown in several illustrations. A complete and fairly detailed balance sheet of the Crenshaw Corporation is now presented to bring together many of the individual features which have been discussed. In studying this corporation balance sheet, however, the student should bear in mind that current practice includes many variations and alternatives in the choice of terminology and the arrangement of items in the statements.

CRENSHAW CORPORATION
Balance Sheet
December 31, 19___

Assets

Current assets:

Cash		$ 855,612	
United States government securities, at cost			
(market value $312,800)		310,000	
Accounts receivable	$1,180,200		
Less: allowance for bad debts	15,000	1,165,200	
Inventories		1,300,800	
Prepaid expenses		125,900	
Total current assets			$3,757,512

Investments:

Bond sinking fund		$ 364,938	
Real estate not used in business		80,000	444,938

Fixed assets:

Land		$ 500,000	
Buildings	$3,482,100		
Less: accumulated depreciation ...	400,000	3,082,100	3,582,100

Other assets:

Organization cost		$ 60,000	
Long-term deposit on lease		50,000	110,000
Total assets			$7,894,550

QUESTIONS

1. Distinguish between the two terms in each of the following pairs:
   a. Long-term notes; bonds
   b. Mortgage bonds; debenture bonds
   c. Fixed-maturity bonds; serial bonds
   d. Coupon bonds; registered bonds

2. Companies X and Y have the same amount of operating income. Determine the amount earned per share of common stock for each of the two companies and explain the source of any difference.

Liabilities and Stockholders' Equity

Current liabilities:

Accounts payable	$1,065,840	
Estimated income taxes payable	384,310	
Dividends payable	10,000	
Bond interest payable	10,000	
Total current liabilities		$1,470,150

Long-term liabilities:

Bonds payable, 4%, due Oct. 1, 1970	$1,000,000	
Less: discount on bonds payable	18,000	982,000
Total liabilities		$2,452,150

Stockholders' equity:

Cumulative 5% preferred stock, $100 par, 8,000 shares authorized and issued	$ 800,000	
Common stock, $1 par, authorized 1,000,000 shares, issued 600,000 shares of which 1,000 shares are held in the treasury	600,000	
Paid-in capital in excess of par value ..	2,400,000	
Total paid-in capital	$3,800,000	

Retained earnings:

Reserve for contingencies	$ 400,000	
Unappropriated retained earnings, of which $8,000 is restricted by reason of treasury stock purchased	1,250,400	1,650,400
Total paid-in capital and retained earnings		$5,450,400
Deduct: treasury stock (at cost)		8,000
Total stockholders' equity		$5,442,400
Total liabilities and stockholders' equity		$7,894,550

	Company X	Company Y
5% debenture bonds	$500,000	$ 200,000
6% cumulative preferred stock, $100 par ..	500,000	300,000
Common stock, $25 stated value	500,000	1,000,000
Retained earnings	250,000	250,000
Operating income, before interest and income taxes (assume a 40% tax rate) ...	300,000	300,000

3. K Company has decided to finance expansion by issuing $10 million of 20-year debenture bonds and will ask a number of underwriters to bid on the bond issue. Discuss the factors that will determine the amount bid by the underwriters for these bonds.

4. What are convertible bonds? Discuss the advantages and disadvantages of convertible bonds from the standpoint of (*a*) the investor and (*b*) the issuing corporation.

5. Determine the average annual interest cost of the following bond issues:

	Company A	Company B
Maturity value of bonds	*$1,000,000*	*$4,000,000*
Contract interest rate	*5%*	*4%*
Price received for bonds on issue date	*103*	*96*
Length of time from issue date to maturity	*10 years*	*10 years*

6. G Company has paid-in capital of $10 million, and retained earnings of $3 million. The company has just issued $1 million in 20-year, 5% bonds. It is proposed that a policy be established of appropriating $50,000 of retained earnings each year to enable the company to retire the bonds at maturity. Evaluate the merits of this proposal in accomplishing the desired result.

7. Discuss the advantages and disadvantages of a call provision in a bond contract from the viewpoint of (*a*) the bondholder and (*b*) the issuing corporation.

PROBLEMS

Group A

21A-1. The Tinkham Company issued, on September 1, 1962, $600,000 in 4 1/2% debenture bonds. Interest is payable semiannually and the bonds mature in 10 years.

    Instructions. Make the necessary adjusting entries as of December 31, 1962 and the journal entry to record the payment of bond interest on March 1, 1963, under each of the following assumptions:
    a. The bonds were issued at 97.
    b. The bonds were issued at 102.

21A-2. The items shown below appear on the Ebbets Company balance sheet as of December 31, 1962.

Current liabilities:		
Interest payable on bonds		*$ 25,000*
Long-term liabilities:		
Bonds payable, 5%, due Apr. 1, 1973 ..	*$2,000,000*	
Discount on bonds payable	*147,600*	*1,852,400*

The bonds are callable on any interest date; on October 1, 1963, the Ebbets Company called $1 million of its bonds at 102.

Instructions

a. Prepare journal entries to record the semiannual interest payment on April 1, 1963.

b. Prepare journal entries to record the call of the bonds and payment of interest on October 1, 1963.

c. Make a journal entry to record the accrual of interest expense as of December 31, 1963.

21A-3. The items listed below appear, with normal balances, on the balance sheet of the Oregon Machine Company at the end of the current year:

Accounts payable	$1,171,000
Accounts receivable	997,500
Accumulated depreciation: buildings	1,390,000
Accumulated depreciation: equipment	2,405,000
Allowance for bad debts	20,000
Bond interest payable	42,500
Bond sinking fund	500,000
Buildings	3,240,000
Cash	624,000
Common stock, no par, stated value $5	1,060,000
Debenture bonds payable, 4 3/4%	2,000,000
Dividends payable	222,500
Earnings retained in business as of Dec. 31	?
Equipment	4,125,000
Income taxes payable	326,000
Inventories (lower of cost or market)	1,386,000
Land	280,000
Long-term advance to supplier	142,000
Marketable securities (at cost; market $180,000)	175,000
Organization costs	75,000
Paid-in capital in excess of par or stated value	975,000
Patents and licenses	320,000
Preferred stock, 6%, cumulative, $50 par	350,000
Premium on bonds payable	23,000
Prepaid expenses	23,500
Research and development in progress	181,000
Reserve for bond retirement	500,000
Reserve for retirement of preferred stock	175,000
Treasury stock, 5,200 shares at cost	49,600

Other data. The company is authorized to issue 10,000 shares of preferred stock and 500,000 shares of common stock. The debenture bonds are due 12 years from balance sheet date.

Instructions. Prepare, in form suitable for publication, a statement of the company's financial position as of the end of the current year. Determine the appropriate amount to insert in place of the question mark for retained earnings, in order to complete the statement.

21A-4. The history of the Fiction Company can be described in two 10-year cycles:

First 10 years: The company was organized by issuing 1,000 shares of common stock at $50 per share, which was the par value. The directors immediately borrowed $100,000 on a 10-year mortgage note, with interest at 5%. The proceeds of this loan were invested in plant estimated to have a service life of 10 years. The balance sheet at the beginning of the 10-year period showed:

FICTION COMPANY
Balance Sheet
At Organization

Assets		*Liabilities and Equity*	
Current assets	*$ 30,000*	*Mortgage payable*	*$100,000*
Land	*20,000*		
Plant	*100,000*	*Capital stock, $50 par*	*50,000*
	$150,000		*$150,000*

The corporation earned $12,000 after interest and income taxes in each of the first 10 years, and distributed dividends in this amount each year to its stockholders. All earnings were reflected as increases in current assets. At the end of the 10-year period, the plant was completely worn out and the mortgage note was paid in full.

Second 10 years: At the beginning of this period, the company issued a new 10-year mortgage note and received $100,000 to finance the construction of a new plant. The company continued to earn $12,000 per year after interest and taxes, which was reflected as an increase in current assets, but paid only $2,000 per year in dividends to stockholders. An appropriation of retained earnings of $10,000 per year was authorized by the directors and entered in an account labeled Reserve for Mortgage Retirement. At the end of the second 10-year period the mortgage note was paid in full, and the directors met to consider the problem of replacing the plant, which was completely worn out.

Instructions
a. Prepare in condensed form the balance sheet of the Fiction Company
(1) At the end of the fifth year of operation
(2) At the end of the tenth year of operation (before payment of the mortgage note)
(3) At the end of the fifteenth year of operation
(4) At the end of the twentieth year of operation, after paying the mortgage note but before replacing the plant
b. Will the company find it necessary to borrow on a new mortgage note to rebuild the plant at the end of the twentieth year? Explain your answer, and discuss the problem of handling the reserve for mortgage retirement after the new plant has been built.

Group B

21B-1. Company R issued $600,000 of 4%, 10-year bonds on January 2, 1963. Interest is payable semiannually on June 30 and December 31. The bonds were sold to an underwriting group at 90.

Company S issued $600,000 of 6%, 10-year bonds on January 2, 1963. Interest is payable semiannually on June 30 and December 31. The bonds were sold to an underwriting group at 110.

Instructions

a. Prepare journal entries, omitting explanations, to record all transactions relating to the bond issues of these two companies during the year 1963.

b. Explain why the average bond interest cost per year is the same for Company R and Company S, despite the difference in the terms of the two bond contracts.

21B-2. Malbro Company is authorized to issue $800,000 in 3%, 12-year debenture bonds dated January 1, 1962. Interest is to be paid semiannually on June 30 and December 31. The bonds were sold to an underwriter at 93, plus accrued interest, on May 1, 1962.

Instructions

a. Prepare all journal entries necessary to record the bond issue and the bond interest cost during the year 1962. (Note that the bonds will be outstanding for a period of 11 years and 8 months.)

b. Prepare a schedule showing the total amount of bond interest cost incurred by the Malbro Company during 1962 and 1963.

21B-3. P Company issued on January 1 at face value $1 million in 5-year, 5% bonds. Interest was payable annually on December 31. On December 31 of each of four years, P Company deposited $184,700 in a sinking fund, on which the trustee was able to earn 4% interest per year. On December 31 of the fifth year the amount was withdrawn from the fund, and sufficient general cash was added to retire the bonds.

X Company issued on January 1 at face value $1 million in 5-year, 5% bonds. Interest was payable annually on December 31. The bonds were callable at par on any interest date. On December 31 of each of the five years following the date of issue, X Company called $200,000 of its bonds and retired them.

Instructions

a. Prepare a schedule showing the accumulation of P Company's sinking fund and the amount of cash required to pay the bonds at maturity. Round all figures to the nearest dollar.

b. Prepare the journal entries that should be made on the books of P Company on December 31 of the fourth and fifth years to record all transactions relating to their bonds.

c. Prepare the journal entries that should appear on the books of X Company on December 31 of each of the five years to reflect the payment of interest and the call of the bonds.

d. Over the five-year period, which company made the largest total cash outlay in connection with its bond issue? Prepare a schedule in support of your answer, showing the expenditures of each company for each of the five years.

21B-4. Turnbull Corporation reported the balances given below at the end of the current year:

Total assets	*$1,160,000*
Current liabilities	*300,000*
Stockholders' equity:	
Capital stock, par $40	*400,000*
Paid-in capital in excess of par	*300,000*
Retained earnings	*160,000*

Other data. The company is planning an expansion of its plant facilities, and a study shows that $800,000 of net funds will be required to finance the expansion. Two proposals are under consideration:

Proposal A. Issue 10,000 shares of common stock at a price of $80 per share.
Proposal B. Borrow $800,000 on a 20-year mortgage note, with interest at 6%.

The assets and liabilities of the Turnbull Corporation have remained relatively constant over the past five years, and during this period the earnings *after* income taxes have averaged 5% of the stockholders' equity. The company expects that its net earnings *before* income taxes will increase by an amount equal to 10% of the new investment in plant facilities.

Past and future income taxes for the company may be estimated by applying the following formula: Taxes = (52% × net income) − $5,500.

Instructions
a. Prove that the company's average net income before taxes during the past five years was $78,125.
b. Prepare a schedule showing the expected net income per share of common stock during the first year of operations following the completion of the $800,000 expansion, under each of the two proposed means of financing. Round off all figures, except per-share earnings, to the nearest thousand dollars.
c. Evaluate the two methods of financing from the viewpoint of a major stockholder of Turnbull Corporation.

22

Investments in bonds, stocks, and mortgages

Security transactions from the viewpoint of investors

In preceding chapters the issuance of securities and such related transactions as the payment of dividends and interest have been considered primarily from the viewpoint of the issuing corporation. In this chapter these transactions are considered from the viewpoint of the investor.

The capital stocks and bonds of nearly all very large corporations are listed on the New York Stock Exchange or on other organized security exchanges. Among the investors in these securities are trust funds, pension funds, universities, banks, insurance companies, industrial corporations, and great numbers of individuals. The stocks and bonds of many smaller companies are not listed on an organized exchange but are bought and sold *over the counter*. At the time of issuance of bonds or stocks, the transaction is between the investor and the issuing corporation (or its underwriting agent). The great daily volume of security transactions, however, consists of the sale of stocks and bonds by investors to other investors. Virtually all these security transactions are made through a stockbroker acting as intermediary.

Listed corporations report to a million owners. When a corporation invites the public to purchase its stocks and bonds, it accepts an obligation to keep the public informed on its financial condition and the profitability of operations. This obligation of full disclosure includes public distribution of financial statements. The Securities and Exchange Commission is a government agency charged with responsibility for determining that corporations with securities listed on stock exchanges make full and fair disclosure of their affairs so that investors have a basis for intelligent investment decisions. The financial pages of the daily newspapers report and discuss security prices and current news of earnings and dividends. Specialized publications such as the *Wall Street Journal* present much more intensive coverage of corporate activities. The flow of corporate accounting data, distributed through these publications to millions of investors, is a vital force in the functioning of our economy; in fact, the successful working of a profit-motivated economy rests upon the quality and dependability of the accounting information being reported.

Listed corporations are audited by certified public accountants. Corporations with securities listed on organized stock exchanges are required to have regular audits of their accounts by independent public accountants. The financial statements distributed each year to stockholders are accompanied by a report by a firm of certified public accountants indicating that an audit has been made and expressing an opinion as to the fairness of the company's financial statements. It is the independent status of the auditing firm that enables investors to place confidence in audited financial statements.

Why do business concerns invest in government bonds?

Many business concerns as well as individuals invest in marketable securities. For example, a recent balance sheet of Standard Oil Company of California shows the following items listed first in the current asset section:

Current assets:	
Cash	*$109,632,517*
U.S. government securities, at cost	*32,338,714*

The action of Standard Oil Company in investing in United States government bonds is in no way unusual. The published balance sheets of a great many corporations show holdings of such securities. These bonds differ from the United States savings bonds owned by many individuals in that they pay interest every six months and may be sold at any time in the securities market without any loss of interest.

Government bonds as current assets. Why does an industrial corporation invest in government bonds and why are these bonds classified as current assets? An answer is suggested by the common practice among businessmen of referring to an investment in government bonds as a "secondary cash reserve." Although accountants dislike to see the word "reserve" used in this manner, the meaning of the expression seems clear. It means that government bonds are just as safe and almost as liquid as cash itself. In the event that cash is needed for any operating purpose, the bonds can be quickly converted into cash; in the meantime, bonds are preferable to cash because of the interest income which they produce. From the viewpoint of creditors as well as that of management, it is often said in appraising a company's financial strength that "cash and government securities" amount to so many dollars. This practice of lumping together cash and government securities reflects the general attitude that these two assets are essentially similar.

A security investment consisting of United States government bonds is a current asset regardless of the maturity date of the bonds and regardless of how long the bonds have been held or how long the company expects to hold them. The important point is that these securities *can* be converted into cash at any time without interfering with the normal operation of the business. A principal purpose of the balance sheet classification of current assets and current liabilities is to aid in portraying short-run debt-paying ability. For this purpose government bonds deserve to be listed immediately after cash because they are even more current than accounts receivable or inventory. To a loan officer in a bank reviewing an application for a loan, there is no more impressive or reassuring asset on the balance sheet of a prospective borrower than a large amount of government bonds.

Investments in other marketable securities

Some corporations choose to invest in bonds and stocks of other corporations as well as in United States government bonds. If these industrial securities are listed on a securities exchange and are not held for the purpose of exercising control over the issuing corporation, they should be classified as current assets. Some accounting authorities have attempted to distinguish between "temporary" and "permanent" investments in marketable securities with the objective of excluding the latter type from current assets. In the opinion of the authors, such a distinction cannot be made consistently in practice and, furthermore, is quite unnecessary. For example, assume that a department store owns 500 shares of the common stock of American Telephone and Telegraph. The store has owned the stock for several years and has no intention of selling it in the near future, so this investment could reasonably be called a permanent one. Of course these shares are not held for the purpose of exercising control over the telephone company, or for any business reason other than that of sound investment. This security investment is a current asset of the highest quality; any analysis of the store's balance sheet for credit purposes would be facilitated by having the AT&T stock listed immediately after cash in the current asset section.

In summary, if security investments are limited to securities of unquestioned marketability (and are not owned for the purpose of bolstering business relations with the issuing corporation), these stocks and bonds may be converted into cash at any time without interfering with normal operations. An expressed intention by management as to near-term sale of the securities is *not* a requisite for classification as a current asset.

Investments for purpose of control. Some corporations buy stocks of other corporations in sufficient quantity that a degree of control may be exercised over the issuing corporation. Sometimes a substantial investment in stock of a customer company may be helpful in maintaining good relations. Investments of this type cannot be sold without disturbing established policies; therefore, such investments are not current assets. They should be carried on the books at cost. On the balance sheet, they should be listed below the current asset section under the heading of Long-term Investments.

Valuation of marketable securities

At current market price. Investments in securities are usually carried at cost, and no gain or loss is recognized until the securities are sold. In current practice the market value of securities is often disclosed in a parenthetical note on the balance sheet, but the securities are nevertheless valued at cost.

Since the current market value of an investment in listed securities can be definitely determined merely by a glance at the financial page of the daily newspaper, some accountants argue that these investments *should* be valued in the balance sheet at current market price regardless of whether this price is above or below cost. Certainly it is true that creditors of a company owning marketable securities will be more interested in the present market value of the securities than in their original cost. There appear to be at least three strong arguments for showing security investments at current market value: (1) the keen interest of creditors in the present market value of security holdings, (2) the availability of current market quotations, which definitely establish present market value for this type of asset, and (3) the fact that the securities can be sold without interfering with the normal operation of the business. Despite these arguments however, market price has not won acceptance in current practice as a basis for balance sheet valuation of security investments.

One argument against market price as a valuation basis is that in a rising market the writing up of the investments account would involve the recording of an unrealized profit. One of the basic concepts in accounting is that gains shall not be recognized until they are realized, and the usual test of realization is the sale of the asset in question. This argument would not hold in the case of losses, however, since accountants often recognize losses on the basis of objective evidence, even though the amount of the loss has not been established through sale of the property. Consequently when the current value of marketable securities declines below cost, many accountants would favor writing down the investment account and charging an expense account entitled Loss from Decline in Market Value of Securities.

At the lower of cost or market. The valuation of investment securities at cost is generally accepted, but accounting theory also treats as acceptable the lower-of-cost-or-market method. The objective of this method of valuation is to give effect to market declines without recognizing market increases, and the result is a most conservative statement of investments in the balance sheet. The lower-of-cost-or-market concept has two alternative interpretations. It may be applied by (1) taking the lower of cost or market for each security owned, or (2) comparing the cost of the total holdings of securities with the market value of the securities as a group. Application of the lower-of-cost-or-market rule to each security individually will produce the lowest possible balance sheet amount for security investments, as shown by the following example:

LOWER OF COST OR MARKET: ALTERNATIVE METHODS

	Cost	Present market price	Lower of cost or market
Adams Corporation stock	$10,000	$ 9,000	$ 9,000
Zenith Corporation stock	15,000	17,000	15,000
Totals	$25,000	$26,000	$24,000

If the lower-of-cost-or-market rule is applied to these two securities individually, the amount to appear in the balance sheet for Investments would be $24,000, which represents the present *market price* of the Adams stock plus the *cost* of the Zenith stock. In other words, the decrease in value of the Adams stock would be recognized but the increase in value of the Zenith stock would be ignored. The alternative application of the lower-of-cost-or-market rule would be made as follows: the cost of the two securities together amounted to $25,000; the present market value of the two stocks is $26,000; the lower of these two totals is the proper amount for the balance sheet and would be labeled as follows in the Current Assets section:

Marketable securities, at lower of cost or market $25,000

Once the carrying value of an investment in securities has been written down to reflect a decline in market price, it is not considered acceptable to restore the amount written off even though the market price afterward recovers to as much as or more than the original cost. To do so would be regarded as recording an unrealized profit. When the security is sold, the gain or loss to be recorded is the difference between the sale price and the adjusted carrying value of the security on the books.

In terms of the usefulness of the balance sheet to creditors and other readers, it seems probable that the lower-of-cost-or-market rule should be applied to the securities holdings as a group rather than on an individual basis. Application of the lower-of-cost-or-market rule on an individual basis leads to an ultraconservative balance sheet valuation, which may mislead rather than inform the reader who is interested in the company's debt-paying ability or in the change in financial position since the preceding balance sheet date. Assume, for example, that a company owned a dozen securities and 11 of them advanced strongly in price during the year while the price of the twelfth security declined below its cost. If the lower-of-cost-or-market rule were applied on an individual basis, the company's balance sheet at the end of the year would show a reduction in the carrying value of securities and the income statement would show a loss from decline in market value of securities. Such reporting seems to have no justification other than conservatism, and conservatism is surely not a virtue when it results in misleading financial statements.

In the past, conservatism was a more important factor than it is today in choosing methods of asset valuation. Accountants have come to accept a realistic statement of values as preferable to deliberate understatement. With this change in viewpoint, the arguments for the lower-of-cost-or-market rule are now often based on grounds of proper measurement of income rather than in terms of balance sheet conservatism. Proper determination of income, in the opinion of many accountants, requires that any part of the cost of an asset which is unrecoverable at the balance sheet date should be deducted from current revenues rather than being carried forward as an asset. If the market price of a security at the balance sheet date has fallen below cost, it may be argued that the excess of cost over market price is unrecoverable. The cogency of such arguments appears to rest upon such issues as the permanence of the market decline and the probability of near-term sale of the investment. Study of published corporate statements suggests that accountants may have overemphasized the idea that marketable securities are "temporary" holdings. If the investment in marketable securities is relatively permanent in nature, the argument for reducing the carrying value of securities to reflect minor declines in market value is not a very convincing one.

Disclosing the basis of valuation in the balance sheet. Because of the variety of methods in use for valuation of investments in securities, the balance sheet should contain a notation as to the valuation method being used. It is also important that the method selected be used consistently from year to year. To illustrate the balance sheet presentation of marketable securities under different valuation methods, the following excerpts are taken from published statements of leading corporations:

United States Steel Corporation:
   United States government securities, at cost ..... $ 317,659,464

Sears, Roebuck and Co.:
   Marketable securities, market value $10,277,541 .. $ 4,503,637

Standard Oil Company (New Jersey):
   Marketable securities, at lower of cost or market .. $1,050,046,546

General Electric Company explains the basis of valuation in a footnote accompanying the balance sheet: "Marketable securities consisted of issues of the United States Government, state and local governments and their agencies and of high-grade short-term commercial paper, carried at the lower of amortized cost or market value on the basis of individual issues. The aggregate quoted market value of these securities was approximately the same as carrying value."

Effect of income tax regulations upon security valuation. Income tax regulations are of course an additional factor influencing the choice of accounting methods. For tax purposes no gain or loss is recognized on an investment in securities until the time of sale. Many businesses which invest in securities prefer to follow this policy for general accounting purposes as well and therefore carry their security investments at cost, unless there is a substantial and apparently permanent decrease in the market value of securities owned.

Determining the cost of investments in stocks and bonds

Emphasis has been placed on the point that cost is the primary basis for valuation of investments as well as for other types of assets. What does the cost of an investment in marketable securities include? Regardless of whether the investment consists of stocks, bonds, mortgages, or similar property, the cost includes any commission paid to a broker. The par value or face value of the security is not used in recording an investment; only the cost is entered in the investments account.

The principal distinction between the recording of an investment in bonds and an investment in stocks is that interest on bonds accrues from day to day. The interest accrued since the last semiannual interest payment date is paid for by the purchaser and should be recorded separately from the cost of the bond itself. Dividends on stock, however, do not accrue and the entire purchase price paid by the investor in stocks is charged to the investments account. For example, assume the purchase of 100 shares of American Airlines 3 1/2% convertible preferred stock at a price of 93 with a broker's commission of $45. The total amount to be paid by the investor would be $9,345, and the following entry would be made:

COST OF INVESTMENT INCLUDES COMMISSION	*Investment in Stocks* 9,345	
	Cash	*9,345*
	Purchased 100 shares of American Airlines convertible preferred stock at 93 plus commission.	

Dividends on this stock are paid quarterly, but regardless of whether the purchase occurs near a dividend date or in the middle of the quarter, no separate charge is made for the dividend.

Income on investments in stocks. Dividends are usually not recorded as income until received. The entry upon receipt of a dividend check consists of a debit to Cash and a credit to Dividends Earned. An alternative method of recognizing income from dividends is to make an entry on the date of record, debiting Dividends Receivable and crediting Dividends Earned. The Dividends Receivable account is then credited when the dividend check is received. However, for the purpose of determining earnings subject to income tax, dividends are not considered income until received, and most investors follow this pattern for all accounting purposes.

Dividends in the form of additional shares of stock are not income to the stockholder, and only a memorandum entry need be made to record the increase in number of shares owned. The *cost basis per share* is decreased, however, because of the larger number of shares comprising the investment after distribution of a stock dividend. As an example, assume that an investor paid $72 a share for 100 shares of stock, a total cost of $7,200. Later he received 20 additional shares as a stock dividend. His cost per share is thereby reduced to $60 a share, computed by dividing his total cost of $7,200 by the 120 shares owned after the dividend.

Purchase of bonds between interest dates. When bonds are purchased between interest dates, the purchaser pays the agreed price for the bond plus the interest accrued since the last interest payment date. By this arrangement the new owner becomes entitled to receive the next semiannual interest payment in its entirety. An account entitled Accrued Bond Interest Receivable should be debited for the amount of interest purchased. For example, assume the purchase of a 6%, $1,000 bond at a price of 106 and accrued interest of $10, plus a broker's commission of $9. The entry is as follows:

SEPARATE ACCOUNT FOR ACCRUED BOND INTEREST PURCHASED	*Investment in Bonds* **1,069**	
	Accrued Bond Interest Receivable **10**	
	Cash	**1,079**
	Purchased 6% bond of XYZ Co. at 106 and accrued interest.	

Four months later at the next semiannual interest payment date, the investor will receive an interest check for $30, which will be recorded as follows:

NOTE PORTION OF INTEREST CHECK EARNED	*Cash* **30**	
	Accrued Bond Interest Receivable	**10**
	Bond Interest Earned	**20**
	Received semiannual interest on XYZ bond.	

This $20 credit to Bond Interest Earned represents the amount actually earned during the four months the bond was owned.

Entries to record bond interest earned each period. If the investor in bonds is to determine bond interest earned each year on an accrual basis, an adjusting entry will be necessary at the balance sheet date for **ENTRIES TO ALLOCATE BOND INTEREST EARNED BY YEARS** any interest earned but not yet received. The following series of entries illustrates the accounting for bond interest earned by a company on a calendar-year basis of accounting. The investment consists of $100,000 face value of 6% bonds with interest dates of February 28 and August 31.

1962				
Dec. 31	Accrued Bond Interest Receivable	. . . .	2,000	
	Bond Interest Earned			2,000
	To accrue four months' interest earned on $100,000 face value of 6% bonds.			
1963				
Feb. 28	Cash		3,000	
	Accrued Bond Interest Receivable			2,000
	Bond Interest Earned			1,000
	Received semiannual bond interest.			
Aug. 31	Cash		3,000	
	Bond Interest Earned			3,000
	Received semiannual bond interest.			
Dec. 31	Accrued Bond Interest Receivable		2,000	
	Bond Interest Earned			2,000
	To accrue four months' interest earned on $100,000 face value of 6% bonds.			

Acquisition of bonds at premium or discount

In the discussion of bonds payable from the viewpoint of the issuing corporation in Chapter 21, emphasis was placed on the point that the issuing company must amortize the premium or discount over the life of the bonds. The position of the *investor in bonds,* however, is very different with respect to the significance of premium or discount. Most investors purchasing bonds above or below par do *not* amortize the premium or discount on these investments, because they do not expect to hold the bonds until maturity. Since bond issues often run for 50 years or more, it is the exception rather than the rule for the investor to hold the bond until it matures. If the investor sells the bond before it matures, the price he receives may be either above or below his cost, according to the current state of the bond market. Under these circumstances there is no assurance that amortization of premium or discount would give any more accurate measurement of investment income than would be obtained by carrying the bonds at cost. A few financial institutions do make a practice of amortizing the premium and discount on their bond investments, presumably on the assumption that the bonds owned will probably be held until maturity.

Amortization of premium on bonds owned. Large institutional investors who purchase bonds at a premium or discount with the intention of holding them until maturity may decide to follow a policy of amortizing or writing off the premium or discount over the remaining life of the bonds. When a bond reaches maturity, only the face value of $1,000 will be paid by the issuing corporation. The value of a bond purchased at a premium will, therefore, tend to decrease toward par as the maturity date approaches, and the carrying value of the bond in the balance sheet can logically be reduced in each successive year.

The income to an investor from a bond purchased at a premium and held until maturity *equals the total interest received minus the premium paid;* consequently, the interest income of each year should be reduced by deducting a portion of the premium paid for the bond. As an example, assume that on January 1, 1963, an investor purchased $100,000 of 6% bonds of the Fox Corporation payable January 1, 1973. Interest is payable on July 1 and January 1. The purchase price was 104 1/2 and the broker's commission $500, making a total cost of $105,000. The $5,000 excess of cost over maturity value is to be written off against the interest received during the 10 years the bonds will be held. Since there are 20 interest periods of six months each, the premium to be amortized each six months is $5,000 ÷ 20, or $250. A check for $3,000 bond interest

INVESTOR'S
ENTRIES
SHOWING
AMORTIZA-
TION OF
PREMIUM

will be received each six months; of this amount $250 may be regarded as recovery of the premium paid and the remaining $2,750 as interest income. The journal entries for the first year the bonds are owned will be as follows:

1963

Jan. 1 Investment in Bonds 105,000
               Cash   105,000
        Purchased 100 six per cent bonds of Fox Corporation
        at 104 1/2 plus commission of $500. Bonds mature
        Jan. 1, 1973.

July 1 Cash 3,000
               Bond Interest Earned   3,000
        Received semiannual bond interest payment.

July 1 Bond Interest Earned 250
               Investment in Bonds   250
        To amortize 1/20 of $5,000 premium.

Dec. 31   *Accrued Bond Interest Receivable* *3,000*
           Bond Interest Earned *3,000*
           To accrue bond interest earned to end of year.

Dec. 31   *Bond Interest Earned* *250*
           Investment in Bonds *250*
           To amortize 1/20 of $5,000 premium.

Dec. 31   *Bond Interest Earned* *5,500*
           Income Summary *5,500*
           To close Bond Interest Income account.

The accrued interest receivable of $3,000 at December 31 will appear in the balance sheet as a current asset, which will be collected January 1 upon receipt of the bond interest check. The bonds will also appear in the current asset section at $104,500, representing the cost of $105,-000 minus the $500 of premium amortized during the year.

The two essential ideas portrayed by this series of entries may be stated as follows: (1) the carrying value of the bonds is gradually being reduced to par by amortizing the premium and (2) the net interest earned each year is equal to the interest received minus the amount of premium amortized.

Amortization of discount on bonds owned. The value of a bond purchased for *less than its face value* will tend to increase to par as the maturity date approaches. In other words, at the maturity date of the bond, the investor will collect more than he paid for the security. This increment in value represents income to the investor in addition to the semiannual interest payments. Amortization of the discount on an investment in bonds means writing up the carrying value of the bonds each year with an off-setting credit to the Bond Interest Earned account. The income from a bond purchased at a discount and held until maturity is equal to the total of the interest payments received plus the amount of the discount.

As an example of the periodic entries for amortization of discount on bond investments, assume that on January 1, 1963, an investor purchased $100,000 face value of 6% bonds of the Bay Corporation payable January 1, 1973. Interest is payable July 1 and January 1. The purchase price was 94 1/2 and the broker's commission $500, making a total cost of $95,000. Since there are 20 interest periods of six months each, the discount to be amortized each six months is $5,000 ÷ 20, or $250. A check for $3,000 bond interest will be received each six months; in addition, the bond interest earned will be increased $250 by writing up the carrying value of the investment.

The journal entries for the first year the bonds are owned will be as follows:

```
1963
Jan.  1   Investment in Bonds .........................  95,000
             Cash ....................................              95,000
          Purchased 100 6% bonds of Bay Corporation at 94 1/2
          plus commission of $500. Bonds mature Jan. 1, 1973.


July  1   Cash .......................................   3,000
             Bond Interest Earned ...................               3,000
          Received semiannual bond interest payment.


July  1   Investment in Bonds .........................     250
             Bond Interest Earned ...................                 250
          To amortize 1/20 of $5,000 discount.


Dec. 31   Accrued Bond Interest Receivable ..............   3,000
             Bond Interest Earned ...................               3,000
          To accrue bond interest earned to end of year.


Dec. 31   Investment in Bonds .........................     250
             Bond Interest Earned ...................                 250
          To amortize 1/20 of $5,000 discount.


Dec. 31   Bond Interest Earned .........................   6,500
             Income Summary ......................                 6,500
          To close Bond Interest Earned account.
```

It is essential to keep in mind that the amortization of premium or discount on an investment in bonds is warranted only if bonds are to be held until maturity. For example, if an investor buys at a discount a bond maturing 40 years from now and sells the bond after holding it only a few years, it is quite possible that the sale price may be less than his cost. The fact that a bond will be paid at par at a distant maturity date does not ensure that its price will move closer to par during each year of its life; bond prices fluctuate with changes in market rates of interest, business activity, and other elements of the economic environment.

Gains and losses from sale of investments in securities

The sale of an investment security is recorded by debiting Cash for the amount received and crediting the investment account for the carrying value of the security. Any difference between the proceeds of sale and the carrying value of the investment is recorded by a debit to Loss on Sale of Investments or by a credit to Gain on Sale of Investments.

Assume that an investment consisting of 100 shares of stock of the Mills Company carried on the books at the cost of $10,000 is sold for $120 a share. The gross sales price is $12,000 but the broker's commission amounts to $100. The entry will be as follows:

SALE OF INVESTMENT IN STOCK

Cash	*11,900*	
Investment in Stocks		*10,000*
Gain on Sale of Investments		*1,900*
Sale of 100 shares of Mills Company stock at $120.		

The next example pertains to a company which follows the practice of valuing its investments at the lower of cost or market. Assume that the 100 shares of Mills Company stock acquired at a cost of $10,000 were subsequently written down to $9,000 to reflect a decline in market price. Later, when the market had recovered, the investment was sold for a net amount of $11,900 after brokerage fees. The entry for the sale is:

GAIN ON SALE OF STOCK INVESTMENT

Cash	*11,900*	
Investment in Stocks		*9,000*
Gain on Sale of Investments		*2,900*
Sold 100 shares of Mills Company stock at $120 a share.		

At the date of sale of an investment in bonds, any interest accrued since the last interest payment date should be recorded. For example, assume that 10 bonds of the Elk Corporation carried on the books at $9,600 are sold at a price of 94 and accrued interest of $50. The commission on the sale is $80. The following entries should be made:

RECORD INTEREST ON BOND INVESTMENT

Accrued Bond Interest Receivable	*50*	
Bond Interest Earned		*50*
To record interest accrued to date of sale.		

. . . THEN RECORD THE SALE TRANS- ACTION

Cash	*9,370*	
Loss on Sale of Investments	*280*	
Investment in Bonds		*9,600*
Accrued Bond Interest Receivable		*50*
Sold 10 bonds of Elk Corporation at 94 and accrued interest.		

Gains and losses on the sale of investments are nonoperating income and should be presented in the income statement below the figure representing net income from operations.

Investments in United States savings bonds

Previous references in this chapter to investments in government bonds have concerned United States Treasury bonds, which are available for purchase by corporations as well as by individuals. Treasury bonds are listed on the stock exchanges, are readily transferable, and may be used as collateral for loans. These United States Treasury bonds should not be confused with the nontransferable, Series E, United States savings bonds, which the government is continually advertising for sale to the public.

The concept of discount on bond investments which we have examined with respect to corporation bonds is also applicable to Series E bonds. These bonds are issued on a discount basis at 75 per cent of their maturity value. No interest payments are made, but the redemption value of the bonds increases at the end of each six-month period from the issue date. Series E bonds, according to present regulations, mature 7 years and 9 months after issuance. If the bonds are held to maturity, the investor will receive $4 for each $3 invested, which represents an investment yield of approximately 3 3/4%, compounded semiannually.

Investments in mortgages and long-term notes

Accounting principles and procedures applicable to investments in mortgages and long-term notes are similar to those for investments in bonds. A mortgage or long-term note is recorded at cost and the cash interest payments received on a monthly or quarterly basis are credited to interest earned.

Mortgages are often acquired at less than face value; in the case of mortgages or notes involving a significant risk of nonpayment, discounts sometimes amount to as much as 20 to 40% or more of the face amount. As an example, an investor purchases for $18,000 a mortgage of $20,000 face amount maturing in five years and paying interest quarterly at the rate of 6% a year. Two alternatives are open with regard to the recognition of income: (1) the mortgage may be carried at cost and only cash interest payments credited to income, or (2) the mortgage investment account may be written up by one-fifth of the discount in each of the five years and this amount credited to interest earned in addition to the cash interest received. Under the first method, the yearly interest earned will be $1,200 (6% $\times$ $20,000), but when the mortgage is collected at the end of the fifth year an additional $2,000 of income (the excess of the face amount over cost) must be recognized. Under the second method calling for the yearly amortization of discount, the annual interest earned would be $1,600, consisting of $1,200 received in cash plus a $400 increase in the carrying value of the investment. The second method will usually give a more meaningful picture of periodic income and is preferable from the viewpoint of accounting theory; both methods are acceptable in the determination of taxable income.

QUESTIONS

1. Why are marketable securities commonly called "secondary cash reserves"?

2. To what extent should the maturity date or the intention of management as to the holding period of an investment in marketable securities influence its classification on the balance sheet?

3. Writing down securities to market value when market is below cost, but refusing to recognize an increase in valuation when market is above cost is inconsistent procedure. What arguments may be given *in favor* of this treatment?

4. "To substitute present market value for cost as a basis for valuing marketable securities would represent a departure from traditional accounting practice." Discuss the case for and against using market value consistently as the basis of valuation in accounting for marketable securities.

5. An investor buys a $1,000, 6%, 10-year bond at 110 and a $1,000, 4%, 10-year bond at 90, both on the date of issue. Compute the average annual interest income that will be earned on these bonds if they are held to maturity.

6. If an investor buys a bond between interest dates he pays, as a part of the purchase price, the accrued interest since the last interest date. On the other hand, if he buys a share of common or preferred stock, there is no "accrued dividend" added to the quoted price. Explain why this difference exists.

7. Z buys a $1,000, 5% bond for 106, five years from the maturity date. After holding the bond for four years, he sells it for 102. Z claims that he has a loss of $40 on the sale. A friend argues that Z has made a gain of $8 on the sale. Explain the difference in viewpoint. With whom do you agree? Why?

PROBLEMS

Group A

22A-1. Selected financial data as of a given date for three companies are shown below:

	Company X	Company Y	Company Z
Cash	$ 80,000	$ 30,000	$ 20,000
Receivables	90,000	80,000	100,000
Inventories	100,000	110,000	90,000
Investments:			
Stock of AB Company, at cost (4,000 of 5,000 shares outstanding	240,000		
Land held for future expansion, at cost			80,000
U.S. Treasury bonds, at cost (market value $159,500)			160,000
Common stock, DuPont Corp., at cost (market value $250,000)		240,000	
Current liabilities	120,000	120,000	120,000

Instructions. Each of the above companies is negotiating a substantial short-term loan. On the basis of the above information, and assuming that the companies are comparable in other significant respects, which firm would you judge to be the best prospect for a grant of short-term credit? Support your answer with a schedule showing the basis for your conclusion.

22A-2. An investor, who maintains records on an accrual basis, completed the transactions shown below during the current year:

Jan. 15. Purchased 1,000 shares of Electronics Corporation common stock at 36 1/2, plus a brokerage commission of $318.

Mar. 1. Purchased 15 Nebraska Highway $1,000, 4%, 10-year bonds, on which interest is payable semiannually on May 1 and November 1. The price paid was 104 plus accrued interest and a commission of $24. These bonds mature 8 years and 8 months from purchase date.

May 3. Received check for interest on the Nebraska Highway bonds. Premium is to be amortized on a straight-line basis.

June 1. Purchased 100 shares of Skyway Airlines 6%, preferred stock, par value $100, at 99 plus commission of $70.

July 10. Received semiannual dividend on Skyway preferred.

July 15. Received dividend of 80 cents per share on Electronics Corporation common stock.

Sept. 1. Purchased, on an interest date, 5% Placer Mining Company 20-year bonds. These bonds have a maturity value of $20,000 and mature in 8 years. Interest is payable semiannually on September 1 and March 1. The purchase price was $19,616, including brokerage commissions.

Nov. 1. Received semiannual interest on the Nebraska Highway bonds and amortized premium to date.

Dec. 1. Received stock dividend of 100 shares of Electronics Corporation common.

Dec. 31. Sold 550 shares of Electronics Corporation common for $17,000, net of commission. Sold 20 shares of Skyway Airlines preferred at 102, less $18 commission and taxes.

Dec. 31. Recorded accrued interest on all bonds held, including amortization to date of any premium or discount.

Instructions. Prepare journal entries to record the above transactions. Show supporting computations as a part of journal entry explanations. Round all computations to the nearest dollar.

22A-3. The following investments were made by the Mutual Insurance Company:

(1) $120,000 in 5%, 10-year, Lane County bonds, purchased 9 years and 4 months prior to their maturity date. The price paid was $124,480 plus accrued interest. The bonds pay interest semiannually.

(2) $120,000 in 4%, 20-year, Marin County bonds, purchased 18 years and 4 months prior to maturity date. The price paid was $106,800 plus accrued interest. These bonds pay interest semiannually.

Instructions

a. Prepare a schedule showing the total amount of interest that will be earned on each of these two investments if held to maturity and the average interest earned per month on each investment.

b. Prepare journal entries to record the purchase of the above two investments and the receipt of interest on the first two interest dates. Any discount or premium is to be amortized on a straight-line basis.

c. State which of these investments yields the higher average rate of return, and explain the basis for your answer.

22A-4. A, B, and C Companies each had certain funds available for temporary investment pending decision as to how this money can be most effectively employed in the business. By coincidence, all three companies made the same investments at approximately the same time, as follows:

> Zerox Corporation common stock, 1,000 shares at 42
> Ascron Corporation 6% preferred stock, 500 shares at 101
> Gerol Corporation 5% bonds, $100,000 maturity value, at 96

The three companies held these investments during a two-year period, receiving $5,000 interest on the bonds each year, regular preferred dividends of $6 per share each year, and dividends on common stock of $1.60 the first year and $1.40 the second year. None of the companies amortizes discount on the Gerol bonds, since there is no intention to hold this investment to maturity.

The securities are all listed on national exchanges, and the market prices at the end of the first and second years were as follows:

	End of 1st year	End of 2d year
Zerox common	48	44 1/2
Ascron preferred	100	98
Gerol bonds	95	98

In arriving at a valuation of investments for financial statement purposes, A Company uses a lower-of-cost-or-market method applied to each security; B Company uses the lower-of-cost-or-market method applied to all investments as a group; and C Company records its investments at market value at year-end, reflecting any resulting gain or loss in an account titled Unrealized Gain or Loss on Marketable Securities.

Instructions

a. Show how these investments would appear on the balance sheets of Companies A, B, and C, respectively, at the end of the first year and at the end of the second year.

b. What amount of revenue from investments would each company report during the first year? During the second year?

c. What balance would appear in the account Unrealized Gain or Loss on Marketable Securities on C's books at the end of each year? In what section of the financial statements would you recommend that this amount be reported by C Company? Why?

Group B

22B-1. (1) Joseph Black purchased 200 shares of Standard Chemical common stock at 36 1/4 plus brokerage fees of $104 on March 31. The company had declared a cash dividend of 80 cents per share on March 20, payable on April 15 to stockholders of record on April 3. On June 30 the company declared a 10% stock dividend. On December 15 the shares were split 2 for 1. On December 20 the company declared a cash dividend of 50 cents per share to stockholders of record on December 30, payable on January 10. On December 31 Black sold 200 shares of the stock at $20 per share, net of commission.

Instructions. Make the necessary journal entries to account for this investment on Black's books, assuming that he keeps accrual records.

(2) Regon Corporation purchased $240,000 of 5%, 10-year state bonds at 94. The bonds mature eight years from the date of purchase. The bonds were sold for 96 1/2 four years from the date of purchase.

Instructions

a. Assuming that the corporation had no intention of holding the bonds to maturity at the time of purchase, determine the total interest income during the four-year period and the gain or loss on disposal.

b. Assuming that the corporation intended to hold the bonds until maturity at the time of purchase, determine the total interest income recorded during the four-year period and the gain or loss on disposal.

22B-2. X Corporation has accumulated funds to finance expansion. Current business conditions, however, make it advisable to postpone the project, and the treasurer is instructed to invest the funds for an indefinite period of time. The transactions below reflect the investments for the current year.

Feb. 1. Purchased for $119,860, including accrued interest, United States Treasury 4% bonds, due in 4 years and 11 months, maturity value $120,000, interest payable on June 30 and December 31.

Feb. 15. Purchased 1,200 shares of Orecal Corp. common stock at 60 5/8 plus a brokerage commission of $386.

Mar. 1. Purchased 80 Public Utility District 4 1/2%, $1,000 bonds, interest payable semiannually on April 1 and October 1. The price paid was 103 plus accrued interest and a commission of $82. These bonds mature six years after the next interest date.

Apr. 1. Received interest on Public Utility District bonds. Premium is to be amortized on these bonds.

May 18. Purchased 500 shares of Sanitary Baking 6% preferred stock, par value $100, callable at 104 at any time within three years. Total price $51,280.

June 30. Received interest on United States Treasury bonds, and sold $50,000 of these bonds at a net price of 98. Because of the small amount involved, did not amortize discount on these bonds.

July 18. Received cash dividend of $1.50 per share on Orecal Co. common stock and a stock dividend of 1 share for each 20 shares held.

Oct. 1. Received interest on Public Utility District bonds; amortized premium to date.

Nov. 15. Sanitary Baking preferred was called at 104. Received check for call price plus the regular annual dividend for the current year. Invested proceeds of this call, plus the amount received from the sale of Treasury bonds on June 30, in Clack County 6% bonds, at face value.

Dec. 31. Recorded accrued interest on all bonds held, including amortization to date of premium on Public Utility District bonds.

Market values of investments at year-end: United States Treasury bonds, 99 1/2; Orecal Corp. stock, 58; Public Utility District bonds, 101 5/8; Clack County bonds, 101.

Instructions

a. Prepare in general journal form the entries necessary to record the above investments. Include explanations only where computations are involved. Round all computations to the nearest dollar.

b. Show how the investments of X Corporation would appear on the balance sheet at the end of the year, assuming the company follows a policy of valuing investments at lower of cost or market in total.

22B-3. The Solem Trust Company has an opening for a promotion in its investment department. The qualifications of the two candidates for the job, Brite and Sharpe, appear equally good. As an aid in making the choice, each man was given $30,000 to invest in corporate bonds. It was understood, though not openly stated, that their performance in investing these funds would be the basis for the promotion decision.

The record of their performance at the end of the current year, as prepared by the assistant to (and brother-in-law of) the president, is as follows:

Brite's Portfolio

Cost	Investment	Interest received
$ 3,780	R & S Co. bonds, $5,000 face value, 3 1/2%, due in 10 years	$ 175
18,600	Ampler Corp. 3% bonds, face value $20,000, due in 4 years	600
7,620	Forco 2 1/2% bonds, $10,000 face value, due in 10 years ..	250
$30,000		$1,025

Return on investment for the year ($1,025 ÷ $30,000): 3.4%

Sharpe's Portfolio

$23,360	Snake Oil Company, 6% bonds, face value $20,000, due in 20 years	$1,200
6,640	Surefind Uranium, 7% bonds, $6,000 face value, due in 4 years	420
$30,000		$1,620

Return on investment for the year ($1,620 ÷ $30,000): 5.4%

On the basis of this record the assistant to the president chose Sharpe for the position. Sharpe's promotion was announced in the company bulletin, where it was read by Astute, a vice-president.

Instructions

a. Explain why Astute should (1) congratulate the assistant to the president for his choice or (2) complain to the president about the decision. Prepare a schedule in support of your conclusion.

b. Assuming that interest rates in general and the financial positions of the companies have not changed since the beginning of the year, make an estimate of the market value, as of the end of the year, of the investment portfolios of Brite and Sharpe. Show the basis for your estimate.

22B-4. Sherry keeps a detailed record of his investments and amortizes discounts and premiums in determining his investment earnings. He held the portfolio shown below throughout the current year:

1,000 shares of White Corporation common stock; cost $212 per share, market value at December 31 $290 per share. Received dividends of $5 per share on March 1, 10% stock dividend on June 1, and $4 per share on December 1 of current year.

$50,000 in 4% Yarbrought County school bonds, maturing eight years from the date of purchase. Purchased for $46,800; market value on December 31, 94 1/2. Received two regular semiannual interest payments during the current year.

$100,000 in 6% Greene Corporation debenture bonds, due 4 years and 2 months from date of purchase. Purchased for $102,500; market value at end of current year, 101 7/8. Received regular semiannual interest payments during current year.

800 shares of Zeder Corporation $6 preferred stock, no par value. Purchased for $78,900; current market value at end of year, 102 3/8. Received regular dividends on March 1 and September 1 of current year.

Instructions

a. Prepare a schedule showing the amount earned during the current year on each of these investments and the rate of return as a percentage of cost and of market value at the end of the year. This schedule may be in columnar form with the following column headings:

Name of security	Cost	Market value	Earnings this year	Rate earned on cost	Rate earned on market value

b. In a friendly discussion with a business associate, Sherry commented on his average return for the year on the total cost of his investment. His friend retorted that return on market value was a better measure of earning performance. Discuss the merits of the percentage earned on cost and the percentage earned on market value as measures of investment success.

23

The voucher system.
Payroll accounting

Control over expenditures

In every business, large or small, a considerable number of expenditures must be made each month for goods and services. Handling these transactions requires such steps as the following:

1. Purchase orders or other authorization for expenditures must be given.

2. Goods and services received must be inspected and approved.

3. Invoices from suppliers must be examined for correctness of prices, extensions, shipping costs, and credit terms.

4. Checks must be issued in payment.

In a very small business it may be possible for the owner or manager to perform all these steps for every transaction. By doing this work personally, he may be assured that the business is getting what it pays for, and that funds are not being disbursed carelessly or fraudulently. As a business grows and the volume of daily transactions increases, it becomes impossible for the owner or manager to give personal attention to each expenditure. When this work is assigned to various employees, a well-designed accounting system is needed to guard against waste and fraud.

Some businesses take great pains to safeguard cash receipts and cash on hand, but quite inconsistently permit a number of employees to incur liabilities by ordering goods or services without any record being made of their actions. When an invoice is received, perhaps a month or more after an expense was incurred, the absence of any record of the expenditure makes it difficult to determine whether the invoice is a proper statement of an amount owed. In this confused situation invoices are apt to be paid without adequate verification. The opportunity exists for a dishonest employee to collaborate with an outsider to arrange for duplicate payment of invoices, for payment of excessive prices, or for payment for goods and services never received. Fraud is particularly likely when an employee has authority to incur expenses and to issue checks in payment as well. Although the spectacular nature of fraud cases causes them to receive wide publicity, it seems probable that when control procedures are lacking the losses from unnecessary and wasteful expenditures may be as great as or greater than the losses from fraud.

To avoid waste and fraud in the incurring of expenditures and the making of cash disbursements in larger organizations, the work of placing orders, verifying invoices, recording liabilities, and issuing checks should be divided among several employees in such a manner that the work of each person serves to prove that of the others. A chain of documentary evidence should be created for each transaction, consisting of written approvals by key employees for the phases of the transaction for which each is responsible.

THE VOUCHER SYSTEM

One method of establishing control over the making of expenditures and the payment of liabilities is the *voucher system.* This system requires that every liability be recorded as soon as it is incurred, and that checks be issued only in payment of approved liabilities. Every purchase is recorded and paid for as an independent transaction, complete in itself, even though a number of purchases may be made from the same supplier during a month.

A written authorization called a *voucher* is prepared for each expenditure, regardless of whether the expenditure covers services, merchandise for resale, or assets for use in the business. A voucher (as illustrated on pages 621 and 622) is attached to each incoming invoice and given an identification number.

The voucher has spaces for listing the data from the invoice and the ledger accounts to be debited and credited in recording the transaction. Space is also provided for approval signatures for each step in the verification and approval of the liability. A completed voucher provides a description of the transaction and also of the work performed in verifying the liability and approving the cash disbursement.

Essential characteristics of a voucher

The form of a voucher will vary from one business to another. Often the voucher is folded lengthwise and supporting business papers such as the invoice and receiving report are attached inside. Regardless of the specific form of the voucher, the following features are usually present:

BROADHILL CORPORATION
Los Angeles, California

Voucher No.

Pay to

Date

Date due

Date of invoice............gross amount $

Invoice number............cash discount

Net amount $

Approval

Dates

Extensions and footings verified

Prices in agreement with purchase order

Quantities in agreement with receiving report

Credit terms in agreement with purchase order

Account distribution & recording approved

(For Accounting Dept.)

Approved for payment

(For Treasurer's Dept.)

1. A separate voucher for every incoming invoice
2. Consecutive numbering of vouchers
3. Name and address of creditor listed on voucher
4. Description of the liability, including amount and terms of payment

REVERSE SIDE OF VOUCHER

Account distribution

Date ....   Amount

Voucher No. ....

Date   ....

Purchases $................

Date due   ....

Transportation in   ....

Repairs   ....

Heat, light, and power   ....

Payee   ....

Advertising   ....

....

Delivery expense   ....

....

Misc. general expense   ....

....

Telephone and telegraph ....

Sales salaries   ....

Amount of invoice $................

Office salaries   ....

Cash discount   ....

Net amount   ....

....

....

Paid by check No.   ....

....

Date of check   ....

Amount of check   ....

Credit vouchers payable
               (total)   ....

Accounting distribution
           by   ....

Entered in voucher
        register by ....

5. Approval signatures for
    a. Verification of invoice
    b. Recording in accounts
    c. Payment of liability
6. Date of check and check number listed on voucher.

When a voucher system is in use, every liability must be recorded in the accounts before it is paid. The entry to record a liability will always include a credit to Vouchers Payable; this account title replaces Accounts Payable. Disbursements of cash, other than from petty cash, will be made only in payment of approved vouchers; consequently, every check issued will be recorded by a debit to Vouchers Payable.

In preceding chapters the payment of expenses such as the monthly telephone bill was handled by an entry debiting Telephone Expense and crediting Cash. However, when a voucher system is in use the receipt and payment of the monthly telephone bill will be recorded by these entries:

1. Upon receipt of the invoice: Debit Telephone Expense; credit Vouchers Payable

2. At time of payment: Debit Vouchers Payable; credit Cash

These two separate entries would be made even though the bill was paid immediately upon receipt. It is fundamental to the successful operation of a voucher system that no cash payment be made except in payment of an approved and recorded voucher. Rigorous compliance with this rule gives assurance that expenditures are recorded in the proper period, and that disbursements are made only after appropriate review by the individuals responsible for the various phases in the verification of a transaction.

Preparing a voucher

The functioning of a voucher system begins with the receipt of an invoice. A clerk prepares a voucher by filling in the appropriate blanks with information taken from the invoice, such as the invoice date, invoice number, and amount, and the creditor's name and address. The voucher with invoice (and possibly receiving report) attached is then sent to the employees responsible for verifying the extensions and footings on the invoice and for comparing prices, quantities, and terms with those specified in the purchase order. When completion of the verification process has been evidenced by approval signatures of the persons performing these steps, the voucher and supporting documents are sent to an employee of the accounting department, who indicates on the voucher the accounts to be debited and credited.

The voucher is now ready to be recorded, but as a further safeguard it is first submitted for the review of the controller or other accounting official. His review provides assurance that the verification procedures have been satisfactorily completed and that the liability is a proper one. After receiving this executive approval the voucher is entered in a book of original entry called a *voucher register*.

The voucher register

The voucher register replaces the purchases journal described in Chapter 8. It may be thought of as an expanded purchases book with additional debit columns for various types of expense and asset accounts.

In comparing the voucher register with a purchases journal, it should be emphasized that the purchases journal is used *only* to record purchases of merchandise on account. Consequently, every entry in a purchases journal consists of a debit to Purchases and a credit to Accounts Payable. The voucher register, on the other hand, is used to record all types of expenditures: for fixed assets, expenses, and payroll as well as for purchases of merchandise. Every entry in the voucher register will consist of a credit to Vouchers Payable, but the debits may affect various asset and expense accounts. Occasionally the entry may require a debit to a liability account; as, for example, when a voucher is prepared to authorize the issuance of a check in payment of an existing mortgage or note payable.

A typical form of voucher register is shown on this and the next page. Notice that columns are provided for the voucher number, the date of entry, the name of the creditor, and the date and number of the check issued in payment. The first money column is a credit column and has the heading of Vouchers Payable; the amount of every voucher is entered in this column. All the other money columns in the voucher register are debit columns, with the exception of one credit column in the Other Gen-

Voucher Register

Voucher no.	Date (19__)		Creditor	Payment Date (19__)	Check no.	Vouchers payable, cr	Purchases, dr	Transportation-in, dr
241	May	1	Black Company	May 10	632	1,000	1,000	
242		2	Midwest Freight	3	627	50		50
243		4	Ames Company	4	628	125		
244		5	1st Natl. Bank	5	629	8,080		
245		5	Rathco, Inc.	6	631	1,200	1,200	
246		5	Midwest Freight	6	630	110		110
286			O. K. Supply Co.			70		
287		30	J. Jones	30	665	210		
288			Black Company			1,176	1,176	
289		31	Midwest Freight	31	666	90		90
290		31	Payroll	31	667	1,865		
						25,875	9,220	640
						(21)	(51)	(52)

eral Ledger Accounts section. Separate columns are provided for accounts frequently debited, such as Purchases and Transportation-in.. At the extreme right of the register, a debit column and a credit column are provided for Other General Ledger Accounts, meaning accounts infrequently used for which special columns are not provided. In this section the account title must be written opposite the amount of each debit and credit. The entries in this section of the voucher register are posted individually and a ledger page (LP) column is provided in which the account number is listed when the individual posting is made.

Each voucher is entered in the voucher register in numerical order as soon as it is prepared and approved. When payment is made the number and date of the check are entered in the columns provided for this purpose. The total amount of unpaid vouchers may be determined from the register at any time merely by listing the "open" items, that is, vouchers for which no entry has yet been made in the Payment columns. The total of the unpaid vouchers appearing in the voucher register should agree with the total of the vouchers in the unpaid vouchers file at the same date.

Adver-tising, dr	Sup-plies, dr	Repairs, dr	Accrued payroll, dr	Other general ledger accounts			
				Account name	LP	Debit	Credit
		125					
				Notes Payable	24	8,000	
				Interest Exp.	79	80	
	70						
		210					
			1,865				
510	470	335	3,800				10,900
(61)	(14)	(74)	(24)				(√)

Posting from the voucher register. All columns of the voucher register are totaled at the end of the month; the equality of debit and credit entries is proved by comparing the combined totals of the two credit columns with the sum of the totals of the various debit columns. After the register has been proved to be in balance, the posting to ledger accounts is begun.

The individual items listed in the Other General Ledger Accounts section are posted as debits and credits to the various accounts indicated, but the total of this column is not posted. The totals of the other debit columns, such as Purchases, Transportation-in, and Advertising, are posted as debits to the accounts named, and the total of the Vouchers Payable column is posted as a credit to the ledger account, Vouchers Payable. The posting of each column total is evidenced by listing the account number in parentheses just below the column total in the voucher register. In the ledger accounts the letters VR are entered to show that the posting came from the voucher register.

The balance of the general ledger account, Vouchers Payable, should be reconciled at the end of the month with the total of the unpaid vouchers shown in the voucher register and also with the total of the vouchers in the unpaid vouchers file.

Paying the voucher within the discount period. After the voucher has been entered in the voucher register, it is placed (with the supporting documents attached) in a tickler file according to the date of required payment. The voucher system emphasizes the required *time for payment* of liabilities rather than the identity of the creditors; for this reason, vouchers are filed by required date of payment. In computing future cash requirements of a business, the amount of a liability and the required date of payment are of basic significance; the identity of the creditor has no bearing on the problem of maintaining a proper cash position.

Cash discount periods generally run from the date of the invoice. Since a voucher is prepared for each invoice, the required date of payment is the last day on which a check can be prepared and mailed to the creditor in time to qualify for the discount.

When the payment date arrives, the voucher is removed from the unpaid file and sent to the cashier, who draws a check for signature by the treasurer. The cashier fills in the check number, amount, and date of payment on the voucher and presents the check and voucher to the treasurer. The treasurer examines the documents, especially the approval signatures, and authorizes the payment of the liability by signing the voucher in the space labeled "Approved for payment." He also signs the check and mails it to the creditor. (Note that the check does not come back into the possession of the employee who prepared it.) The voucher is forwarded to the accounting department, which will record the issuance of the check and also note in the voucher register the payment of the voucher.

The check register

A check register is merely a simplified version of the cash payments journal illustrated in Chapter 8. When a voucher system is in use, checks are issued only in payment of approved and recorded vouchers. Consequently, every check issued is recorded by a debit to Vouchers Payable and a credit to Cash. The check register therefore contains a special column for debits to Vouchers Payable and a Cash credit column. The only other money column needed in this compact record is for credits to Purchase Discounts when invoices are paid within the cash discount period. Shown below is a check register with entries corresponding to the payments listed in the voucher register on pages 624 and 625.

The check register provides a chronological record of all checks issued. All entries in the check register are serially numbered and a separate line is used for each check. To look up the details of a transaction involving a payment of cash is therefore quite easy if one knows either the date or the serial number of the check.

To record the payment of a voucher, an entry is made in the check register, and a notation of the check number and date is placed on the appropriate line in the voucher register. At the end of the month the column totals of the check register are posted as for other special journals; this posting consists of a debit to the Vouchers Payable account for the total of the vouchers paid during the month and a corresponding credit to the Cash account. The symbol CkR is placed in the ledger accounts to indicate that a posting came from the check register.

CHECKS ISSUED ONLY IN PAYMENT OF APPROVED VOUCHERS

Check Register

Check no.	Date (19___)		Payee	Voucher no.	Vouchers payable, dr	Purchase discount, cr	Cash, cr
627	May	3	Midwest Freight	242	50		50
628		4	Ames Company	243	125		125
629		5	1st National Bank	244	8,080		8,080
630		6	Midwest Freight	246	110		110
631		6	Rathco, Inc.	245	1,200		1,200
632		10	Black Company	241	1,000	20	980
665		30	J. Jones	287	210		210
666		31	Midwest Freight	289	90		90
667		31	Payroll	290	1,865		1,865
					23,660	240	23,420
					(21)	(52)	(1)

Throughout this chapter it is assumed that purchase invoices are recorded at the gross amount and that purchase discounts obtained through prompt payment are reflected in the check register. However, the voucher system is adaptable to the recording of purchase invoices at either the gross amount or the net discounted amount. (These alternative methods of recording purchase invoices were discussed in Chapter 7.) If invoices are to be recorded net, some slight changes will be required in the columnar arrangement illustrated for the voucher register and the check register.

Illustration of use of voucher register and check register. The use of

SOME
SAMPLE
ENTRIES

the voucher register and the check register in handling typical transactions may be further clarified by the following examples:

June 2.   Paid *Morning Times* for advertising.

Voucher Register	*Check Register*

Advertising Expense .... *xxx*
    Vouchers Payable ..   *xxx*
(Also enter check number and
date in Payment column.)
	Vouchers Payable .... *xxx*
	    Cash .... *xxx*

June 3.   Received shipment of merchandise from Cross Company, terms 2/10, n/30.

Voucher Register	*Check Register*
Purchases .... *xxx* *Vouchers Payable* ... *xxx*	*(No entry until payment* *is made.)*

June 12.   Paid Cross Company invoice of June 3; took discount.

Voucher Register	*Check Register*

(Enter check number and date
in Payment column.)
	Vouchers Payable .... *xxx*
	    Purchase Discount .. *xxx*
	    Cash .... *xxx*

June 13.   Replenished petty cash fund.

Voucher Register	*Check Register*

Various expense accounts .. *xxx*
    Vouchers Payable ...   *xxx*
(Enter check number and
date in Payment column.)
	Vouchers Payable .... *xxx*
	    Cash .... *xxx*

Check and remittance advice. The check used in payment of a voucher often has a remittance advice attached informing the creditor as to the particular invoice being paid. A combination check and remittance advice, which is often prepared in duplicate or triplicate, is illustrated on page 629.

COM-
BINED
CHECK
AND
REMIT-
TANCE
ADVICE

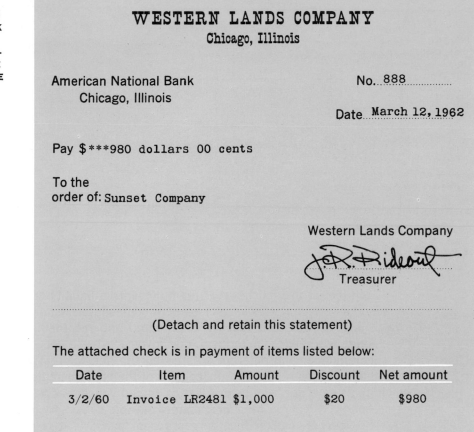

WESTERN LANDS COMPANY

Chicago, Illinois

American National Bank
Chicago, Illinois

No. 888

Date March 12, 1962

Pay $***980 dollars 00 cents

To the
order of: Sunset Company

Western Lands Company

J. R. Rideout

Treasurer

(Detach and retain this statement)

The attached check is in payment of items listed below:

Date	Item	Amount	Discount	Net amount
3/2/60	Invoice LR2481	$1,000	$20	$980

Filing paid vouchers. After the payment has been recorded in the check register and noted in the voucher register, the paid voucher is placed in numerical order in a paid vouchers file. Many companies prepare a duplicate copy of the check and remittance advice for filing with the paid voucher. The paid vouchers file then contains a complete set of documents describing and supporting every disbursement of cash.

Special considerations of the voucher register

As a subsidiary ledger. When a voucher system is used to control liabilities and cash disbursements, there is no need to maintain an accounts payable subsidiary ledger such as the one described in Chapter 8. Since the traditional form of accounts payable ledger contains a separate account with every creditor, it requires a great deal of detailed posting and recording work. The elimination of this costly subsidiary ledger is one of the major savings to be achieved by adopting a voucher system. But exactly how is it possible for a company to get along without a separate ledger for accounts payable?

CREDITOR
INDEX CARD
FOR
VOUCHERS

Creditor Rogers Machine Company

900 Alameda Street, Los Angeles, California

Date 196__	Voucher number	Date	Voucher number	Date	Voucher number
Apr. 4	4–32				
May 7	5–39				
Aug. 12	8–57				
Aug. 20	8–83				

Each line of the voucher register represents a liability account with an individual creditor. This liability account comes into existence when an invoice is received and a voucher is prepared and recorded, describing the amount owed under the terms of that invoice. When a voucher is paid, the check number and date are entered on the line for that voucher to show that the liability is ended. Inspection of the voucher register reveals which items have not been paid. A list of unpaid vouchers corresponds to a trial balance prepared from an accounts payable subsidiary ledger.

NOTE
HANDLING
OF
PURCHASE
RETURNS

The voucher register thus serves a dual purpose; it is primarily a book of original entry, but it also serves as the equivalent of a subsidiary ledger of liability accounts. However, the voucher register does not classify invoices by creditors; it does not show the total amount owed to a given

Voucher Register

Voucher no.	Date (19__)		Creditor	Payment		Vouchers payable, cr
				Date (19__)	Check no.	
621	Oct.	2	Barnard Co.	See vou. No. 633		2,800
633	Oct.	8	Barnard Co.			2,000
						4,800
						(21)

creditor with several invoices outstanding. Neither does it show the total purchases from a given supplier over a period of time. Some companies consider it important to maintain a record of the total business done with each supplier. For this purpose a memorandum card file may be established with a card for each creditor showing the dates and numbers of vouchers payable to that supplier. A creditor index card of this type is illustrated on page 630. However, the maintenance of a card file of vouchers classified by creditor requires much of the same detailed work involved in maintaining an accounts payable subsidiary ledger.

Handling purchase returns and allowances. The following example illustrates one of the several common methods for handling purchases returns and allowances under a voucher system.

Assume that on October 2 an invoice in the amount of $2,800 was received from a supplier, Barnard Company. Voucher No. 621 was prepared and recorded in the voucher register, as illustrated below. Shortly thereafter some of the merchandise was returned to Barnard Company, and on October 8 a credit memorandum for $800 was received.

A new voucher (No. 633) was prepared in the amount of $2,000, and the original voucher (No. 621 for $2,800) was canceled, marked with a reference to the replacement voucher, and placed in the paid vouchers file

Vouchers Payable (21)			
Oct. 8	2,800	Oct. 31	4,800

Purchases (51)		
Oct. 31	2,800	

Purchase Returns & Allowances (52)		
	Oct. 8	800

Purchases, dr	Transpor-tation-in, dr	Other general ledger accounts			
		Account name	LP	Debit	Credit
2,800					
		Vouchers Payable	21	2,800	
		Purchase Returns	52		800
2,800				2,800	800
(51)				(√)	(√)

In the voucher register the new voucher is recorded as a credit of $2,000 to Vouchers Payable in the Vouchers Payable column and as a debit of $2,800 to Vouchers Payable in the Other General Ledger Accounts section. A credit of $800 to Purchases Returns and Allowances is also recorded in the Other General Ledger Accounts section. In the Payment column of the register, a notation is entered on the line for the old voucher, "See voucher No. 633." To make this procedure clear, the illustrated voucher register on page 631 contains only the transactions with the Barnard Company; posting to the ledger accounts is also shown.

Making partial payments. If it is known at the time an invoice is received that payment will be made in two or more installments, a separate voucher should be prepared for each installment. However, if the use of partial payments is decided upon after a single voucher for the entire amount of the invoice has been recorded, the original voucher should be canceled and new vouchers prepared for each expected installment payment.

For example, assume that voucher No. 312 was prepared and recorded on May 5, in the amount of $10,000, as shown in the illustration on this page. On May 12, after discussions with the creditor, a decision was reached to pay $2,000 at once and to pay the remaining $8,000 a few weeks later. The transaction did not involve cash discounts. Two new vouchers should be prepared: voucher No. 335 for $2,000 and voucher No. 336 for $8,000. These new vouchers are recorded in the voucher register by credits in the Vouchers Payable column and debits to the Vouchers Payable account in the Other General Ledger Accounts section. A reference to the new vouchers, "See vouchers Nos. 335 and 336," is entered in the Payment column opposite the original voucher. Also on May 12, check No. 906 for $2,000 is issued and recorded in the check register (see top of page 633). The date and number of the check are both listed in the voucher register opposite voucher No. 335.

PROCE-
DURES FOR
PARTIAL
PAYMENT OF
VOUCHERS

Voucher Register

Voucher no.	Date (19___)		Creditor	Payment		
				Date (19___)		Check no.
312	May	5	Auto Supply Co.	See Vou. Nos. 335 & 336		
335	May	12	Auto Supply Co.	May	12	906
336		12	Auto Supply Co.			

		Check Register				
Check no.	Date (19___)	Payee	Voucher no.	Vouchers payable Debit	Purchase discount Credit	Cash Credit
906	May 12	Auto Supply Co.	335	2,000		2,000

Issuing notes payable. Occasionally the liability reflected by a voucher will be met by issuing a note to the creditor rather than by writing a check. To record issuance of a note under these circumstances, the following general journal entry may be made:

<table>
<tr><td>TO SETTLE A
VOUCHER BY
ISSUANCE
OF NOTE</td><td>Vouchers Payable xxx
    Notes Payable   xxx
To record issuance of a 90-day, 6% note in settlement of
voucher No. 825.</td></tr>
</table>

In the Paid column of the voucher register, a notation should be made "Paid by note, see JE dated _____." The voucher itself should be marked "Canceled," with a notation concerning the issuance of the note, and placed in the paid vouchers file.

When the note matures a new voucher must be prepared to authorize the cash disbursement to pay the note. In recording this new voucher in the voucher register, the debit entries to Notes Payable and to Interest Expense will be entered in the Other General Ledger Accounts section.

Correcting errors in the voucher register. If an error in the voucher register is discovered *before* the posting work is performed at the end

Vouchers payable Credit	Purchases Debit	Other general ledger accounts			
				Amount	
		Account name	LP	Debit	Credit
10,000	10,000				
2,000 8,000		Vouchers Payable	21	10,000	

of the month, the erroneous entry may be canceled by drawing a line through it and a new voucher prepared and recorded. The original voucher should be marked with the word "Canceled" and a reference to the number of the replacement voucher.

If an error in the voucher register is not discovered until after the register has been posted, a general journal entry may be made to reverse the erroneous entry. A reference to the adjusting journal entry should be made in the payment column of the voucher register. A new voucher can then be prepared and recorded in the voucher register.

Presentation of liability in the balance sheet

Although the liability account title Vouchers Payable occasionally appears on a balance sheet, it is better practice to use the more widely understood term Accounts Payable.

A "voucher system" without vouchers

One interesting variation of the system described in this chapter is to use a voucher register, but not to prepare vouchers. Invoices are assigned consecutive numbers as they are received, and entered in the voucher register, which is usually given the name of invoice register. As each invoice is verified as to quantities, prices, extensions, and other aspects of the transaction, approvals are noted on the invoice itself. At the time of payment, the invoice is transferred from an unpaid invoices file to a paid invoices file. The invoice register is footed and posted at the end of the month in the same manner as a voucher register. The use of a check register follows the pattern previously described, and the review of documents by executives before approving an invoice or issuing a check may correspond to the control procedures described for the voucher system.

Appraisal of the voucher system

The voucher system is widely used, and it is particularly common in large organizations which have given serious study to the problem of internal control. Perhaps the greatest single advantage of the voucher system is the assurance that every expenditure of the business is systematically reviewed and verified before payment is made. Executives are able to make rapid but effective review of expenditures by relying upon the approval signatures of key employees, who assume personal responsibility for the propriety of the expenditure.

Other advantages of the voucher system include the following:

1. Since invoices are recorded immediately upon receipt, expenditures are charged to appropriate expense or asset accounts in the period incurred. Also, the record of liabilities is current and complete.

2. A complete history of every expenditure and the nature of the verification made is readily available by looking up the paid voucher.

3. Orderly payment of bills in time to take advantage of cash discounts is facilitated.

4. Detailed bookkeeping work is reduced by elimination of the accounts payable subsidiary ledgers.

5. Verification and payment of each invoice on an individual basis provides clearer records and less opportunity for error and fraud than when payments of round amount are made against an accumulation of invoices from a supplier.

The disadvantages of the voucher system are (1) the lack of any comprehensive record of business done with particular suppliers and (2) the somewhat cumbersome procedures necessary to handle partial payments, purchase returns and allowances, and corrections of errors.

PAYROLL ACCOUNTING

Accurate detailed payroll records are essential for several reasons. These records provide a basis for maintaining satisfactory relations with employees; they provide significant information as to operating costs; and they enable employers to meet their obligations under Federal and state laws concerning payroll taxes. Social security legislation requiring payroll deductions and taxes on payrolls has had a considerable effect on payroll records and procedures. Employers are also required to withhold a portion of employees' earnings for payment of Federal income taxes. Another factor augmenting the problems of payroll accounting has been the trend toward withholding specified sums from employees' earnings for a variety of purposes such as union dues, insurance premiums, and purchase of savings bonds.

Employers engaged in interstate commerce are required by the Federal Fair Labor Standards Act (also known as the Wages and Hours Law) to pay overtime at a minimum rate of 1 1/2 times the regular rate for hours worked in excess of 40 per week. Many companies also pay overtime premium rates for night shifts and for work on Sundays and holidays. Since wages earned are now commonly based on hours worked at various rates, the function of timekeeping has become of increased importance. Time clocks and time cards are widely used in compiling the detailed information required for payroll purposes.

A distinction must be drawn between employees and independent contractors. Public accountants, architects, attorneys, and other persons who render services to a business for a fee but are not controlled or directed by the client are not employees but independent contractors, and the amounts paid to them are not subject to payroll taxes.

Deductions from earnings of employees

The take-home pay of most employees is considerably less than the gross earnings. Major factors explaining this difference between the amount earned and the amount received are social security taxes and Federal income taxes withheld.

Federal Insurance Contributions Act taxes. Under the terms of the Social Security Act, qualified workers in covered industries who retire after reaching the age of sixty-five shall receive monthly retirement benefits. Benefits are also provided for the family of a worker who dies before or after reaching this retirement age. Funds for the operation of this program are obtained through taxes levied under the Federal Insurance Contributions Act, often referred to as F.I.C.A. taxes.

Employers are required by the Federal Insurance Contributions Act to withhold a portion of each employee's earnings as a contribution to the social security program. For illustrative purposes and convenience in working problems we shall assume the rate of tax is 3% of the first $4,800 of wages received in each calendar year. The law calls for higher rates to be imposed in future years. Wages in excess of $4,800 paid to a worker in one calendar year are not subject to the tax. Each employee is assigned a social security number, which is used by the employer in maintaining individual records of amounts earned and withheld. Within a month after the close of the year, the employer must furnish each employee with a statement showing the total amount of social security tax withheld.*

Federal income tax. Our pay-as-you-go system of Federal income tax requires employers to withhold a portion of the earnings of their employees. The amount withheld depends upon the amount of the earnings and upon the number of exemptions allowed the employee. The employee is entitled to one exemption for himself, and an additional exemption for each person qualifying as a dependent. Persons over sixty-five or blind are entitled to additional exemptions. (More extensive consideration of exemptions and of other aspects of Federal income taxes will be found in Chapter 27.) A withholding exemption certificate must be prepared by each employee, stating the number of exemptions to which he is entitled; this certificate is given to the employer so that he will be able to compute the proper amount of tax to be withheld. As a matter of convenience to employers, the government provides withholding tax tables which indicate the amount to withhold for any amount of earnings and any number of exemptions.

States or cities which levy income taxes may also require the employer to withhold the tax from employees' earnings, but as such situations are not common they will not be discussed here.

Other deductions from employees' earnings. Programs of unemployment compensation insurance are found in every state, but they are generally financed by taxes on employers rather than on employees. In a few states unemployment insurance taxes are levied on employees and such taxes are withheld by employers from employees' earnings.

In addition to the compulsory deductions for taxes, many other deductions are voluntarily authorized by employees. Union dues, insurance premiums, and savings bond purchases have already been mentioned as examples of payroll deductions. Others include charitable contributions,

---

* Recent revision of Social Security taxes has set the rates at 3 5/8% each on employees and employers, or a total of 7 1/4% of the first $4,800 of taxable wages paid each employee in a calendar year.

supplementary retirement programs and pension plans, and repayments of payroll advances or other loans.

Employer's responsibility for amounts withheld. When an employer withholds a portion of an employee's earnings for any reason, he must maintain accounting records which will enable him to file required reports and make designated payments of the funds withheld. From the employer's viewpoint, most amounts withheld from employees' earnings represent current liabilities. In other words, the employer must pay to the government or some other agency the amounts which he withholds from the employee's earnings. An exception would be the deductions made from an employee's pay to liquidate a previous loan to the employee. A statement of earnings and deductions is usually prepared by the employer and presented to the employee with each pay check or pay envelope to explain how the net pay was determined.

Payroll records and procedures

Although payroll records and procedures vary greatly according to the number of employees and the extent of mechanization in processing payroll data, there are a few fundamental steps common to payroll work in most organizations. One of these steps taken at the end of each pay period is the preparation of a payroll showing the names and earnings of all employees. The information entered in this payroll record will include the authorized rates of pay for each employee and the number of hours worked, taken from time cards or similar documents. After separating the regular hours from overtime hours and applying appropriate pay rates for each category, the total taxable earnings are determined. F.I.C.A. tax, Federal income tax, and any items authorized by the employee are then deducted to arrive at the net amount payable. When the computation of the payroll sheet has been completed, the next step is to reflect the expense and the related liability in the ledger accounts. A general journal entry such as the following may be made to bring into the accounts the data summarized on the payroll.

ENTRY TO RECORD PAYROLL	*Sales Salaries Expense* 1,200	
	Office Salaries Expense 800	
	F.I.C.A. Taxes Payable	*60*
	Liability for Income Tax Withheld	*220*
	Group Insurance Payments Withheld	*10*
	Accrued Payroll	*1,710*
	To record the payroll and related deductions for the pay period ended January 15.	

The two debits to expense accounts indicate that the business has incurred a total salary expense of $2,000; however, only $1,710 of this amount will be paid to the employees. The remaining $290 (consisting of deductions for taxes and insurance premiums withheld) is lodged in liability accounts. Payment of these liabilities will be made at various later dates.

Payment of employees. The preceding section illustrated the recording of the payroll and showed the sum of $1,710 in a current liability account entitled Accrued Payroll. The procedures for the actual payment to employees to discharge this liability will depend upon whether the company pays salaries by checks on the regular bank account, by checks drawn on a special bank account, or in cash. These payment procedures also depend on whether a voucher system is in use.

The advantages of establishing a separate payroll bank account were discussed in Chapter 9. At the close of each pay period, a check is drawn on the general bank account for the entire amount of the payroll and deposited in the payroll bank account. Pay checks to individual employees are then drawn on the payroll bank account, which is immediately reduced to zero. If the voucher system is in use, a voucher for the payroll would be prepared and recorded in the voucher register as a debit to Payroll Bank Account and a credit to Vouchers Payable in the amount of $1,710.[1] The transfer of the funds would then be carried out by issuing a check on the general bank account and recording this disbursement in the check register by a debit to Vouchers Payable and a credit to Cash.

Payment of employees in cash. Payment of salaries in cash affords less internal control than the use of checks, but it is preferred by some companies in locations where banks or other check-cashing facilities are not readily available. The recording procedures do not differ significantly from those previously described; a voucher is prepared for the amount of the payroll, and a single check drawn and cashed to obtain the cash to fill the individual pay envelopes. As previously mentioned, a statement of earnings and deductions is usually furnished to the employee each payday. When payment is made by check, this information may be printed on a stub attached to the pay check. When wages are paid in cash, the information is usually printed on the pay envelope.

Withholding statement. By January 31 each year, employers are required to furnish every employee with a withholding statement (Form W-2). This form shows the gross earnings for the preceding calendar year, and the amounts withheld for F.I.C.A. tax and income tax. The employer sends one copy of this form to the Director of Internal Revenue and also gives two copies to the employee. When the employee files his Federal income tax return, he must attach a copy of the withholding statement.

Individual earnings records for employees. To facilitate preparation of the withholding statements and to determine the amount of F.I.C.A. tax to be withheld for each employee, the employer is required to maintain an

---

[1] No vouchers need be prepared at this time for the $290 of liabilities resulting from deductions. These liabilities are accumulated in ledger accounts until the end of the quarter. Vouchers will be prepared prior to the time for payment of these liabilities.

individual record of earnings and deductions for each employee. This record shows for each employee the total compensation for each pay period, any portion not subject to tax, and the amount of tax withheld. These employees' earnings records are also used in preparing the quarterly and annual reports of earnings and deductions which the employer must file with Federal and state tax authorities.

Payroll taxes on the employer

The discussion of payroll taxes up to this point has dealt with taxes levied on the employee and withheld from his pay. From the viewpoint of the employer, such taxes are significant because he must account for and remit the amounts withheld to the appropriate government offices. Payroll taxes are also levied on the *employer;* these taxes are expenses of the business and are recorded by debits to expense accounts, just as in the case of property taxes or license fees for doing business.

F.I.C.A. tax. The employer is taxed to help finance the social security program; currently the tax rate is 3% of the first $4,800 of gross earnings by each employee in each calendar year. The rate of tax corresponds to that levied on employees, and the same schedule of future increases is applicable.

Federal unemployment insurance tax. Employers are also subject to a Federal unemployment insurance tax on the first $3,000 of wages paid to each covered employee each year.* However, the Federal law provides that 90% of this tax is to be remitted by employers directly to state governments which carry out the Federal-state unemployment insurance program. If we assume a Federal tax of 3%, the effective rate is only 0.3%; the other 2.7% is paid to the state. Under this assumption, the tax rates may therefore be stated as follows:

Federal tax	*0.3%*
State tax	*2.7%*
Total	*3.0%*

Only employers with four or more employees are subject to the Federal unemployment insurance tax, which is not levied on employees. Payments to unemployed persons are made by the state governments, not by the Federal government.

State unemployment compensation taxes. All states participate in the Federal-state unemployment insurance program. Although the state laws vary somewhat, the division rate mentioned previously is the basic rate in general use. Most states have a merit-rating plan which permits a reduction in the tax rate for employers who establish a record of stable employment.

* Although the tax has recently been raised to 3.5%, the 3% rate is retained in this illustration and in the related problems to simplify the calculations required.

Accounting entry for employer's payroll taxes. The entry to record the employer's payroll taxes is usually made at the same time the payroll is recorded. For the payroll illustrated on page 637, the entry for all three of the payroll taxes on the employer is as follows:

Payroll Taxes Expense 120		
F.I.C.A. Taxes Payable		*60*
State Unemployment Taxes Payable		*54*
Federal Unemployment Taxes Payable		*6*
To record payroll taxes on employer for pay period ended January 15.		

Accrual of payroll taxes at year-end. Payroll taxes are levied only on wages actually *paid,* but under the accrual basis of accounting both wages and the taxes on such wages are logically an expense of the period in which the wages are earned by employees. If an adjusting entry is made at December 31 to accrue wages earned by employees but not payable to them until sometime in January, an entry should also be made to accrue the payroll taxes on such wages. No adjusting entry is needed for taxes to be withheld from employees' pay because taxes levied on employees are not an expense of the business.

Statement presentation. The payroll taxes levied on the employer and the taxes withheld from employees are current liabilities of the business until payment to the government is made. The following accounts are, therefore, classified in the balance sheet as current liabilities: F.I.C.A. Taxes Payable, Federal Unemployment Taxes Payable, State Unemployment Taxes Payable, and Liability for Income Taxes Withheld.

Payroll taxes expense appears in the income statement: it may be apportioned between selling expenses and general expenses on the basis of the amount of payroll originating in each functional division. Thus, payroll tax on salaries of salesmen is classified as a selling expense, and payroll tax on office salaries is classified as a general expense.

Payment of payroll taxes. Four times a year the employer is required to remit to the government the amounts withheld from employees' pay for income taxes and F.I.C.A. taxes. The F.I.C.A. tax on the employer is also payable at these dates and is reported on the same tax form. These payments are made during the month following the close of each quarter of the year. If the total of the amounts withheld from employees plus the F.I.C.A. tax on the employer exceeds $100 during the first or second month of the quarter, the amount must be deposited by the employer with the Federal Reserve bank by the fifteenth of the following month.

The employer must file his Federal unemployment tax return by January 31 each year for the preceding calendar year. Most states require employers to file tax returns and to make payment of the state unemployment compensation tax on a quarterly basis.

QUESTIONS *

1. Explain how a purchase order, receiving report, voucher, and check constitute a chain of documentary evidence that facilitates control over business expenditures.

2. The following column totals appear in a voucher register at the end of the month: transportation-in, $1,280; selling expense control, $6,020; general expense control, $4,210; vouchers payable, $61,750; accrued payroll, $15,640; merchandise purchases, $18,440; other general ledger accounts, $16,160 (notes payable, $16,000 and interest expense, $160). Prepare in general journal form an entry summarizing the voucher transactions for the month.

3. The following column totals appear in a check register at the end of the month: cash, $11,710; vouchers payable, $11,390; cash discounts not taken, $320. Prepare a general journal entry to summarize cash disbursements for the month. Explain how the company handles cash discounts on purchases.

4. "The voucher register serves as a book of original entry and as a subsidiary ledger at one and the same time." Explain the disadvantages of the voucher register as a subsidiary ledger record.

5. G Company buys almost entirely from firms offering cash discounts for payment within 10 days after the end of the month in which a charge is billed. A voucher is prepared for each supplier; invoices from that supplier are noted on the voucher jacket as they are received, and are filed with the voucher. At the end of each month the voucher for each firm is entered in the voucher register and a lump-sum check is drawn for the amount of all invoices received from that firm during the month. What advantages and disadvantages do you see in this system?

6. In May, R Company recorded voucher No. 106 to X Company for $1,500, covering the purchase of equipment. The voucher remained unpaid at the end of May, and in June it was discovered that the invoice had been incorrectly priced; the amount should have been $1,750. Explain how this error should be straightened out in the accounting records.

7. Explain how the following would be handled in a voucher system:

    a. Return of merchandise to supplier in the same month as purchase but after original invoice has been entered in voucher register.

    b. Return of merchandise to supplier in the month following purchase.

8. Explain which of the following taxes relating to an employee's wages are borne by the employee and which by the employer:

    a. F.I.C.A. taxes

    b. Federal unemployment compensation taxes

    c. State unemployment compensation taxes

    d. Federal income taxes

9. Jones receives a salary of $6,000 per year from H Company. Under the merit rating system in the state, H Company is subject to a state unemployment tax rate of 0.5% on all wages up to $3,000 per year. F.I.C.A. taxes are 3% on wages

---

* In all questions and problems for this chapter, assume an FICA tax rate of 3% for both employers and employees on the first $4,800 of wages paid each employee each year. Also, for the employer, assume a 3% rate for the Federal unemployment insurance tax applicable to the first $3,000 of wages paid to each covered employee each year.

up to $4,800, and Federal income taxes of $720 were withheld from Jones's salary during the year. Prepare in general journal form an entry summarizing the payroll transactions for employee Jones for the current year.

10. Explain when (in what month) the following taxes are paid by the employer:

    a. Federal income taxes withheld

    b. F.I.C.A. taxes

    c. State unemployment compensation taxes

    d. Federal unemployment compensation taxes

PROBLEMS

Group A

23A-1. *Instructions.* Vollum Company uses a voucher system for all cash expenditures. Following the form indicated in the example, indicate how the transactions given below would be recorded by the company.

    Example. Purchased supplies from X Company; paid invoice in full.

Voucher Register		*Check Register*		*General Journal*
Supplies on Hand ...... *xx*		*Vouchers Payable* ...... *xx*		*No entry*
Vouchers Payable .. *xx*		*Cash* .... *xx*		
(Enter check number and date of payment.)				

    Data

    (1) Purchased merchandise from R Company, terms 2/10, n/30, and paid invoice within 10 days.

    (2) Received credit memorandum from R Company for the cost of merchandise returned after invoice had been paid. Vollum Co. will treat this as an account receivable from R Company.

    (3) Purchased equipment from J Company on 30-day open account.

    (4) Made a partial payment on the equipment purchase from J Company, and gave a six-month note for the balance.

    (5) Paid the J Company note plus accrued interest.

    (6) Recorded accrual of monthly payroll. Amounts were withheld for income taxes and F.I.C.A. taxes. A single voucher was prepared covering the total payroll.

    (7) Drew a single check for payroll, to be deposited in a payroll bank account.

    (8) Purchased merchandise from M Company, terms net 60 days.

    (9) Drew a check to reimburse petty cash fund; all expenditures are chargeable to Miscellaneous Expense.

    (10) Recorded the company's share of F.I.C.A. taxes and state and Federal unemployment taxes (charge Payroll Tax Expense). Made monthly deposit of F.I.C.A. taxes and withheld income taxes; paid state unemployment taxes due for the past quarter.

23A-2. McBroom Company has six employees; two are employed on a monthly salary, and four are paid an hourly rate with provision for time and one-half for overtime. The basic data for the July 31 payroll is given below:

Employee	Hours Reg.	Hours OT	Pay rate	Com- pensation to June 30	Gross pay due	Fed. inc. tax wh.
Able	160	10	$ 2.50 hr	$2,600	$437.50	$47.40
Baker	160		3.00 hr	2,700	480.00	78.20
Cass	160	22	1.75 hr	2,650	337.75	21.20
Dun	Salary		600.00 mo	3,600	600.00	91.60
Eck	160		2.00 hr	2,800	320.00	18.30
Fager	Salary		750.00 mo	4,500	750.00	83.20

Other data. Compensation of Dun and Fager is considered an administrative expense; the balance of the earnings is chargeable to Shop Wages. Payroll taxes apply as follows: F.I.C.A., 3% up to maximum of $4,800; state unemployment, 2.7% up to maximum of $3,000; Federal unemployment, 0.3% up to maximum of $3,000. McBroom Company has group insurance and a supplementary retirement plan under which each employee contributes 5% of his gross pay, and the company matches this contribution. Both employees' and employer's contributions are deposited with the Standard Insurance Company at the end of each month.

Instructions

a. Prepare a payroll record for July, using the following columns:

Employee	Gross pay	Amount subject to Unemploy- ment taxes	Amount subject to F.I.C.A. taxes	Federal income tax withheld	F.I.C.A. tax withheld	Retirement deduction	Net pay due

b. Explain how the gross pay for Cass was computed for the month of July.

c. Explain why the Federal income taxes withheld for Fager are less than those withheld for Dun, despite the fact that Fager received a higher gross compensation.

d. Prepare in general journal form the entry to record the payroll for the month of July.

e. Prepare in general journal form the entry to record the employer's payroll taxes and insurance plan contributions for the month of July.

23A-3. Leebor Company was organized late in September and began business on October 1. The company's accounting system was designed by a firm of CPAs and included a voucher system for controlling cash payments. Small payments were made from a petty cash fund, and the semimonthly payroll was deposited in a special payroll bank account, on which individual pay checks were written. In the general ledger control accounts for selling expenses and for general expenses were used; the individual expense accounts were maintained in subsidiary ledgers as follows:

Selling expense control: General expense control:
Acct. 200   Advertising   Acct. 400   Administrative salaries
      210   Sales salaries   405   Building expense
      220   Delivery expense   415   Payroll taxes
      230   Miscellaneous   425   Miscellaneous

Below are described certain transactions of the Leebor Company during the month of October:

Oct. 1. Issued voucher 10-1 to establish a petty cash fund of $300, and wrote check No. 1 to set up the fund.

Oct. 2. Rent on the building for October was $600. Issued voucher 10-2 and check No. 2 payable to Ace Realty Co.

Oct. 3. Invoice for merchandise purchased from Crane Supply was received, total amount $8,400. Of the total, $250 was for freight; the balance was subject to terms 2/10, n/30. Issued voucher 10-3.

Oct. 7. Received bill for advertising from The Herald in the amount of $280; issued voucher 10-4, and check No. 3 in payment.

Oct. 12. Purchased office equipment from Valley Company for $1,800. Voucher 10-5 was issued for the down payment of $360, and voucher 10-6 for the balance, which is due in 60 days. Wrote check No. 4 to cover the down payment.

Oct. 12. Paid voucher 10-3, taking the cash discount; check No. 5.

Oct. 15. Purchased merchandise from Black Company for $3,750, terms 3/5, n/30. Received bill from Midway Express for $124 freight charges. Issued vouchers 10-7 and 10-8 to cover these bills.

Oct. 18. Returned $750 of merchandise to Black Company because it was not the model ordered. Issued voucher 10-9 to replace 10-7.

Oct. 20. Issued check No. 6 in payment of voucher 10-9, taking the cash discount.

Oct. 25. Issued voucher 10-10 and check 7 in payment (principal and interest) of a $12,000, 30-day, 6% note given to Citizens Bank on September 25.

Oct. 26. Received invoice for building repairs from Twin Oaks Lumber Co., amount $172. Issued voucher 10-11.

Oct. 28. Received invoices for October utilities. Issued voucher 10-12 to Ace Gas & Electric for $185, and voucher 10-13 to Pacific Telephone Co. for $23.

Oct. 30. Received invoice for merchandise purchased from Abar Company, $2,700, terms 30 days net, and issued voucher 10-14.

Oct. 31. Reimbursement of petty cash fund was authorized on voucher 10-15. Expenditures from the fund during October were: delivery expense, $24; general office expense, $36; sales supplies, $48; contributions, $25; building maintenance, $35; advertising, $20; salary advances, $75.

Oct. 31. Prepared voucher 10-16 for monthly payroll. Total wages were as follows: deliveryman, $300; sales employees, $2,400; office employees, $1,950; building custodian, $350. Withholdings were made for: salary advances, $75; F.I.C.A. taxes, $150; Federal income taxes, $625. The company is subject to state unemployment taxes of 2.7% on all wages, to normal Federal unemployment tax on all wages, and to matching payments of F.I.C.A. taxes. Record employer's payroll taxes in general journal, all other parts of this transaction in voucher register.

Oct. 31. Checks Nos. 8 and 9 were issued in payment of vouchers 10-15 and 10-16, respectively. Check No. 8 is payable to petty cash fund and check 9 to payroll account.

Instructions

a. Record the October transactions in a voucher register, a check register, and a general journal. Set up the voucher register with columns as shown below.

Voucher no.	Date	Creditor	Payment		Vouchers payable	Purchases	Transportation-in
			Date	Check no.			

Selling expense control		General expense control		Other accounts		
Account no.	Amount	Account no.	Amount	Title	Amount	
					Debit	Credit

Use the following columns in the check register:

Date	Payee	Check no.	Voucher no.	Vouchers payable	Purchase discounts	Cash

b. Total the voucher register and the check register and post from all journals to the following general ledger accounts: Vouchers Payable, Purchases, Selling Expense Control, General Expense Control. Post also to all subsidiary ledger expense accounts.

c. Prepare a schedule summarizing the subsidiary ledgers for selling and administrative expenses and proving the October 31 balances in the control accounts.

d. Prepare a schedule of outstanding vouchers at October 31 to substantiate the balance in the Vouchers Payable account.

23A-4. Orthram Company employs a standard voucher system. Below are described selected transactions of the company for the month of October:

Oct. 1. Purchased merchandise as follows:
Blake Company, terms net 30 days, $3,250
Karp Company, terms 2/10, n/30, $2,800

Oct. 2. Received invoice for purchase of office equipment from Burt & Sons, invoice price $650, plus $30 transportation charges.

Oct. 9. Gave Blake Company a 60-day, 5% note in payment of the purchase of October 1.

Oct. 11. Paid all but $800 of the October 1 invoice of Karp Company, taking the cash discount on the amount paid. The $800 portion of the invoice is in dispute.

Oct. 15. Received an allowance of $100 on the purchase of office equipment from Burt and Sons on October 2 because it was not the latest model, as ordered.

Oct. 18. Sales display equipment was purchased from Standard Equipment Company for $9,000. Cash payment of $3,000 was made, with the balance to be paid in two equal installments due in 30 and 60 days, respectively.

Oct. 20. Paid $400 in full settlement of amount due Karp Company on October 1 invoice. Received their credit memorandum for the remaining $400.

Oct. 23. Purchased $10,000 in Noma Water District 4% bonds, due in nine months, as a short-term investment. Price 101 1/2 plus accrued interest for three months. Gave check in payment to Waltham Company.

Oct. 25. Drew check for $820 in favor of L. Kulp as a refund for merchandise returned by him.

Oct. 26. Drew check for $645 to State Unemployment Commission in payment of state unemployment taxes for the quarter ended on September 30.

Oct. 30. Monthly payroll for office salaries was recorded as follows: Salaries, $7,000; income taxes withheld, $1,020; F.I.C.A. taxes withheld, $164; amounts withheld for Blue Cross hospitalization plan, $156. Employer's taxes are: state unemployment, $81; Federal unemployment, $9; F.I.C.A. tax, $164. (Record payroll and employer's taxes in the general journal.)

Oct. 31. Drew check to Payroll account for October payroll.

Instructions. Record the above transactions in the following journals (use columns as indicated):

Voucher register:

Date	Voucher no.	Creditor	Payment		Vouchers payable	Purchases	Accrued payroll
			Date	Check no.			

Other accounts		
Title	Debit	Credit

Check register:

Date	Check no.	Payee	Voucher no.	Vouchers payable	Purchase discount	Cash

General Journal: Debit and credit

(Number vouchers and checks consecutively, starting with voucher No. 10 and check No. 100.)

Group B

23B-1. Cole Company uses a voucher system for all major expenditures. Selected transactions for May are presented below. As of April 30 one voucher, No. D26, was outstanding.

(1) Drew a check to establish a petty cash fund.

(2) Gave a 60-day, 6% note in settlement of voucher No. D26.

(3) Paid a note, plus accrued interest, in favor of the Citizens Bank.

(4) Purchased merchandise from J Company, terms 3/15, n/30.

(5) Purchased equipment, making a down payment and agreeing to pay the balance in 60 days.

(6) Received a credit memorandum from J Company for the return of a portion of the merchandise purchased from them.

(7) Made several small cash payments from the petty cash fund; all are chargeable to Office Expense.

(8) Advanced (by check) travel expenses to officer making a business trip.

(9) Paid invoice from J Company, taking the discount.

(10) Drew check to reimburse petty cash fund for office expenses and delivery expense.

(11) Reimbursed officer by check for trip expenses incurred by him in excess of the amount advanced.

(12) Declared cash dividend on outstanding shares of stock.

(13) Deposited total amount of dividend in a special bank account against which individual dividend checks will be drawn.

Instructions. Using the form described in problem 23A-1, indicate how each of these transactions would be recorded by the company in the voucher register, the check register, and the general journal.

23B-2. Arco Machine Company operates two major shops, a machine shop and a chemical milling shop. Below is summarized the payroll data for the month of May:

	Total wages	Income tax withheld	Amount subject to		Workmen's compensation rates	Man-hours worked
			F.I.C.A. tax	Unemployment tax		
Machine shop wages	$125,000	$11,294	$76,000	$52,000	$1.00 per $100 of wages	64,000
Chemical milling shop wages	65,500	7,162	32,000	27,000	1.60 per $100 of wages	26,000

The following accounts applicable to payroll are carried by the company:

Expense accounts	Account numbers	
	Machine shop	Chem. mill. shop
Factory wage expense	M-100	CM-100
Payroll tax expense	M-120	CM-120
Workmen's compensation insurance	M-130	CM-130
Vacation allowance	M-140	CM-140

Balance sheet accounts	Account number
Accrued payroll	L-125
Income taxes withheld	L-126
F.I.C.A. taxes payable	L-127
State unemployment tax payable	L-128
Federal unemployment tax payable	L-129
Estimated vacation allowance payable	L-130
Prepaid insurance: workmen's compensation ..	CA-10

The company is subject to the following payroll tax rates: F.I.C.A. taxes, 3% on employee and employer; state unemployment, 2.7% on employer; Federal unemployment, 0.3% on employer. A two-week vacation is allowed all full-time employees each year. The company provides for this by a charge of 4% of total wages in each pay period to vacation allowance expense. The company carries workmen's compensation insurance on its employees, at rates scheduled above. The premium is paid one year in advance on February 1; this amount is then amortized at the time the payroll is recorded, using the appropriate departmental rates.

Instructions

a. Prepare in general journal form the entry to record the payroll for the month of May. (Account numbers may be used in lieu of account titles.)

b. Prepare in general journal form the entry to record the employer's liabilities for payroll taxes, vacation allowance, and the amortization of prepaid workmen's compensation insurance. (Account numbers may be used in lieu of account titles.)

c. Compute for each department the average cost per man-hour for all fringe benefits (including payroll taxes) over and above wages.

23B-3. Hodel Company has been in business for one year. The post-closing trial balance at the end of last year is given below:

HODEL COMPANY
Post-closing Trial Balance
December 31, 19＿

Cash	$12,600
Marketable securities	5,800
Inventories, Dec. 31	27,500
Prepaid insurance	800
Equipment	18,000

Accumulated depreciation: equipment	....	$ 1,800
Vouchers payable	....	980
Income taxes withheld	....	914
F.I.C.A. taxes payable	....	484
State unemployment taxes payable	....	94
Federal unemployment taxes payable	....	220
Capital stock	....	50,000
Retained earnings	....	10,208
	$64,700	$64,700

Other data. Below are listed the books of original entry, with money columns as indicated, used by the Hodel Company:

General journal: Debit, Credit.

Cash receipts: Cash, Sales, Other accounts (credit).

Check register: Vouchers payable, Cash discounts not taken (debit), Cash.

Voucher register: Vouchers payable, Purchases, Transportation-in, Selling expense, Administrative expense, Other accounts (debit and credit).

In addition to the above accounts, the following income and expense accounts appear in the general ledger:

Sales	Selling expense
Purchases	Administrative expense
Transportation-in	Cash discounts not taken
Purchase returns and allowances	Gain or loss on sale of securities

The company follows the practice of recording all merchandise purchases net of available cash discounts. It may be assumed that employer's payroll tax rates are as follows: F.I.C.A., 3%; state unemployment, 1.8%; Federal unemployment, 0.3%.

Transactions for the month of January of the current year are shown below.

Jan. 2. Check for $1,000 to Ramer Co. in payment of voucher L-18 recorded in December of last year. The amount appears on the voucher record as $980, net of 2% cash discount, but payment was not made within the discount period.

Jan. 5. Drew voucher and check to deposit income tax and F.I.C.A. tax withholdings as of December 31 in the First National Bank.

Jan. 8. Purchased merchandise as follows:
Beagle Company: $8,400, terms 2/10, n/30;
Rosco Corporation: $12,000, terms 3/15, n/60.

Jan. 9. Received bill from Coastal Freightways for transportation charges on merchandise purchased, $830.

Jan. 12. Returned merchandise with an original invoice cost of $300 to Rosco Corporation for credit. (*Note:* Since the purchase (Jan. 8) was recorded net of the cash discount, this must be taken into account in recording the return. Draw a new voucher for the revised amount due Rosco Corporation.)

Jan. 15. Summary of cash sales to date, $19,200.

Jan. 16. Vouchers to state treasurer for $94, and to Director of Internal Revenue for $220 in payment of quarterly state and annual Federal unemployment taxes accrued as of December 31. Payment is made.

Jan. 20. Purchased public liability insurance for one year from Greene Agency and received invoice for premium of $140.

Jan. 22. Paid invoices for merchandise purchased on January 8 from Beagle Company and Rosco Corporation. Discount has been missed on the Beagle Company purchase.

Jan. 25. The following invoices were received:
KWAX-TV, spot advertising, $480.
Public Utility Co., services for January, $120. (Charge 60% to administrative and 40% to selling expenses.)
Burns Realty, building rental for January, $600. (Charge 90% to selling expense and 10% to administrative expense.)

Jan. 26. Sold marketable securities costing $3,200 for $3,500, net of brokerage fees and other sales costs.

Jan. 28. Received invoice from Reed Company for merchandise, $1,300, terms 2/10, n/30, plus freight charge of $65, total $1,365. (Cash discount is not allowed on the freight.)

Jan. 31. Prepare voucher for the monthly payroll: sales salaries, $8,000; administrative salaries, $4,000. Income taxes withheld were $972, and employees' share of F.I.C.A. taxes totaled $360. The entire amount of salaries was subject to employer's F.I.C.A. and unemployment taxes. Payroll taxes may be allocated between selling and administrative expense in proportion to salaries. (Record the accrual of the employer's share of payroll taxes in the general journal. Record the payroll directly in the voucher register.)

Jan. 31. Drew check to Payroll Account in the First National Bank for the total amount due employees for the month.

Jan. 31. Summary of cash sales to date, $23,800.

Instructions

a. Record the January transactions in the four journals. Use consecutive voucher numbers beginning with A-1, A-2, etc., and successive check numbers beginning with No. 1.

b. Enter the December 31 balances in general ledger T accounts, and post all journal information for January to the accounts. Expense detail is not an element of this problem; all expenses may be charged to the two control accounts, selling expense and administrative expense.

c. Prepare a general ledger trial balance as of January 31.

d. Summarize the unpaid vouchers at January 31 to show that they agree in total with the balance in the Vouchers Payable account in the general ledger.

23B-4. Zeebax Company employs a variation of a standard voucher system. As bills and invoices come into the company, they are attached to a voucher form, along with supporting documents, and approved for payment by a responsible person. When a voucher has been approved, it is assigned a number and filed according to the date that payment is to be made. Each morning a clerk withdraws the vouchers to be paid on that day, makes out the checks, and enters the transactions in a single journal, which serves the function of both the voucher register and the check register.

Instructions

a. Prepare a voucher payment journal with columns as shown below.

Date	Creditor	Voucher no.	Check no.	Cash	Purchases	Trans-portation-in	Accrued payroll	Other accounts	
								Debit	Credit

Record the payment of the following approved vouchers.

Nov. 12. Purchase of merchandise from R Company in the amount of $3,200, terms 2/10, n/30, is approved for payment within discount period; voucher No. 125; check No. K23.

Nov. 21. Paid one month's rent on the building in advance, $450; voucher No. 129; check No. K30 to Y. Waite.

Nov. 27. Paid accrued payroll for week ending November 27; check drawn to payroll bank account in amount of $4,600; voucher No. 141; check No. K37.

b. At the end of each month the vouchers in the unpaid voucher file are summarized and a journal entry is made to record the outstanding liabilities. Prepare a general journal entry to record the following vouchers which were outstanding at the end of November.

No. 146   Consolidated Trucking, freight on incoming merchandise, $370

No. 148   Que Company, merchandise, terms net 30 days, $2,350

No. 150   Pacific Telephone Co., bill for November, $38

c. The three vouchers described in (*b*) are paid on December 6. Illustrate the procedure you would recommend that the company use, by recording the payment of these vouchers (check Nos. L5, L6, and L7) in the voucher payment journal. Draw double lines under the transactions recorded for November to separate them from the December entries.

d. Can you see any advantages or disadvantages to this system in comparison with a standard voucher system? Explain.

24

Control and decision making. Departmental operations

The need for departmental information

When a number of essentially different activities are carried on within a single business entity, organization along departmental lines is a natural development. A manager is usually put in charge of each segment of business operations, and personnel and resources are assigned to enable him to carry out his responsibility. In addition, he may draw upon the general resources and staff talent of the firm for such services as accounting, financing, legal advice, advertising and promotional backing, transportation, and storage.

This sort of organizational subdivision creates a need for information about the operating results of each department so that general management can determine the relative profitability of the various departments and the manner in which departmental personnel are performing their assignments. Departmental information also provides a basis for intelligent planning and for evaluating the effect of new ideas and procedures.

To serve these managerial functions, a procedure for measuring revenues realized by and expenses attributable to each department is required. This is the process described by the term *departmental accounting.*

The managerial viewpoint

The details of departmental revenues and expenses are not usually made available to the public, on the grounds that such information would be of considerable aid to competitors. Departmental accounting information, therefore, is designed to serve the needs of internal management, and we might ask, what use is made of such information?

1. **As a basis for allocating resources and effort.** Management wants

to know how various departments are doing as a guide in allocating the resources and talent of the firm as a whole to those areas that have the greatest profit potential. If Department A is producing larger profits than Department B, this may indicate that greater effort should be made to expand and develop the activities in the more profitable department.

2. **As a basis for taking remedial action.** A well-designed accounting system will throw a spotlight on troubled areas. A manager who is not doing a good job should be replaced; costs that are out of line should be controlled; an unsuccessful department should be revamped or perhaps dropped altogether. Pointing up the areas that need managerial attention is an important function of accounting.

3. **As a basis for pricing decisions.** The idea that prices are determined by finding costs and adding a required margin of profit contains a grain of truth too often magnified to balloon proportions. For the average firm, prices are set by the market, and management's ability to exercise control over prices is severely limited by the actions of competitors and firms selling substitute products. It is a truism, however, that over the long run a firm must either set its asking prices high enough to cover all costs of operation plus a reasonable return on its investment or face extinction. If we are careful not to attribute too much to the statement, therefore, it may be said that departmental cost information is a factor in pricing decisions.

This is not a complete list of the uses that might be made of departmental accounting information. It serves to indicate, however, that we must keep the decision-making objective in mind in allocating revenues and costs among departments.

Collecting departmental data

Two basic approaches may be used in developing departmental information:

1. *Establish separate departmental accounts for each item of revenue and expense and identify each charge or credit with the department involved.* This method is easily adapted for accounts such as sales, purchases, and inventories, which can be readily identified with particular departments. For example, a business having six departments would use six sales accounts, six purchase accounts, and six inventory accounts, one for each department. If the number of departments is very large it may be advisable to use a control account in the general ledger and to put departmental accounts in a subsidiary ledger.

2. *Maintain only one general ledger account for a particular item of revenue or expense, and distribute the total amount among the various departments at the end of the accounting period.* When this procedure is used, distribution by departments is made on a work sheet rather than in the ledger accounts. For example, building rental might be charged to a single

expense account and the total allocated among departments only for statement purposes.

Some companies carry departmentalization of operating results only as far as gross profit on sales by departments; others extend the process to include certain operating expenses but not others; a few go so far as to apportion all expenses among departments and compute net income on a departmental basis.

In the remainder of this chapter we shall consider some of the problems and issues that arise in developing and using departmental information. As a basis for discussion and to illustrate procedures, we shall use a set of facts relating to a hypothetical business, the Moss Corporation. We shall assume that the Moss Corporation has only two operating departments, designated A and B. This will enable us to focus on the issues without bogging down in a mass of detail. The principles discussed, however, are applicable to more complex situations and to cases involving any number of departments.

Departmental gross profit on sales

In a mercantile business a figure of extreme interest to management is the total gross margin realized over and above the cost of merchandise sold in any department. Gross profit on sales is a function of two variables: the volume of goods sold and the margin of gross profit earned on each dollar of sales. The same total dollar gross profit may be realized from a large volume of sales made at a low margin, or from a smaller volume of sales made at a higher margin of gross profit.

Within any given business, department managers are constantly making decisions that affect the gross profit margin, in the hope of maintaining a sales volume that will maximize the total dollar gross profit realized by their department. This is not to say that operating expenses may be ignored; obviously the ultimate objective is net, not gross profits. Departmental gross profit is significant because it is an element of net income subject to considerable managerial control, and because it can be measured with a relatively high degree of accuracy.

Departmental net revenues. The first step in arriving at departmental gross profit is to departmentalize revenues. To illustrate, assume the Moss Corporation maintains in its general ledger separate departmental sales and contrasales accounts as follows:

Sales: Department A	Sales: Department B
Sales Returns: Department A	Sales Returns: Department B
Sales Discounts: Department A	Sales Discounts: Department B

As a convenient means of accumulating departmental data, special columns may be added to the various journals. For example, the Moss Corporation's sales journal and cash receipts journal for a typical month might appear as follows:

Sales Journal

Date	Invoice no.	Account debited	PR	Accounts receivable, dr	Cash, dr	Sales Dept. A, cr	Sales Dept. B, cr
19__							
Aug. 1	100	Abar Co.	√	700		700	
		Cash Sales			1,180	470	710
2	101	Jones & Elb	√	1,500			1,500
	102	Craig Co.	√	800		600	200
		Cash Sales			1,410	920	490
31		Totals		50,200	4,900	32,600	22,500
				(5)	(√)	(200)	(300)

Cash Receipts Journal

Date	Account credited	PR	General, cr	Cash sales, cr	Accounts receivable, cr	Sales disc. Dept. A, dr	Sales disc. Dept. B, dr	Cash, dr
19__								
Aug. 1	Cash Sales			1,180				1,180
	High Co.	√			1,000	15	5	980
2	Cash Sales			1,410				1,410
	Low Co.	√			4,000	60	20	3,920
3	Interest Income	701	600					600
31	Totals		8,600	4,900	34,800	520	270	47,510
			(√)	(5)	(√)	(201)	(301)	(1)

The amount of credit sales applicable to each department may be computed from the original sales invoice. If cash registers are used, the division of cash sales by departments may be made at the time each sale is rung up; daily totals by departments will thus be available on the cash register tapes.

In the illustrative journals, cash sales have been recorded in both the sales and cash receipts journals. This procedure makes it possible to omit departmental sales columns in the cash receipts journal, since the distribution of sales by departments is made in the sales journal. The totals of the Cash debit column in the sales journal ($4,900) and the Cash Sales credit column in the cash receipts journal ($4,900) exactly offset and need not be posted. The net effect is that all cash receipts are posted in total from the cash receipts journal, and all credits to departmental sales accounts are posted in total from the sales journal.

If there are a large number of departments in a business, using a separate journal column for each departmental account would result in journals of almost unmanageable size. In such cases it is more efficient to analyze duplicate copies of sales invoices by departments, posting the totals directly to the departmental accounts in the ledger. The trend in modern accounting systems is to avoid journals with numerous columns by using various machine methods of sorting, classifying, and summarizing original data prior to recording in journals.

Regardless of the system used, the basic procedures are: (1) See that data by departments are entered on original invoices, credit memorandums, cash register tapes, etc.; (2) sort and accumulate these individual transaction figures to arrive at subtotals for each departmental account; (3) enter this information in ledger accounts. The objective of any departmental accounting system is to do this accurately and with a minimum expenditure of time and effort.

Since separate departmental accounts for sales, sales returns, and sales discounts were used by the Moss Corporation, a report of departmental net sales may be prepared directly from the balances in these **NET SALES** accounts. The results for the current year are summarized below (paren- **BY DEPART-** theses indicate deductions). **MENTS**

	Total	Department A	Department B

MOSS CORPORATION
Departmental Net Sales
Current Year

	Total	Department A	Department B
Sales	$500,000	$320,000	$180,000
Less: sales returns	(5,000)	(2,300)	(2,700)
Sales discounts	(8,000)	(6,000)	(2,000)
Net Sales	$487,000	$311,700	$175,300

Distributing sales and sales returns by departments at the time the transactions are recorded usually causes little difficulty. However it is not always convenient to determine the amount of cash discount applicable to each department at the time the customer pays his account if payment covers sales from more than one department. For example, suppose that a customer takes a 2% cash discount on a billing of $4,000. The person who records this entry must refer back to the invoices to discover that this payment covers sales of $3,000 from Department A and $1,000 from Department B, and that therefore the total cash discount of $80 must be split $60 to Department A and $20 to Department B. The accountant may feel that the accuracy attained through this analysis is not worth the time required to make it. The alternative is to record sales discounts in a single account and distribute the amount among departments on some reasonable basis, such as departmental sales. This should produce reasonably accurate results unless the per cent discount offered by the various departments differs or the customers of one department are less inclined to take the discounts than customers of another department.

A comparison of the Moss Corporation's actual sales discounts by departments and the allocation that would have been made if sales discounts had been distributed on the basis of departmental sales appears in the following schedule:

	Sales	Per cent of total	Allocation of sales discounts	Actual sales discounts
Department A	$320,000	64	$5,120	$6,000
Department B	180,000	36	2,880	2,000
Total	$500,000	100	$8,000	$8,000

Note that Department A's sales were 64% and Department B's 36% of total sales. The total sales discount of $8,000 is therefore allocated in the same proportion, that is, 64% to Department A and 36% to Department B. The discrepancy between allocated sales discounts and actual departmental division presumably arises because Department A customers took a greater proportion of the discounts available to them.

Departmental cost of sales. We shall assume that the Moss Corporation keeps separate departmental accounts for each element of cost of sales as follows:

Inventory: Department A   Inventory: Department B
Purchases: Department A   Purchases: Department B
Purchase Returns: Department A   Purchase Returns: Department B
Purchase Discounts: Department A   Purchase Discounts: Department B
Freight-in: Department A   Freight-in: Department B

Separate columns for departmental purchases, purchase returns, and freight-in are used in the voucher register to accumulate the charges in these accounts. Similarly, separate columns for departmental purchase discounts appear in the cash disbursements journal. The department for which purchases are made is shown on the purchase order, and the amount applicable to each department is computed at the time invoices are received. Inventories are taken separately in each department. When purchases for both departments are combined on one order and shipment, an analysis of transportation charges and purchase discounts is made in order to charge or credit the appropriate department.

A schedule summarizing the cost of goods sold by departments for the current year would appear as follows:

	Total	Department A	Department B
MOSS CORPORATION *Departmental Cost of Goods Sold* *Current Year*			
Beginning inventory	$ 70,000	$ 28,000	$ 42,000
Purchases	360,000	205,200	154,800
Purchase returns	(10,000)	(5,700)	(4,300)
Purchase discounts	(6,100)	(3,000)	(3,100)
Freight-in	17,000	4,800	12,200
Total merchandise available	$430,900	$229,300	$201,600
Less: ending inventory	90,000	36,000	54,000
Cost of goods sold	$340,900	$193,300	$147,600

Inventories, purchases, and purchase returns are readily identified by department. The problems involved in dividing purchase discounts at the time payment is made are similar to those for sales discounts. Recording purchases net of the discount is the simplest solution. If this is not done and if direct analysis is not feasible, some basis of allocation, such as departmental purchases, would be a reasonable solution. Note in the Moss Corporation statement, however, that the $3,100 purchase discounts taken by Department B were larger in relation to purchases than discounts taken by Department A. This might occur because more of Department B's suppliers offered cash discounts.

Freight-in poses a similar problem. Transportation charges are an element of the cost of merchandise purchased and must therefore be added to departmental purchases to determine cost of goods sold. Strict accuracy requires that departmental charges be segregated at the time freight bills are received. If a separation of transportation charges at the time of billing is impractical, again some method of allocation is necessary. Since transportation charges vary with the manner of shipment, distance shipped, and the value, bulk, and weight of the goods, it is likely that a simple basis of allocation, such as dollar purchases in each department, will produce imperfect results. It may be possible to study the relationship between freight charges and invoice prices by departments over a period of time to arrive at a basis of allocation that can be used if occasional tests are made to see that relationships have not changed.

Working papers: gross profit by departments. An expanded form of working papers, shown on page 660, is used when gross profits are determined on a departmental basis. In the illustration only selected accounts have been included; most balance sheet accounts and the details of operating expenses were deliberately omitted. Note that the departmental net sales and cost of sales accounts are extended into special departmental columns in the income statement section of the working papers; the balancing figure in these columns is thus departmental gross profit.

Two "nondepartmental" columns in the income statement section are used to accumulate both the sum of the departmental gross profits and items of miscellaneous revenue and operating expenses that are not departmentalized. When these amounts are combined, the difference between the debit and credit totals in the nondepartmental columns is the net income for the business as a whole. A provision of $7,500 for income taxes has been made, so that only the net income after taxes appears on the illustrative working papers.

Income statement: gross profit by departments. An income statement for the Moss Corporation, departmentalized only through the gross profit figures, is illustrated on page 662. If the number of departments were larger, a horizontal expansion of the income statement in this fashion might become unwieldy, in which case separate statements of gross profit on sales for each department might be prepared and attached to the income statement for the business as a whole.

It is evident that Department A contributes a greater proportion of Moss Corporation's gross profit than Department B. By studying the reasons for this difference, management may be led to make changes in buying policies, selling prices, or the personnel of Department B in an effort to improve its performance. Whether Department A contributes more than B to the net profit of the business, however, depends on the amount of operating expenses attributable to each department.

Apportioning expenses to departments

An analysis of expenses by departments provides information about the cost of departmental operations and makes it possible to prepare an income statement showing departmental *net,* as well as gross, income. The mechanics of expense apportionment are similar to those used in departmentalizing revenues and cost of goods sold. The theoretical issues are more troublesome, however, because the relation between various expenses and the activities of a given department is not always clear.

To understand the nature of these difficulties, it is helpful to know something about the problem of expense classification, the tests used in relating expenses to departmental activities, and the problem of joint costs—all of which are discussed briefly in the following sections:

Expense classification. There are two basic approaches to the classification of expenses. Under an *object of expenditure* classification, expenses are grouped according to the nature of the cost incurred, such as salaries, advertising, taxes, depreciation, etc. This classification is convenient for record-keeping purposes, but it may not serve well as a basis for allocating expenses among departments. Under a *functional* classifi-

MOSS CORPORATION
Working Papers
Current Year

Account titles	Adjusted trial balance		Department A	
	Dr	Cr	Dr	Cr
Beginning inventory:				
Dept. A	28,000		28,000	
Dept. B	42,000			
~~	~~~~~~	~~~~~~	~~~~~~	~~~~~~
Sales:				
Dept. A		320,000		320,000
Dept. B		180,000		
Sales returns:				
Dept. A	2,300		2,300	
Dept. B	2,700			
Sales discounts:				
Dept. A	6,000		6,000	
Dept. B	2,000			
Purchases:				
Dept. A	205,200		205,200	
Dept. B	154,800			
Purchase returns:				
Dept. A		5,700		5,700
Dept. B		4,300		
Purchase discounts:				
Dept. A		3,000		3,000
Dept. B		3,100		
Freight-in:				
Dept. A	4,800		4,800	
Dept. B	12,200			
Interest income		4,400		
Operating expenses (details omitted)	125,500			
Ending inventory:				
Dept. A				36,000
Dept. B				
	997,800	997,800	246,300	364,700
Gross profit on sales			118,400	
			364,700	364,700
Estimated income taxes				
Net income				

* Various asset, liability, and owners' equity accounts are not shown but are included in totals.

Income statement				Balance sheet	
Department B		Nondepartmental			
Dr	Cr	Dr	Cr	Dr	Cr
42,000					
	180,000				
2,700					
2,000					
154,800					
	4,300				
	3,100				
12,200					
			4,400		
		125,500			
				36,000	
	54,000			54,000	
213,700	241,400				
27,700			146,100		
241,400	241,400	125,500	150,500	486,700	461,700
		7,500			7,500
		17,500			17,500
		150,500	150,500	486,700	486,700

MOSS CORPORATION
Income Statement, Current Year

	Total	Department A	Department B
Sales revenues:			
Sales	$500,000	$320,000	$180,000
Less: Sales returns and allowances ...... $ 5,000		$ 2,300	$ 2,700
Sales discounts 8,000	13,000	6,000 8,300	2,000 4,700
Net sales	$487,000	$311,700	$175,300
Cost of goods sold:			
Beginning inventory	$ 70,000	$ 28,000	$ 42,000
Purchases $360,000		$205,200	$154,800
Freight-in 17,000		4,800	12,200
Purchases returns and allowances ...... (10,000)		(5,700)	(4,300)
Purchase discounts .... (6,100)	360,900	(3,000) 201,300	(3,100) 159,600
Merchandise available	$430,900	$229,300	$201,600
Less: ending inventory	90,000	36,000	54,000
Cost of goods sold	$340,900	$193,300	$147,600
Gross profit on sales	$146,100	$118,400	$ 27,700
Operating expenses (details omitted)	125,500		
Operating income	$ 20,600		
Interest earned	4,400		
Net income before income taxes	$ 25,000		
Provision for income taxes	7,500		
Net income	$ 17,500		

cation system, expenses are identified with various functions performed in carrying out the objectives of a business. These two approaches are not mutually exclusive; they are often used in various combinations.

For example, in a very simple object of expenditure classification system, all supplies used would be charged to a single expense account. A slight improvement would be to identify the selling function and the administrative function, and to classify office supplies as an administrative expense and sales supplies as a selling expense. A more elaborate functional classification system might identify the cost of supplies used in performing such functions as advertising, delivery, building maintenance, etc.

A functional classification system is useful because it relates expenses to particular business functions or activities, and the basis used in apportioning expenses by departments is usually some measure of the amount of services used by a given department. Combining all the costs of performing a function makes it easier to find a common basis for allocation and reduces the number of computations required. For example, if delivery expenses of all kinds are accumulated in one total, a single distribution by departments may be made on the basis of a measure (number of delivery orders, packages delivered, miles driven) of the amount of delivery services used by each department.

EXPENSES CLASSIFIED BY FUNCTION What are the functional divisions of the typical nonmanufacturing business? A number of alternative functional groupings are possible, but for illustrative purposes let us identify six broad business functions and classify the Moss Corporation's operating expenses as follows:

MOSS CORPORATION
Functional Classification of Expenses
Current Year

Sales force expenses: all compensation and payroll-related costs of persons engaged in direct selling	$ 27,000
Advertising and promotion: all expenses incurred to advertise and promote the sale of products	18,000
Building expense: all costs relating to the occupancy of the building in which business is conducted	16,000
Buying expense: compensation of departmental buyers, travel expense, handling and pricing of merchandise	26,800
Delivery expense: expenses of delivery truck, compensation of driver, and all transportation charges on outbound goods	12,000
Administrative expenses: compensation of administrative, office, and clerical employees, and other general expenses such as insurance, credit and collection, accounting	25,700
Total operating expenses	*$125,500*

Within each of these major classifications, a business might maintain a number of expense accounts on an *object of expenditure* basis. For example, the total Sales Force Expense might be subdivided:

Sales force expenses:

Salesmen's salaries	Secretarial help: salesmen
Salesmen's commissions	Payroll taxes: sales force
Salesmen's travel expenses	Sales training expense

A complete enumeration of expense accounts in all six functional categories would involve a considerable amount of detail. Even a medium-sized company may have as many as 100 individual expense accounts. For purposes of illustration, therefore, we shall assume that the major functional accounts are control accounts, supported by a number of individual subsidiary expense accounts, the details of which need not concern us in our present discussion.

Direct versus indirect expenses. Within each of the six functional categories adopted for illustrative purposes there will be some expenses that can be clearly identified with a particular department of the business, and other expenses whose relationship to individual departments is difficult to trace. *Direct expenses* are those which may be identified by department, in the sense that if the department did not exist, the portion of the expense assignable to it would not be incurred. *Indirect expenses* are incurred for the benefit of the business as a whole; they cannot be identified readily with the activities of a given department. These would, for the most part, continue even though a particular department were discontinued.

Some direct expenses may be charged directly to separate departmental expense accounts at the time they are incurred. For example, the salaries of sales personnel assigned to Department A might be charged to a special account, Sales Salaries: Department A; those for Department B would be treated similarly. This procedure is similar to that illustrated in the case of departmental sales, purchases, inventories, etc.

Other expenses, even though they are direct in nature, may be more conveniently charged to a single account and divided among the departments at the end of the accounting period by allocation. For example, insurance on inventories is a direct expense, since the cost of the insurance on the inventories in any department would disappear if the department did not exist. However, the most convenient procedure may be to charge the expired premiums to a single insurance expense account within the administrative expense classification. Then at the end of each period the amount of insurance expense applicable to each department may be determined on the basis of the average inventory in each.

Indirect expenses, by their very nature, can be assigned to departments only by a process of allocation. For example, the salary of the president of the company is an expense not directly related to the activities of any particular department. If it is to be apportioned among the departments, some method of allocation is necessary.

Responsibility versus benefit tests. For the most part expense allocations rest on two criteria: benefit and responsibility. Under the *benefit test* expenses are assigned on the basis of the relative benefits that accrue to the various departments as the result of an expenditure for services. Under the *responsibility test* expenses are assigned to the department primarily responsible for incurring the expense. In some cases responsibility and benefit coincide; in others they are at variance. For example, a given department is both responsible for and benefits from the services of sales personnel assigned to it. On the other hand, the responsibility for incurring advertising expense might be traced to one department, but some part of the benefits from such advertising may accrue to other departments. Suppose, for example, that only the products of one department were advertised. Customers attracted by these advertisements would no doubt visit other departments and make purchases, thus bestowing on these departments the benefits of advertising for which only one department was responsible.

It is seldom possible to follow one or the other test consistently in allocating costs among departments. In general, however, the responsibility test can be more objectively applied and thus is likely to give more meaningful results; benefits are difficult to trace.

Planned effort versus results. One purpose of allocating expenses among departments is to observe the effect of past plans and decisions. This involves a study of the relationship between results obtained (sales) and efforts incurred (expenses). A primary objective in departmentalizing expenses, therefore, is to measure the cost of *planned effort* independently of the results obtained from such efforts.

Suppose, for example, that a buyer makes purchases for two departments, A and B. It is agreed that he shall increase the number of buying trips he makes during the year in order to keep up with rapid changes in the style of products sold in Department A and to improve the performance of that department. Management would have a keen interest in the next departmental income statement to see whether this decision produced the desired results. If travel expenses are allocated on the basis of sales in each department (results) the information on a departmental income statement may be misleading. Suppose, for example, that sales in Department A did *not* increase. The increased travel expenses would be divided between both departments, and Department A's net income would not fully show that results were not commensurate with increased costs. If the cost of the extra buying trips were charged on the basis of planned buying effort, however, the entire increase in travel expenses would be charged against Department A, and departmental net income would fully reflect the effect of the decision to spend more on travel. This illustrates the importance of making expense allocations on the basis of planned effort rather than of results obtained.

Joint versus common costs. One of the problems that plagues the accountant in his attempt to allocate expenses is the existence of *joint costs.* Simply stated, a joint cost is the single cost inevitably incurred in obtaining two or more essentially different services or products. It is to be distinguished from a *common cost,* which is the single cost of obtaining two or more essentially similar services or products. In both cases a lump-sum cost is involved; the distinguishing characteristic is whether the units of service or product are similar or different in nature.

To illustrate, assume that an expense of $10,000 has been incurred in renting a building that is two stories high and has a total floor space of 20,000 square feet. If the building is to be used as a warehouse, the rental payment is a common cost since there is no material difference between a square foot of floor space in the middle of the first floor and a similar amount of space in the corner of the second floor. For warehousing purposes one square foot of space is equivalent to another. If Department A's merchandise is stored on the first floor and Department B's on the second floor, it would seem reasonable to allocate the rental cost one-half to each, or at a rate of 50 cents per square foot occupied. Dividing a common cost by the number of similar units produces a meaningful average cost per unit.

Now suppose that the same building is to be used, not as a warehouse but as a retail department store. Units of space in different locations throughout the building are now *essentially different* in nature, because the buying habits of customers are influenced by the location of the merchandise offered for sale. Space near the entrance on the first floor is more valuable than space in the far corner of the second floor. The building rental of $10,000 has become a joint cost; since each square foot of space is different, allocation between departments on the basis of the amount of space occupied is no longer reasonable. This would become apparent if we were to sublease the building to two different businesses with business A to occupy the first floor and business B the second floor. We would expect business A to pay a higher rental than business B in recognition of the difference in the relative value of the space.

If joint costs cannot be reasonably allocated on the basis of units of service or product, since various units are significantly different, how is the problem to be solved? Unfortunately there *is* no very satisfactory solution. The usual approach is to allocate the joint cost on the basis of the estimated relative value of the units of service or product. For example, if it were estimated that, for retail purposes, the 10,000 square feet of floor space on the first floor were twice as valuable as the 10,000 square feet on the second floor, two-thirds of the rental cost should be allocated to the department occupying the first floor and one-third to the department on the second floor. This is a better indication of relative cost than allocation on a square-footage basis, but it is a somewhat arbitrary determination at best.

Unfortunately, joint costs occur frequently in businesses of all types. In a later chapter we shall see that they create similar problems in dealing with manufacturing costs. For the present, remember two fundamentals: the allocation of joint costs on the basis of relative values is preferable to allocation on the basis of unlike physical units, and any allocation should be viewed as a rough estimate.

Illustration of expense allocation

Let us consider now the reasoning that might be employed in allocating the operating expenses of the Moss Corporation between Departments A and B.

A first step is to determine which expenses are direct and which are indirect. A summary of this analysis appears in Schedule A on page 668. Note that sales force expenses of $27,000 were all direct expenses, building expenses were all indirect, and in the other expense categories some expenses were direct and some indirect.

The next step is to allocate the indirect expenses in each of the six functional classifications between Departments A and B on the basis of some reasonable measure of responsibility or benefit. A summary of the result of this allocation appears in Schedule B.

Finally, a summary of the total operating expenses, both direct and indirect, and their allocation by departments appears in Schedule C.

The following comments explain how the allocation was made:

1. **Sales force expenses.** Moss Corporation's sales personnel work exclusively in one or the other of the departments. This is an example of a direct expense clearly identified with the departments involved, and thus charged to departments on the basis of the personnel involved. If a sales manager, or one or more of the salesmen, had divided his time between the two departments, we would face the problem of determining the amount of time, and perhaps the relative value of the time spent in each, to arrive at a satisfactory basis for dividing this expense.

2. **Advertising and promotion.** The Moss Corporation advertises primarily through newspapers with occasional spot advertisements on radio and television. The $8,000 of direct expenses represents the cost of newspaper lineage and time purchased to advertise specific products identified with each department. Indirect expenses of $10,000 include the cost of administering the advertising program, plus advertising applicable to the business as a whole. Indirect expenses were allocated in proportion to the direct departmental advertising costs, as follows:

	Direct expense	Per cent	Indirect expense allocation
Department A	$5,000	62.5	$ 6,250
Department B	3,000	37.5	3,750
Total	$8,000	100.0	$10,000

3. **Building expense.** The Moss Corporation operates in a two-story

MOSS CORPORATION
Operating Expense Analysis, by Departments
Current Year

Schedule A: Division of Expenses into Direct and Indirect

Operating expense	Total expense	Direct expense Department A	Direct expense Department B	Indirect expense
Sales force expenses	$ 27,000	$16,900	$10,100	
Advertising and promotion	18,000	5,000	3,000	$10,000
Building expenses	16,000			16,000
Buying expenses	26,800	14,000	7,800	5,000
Delivery expenses	12,000		2,000	10,000
Administrative expenses	25,700	3,100	2,600	20,000
Totals	$125,500	$39,000	$25,500	$61,000

Schedule B: Allocation of Indirect Expenses

	Indirect expenses	Basis of allocation	Department A	Department B
Sales force expenses				
Advertising and promotion	$10,000	Direct advertising	$ 6,250	$ 3,750
Building expenses	16,000	Value of space	9,600	6,400
Buying expenses	5,000	Purchases	2,750	2,250
Delivery expenses	10,000	Deliveries made	3,000	7,000
Administrative expenses	20,000	Sales	12,800	7,200
Totals	$61,000		$34,400	$26,600

Schedule C: Summary of Expense Allocation

	Total expense	Department A Total	Department A Direct	Department A Indirect	Department B Total	Department B Direct	Department B Indirect
Sales force expenses	$ 27,000	$16,900	$16,900		$10,100	$10,100	
Advertising and promotion	18,000	11,250	5,000	$ 6,250	6,750	3,000	$ 3,750
Building expenses	16,000	9,600		9,600	6,400		6,400
Buying expenses	26,800	16,750	14,000	2,750	10,050	7,800	2,250
Delivery expenses	12,000	3,000		3,000	9,000	2,000	7,000
Administrative expenses	25,700	15,900	3,100	12,800	9,800	2,600	7,200
Totals	$125,500	$73,400	$39,000	$34,400	$52,100	$25,500	$26,600

building. Department A and the general offices are on the first floor; Department B and warehouse space are on the second. Because this is a merchandising operation, the total cost of building occupancy is a joint cost. Therefore, although the total space occupied by the two departments is approximately equal, an estimate of the relative value of the space assigned to each department indicates that Department A should be charged with 60% and Department B with 40% of the building expenses.

The cost of office and warehouse space might have been determined separately and allocated between the two departments on some separate basis. Because space value can only be estimated, however, this additional refinement would add nothing to the significance of the figures.

An arbitrary assignment, based on judgment, is not as soul-satisfying as a precise statistical computation carried out to the last penny. The wise accountant, however, honors a rule of long standing in the engineering profession: the accuracy of an answer is no better than the least accurate figure entering into the computation; guesses are not improved by carrying them out to three places beyond the decimal point.

4. **Buying expenses.** The compensation of departmental buyers, their travel expenses, and certain merchandise handling costs, a total of $21,800, were considered direct expenses and assigned to the two departments on the basis of the personnel involved and expense accounts submitted by them. The remaining $5,000 of indirect buying expenses was allocated on the basis of departmental purchases:

	Purchases	Per cent	Indirect buying expense
Department A	$199,500	53	$2,750
Department B	150,500	47	2,250
Total	$350,000	100	$5,000

The possible defects of purchases as an allocation basis are obvious; there is no necessary reason why the cost of buying or handling an item of large dollar value is significantly greater than for a less costly item.

5. **Delivery expenses.** Department B shipped certain merchandise by common carrier at a cost of $2,000, a direct expense of this department. The $10,000 balance of the cost of maintaining a delivery service was common to both departments. A study covering several months of typical operation showed that on the average 70% of all delivery requests originated in Department B; therefore, 30% ($3,000) of the indirect delivery expense was charged to Department A, and 70% ($7,000) to Department B.

6. **Administrative expenses.** Two direct expenses were included in the administrative expense category; the remainder were indirect:

	Total	*Department A*	*Department B*
Direct administrative expenses:			
Bad debts	$ 3,700	$ 2,300	$1,400
Insurance on inventories	2,000	800	1,200
Total direct expenses	$ 5,700	$ 3,100	$2,600
Indirect administrative expenses	20,000	12,800	7,200
Total administrative expenses	$25,700	$15,900	$9,800

The division of the $3,700 provision for bad debts was made on the basis of an analysis of accounts charged off during the period. If this had not been feasible, allocation on the basis of credit sales in each department would have been reasonable.

Insurance on inventories of $2,000 was charged to the departments on the basis of the average inventory in each department:

	Total	*Department A*	*Department B*
Beginning inventory	$ 70,000	$28,000	$42,000
Ending inventory	90,000	36,000	54,000
Total	$160,000	$64,000	$96,000
Average (divide by 2)	$ 80,000	$32,000	$48,000
Per cent	100%	40%	60%
Allocation of insurance cost	$ 2,000	$ 800	$ 1,200

Indirect administrative expenses of $20,000 were allocated on the basis of sales, for want of a more reasonable basis:

	Sales	*Per cent*	*Indirect administrative expenses*
Department A	$311,700	64	$12,800
Department B	175,300	36	7,200
Total	$487,000	100	$20,000

Departmental net income statement

On the basis of departmental data developed thus far, we can now prepare a statement showing the net income of each department.

MOSS CORPORATION
Departmental Income Statement
Current Year

	Total	Department A	Department B
Net sales	$487,000	$311,700	$175,300
Cost of goods sold	340,900	193,300	147,600
Gross profit on sales	$146,100	$118,400	$ 27,700
Operating expenses:			
Sales force expenses	$ 27,000	$ 16,900	$ 10,100
Advertising and promotion	18,000	11,250	6,750
Building expense	16,000	9,600	6,400
Buying expenses	26,800	16,750	10,050
Delivery expenses	12,000	3,000	9,000
Administrative expenses	25,700	15,900	9,800
Total operating expenses	$125,500	$ 73,400	$ 52,100
Net operating income (or loss)	$ 20,000	$ 15,000	$(24,400)
Interest earned	4,400		4,400
Net income (or loss) before income taxes ..	$ 25,000	$ 45,000	$(20,000)
Provision for income taxes (or credit)	7,500	13,500	(6,000)
Net income (or loss)	$ 17,500	$ 31,500	$(14,000)

A comment on two items is in order. Interest earned arises in connection with certain notes receivable taken in payment of sales in Department B; therefore the entire amount is allocable to that department. Income taxes were computed at an assumed rate of 30%. To reflect clearly the relationship between income taxes and operating results, the provision for income taxes charged to Department A is a full 30% of the income of that department, and this is offset by a credit equal to 30% of the loss reported in Department B.

When is a department unprofitable? The first reaction of management, confronted with the departmental income statement of the Moss Corporation, might be that the company would be better off if Department B were dropped. The statement appears to indicate that net income would have been $31,500 rather than $17,500 were it not for the existence of Department B. Is this true?

If we could, with a wave of the hand, blot Department B out of existence, the income statement of the Moss Corporation for the current year would probably appear as follows:

MOSS CORPORATION
Income Statement Reflecting Discontinuance of Department B
Current Year

Net Sales		$311,700
Cost of goods sold		193,300
Gross profit on sales		$118,400
Operating expenses:		
Direct expenses of Department A	$39,000	
Indirect expenses (total)	61,000	100,000
Net income before income taxes		$ 18,400
Provision for income taxes (30%)		5,520
Net income		$ 12,880

Instead of improving the company's showing, the result is a *decrease* in income of $4,620 ($17,500 − $12,880). Apparently the information in the departmental income statement is misleading in this respect.

The answer to this paradox is that the discontinuance of Department B would eliminate the entire gross profit on sales earned in that department but not all the expenses that were allocated to Department B.

An explanation of the estimated decline in net income of $4,620, shown above, might be put in statement form as shown on page 673.

It is apparent from this statement that reducing expenses $25,500 and eliminating $1,980 in income taxes are not sufficient to offset the decrease in income of $32,100 that would follow from the discontinuance of Department B.

If the effect on expenses shown on this statement is compared with the expenses allocated to Department B as shown on Schedule C on page 668, you will see that only direct expenses of $25,500 were assumed to be eliminated as a result of the discontinuance of this department. This is no coincidence, since direct expenses were defined as costs relating to the activities of a particular department that would be largely eliminated if the department did not exist. Thus compensation of sales and buying personnel, cost of advertising space, outbound transportation paid to carriers, bad debts, and insurance on inventories would presumably disappear along with Department B.

The $26,600 of expenses that would *not* be eliminated is the amount of indirect expenses assigned to Department B. The assumption that *indirect* costs would remain unchanged is reasonable for general purposes but, realistically, some reduction in indirect costs would probably occur if Department B were eliminated. The change in indirect costs that follows from departmental changes will depend to some extent on the alternatives that are being considered. For example, the indirect expense, Building Expense, would continue largely unchanged whether Department

MOSS CORPORATION
Estimated Effect of Discontinuing Department B
Current Year

	Depart- ment B share	Assuming discontinuance of department		
		Not eliminated	Eliminated	Effect on net income *
Effect on income:				
Gross profit on sales	$27,700		$27,700	
Interest earned	4,400		4,400	
Total	$32,100			$(32,100)
Effect on expenses:				
Sales force expenses	$10,100		$10,100	
Advertising expense	6,750	$ 3,750	3,000	
Building expense	6,400	6,400		
Buying expense	10,050	2,250	7,800	
Delivery expense	9,000	7,000	2,000	
Administrative expense	9,800	7,200	2,600	
Total	$52,100	$26,600		25,500
Effect on net income before income taxes				$ (6,600)
Reduction in income taxes (30% of $6,600)				1,980
Reduction in net income				$ (4,620)

* Parentheses indicate decrease.

B existed or not, since the company owns the entire building. However, if the company were to drop Department B and reduce the scale of its activities, it might rent the second floor space to outsiders and thus reduce occupancy cost. On the other hand, if the question were whether Department B should be reorganized or a new kind of operation substituted for it, building expenses and other indirect costs would probably not change by an amount large enough to influence the decision.

There is considerable wisdom in the phrase "different costs for different purposes." The allocation of costs for one purpose may not produce results that are significant for a different kind of decision; special cost studies are often necessary to answer particular questions.

Departmental contribution to overhead

We have seen that gross profits by departments can be determined with good assurance that the results are meaningful and useful. We have seen also that the division of direct expenses among departments is a fairly straightforward process. Sales revenues, cost of goods sold, and direct expenses are all operating elements that, in general, relate clearly to the existence of the department and its activities.

On the other hand, most indirect expenses are costs associated with the business as a whole, and in general they lie outside the control of department managers. Because of their indirect relationship to departmental activities, any basis of allocation used is somewhat arbitrary and the proper interpretation of the results is often in doubt.

Because of these factors, some accountants argue that the important benefits of departmental accounting can be gained by stopping short of a full allocation of all expenses by departments. They urge that each department be credited with revenues and charged with costs and expenses that, in the opinion of management, would disappear if the department did not exist. This approach leads to a departmental income statement showing the contribution of each department to the general overhead or indirect expenses of the business.

Such a statement, using figures previously developed for the Moss Corporation, is illustrated on page 675.

In contrast to the departmental net income statement on page 671, which shows that Department B suffered a net loss of $14,000, this statement shows that this department contributed $6,600 (before income taxes) to the general overhead of the business. This figure agrees with the estimated reduction in net income *before taxes* if Department B were discontinued, as shown on page 673.

The performance of department managers can be better judged by their contribution to general overhead than by the *net* income or loss per department, since to a large extent indirect expenses are outside the control of department managers. Furthermore, so long as a department is covering its direct costs it is probably contributing to the ultimate profitability of the business as a whole.

Working papers: expense allocation. The basic format of the working papers for a departmentalized business, illustrated on page 660, may still be used when all or a part of the operating expenses are apportioned among departments. The amount of each expense item is extended into the proper departmental columns in the same manner as the single operating expense figure in the illustration. The difference between the departmental debit and credit columns in the income statement section will be the net income per department, or the contribution to overhead per department, depending on the circumstances. If only direct expenses are departmentalized, indirect expenses will be extended directly into the nondepartmental column, the contribution to overhead by all departments will be carried into the nondepartmental column, and the work sheet completed in the usual manner. If all items of revenue and expense are departmentalized, the nondepartmental columns may be omitted.

MOSS CORPORATION
Departmental Income Statement: Contribution to Overhead Basis
Current Year

	Total	Department A	Department B
Net sales	$487,000	$311,700	$175,300
Cost of goods sold	340,900	193,300	147,600
Gross profit on sales	$146,100	$118,400	$ 27,700
Interest earned	4,400		4,400
Total gross profit and other income	$150,500	$118,400	$ 32,100
Direct departmental expenses:			
Sales force expenses	$ 27,000	$ 16,900	$ 10,100
Advertising and promotion	8,000	5,000	3,000
Buying expenses	21,800	14,000	7,800
Delivery expenses	2,000		2,000
Administrative expenses	5,700	3,100	2,600
Total direct expenses	$ 64,500	$ 39,000	$ 25,500
Contribution to indirect expenses	$ 86,000	$ 79,400	$ 6,600
Indirect expenses:			

Advertising & promotion	$10,000	
Building expenses	16,000	
Buying expenses	5,000	
Delivery expenses	10,000	
Administrative expenses	20,000	

Total indirect expenses	$ 61,000
Net income before income taxes	$ 25,000
Provision for income taxes	7,500
Net income	$ 17,500

Separate expense distribution analysis schedules similar to those illustrated on page 668 are usually prepared in advance to support the amount of each departmental expense item shown on working papers and the departmental income statement.

QUESTIONS

1. As the general manager of the local bookstore, you are trying to convince the board of directors that gross profits should be determined for each of the three departments: textbooks, general books, and merchandise. Explain the advantages of departmental gross profit figures and how you would use them in a managerial capacity.

2. The manager of a department of a retail store states: "We determine our selling prices by adding 50% to our costs."

    a. If the manager's statement is factual, what rate of gross profit per dollar of sales would the company realize in this department?

    b. Assume that the actual realized gross profit in this department for a given period was 28% of net sales. What reasons can you give for this?

3. **a.** Explain the distinction between direct expenses and indirect expenses in departmental accounting.

    b. May an expense that is divided among departments on the basis of an apportionment or allocation be a direct expense?

4. **a.** What is the distinction between an "object of expenditure" and a "functional" classification of expense accounts?

    b. Suppose that W Company has the following insurance policies: casualty insurance on delivery trucks, public liability insurance, fidelity bonds on office personnel, fire insurance on buildings and equipment, fire insurance on merchandise, and workmen's compensation insurance. Explain how expired premiums would be treated under an object of expenditure and under a functional classification system.

5. A retail company, operating in a one-story building and having three merchandising departments, allocates building occupancy expenses among departments on the basis of sales. What is your opinion of this procedure? Explain.

6. Avon Company has three operating departments, but all purchases are made through a single purchasing agent. Departmental requisitions for merchandise are often combined into a single order and shipment. Discuss the problems that might arise in departmentalizing purchase discounts and transportation-in under these circumstances.

7. After examining a departmental income statement, the manager of one department complains that the amount of income taxes allocated to his department is greater than the amount that the business as a whole will have to pay, and he feels that this is entirely unreasonable. Explain how this could happen, and whether or not you agree with the department manager's view.

PROBLEMS

Group A

24A-1. The Ronsine Company operates a retail business in a three-story building. Each floor has usable space of 20,000 square feet. The occupancy cost for the building per year averages $48,000. There are a number of separate departments in the store, and departmental income statements are prepared each year. Department A occupies 4,000 square feet of space on the first floor. Department M occupies 6,400 square feet of space on the third floor.

    In allocating occupancy cost among the various departments, the bookkeeper has determined that the average occupancy cost per square foot is 80 cents ($48,000 ÷ 60,000), and so he has charged Department A with $3,200 of occupancy cost and Department M with $5,120, on the basis of space occupied.

    Roberts, the manager of Department M, feels that this allocation is unreasonable. He has made a study of rental prices being charged for similar property in the area and finds the following:

	Average yearly rental, per square foot
First-floor space	$2.00
Second-floor space	1.20
Third-floor space	0.80

On the basis of this evidence, Roberts argues that the charge to his department should be modified.

Instructions
a. Comment on the validity of Roberts' position.
b. On the basis of Roberts' findings, how much occupancy cost per year should be charged to Department A and to Department M? Show computations.

24A-2. The trial balance of the Dravo Corporation at the end of the calendar year is:

DRAVO CORPORATION
Trial Balance
December 31, 19___

Cash	$ 46,500	
Accounts receivable	56,700	
Allowance for bad debts		$ 3,100
Prepaid expenses		
Inventory: Jan. 1, Department X	36,800	
Inventory: Jan. 1, Department Y	18,200	
Land	40,000	
Buildings	250,000	
Allowance for depreciation: buildings ...		87,500
Equipment	94,000	
Allowance for depreciation: equipment ..		37,600
Notes payable		40,000
Accounts payable		35,900
Accrued expenses		16,200
Common stock		100,000
Retained earnings		132,600
Sales: Department X		320,000
Sales: Department Y		480,000
Sales returns & allowances: Dept. X	13,400	
Sales returns & allowances: Dept. Y	16,100	
Sales discounts	15,200	
Purchases: Department X	175,000	
Purchases: Department Y	325,000	
Purchase returns & allowances: Dept. X .		17,500
Purchase returns & allowances: Dept. Y .		21,200
Purchase discounts		11,200
Transportation-in	26,400	
Selling expense control	110,400	
Administrative expense control	87,500	
Gain on sale of land		8,400
	$1,311,200	$1,311,200

Other data

(*a*) Inventories at December 31 were: Department X, $40,000; Department Y, $22,000.

(*b*) Certain expenditures that had been charged to expense during the period were applicable to future operations:

Charged to selling expenses $4,200
Charged to administrative expenses $2,300

(*c*) The allowance for bad debts should be increased by 1 1/2% of December sales, which were: Department X, $34,000; Department Y, $48,000. Bad debts is classed as an administrative expense.

(*d*) Depreciation has not been recorded. Depreciation on buildings is at the rate of 3% per year. Depreciation on equipment is computed at a declining balance rate of 20%. Of the total depreciation expense, two-thirds is applicable to selling expense and one-third to administrative expense.

(*e*) Sales discounts are to be allocated on the basis of departmental gross sales.

(*f*) Purchase discounts are to be allocated in proportion to departmental purchases.

(*g*) A study of freight bills for the month of July showed that, of the total transportation-in for that month, $2,100 was applicable to Department X purchases and $900 to Department Y purchases. The transportation-in for the year is to be apportioned in the same ratio.

(*h*) Income taxes are estimated at 40% of net book income, except for the gain on the sale of land, on which the tax is 25%.

Instructions

a. Prepare year-end working papers for the Dravo Corporation, showing the determination of gross profits by departments.

b. Which department has the highest rate of gross profit per dollar of sales?

24A-3. The summarized adjusted trial balance of the Funk Company for the fiscal year ended January 31, 19___ is shown below:

FUNK COMPANY
Trial Balance
January 31, 19___

Administrative expense: Dept. A	$ 11,700	
Administrative expense: Dept. B	5,900	
Administrative expense: indirect	25,400	
Advertising expense: Dept. A	12,400	
Advertising expense: Dept. B	16,200	
Advertising expense: indirect	12,000	
Allowance for depreciation		$ 93,000
Buildings and equipment	270,000	
Bldg. occupancy expense: Dept. A	2,800	
Bldg. occupancy expense: Dept. B		
Bldg. occupancy expense: indirect	15,200	
Buying expenses: Dept. A	10,300	
Buying expenses: Dept. B	5,600	

Buying expenses: indirect	9,700	
Capital stock		100,000
Cost of goods sold: Dept. A	225,000	
Cost of goods sold: Dept. B	150,000	
Current assets	126,000	
Current liabilities		63,400
Goodwill	50,000	
Interest expense	5,500	
Interest income: Dept. A		300
Interest income: Dept. B		900
Land	60,000	
Long-term notes payable		80,000
Loss on sale of investment	7,000	
Net sales: Dept. A		360,000
Net sales: Dept. B		220,000
Retained earnings		138,100
Sales salaries: Dept. A	18,000	
Sales salaries: Dept. B	9,000	
Sales salaries: indirect	8,000	
	$1,055,700	$1,055,700

No provision has been made for income taxes. It is estimated that they will amount to 45% of net income excluding the effect of the loss on the sale of investments, which is not deductible for tax purposes in the current year.

Instructions. Prepare year-end working papers (10-column) from which a departmental income statement and a balance sheet could be prepared. The Funk Company is interested in knowing the contribution that each department makes toward the indirect overhead of the business.

Since there are no adjustments other than income taxes, the working papers may start with the adjusted trial balance. Allow two columns each for the following: Income statement: Dept. A, Income statement: Dept. B, Unallocated revenues and expenses, and Balance sheet.

24A-4. Greene Company has four operating departments. At the end of the current year the controller has computed departmental results in three ways, showing net income by departments, the departmental contribution to indirect expenses, and the gross margin on sales for each department as shown below:

	Total	Departments A	B	C	D
Departmental net income	$ 15,000	$ 63,000	$(4,000)	$(18,000)	$(26,000)
Departmental contribution to indirect expenses	85,000	98,000	14,000	(8,000)	(19,000)
Departmental gross margin on sales	168,000	128,000	36,000	9,600	(5,600)
Gross profit as a percentage of sales	24%	40%	20%	8%	(7%)

( ) = *loss.*

Instructions

a. On the basis of the above information, prepare a departmental income statement for the Greene Company. It will be necessary to compute the following amounts: sales, cost of sales, direct expenses, and indirect expenses. (*Hint:* Gross margin on sales is given in total and by departments. Also the percentage of gross margin on sales is given for the company as a whole and for each department. From this information sales can be computed.)

b. What conclusions would you reach about the operations of Departments B, C, and D on the basis of the statement prepared in (*a*)? Should any of these departments be discontinued? Explain your reasoning.

24A-5. The Wixon Company operates a retail business having three departments. Departmental expense accounts are maintained for some expenses, the rest are apportioned at the end of each accounting period. The operating expenses for the current year were as follows:

	Departmental expense accounts			Unassigned expenses
	Dept. R	Dept. S	Dept. T	
Sales salaries	$19,200	$17,300	$11,500	
Salaries: other				$25,000
Building rental				9,600
Advertising	1,800	1,200	600	1,500
Supplies used	750	800	620	
Payroll taxes				2,920
Insurance expense				900
Heat and light				1,680
Depreciation on equipment				1,625
Miscellaneous expenses	300	200	180	1,000

Other data

	Dept. R	Dept. S	Dept. T
Net sales	$200,000	$120,000	$80,000
Cost of sales	156,000	83,700	50,300
Equipment (original cost)	3,640	3,900	5,460
Value of floor space	50%	30%	20%
Floor space (square feet)	1,600	1,600	800
Average inventory	$ 15,860	$ 19,500	$29,640

Unassigned expenses are apportioned among the departments on the bases given below. Round all expense apportionments to the nearest dollar.

Unassigned expense	Basis of apportionment
Salaries: other	Gross profit margin
Building rental	Value of floor space occupied
Advertising	Direct departmental advertising
Payroll taxes	Salaries, both direct and apportioned
Insurance expense	Sum of equipment and average inventories
Heat and light	Square feet of floor space
Miscellaneous expense	Sales

Instructions

a. Prepare a schedule showing the allocation of operating expenses among the three departments. Use four money columns headed: Total, Department R, Department S, and Department T. Show all computations necessary to arrive at departmental apportionments in supporting footnotes.

b. Prepare a summarized departmental net income statement for the Wixon Company, using the same column headings. Show summary figures for both total and departmental operating expenses, using totals from the schedule in (*a*).

24A-6. Refer to the data given for the Wixon Company in problem 24A-5. The management of the company is quite disappointed in the net income of $3,380 realized in Department R on sales of $200,000. They are considering a proposal to lease this department, under an agreement whereby the Wixon Company would receive a flat 6% of departmental sales realized by the lessee.

You have been asked to determine whether the Wixon Company would gain by accepting this proposal. It is assumed that if the department were operated on a lease basis, the sales would remain unchanged.

The following managerial estimates are to be used as a basis for your study of the effect of discontinuing the operation of Department R:

(1) It is assumed that expenses charged directly to departmental expense accounts would disappear with the discontinuance of the department.

(2) Salaries: other, would be cut by $4,500. Insurance expense in Department R would be reduced by 20%. Equipment in this department would be sold to the lessee at book value, and the depreciation therefore eliminated.

(3) These expenses would remain unchanged: building rental, heat and light.

Instructions

a. Prepare a schedule showing the net advantage or disadvantage to the Wixon Company from the discontinuation of Department R and its lease for 6% of departmental sales.

b. Write a brief statement of your recommendation to management, explaining the reasons for your conclusion.

Group B

24B-1. Reed Company offers its customers a 2% cash discount on all cash sales and charges a financing charge of 1/2% per month on all account balances that are not paid within 30 days of the invoice date. Cash discounts are allocated directly to its three operating departments at the time of sale. Financing-charge revenues are apportioned among departments on the basis of credit sales.

This data is taken from the Reed Company accounts for the current year:

	Total	Dept. A	Dept. B	Dept. C
Sales	$400,000	$80,000	$260,000	$60,000
Financing-charge revenue	3,300			
Sales discounts	(2,000)	(1,000)	(800)	(200)
Net revenues	$401,300			

Instructions

a. Determine the amount of credit sales for each of the three departments.

b. Determine the amount of financing charges that will be credited to each department.

c. Comment on the validity of the method used by this company in apportioning financing charges among departments. Explain why you think it will or will not produce accurate results.

24B-2. The Burrell Company has suffered operating losses in recent years. At the beginning of the current year, the company organized its operations on a departmental basis in an attempt to improve the situation. Burr took charge of Department S, and Rell became the manager of Department T. At that time Burr promised that his department would contribute a larger gross profit during the current year than Rell's. Rell countered with a friendly wager (a steak dinner) that his department would show the larger gross profit.

The trial balance prepared at the end of the year is given below.

BURRELL COMPANY
Trial Balance
End of Current Year

Cash	$ 24,300	
Accounts receivable	31,000	
Allowance for bad debts		$ 2,800
Prepaid expenses	1,800	
Inventory, Jan. 1: Dept. S	28,980	
Inventory, Jan. 1: Dept. T	22,820	
Equipment and fixtures	52,000	
Allow. for depreciation: Equip. & Fixt.		18,000
Long-term investments	20,000	
Accounts payable		30,000
Accrued expenses		15,000
Common stock		70,000
Retained earnings	900	
Sales: Department S		220,000
Sales: Department T		180,000
Sales returns: Dept. S	20,000	
Sales returns: Dept. T	9,000	
Sales discounts	8,000	
Purchases: Dept. S	110,000	
Purchases: Dept. T	90,000	

Purchase returns: Dept. S		*5,600*
Purchase returns: Dept. T		*3,400*
Purchase discounts		*3,600*
Freight-in on purchases	*21,000*	
Selling expense control	*60,000*	
Administrative expense control	*50,000*	
Dividend and interest revenue		*1,400*
	$549,800	*$549,800*

Other data

(*a*) Inventories at the end of the year were: Department S, $18,260; Department T, $14,360.

(*b*) The company rents its building. At the end of the year $2,500 of rent is due and unpaid. Of this amount, $2,000 is treated as a selling expense and $500 as an administrative expense.

(*c*) Accounts receivable totaling $700 are definitely uncollectible and should be written off.

(*d*) Equipment costing $2,000 was scrapped during the year. The equipment was fully depreciated.

(*e*) Sales discounts should be allocated between departments in proportion to gross sales.

(*f*) Purchase discounts should be allocated on the basis of gross purchases.

(*g*) A study of freight bills over a six-month period indicates that the freight charges applicable to Department S are, on the average, twice as large as those applicable to Department T.

(*h*) Income taxes are estimated at 30% of taxable income. Taxable income is the same as book income except that the company is entitled to deduct, in determining taxable income, 85% of dividends received from domestic corporations. During the year $1,000 of such dividends were received.

Instructions

a. Prepare year-end working papers for the Burrell Company. Include six income statement columns in your work sheet: two for Department S, two for Department T, and two for nondepartmental items. Determine gross profit by departments.

b. Does Burr or Rell have to buy the steak dinner? Explain.

c. Prepare a schedule showing which of the two departments produced the higher *rate* of gross profit per dollar of net sales.

24B-3. At the end of the month of June, the summarized adjusted trial balance shown below was prepared from the records of Duncan and Webb, a retailing partnership.

Administrative expenses	*$ 26,000*	
Advertising expenses	*17,600*	
Allowance for depreciation		*$147,000*
Buildings and equipment	*350,000*	
Buying expenses	*20,000*	
Cost of goods sold: Dept. D	*115,000*	
Cost of goods sold: Dept. W	*65,000*	

Current assets	$ 98,000	
Current liabilities		$ 45,000
Duncan, capital		87,000
Interest expense	600	
Land	25,000	
Mortgage payable		120,000
Net sales: Dept. D		190,000
Net sales: Dept. W		110,000
Occupancy expenses	22,000	
Selling expenses	28,400	
Service charges: Dept. D		1,200
Service charges: Dept. W		1,700
Webb, capital		65,700
	$767,600	$767,600

Other data. The partners have agreed that monthly income statements shall show the contribution of each department over and above the direct costs of departmental operations. An analysis of operating expenses during June indicates that the following amounts in each class of expense are directly chargeable to the departments:

	Direct expense	
	Department D	Department W
Administrative expenses	$ 6,700	$3,500
Advertising expenses	7,000	5,000
Buying expenses	7,300	5,600
Occupancy expense	500	1,000
Selling expense	11,800	7,200

The partnership agreement provides that net income shall be divided between the partners as follows: Duncan is to be credited with 10% of the excess of revenues over direct costs in Department D; Webb is to be credited with 10% of the excess of revenues over direct costs in Department W; any remainder shall be divided equally.

Instructions

a. Prepare working papers as of the end of June for the partnership, showing the contribution of each department to the indirect operating expenses of the business. Ten columns will be required in the working papers. Allow two columns each to: Adjusted trial balance, Department D, Department W, Unallocated, and Balance sheet.

b. Prepare a schedule showing the division of the June net income between the two partners.

24B-4. J. Appleseed owns an apple orchard, from which he harvested and sold during the current year 200,000 pounds of apples. The price received varied in accordance with the grade of apple as shown in the table below.

Grade	Pounds	Price per pound	Receipts
Superior	40,000	$0.24	$ 9,600
Medium	100,000	0.108	10,800
Cooking	60,000	0.06	3,600
	200,000		$24,000

Appleseed's expenses for the year, as taken from his accounting records, are given below.

		Dollars	Per pound
Growing expenses		$ 5,000	$0.025
Harvesting expenses		7,000	0.035
Packing & shipping:			
Superior	$2,000		0.05
Medium	4,000		0.04
Cooking	1,800	7,800	0.03
Total expenses		$19,800	

Appleseed asked a friend, who was taking an accounting course at a nearby university, to determine his income from each grade of apple. The friend gave him the statement shown below:

	Total	Superior	Medium	Cooking
Sales	$24,000	$9,600	$10,800	$ 3,600
Expenses:				
Growing	$ 5,000	$1,000	$ 2,500	$ 1,500
Harvesting	7,000	1,400	3,500	2,100
Packing & shipping ...	7,800	2,000	4,000	1,800
Total expenses	$19,800	$4,400	$10,000	$ 5,400
Net income (or loss)	$ 4,200	$5,200	$ 800	$(1,800)

After studying this statement, Appleseed remarked to a neighbor, "I made money on my superiors and about broke even on the mediums, but I should have dumped the cooking apples in the river; they cost me more than I got from them!"

Instructions. Do you agree? Discuss. What kind of statement of income per grade of apple would you have prepared for Appleseed? Illustrate.

24B-5. Refer to the adjusted trial balance of the Funk Company that appears in problem 24A-3. Assume that the company wishes to prepare a departmental income statement showing *net income* by departments. The bases for allocating indirect expenses between the two departments have been agreed upon as shown below.

Sales salaries: number of employees. There were five employees in Department A and three in Department B.

Advertising: column inches of advertising. Of the total inches placed, 6,240 are chargeable to Department A and 8,160 to Department B.

Building occupancy: value of space occupied. It is estimated that the value of the space occupied by Department A is five-eighths of the total value of all the space in the building.

Buying expense: one-fourth to Department B; three-fourths to Department A.

Administrative: in proportion to sales in each department.

Interest expense: in the same ratio as occupancy cost, since most of the interest is on debt incurred in connection with the purchase of the building.

Instructions

a. Prepare a schedule showing the allocation of indirect expenses between departments. In making apportionments, round all figures to the nearest dollar.

b. Prepare a schedule showing a summary of operating expenses (both direct and indirect) by departments.

c. Prepare a condensed income statement showing the net income by departments. Use three columns: Total, Department A, and Department B. Show operating expenses in total only, using figures from the schedule prepared in (*b*) above. Income taxes may be allocated on the basis of departmental net income. Loss on the sale of investments may be shown as a final deduction and need not be allocated to the two departments.

24B-6. The condensed income statement given below reflects the operating results of the Dykstra Company for the current year.

DYKSTRA COMPANY
Condensed Income Statement
Current Year

	Total	Department K	Department T
Net sales	$980,000	$400,000	$580,000
Cost of goods sold	725,000	310,000	415,000
Gross profit on sales	$255,000	$ 90,000	$165,000
Financing and service charges	12,000	8,000	4,000
Gross profit and other income	$267,000	$ 98,000	$169,000
Operating expenses:			
Buying expenses	$ 21,600	$ 11,600	$ 10,000
Warehousing & stock control	13,500	8,300	5,200
Building occupancy	29,000	16,000	13,000
Advertising & promotion	27,500	16,000	11,500
Sales force	43,100	23,100	20,000
Delivery expense	24,300	15,000	9,300
Credit & collection expense	16,000	10,000	6,000

General administrative expense	*42,000*	*18,000*	*24,000*
Total operating expense	*$217,000*	*$118,000*	*$ 99,000*
Net income before income taxes	*$ 50,000*	*$ (20,000)*	*$ 70,000*
Provision for income taxes	*20,500*	*(8,200)*	*28,700*
Net income	*$ 29,500*	*$ (11,800)*	*$ 41,300*

A major stockholder of the company argues that Department K should be discontinued, since this department has been operating at a comparable loss for the last several years. The president of the company reports that he has an offer from a noncompeting firm to rent the space occupied by Department K for $2,000 per month on a long-term lease.

An analysis of operating expenses indicates that if Department K were dropped the following changes in expenses could be expected:

The portion of sales force and delivery expenses now allocated to Department K would completely disappear. Building occupancy expense would remain unchanged. The remaining classes of expense would be reduced by varying percentages (of the total expense) as follows: buying expense, 50%; warehouse and stock control, 60%; advertising and promotion, 40%; credit and collection, 30%; general administrative, 10%.

Instructions. You have been asked by management to make a recommendation on the basis of this information.

a. Prepare a schedule showing the net advantage or disadvantage (before income taxes) to the Dykstra Company of discontinuing Department K and accepting the rental proposal. What do you recommend?

b. Compute the net income that the Dykstra Company would have realized this year if the rental proposal had been accepted at the beginning of the year and if all assumptions as to changes in operating expenses had been accurate. Income taxes are estimated to be 30% on the first $25,000 of net income and 52% on all net income over $25,000.

25

Accounting for manufacturing concerns

Additional accounting problems faced by the manufacturer

In preceding chapters of this book we have considered accounting principles and procedures applicable to nonmanufacturing concerns; that is, to merchandising and service organizations. Although these same accounting principles and procedures are used by manufacturing concerns as well, a company that is engaged in manufacturing requires some additional accounting techniques to control and report factory production costs.

A typical manufacturing business buys raw materials and processes them into finished goods. The raw materials purchased by an aircraft manufacturer, for example, include sheet aluminum, jet engines, and a variety of instruments. The completed airplane assembled from these components represents the "finished goods" of the airplane manufacturer. The terms *raw materials* and *finished goods* are defined from the viewpoint of the particular manufacturer. Sheet aluminum, for example, is a raw material from the viewpoint of the aircraft company, but a finished good from the viewpoint of the aluminum manufacturer.

The processing of raw materials by the manufacturer requires expenditures for factory labor and a variety of other factory costs, such as electrical power, machinery repairs, and factory supervision. These production costs are added to the cost of the raw materials in determining the cost of the finished goods. Consequently, accounting records must be expanded for a manufacturing business to include ledger accounts for these various types of factory costs, and the financial statements also must be designed to reflect the costs of manufacturing. The accounting problems of merchandising concerns are often less involved than those of manufacturing companies; the retailer or wholesaler has as a major function the distribution of finished goods, whereas the manufacturer has two major functions: the production of finished goods, and the sale of the goods produced. Much of the accounting work for a manufacturing company pertains to production costs; however, the manufacturer also incurs general administrative expenses and selling expenses comparable to those of a trading concern.

Determining the cost of goods sold. The principal difference in accounting for a merchandising business and for a manufacturing concern is found in computing the cost of goods sold. In a merchandising business the cost of goods sold is computed as follows:

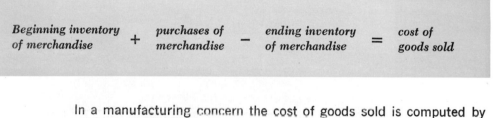

Beginning inventory of merchandise + *purchases of merchandise* − *ending inventory of merchandise* = *cost of goods sold*

In a manufacturing concern the cost of goods sold is computed by a parallel computation, as follows:

Beginning inventory of finished goods + *cost of goods manufactured* − *ending inventory of finished goods* = *cost of goods sold*

Comparison of these two similar computations shows that the cost of goods manufactured in a manufacturing company is in a sense the equivalent of purchases of merchandise in a merchandising business. This point is further emphasized by a comparison of the income statement of a merchandising company and that of a manufacturing concern.

Comparison of income statements for manufacturing and merchandising concerns. The treatment of sales, selling expenses, general administrative expenses, and income taxes is just the same on the income statement of a manufacturing company as for a merchandising concern. The only point of difference in the following two income statements lies within the cost of goods sold section, with the item of Purchases in the one statement being replaced by the item of Cost of Goods Manufactured in the other statement.

A MERCHANDISING COMPANY
Income Statement
For the Year Ended December 31, 1963

Sales		$100,000
Cost of goods sold:		
Inventory of merchandise, Dec. 31, 1962	$30,000	
→ PURCHASES	60,000	
Cost of goods available for sale	$90,000	
Deduct: inventory of merchandise, Dec. 31, 1963	25,000	
Cost of goods sold		65,000
Gross profit on sales		$ 35,000
Operating expenses:		
Selling expenses	$10,000	
General administrative expenses	15,000	25,000
Net income		$ 10,000

A MANUFACTURING COMPANY
Exhibit A
Income Statement
For the Year Ended December 31, 1963

Sales		$100,000
Cost of goods sold:		
Inventory of finished goods, Dec. 31, 1962	$30,000	
→ COST OF GOODS MANUFACTURED (per Exhibit B) ..	60,000	
Cost of goods available for sale	$90,000	
Deduct: inventory of finished goods, Dec. 31, 1963	25,000	
Cost of goods sold		65,000
Gross profit on sales		$ 35,000
Operating expenses:		
Selling expenses	$10,000	
General administrative expenses	15,000	25,000
Net income		$ 10,000

Statement of cost of goods manufactured. The principal new element in the illustrated income statement for a manufacturing company is the item: "Cost of Goods Manufactured ... $60,000." This amount was determined from the *statement of cost of goods manufactured,* a financial statement prepared to accompany and support the income statement, shown below.

A MANUFACTURING COMPANY

Exhibit B

Statement of Cost of Goods Manufactured
For the Year Ended December 31, 1963

Goods in process inventory, Dec. 31, 1962		$ 7,000
Raw materials:		
Raw materials inventory, Dec. 31, 1962	$ 5,000	
Purchases $10,000		
Deduct: purchase returns & allowances 300	9,700	
Transportation-in	500	
Cost of raw materials available for use	$15,200	
Deduct: raw materials inventory, Dec. 31, 1963	4,200	
Cost of raw materials used	$11,000	
Direct labor	23,000	
Factory overhead:		
Indirect labor .... $ 6,000		
Supervisory salaries 10,000		
Heat, light, & power 1,800		
Repairs & maintenance 1,200		
Property taxes 1,800		
Insurance expense 1,500		
Depreciation of factory building 600		
Depreciation of machinery & equipment 300		
Amortization of patents 200		
Factory supplies expense 800		
Miscellaneous factory expense 800		
Total factory overhead	25,000	
Total manufacturing costs		59,000
Total cost of goods in process during the period		$66,000
Deduct: goods in process inventory, Dec. 31, 1963		6,000
Cost of goods manufactured		$60,000

Observe that the final amount of $60,000 on the cost of goods manufactured statement is carried forward to the income statement and is used in determining the cost of goods sold, as illustrated in the statements on page 690.

Manufacturing costs

To gain a better understanding of how the cost of goods manufactured is determined, we must now examine the nature of the costs incurred in a manufacturing plant. To paint a clear picture of the major elements of

FUNCTIONAL
DIVISIONS
OF A MANU-
FACTURING
COMPANY

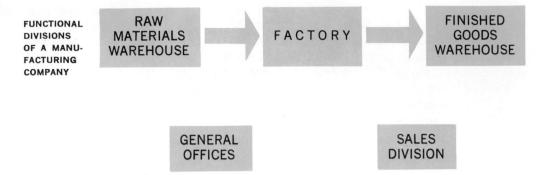

manufacturing cost and to distinguish sharply between manufacturing cost on the one hand and administrative and selling expenses on the other, assume that our hypothetical manufacturing company owns five separate buildings, each used exclusively for a single function of the business. These five buildings, as shown in the accompanying sketch, consist of (1) a raw materials warehouse, (2) a factory building, (3) a finished goods warehouse, (4) a general office building, and (5) a building housing the sales division of the company.

The raw materials received from suppliers are first placed in the raw materials warehouse; as these raw materials are needed in the production process they are moved into the factory, as shown by the arrow connecting these two buildings. In the factory building the raw materials are converted (cut up, processed, and assembled) into finished goods. Each unit of finished product is moved immediately upon completion out of the factory into the finished goods warehouse. As sales orders are obtained from customers, shipments are made from the finished goods warehouse.

Now let us concentrate our attention upon the factory building, for it is here that all manufacturing costs are incurred. These costs are classified into three groups:

1. *Raw materials cost*
2. *Direct labor*
3. *Factory overhead*

Each unit of finished goods leaving the factory includes these elements of manufacturing cost. Each of the three cost elements will now be discussed in some detail.[1]

---

[1] The Committee on Terminology of the American Institute of Certified Public Accountants has recommended that ". . . items entering into the computation of cost of manufacturing, such as material, labor, and overhead, should be described as costs and not as expenses."

Raw materials. The cost of raw materials (also called *direct materials*) represents the delivered cost of materials which enter into and become part of the finished product. In thinking about the elements of manufacturing cost during a given period, we are interested in the cost of raw materials *used* rather than the amount of raw materials purchased. Purchases of raw materials flow into the raw materials warehouse, but the consumption or use of raw materials consists of the materials moved from the raw materials warehouse into the factory to be processed. The computation of the cost of raw materials used was illustrated in the statement of cost of goods manufactured on page 691. The raw materials section of that statement is presented again at this point to emphasize the flow of cost for materials.

<table>
<tr><td>COMPUTING
THE COST
OF RAW
MATERIALS
USED</td><td>

Raw materials:

Raw materials inventory, Dec. 31, 1962		*$ 5,000*
Purchases	*$10,000*	
Less: purchase returns & allowances	*300*	*9,700*
Transportation-in		*500*
Cost of raw materials available for use		*$15,200*
Less: raw materials inventory, Dec. 31, 1963		*4,200*
Cost of raw materials used		*$11,000*

</td></tr>
</table>

Since the cost of raw materials used is computed by subtracting the amount of raw materials on hand at the end of the period from the total of the beginning inventory plus the purchases of the period, any raw materials which were stolen, spoiled, or lost will be included in the residual amount labeled Cost of Raw Materials Used. Inability to spotlight shortages or wastage of materials is one of the weaknesses inherent in the periodic inventory method.

LEDGER
ACCOUNTS
FOR RAW
MATERIALS
    In order to have the information for computing the cost of raw materials used readily available in the accounting records, the following ledger accounts are maintained:

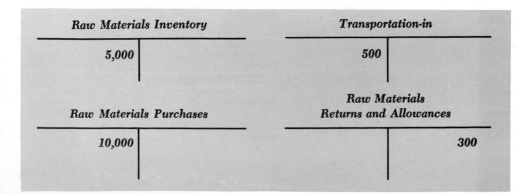

The Raw Materials Inventory account is used only at the end of the year, when a physical count of raw materials on hand is made, and the cost of these materials on hand is recorded by a debit to the Inventory account. The offsetting credit is made to the Manufacturing account, which will be explained later in this chapter. The other three accounts illustrated are used throughout the year to accumulate (1) the purchases of raw materials, (2) the transportation charges on inbound shipments of raw materials, and (3) the returns to suppliers of unsatisfactory or excessive raw materials.

Direct labor cost. The second major element of manufacturing costs is called direct labor and consists of the wages paid to factory employees who work directly on the product being manufactured. Direct labor costs include the payroll costs of machine operators, assemblers, and those who work on the product by hand or with tools, but not the wages of indirect workers such as plant watchmen, janitors, timekeepers, and supervisors.

What is the reason for separating the costs of direct labor and indirect labor? Direct labor is expended in converting raw materials into finished goods. If factory output is to be increased, it will be necessary to employ more direct labor and direct labor costs will rise. If factory output is to be reduced, any existing hours of overtime will be reduced and workers may be discharged. Direct labor costs vary directly with changes in the level of output; consequently, in planning operations for future periods, management can estimate the direct labor cost required for any desired volume of production.

Indirect labor, on the other hand, is much less inclined to rise and fall with changes in factory output. An increase or decrease of 10%, for example, in the number of units being produced will ordinarily not cause any change in the salary of the factory superintendent or in the number of janitors or guards. A large change in the volume of production will, of course, have some impact upon indirect labor costs.

Factory overhead. Factory overhead includes all costs incurred in the factory other than the costs of raw material and direct labor. Included in factory overhead are such costs as the following:

1. Indirect labor
    a. Supervision
    b. Timekeeping
    c. Janitorial and maintenance
    d. Production scheduling
    e. Plant protection service
2. Occupancy cost
    a. Depreciation of building
    b. Insurance on building
    c. Property taxes on land and building

   d. Repairs to building
   e. Heat, light, and power
3. Machinery and equipment costs
   a. Depreciation of machinery and equipment
   b. Insurance on machinery and equipment
   c. Property taxes on machinery and equipment
   d. Repairs and maintenance of machinery and equipment

This is not a complete list of factory overhead costs; in fact, it is the impossibility of preparing a complete list that leads accountants to define factory overhead as *all* costs incurred in the factory other than raw material and direct labor. A significant characteristic of factory overhead is that these costs cannot be directly related to units of product as can the costs of direct labor and direct material. In a factory producing two different products such as radios and television sets, it is possible to measure fairly accurately the costs of raw material and direct labor applied to each product, but the nature of factory overhead costs (such as insurance and repairs to buildings) is such that they cannot be associated directly with the particular articles being produced. For this reason, raw materials and direct labor are sometimes referred to as the *direct costs* or *prime costs* of manufacturing in contrast to factory overhead, which may be regarded as an *indirect cost.* Alternative titles for factory overhead include indirect manufacturing cost, factory burden, manufacturing burden, and manufacturing overhead.

Certain expenses such as insurance, property taxes, telephone, and salaries of executives may be applicable in part to factory operations and in part to administrative and selling divisions of the company. In such cases the expense may be apportioned among factory overhead, general administrative expense, and selling expense accounts at the time incurred, or as an alternative, the expense may be recorded in a single ledger account and the apportionment made in the working papers, as illustrated later in this chapter.

The flow of costs in a manufacturing business

The sketch on page 696 emphasizes the flow of costs in a manufacturing business and some of the principal concepts appearing in the financial statements.

Product costs and period costs. *Product costs* are manufacturing costs which become part of the carrying value of goods in process and finished goods inventories. To the extent that goods manufactured this year are not sold immediately but are held in inventory for sale in future periods, the costs of manufacturing these goods are carried as assets rather than being deducted from revenues in the period incurred.

Period costs traditionally have consisted of general and administrative expenses and of selling expenses. These expenses are "costs of the

The cost of raw materials used consists of:
  Beginning inventory of raw materials
  Plus the delivered cost of purchases
  Minus the ending inventory of raw materials

Factory costs consist of:
  1. Cost of raw materials used
  2. Direct labor
  3. Factory overhead

Cost of goods manufactured refers to the cost of units completed and moved out of the factory.

Cost of goods sold consists of:
  Beginning inventory of finished goods
  Plus cost of goods manufactured
  Minus ending inventory of finished goods

Shipments of finished goods to customers are made from the finished goods warehouse.

period" because they are deducted from revenues in the period incurred. This immediate charge to expense is based on the assumption that the benefits are received in the same period the expenditures are made. It is not always easy to decide whether a particular cost pertains primarily to the factory and should be treated as a product cost, or is of an administrative character and should not be included in the cost of goods manufactured. For example, the costs of maintaining a cost accounting department, a personnel department, and guard service are treated by some companies as factory overhead (product costs) and by other companies as general and administrative overhead (period costs).

Full costing and direct costing. Traditionally, all costs pertaining to the manufacturing division of the business have been treated as product costs, but in recent years the concept of *direct costing* has received some support. Direct costing limits product costs to raw material, direct labor, and that portion of factory overhead which is believed to vary directly with changes in the level of factory output. In other words, the fixed elements of factory overhead which continue regardless of decreases in quantity of units produced are treated as period costs and not included in the valuation of inventories. As a result, inventories of finished goods and work in process would appear at lower valuations in the balance sheet if direct costing were adopted. Net income would be reduced in the year in which direct costing was adopted because many costs normally converted into inventory values would be treated as expenses of the period. Although direct costing may be very useful in making internal studies for use by management, most accounting authorities object to its use in preparing financial statements for distribution to outsiders. Throughout this chapter, the "full cost" concept is used; full cost as opposed to direct costing means that all elements of factory overhead are included as part of the cost of goods manufactured.

Additional ledger accounts needed by a manufacturing company

The next step in studying the accounting techniques for determining the costs of goods manufactured is consideration of the additional ledger accounts required by a manufacturing concern to reflect costs of production. No special consideration needs to be given to the ledger accounts for sales, cost of goods sold, selling expenses, and general administrative expenses, because these accounts are handled in the same manner as in a retail or wholesale business.

Current asset accounts. In place of the single inventory account found on the balance sheet of a retail or wholesale business, a manufacturing concern has three separate inventory accounts. These accounts consist of:

1. *Raw materials inventory.* This account represents the unused portion of the raw materials purchased. The amount is determined at year-end by taking a physical count of the raw materials which have not yet been placed in production. In our earlier example of the company with five buildings, this inventory would be located in the raw materials warehouse. As a matter of convenience, factory supplies on hand (oil, grease, sweeping compounds) acquired for use in maintaining and servicing the factory building and machinery are often merged with raw materials. Some companies insist upon a separate accounting for supplies, because, unlike raw materials, the quantity of supplies used does not vary directly with the number of units produced. A choice between these alternative methods often hinges on the relative importance of supplies in the particular business.

2. *Goods in process inventory.* This inventory consists of the partially completed goods on hand in the factory at year-end, determined by a physical count. The costing of these partially manufactured goods is accomplished by estimating the costs of the raw materials, direct labor, and factory overhead associated with these units. The goods in process inventory appears on the balance sheet as a current asset and also ap-

pears on the statement of cost of goods manufactured (page 691). To compute the cost of goods manufactured in a given year, start with the inventory of partially completed goods on hand January 1, add the manufacturing costs for the current year, and deduct the costs incurred on the partially completed units in the factory at December 31.

3. *Finished goods inventory.* This account shows the amount of finished goods on hand and awaiting sale to customers as of the end of the year. The costs of these finished units are composed of the factory costs of raw material, direct labor, and factory overhead. The method of pricing finished goods will be discussed later in this chapter. In the balance sheet, the finished goods inventory appears as a current asset; it is also used in computing the cost of goods sold in the income statement.

Plant and equipment accounts. Manufacturing concerns have generally found it necessary to invest a larger part of their total capital in plant and equipment than have merchandising companies; in recent years the trend toward greater mechanization of production has led to particularly heavy investment in manufacturing facilities. Depreciation of the plant and equipment is one of the more important expenses included in factory overhead; the cost of the plant is thereby gradually transformed into the cost of goods manufactured.

Because of the great variety of items of manufacturing equipment, it is customary to maintain a subsidiary plant ledger as described in Chapter 14. On the balance sheet the caption of Plant and Equipment, or Machinery and Equipment, is often used to summarize all types of productive facilities.

Research and development costs. Intangible assets (see Chapter 14), such as patents and deferred costs of research and development, are also commonly found on the balance sheets of manufacturing concerns. In recent years success in the field of manufacturing seems to have been closely related to leadership in research and development of new products. In many organizations, the heavy cost of maintaining large research departments has been treated as current expense deducted from revenues in the period in which incurred. Other companies have charged research and development costs to asset accounts such as Deferred Research and Development Costs. Assets of this type are amortized over the years in which they contribute to revenues: through the process of amortization these costs become part of the cost of goods manufactured.

A policy of capitalizing research and development costs is entirely acceptable in terms of accounting theory. The opposing arguments for immediately charging research costs to expense include convenience and conservatism. Many manufacturing companies find that continuous operation of a research program is necessary merely to maintain a competitive position in the industry; as a consequence, these companies regard research expenditures as "period costs" to be deducted from revenue in the year incurred.

Raw material, direct labor, and factory overhead. The accounts required for recording the three major elements of production cost have already been indicated. In recording factory overhead a separate account must be created for each type of indirect manufacturing cost (Depreciation of Machinery, Repairs, Timekeeping, etc.) as indicated on page 694. If there are a great many of these factory overhead accounts, it is convenient to transfer them to a subsidiary ledger which will be controlled by a general ledger account entitled Factory Overhead.

The manufacturing account. Last in our list of ledger accounts peculiar to a manufacturing business is a summary account called *Manufacturing,* which is used at the end of each period to summarize the various elements of factory cost and to determine the cost of goods manufactured. The balance of this account represents the cost of goods manufactured during the period. The Manufacturing account is closed by transferring its debit balance to the Income Summary account, as shown by the following illustration.

NOTE KINDS
OF COSTS
SUMMARIZED
IN MANU-
FACTURING
ACCOUNT

		Manufacturing			
1963			*1963*		
Dec. 31	*Goods in process inventory Dec. 31, 1902*	*7,000*	*Dec. 31*	*Goods in process inventory Dec. 31, 1063*	*6,000*
31	*Raw materials inventory Dec. 31, 1962*	*5,000*	*31*	*Raw materials inventory Dec. 31, 1963*	*4,200*
31	*Raw materials purchases*	*10,000*	*31*	*Raw mat. purchases ret. & all.*	*300*
31	*Transportation-in*	*500*	*31*	*Cost of goods manufactured, to Income Summary*	*60,000*
31	*Direct labor*	*23,000*			
31	*Factory overhead (total)*	*25,000*			
		70,500			*70,500*

		Income Summary			
1963			*1963*		
Dec. 31	*Finished goods inventory Dec. 31, 1962*	*30,000*	*Dec. 31*	*Finished goods inventory Dec. 31, 1963*	*25,000*
31	*Cost of goods manufactured*	*60,000*			

A distinction is necessary between the phrases *cost of goods manufactured* and *total manufacturing cost.* Cost of goods manufactured means the cost of the units which are completed during the period and transferred from the factory to the warehouse for finished goods. Total manufacturing costs, on the other hand, include the cost of raw materials used, direct labor, and factory overhead for the period regardless of whether the units worked on have been completed or are still in process at the end of the period. As an extreme example, consider a manufacturing plant engaged in the construction of a single huge airplane. During the first year of work on the plane the manufacturing costs are as follows:

COMPARE "TOTAL MANUFACTURING COST" WITH "COST OF GOODS MANUFACTURED"

Cost of raw materials used	$ 300,000
Direct labor	700,000
Factory overhead	1,000,000
Total manufacturing cost	$2,000,000
Less: inventory of goods in process (ending)	2,000,000
Cost of goods manufactured	$ 000

The cost of goods manufactured was zero in the above illustration because no units were completed during the year, and we have defined the term *cost of goods manufactured* to mean the manufacturing cost of units that have been completed and moved out of the factory during the year.

Working papers for a manufacturing business

The work sheet for a merchandising concern illustrated in Chapter 5 can be adapted for use in a manufacturing company merely by adding a pair of columns for the data which will appear in the statement of cost of goods manufactured. Illustrative working papers for the Overland Manufacturing Corporation are presented on pages 702 to 705. As a means of simplifying the illustration, it is assumed that all adjusting entries were made before the trial balance was entered on the work sheet. The Adjustments columns are, therefore, omitted and the illustration begins with an Adjusted Trial Balance. Adjusting entries for a manufacturing business do not differ significantly from those previously described for a mercantile business.

Notice that the Heat, Light, and Power expense account with a balance of $6,000 has been apportioned as follows: to the Manufacturing columns $4,800; to the Income Statement columns $1,200, which is subdivided into $900 of general and administrative expense and $300 of selling expense. This subdivision is indicated by entering the letters G and S after these two amounts in the Income Statement columns. Similarly the Depreciation Expense: Buildings account and the Taxes and Insurance Expense account are apportioned in the working papers to the manufacturing, general administrative, and selling divisions of the company. This procedure of apportioning expense accounts in the working papers avoids the necessity for carrying additional accounts in the ledger; it is similar to the procedure illustrated in Chapter 24 for apportioning expenses by departments.

Treatment of inventories in the working papers. Since the Manufacturing columns are the distinctive feature of this work sheet, they require close study, especially the handling of the inventory accounts.

1. The beginning inventory of raw materials and the beginning inventory of goods in process have become part of the cost of goods manufactured and are, therefore, carried from the Adjusted Trial Balance to the Manufacturing debit column.

2. The ending inventories of raw materials and of goods in process must be recorded as assets and must be shown as a deduction in determining the cost of goods manufactured. This step requires the listing of the two inventories as debits in the balance sheet columns and as credits in the Manufacturing columns.

The nature of the Manufacturing columns may be clarified by a brief summary of the items placed in each column. The debit column includes the beginning inventories of raw materials and goods in process plus all the manufacturing costs of the period. The credit column contains credits for the ending inventories of raw materials and goods in process, and for offset accounts such as Raw Materials Returns and Allowances. The total of the amounts in the debit column exceeds the total of the credit column by $371,800. This debit balance represents the cost of goods manufactured and is extended to the Income Statement columns as a deduction from the revenues of the period.

Notice that the beginning and ending inventories of finished goods appear in the Income Statement columns but not in the Manufacturing columns. The illustration earlier in this chapter of separate buildings for factory operations and for the storage of finished goods was designed to emphasize that changes in the quantity of finished goods on hand are not a factor in computing the cost of goods that are manufactured in the factory.

Financial statements

Four financial statements for the Overland Manufacturing Corporation prepared from the illustrated work sheet on pages 702 to 705 are presented on pages 706 to 708. These statements are the balance sheet (Exhibit A, page 706), statement of retained earnings (Exhibit B, page 707), income statement (Exhibit C, pages 707 and 708), and statement of costs of goods manufactured (Exhibit D, page 708).

OVERLAND MANUFACTURING CORPORATION
Working Papers
For the Year Ended December 31, 1963

	Adjusted trial balance		Manufacturing	
	Dr	Cr	Dr	Cr
Cash	30,000			
Accounts receivable	40,000			
Allowance for bad debts		1,000		
Inventories, Dec. 31, 1962:				
Finished goods inventory	55,000			
Goods in process inventory	18,000		18,000	
Raw materials inventory	10,000		10,000	
Unexpired insurance	600			
Land	30,000			
Buildings	100,000			
Accumulated depreciation: Bldgs.		54,000		
Machinery & equipment	50,000			
Accumulated depreciation: M & E		20,000		
Furniture & fixtures	4,000			
Accumulated depreciation: F & F		1,200		
Patents	8,000			
Deferred research & developm't cost	12,000			
Accounts payable		43,200		
Accrued wages payable		800		
Federal income taxes payable		8,600		
Mortgage payable		80,000		
Capital stock		50,000		
Paid-in capital in excess of par		50,000		
Retained earnings (beginning)		48,200		
Dividends	6,000			
Sales		502,500		
Sales returns & allowances	2,500			
Raw materials purchases	100,000		100,000	
Purchase returns & allowances		1,000		1,000
Transportation-in	2,000		2,000	
Direct labor	171,750		171,750	
Indirect labor	67,250		67,250	
Heat, light, & power	6,000		4,800	
Property taxes & insurance	4,000		3,200	
Depreciation: buildings	2,500		2,000	
Totals forward	719,600	860,500	379,000	1,000

Income statement		Retained earnings		Balance sheet	
Dr	Cr	Dr	Cr	Dr	Cr
				30,000	
				40,000	
					1,000
55,000					
				600	
				30,000	
				100,000	
					54,000
				50,000	
					20,000
				4,000	
					1,200
				8,000	
				12,000	
					43,200
					800
					8,600
					80,000
					50,000
					50,000
			48,200		
		6,000			
	502,500				
2,500					
900G					
300S					
600G					
200S					
400G					
100S					
60,000	502,500	6,000	48,200	274,600	308,800

	Adjusted trial balance		Manufacturing	
	Dr	**Cr**	**Dr**	**Cr**
Totals brought forward	719,600	860,500	379,000	1,000
Depreciation: M & E	5,000		5,000	
Amortization of patents	2,800		2,800	
Research & development cost	8,000		8,000	
Miscellaneous factory cost	10,000		10,000	
Depreciation: F & F	400			
Advertising	14,000			
Sales salaries	32,000			
Miscellaneous selling expense	2,800			
Administrative salaries	40,000			
Office salaries	5,000			
Telephone & Telegraph	1,800			
Bad debts expense	2,700			
Miscellaneous general expense	2,800			
Interest expense	5,000			
Federal income taxes	8,600			
	860,500	860,500		
Inventories, Dec. 31, 1963:				
Finished goods inventory				
Goods in process inventory				20,000
Raw materials inventory				12,000
Cost of goods manufactured				371,800
			404,800	404,800
Net income				
Retained earnings (ending)				

Income statement		Retained earnings		Balance sheet	
Dr	Cr	Dr	Cr	Dr	Cr
60,000	502,500	6,000	48,200	274,600	308,800
400					
14,000					
32,000					
2,800					
40,000					
5,000					
1,800					
2,700					
2,800					
5,000					
8,600					
	62,800			62,800	
				20,000	
				12,000	
371,800					
18,400			18,400		
565,300	565,300				
		60,600			60,600
		66,600	66,600	369,400	369,400

OVERLAND MANUFACTURING CORPORATION   *Exhibit A*
Balance Sheet
December 31, 1963
Assets

Current assets:
Cash		$30,000
Accounts receivable	$40,000	
Less: allowance for bad debts	1,000	39,000
Inventories:		
Finished goods		62,800
Goods in process		20,000
Raw materials		12,000
Unexpired insurance		600
Total current assets		$164,400

Plant and equipment:

	Cost	Accumulated depreciation	Book value	
Land	$ 30,000		$30,000	
Buildings	100,000	$54,000	46,000	
Machinery & equipment	50,000	20,000	30,000	
Furniture & fixtures	4,000	1,200	2,800	
	$184,000	$75,200		108,800

Intangible assets:
Patents	$ 8,000	
Research and development	12,000	20,000
Total assets		$293,200

Liabilities and Stockholders' Equity

Current liabilities:
Accounts payable	$43,200	
Accrued wages payable	800	
Federal income tax payable	8,600	
Total current liabilities		$ 52,600

Mortgage payable, due 1975 80,000

Stockholders' equity:
Capital stock, par value $5,		
authorized and issued 10,000 shares	$50,000	
Additional paid-in capital	50,000	
Retained earnings, per Exhibit B	60,600	160,600
Total liabilities and stockholders' equity		$293,200

OVERLAND MANUFACTURING CORPORATION   Exhibit B
Statement of Retained Earnings
For the Year Ended December 31, 1963

Retained earnings at Dec. 31, 1962	$48,200
Net income for the year, per Exhibit C	18,400
Total	$66,600
Less: dividends	6,000
Retained earnings at Dec. 31, 1963	$60,600

OVERLAND MANUFACTURING CORPORATION   Exhibit C
Income Statement
For the Year Ended December 31, 1963

Gross sales		$502,500
Less: sales returns & allowances		2,500
Net sales		$500,000
Cost of goods sold:		
Finished goods inventory, Dec. 31, 1962	$ 55,000	
Cost of goods manufactured, per Exhibit D	371,800	
Total cost of finished goods available for sale	$426,800	
Less: finished goods inventory, Dec. 31, 1963	62,800	
Cost of goods sold		364,000
Gross profit on sales		$136,000
Operating expenses:		
Selling expenses:		
Advertising	$14,000	
Sales salaries	32,000	
Miscellaneous selling expense	2,800	
Heat, light, & power	300	
Property, taxes & insurance	200	
Depreciation: buildings	100	
Total selling expenses		$ 49,400
General and administrative expenses:		
Administrative salaries	$40,000	
Office salaries	5,000	
Telephone & telegraph	1,800	
Bad debts	2,700	
Miscellaneous general expense	2,800	
Heat, light & power	900	
Property taxes & insurance	600	
Depreciation: buildings	400	
Depreciation: furniture & fixtures	400	

Total general & administrative expenses	$ 54,600	104,000
Net income from operations		$ 32,000
Less: interest expense		5,000
Net income before Federal income taxes		$ 27,000
Federal income taxes		8,600
Net income		$ 18,400

OVERLAND MANUFACTURING CORPORATION   Exhibit D
Statement of Cost of Goods Manufactured
For the Year Ended December 31, 1963

Goods in process inventory, Dec. 31, 1962			$ 18,000
Raw materials:			
Inventory, Dec. 31, 1962		$ 10,000	
Purchases	$100,000		
Less: purchase returns & allowances	1,000	99,000	
Transportation-in		2,000	
Cost of raw materials available for use		$111,000	
Less: raw materials inventory, Dec. 31, 1963		12,000	
Cost of raw materials used		$ 99,000	
Direct labor		171,750	
Factory overhead:			
Indirect labor	$ 67,250		
Heat, light, & power	4,800		
Property taxes & insurance	3,200		
Depreciation: buildings	2,000		
Depreciation: machinery & equipment	5,000		
Amortization of patents	2,800		
Research & development cost	8,000		
Miscellaneous factory cost	10,000		
Total factory overhead		103,050	
Total manufacturing cost			373,800
Total of goods in process during the period			$391,800
Less: goods in process inventory, Dec. 31, 1963			20,000
Cost of goods manufactured			$371,800

Closing the books

The entries to close the books of a manufacturing concern can be taken directly from the work sheet. A Manufacturing account is opened by debiting it with the total of all the amounts listed in the Manufacturing debit column of the work sheet. A second entry is made crediting the Manufacturing account with the total of all the accounts listed in the Manufacturing credit column. These two entries serve to close out all the operating accounts used in computing the cost of goods manufactured.

1963
Dec. 31   *Manufacturing* 404,800
    Goods in Process Inventory, Dec. 31, 1962 .. *18,000*
    Raw Materials Inventory, Dec. 31, 1962 .... *10,000*
    Raw Materials Purchases *100,000*
    Transportation-in *2,000*
    Direct Labor *171,750*
    Indirect Labor *67,250*
    Heat, Light, & Power *4,800*
    Property Taxes & Insurance *3,200*
    Depreciation: Buildings *2,000*
    Depreciation: Machinery & Equipment *5,000*
    Amortization of Patents *2,800*
    Research & Development Cost *8,000*
    Miscellaneous Factory Cost *10,000*
  To close the manufacturing cost accounts into the
  summary account Manufacturing.

Dec. 31   *Purchase Returns & Allowances* *1,000*
    Goods in Process Inventory, Dec. 31, 1963 .... *20,000*
    Raw Materials Inventory, Dec. 31, 1963 .... *12,000*
    Manufacturing *33,000*
  To close the manufacturing accounts with credit
  balances and to record the ending inventories.

The next step in the closing procedure is to transfer the balance of the Manufacturing account to the Income Summary. Notice that this balance is the cost of goods manufactured.

1963
Dec. 31   *Income Summary* 371,800
    Manufacturing *371,800*
  To close the Manufacturing account.

The next closing entries consist of debiting and crediting the Income Summary account with all the items listed in the Income Statement columns of the work sheet. Although certain expense accounts, such as Heat, Light, and Power, were apportioned in the work sheet between general expense ($900) and selling expense ($300), the closing entry transfers the combined amount of $1,200 to the Income Summary account.

1963
Dec. 31   Income Summary 175,100
    Finished Goods Inventory, Dec. 31, 1962 ... 55,000
    Sales Returns & Allowances 2,500
    Heat, Light, & Power 1,200
    Property, Taxes & Insurance 800
    Depreciation: Buildings 500
    Depreciation: Furniture & Fixtures 400
    Advertising 14,000
    Sales Salaries 32,000
    Miscellaneous Selling Expense 2,800
    Administrative Salaries 40,000
    Office Salaries 5,000
    Telephone & Telegraph 1,800
    Bad Debts Expense 2,700
    Miscellaneous General Expense 2,800
    Interest Expense 5,000
    Federal Income Taxes 8,600
   To close the income statement accounts with debit
   balances.

Dec. 31   Sales 502,500
   Finished Goods Inventory, Dec. 31, 1963 62,800
    Income Summary 565,300
   To close the Sales account and to record the ending
   inventory of finished goods.

The preceding entries have produced in the Income Summary account a credit balance of $18,400, which represents the net income for the year. The closing process is completed by transferring the net income and the balance in the Dividends account to Retained Earnings.

1963
Dec. 31   Income Summary 18,400
    Retained Earnings 18,400
   To transfer the net income for the period to Retained
   Earnings.

  31   Retained Earnings 6,000
    Dividends 6,000
   To close the Dividends account to Retained Earnings.

Valuation of inventories in a manufacturing concern

Under the periodic method of inventory described in this chapter, a manufacturing concern determines inventory amounts on the basis of a physical count of raw materials, goods in process, and finished goods at the end of each accounting period. When the physical quantity of raw materials on hand has been established, the raw materials inventory is costed in the same manner as an inventory of merchandise in a trading concern. Cost is readily determinable by reference to purchase invoices. If the raw materials inventory is to be costed at the lower of cost or market, the "market" prices to be used are the current replacement costs for the materials on hand.

Costing the inventory of goods in process and the inventory of finished goods is usually a more difficult process. Cost can not be determined merely by pulling a purchase invoice out of the files. If a manufacturing plant produces only a single product, the cost per unit for the finished goods inventory can be computed by dividing the cost of goods manufactured by the number of units produced. For example, if the cost of goods manufactured were $100,000 in a given year, during which the factory turned out 1,000 identical units, the cost per unit would be $100. Most factories, however, produce more than one product, and the unit cost of each product must be determined by deriving from the accounting records the approximate amount of raw material, direct labor, and factory overhead applicable to each unit. In this situation the determination of cost of a unit of the work in process at the year-end requires the following steps:

1. Estimate the cost of the raw materials in the partially completed units.
2. Add the estimated direct labor cost incurred.
3. Add an appropriate amount of factory overhead.

This same procedure of computing a total cost by combining the three elements of manufacturing cost is followed in costing the finished goods inventory.

The raw material cost included in a unit of goods in process or a unit of finished goods may be established by inspection or by reference to the engineering specification for the article. The cost of the direct labor embodied in each unit may be estimated on the basis of tests and observations by supervisors of the direct labor time required per unit of output. In other words, both raw material cost and direct labor cost are directly associated with units of product.

The third element of manufacturing cost to be included in costing the inventory of goods in process is factory overhead, and this cost element is *not* directly related to units of output. Factory overhead, however, is usually related to the amount of direct labor. A factory overhead rate may, therefore, be computed by dividing the total factory overhead for the period by the total direct labor cost for the same period. The resulting factory overhead rate is then applied to the direct labor cost of the goods in process to determine the amount of factory overhead to be included in the inventory cost. In the illustrated statements of the Overland Manufacturing Corporation, the following amounts appear on the statement of cost of goods manufactured on page 708:

Direct labor cost	$171,750
Factory overhead	103,050

NOTE COST ELEMENTS IN INVENTORIES   The *factory overhead rate* is $103,050 ÷ $171,750, or 60%. This 60% rate was used in determining the ending inventories of goods in process and of finished goods, as shown by the following illustration:

Goods in Process Inventory

	Raw materials	Direct labor	Factory overhead (60%)	Total unit cost	Units in inventory	Total cost of inventory
Product X	$ 8	$10	$ 6	$ 24	500	$12,000
Product Y	20	50	30	100	80	8,000
Total						$20,000

Finished Goods Inventory

	Direct costs		Factory overhead (60%)	Total unit cost	Units in inventory	Total cost of inventory
	Raw materials	Direct labor				
Product X	$ 8	$ 20	$12	$ 40	820	$32,800
Product Y	60	150	90	300	100	30,000
Total						$62,800

Cost accounting and perpetual inventories

The periodic method of inventory and the related accounting procedures described in this chapter are used by many small manufacturing concerns, but these procedures have serious deficiencies and they do not constitute a cost accounting system. The shortcomings inherent in the use of periodic inventories by a manufacturing concern include the following:

1. The estimates used in computing the inventories of goods in process and finished goods are rough and inexact. Any inaccuracy in costing the inventories causes a corresponding error in net income for the period.

2. Taking and costing inventories is so time-consuming that it usually is done only once a year; consequently, operating statements are not available to management at sufficiently frequent intervals.

3. Cost data available to management are not sufficiently detailed to afford a sound basis for control of operations.

The greater the number of products being manufactured, the more critical these deficiencies become. Management needs detailed day-to-day information on the costs of each product being manufactured. Decision making with respect to possible discontinuance of certain products or increases in the output of other articles requires current detailed reporting of cost data. An accurate determination of costs for individual products is also very useful in setting selling prices. Many progressive manufacturing concerns achieve control of costs and operations by the preparation of budgets which indicate far in advance what the outlays for material, labor, and factory overhead *should* be. The accounting records and procedures are so designed as to provide a steady flow of reports summarizing actual cost results for comparison with the budgeted figures. A key step in providing the cost information needed by management for planning and controlling manufacturing operations with optimum efficiency is the maintenance of perpetual inventories.

Cost accounting is a specialized field of accounting, with the objective of providing management with means of planning and controlling manufacturing operations. A cost accounting system is characterized by the maintenance of perpetual inventories and by the development of cost figures for each unit of product manufactured. An introduction to the subject of cost accounting is presented in the following chapter.

QUESTIONS

1. Name and describe the nature of the three main elements of manufacturing cost.

2. Explain the distinction between "product" and "period" costs under the "full cost" concept. Why is this distinction made?

3. Into which of the three elements of manufacturing cost would each of the following be classified?

    a. Cost of preparing the factory payroll

    b. Wages paid to persons who inspect finished product for imperfections

    c. Cost of subscription to trade magazine for the engineering department

    d. Oil and grease used in machinery maintenance

    e. Foam-rubber padding used in manufacture of furniture

    f. Unemployment compensation tax paid on wages of machine operators

4. What is the purpose of the Manufacturing Summary account?

5. Distinguish between cost of goods manufactured and total manufacturing cost.

6. When a given expense is applicable partly to manufacturing and partly to the administrative or selling functions, how is this allocation handled in the working papers? Discuss a possible alternative method.

7. Explain how the ending inventories of raw materials, goods in process, and finished goods are determined under a physical inventory system, and when they are entered in the accounts.

8. What are the major shortcomings of the periodic inventory method for a manufacturing concern?

PROBLEMS

Group A

25A-1. *Instructions.* On the basis of the information given below, taken from the books of Barren Corporation, prepare a schedule of costs of goods sold for the month of August.

    Data

Inventories:	Aug. 1	Aug. 31
Raw materials	$16,720	$23,100
Finished goods	24,650	18,900
Goods in process	9,600	21,500

	Month of August
Direct labor	$125,300
General expense control	62,370
Factory overhead control	78,430
Raw material purchase returns	3,600
Selling expense control	49,350
Transportation-in on raw materials	11,740
Raw material purchase discounts	1,720
Purchases of raw materials	86,000

25A-2. The account balances listed below were taken from the adjusted trial balance prepared from the records of the Mencel Corporation on August 31. The assistant controller noted, in a report on inventory changes since August 1, that "the inventory of raw materials is down 10%; our work in process inventory has been cut in half; and the finished goods inventory has risen 20%."

Account	Balance, Aug. 31
Administrative expense control	$ 48,720
Direct labor	83,000
Finished goods inventory, Aug. 1	31,600
Interest revenues	1,800
Manufacturing overhead control	66,400
Purchases of raw materials	102,000
Purchase returns and allowances	8,500
Raw materials inventory, Aug. 1	64,300
Sales	342,000
Sales discounts allowed	7,800
Selling expense control	33,250
Work in process inventory, Aug. 1	24,300

Instructions. On the basis of this information, make all closing entries as of August 31.

25A-3. The accounts shown below appear on the books of the Genor Manufacturing Company at the close of its current fiscal year ending April 30. All amounts relate solely to manufacturing activities.

Direct labor	$136,000
Transportation-in	7,960
Heat, light, and power	8,640
Property taxes and insurance	5,400
Depreciation expense: buildings	7,500
Raw materials purchases	106,700
Depreciation expense: equipment	5,200
Research and development cost	12,460
Raw materials returns and allowances	5,400
Indirect labor	28,200
Supervisory salaries	18,000
General factory expense	4,120
Raw materials inventory, beginning of year	21,570
Goods in process inventory, beginning of year	32,600
Maintenance and repair expense	8,400

Inventories taken at April 30 indicate that raw materials on hand cost $18,430, and that $15,000 of direct labor and $18,300 of direct materials have been applied to the unfinished goods in process at the end of the current fiscal year.

Instructions

a. Prepare a schedule of factory overhead for the year.

b. Determine the cost of the ending inventory of goods in process, assuming that the amount of overhead applicable to the inventory is related to direct labor cost.

c. Prepare a statement of cost of goods manufactured. Factory overhead may be shown as a single total figure as determined in (a).

25A-4. On December 31, 1962, the trial balance given below was prepared from the records of the Harwood Manufacturing Company:

Cash	$ 86,400	
Accounts receivable	54,300	
Allowance for bad debts		$ 1,700
Inventories, Jan. 1, 1962:		
Raw materials	15,800	
Goods in process	21,300	
Finished goods	32,450	
Supplies on hand	14,620	
Unexpired insurance	5,700	
Land	25,000	
Buildings	340,000	
Accumulated depreciation: buildings		83,600
Equipment	280,000	
Accumulated depreciation: equipment ...		112,000
Patents	37,500	
Accounts payable		62,580
Accrued expenses		34,630
Mortgage payable		150,000
Capital stock		300,000
Retained earnings, Jan. 1, 1962		74,690
Dividends	18,000	
Sales		996,000
Sales returns and allowances	7,200	
Sales discounts	16,300	
Purchases: raw materials	276,000	
Purchase returns and allowances		12,300
Purchase discounts		4,190
Transportation-in	22,960	
Direct labor	243,000	
Indirect labor	87,920	
Building occupancy expense	36,600	
Equipment depreciation and maintenance	11,000	
Taxes and insurance	7,600	
General factory expense	15,400	
Advertising	21,000	
Sales salaries	45,200	
General selling expense	8,400	
Administrative salaries	56,000	
Office expense	25,700	
Miscellaneous general expense	12,540	
Interest expense	9,000	
Interest revenue		1,200
	$1,832,890	$1,832,890

Other data. The following information has been compiled as a basis for adjusting entries:

(a) Inventories, Dec. 31, 1962:

Raw materials	*$23,700*
Goods in process	*30,500*
Finished goods	*41,300*

(b) Supplies used during the year: manufacturing supplies, $4,300; selling supplies, $3,800; office and administrative supplies, $2,400. (Use a single expense account and make the allocation on the working papers.)

(c) Unexpired insurance at December 31, 1962: $2,300.

(d) Salaries and wages due but unpaid at year-end: direct labor, $8,700; indirect labor, $4,200; sales salaries, $2,700; administrative salaries, $3,300.

(e) Depreciation on building (charge Building Occupancy), $8,400.

(f) Depreciation on equipment (charge Equipment Depreciation and Maintenance), $14,000.

(g) The average remaining life of patents held was five years from the beginning of 1962.

(h) The provision for uncollectible receivables has been charged to Miscellaneous General Expense. An analysis of receivables at year-end indicates that an adequate allowance would be $3,100.

(i) The following expenses are allocated as indicated:

	Factory	*Selling*	*Adminis-trative*
Building occupancy	*70%*	*20%*	*10%*
Equipment depreciation and			
maintenance	*60%*	*10%*	*30%*
Taxes and insurance	*40%*	*25%*	*35%*

(j) The provision for income taxes for the current year has been estimated at $33,000.

(k) On December 28, 1962, a customer paid a $12,000 invoice and was allowed a 2% cash discount. The bookkeeper, in recording the transaction, credited Accounts Receivable for $11,760.

Instructions

a. Prepare working papers. When listing the accounts and amounts in the trial balance, allow two lines for the following accounts: Building occupancy expense, Equipment depreciation and maintenance, Taxes and insurance, Supplies used.

b. Prepare a schedule of cost of goods manufactured.

c. Prepare an income statement.

d. Prepare a balance sheet. Include a statement of retained earnings in the stockholders' equity section.

e. Assuming that all adjusting entries have been made and recorded in the ledger accounts, prepare the entries necessary to close the books at December 31, 1962.

25A-5. *Instructions.* On the basis of the information given below and the data that can be derived from it, prepare a statement of cost of goods manufactured for the Glass Company for the quarter ended March 31 of the current year.

Data

For the quarter ended March 31:

Cost of goods manufactured $712,100

Factory overhead 131,040

Beginning inventories, Jan. 1:

Raw materials 48,500

Goods in process 36,200

Finished goods 39,700

Ending inventories, Mar. 31:

	Raw materials	Goods in process	Finished goods
Materials	$45,716	$16,340	$ 47,800
Labor		21,000	35,400
Overhead		?	21,240
	$45,716	?	$104,440

The company paid transportation costs on materials purchased of $28,640; it received credit of $19,460 for materials returned to suppliers.

Group B

25B-1. *Instructions.* The two closing entries shown below appear on the books of Haskins Tool Company at the close of the current year. From this information, prepare a statement of cost of goods manufactured for the year.

Data

Manufacturing 140,002

Raw Materials Inventory 9,216

Goods in Process Inventory 8,732

Purchases of Raw Materials 72,379

Transportation-in 2,752

Direct Labor 19,066

Indirect Labor 20,345

Factory Lease Expense 2,750

Occupancy Cost 1,823

Machinery Repairs and Maintenance 1,234

Taxes and Insurance 748

Depreciation: Machinery 957

Purchase Returns and Allowances 2,348

Purchase Discounts 1,184

Raw Materials Inventory 9,743

Goods in Process Inventory 5,462

Manufacturing 18,737

25B-2. On November 1 the inventories of the Willcox Company were: raw materials, $5,400; goods in process, $3,200; and finished goods, $8,300. On November 30 the cost accountant reports that total manufacturing costs for the month were as follows: raw materials used, $184,600; direct labor, $180,000; factory overhead, $126,000.

Willcox Company manufactures a product in three models, designated K, L, and M. Unit costs information for each model for November is:

Product	Raw material cost	Direct labor cost
K	$1.50	$2.60
L	3.00	3.00
M	4.60	3.40

Overhead is allocated to products on the basis of its relation to direct labor cost. At the end of November, physical inventories were taken. The ending inventory of raw materials totaled $4,380. The ending inventories of goods in process and finished goods, by models, were as follows:

	Units of Product		
	K	L	M
In process, fully complete as to materials, and 50% complete as to labor and overhead	300	200	100
Finished product	1,000	800	500

Instructions
a. Determine the valuation of the ending inventories of goods in-process and finished goods at cost.
b. Compute the cost of goods manufactured for November.
c. Compute the cost of goods sold for November.

25B-3. At the end of September the bookkeeper of the Barker Manufacturing Company reported the results shown below for the month of September:

Cost of goods manufactured	$128,640
Cost of goods sold	131,000
Net income	34,000

The company auditor, after reviewing the records, reports that he has discovered the following errors:

(1) The inventory of raw materials on hand at September 30 did not include

materials costing $900 which were on hand but were inadvertently missed in taking the inventory.

(2) The following expenses, which apply in part to selling and administrative functions, were charged entirely to factory overhead:

	Total	Manu-facturing	Selling	Adminis-trative
Building occupancy ...	$22,700	$12,800	$3,200	$6,700
Taxes and insurance ...	4,200	3,000	200	1,000

(3) Sales returns and allowances of $1,300 were treated as a part of factory overhead.

(4) Research and development costs of $3,000, charged to expense during the month of September, are applicable to future production.

(5) As the result of the above errors, the goods in process inventory at September 30 was overstated by $1,700, and the finished goods inventory was overstated by $2,300.

Instructions

a. Determine the proper amount of the cost of goods manufactured, the cost of goods sold, and the net income for the Barker Company. Set up a working paper with three columns headed: Cost of goods manufactured, Cost of goods sold, and Net income, and enter the amounts of each as determined by the bookkeeper. In the space below, explain the effect of each of the above errors, and show the amount that should be added to or subtracted from the bookkeeper's figures to arrive at the corrected totals.

b. Did the company's finished goods inventory, as corrected, increase or decrease during September, and by what amount?

25B-4. The adjusted trial balance taken from the records of the Drybo Manufacturing Company on September 30, 1962, the end of its fiscal year, is given below.

DRYBO MANUFACTURING COMPANY
Adjusted Trial Balance
September 30, 1962

Cash	$ 27,600	
Accounts receivable	43,800	
Allowance for bad debts		$ 2,800
Raw materials inventory, Oct. 1, 1961	23,400	
Goods in process inventory, Oct. 1, 1961	16,200	
Finished goods inventory, Oct. 1, 1961	9,500	
Prepaid expenses	4,300	
Factory machinery	270,000	

Accumulated depreciation: factory machinery		65,000
Sales and office equipment	128,000	
Accumulated depreciation: sales & office equipment		48,000
Research and development cost	15,400	
Accounts payable		32,400
Accrued expenses		18,800
Income taxes payable		25,700
Capital stock		200,000
Additional paid in capital		40,000
Retained earnings, Oct. 1, 1961		72,500
Loss on sale of factory machinery	20,000	
Sales		845,000
Sales returns	6,200	
Raw material purchases	173,500	
Purchase returns		8,700
Transportation-in	24,300	
Direct labor	286,200	
Factory overhead (control)	134,700	
Selling expense (control)	86,200	
Administrative expense (control)	63,900	
Provision for income taxes	25,700	
	$1,358,900	$1,358,900

Inventories at September 30, 1962, were as follows:

Raw materials inventory	$18,200
Goods in process inventory	23,300
Finished goods inventory	12,600

Instructions. Prepare
  a. Working papers
  b. Statement of cost of goods manufactured
  c. Income statement
  d. Balance sheet (including retained earnings statement)

25B-5. The Springfield plant of Akre Industries manufactures a standard subassembly which it sells under an annual contract at a fixed price. The plant manager has prepared a manufacturing budget for the current year which calls for the production of 15,000 units at an average unit cost of $75; this is composed of raw material cost $24, direct labor cost $30, and factory overhead $21.

The plant had no inventory of work in process at the beginning of the year. During the current year 20,000 units of product were put into production, and 14,000 units were completely finished. The 6,000 units in process at the end of the year were fully complete as to materials but were only 50% completed, on the average, as to labor and factory overhead.

The cost data shown below were taken from the plant records at the end of the current year:

Raw materials inventory, beginning of year	$ 60,000
Raw materials inventory, end of year	40,000
Raw material purchases (net)	380,000
Direct labor	510,000
Indirect labor	182,000
Factory supplies used	28,000
Repairs and maintenance	24,000
Patent royalties	30,000
Building occupancy cost	86,000
Equipment depreciation	16,000
General factory overhead	42,000

Instructions

a. Determine the unit costs of product completed during the current year in terms of each of the three cost elements: raw materials, direct labor, and overhead. (Hint: In order to do this, it will be necessary to estimate the total production for the year in terms of units of completed product.)

b. Determine a reasonable valuation for the ending inventory of goods in process at the end of the current year.

c. Write a brief report explaining the difference between actual unit costs and those expected at the beginning of the year.

26

Cost accounting: a tool of management

Cost accounting serves two important managerial objectives: to determine product costs, and to control the cost of business operations.

Product costs are determined by relating prices paid for materials, labor, and overhead expenses to some unit of output or accomplishment. Product cost information has some influence on pricing decisions; it also provides a basis for inventory valuation needed to measure periodic business income.

Controlling costs is a part of management's general responsibility for carrying on the functions of a business efficiently and economically. Knowing the cost of making a product, performing a manufacturing operation, or carrying on some function of a business is a starting point in control. By comparing detailed cost data with budgets, standards, or other yardsticks, management finds a basis for controlling costs and planning operations.

A *cost accounting system* is a method of developing cost information within the framework of general ledger accounts. Because cost accounting is more highly developed in manufacturing industries, we shall focus our attention on manufacturing costs. The need for cost information, however, is much broader than this. Many of the procedures used to obtain manufacturing costs are applicable to a variety of cost problems and have been used by retailers, wholesalers, and such service organizations as hospitals, public utilities, and banks, to determine the cost of performing various service functions.

Problems of cost determination

A common misconception about accounting figures is that the cost of any product or unit of output can be measured with precision.

There are two basic reasons why it is usually impossible to determine *the cost* of anything with a high degree of accuracy: First, the relationship between the costs incurred and the output produced is often difficult to establish. Secondly, a number of different relationships may be found, each useful for different purposes, but none of which can really claim to be *the* cost. Let us consider these two problems briefly:

Relating costs to output. The process of relating costs to units of output has two stages. The first stage, common to all phases of accounting, is to measure the cost of all resources used up in the total productive effort of a given accounting period. Dividing the cost of asset services among accounting periods is more a matter of judgment than arithmetic. For example, raw materials and supplies are purchased at different unit prices. Determining which prices are applicable to materials and supplies used during the period, and which to materials and supplies on hand for future use requires some rather arbitrary assumptions (such as fifo, lifo, or weighted average). The services of long-lived assets, such as plant and equipment, are purchased in "bundles" and used up over a number of accounting periods. Both the total service life of such assets and the relative amount and value of services withdrawn from the bundle each period are uncertain. The portion of the total cost of the asset to be charged against the production of any given accounting period is therefore, at best, an educated guess. The total cost (materials, labor, and overhead) for any accounting period is affected by these estimates and the choice of procedures adopted in resolving these uncertainties. The point is that even total cost is not a precise figure.

The second stage in cost accounting is to relate total manufacturing cost to the output of any given accounting period. This, also, is a process fraught with difficulties. Almost all total cost figures include elements of common or joint costs which cannot be traced directly to any given unit of output and which must therefore be assigned or allocated on some reasonable, but necessarily arbitrary, basis. For example, some part of the cost of a barrel of crude oil is clearly a part of the cost of each product (gasoline, fuel oil, lubricating oil) that emerges from the refinery, but no one can determine exactly how the cost of crude oil should be divided among these products. Similarly, some part of the salary of the plant manager is a cost of operating each department within the plant, but the precise portion cannot be determined for any particular department. Is the cost of training a new employee chargeable to his production during the training period, or to production after he is fully trained? Resolving these issues and assigning such costs to products or processes is the distinguishing feature of cost accounting.

Different costs for different purposes. The second reason why it is meaningless to talk about *the* cost of anything is that for different purposes different relationships between costs and output may be useful. In reporting on the over-all position and progress of a business, cost information is needed primarily to determine the valuation of raw materials, goods in process, and finished goods inventories on the balance sheet, and the cost of goods sold figure on the income statement. For these purposes total manufacturing costs are usually associated with the flow of products through the factory to determine the "full" cost of products sold and those on hand at the end of the accounting period.

Cost information is also used, however, as a basis for managerial decisions. For these purposes certain portions of the total cost figure may not be significant. For example, consider the cost of heating a factory building. In arriving at inventory valuation and cost of goods sold, some portion of the heating cost must be allocated to the various operations and in turn to the production of the period. If the decision is whether or not to shut down the plant, only the cost of stand-by heating is a significant factor. In a study of the operating efficiency of factory foremen, the cost of heating the building is largely outside their control and should be ignored. If we are planning the addition of a wing to the building, the *change* in the heating cost as a result of the addition is the significant cost figure. Thus for some purposes the entire heating cost is useful, for some only a part of the heating cost is relevant, and for still other purposes this cost may be omitted altogether.

If cost data are to be used intelligently, the user must understand that any cost figure has inherent limitations and that no single method of arriving at cost will serve equally well all the varied purposes for which such information is needed. Most cost systems are designed to meet the general purpose of income determination and to develop in the accounts the basic data from which cost studies for special purposes can proceed. In the balance of this chapter the basic techniques of cost accounting will be briefly described.

Flow of costs through perpetual inventories

In the previous chapter we saw that even when periodic inventories are used, certain over-all cost information can be obtained. Under the periodic inventory system, however, much potentially useful information is buried in totals, cost data are available only at infrequent intervals, and the details of product or departmental costs are not available. The first step in setting up a cost system, therefore, is to establish perpetual inventories.

The cost elements that enter into the valuation of inventories are called *product costs;* costs that are charged against revenues in the period in which they are incurred are called *period costs.* In the typical manufacturing company product costs are limited to manufacturing costs, as distinguished from selling, general administrative, and financial expenses. The flow of costs through perpetual inventories is therefore usually limited to direct materials, direct labor, and factory overhead.

Three perpetual inventory accounts are used to trace the flow of costs to the flow of product through the manufacturing operations:

1. Stores (raw materials and factory supplies)
2. Goods in process (product in the process of manufacture)
3. Finished goods (completed product)

As an aid in visualizing basic cost flows, a diagram is given below. The arrows show the flow of costs through the perpetual inventory accounts; arrows connecting two items indicate the two sides of an accounting entry. Thus the use of raw materials reduces the Stores Inventory account and increases the Goods in Process Inventory. Some items are not connected with arrows because the accounts appearing in the diagram are not complete. For example, the debit to Stores Inventory for materials and supplies purchased is offset by a credit to Vouchers Payable, which is not included on the diagram.

Note that when all the indicated entries have been made, the balance in the Stores Inventory, Goods in Process Inventory, and Finished Goods Inventory accounts represent the dollar valuation of these inventories.

Even under a perpetual inventory system it will be advisable to take a physical inventory at various times to verify the accuracy of the book figure and to disclose losses due to waste, theft, or breakage that for one reason or another are not recorded in the accounts.

ARROWS
SHOW FLOW
OF COSTS

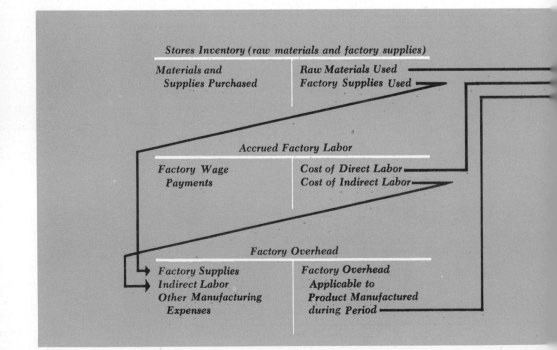

Two basic types of cost systems

There are two distinct types of formal cost systems; an end product of each is the average unit cost of physical output.

Under a *job order cost system,* the focal point of costing is a particular quantity of finished product known as a *job* or *lot.* The cost of raw materials, direct labor, and factory overhead applicable to each job is compiled and divided by the number of finished units in the job to arrive at average unit cost.

The following summary report on a completed job is illustrative:

THE COST OF ONE JOB OR LOT

Job Order Cost Sheet

. Job No. 101	Product A	Units completed: 1,000

Direct materials used $17,500
Direct labor cost applicable to this job 30,000
Factory overhead applicable to this job 22,500

Total cost of job No. 101 .... $70,000
Average cost per unit ($70,000 ÷ 1,000) .... $ 70

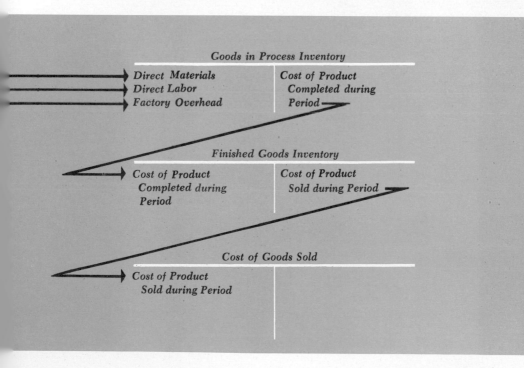

Goods in Process Inventory

Direct Materials
Direct Labor
Factory Overhead

Cost of Product
Completed during
Period

Finished Goods Inventory

Cost of Product
Completed during
Period

Cost of Product
Sold during Period

Cost of Goods Sold

Cost of Product
Sold during Period

Under a *process cost system,* the focal points in costing are the various departments or processes in the production cycle. First the cost of raw materials, labor, and factory overhead applicable to each department or process for *a given period of time* is compiled. Then the average cost of running a unit of product through each department is determined by dividing the total departmental cost by the number of units processed during the period.

When a product moves through two or more departments, the total unit cost of finished product is built up by tracing the costs incurred in each department to the product as it moves from process to process. The following process cost accounts for two departments illustrate how this is done.

BUILD-UP OF COSTS IN TWO PROCESSES

Goods in Process, Department X

Raw material cost	$ 4,000	Transferred to Dept. Y, 1,000	
Departmental labor	5,000	units @ $12	$12,000
Factory overhead applicable			
to department	3,000		
	$12,000		
Units produced	1,000		
Unit cost ($12,000 ÷ 1,000)	$ 12		

Goods in Process, Department Y

From Dept. X (1,000 units		Transferred to finished goods	
@ $12)	$12,000	inventory, 1,000 units @	
Materials added	1,200	$24	$24,000
Departmental labor	6,000		
Factory overhead applicable			
to department	4,800		
	$24,000		
Units produced	1,000		
Unit cost ($24,000 ÷ 1,000)	$ 24		

Each kind of cost system (job order and process) has advantages in particular manufacturing situations. Both are widely used; sometimes a combination of the two systems is found within the same company. In the sections that follow we shall examine briefly the basic structure of the two systems.

JOB ORDER COST SYSTEM

When should job order costs be used?

In general, a job order cost system is applicable when each product or lot of product is significantly different. It is the only system possible in the construction industry, for example, since each construction project is to some extent unique. Job order cost systems are also used in the machine tool, job printing, and motion picture industries for similar reasons.

An essential requirement of a job order system is that each specific lot of product can be identified in each step of the manufacturing operation. Through the use of various subsidiary detailed cost records, the cost of raw materials, direct labor, and factory overhead applicable to each job is recorded on a *job cost sheet*, so that when the job is finished the total and per unit cost of the job can be computed.

Job order cost flow chart

A flow chart showing the accounts used in a simple job order cost system, together with lines indicating the flow of data from one account to another, appears on pages 730 and 731. We shall use the figures in this illustration to outline the essential features of job order costing.

The flow chart contains figures representing one month's operations for a hypothetical manufacturing company. The company manufactures three products, identified as Product A, Product B, and Product C. Three kinds of raw materials (Materials X, Y, and Z) are used in the manufacturing process. Each of the three perpetual inventory accounts (Stores, Goods in Process, Finished Goods) is supported by subsidiary ledger records in which the details of the flow of costs are recorded.

Stores (materials and supplies). Accounting for the purchase and use of materials and supplies is a straightforward application of the use of perpetual inventories. The summary entries in the Stores Inventory control account are matched by detailed entries in the subsidiary ledger accounts as follows:

1. The $17,000 beginning balance in the Store Inventory control account is equal to the beginning balances in the subsidiary stores ledger accounts.

2. The record in the subsidiary ledger accounts for the quantity and cost of materials purchased is made from information on suppliers' invoices. The stores purchased ($58,000) was posted in total from the voucher register.

3. Materials and factory supplies are issued on the basis of *requisitions,* which show the quantity needed and the identity of the job on which raw materials are to be used or the factory overhead account to which supplies should be charged.

**JOB ORDER
FLOW
CHART:
BASIC
REFERENCE**

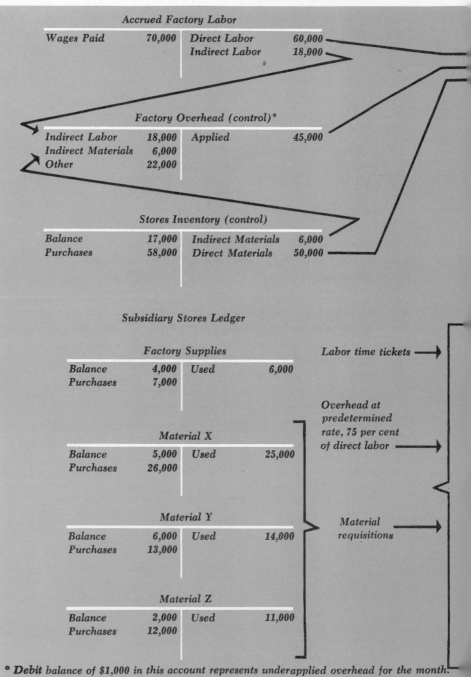

Accrued Factory Labor

Wages Paid	70,000	Direct Labor	60,000
		Indirect Labor	18,000

Factory Overhead (control)°

Indirect Labor	18,000	Applied	45,000
Indirect Materials	6,000		
Other	22,000		

Stores Inventory (control)

Balance	17,000	Indirect Materials	6,000
Purchases	58,000	Direct Materials	50,000

Subsidiary Stores Ledger

Factory Supplies

Balance	4,000	Used	6,000
Purchases	7,000		

Labor time tickets ⟶

Overhead at
predetermined
rate, 75 per cent
of direct labor ⟶

Material X

Balance	5,000	Used	25,000
Purchases	26,000		

Material Y

Balance	6,000	Used	14,000
Purchases	13,000		

Material
requisitions ⟶

Material Z

Balance	2,000	Used	11,000
Purchases	12,000		

° **Debit** *balance of $1,000 in this account represents underapplied overhead for the month.*

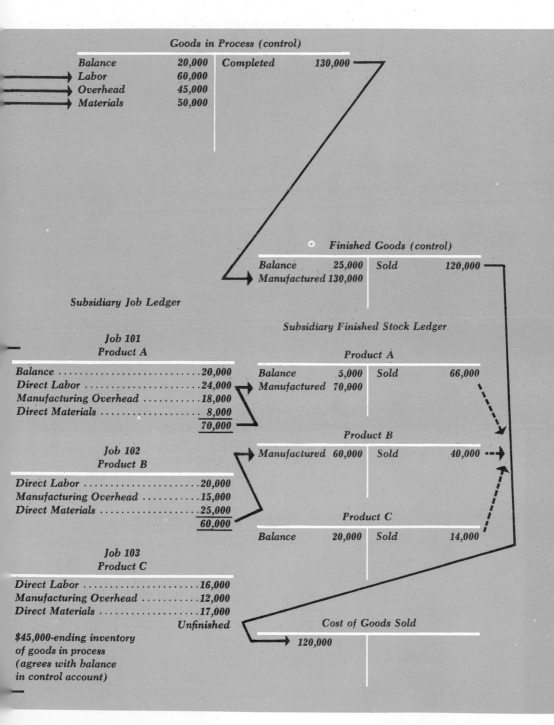

Goods in Process (control)

Balance	20,000	Completed	130,000
Labor	60,000		
Overhead	45,000		
Materials	50,000		

Finished Goods (control)

| Balance | 25,000 | Sold | 120,000 |
| Manufactured | 130,000 | | |

Subsidiary Job Ledger

Job 101
Product A

Balance	20,000
Direct Labor	24,000
Manufacturing Overhead	18,000
Direct Materials	8,000
	70,000

Job 102
Product B

Direct Labor	20,000
Manufacturing Overhead	15,000
Direct Materials	25,000
	60,000

Job 103
Product C

Direct Labor	16,000
Manufacturing Overhead	12,000
Direct Materials	17,000
	Unfinished

$45,000-ending inventory
of goods in process
(agrees with balance
in control account)

Subsidiary Finished Stock Ledger

Product A

| Balance | 5,000 | Sold | 66,000 |
| Manufactured | 70,000 | | |

Product B

| Manufactured | 60,000 | Sold | 40,000 |

Product C

| Balance | 20,000 | Sold | 14,000 |

Cost of Goods Sold

| 120,000 | |

4. The stores clerk refers to individual stores ledger cards to get the cost of each item requisitioned, and enters this on the requisition form. Since purchases are at different prices, costing stores used requires some systematic cost flow assumption such as lifo, fifo, or weighted average. A summary of the stores requisitions for the month becomes the basis for the entry crediting Stores Inventory ($56,000) and charging Goods in Process ($50,000) and Factory Overhead ($6,000) with the cost of material and supplies used.

DETAILED STORES RECORD FOR MATERIAL "X"

In the cost flow diagram, subsidiary stores ledger accounts are shown in T-account form; in practice they would contain more detailed unit cost information. An illustrative stores ledger card, showing the record for Material X during the month, appears below:

Stores Ledger Card
Material X

Ref no.*	Received			Issued			Balance	
	Quantity	Unit cost	Amount	Quantity	Unit cost †	Amount	Quantity	Balance
Balance							2,500	$ 5,000
47	5,000	$2.20	$11,000				7,500	16,000
3				2,500	$2.00	$5,000		
				4,000	2.20	8,800	1,000	2,200
98	7,500	2.00	15,000				8,500	17,200
6				1,000	2.20	2,200		
				4,500	2.00	9,000	3,000	6,000

* *Identifying number of invoice or requisition from which data were taken*
† *Fifo basis*

Factory labor. Payment of factory employees usually occurs after the services have been performed. During the pay period, detailed records of time, rates of pay, and the jobs on which employees worked must be kept in order to compile the necessary cost data. The wages earned by employees who work directly on job production are charged to each job. The wages earned by employees whose work is not directly associated with any particular job or quantity of product are charged to factory overhead.

A number of mechanical means have been devised for compiling payroll information. A common system, which is illustrative, is to prepare *time tickets* for each employee, showing the time worked on each job, the rates of pay, and the total cost chargeable to each job. These tickets, summarized periodically, become the basis for preparing the payroll and paying factory employees. They also become the basis for entries on various job cost sheets showing the direct labor cost incurred.

In the cost flow diagram on pages 730 and 731, $60,000 of direct labor was charged to the three jobs in process and $18,000 of indirect labor was charged to factory overhead. Of the total wage cost of $78,000, only $70,000 was actually paid during the period. The balance of $8,000 in the Accrued Factory Labor account represents the liability for unpaid wages at the end of the month.

Factory overhead. Included in this category are all manufacturing costs other than direct labor and direct materials. The Factory Overhead account is usually a control account; details of individual manufacturing expenses are kept in subsidiary ledger or expense analysis records. The source of individual overhead charges varies. Indirect labor charges are summarized from payroll records; factory supplies used are summarized from stores requisitions. Charges for such current services as electricity and water are posted from the voucher register. Depreciation on plant and equipment, the expiration of prepaid expenses, and overhead expenses resulting from accrued liabilities (for example, property taxes) are recorded as adjusting entries.

The problem in dealing with factory overhead lies not so much in computing total overhead cost as in relating overhead costs to output. Dividing total overhead cost by the number of units or lots of product will not ordinarily produce a meaningful figure, since various units or lots of product are significantly different. A more promising idea is to relate overhead costs, which cannot be directly identified with any particular quantity of output, and some other cost factor that *can* be so identified. Many overhead costs either are a function of time (for example, building rent, foreman's salary) or tend to vary with the amount of labor or machine time involved in manufacture. For these reasons charging factory overhead against various jobs in proportion to the amount of direct labor cost, direct labor hours, or machine hours is a reasonable and a widely used procedure.

Assume for the moment that direct labor cost is the basis chosen for overhead apportionment. Since actual factory overhead and actual direct labor cost will not be known until the end of an accounting period, the factory overhead rate is predetermined by making an advanced estimate of each factor. For example, if factory overhead for the year is estimated to be $540,000 and direct labor cost is estimated at $720,000, the factory overhead rate will be 75% of direct labor cost. For every dollar of direct labor cost incurred on a job, 75 cents of factory overhead will be charged or applied.

Actual overhead cost will be accumulated in the Factory Overhead control account. As manufacturing proceeds and direct labor cost is charged against jobs, overhead will also be applied to jobs at the predetermined rate. The total amount of applied overhead will be debited to

Goods in Process and credited to Factory Overhead.[1] In the flow diagram on page 731, the total direct labor charged against jobs during the month was $60,000 and 75% of this amount, or $45,000, was applied as the overhead cost applicable to these jobs.

Over- or underapplied overhead. We should not expect that applied overhead will ever exactly equal actual overhead, since the predetermined overhead rate was based on estimates. A debit balance in the Factory Overhead account at the end of a period indicates that actual expenses exceeded overhead applied to jobs; a credit balance shows that overhead applied was greater than actual expense.

What is the significance of the amount of over- or underapplied overhead at the end of any period? This is a major issue in cost accounting, which can be discussed only briefly here. Basically there are two interpretations, each leading to a different procedure:

1. *There has been an error in allocating actual overhead against the production of the period.* This interpretation suggests that the error should be corrected by apportioning over- or underapplied overhead among the Goods in Process Inventory, the Finished Goods Inventory, and Cost of Goods Sold on some reasonable basis to restate them at "actual" cost. Often the entire amount is charged to Cost of Goods Sold, on the ground that most of the error applied to goods sold during the period.

2. *Actual overhead incurred during the period differs from the normal overhead absorbed by the production of the period.* Under this interpretation, inventories are priced on the basis of predetermined overhead rates, and any balance of over- or underapplied overhead is charged to Income Summary as a special adjustment reflecting *abnormal* conditions of that period.

Since the bases used in applying overhead (direct labor, machine hours) vary with production and many elements of overhead do not, overhead will tend to be *underapplied* during months of low production, and *overapplied* during months of high production. To avoid variations in unit product costs due to monthly variations in volume of output, the difference between actual and applied overhead is usually carried forward from month to month, and the overapplied overhead of one month offset against the underapplied overhead of another. At the end of the year, any net balance of over- or underapplied overhead is then handled in accordance with one of the two basic interpretations described above.

Goods in process. The Goods in Process Inventory is charged with the cost of direct materials, direct labor, and an estimate of overhead expenses applicable to all jobs. The supporting subsidiary ledger records for this control account are the job cost sheets relating to each job in process

[1] Some accountants feel that actual overhead charges and applied overhead credits should not be mixed in the same account. Therefore they credit applied overhead to a special account called Applied Factory Overhead which has a credit balance until closed at the end of an accounting period.

during the period. In the cost flow diagram on pages 730 and 731, note the relation between entries in the control account and the subsidiary ledger accounts, summarized below:

Goods in Process, Control Account		Job Cost Sheets		
Beginning balance	$ 20,000	Job No. 101	Balance	$20,000
		Job No. 101	Labor	24,000
Direct labor on jobs	60,000	Job No. 102	Labor	20,000
		Job No. 103	Labor	16,000
Factory overhead applied to		Job No. 101	Overhead	18,000
jobs	45,000	Job No. 102	Overhead	15,000
		Job No. 103	Overhead	12,000
		Job No. 101	Materials	8,000
Raw materials used on jobs	50,000	Job No. 102	Materials	25,000
		Job No. 103	Materials	17,000
Total	$175,000			
		Job No. 101	Complete cost .	70,000
Cost of jobs completed	130,000	Job No. 102	Complete cost .	60,000
Ending balance	$ 45,000	Job No. 103	Unfinished	45,000

Finished goods inventory. When a production job is completed, the data on the job cost sheet are summarized and the total cost of that job becomes the basis for an entry crediting Goods in Process Inventory and debiting Finished Goods Inventory. Stock ledger cards are maintained as subsidiary ledger records for each type of finished product.

When finished product is sold, information on the stock ledger cards becomes the basis for removing the cost of these products from the Finished Goods Inventory account and charging the Cost of Goods Sold account. Once more some flow assumption is required.

STOCK
LEDGER
SUPPORTS
ENTRIES IN
CONTROL
ACCOUNT The relation between entries in the Finished Goods Inventory control account and the Finished Stock subsidiary ledger, as shown on the cost flow diagram on page 731, is summarized in the following schedule:

Finished Goods, Control Account		Stock Ledger		
Beginning balance	$ 25,000	Product A	Balance	$ 5,000
		Product B	Balance	20,000
Manufactured during period	130,000	Product A (job No. 101)		70,000
Total	$155,000	Product B (job No. 102)		60,000

Cost of goods sold during the period	120,000	Product A	66,000
		Product B	40,000
		Product C	14,000
Balance on hand at end of period	$ 35,000	Product A	9,000
		Product B	20,000
		Product C	6,000

PROCESS COST SYSTEM

In many industries the production of a large volume of standard products on a relatively continuous basis is the typical situation. The natural point on which to focus cost information in such situations is a manufacturing operation or process. A process cost system is a method of accumulating cost information in the accounts by department or operation.

Process costs are particularly suitable for mass-production operations of all types, and they are used in such industries as textiles, cement, cigarettes, dairy products, appliances, and lumber. Furthermore, the process cost approach may be used in the analysis of nonmanufacturing costs. Distribution activities may be divided into such functions as sales visitations, receipt of orders, filling orders, packing and shipping, and the cost per unit of output computed for any given period of time. Thus the process cost approach has a much wider application than job order costing.

Characteristics of a process cost system

In a process cost system no attempt is made to determine the cost of particular lots of product as they travel through the factory. Instead the cost of materials, labor, and overhead during any given time period (such as a month) are traced to various manufacturing departments or cost centers. The costs incurred in each process are accumulated in separate goods in process accounts, and a record is kept of the units processed in that operation each period. The cost report of each department shows the average per unit cost of processing output during the period, and this figure becomes the basis for tracing the flow of costs through the various goods in process accounts and finally to finished goods inventory and cost of goods sold.

In a very simple situation, only one product is processed in each department. Process costs can be used, however, when more than one product is involved. In such cases, charges for materials and direct labor are identified with individual products or models and accumulated separately in each department's cost reports. Since all products utilize departmental machinery and other indirect services, these costs may be divided among various products on the basis of their relative usage of departmental facilities. To simplify the illustrations, we shall assume the manufacturing of a single product throughout the discussion which follows.

Direct and indirect process costs

Whether a given process cost is direct or indirect depends, not on its relation to a particular quantity or lot of product, but on its relation to the operations of a department or process. Direct process costs are those associated with the operations of a particular process. Costs that are common to several processes are treated as a part of general factory overhead.

Materials and labor. The cost of materials and supplies used, and the wages of departmental personnel can usually be traced directly to the operations of each department; if not, they become an element of overhead. Note that direct departmental costs are not necessarily variable in relation to output. For example, a department foreman's salary is a direct cost of the department in which he works, but his salary is a fixed cost in relation to variations in the output of that department.

Factory overhead. The simplest method of handling factory overhead in a process cost system is to allocate actual overhead expenses among the various processes at the end of each period. If this is done, goods processed during any given period are charged with the actual overhead incurred and there is no balance in the factory overhead account at the end of the period.

Alternatively, departmental overhead rates may be predetermined by setting up a factory overhead budget for each department at the beginning of the period. Overhead is then charged to departments in proportion to labor cost, labor hours, machine hours, or some other basis. To illustrate, suppose the following estimates are made in a budget drawn up at the beginning of the year:

Budget for the Year		
	Dept. H	*Dept. B*
Estimated factory overhead	$100,000	$150,000
Estimated direct labor hours	40,000	200,000
Predetermined factory overhead rate		
per hour	$2.50	$0.75

Factory overhead would be applied to goods processed in Department H at $2.50 and in Department B at 75 cents per hour during the year.

A further refinement in overhead accounting is to set up special overhead cost accounts for one or more service departments, that is, departments that do not actually process raw materials directly. For example, a power department might be established, and all costs of producing power for the factory charged to this department. A maintenance department, to which would be charged wages, supplies, and overhead applicable to the maintenance function, is another possible example. The cost of operating these service departments would in turn be charged to operating departments in proportion to their relative use of the service.

USE OF SERVICE DEPART-MENT TO ALLOCATE COSTS   To illustrate, suppose that a maintenance department is set up, a record is kept of maintenance work done for each processing department, and an hourly charge made to each process department. The Maintenance Department account for a month might appear as follows:

Maintenance Department			
Wages	*$1,500*	*Charged to Dept. A, 600 hr @ $2*	*$1,200*
Supplies	*900*	*Charged to Dept. B, 800 hr @ 2*	*1,600*
Portion of various factory		*Charged to Dept. C, 200 hr @ 2*	*400*
expenses applicable to			
maintenance dept.	*800*		
	$3,200		*$3,200*

A total of 1,600 hours of maintenance work was done during the month for three operating departments (A, B, and C) at a cost of $3,200. Each department is therefore charged with an average hourly cost of $2 per hour ($3,200 ÷ 1,600 hours). Alternatively, maintenance cost and departmental hours might have been estimated at the beginning of the year to arrive at a predetermined hourly rate for maintenance work.

Over- or underapplied overhead. When predetermined rates are used in applying factory overhead or service department costs to operating departments, a balance of under- or overapplied overhead will usually appear in the overhead account at the end of the period. This represents the difference between actual overhead incurred and overhead charged against the production of the period. The problem of disposing of this balance was discussed earlier in connection with job order costs.

In modern cost accounting, there is a tendency to accept predetermined overhead rates, set on the basis of careful estimates, as a reasonable basis for product costing and inventory valuation. Over- or underapplied overhead is usually viewed as an indication of abnormal conditions during the period and treated as an adjustment of net income, either through the Cost of Goods Sold or Income Summary accounts.

Flow of costs in a process cost system

To illustrate the main features of a process cost system, let us assume a very simple manufacturing situation. The Sharp Manufacturing Company

makes a popular kitchen knife. The company has three processing departments. In the Blade Department, the blades are stamped, honed, and
drilled for attachment to the handle. In the Handle Department the handles
are lathed, sanded, and varnished. In the Assembly Department the handles
and blades are riveted together, the trademark is stamped on both handle
and blade, and finished knives are packed one dozen to a box for shipment.
The standard unit of product is one dozen knives, which sells for $3.

The cost flow diagram on pages 740 and 741 shows the basic process
cost accounts and a summary of the cost entries for the month of July.
Each major step in the process will now be examined briefly to demonstrate
the process costing under these simple conditions.

Materials and supplies. There was a $4,000 balance in the Stores
Inventory at the beginning of the period. During the month of July purchases of factory materials and supplies were charged to the Stores In
ventory in the amount of $34,000. At the end of July a summary of ma-
terials requisitioned by each department and general factory supplies used
by all departments became the basis for the following entry:

END-OF- MONTH ENTRY: STORES USED	*Goods in Process: Handle Dept.*	*6,600*
	Goods in Process: Blade Dept.	*21,000*
	Goods in Process: Assembly Dept.	*3,600*
	Factory Overhead	*2,000*
	Stores Inventory	*33,200*

Factory labor. On the basis of departmental payroll records, the total
cost of labor used in each department during July was determined. The
wages of personnel (such as the factory superintendent, cost accountant,
general maintenance employees) whose work is applicable to all departments were charged to Factory Overhead. The entry summarizing the payroll (ignoring various withholdings from wages) would be:

END-OF- MONTH ENTRY: FACTORY LABOR	*Goods in Process: Handle Dept.*	*10,500*
	Goods in Process: Blade Dept.	*16,400*
	Goods in Process: Assembly Dept.	*12,000*
	Factory Overhead	*5,100*
	Accrued Factory Payroll	*44,000*

Payments to employees during the period amounted to $37,800,
leaving a credit balance of $6,200 in the accrued factory payroll account,
which represents wages payable at the end of July.

Factory overhead. The Sharp Company prepares a departmental factory overhead budget at the beginning of each year, and factory overhead

is applied to departmental work in process accounts on the basis of departmental labor cost at the following rates:

Handle Dept.	80% of direct labor cost
Blade Dept.	75% of direct labor cost
Assembly Dept.	66 2/3% of direct labor cost

The entry charging the departmental goods in process accounts for their share of factory overhead, at these predetermined rates, may be summarized as follows:

Goods in Process: Handle Dept.	8,400	
Goods in Process: Blade Dept.	12,300	
Goods in Process: Assembly Dept.	8,000	
Factory Overhead		28,700

COMPARE WITH JOB ORDER FLOW CHART, PAGES 730 AND 731

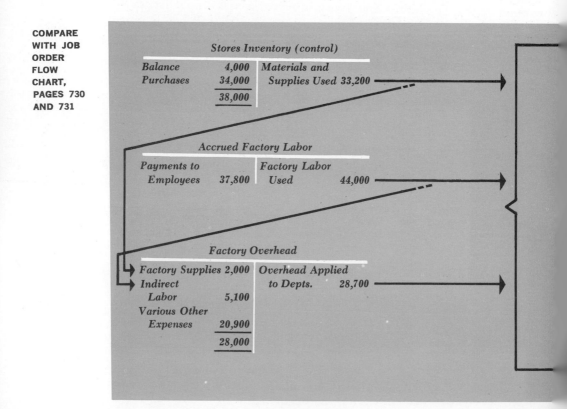

Actual overhead for the month of July totaled $28,000, leaving a credit balance of $700 in the Factory Overhead account, representing overapplied overhead for the month. This amount would be carried forward month by month, and an adjustment to close out the balance would be required at the end of the year.

Determining unit costs

If all materials in any particular department are completely processed during the period, computing unit costs is a simple matter of dividing departmental costs by the number of units processed. In some cases, however, there will be unfinished products remaining in production departments at the end of an accounting period. The total costs incurred in each department for the period must then be allocated between the goods that have been completed and transferred out of the department and the goods that are left in various stages of the process at the end of the period. Obviously, total costs cannot be divided by a number of units of product, some of which are complete and some of which are only partly finished, to obtain a meaningful unit cost figure. If completed and partly completed

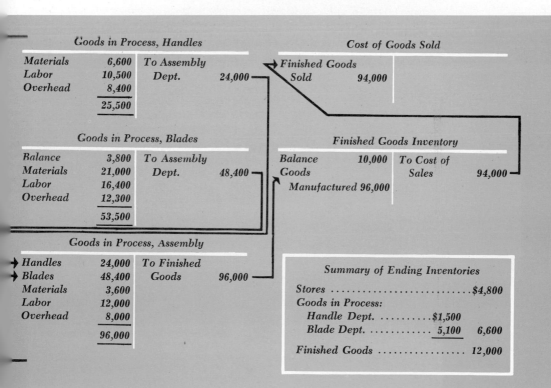

units of product are expressed in *equivalent units* of completed product, however, this difficulty is overcome.

The procedure will be illustrated, using the data that appear in the cost flow diagram on page 741. The costs incurred in the three processing departments during July appear in the departmental goods in process **PRODUCTION** accounts. Supplementary production reports show the units of product **REPORT FOR** processed in each department for July as follows:
JULY

	Handle Dept.	Blade Dept.	Assembly Dept.
Units in process on July 1	. . .	4,000	. . .
Units started during July	44,000	42,000	40,000
Total	44,000	46,000	40,000
Less: units in process on July 31	4,000	6,000	. . .
Completed production for July	40,000	40,000	40,000

Using this information, let us now consider the problem of determining unit costs in each of the three operating departments:

Handle department. On the basis of cost and unit production data, a cost report for the Handle Department for the month of July might appear as follows:

HOW ARE
MISSING
FIGURES
COMPUTED?

HANDLE DEPARTMENT
Cost Report for July (Incomplete)

	Cost	Units (doz.)
Input:		
Units in process at beginning of month ..	. . .	. . .
Materials requisitioned	$ 6,600 ⎤	
Labor cost	10,500 ⎬	44,000
Overhead applied	8,400 ⎦	
Total input	$25,500	44,000
Output:		
Transferred to Assembly Department ..	P	40,000
In process at the end of the month	P	4,000
	$25,500	44,000

The question marks indicate missing data that can be supplied only when units costs have been computed. We cannot divide the total costs of $25,500 incurred in the Handle Department by the 44,000 units processed in this department, because 40,000 of these units were completed during the month and 4,000 were only partially finished at month's end. To compute the equivalent production in terms of completed units we must estimate the stage of completion (on the average) of the units in process with respect to materials, labor, and overhead. A very rough assumption would be that on the average 50% of these costs had been applied to the 4,000 units of unfinished product. In this case the ending inventory of goods in process would represent the equivalent of 2,000 units (50% of 4,000) of completed production, and the total production of the department, expressed in terms of completed units, would be 42,000 (that is, 40,000 units finished, and 4,000 units unfinished and on the average one-half completed).

This rough computation of equivalent units may be refined by considering differences in the state of completion with respect to *materials* and with respect to *processing costs* (that is, labor and overhead). In a few cases material may be put into production evenly, so that units half-finished have one-half of the material in them; a more common situation, however, is to have material put into production at the beginning of a process. In this case *all* material cost has been incurred on units that are only half-finished at the end of the period.

COMPUTATION OF AVERAGE UNIT COSTS

In the Handle Department, all material for the handles is requisitioned as a starting point in production. Therefore equivalent production would be computed separately for material and for labor and overhead, as follows:

HANDLE DEPARTMENT
Computation of Equivalent Production
Month of July

	Materials	Labor and Overhead
Units completed	40,000	40,000
Add: units in process at end of July (4,000):		
Material equivalent (4,000 × 100%)	4,000	
Labor and overhead equivalent (4,000 × 50%)		2,000
Equivalent production (in terms of finished units)	44,000	42,000

The unit costs in the Handle Department may then be determined as follows:

	Total cost	Units: equivalent production	Unit cost
Material	$ 6,600	44,000	$0.15
Labor	10,500	42,000	0.25
Overhead	8,400	42,000	0.20
	$25,500		$0.60

The cost of the 40,000 units transferred to the Assembly Department may now be computed as $24,000 (40,000 × $0.60). This leaves a $1,500 ($25,500 − $24,000) balance in the Goods in Process account for this department, which may be verified as follows:

COMPOSI-
TION OF
GOODS IN
PROCESS
BALANCE

HANDLE DEPARTMENT
Goods in Process Inventory
(4,000 units: 100% complete as to material, 50% processed)

Material (4,000 × 100% × 0.15) .... $ 600
Labor (4,000 × 50% × 0.25) 500
Overhead (4,000 × 50% × 0.20) 400

Ending inventory of goods in process $1,500

Blade department. In the Blade Department an additional feature has been introduced: the existence of a beginning as well as an ending inventory of unfinished product. The essential reasoning in obtaining unit costs in this situation is unchanged, however. On the basis of cost and unit production data, the cost report for the Blade Department for July would appear thus:

WHAT IN-
FORMATION
IS NEEDED
TO COM-
PLETE
REPORT?

BLADE DEPARTMENT
Cost Report for July (Incomplete)

	Cost	Units (doz.)
Input:		
Units in process at beginning of month ..	$ 3,800	4,000
Materials requisitioned	21,000 ⎤	
Labor cost	16,400 ⎬	42,000
Overhead applied	12,300 ⎦	
Total input	$53,500	46,000

Output:		
Transferred to Assembly Department ...	P	*40,000*
In process at the end of the month	P	*6,000*
	$53,500	*46,000*

Once more, the data to be inserted in place of the question marks can be derived only on the basis of unit cost information. Since blade materials enter production at the beginning of the process, both the beginning and ending goods in process inventories are fully complete as to materials. We shall assume that goods in process are on the average 50% complete as to processing costs (labor and overhead).

COMPUTA-TION OF AVERAGE UNIT COSTS

The following schedules Illustrate the computation of equivalent production and unit costs in the Blade Department:

BLADE DEPARTMENT
Computation of Equivalent Production
Month of July

	Materials	Labor and overhead
Units completed during July	*40,000*	*40,000*
Deduct: units in process at start of month (4,000):		
Material equivalent (4,000 × 100%)	*4,000*	
Labor and overhead equivalent (4,000 × 50%) ..		*2,000*
	36,000	*38,000*
Add: units in process at end of month (6,000):		
Material equivalent (6,000 × 100%)	*6,000*	
Labor and overhead equivalent (6,000 × 50%) ..		*3,000*
Equivalent production (expressed in finished units) ..	*42,000*	*41,000*

Unit costs: July

	Total cost	Units: equivalent production	Unit cost
Material	*$21,000*	*42,000*	*$0.50*
Labor	*16,400*	*41,000*	*0.40*
Overhead	*12,300*	*41,000*	*0.30*
	$49,700		*$1.20*

The reasoning behind the computation of equivalent production may be stated as follows: the equivalent finished units in the beginning inventory of goods in process must be subtracted from units completed during the period, because the cost of this production is included in the $3,800 carried forward from the previous month. The equivalent finished units in the ending inventory must then be added, because the cost of this productive effort is included in the department cost for the current period. The result is the equivalent production of finished units during the current period, and this may be divided into the costs incurred during the period to derive a unit production cost for July.

In computing the cost of the 40,000 units transferred out, it is necessary to make some assumption as to which units are involved. A first-in-first-out assumption has been used in this illustration. This means that the 40,000 units transferred to the Assembly Department consist of 4,000 units in process at the beginning of the period, and 36,000 units that were started and finished during the period. The cost of the goods transferred would be computed as follows:

COST OF TRANSFERRED UNITS, FIFO BASIS

BLADE DEPARTMENT
Department Cost Report
Month of July

Beginning inventory in process (4,000 units):
Cost brought forward from previous month		$ 3,800	
Cost to complete during July:			
Material	$000		
Labor (4,000 × 50% × 0.40)	800		
Overhead (4,000 × 50% × 0.30)	600	1,400	$ 5,200
Goods started and finished during July (36,000 units):			
Material (36,000 × 0.50)		$18,000	
Labor (36,000 × 0.40)		14,400	
Overhead (36,000 × 0.30)		10,800	43,200
Cost of units transferred to Assembly Department			$48,400

The total costs in the Blade Department (including the beginning inventory) were $53,500. Subtracting the $48,400 cost of transferred product leaves a balance in the Goods in Process account of $5,100. That this does represent the cost of the ending inventory may be verified:

ENDING INVENTORY VERIFIED

BLADE DEPARTMENT
Ending Inventory of Goods in Process
(6,000 units: 100% complete as to materials; 50% processed)

Material (6,000 × 100% × 0.50)	$3,000	
Labor (6,000 × 50% × 0.40)	1,200	
Overhead (6,000 × 50% × 0.30)	900	
Ending inventory	$5,100	

Assembly department. There is neither a beginning nor an ending inventory of goods in process in the Assembly Department. Therefore the unit cost in this department may be determined by dividing each cost element by the 40,000 units started, completed, and transferred to Finished Goods Inventory during the month:

<table>
<tr><td rowspan="2">SUMMARY
OF
ASSEMBLY
DEPART-
MENT COSTS</td><td colspan="4" align="center">*ASSEMBLY DEPARTMENT*
Unit Costs
Month of July</td></tr>
<tr><td></td><td align="center">*Total*
cost</td><td align="center">*Equivalent*
units
completed</td><td align="center">*Unit*
cost</td></tr>
<tr><td></td><td>*Handles* ....</td><td>$24,000</td><td rowspan="5" align="center">40,000</td><td>$0.60</td></tr>
<tr><td></td><td>*Blades* ....</td><td>48,400</td><td>1.21</td></tr>
<tr><td></td><td>*Materials* ....</td><td>3,600</td><td>0.09</td></tr>
<tr><td></td><td>*Labor* ....</td><td>12,000</td><td>0.30</td></tr>
<tr><td></td><td>*Overhead* ....</td><td>8,000</td><td>0.20</td></tr>
<tr><td></td><td>*Total* ....</td><td>$96,000</td><td></td><td>$2.40</td></tr>
</table>

Summary of cost systems

Several simplifying assumptions have been made in developing these illustrations of job order and process cost systems; nevertheless, the essential features of the two basic types of cost systems are contained in the illustrations. Both job order and process systems are essentially devices for collecting cost information. A process cost system produces information about the average cost of putting a unit of product through various manufacturing operations for a given time period. A job order cost system produces information about the cost of manufacturing a particular unit or lot of product. A job order cost system usually involves more detailed cost accounting work and in return gives more specific cost information. On the other hand, a process cost system involves less detailed accounting work and accumulates costs in terms of departmental responsibility.

DIRECT COSTING VERSUS FULL COSTING

The previous discussion of cost accounting methods has been based on the assumption that the total manufacturing costs incurred in any given period should be traced to the production (both in terms of finished and partially finished product) of that period. In both the job order and process systems illustrated the entire manufacturing costs were allocated among the goods in process inventory, the finished goods inventory, and the cost of goods sold. This procedure is based on what is known as the *full cost* assumption. An alternative assumption, *direct costing* has received considerable attention in recent years.

Under direct costing:

1. All manufacturing costs are first divided into those which are "variable," that is, which vary in direct proportion with changes in the number of units produced, and those which are "fixed," that is, which remain unchanged despite variations in the number of units produced. Raw materials and the wages of factory employees who work directly on the manufacture of products are examples of variable costs. Depreciation on the factory building is an example of a fixed cost.

2. Variable manufacturing costs are traced directly to production and become a part of the figures for ending inventories of goods in process and finished goods and cost of goods sold.

3. Fixed manufacturing costs are treated as period costs and are charged against revenues in the period in which they are incurred.

Illustration of direct costing

To illustrate the differences between direct and full costing, let us compare the income statements that would result under each method using the following assumed data:

Production	40,000	units
Sales	30,000	units
Sales price per unit	$3.00	
Variable costs (per unit):		
Material	$0.60	
Labor	0.80	$1.60 variable manufacturing cost
Factory overhead ...	0.20	
Selling expense	0.15	
Fixed costs (total):		
Factory overhead ...	$12,000	
Selling	9,000	
Administrative	7,500	

FIXED COSTS EXCLUDED FROM INVENTORY   An income statement based on these data, with the direct cost assumption used in compiling costs, would appear as follows:

Income Statement
(Direct costing)

Sales revenues (30,000 units × $3.00)	$90,000
Variable cost of goods sold (30,000 units × $1.60)	48,000
Manufacturing margin	$42,000
Variable selling expenses (30,000 units × $0.15)	4,500
Marginal income	$37,500

Period costs:
Factory overhead (fixed portion) $12,000
Selling expenses (fixed portion) 9,000
Administrative expenses 7,500   28,500

Net operating income .... $ 9,000

FIXED COSTS INCLUDED IN INVENTORY   This may be compared with an income statement using the same data but following the traditional full cost assumption in compiling costs:

Income Statement
(Full costing)

Sales revenues (30,000 units × $3.00) $90,000
Cost of goods sold ° 57,000

Gross margin on sales $33,000
Selling expenses $13,500
Administrative expenses 7,500   21,000

Net operating income $12,000

  ° Computation of cost of goods sold:
    Direct production costs (40,000 units × $1.60) $64,000
    Indirect factory overhead 12,000

    Full cost of production (40,000 units) $76,000
    Less: ending inventory (10,000 ÷ 40,000 × $76,000) 19,000

    Cost of goods sold $57,000

A comparison of these two statements shows that there is a difference of $3,000 in the net income computed under the two assumptions:

WHY DID DIRECT COSTING REDUCE NET INCOME?

Net income, full costing $12,000
Net income, direct costing 9,000

Difference .... $ 3,000

This difference may be analyzed as follows:
Under direct costing the entire fixed factory overhead is charged against revenues in the current period $12,000
Under full costing the fixed factory overhead is apportioned between the ending inventory and the cost of goods sold during the current period. The portion applicable to cost of goods sold may be computed as follows:

$$\frac{30,000 \; units \; sold}{40,000 \; units \; produced} \times \$12,000 \; fixed \; overhead \; \dots \dots \quad 9,000$$

Difference .... $ 3,000

Effect of direct costing on net income and inventory valuation

In general, the difference between the results produced under direct cost-ing and full costing will stem from the amount of fixed costs allocated to the ending inventories. When inventories are increasing (that is, production exceeds sales) direct costing will result in a smaller net income than full costing. When inventories are decreasing (that is, sales exceed produc-tion) direct costing will result in a larger net income than full costing.

Proponents of direct costing argue that fixed costs are not a part of the cost of goods produced during a given period but are the cost of having the capacity to produce. They believe that such capacity costs are there-fore chargeable against the revenues of the period, without regard to variations in the amount of product produced. Critics of direct costing point out that fixed costs are no less essential in the production of goods than variable costs, and that net income from the sale of any unit of product emerges only after recovery of the total cost of bringing that product to the point of sale.

Segregating variable and fixed costs in the accounts produces data that are undoubtedly useful to management in studying cost-volume-profit relationships. On the other hand, including only variable costs in inven-tories understates the valuation of goods on hand and makes direct costing of doubtful validity for periodic income measurement purposes. For this reason, direct costing is not a generally accepted procedure for income determination in published financial statements.

STANDARD COSTS

Thus far in this chapter we have confined our discussion to actual historical cost information. Additional kinds of cost information can be obtained by introducing standard costs into a cost accounting system. A *standard cost* is the cost that *should be* incurred to produce a given product or to perform a particular operation under a normal condition and normal operating efficiency.

The basic objective of standard costing is to compare standard costs (what costs should be) with actual costs (what costs were) to isolate dif-ferences as a basis for study and possible remedial action. For example, if the standard production cost per unit of product is $6.00 and the actual cost for a given period is $6.80 per unit, management would be interested in knowing the reasons for the 80-cent excess. Standard cost procedure (which may be used in connection with either job order or process cost systems) is designed to produce detailed information about such differences and the causes behind them.

Cost variances

Under standard cost procedures, the costs charged to the work in process inventory, and through this inventory account into finished goods and cost of sales, are the standard costs of raw materials, labor, and overhead, not the actual costs. Any differences between the actual manufacturing costs incurred and the standard cost of goods produced are accumulated in a number of *variance accounts.*

For example, if the actual cost of raw materials used is $3,000 and the standard cost is $2,700, there is a $300 variance between actual and standard material costs. This is an *unfavorable* variance; that is, the actual cost exceeds the standard cost. In establishing the standard material cost for each unit of product, two factors were considered: (1) the quantity of material that should be used in making each finished product, and (2) the prices that should have been paid in acquiring this quantity of material. Therefore, the total material cost variance of $300 may result from differences between standard and actual material usage, or between standard and actual prices paid for materials, or from some combination of both factors. An analysis of these factors might produce the following journal entry summarizing material usage and isolating the causes of the variance:

WHY WAS
ACTUAL
MATERIAL
COST
"HIGHER"
THAN
STANDARD?

Goods in Process Inventory (standard cost)	2,700	
Material Quantity Variance	700	
Material Price Variance		400
Stores Inventory (actual cost)		3,000

It is apparent from this entry that a greater quantity of material was used than standard, resulting in an unfavorable quantity variance of $700. Prices paid for materials, however, were somewhat less than standard cost, with the result that there was a favorable material price variance during the period of $400.

Similarly in the case of labor cost, if the accrued payroll for the period is $4,000 and the standard labor cost for units produced during the period is $4,500, there is a $500 *favorable* labor variance for the period, since the standard costs of units produced is greater than the actual labor costs incurred. Labor cost standards are also a product of two variables: (1) the hours of labor that should be used in making a unit of product, and (2) the wage rate that should be paid for that labor. An analysis of the total $500 labor variance will indicate whether the variance was due to the fact that more or less than standard time was required in production, or that more or less than standard wage rates were paid, or some combination of both these factors. The entry summarizing labor costs for the period might be:

WHY WAS
ACTUAL
LABOR COST
"LESS"
THAN
STANDARD?

Goods in Process (standard labor cost) 4,500		
Labor Rate Variance 300		
Labor Usage Variance	800	
Accrued Payroll (actual labor cost)	4,000	

This entry indicates that fewer labor hours than standard were required for current production, resulting in a favorable labor usage variance of $800. On the other hand the wage rates paid during the period were higher than standard, which resulted in an unfavorable labor rate variance of $300.

The difference between the actual overhead costs incurred during the period and the standard overhead cost charged against units produced during the period is the total amount of overhead variance. Since the relationship between overhead and production is more uncertain than in the case of materials and direct labor, an analysis of this variance is a complex undertaking. The standard overhead cost is applied to goods in process inventory on the basis of a predetermined overhead rate. This overhead rate is based on a careful study of what overhead costs should be at various levels of output. The difference between the actual expenses and standard expenses may be analyzed into two general variances: the difference between actual expenses and expenses budgeted for the level of output experienced (called the controllable variance); and the difference between the budgeted expenses and the standard expenses (called the volume variance). A discussion of the analyses necessary to determine these variances is beyond the scope of this introductory discussion of cost accounting.

QUESTIONS

1. There are two stages in the process of determining unit production costs. What are these two stages? Discuss the nature of the problems that arise in each.

2. Distinguish a *process cost* system from a *job order cost* system. What factors should be taken into account in deciding which system to use in any given manufacturing situation?

3. What is meant by the phrase, "different costs for different purposes"? Illustrate by explaining how factory superintendent's salary expense might be treated differently, as a cost, for different purposes.

4. What is the source of the information entered in each section (received, issued, balance) of a stores ledger card? A finished stock ledger card?

5. Describe the information that is entered on a job cost sheet and its source. For what general ledger control account do job cost sheets constitute supporting detail?

6. X Company applies factory overhead on the basis of direct labor hours. At the end of the current year, the factory overhead account has a credit balance. What are the possible explanations for this? What disposition should be made of this balance?

7. What is the purpose of setting up special cost accounts for one or more service departments, in conjunction with a cost accounting system? Give some examples of possible service departments.

8. Explain what is meant by the term *equivalent production*. Why is such a concept necessary in order to compute average unit costs?

9. During the current year Company C increased its inventory of finished product. Would you expect that net income computed under the direct cost assumption would be smaller or larger than income computed under a full cost assumption? Explain the source of the difference.

10. What is the basic objective behind the use of standard costs in either a job order or a process cost system?

PROBLEMS

Group A

26A-1. At the end of July, the following balances appeared on the post-closing trial balance of the Willamette Manufacturing Company:

Stores inventory	*$ 8,400*
Goods in process inventory	*12,600*
Finished goods inventory	*18,300*
Factory overhead (credit bal.)	*(1,200)*

Other data. The information given below relates to transactions and events during the month of August:

(1) Materials and supplies purchased on open account, $26,200

(2) Wage costs incurred: direct labor, $38,000; indirect labor, $18,400

(3) Stores requisitions: raw materials, $16,800; factory supplies, $6,700

(4) Depreciation on factory plant and equipment, $2,600

(5) Expenses incurred during the month:

	Factory	*Selling & adm. exp.*
Accounts payable	*$3,000*	*$ 8,700*
Accrued liabilities (other than wages)	*2,700*	*12,100*

Factory overhead is applied to production at the rate of 80% of direct labor cost.

(6) Ending inventory of goods in process, 10% of production costs incurred during the month of August

(7) Ending inventory of finished goods, 20% of the cost of goods manufactured during the month of August

(8) Sale of finished production, on open account, $120,000

Instructions

a. Prepare general journal entries to record the transactions and events during the month of August. Show supporting computations where necessary. Use a single control account for factory overhead and for selling and administrative expense.

b. Prepare, in condensed form, the August income statement for the Willamette Manufacturing Company.

c. Compute the amount of over- or underapplied factory overhead as of August 31.

26A-2. The Springfield Manufacturing Company makes standard metal parts in large quantities, and uses a process cost system. One of its processing departments is the Machining Department. During the month of April, the following charges were made to the Goods in Process account for this department:

Machining Department: Goods in Process

Beginning inventory	*14,750*	
Materials	*36,800*	
Direct labor	*22,500*	
Factory overhead (110% of		
direct labor cost)	*24,750*	

The production report for this department for the month of April is as follows:

	Units
Units in process Apr. 1 (100% complete as to materials; 50% complete as to labor and overhead)	*10,000*
Units put into process in April	*50,000*
Total units to account for	*60,000*
Units transferred to Assembly Department during April	*40,000*
Units in process on Apr. 30 (80% complete as to materials; 50% complete as to labor and overhead)	*20,000*
Total units accounted for	*60,000*

Instructions

a. Compute the unit costs for materials, labor, and overhead for this department for the month of April.

b. Make the journal entry necessary to transfer finished product from the Machining to the Assembly Department for April. Show how you determined the cost of the units transferred. (You may use a first-in, first-out assumption.)

c. Prepare a schedule showing the computation of the cost of the ending inventory of goods in process.

26A-3. At May 1 the balances shown below appear in the ledger of the Richins Manufacturing Company:

	Debit	Credit
Cash	$ 20,000	
Receivables	58,000	
Stores inventory	46,000	
Goods in process: blending department		
Goods in process: cooking department		
Finished goods inventory	24,000	
Machinery and equipment	200,000	
Allowance for depreciation: mach. & equip. ...		$ 56,000
Accounts payable		52,000
Accrued liabilities		34,000
Common stock		120,000
Retained earnings		86,000
	$348,000	$348,000

Other data. The company manufactures a special ingredient used in the composition of certain plastics and sells it in gallon containers, after blending and cooking the raw materials. The company's transactions during May are summarized below.

(1) Materials were purchased on open account in the amount of $85,000.

(2) Stores were requisitioned as follows: blending department $66,000; cooking department $8,100; general factory supplies $14,000.

(3) Total payroll for the month: blending department labor $18,000; cooking department labor $20,000; indirect factory labor $27,000; administrative and sales salaries $24,000.

(4) Cash disbursements: on accounts payable $80,000; on accrued liabilities $98,000; in payment of administrative and selling expenses $17,000.

(5) Building rental for the month was paid, $15,000. Of this amount 80% is chargeable as a manufacturing expense and 20% as administrative expense.

(6) Depreciation on equipment: 1% of balance at beginning of the month; 90% allocated to manufacturing and 10% to selling and administration.

(7) Factory overhead is applied at the following rates: blending department, 125% of direct labor cost; cooking department, 150% of direct labor cost.

(8) Sales on open account, $200,000.

(9) Collected on receivables, $215,600. This is the cash received after customers had deducted $4,400 of sales discounts from the amount billed them.

(10) In the blending department 11,000 gallons were put into production. During May, 9,000 gallons were transferred to the cooking department; 2,000 gallons remained in process, 100% complete as to materials and 50% complete as to processing costs.

(11) In the cooking department 9,000 gallons were transferred in during May. Of this, 7,000 gallons were transferred to finished goods, and 2,000 gallons were left in process at the end of the month. Since the material is cooked in sealed containers, the product in process in this department was 100% complete as to materials, and 50% complete as to processing.

(12) Ending inventory of finished goods: 1,000 gallons, to be priced on a fifo basis.

Instructions

a. Prepare general journal entries to record the summarized transactions for the month. Entries may be made without explanations, but any necessary supporting computations should be shown clearly below the journal entry to which they apply.

b. Post the entries in (*a*) to general ledger accounts. You may use single control accounts for factory overhead and for selling and administrative expenses.

c. Prepare a trial balance as of May 30 and a computation of the net operating income for the month. Over- or underapplied overhead may be treated as an adjustment of the cost of sales account.

26A-4. The Ballaine Manufacturing Company makes a standard product. Materials, labor, and overhead are charged to work in process at the end of each month on the basis of actual costs incurred in each period. At the end of the current year, Ballaine received the following report showing unit costs for each of the four quarters of the year:

	1st quarter	*2d quarter*	*3d quarter*	*4th quarter*
Materials	$10,600	$ 39,000	$ 28,700	$ 20,900
Direct labor	21,000	80,800	58,700	40,200
Fixed overhead	25,000	23,000	24,000	24,000
Variable overhead	13,600	47,000	38,500	25,670
Total mfg. cost	$70,200	$189,800	$149,900	$110,770
Units produced	10,000	40,000	30,000	20,000
Unit cost	$7.02	$4.75	$4.99	$5.53

Ballaine is concerned about the wide variation in unit costs; he notes that the unit costs for the first quarter are $7.02 per unit, while unit costs in the second quarter were $4.75. He asks the controller to study the problem and present a proposal for a different method of computing costs. The controller, noting that the primary reason for the cost variation is the fluctuation in production, suggests that if overhead were applied against production on the basis of a yearly estimate of direct labor costs, the quarterly unit cost figures would become more comparable.

Instructions

a. Prepare a schedule showing the unit costs that would have resulted for each quarter's production if overhead had been applied to production during the year as a function of direct labor cost.

b. Compute the amount of over- or underapplied overhead that would have resulted in each quarter during the year.

c. Write a brief statement explaining the reason for the difference between the unit cost figures shown above, and those in the schedule prepared in (*a*).

d. Early in the first quarter of the year the company had received an offer from an exporter to buy 5,000 units of their product at a special price of $4.70 per unit. The company's normal selling price is $6 per unit. Since the company's total unit costs had never been as low as $4.70, the president refused the offer. On the basis of the information that you have, would you have made the same decision? Why?

26A-5. At the beginning of the current year, the Walton Company established a branch plant to manufacture a patented fuel gauge for buried oil tanks. During the year the branch sold 50,000 units at an average price of $4 per unit. At the end of the year there were 6,000 finished units on hand, and 4,000 units in process that were complete as to materials, but only 50% complete as to labor and overhead costs.

The branch reported the following costs charged into the goods in process account during the year:

Materials	$45,000
Labor	46,400
Variable overhead	14,500
Fixed overhead	37,700

The following analysis of branch operating expenses for the year has been prepared:

	Fixed	Variable (per unit sold)
Selling expenses	$20,000	$0.50
Administrative expenses	24,000	0.10

The plant manager has prepared an income statement for the year showing an operating income for the branch of $3,500, based on a full costing assumption. The company controller, who is an advocate of direct costing, insists that on a direct costing basis the branch plant did not cover the fixed costs incurred for the year.

Instructions

a. Prepare an income statement, under a full cost assumption, showing the computation of operating income as it must have been made by the plant manager. Attach supporting schedules showing the computation of the ending inventories of finished goods and goods in process.

b. Prepare an income statement such as the controller had in mind, using the direct costing assumption. Show the determination of ending inventories under the direct costing assumption.

c. Explain the reason for the difference between the plant manager's and the controller's computation of operating income for the year.

Group B

26B-1. At the beginning of the current month, the following inventories appeared on the records of the Reithel Company: materials and supplies, $41,200; goods in process, $10,600; finished product, $26,400.

Below is a summary of transactions and events during the month:

(1) Total accrued payroll for the month:

Direct labor (36,000 hours)	$66,300
Indirect labor	29,000
Selling & administrative salaries	20,000

(2) Materials and supplies purchased, $56,000.

(3) Depreciation on buildings and equipment, $4,000 (80% related to manufacturing and 20% to selling and administrative functions).

(4) Write-off of prepaid expenses: to manufacturing expense, $800; to selling and administrative expenses, $500.

(5) Requisitions for the month: raw materials, $53,700; factory supplies, $17,500; sales and general supplies, $2,100.

(6) Creditors' bills for expense items: factory expenses, $8,400; administrative expenses, $4,600.

(7) Factory overhead is applied on the basis of direct labor hours. At the beginning of the year the manufacturing expense budget was set at $800,000. It was estimated that 500,000 direct labor hours would be used during the year.

(8) Two production orders were uncompleted at month-end:

	Job 105	Job 108
Materials	$1,800	$2,700
Labor and overhead	4,400	5,900

(9) All the finished product in the beginning inventory was sold, and 80% of the current month's production was sold.

(10) The average selling price of goods sold was 150% of their manufacturing cost. All sales were on open account.

Instructions

a. Prepare general journal entries summarizing the transactions of the Reithel Company for the month. Show supporting computations, where necessary. Use a single control account for selling and administrative expenses, and for factory overhead.

b. Prepare in condensed form a statement of operating income for the month. Assume that over- or underapplied overhead is closed to cost of sales at the end of each month.

26B-2. The Orta Company commenced operations on September 1, after having been closed down for two weeks for employee vacations. One of the company's primary products is Orta-Grow, which is processed successively in Department X and Department Y. The production report for this product for the month of September is given below.

	Department X	Department Y
Production Report: Orta-Grow		
Units in process, Sept. 1		
Units put into process during Sept.	20,000	17,000
Units completed and transferred:		
To Department Y	17,000	
To finished goods inventory		16,000
Units in process, Sept. 30, on the average one-half completed	3,000	1,000

	Department X	Department Y
Manufacturing Costs: Orta-Grow		
Raw materials	$ 8,325	$ 990
Direct labor	4,440	4,950
Factory overhead	2,775	3,300
	$15,540	$9,240

Instructions

a. Compute the equivalent production of Orta-Grow for each department during September.

b. Determine unit costs for Departments X and Y for September.

c. Make the journal entries necessary to record the transfer of product moving out of Departments X and Y during September.

26B-3. The fiscal year of the Koplin Company closes on June 30. On June 1 the balances shown below appeared in the company's accounts:

	Debit	Credit
Cash	$ 85,000	
Receivables	126,000	
Allowance for bad debts		$ 6,000
Stores inventory	48,000	
Goods in process inventory	12,000	
Finished goods inventory	54,000	
Plant and equipment	400,000	
Allowance for depr.: plant & equip.		180,000
Accounts payable		95,000
Accrued liabilities		46,000
Common stock ($25 par)		250,000
Retained earnings.		68,500
Sales		860,000
Cost of goods sold	580,000	
Factory overhead		1,500
Selling & administrative expenses	202,000	
	$1,507,000	$1,507,000

Other data. Transactions and adjustments during the month of June are summarized below:

(1) Creditors' bills for the month: stores, $32,000; factory expenses, $11,000; general expenses, $15,000.

(2) Accrued payroll for the month: charged to jobs, $28,000; indirect labor, $16,000; sales and office salaries, $22,000.

(3) Material requisitions: for production jobs, $24,000; factory supplies, $7,200; sales and office supplies, $3,800.

(4) Overhead was applied to factory jobs at 150% of direct labor cost.

(5) Sales on open account, $120,000.

(6) Total cost of jobs completed during June, $86,000.

(7) Total cost of product sold during June, $98,000.

(8) Cost of finished product given away for sales promotion and advertising purposes, $1,100.

(9) Cash received from customers, $160,000.

(10) Cash disbursements: on accounts payable, $88,000; on accrued liabilities, $92,000.

(11) Depreciation on plant and equipment, $3,600 (3/4 applicable to manufacturing, 1/4 to sales and administration).

(12) Provision for bad debts: 1% of total monthly sales. Accounts receivable written off as uncollectible, $2,000.

(13) Finished product returned by customers for credit, $7,000 (Debit directly to Sales). Goods returned, which cost $5,000, are resalable.

(14) Balance of under- or overapplied overhead for the year was closed to cost of goods sold.

(15) Estimated income taxes provided at 40% of net income. (Show computation of taxable income in supporting schedule.)

Instructions

a. Record the initial account balances (as of June 1) in T accounts.

b. Record all transactions and adjustments directly in T accounts, using the identifying number to cross-reference the entries.

c. Prepare an adjusted trial balance as of June 30.

26B-4. The Kyle Company has an automatic sprinkler system for fire protection. Shortly after the end of August, the system went off by accident and sprayed water on the accounting records, smearing some of the pages and figures so that they cannot be read. A fragment of the adjusted trial balance taken at August 31 is available:

Accounts receivable	*$30,000*
Stores inventory	*11,400*
Goods in process	*28,000*
Finished goods	*14,200*
Accrued payroll	*10,300*

In the general ledger accounts given below, the bookkeeper has inserted a letter (A, B, C, etc.) in the spots where figures are blurred beyond recognition.

Stores Inventory

Aug.	*1*	*Balance*	*18,300*	*Aug. 31 Requisitions*	*72,000*
	31	*Purchases*	*A*		

Goods in Process

Aug.	*1*	*Balance*	*5,000*	*Aug. 31 Production*	*D*
	31	*Raw materials*	*B*		
	31	*Direct labor*	*51,000*		
	31	*Overhead*	*C*		

Finished Goods

Aug. 1	Balance	17,000	Aug. 31	Goods sold		F
31	August production	E				

Accounts Receivable

Aug. 1	Balance	40,000	Aug. 31	Collections		G
31	Customer charges	180,000				

Accrued Payroll

Aug. 31	Wage payments	59,900	Aug. 1	Balance	6,800
			31	August payroll	H

Sales

		Aug. 31	Sales	I

Cost of Goods Sold

Aug. 31	Cost of sales	J	

Factory Overhead

Aug. 31	Indirect material	3,600	Aug. 31	Applied (80% of	
31	Indirect labor	K		direct labor cost)	L
31	Other	24,000			

Instructions

a. List the letters (from A to L) in the above accounts, and determine the amount that belongs in the space occupied by each.

b. Reconstruct in general journal form as many of the summary entries for the month of August as you can determine from the fragmentary information given.

26B-5. The Simpson Stapler Company manufactures an industrial stapling machine and uses standard costs in a process cost system. The *standard* unit cost of each stapler, established at the beginning of the year was:

	Cost per unit
Materials	$ 3.20
Labor	4.50
Overhead	3.60
	$11.30

On July 1 there were 1,000 staplers in process, to which all the materials and one-half of the conversion costs (labor and overhead) had been applied. During July, 10,400 staplers were transferred to finished stock. On July 31 there were 600 staplers in process, 50% complete as to conversion costs and 100% complete as to materials.

All costs are charged into work in process at standard cost, and separate price and quantity variance accounts are established to account for the difference between actual and standard cost.

Actual costs incurred during July were: materials used, $30,600; direct labor, $47,295; factory overhead, $38,600.

The Material Price Variance account had a debit balance of $1,800 at the end of July, and the Labor Usage Variance account had a credit balance of $900.

Instructions

a. Compute the equivalent production of finished staplers during July.

b. Make general journal entries summarizing all transactions involving the Goods in Process account during July. Note that all charges to goods in process will be at standard cost, and that it will be necessary to compute the *materials usage variance*, the *labor rate variance*, and the *overhead variance*, since these amounts are not given. Show supporting computations for each journal entry.

c. Prepare a schedule reconciling standard cost of production with actual cost of production during July. Start with the standard cost of production as determined in (*b*), add favorable variances from standard, and deduct unfavorable variances from standard to arrive at actual costs.

27

Accounting for taxes

Nature and importance of taxes

Taxes levied on business entities by Federal, state, and local governmental units are a significant part of the cost of operating a business enterprise. In terms of revenue, the three most important kinds of taxes in the United States are income taxes, sales taxes, and property taxes. The income tax is the major source of revenue for the Federal government. Most states rely heavily on sales taxes, although a few depend almost entirely upon income or property taxes. The property tax is the mainstay of local governmental units such as counties, cities, school districts, etc.

The amount of tax due is often determined from information contained in accounting records. Sales and various excise taxes are based on sales revenues. Income taxes are levied on taxable income which, though not necessarily the same as accounting income, is computed from accounting data. Property taxes are based on assessed value, determined by appraisal but influenced to some extent by accounting valuations, particularly in the case of inventories and equipment.

The accountant is not only involved in computing and paying taxes but is concerned with their effect on financial position and net income. Some taxes are paid in advance and are therefore treated as assets to be amortized over future periods; others accrue and must be shown as liabilities. Taxes, other than those levied on net income, are generally treated as a part of the operating costs of a business and are recorded and allocated in the same way as other costs of doing business.

Although taxes are an involuntary contribution by the taxpayer, they are not entirely uncontrollable. Businessmen may legally alter their tax costs by the kind of business in which they engage, the way in which they draw contracts and arrange transactions, and by their choice of plant location, form of business organization, kinds of financing, and alternative accounting procedures. It is perhaps unfortunate that taxes have become such an important factor in business decisions which, ideally, should be based on other considerations, but we must recognize this fact if we are to understand fully how business decisions are made.

The body of knowledge required to be well informed in matters of taxation is such that it has become a special field among professional men in accounting and law. Some general knowledge of our tax laws and how they operate, however, is a useful background in understanding accounting and the use of accounting data by businessmen. The remainder of this chapter will be devoted to a brief, and necessarily general, discussion of income taxes, property taxes, and sales taxes.

FEDERAL INCOME TAX

The present Federal income tax dates from the passage of the Sixteenth Amendment to the Constitution in 1913.[1] This amendment, only 30 words in length,[2] removed all questions of the constitutionality of income taxes and paved the way for the more than 45 revenue acts passed by Congress since that date. In 1939 these tax laws were first combined into what is known as the Internal Revenue Code. The administration and enforcement of the tax laws are duties of the Treasury Department, operating through a division known as the Internal Revenue Service. The Treasury Department publishes its interpretation of the tax laws in Treasury regulations; the final word in interpretation lies with the Federal courts.

Classes of taxpayers

In the eyes of the income tax law, there are four major classes of taxpayers: individuals, corporations, estates, and trusts. Proprietorships and partnerships are not taxed as business units; their income is taxed directly to the individual proprietor or partners, whether or not actually withdrawn from the business. A proprietor reports his business income on a separate schedule and attaches it to his personal tax return. A partner includes on his personal return his share of partnership income. However, the partnership must file an information return showing total partnership net income and the share of each partner.

A corporation is a separate taxable entity; it must file a tax return and pay a tax on its annual taxable income. In addition, individual stockholders must report dividends received as part of their personal taxable

[1] A Federal income tax was proposed as early as 1815, and an income tax law was actually passed and income taxes collected during the Civil War. This law was upheld by the Supreme Court, but it was repealed when the need for revenues subsided after the war. In 1894 a new income tax law was passed, but the Supreme Court declared this law invalid on constitutional grounds.

[2] It reads: "The Congress shall have power to lay and collect taxes on incomes, from whatever source derived, without apportionment among the several States, and without regard to any census or enumeration."

income. This has led to the charge that there is "double taxation" of corporate income—once to the corporation and again when it is distributed to stockholders. The validity of this charge depends on whether corporations are able to pass on the income tax to their customers through higher prices, and the evidence as well as opinion on this point is conflicting.

Tax rates

All taxes may be characterized as proportional, regressive, or progressive with respect to any given base. A *proportional* tax remains a constant percentage of the base no matter how that base changes. For example, a 2% sales tax remains a constant percentage of gross sales regardless of changes in the sales figure. A *regressive* tax becomes a smaller percentage of the base as the base increases. A business license tax of $500, for example, is regressive with respect to income, since the larger the income the smaller the tax as a percentage of income. A *progressive* tax becomes a larger portion of the base as that base increases. Federal income taxes are progressive with respect to taxable net income, as may be seen from the following schedule of rates for a recent year:

For Unmarried Individuals		For Corporations	
Taxable income	*Amount of tax*	*Taxable income*	*Amount of tax*
$0– $2,000	20%	$0–$25,000	30%
2– 4,000	$400 plus 22% of amount over $2,000	Over $25,000	$7,500 plus
4– 6,000	840 plus 26% of amount over 4,000		52% of amount
6– 8,000	1,360 plus 30% of amount over 6,000		over $25,000
8– 10,000	1,960 plus 34% of amount over 8,000		
10– 12,000	2,640 plus 38% of amount over 10,000		
12– 14,000	3,400 plus 43% of amount over 12,000		
14– 16,000	4,260 plus 47% of amount over 14,000		
16– 18,000	5,200 plus 50% of amount over 16,000		
18– 20,000	6,200 plus 53% of amount over 18,000		
20– 22,000	7,260 plus 56% of amount over 20,000		
22– 26,000	8,380 plus 59% of amount over 22,000		
26– 32,000	10,740 plus 62% of amount over 26,000		
32– 38,000	14,460 plus 65% of amount over 32,000		
38– 44,000	18,360 plus 69% of amount over 38,000		
44– 50,000	22,500 plus 72% of amount over 44,000		
50– 60,000	26,820 plus 75% of amount over 50,000		
60– 70,000	34,320 plus 78% of amount over 60,000		
70– 80,000	42,120 plus 81% of amount over 70,000		
80– 90,000	50,220 plus 84% of amount over 80,000		
90–100,000	58,620 plus 87% of amount over 90,000		
100–150,000	67,320 plus 89% of amount over 100,000		
150–200,000	111,820 plus 90% of amount over 150,000		
200,000 and over	156,820 plus 91% of amount over 200,000		

In any analysis of tax costs, it is important to distinguish the *marginal* rate of tax from the *average* rate. This distinction may be illustrated as follows: If a corporation has a taxable income of $50,000, its income tax will be $20,500, an average tax rate of 41% of taxable income. On the last dollar of income, however, the tax was 52 cents, since the corporation is subject to a marginal tax rate of 52% on all income over $25,000.

An even wider discrepancy between average and marginal tax rates may exist in the case of individual taxpayers. To illustrate, assume that Mr. Jones, an unmarried executive earning $50,000 per year, is considering a change to a more responsible position that pays $10,000 more per year in salary. Using the tax rates illustrated, Mr. Jones now pays Federal income taxes of $26,820, an average of 54% of his taxable income. His marginal tax rate on all income over $50,000, however, is 75%. Therefore, he will be able to keep only $2,500 out of the extra $10,000 of compensation; this may influence heavily his decision to make the change.

Married taxpayers. A special schedule of tax rates applies to married individuals who combine their income and deductions on a single *joint return.* This provision was introduced to equalize the tax load for families in different states. Certain states whose laws are based on Spanish rather than English law have what are known as "community property" laws, under which a husband and wife are deemed to own one-half of any income earned by either. This meant that married couples living in these states could usually reduce their income taxes by assigning half of their combined income to the husband and half to the wife and filing separate income tax returns, thus subjecting each one-half of the income to lower marginal tax rates. To remove this inequity, in 1948 Congress made "income splitting" permissible for all married persons in all states. The procedure is to allow married couples first to figure the tax on one-half of their combined taxable income, and then compute the tax due by doubling this amount. As a result married couples with large incomes enjoy a considerable tax advantage over single individuals having the same taxable income. Special tax rate schedules for married persons are available so that the tax can be computed directly from the taxable income shown on the joint return.

Head of household rates. Certain persons who qualify as the head of a household are entitled to use still another schedule of tax rates that are higher than those for married persons but less than those for unmarried persons. This treatment extends a part of the income-splitting benefits allowed to married persons to an unmarried person who maintains a household in which he and his children or other dependents live.

Accounting methods

The student who has progressed this far in his study of accounting is well aware that business income is not a precise calculation. Various accounting procedures result in different net income figures, and matters of judgment that allow for varying results are always present. This lack of precision carries over into the determination of taxable income. The tax law and Treasury regulations specify certain procedures that must be followed and set rules governing the adoption of optional accounting procedures. In general, taxpayers have the option of using either the cash basis or the accrual basis of computing income, subject to Treasury Department approval.

Cash basis. Strictly speaking, the cash basis of measuring income is just what the title implies: income is recognized when cash is received, and expenses are recorded when they are paid. This method does not reflect income in the accounting sense, but with some modifications it is allowed for income tax purposes because it is simple, requires a minimum of records, and produces reasonably satisfactory results for individuals not engaged in business and for simple businesses in which receivables, payables, and inventories are not a major factor.

The cash basis allowed for tax purposes varies in two important ways from a simple compilation of cash receipts and disbursements. On the expenditure side, the taxpayer who buys property having a service life of more than one year is not allowed to deduct the entire cost in the year of purchase but must treat it as an asset and deduct depreciation each year. Other major items of prepaid expenses, such as rent paid in advance or insurance premiums covering more than one year, must be treated similarly. Thus expenses paid *in advance* are deductible only when they are incurred, but expenses paid *after* they are incurred are deductible in the year of payment.

On the revenue side, a cash basis taxpayer must report revenue when it has been *constructively received,* even though the cash is not yet in his possession. Constructive receipt means that the revenue is so much within the control of the taxpayer as to be equivalent to receipt. For example, if a taxpayer has a savings account, the interest on that account is constructively received for income tax purposes, even though he does not actually draw it out. Similarly a salary check received on December 31 is constructively received even though it is not cashed until January 2.

From the taxpayer's viewpoint, choosing between the cash and accrual methods is not entirely a matter of deciding which provides the best measure of business income. There is a tendency for taxpayers to elect the cash basis wherever possible in order to postpone the recognition of taxable income and payment of the tax. In this way they have the interest-free use of funds that would otherwise be paid in taxes. To prevent the undue use of the cash basis for this reason, the government may legally insist on a conversion from cash to accrual method when it can be shown that income is not clearly reflected on a cash basis.

Accrual basis. The accrual method of determining income has been discussed throughout the preceding chapters of this book. Revenue is recognized when it is realized, and expenses are recognized when incurred, without regard to the time of receipt or payment. Any taxpayer who maintains a set of accounting records may elect to use the accrual basis. When the production, purchase, or sale of merchandise is a significant factor in a business, the accrual method is mandatory.

Accounting income versus taxable income. Even when the accrual method is used, differences arise between accounting income and taxable income. Some items of accounting income are not included in taxable income; for example, interest received on state or municipal bonds is not taxed by the Federal government. Some expenses are not deductible; for example, amounts spent for lobbying to promote or defeat legislation. Special deductions are allowed to some taxpayers; for example, depletion expense in excess of actual cost is allowed taxpayers in the oil and mining industries. Finally, timing of certain items of revenue and expense allowed for tax purposes may differ from that appropriate for general accounting purposes. For example, rental income received for several years in advance is taxable in the year of receipt, although for accounting purposes it would be prorated over the rental period.

As a matter of bookkeeping convenience, accounting records for many businesses are kept on a "tax" basis, that is, where there are differences between accounting income and taxable income, accounting principles give way to tax laws. If the differences are not material, this procedure is warranted as a means of simplifying the keeping of tax accounting records. The objectives in defining taxable income, however, differ to some extent from those governing the measurement of accounting income. Rather than permit misinformation to creep into accounting records as the result of special provisions of the tax laws, it is preferable to maintain accounting records to meet the need for relevant information about business activities and to adjust such data to arrive at taxable income. A schedule in which differences between taxable income and book income may be explained is provided on tax return forms.

The income tax formula for individuals

The income tax forms supplied by the government contain a convenient outline of the tax computation to guide taxpayers to the proper determination of their tax. In studying the elements of the tax determination, however, it is helpful to visualize the computation in terms of the tax formula. The formula, applicable to all taxpayers other than corporations, estates, and trusts, is as follows:

BASIC FEDERAL INCOME TAX FORMULA			
Gross income			*xxx*
Less: deductions (generally of a business nature) to arrive at adjusted gross income			*xxx*
Adjusted gross income			*xxx*
Less: deductions from adjusted gross income:			
Itemized deductions (generally of a personal nature) or standard deduction		*xxx*	
Personal exemptions		*xxx*	*xxx*
Taxable income			*xxx*

Tax computed on taxable income	*xxx*
Less: tax credits	*xxx*
Amount of tax liability	*xxx*

Gross income. Gross income for tax purposes is all income not excluded by law. It includes income from business, compensation for services, gains on the sale or exchange of property, interest, rents, royalties, dividends, and, to cover any other possibilities, the law contains the phrase "all income from whatever source derived." To determine whether any given item is included in gross income, two tests may be applied: (1) Is it income (as distinguished, for example, from a return of capital)? (2) Is there a provision in the law excluding this from taxation? If the answer to the first question is yes, and to the second no, the item must be included in gross income.

In practice it is often necessary to refer to the law, Treasury regulations, and court decisions to determine whether a particular item is or is not included in gross income. Some idea of the major items that are included or excluded, however, may be gained from the following tabulation, which is illustrative only and does not represent a complete enumeration.

WHAT DOES GROSS INCOME INCLUDE?

Examples of Items Included in and Excluded from Gross Income

Included in Gross Income	Excluded from Gross Income by Statute
Compensation for services in all forms; wages, salaries, bonuses, commissions, tips, gratuities; fair market value of noncash compensation	Interest on state and municipal obligations
	Gifts, inheritances, and bequests
Rents and royalties	Life insurance proceeds received because of the death of the insured
Taxable gains from the sale of real estate, securities, and other property	Amounts received from workmen's compensation insurance and as damages or reimbursement of medical costs in connection with bodily injury or sickness; also benefits to compensate for loss of wages during illness, under certain conditions, up to $100 per week
Taxpayer's share of income from business or profession, conducted as a proprietorship or partnership	
Taxpayer's share of income from estates or trusts	
All pensions to the extent that the amount received exceeds a proportionate share of the taxpayer's cost	Social security benefits and the portion of receipts from annuities that represent return of cost

Contest prizes

Gambling winnings

Cancellation of indebtedness for consideration

Periodic alimony payments received by taxpayer

Dividends and interest income

Income from illegal activities

GI benefits and military bonuses received from state or Federal governments; certain military pay while in combat zone; pensions and disability compensation to war veterans and their families

Compensation for damages relating to personal or family rights

Income earned by United States citizens from sources outside the United States, after 18 months abroad, and up to $20,000 per year

First $50 of dividend income from United States corporations

Capital gains and losses. Certain kinds of property are defined under the tax law as *capital assets,*[3] and gains or losses from the sale or exchange of such assets are granted special treatment for income tax purposes. Because long-term capital gains are taxed at one-half or less than one-half of the rates applicable to ordinary income, there is a strong incentive for taxpayers to arrange their business and personal affairs so that whenever possible income will be realized in the form of capital gains. The government's efforts to keep such arrangements within bounds have been exceeded only by the collective ingenuity of taxpayers in making income appear in the form of capital gains. This tugging and hauling between lawmakers and taxpayers has made the general area of capital gains taxation one of the most complex in the income tax laws. In a brief summary, we can only outline the general features of this phase of income taxation.

Amount of gain or loss. The tax gain (or loss) from the sale or exchange of capital assets is the difference between the selling price and the *basis* of property sold. Basis rules are complicated; tax basis depends, among other things, on how the property was acquired, whether it is personal or business property, and in some cases whether it is sold at a gain or at a loss. In general, the basis of purchased property is its cost, reduced by any depreciation that has been allowed for tax purposes. Two examples of exceptions to this general rule are property acquired by gift and that acquired by inheritance. The basis of property acquired by gift

---

[3] Capital assets are actually defined in the law by "exclusion"; that is, the law (IRC 1221) states that capital assets are all items of property *except* (*a*) inventories in a trade or business; (*b*) trade accounts and notes receivable; (*c*) copyrights, literary, musical, or artistic compositions in the hands of their creator; (*d*) any government obligations due within one year and issued at a discount; and (*e*) real or depreciable property in a trade or business.

is usually the same as the basis of that property in the hands of the donor. The basis of property acquired by inheritance is its fair market value at the date of death, with certain exceptions. Thus if Able buys land for $1,000 and later, when it is worth $3,000, gives it to Baker, the basis of the property in Baker's hands is $1,000 and Baker has a taxable gain of $2,000 if he sells the land for $3,000. On the other hand, if Able dies, leaving the property to Baker in his will, the basis of the property to Baker is $3,000, market value at date of death; in this case, Baker would have no taxable gain if he sold the property for $3,000.

Long term versus short term. Long and short are relative terms; in income taxation the dividing line is six months. Long-term capital gains or losses result from the sale or exchange of capital assets held for more than six months; short-term for those held six months or less.

Short-term gains must be reported in full and are taxed as ordinary income. Only one-half of long-term gains are included in adjusted gross income, and the maximum rate of tax applicable to the total gain is 25%. For example, suppose that a taxpayer subject to a marginal tax rate of 30% has a $1,000 long-term capital gain. He would include $500 in adjusted gross income and pay a $150 (30% × $500) tax on the gain. In effect the tax rate applicable to his $1,000 long-term gain is 15%, one-half of his marginal rate. On the other hand, suppose the same taxpayer has a marginal tax rate of 80%. If he were to include $500 (one-half of the long-term gain) in adjusted gross income and apply the 80% mar ginal rate, his tax would be $400, or 40% of the total $1,000 gain. The law, however, sets the maximum rate at 25%, and therefore the taxpayer would be entitled to compute his tax as 25% of $1,000, or $250. In this case the rate applicable to the long-term capital gain is *less* than one-half of his marginal rate of tax.

Capital *losses,* either long-term, short-term, or a combination of both, may be deducted from other gross income up to a maximum of $1,000 or the taxable income for the year, whichever is smaller.

Long- and short-term transactions must be combined in a certain way in arriving at taxable income. First, all long-term gains and long-term losses must be offset against each other to produce a net long-term gain or loss. Short-term gains and losses must be similarly combined. When this has been done a number of possible situations exist:

1. *Both a net long-term gain and a net short-term gain.* In this case the two items are treated separately: the short-term gain is included in gross income and treated as ordinary income; only one-half of the long-term gain is included in adjusted gross income.

2. *Losses (of either type) greater than gains (of either type); or both long-term and short-term losses.* In this case the capital losses are combined into one figure and, up to $1,000, may be deducted to arrive at adjusted gross income. Any amount not deducted in a given year may be carried over and applied over the next five years as a short-term (by definition) capital loss.

3. *Gains (of either type) greater than losses (of either type).* Long-term and short-term must be offset to produce a net capital gain that is either long-term or short-term in nature, depending on the characteristic of the dominant gain.

These rules may be illustrated as follows:

Case 1	*Case 2(a)*	*Case 2(b)*
Net LTCG $2,000	*Net LTCG* $2,000	*Net LTCL* $2,000
Net STCG 800	*Net STCL* 2,900	*Net STCL* 3,000
	Total capital loss .... $ 900	*Total capital loss* $5,000
Result: Reported separately. All of STCG included in gross income; one-half of LTCG included in adjusted gross income.	*Result: All deductible to arrive at adjusted gross income.*	*Result: $1,000 deductible to arrive at adjusted gross income. Balance carried over to future years.*

Case 3(a)	*Case 3(b)*
Net LTCG $3,000	*Net LTCL* $2,600
Net STCL 1,800	*Net STCG* 3,000
Total capital gain (long-term) ... $1,200	*Total capital gain (short-term in nature)* ...... $ 400
Result: $600 included in adjusted gross income.	*Result: Included in gross income in full and taxed as ordinary income.*

Business plant and equipment. Real or depreciable property used in a trade or business is *not* a capital asset under the tax law. Thus any losses realized on such property are fully deductible. However, any gains from the sale of real or depreciable property held over six months are treated as long-term capital gains, giving business taxpayers the full benefit of the 50% long-term capital gain deduction.

Deductions to arrive at adjusted gross income. The deductions from gross income allowed in computing adjusted gross income may be classified as follows :

1. *Business expenses.* These include all ordinary and necessary expenses of carrying on a trade, business, or profession (other than as an employee). In the actual tax computation, business expenses are deducted from business revenues, and net business income is then included in adjusted gross income.
2. *Employees' expenses.* Certain limited expenses incurred by employees in connection with their employment are allowed as a deduction:

a. *Reimbursed expenses.* Expenses for which the employee was reimbursed by his employer. The reimbursement must be included in gross income, so that a reimbursement larger than the actual expense becomes a part of taxable income.

b. *Travel expenses.* If an employee is away from home (absent from his residence overnight) performing his duties as an employee, he may deduct all ordinary and necessary expenses such as transportation, meals, and lodging. Transportation expenses incurred by an employee in connection with his duties as an employee may be deducted in any case.

c. *"Outside salesmen" expenses.* A person engaged principally in soliciting business for his employer at places other than the employer's place of business qualifies as an outside salesman. He is allowed to deduct such expenses as telephone, telegraph, secretarial help, and entertainment, in addition to the expenses mentioned in (*a*) and (*b*) above.

3. *Expenses attributable to rents and royalties.* Expenses, such as depreciation, property taxes, repairs, maintenance, interest on indebtedness related to property, and any other expense incurred in connection with the earning of rental or royalty income, are allowed as a deduction. This means that *net income* derived from rents and royalties is included in adjusted gross income.

4. *Losses from the sale or exchange of property.* It property has been acquired for the production of income,[4] the loss resulting from its sale or exchange may be deducted against other items of gross income, up to $1,000 in any one year or the amount of taxable income, whichever is less. Losses from the sale of capital assets must first be offset against capital gains, as described earlier.

5. *Long-term capital gain deduction.* One-half of long-term capital gains is a deduction to arrive at adjusted gross income.

Deductions from adjusted gross income. The individual taxpayer has an option with respect to deductions *from* adjusted gross income. He may choose to take an unidentified standard deduction, or he may choose to itemize his deductions, in which case he may deduct a number of expenses specified in the law as itemized deductions.

The standard deduction. The standard deduction is equal to 10% of adjusted gross income, with a maximum deduction of $1,000. For example, if a taxpayer has adjusted gross income of $8,000, his standard deduction is $800. If he has adjusted gross income of $25,000, his standard deduction is $1,000, the legal limit.

The existence of the standard deduction explains in part the im-

---

[4] Losses arising from the sale of personal property, such as a home or personal automobile, are not deductible. On the other hand, gains from the sale of personal property are taxable. This appears inconsistent, until one realizes that a loss on the sale of personal property usually reflects depreciation through use, which is a personal expense.

portance of the distinction between deductions *to arrive at* and deductions *from* adjusted gross income. Deductions to arrive at adjusted gross do not affect the decision to take the standard deduction. However, deductions from adjusted gross income (other than personal exemptions) are relinquished if the standard deduction is taken.

Itemized deductions. Some of the common itemized deductions are discussed below:

1. *Interest.* Interest on any loan, installment contract, or other indebtedness is deductible as an itemized deduction.

2. *Taxes.* In general, all state and local taxes (with the exception of estate, gift, and inheritance taxes) are deductible by the person on whom they are imposed. No Federal taxes are deductible. In addition, the necessary cost of determining or collecting a refund of any tax is deductible.

3. *Contributions.* Contributions by individuals to recognized charitable, religious, educational, and certain other nonprofit organizations are deductible, within certain limits. If contributions to churches, hospitals, and educational institutions (known as CHE contributions) are at least 10% of adjusted gross income, the limit is 30%. Otherwise the limit is 20% of adjusted gross plus the amount of CHE contributions.

4. *Medical expenses.* Medical and dental expenses of the taxpayer and his family are deductible to the extent that they exceed 3% of adjusted gross income, subject to certain maximum limits. Medical expenses include the cost of medicine and drugs in excess of 1% of adjusted gross income. To illustrate: if a taxpayer has $6,000 adjusted gross income, drug expenses of $100, and other medical expenses of $300, his medical deduction is $160. [Drugs $100 − $60 (1% of adjusted gross income) = $40, plus other medical expenses of $300 = $340, less $180 (3% of adjusted gross income) = $160.] If the taxpayer or his wife is sixty-five years of age or over, the 3% limitation is dropped.

5. *Casualty losses.* Losses from fire, storm, shipwreck, theft, or other casualty of unexpected or unusual cause are allowed as itemized deductions, up to the amount of the tax basis of the property involved.

6. *Expenses related to the production of income.* In this category are included any necessary expenses in producing or collecting income or for the management, conservation, or maintenance of income-producing property, other than those deductible to arrive at adjusted gross income.

Since the law is general rather than specific in this area, many rules about the deductibility of specific items result from past court cases. Examples of allowable deductions are: union dues, the cost of uniforms and work clothes when required by employment and if not suitable for off-duty wear, rental of safety deposit box in which securities are kept. Examples of nondeductible items: cost of going to and from work, campaign expenses of candidates seeking election.

7. *Net operating loss carry-over.* Taxable income may be either positive or negative. If positive income were taxed and no allowance made for operating losses, a taxpayer whose business income fluctuated between

income and loss would pay a relatively higher tax than one having a steady income averaging the same amount. Therefore, the tax law allows the carry-over of net operating losses as an offset against the income of other years. At the present time a loss must be carried back against the income of the three preceding years, and then forward against the income of five succeeding years. Thus the taxpayer has a total of eight years in which to average losses against income.

Personal exemptions. In addition to itemized deductions, a deduction from adjusted gross income is allowed for personal exemptions. One exemption each is allowed for the taxpayer, his spouse (if a joint return is filed), and each person who qualifies as a dependent of the taxpayer. In recent years the amount of each personal exemption has been $600.

The term *dependent* has a particular meaning under the law. Briefly but incompletely stated, a dependent is a person who (1) receives over one-half of his support from the taxpayer, (2) is either closely related to the taxpayer or lives in his home, and (3) has gross income during the year of less than $600, unless he or she is a child of the taxpayer who is under nineteen years of age or a full-time student.[5]

A taxpayer and his spouse may each claim an additional exemption if he or she is blind, or if either is sixty-five years of age or over. These extra exemptions do not apply to dependents.

Tax returns and payment of the tax. Every individual who has gross income in excess of the amount of his own personal exemption (or two exemptions in the case of persons over sixty-five) must file an income tax return within 3 1/2 months after the close of the taxable year. On the calendar-year basis, applicable to most taxpayers, the due date is thus April 15. If a set of accounting records is kept, a taxpayer may elect to report and pay income taxes on the basis of any twelve-month fiscal year.

Since 1943, the payment of Federal income taxes has been on a "pay as you go" basis. The procedure by which employers withhold income taxes from the wages of employees has been discussed in a previous chapter. To equalize the treatment of employees and self-employed persons, the tax law requires persons who have income in excess of a given amount, from which no withholdings have been made, to file a Declaration of Estimated Income Tax and to pay estimated taxes in quarterly installments. An under- or overpayment is adjusted when the tax return is filed at the regular time. This provision also applies to employees having large incomes, since the withholding provisions do not require adequate payroll deductions against incomes over $10,000 per year. Persons who do not comply with these requirements are subject to a penalty equivalent to an interest charge on the tax not paid at the proper time, with allowances made for reasonable errors in forecasting income.

---

[5] A child under nineteen or a full-time student who qualifies as a dependent in all other respects but who earns over $600 in any one year has, in effect, two personal exemptions. One may be taken by the taxpayer who claims him as a dependent. The other he will claim for himself on his own personal tax return.

Tax credits. When the tax liability on net taxable income has been computed, the final step in arriving at the amount of tax due is to deduct certain credits against the tax. The most common tax credits are:

1. *Taxes withheld or paid on declared estimates.* The taxpayer takes credit for all taxes withheld from his salary and for any quarterly payments made on the basis of his Declaration of Estimated Income Tax.

2. *Dividend credit.* A tax credit is allowed equal to 4% of any dividends (from United States corporations) included in gross income. This is a concession to the argument that corporate income is hit relatively heavily by both the corporate income tax and personal taxes on dividends received by stockholders. For example, a husband and wife who hold stock jointly and receive $600 in dividends will first exclude $100 ($50 each) of these dividends, and include $500 in gross income. Then they may take a credit of $20 (4% of $500) against their personal income tax.

3. *Retirement income credit.* A person aged sixty-five or over who receives retirement income is entitled to a tax credit of 20% of all retirement income up to $1,200 per year, or a maximum credit of $240 against his income tax. Retirement income in general is income from pensions, interest, rents, and dividends. The provision was made to compensate somewhat for the fact that social security benefits are not taxable.

4. *Miscellaneous.* Certain other tax credits, not of general applicability, are allowed. An example is the credit for taxes paid to foreign countries on income taxed by the United States.

Illustrative individual income tax computation. The following demonstration, based on assumed data for a hypothetical taxpayer, illustrates the main features of the individual Federal income tax computation:

Statement of facts. Mr. M. J. Bricker is married and provides over one-half of the support of a son and daughter. The son, aged twenty, is a full-time student at the state university, and earned $800 in part-time work during the current year. The daughter is fifteen years of age and had income of $200 from baby sitting. Neither Mr. nor Mrs. Bricker is sixty-five years of age or over, or blind. Mr. Bricker is a practicing attorney. Mrs. Bricker works part time as a secretary for an insurance company. This information is from the business and personal records of the family:

NOTE SUPPORTING COMPUTATIONS IN SCHEDULES A TO F

Income:

Net income from law practice (gross fees $50,000; operating expenses $30,000)	$20,000
Mrs. Bricker's salary (income taxes withheld $475)	2,700
Interest on state bonds	250
Interest credited to savings accounts	220
Dividends received (on stock owned by Mr. Bricker)	1,200
Dividends received (on stock inherited by Mrs. Bricker)	500
Gain on sale of stock (stock purchased several years ago by Mr. Bricker for $1,600; sold for $2,400, net of brokerage fees)	800

Expenditures:

Contributions to church and university	$ 3,000
Other contributions to recognized nonprofit organizations	800
Interest paid on mortgage on residence	912
Property taxes paid on residence	480
State taxes paid:	
Sales tax	240
Automobile license	20
Gasoline tax	40
Family medical expenses:	
Doctor and hospital fees	800
Drugs and medicine	300
Travel expenses incurred by Mrs. Bricker on trip for employer	120
Damage to auto in accident (Damage $400, insurance recovery $300) ..	100
Payments during the year on declaration of estimated income tax	3,000

The computation of the Brickers' income tax on a joint return might appear as follows, in summary form:

MR. AND MRS. M. J. BRICKER
Illustrative Income Tax Computation
(See Schedules A to F for details)

Schedule:

A	Gross income		$55,320
B	Deductions to arrive at adjusted gross income		30,520
	Adjusted gross income		$24,800
	Deductions from adjusted gross income:		
C	Itemized deductions	$5,700	
D	Personal exemptions	2,400	8,100
	Taxable income		$16,700
E	Amount of tax		$ 4,158
F	Tax credits		3,539
	Amount of tax due		$ 619

Schedule A: Gross Income

Income from law practice	$50,000
Dividends (Mr. Bricker $1,200 less $50 exclusion; Mrs. Bricker $500	
less $50 exclusion)	1,600
Mrs. Bricker's salary	2,700
Interest income on savings	220
Long-term capital gain (on sale of stock held over six months)......	800
Total gross income	$55,320

Schedule B: Deductions to Arrive at Adjusted Gross Income

Operating expenses of law practice	$30,000
Travel expenses by Mrs. Bricker in connection with employer's business	120
Long-term capital gain deduction (50% of $800)	400
Total deductions to arrive at adjusted gross income	$30,520

Schedule C: Itemized Deductions

Contributions (CHE contributions are over 10% of adjusted gross income, so limit is 30%; total contributions are within this limit) ..		$3,800
Interest on mortgage		912
Property taxes		480
State taxes (sales tax, $240; automobile license, $20; gasoline tax, $40)		300
Medical expenses:		
Drugs in excess of 1% of adjusted gross income	$ 52	
Doctor and hospital expenses	800	
Total	$852	
Less: 3% of adjusted gross income	744	108
Casualty loss (damage to auto not covered by insurance)		100
Total itemized deductions		$5,700

Schedule D: Personal Exemptions

Mr. Bricker	1
Mrs. Bricker	1
Dependents:	
Daughter	1
Son (since he is a student, earnings over $600 do not disqualify him as a dependent)	1
Total personal exemptions	4
Amount of personal exemption ($600 × 4)	$2,400

Schedule E: Tax Computation

Taxable income		$16,700
One-half of taxable income (income splitting on joint return)		$ 8,350 *
Tax on $8,000 (from rate schedule)	$1,960	
Tax on $350 at marginal rate of 34%	119	
One-half of total tax	$2,079	
Multiply by	2	
Total income tax liability		$ 4,158

Schedule F: Credits against the Tax

Withheld from Mrs. Bricker's salary	$ 475
Payments by Mr. Bricker on declaration of estimated tax	3,000
Dividend credit (4% of $1,600)	64
Total tax credits	$3,539

* Special tables are available from which the joint-return tax on taxable income of $16,700 can be read directly. The income splitting shown in this computation is taken into account in the figures in such tables.

Partnerships

The Federal income tax law generally follows a "conduit" theory of partnership income; that is, partnerships are treated as a conduit through which taxable income flows to the partners. An information return must be filed by all partnerships showing the determination of net income and the share of each partner. Under the conduit philosophy, certain items of partnership income and deductions are segregated, and each partner is required to treat his share of each of these items as if he had received or paid them personally. In general, segregated items are those granted special tax treatment; they include tax-exempt interest, all capital gains and losses, charitable contributions, and dividends received. Any salaries actually paid to partners may be deducted in arriving at partnership taxable income, but must be reported by the individual partners on their personal returns.

ELEMENTS OF PARTNERSHIP INCOME

To illustrate, assume that the AB Partnership has partnership taxable income of $50,000, *after* salaries of $6,000 each to partners A and B, and that the share of partnership income and segregated items is as follows:

	Total	A's share	B's share
Partnership taxable income	$50,000	$30,000	$20,000
Long-term capital gain	1,000	600	400
Short-term capital gains	2,000	1,200	800
Dividends received	4,000	2,400	1,600
Contributions	(3,000)	(1,800)	(1,200)
Tax-exempt interest received	800	480	320
Total partnership income per books	$54,800	$32,880	$21,920

In his personal income tax return, Partner B, for example, would combine the following items with his own personal income and deductions: Salary received $6,000; income from partnership $20,000; long-term capital gain (subject to 50% deduction) $200; short-term capital gain $800; dividends received (net of $50 exclusion) $1,550; contributions (itemized deduction) $1,200. The tax-exempt interest is excluded from B's gross income. B's personal income tax would then be computed in the manner previously illustrated.

Corporations

The ordinary business corporation is a taxable entity and is subject to a tax at special rates on its net taxable income. Corporate taxable income in general is computed in the same manner as for individuals, with the following major differences:

1. Corporations are not entitled to certain deductions of a personal nature allowed to individuals. Examples are medical expenses, the standard deduction, and personal exemptions. Because there is no standard deduction, the concept of adjusted gross income is not applicable to corporations.

2. The dividend exclusion and 4% tax credit are not applicable to corporations. Instead, a corporation may take, as a special deduction to arrive at taxable income, 85% of dividends received from domestic corporations. This means in effect that only 15% of intercorporate dividends are taxed to the receiving corporation.

3. Corporations may deduct capital losses only as an offset against capital gains. If capital losses exceed gains, no deduction for the loss is allowed in the current year. It may, however, be carried over and offset against any taxable capital gains during the succeeding five years.

4. Corporations are not entitled to the 50% deduction for long-term capital gains. The corporation is, however, subject to a maximum tax rate of 25% on the total amount of all net long-term capital gains.

5. The limit on the deductibility of charitable contributions for corporations is 5% of taxable income, computed without the deduction of charitable contributions. Contributions in excess of the limit may be carried forward for two succeeding years and deducted, if total contributions (including those carried forward) in those years are within the 5% limit.

NOTE DIFFERENCE BETWEEN ACCOUNTING AND TAXABLE INCOME

Corporate tax returns must be filed 2 1/2 months after the end of the taxable year. A corporation whose tax is expected to be over $100,000 in any given year is required to prepay the tax partially by making certain advance payments on the amount of estimated tax in excess of $100,000.

To illustrate some of the features of the income tax law as it applies to corporations, a tax computation for a hypothetical corporation is:

HYPOTHETICAL CORPORATION
Illustrative Tax Computation

Revenues:		
Sales revenues		$200,000
Dividends received from domestic corporations		10,000
		$210,000
Expenses:		
Cost of goods sold	$118,000	
Other operating expenses	50,000	168,000
Net income per books		$ 42,000
Add back (items not deductible for tax purposes):		
Capital loss deducted as part of operating expenses		3,000
Charitable contributions in excess of 5% limit		1,200
		$ 46,200

Special deductions:	
Dividends received credit (85% of $10,000)	8,500
Net taxable income	$ 37,700
Tax computation:	
Tax on first $25,000 of income at 30%	$ 7,500
Tax on income over $25,000 ($12,700 × 52%)	6,604
Total tax due	$ 14,104

Taxes as a factor in business decisions

Income taxation has become so complex that detailed tax planning must be left to experts. However, businessmen should learn to recognize areas of decision in which income tax considerations may be significant.

Form of organization. Corporations are taxed at rates ranging from 30 to 52%, may deduct salaries paid to owners as an expense, but may not deduct dividends paid to stockholders. Stockholders must pay a tax on dividend income. Owners of unincorporated businesses, on the other hand, are taxed on their share of the annual taxable income, whether or not they withdraw anything from the business.

Since retained earnings have been taxed only at corporate rates, a corporation may offer a tax saving whenever a stockholder's marginal tax rate is greater than that of the corporation. For example, suppose that Able, a proprietor, has business income of $50,000, files a joint return, and takes the standard deduction. His Federal incomes taxes (using rates shown on page 765) would be $19,002. Now suppose that Able incorporates his business and draws a salary of $20,000 as president. The corporation has $30,000 taxable income, after salary expense, and pays income taxes of $10,100. Able's tax on his $20,000 salary would be $4,532. Thus the combined corporate and individual tax is $14,632, or $4,370 less than Able's taxes as an individual proprietor. Of course, if the corporation pays dividends, Able will be subject to tax on these. Also if the stock increases in value because of reinvested earnings and Able sells at a gain, he would have to pay a capital gains tax. These and other factors must be given careful consideration in assessing the relative advantages of a given form of business organization. Adding to the complexity is the fact that under certain conditions partnerships may choose to be taxed as corporations and small, closely held corporations may choose to be taxed as partnerships.

Accounting procedures. Taxpayers gain by postponing the recognition of taxable income. Even though all income must be reported at some time, a postponement represents an interest-free loan to the extent that taxes are deferred. A number of alternative accounting procedures operate to defer taxable income. For example, during periods of rising prices the lifo method of inventory pricing will result in charging higher current costs against revenues, thus reducing taxable income. Depreciation methods (such as the sum-of-the-years'-digits method) that produce high charges in early years of service life and smaller charges in later years have the same effect. The cash basis of accounting postpones the recognition of taxable income and also allows a taxpayer to control income by timing the receipt and expenditure of cash, particularly in months near the end of any taxable year.

A policy of postponing income and accelerating deductions may boomerang if tax rates rise in later years. Companies taking maximum depreciation deductions during the 1930s presumably regretted their decision when confronted with higher tax rates during World War II.

Financial planning. Taxable income computed on the accrual basis is not necessarily matched by an inflow of spendable funds. A healthy profit picture accompanied by a tight cash position is not unusual at the end of a successful year. Income taxes are a substantial cash drain and an important factor in planning cash requirements. This is true even for unincorporated businesses because money to pay taxes often must be withdrawn by the owners.

Different forms of financing produce different tax costs. Interest on debt, for example, is fully deductible while dividends on preferred or common stocks are not. This factor operates as a strong incentive to finance expansion by borrowing. Suppose that a company needs $100,000 and can expect to earn 12% on the investment of these funds in productive assets. If the company issues $100,000 in 6% preferred stock it will earn, after taxes, $5,760 (12,000 less 52% of $12,000), an amount $240 less than the $6,000 preferred dividend requirements. If the company borrows the $100,000 at 6% its taxable income will be $6,000 ($12,000 earnings less interest expense of $6,000). The tax on this amount at 52% would be $3,120, leaving income of $2,880 available for common stockholders or for reinvestment in the business.

Form of transactions. A transaction, undertaken solely to save taxes and having no business purpose, may be declared legally ineffective and income taxes assessed as if it had not occurred. However, many transactions that have a business purpose may be arranged to alter the tax result. For example, when real property is sold under an installment contract, the gain may be prorated for tax purposes over the period during which installment payments are received. In order to qualify, however, the payments received during the first year must not exceed 30% of the net selling price. By arranging the down payment within these limits, the tax is postponed to correspond more closely with the receipt of cash.

PROPERTY TAXES

Property taxes are an *ad valorem* tax, that is, they are based upon the assessed value of the property. Legally all property falls into two classes, *real* and *personal*, and different rates of tax may be levied on each class. Real property includes land and all growth or structures permanently attached to the land, such as buildings, trees, sewers, and sidewalks. All property other than real property is personal property; it includes business inventories, equipment, and intangibles such as stocks, bonds, receivables, bank deposits, and other claims or rights.

Assessed value and rates

The total amount of property taxes levied by a governmental unit is a product of the assessed value of all property within its jurisdiction and the tax rate. Tax rates are based on advance estimates of revenue needs and total assessed value. Thus if the assessed value of all property within a city is $200 million and the city budget is $5 million, the tax rate necessary to balance the budget would be $25 per $1,000 of assessed valuation. This tax rate would be described as 25 *mills* (1/10 of a cent) per $1 of assessed valuation.

For reasons that are not entirely clear, most local governments establish assessed value at some fraction of fair market value. For example, if all property is to be assessed at 25% of fair market value, a given property worth $20,000 would have an assessed valuation of $5,000. If all property were assessed at actual value, property taxes would be identical; the assessed value would simply be higher and the millage rate correspondingly lower.

Property is often subject to taxes levied by more than one jurisdiction. For example, a single piece of land may be within a school district, a city, and a county and may be subject to taxes by all three governmental units. Usually, in order to minimize the effort and expense of levying and collecting such taxes, the property is assessed by the county, and all taxes are collected by the county and distributed among the various taxing units.

Property tax dates

Three dates are significant in connection with property taxes, although in some cases two or more of the three may coincide. The *assessment date* is the date as of which the assessed valuation of the property is determined. The *lien date* is the date the tax becomes a charge or a lien against the property. The *payment date* varies greatly among various governmental units, but typically the taxpayer may pay his tax in a lump sum (in which case he may get a cash discount) or in installments throughout the tax year. Penalties may be levied on taxes that are past due, and if taxes are delinquent for a specified time the property may be seized by the government and sold to recover taxes due and unpaid.

Accounting for property taxes

Legally property taxes do not accrue in the same way that interest, for example, accrues; rather they attach to property as of a particular moment in time, the lien date. Economically, however, property taxes are a payment for the right to use and enjoy property throughout the fiscal year of the taxing authority. Accounting for property taxes is responsive to both these viewpoints. Since the tax comes into existence at the lien date, the appropriate entry at this time (assuming for example that the lien date is July 1) is as follows:

> July 1   Deferred Property Taxes 1,200
>   Property Taxes Payable   1,200
>   To recognize the liability for property taxes
> for the period July 1 to June 30.

Property tax expense should be prorated and charged against revenues over the fiscal year of the taxing unit, in this case July 1 to June 30. The entry at the end of each month would thus be:

> Property Tax Expense 100
>   Deferred Property Taxes   100
> To record property tax expense for the month.

When the tax is paid, either in total or in installments, the liability account Property Taxes Payable is debited. In the above example, if the entire taxes were paid on November 30, the only balance sheet item left at the end of the calendar year would be the asset account Deferred Property Taxes, $600. This balance represents the tax expense paid in advance for the succeeding six-month period.

In some jurisdictions the exact amount of property tax is not known on the lien date. In this case an estimate can be made, based on last year's tax and any information available as to changes in assessed valuation or tax rates. When the tax bill is received the amount of Deferred Property Taxes, Property Taxes Payable, and the monthly charge to Property Tax Expense can be adjusted accordingly.

Property taxes added to the valuation of property

In some cases taxes paid in connection with property represent not an expense of the period but an addition to the cost of the property.

One such case arises when delinquent taxes are paid on property that is purchased. Since such taxes are a lien against the property, they were presumably taken into account in arriving at the purchase price and are in effect an adjustment of that price. For example, if a buyer feels that a piece of land is worth $10,000 but finds that it is subject to $800 in delinquent taxes, he will agree to pay only $9,200 to the seller. The cost of the property for accounting purposes, however, is $10,000—the $9,200 cash price plus the $800 of delinquent taxes that must be paid in order to get a clear title to the property. All subsequent taxes are an expense, a cost of using the property for current productive purposes.

A similar situation arises in the case of *special assessments* levied by governmental units as reimbursement for improvements on or adjacent to real property. For example, suppose a buyer purchases an unimproved lot for $500. The city then puts in streets, sidewalks, sewers, and water mains, and assesses $1,300, the cost of these improvements, against the benefited property. The assessment should be added to the cost of the lot; the investment in the improved property is a total of $1,800. In the typical case, these improvements are permanent, since costs of upkeep and repair will be met out of the general revenues of the city.

SALES AND EXCISE TAXES

A flat rate tax based on retail sales within their boundaries is levied by many states and a number of cities. Typically certain classes of sales are exempt, notably food and commodities, such as gasoline and cigarettes, already subject to special excise taxes. To restrict the practice of purchasing outside the state to avoid the tax, some states levy a supplementary *use tax*, applicable to goods purchased outside the state and brought in.

Typically a sales tax is imposed on the consumer, but the seller must collect the tax, file tax returns at times specified by law, and remit a percentage of his reported sales. The actual tax collected by the seller from his customers may be greater or less than the amount due because no tax is collected on sales under a certain amount and, due to rounding of pennies, the tax is not always the exact specified percentage of individual sales.

Accounting for sales taxes

Since the seller is merely a conduit for sales taxes, he logically should record a liability at the time of the sale as follows:

SALES TAX RECORDED AT TIME OF SALE	*Accounts Receivable (or Cash)* *1,030*	
	Sales Tax Payable	*30*
	Sales	*1,000*
	To record sale of $1,000 subject to 3% sales tax.	

A special column in the sales journal may be used to accumulate sales taxes payable. An adjustment would be made for any discrepancy between the total sales tax accrued and the actual amount of the liability based on total sales.

Where it is not convenient to set up the sales tax liability at the time of sale, an alternative procedure is to credit sales with the entire amount to be collected, including the sales tax, and to make an adjustment at the end of each period to reflect sales tax payable. For example, suppose that the total recorded sales for the period under this method were $267,800. Since the Sales account includes both the sale price and the 3% sales tax, it is apparent that $267,800 is 103% of the actual sales figure. Actual sales are $260,000 ($267,800 ÷ 1.03) and the amount of sales tax due is $7,800. (Proof: 3% of $260,000 = $7,800.) The entry to record the liability for sales taxes would be:

SALES TAX RECORDED AS ADJUSTMENT OF SALES

Sales *7,800*
      Sales Tax Payable *7,800*
To remove sales taxes of 3% on $260,000 of sales from the Sales account, and reflect as a liability.

Any discrepancy between the tax due and the amount actually collected from customers, under this method, would be automatically absorbed in the net sales figure. Where not all classes of sales are subject to the tax, it will be necessary to keep a record of taxable and nontaxable sales.

Federal excise taxes

The Federal government levies a form of sales tax known as an *excise* tax, on certain sales at retail (for example, jewelry and entertainment admissions) and upon sales by manufacturers (for example, automobiles, cigarettes, liquor). These taxes may be, and usually are, passed on to the customer in the price of the product. Since these are taxes on particular products, it is usually most convenient to record the tax liability at the time of sale.

QUESTIONS

1. What is meant by the terms *progressive, regressive,* and *proportional* in connection with taxes? Give an example to illustrate each.

2. Explain the difference between the marginal rate and the average rate of a tax. What is the *marginal* income tax rate for a single individual having a taxable income of $100,000? What is the *average* rate of tax? (Use the table on page 765.)

3. What is meant by the term "income splitting" with reference to a married couple who file a joint return? Doran, a bachelor, expects to have a taxable income of $16,600 this year. What amount of Federal income tax would he save if he were to get married before the end of the year?

4. Q is a doctor who files his tax return on the cash basis. During the current year he collected $8,000 from patients for medical services rendered in prior years, and billed patients $28,000 for services rendered this year. He has accounts receivable of $9,400 at the end of the period. What is the amount of gross income he should report on his Federal income tax return for the current year?

5. R is a cash basis taxpayer. During December of the current year dividends were declared on stock that he owned; he received the dividend check on December 30 and deposited it in his bank account on January 4 of the following year. He paid a year's rent on certain business property on December 31 of the current year. How would these items be handled in his Federal income tax return for the current year?

6. Assuming that a taxpayer uses the accrual basis of accounting, why would his accounting income ever differ from his taxable income? State three general sources of difference.

7. Why does it make any difference in computing the amount of income tax whether a deduction is allowable to arrive at adjusted gross income, or from adjusted gross income? Give an example of an expenditure that might result in either kind of deduction, depending on the circumstances of the case, and explain.

8. T purchased certain shares of stock for $2,000 in 1960. In 1961, when the stock was worth $5,000, he gave it to W; in 1962 W died and the stock, now worth $6,000, passed by will to S. What amount of gain would have been reported for income tax purposes if the stock had been sold for $7,500 in 1960? In 1961? In 1962?

9. Why is postponement of income taxes an economic advantage? Give two examples of permissible procedures that result in a postponement of the payment of income taxes.

10. What is a net operating loss carry-over? What is the purpose of this provision of the income tax law?

11. The total assessed valuation in a certain city is $63 million. The city budget shows that $1,278,900 in tax revenues is needed for operations during the coming year. What will the tax rate be, in mills, for the coming fiscal year? A resident owning property that is assessed at $15,000 will pay how much in city taxes?

12. J. Ryersee purchased certain land to be used as a building site. He paid $3,000 down, gave an interest-bearing note for $7,500, and paid $1,200 to the county treasurer for property taxes. Of the property taxes, $950 represented delinquent taxes on the land and $250 represented the taxes for the year following the date of purchase. Shortly after the date of purchase, Ryersee paid $650 as a special assessment for paving the streets that surrounded the property. At what cost should Ryersee record the property in his books?

PROBLEMS

Group A

27A-1. *Case A.* Avery has total income this year of $18,000; income excluded for Federal income tax purposes of $800; deductions to arrive at adjusted gross income of $1,300; personal exemptions of $2,400; and itemized deductions of $870.

Instructions. Determine the amount of Avery's adjusted gross income and his taxable income for the year.

Case B. Bray files his Federal income tax return on a cash basis. During the current year he had net income from his business (computed on an accrual basis) of $21,600. Bray's business has no inventories. Between the beginning and the end of the current year, receivables relating to revenues increased by $3,000, and payables relating to operating expenses decreased by $1,700. Included in the reported business income is $300 of interest received on municipal bonds. Bray has a personal savings account to which $180 in interest was credited during the year, none of which was withdrawn by him. Bray has $3,000 in personal exemptions, $1,700 in itemized deductions, and $340 in deductions to arrive at adjusted gross income (in addition to business expenses already taken into account in computing his business income).

Instructions. Determine the amount of adjusted gross income and taxable income Bray should report for Federal income tax purposes.

27A-2. Kell & Sons keep their accounts on a calendar year. Financial statements are prepared monthly. The fiscal year of the local governmental units runs from July 1 to June 30. Property is assessed on March 1; the lien date is July 1; and payment, if made before October 30, is subject to a 2% cash discount.

On January 1, 1962, the company had on its books prepaid property taxes in the amount of $2,700. The assessment by local governmental units was 62 mills on 30% of the property valuation. The valuation of all Kell & Sons property is $300,000. The company follows a policy of setting up the full liability for property taxes, net of discount, on the lien date. Taxes were paid in full on October 20, 1962.

Instructions

a. Prepare in general journal form the following entries relating to property taxes that would be made by Kell & Sons:

(1) Monthly adjustments for property taxes on January 31, 1962
(2) Entry on July 1, 1962
(3) Payment of tax on October 20, 1962
(4) Monthly adjustment for property taxes on November 30, 1962

b. What will be the balances in the balance sheet accounts relating to property taxes on the following dates?

(1) May 1, 1962
(2) August 1, 1962
(3) November 1, 1962
(4) December 31, 1962

27A-3. Louis B. Major, aged sixty-six, and Mrs. Major, aged fifty-eight, file a joint return. They furnish over one-half the support of their son, Scott, who earned $1,200 and is attending college full time; and of Mrs. Major's mother, aged eighty, who has no income. Various receipts and expenditures of Mr. and Mrs. Major are listed below:

Mr. Major

Receipts:

Withdrawals from business (sales $130,000; cost of goods sold $76,500; operating expenses $28,500)	$15,000
Cash dividends on stock	1,625
Gain on sale of stock: stock purchased on Mar. 30 and sold on Nov. 15 of current year	2,600
Interest on school district bonds	850

Disbursements:

Charitable contributions	680
Property taxes on residence	520
Insurance on residence	120
Auto license	20
State gasoline tax	50
State sales tax	120
Medical expenses:	
Drugs	90
Doctor, dental, and hospital bills (all for Mr. and Mrs. Major) *	820
Windstorm damage to residence $500; insurance recovery $400	100
Interest on personal loan	60
Payments on declaration of estimated tax	6,000
Federal excise tax on new family car	150

* Since Mr. Major is over 65, the 3% medical expense exclusion does not apply (see page 774).

Mrs. Major

Receipts:

Rental of apartment building	$ 9,650
Dividends on stocks held	600
Received from sale of stock purchased for $1,800 five months previously	1,100

Disbursements:

Apartment building: (Depreciation basis is $60,000; depreciation rate 5%)	
Interest on mortgage	$ 780
Property taxes	830
Insurance (one year)	85
Repairs and maintenance	1,260
Charitable contributions	200

Instructions. Compute Mr. and Mrs. Major's income tax liability for the current year. Use the rates on page 765, remembering the income-splitting provision on a joint return.

27A-4. Cramer and Suger are partners in a wholesale coffee distributorship. The following information is taken from the partnership tax return:

	Total	Share of Cramer	Share of Suger
Partnership taxable income	$46,000	$32,200	$13,800
Long-term capital gain	3,600	2,520	1,080
Short-term capital gain	1,500	1,050	450
Short-term capital loss	(2,300)	(1,610)	(690)
Dividends received	750	525	225
Charitable contributions	(1,340)	(938)	(402)
Interest on state freeway bonds	370	259	111
Salaries to partners	18,000	6,000	12,000
Partnership net income per books (before partners' salaries)...................	$66,580	$40,006	$26,574

Suger is single, aged forty-two, and provides over one-half the support of his brother. The brother is a student, lives with his parents, and earned $550 during the year. Suger has a savings account to which interest of $180 was credited during the year, but he did not draw this out. He received dividends from personal stockholdings of $300.

Suger was in an auto accident while on a vacation trip during the year. Damages to his car were $890 and he incurred hospital and doctor bills of $2,612. Although the other driver was at fault, he was uninsured and Suger was unable to collect. Suger, himself, carries only public liability insurance.

Suger uses his car 50% of the time in his business. It cost $4,200, has an estimated life of five years, and salvage value at the end of this time of $700. He spent $240 on gasoline, including $50 in state gas taxes; $24 for license; $61 insurance; and $115 on other recurring expenses in maintaining the car. One-half of the auto expenses may be taken as a business expense.

Suger paid life insurance premiums of $360, made charitable contributions of $2,300, and paid $6,200 on his declaration of estimated income tax during the year.

Instructions. Compute the amount of Suger's Federal income tax liability, using the rate schedule on page 765. Prepare the computation in outline form and show all details in subsidiary schedules. (It is permissible in computing Federal income taxes to round all figures to the nearest dollar.)

27A-5. The information given below has been taken from the records of the Xena Corporation:

Sales	$836,000
Sales returns and allowances	8,670
Cost of goods sold	573,290
Officers' salaries expense	42,000
Dividends declared	25,000
Dividends received (on stock of domestic subsidiary corporation)	18,000

Other administrative expenses (including charitable contri-

butions of $7,600) $62,180

Selling expenses 78,300

Gain on sale of capital asset, acquired five years ago 12,420

Loss on sale of capital asset (acquired three months prior

to sale) 4,180

Instructions. On the basis of this information, prepare an income statement for the Xena Corporation. The company reports gains and losses on the sale of assets on the income statement.

In a separate schedule, show your computation of the provision for Federal income taxes for the year (rounding the provision to the nearest dollar). Use the corporation tax rate schedule given on page 765. *Note:* The limit on the deduction of charitable contributions is $5,270.

Group B

27B-1. *Instructions*

a. State for each of the following items whether, for Federal income tax purposes, it should be included in gross income or excluded from gross income.

(1) Tips received by a waiter

(2) Value of trip to Bermuda, given as a prize in a sales contest by an employer

(3) Proceeds of life insurance policy received on death of a parent

(4) Inheritance received on death of rich uncle

(5) Dividends on stock of Atlanta Paper Company

(6) Value of automobile won as a prize in a television quiz contest

(7) Value of United States Treasury bonds received as a gift

(8) Gain on the sale of personal residence

b. State for each of the following items whether, for Federal income tax purposes, it should be (1) deducted to arrive at adjusted gross income; (2) deducted from adjusted gross income; or (3) not deducted.

(1) Interest paid on mortgage covering rental property

(2) Expenses incurred by employee in connection with his job, for which he is reimbursed by employer

(3) Rent expense paid on personal residence

(4) Interest paid on mortgage covering personal residence

(5) Damage in storm to motorboat used for pleasure

(6) Carry forward of unused operating loss from previous year

(7) Loss on the sale of corporation bonds, by owner

(8) State sales tax paid on purchase of family automobile

(9) Fee paid for assistance in contesting additional income taxes assessed by Internal Revenue Service

27B-2. The Hardwood Furniture Company operates in a state that levies a 3% retail sales tax. The tax is imposed on all sales except those to schools and governmental organizations. The seller is required to collect the tax on each sale, to refund the tax on all returns, and to remit to the state government 3% of tax-

able net sales, less 10% of the tax, which the company may retain as a commission for its collection services. The Hardwood Furniture Company records
all sales and sales returns at the gross amount, including any applicable sales
tax. During the first three months of the current year, the amount credited to
Sales was $162,435.80 and the amount debited to Sales Returns was $2,646.51.
An analysis of invoices showed that nontaxable sales amounted to $16,420.50,
which were included in the sales total. There were no returns on these sales.

   Instructions. Compute the amount of sales tax liability as of the end of the
three-month period. Make the journal entry necessary to adjust the accounts
and establish this liability on the books.

27B-3. The Federal income tax information relating to an individual taxpayer given below
may be presumed to be accurately compiled:

Tax credits	*$1,100*
Deductions to arrive at adjusted gross income	*700*
Total ordinary income (including $800 from sources not	
subject to Federal income tax)	*8,800*
Itemized deductions	*670*
Long-term capital gain	*2,400*
Short-term capital loss	*600*

   Instructions
   a. Using these data, compute the income tax due, assuming that the taxpayer is married and has three dependents.
   b. Compute the income tax due, assuming that the taxpayer is an unmarried individual.

27B-4. *Instructions*
   a. Each of the following six cases represents a possible situation with respect to capital gains and losses. Assume that a taxpayer, Vernon Snow, has
salary income of $6,000 in addition to the items shown in each situation below.
Compute his adjusted gross income in each case:
   (1) Long-term capital gain $7,000; long-term capital loss $3,000; short-
term capital gain $5,000; short-term capital loss $2,500
   (2) Long-term capital gain $2,000; long-term capital loss $4,000; short-
term capital gain $800; short-term capital loss $3,500
   (3) Long-term capital gain $3,000; short-term capital loss $6,000
   (4) Long-term capital loss $3,000; short-term capital gain $4,800
   (5) Long-term capital gain $900; long-term capital loss $400; short-term
capital loss $1,100
   (6) Long-term capital gain $4,500; short-term capital loss $2,000
   b. Dykstra is single, has a net long-term capital gain of $10,000 in the
current year, and uses the standard deduction. Compute the amount of his
Federal income tax under each of the following conditions:
   (1) Ordinary income $33,600
   (2) Ordinary income $10,600
   Hint: Remember that the tax on long-term capital gains cannot exceed
25% of the gain.

27B-5. Huff, a bachelor, operates a business as a single proprietorship. During the current year the net income per books was $65,000. Huff withdrew $45,000 from the business. He has no outside income, and takes the standard deduction in his Federal income tax return.

At the end of the year, Huff is considering the possibility of incorporating his business. He would own all the capital stock except for a few qualifying shares. If the business had been incorporated during the current year, Huff would have paid himself a salary of $25,000 as president and would have received $20,000 in dividends on the common stock.

Instructions. (Round all figures to the nearest dollar.)

a. Compute the amount of tax that Huff would have to report this year on his personal Federal income tax return.

b. Compute the amount of tax that Huff would have reported had the business been incorporated, under the assumptions stated above.

c. Determine the amount after taxes that Huff would have left out of the $45,000 that he drew from the business under assumptions (*a*) and (*b*). Which form of business organization leaves him the greatest amount of cash after taxes?

d. Compare the total taxes that Huff would pay this year as a proprietor with the total of his personal taxes plus the tax that would be paid by the corporation under the above assumptions.

28

Analysis of financial statements. Statement of sources and applications of funds

The financial affairs of any business are of interest to a number of different groups: management, creditors, investors, and governmental agencies. Despite a considerable common interest, each group will place a greater emphasis on particular aspects of the total financial picture.

Investors are primarily interested in the earnings record of a company and its prospects for future growth and success. Creditors attempt to gauge a firm's ability to pay debts as they fall due. Management is interested in the long-run stability of the business and the efficiency of its operations; the executives view financial statements as the instrument panel of the business, which tells how things are running and warns them of conditions that require remedial action.

FINANCIAL STATEMENT ANALYSIS

Many complete books have been written on financial statement analysis; the subject encompasses the entire interpretive phase of accounting. In this chapter the discussion will be limited to the kind of analysis that can be made by "outsiders" who do not have access to the complete accounting records. Investors must rely to a considerable extent on financial statements in published annual and quarterly reports. In the case of large publicly held corporations, certain statements that must be filed with public agencies such as the Securities and Exchange Commission are available. Financial information for most sizable corporations is also published in such reference books as Moody's *Manual of Investments* and Standard & Poor's *Corporation Records.* Bankers are usually able to get more detailed information, such as a copy of the report prepared by an independent auditor, by requesting it as a condition for granting a loan. Trade creditors may obtain financial information for businesses of almost any size from such mercantile agencies as Dun and Bradstreet. Each of these groups seeks in the available financial statements and supplementary data the answers to the questions that most concern them.

Tools of analysis

Few figures on a financial statement are highly significant in and of themselves. It is their relationship to other quantities, or the amount and direction of change since a previous date, that is important. Analysis is largely a matter of establishing significant relationships and pointing up changes and trends. There are three widely used analytical techniques:

1. **Dollar and percentage changes.** The change in financial data over time is best exhibited in statements showing data for a series of years in adjacent columns. Such statements are called *comparative* financial statements. A highly condensed comparative balance sheet might appear as follows:

CONDENSED THREE-YEAR BALANCE SHEET DATA

X CORPORATION
Comparative Balance Sheet
As of December 31, 1960, 1961, 1962
(In thousands of dollars)

	1962	1961	1960
Assets:			
Current assets	$180	$150	$120
Plant and equipment	450	300	345
Total assets	$630	$450	$465
Liabilities & Stockholders' Equity:			
Current liabilities	$ 60	$ 80	$120
Long-term liabilities	200	100	
Capital stock	300	300	300
Retained earnings (deficit)	70	(30)	45
Total liabilities & stockholders' equity	$630	$450	$465

The usefulness of comparative financial statements covering two or more annual periods is well recognized. It is not uncommon to find in published annual reports comparative financial statements covering a period as long as 10 years. By observing the change in various items period by period, the analyst may gain valuable clues as to important trends affecting the business.

The dollar amount of change from year to year is of some interest;

reducing this to percentage terms adds perspective. For example, if sales this year have increased by $100,000, the fact that this is an increase of 10% over last year's sales of $1 million puts it in a different perspective than if it represented a 1% increase over sales of $10 million for the prior year. Observing the direction of a change provides some indication of the trend of change over a period of time, and this may be helpful in estimating future changes.

The dollar amount of any change is the difference between the amount for a *base* year and for a *comparison* year. The percentage change is com-

DOLLAR AND PERCENTAGE CHANGES
puted by dividing the amount of the change between years by the amount for the base year. This is illustrated in the following tabulation, using data from the comparative statement on page 795.

| | In thousands | | | Increase or (decrease) | | | |
| | | | | 1962 over 1961 | | 1961 over 1960 | |
	1962	1961	1960	Amount	Per cent	Amount	Per cent
Current assets	$180	$150	$120	$30	20%	$30	25%
Current liabilities	$ 60	$ 80	$120	($20)	(25%)	($40)	(33.3%)

Note that although current assets increased $30,000 in both 1961 and 1962, the percentage of change differs because of the shift in the base year from 1960 to 1961.

In some cases it may be useful to compare changes over one or more periods of time in relation to a single base year. Trend percentages, a con-

PERCENTAGE CHANGE FROM A BASE YEAR
venient means of indicating changes in relation to a single base year, are computed by dividing the amount for any comparison year by the amount for a chosen base year. To illustrate, trend percentages for the same balance sheet amounts, using 1960 as the base year, would be:

| | Amount in thousands | | | Trend percentages Base year 1960 | | |
	1962	1961	1960	1962	1961	1960
Current assets	$180	$150	$120	150%	125%	100%
Current liabilities	$ 60	$ 80	$120	50%	66.7%	100%

When trend percentages are available the percentage change between the base year and any comparison year may be determined by subtracting 100% from the trend percentage for the comparison year. For example, the percentage *increase* in current assets between 1960 and 1962 was 50% (150% − 100%). Similarly the percentage *decrease* in current liabilities between 1960 and 1961 was 33.3% (66.7% − 100%).

The computation of percentage changes is not appropriate in two situations. One is when the base-year amount is zero. Any increase or decrease from zero is infinite in percentage terms and therefore not meaningful. The other is when the base-year amount is negative. The following examples are illustrative:

Situation	Retained earnings or (deficit)		Increase or (decrease)	
	Comparison year	Base year	Amount	Per cent
1	$200	$ 50	$150	300%
2	50	200	(150)	(75%)
3	0	200	(200)	100%
4	200	0	200	. . .
5	(50)	0	(50)	. . .
6	50	(200)	250	. . .
7	(50)	200	(250)	(125%)
8	(50)	(200)	150	. . .

Knowing what relationships to look for and how to interpret them is the essence of statement analysis. To the casual observer an increase of 30% in inventories may simply mean that the company has increased its investment in this kind of asset. The experienced analyst will relate this increase in inventories to the change in the volume of business, to changes in other current assets, and to changes in the relationship between current assets and liabilities. If, for example, the volume of sales has increased 100%, an increase of 30% in inventories actually indicates a smaller investment in merchandise in relation to the amount of business being done.

2. **Component percentages.** The phrase "a piece of pie" is subject to varying interpretations until it is known whether the piece represents one-sixth or one-half of the total pie. The percentage relationship between any particular financial item and a significant total that includes this item is known as a *component percentage;* this is often a useful means of showing relationships or the relative importance of the item in question. Thus if inventories are 50% of total current assets, they are a far more significant factor in the current position of a company than if they are only 10% of current assets.

One application of component percentages is to express each asset group on the balance sheet as a percentage of total assets. This shows quickly the relative importance of current and noncurrent assets, and the relative amount of financing obtained from current creditors, long-term creditors, and stockholders.

Another application is to express all items on an income statement as a percentage of net sales. Such a statement is sometimes called a *common size* income statement. A highly condensed common size income statement might be prepared as follows:

Income Statement: Component Percentages

	1963	1962
Net sales	100.0%	100.0%
Cost of goods sold	70.0	60.0
Gross profit on sales	30.0%	40.0%
Operating expenses	20.0	25.0
Net income	10.0%	15.0%

We see at once that the decline in the gross profit rate from 40 to 30% was only partially offset by the decrease in operating expenses as a percentage of sales, causing net income to decrease from 15 to 10% of sales.

Now let us look at the actual dollar figures on which the above common size statement was based:

Same Income Statement: Dollars

	1963	1962
Net sales	$500,000	$200,000
Cost of goods sold	350,000	120,000
Gross profit on sales	$150,000	$ 80,000
Operating expenses	100,000	50,000
Net income	$ 50,000	$ 30,000

An entirely different impression emerges. It is true that sales increased faster than net income, but net income improved significantly in 1963, a fact not apparent from a review of component percentages alone. This points up an important limitation in the use of component percentages. Changes in the component percentage may result from a change in the component, in the total, or in both. Reverting to our previous analogy, it is important to know not only the relative size of a piece of pie, but also the size of the pie; 10% of a large pie may be a bigger piece than 15% of a smaller pie.

3. **Ratios.** A ratio is a simple mathematical expression of the relationship of one item to another. Ratios may be expressed in a number of ways. For example, if we wish to clarify the relationship between sales of $800,000 and net income of $40,000, we may state: (a) the ratio of sales to net income is 20 to 1 (or 20:1); (b) for every $1 of sales the company has an average net income of 5 cents; (c) net income is 1/20 of sales. In each case the ratio is merely a means of describing the relationship between sales and net income in a simple and understandable form.

In order to compute a meaningful and useful ratio, there must be a significant relationship between the two figures. A wide variety of ratios have been proposed by various analysts. At times, in fact, the analysis of financial statements and the computation of ratios have been treated as if they were one and the same thing. A ratio focuses attention on a relationship which is significant, but a full interpretation of the ratio usually requires further investigation of the underlying data. Ratios are an aid to analysis and interpretation; they do not substitute for thinking in the analytical process.

Standards of comparison

In using dollar and percentage changes, component percentages, and ratios, the analyst constantly seeks some standard of comparison against which to judge whether the relationships that he has found are favorable or unfavorable. Two such standards are the past performance of the company and the performance of other companies in the same industry.

Past performance of the company. Comparing analytical data for a current period with similar computations for prior years affords some basis for judging whether the position of the business is improving or worsening. This comparison of data over time is sometimes called *horizontal* or *dynamic* analysis, to express the idea of reviewing data for a number of periods. It is distinguished from *vertical* or *static* analysis, which refers to the review of the financial information for only one annual accounting period.

In addition to determining whether the situation is improving or getting worse, horizontal analysis may aid in making estimates of future prospects. Since changes may reverse their direction at any time, however, projecting past trends into the future is always a somewhat risky statistical pastime.

A weakness of horizontal analysis is that comparison with the past does not afford any basis for evaluation in absolute terms. The fact that net income was 2% of sales last year and is 2.5% of sales this year indicates improvement; if there is evidence that net income *should be* 10% of sales, the record for both years is unfavorable.

Industry standards. The limitations of horizontal analysis may be overcome to some extent by finding some other standard of performance as a yardstick against which to measure the record of any particular firm. The yardstick may be a comparable company, the average record of several companies in the same industry, or an arbitrary standard based upon the past experience of the analyst.

Suppose that X Company suffers a 5% drop in its sales during the current year. The discovery that the sales of all companies in the same industry fell an average of 20% would indicate that this was a favorable rather than an unfavorable performance. Assume that Y Company's net income is 1% of net sales. This would be a grossly substandard performance if Y is an automobile company; but it would be a satisfactory record if Y is a meat-packing concern.

There are a number of important pitfalls in using the record of other companies or industry averages as a standard of comparison. They all add up to the question of true comparability. The term "industry" is difficult to define, and companies that fall roughly within the same industry may not be comparable in many respects. One company may engage only in the marketing of oil products, another may be a fully integrated producer from the well to the gas pump, yet both are in the "oil industry."

Companies with materially different modes of operation are not comparable. For example, a comparison of investment in plant and sales is meaningless if one company leases and the other owns its operating plant.

Differences in accounting procedures may destroy the comparability of financial data for two companies. For example, the understatement of inventories on the balance sheet of a company using lifo may be so serious as to destroy the significance of comparisons with companies whose inventories are valued on a current cost basis.

Despite these limitations, studying comparative performances is a useful method of analysis if carefully and intelligently done.

Illustrative analysis

With this preliminary discussion of analytical procedures as a background, the remainder of our discussion can best proceed within the framework of an illustrative set of financial statements. Assume that we have available the following comparative financial statements of the Weaver Company, together with a computation of increases and decreases and component percentages, where applicable:

Schedule A, Comparative Balance Sheet as of December 31, 1962 and 1963

Schedule B, Comparative Income Statement for 1962 and 1963

Schedule C, Comparative Statement of Retained Earnings for 1962 and 1963

Schedule A

WEAVER COMPANY
Condensed Comparative Balance Sheet *
As of December 31, 1962 and 1963

	1963	1962	Increase or (decrease) Dollars	Increase or (decrease) Per cent	Per cent of total assets 1963	Per cent of total assets 1962
Assets						
Current assets	$390,000	$288,000	$102,000	35.4	41.0	33.6
Plant and equipment (net)	500,000	467,000	33,000	7.1	52.7	54.2
Other assets	60,000	105,000	(45,000)	(42.8)	6.3	12.2
	$950,000	$860,000	$ 90,000	10.5	100.0	100.0

Liabilities and Stockholders' Equity

Liabilities:						
Current liabilities	$147,400	$ 94,000	$ 53,400	56.8	15.5	10.9
Long-term liabilities ..	200,000	250,000	(50,000)	(20.0)	21.1	29.1
Total liabilities	$347,400	$344,000	$ 3,400	1.0	36.6	40.0
Stockholders' Equity:						
6% preferred stock ..	$100,000	$100,000			10.5	11.6
Common stock ($50 par)	280,000	200,000	$ 80,000	40.0	29.5	23.2
Retained earnings	222,600	216,000	6,600	3.0	23.4	25.2
Total stockholders' equity	$602,600	$516,000	$ 86,600	16.8	63.4	60.0
Total liabilities and stockholders' equity .	$950,000	$860,000	$ 90,000	10.5	100.0	100.0

* In order to focus attention on important subtotals, this statement is highly condensed and does not show individual asset and liability items. These details will be introduced as needed in the text discussion. For example, a list of the Weaver Company's current assets and current liabilities appears on page 811.

Schedule B

WEAVER COMPANY
Comparative Income Statement
For the Years 1962 and 1963

	1963	1962	Increase or (decrease)		Per cent of net sales	
			Dollars	Per cent	1963	1962
Net sales	$900,000	$750,000	$150,000	20.0	100.0	100.0
Cost of goods sold	585,000	468,800	116,200	24.9	65.0	62.5
Gross profit on sales	$315,000	$281,200	$ 33,800	12.0	35.0	37.5
Operating expenses:						
Selling expenses	$117,000	$ 75,000	$ 42,000	56.0	13.0	10.0
Administrative expenses	126,000	94,500	31,500	33.3	14.0	12.6
Total expenses	$243,000	$169,500	$ 73,500	43.4	27.0	22.6
Net operating income ...	$ 72,000	$111,700	$(39,700)	(35.6)	8.0	14.9
Interest expense	12,000	15,000	(3,000)	(20.0)	1.3	2.0
Net income before income taxes	$ 60,000	$ 96,700	$(36,700)	(38.0)	6.7	12.9
Provision for income taxes	23,400	44,200	(13,900)	(31.8)	2.6	5.9
Net income	$ 36,600	$ 52,500	$(22,800)	(43.5)	4.1	7.0

Schedule C				
WEAVER COMPANY				
Statement of Retained Earnings				
Years Ended December 31, 1962 and 1963				

	1963	1962	Increase or (decrease)	
			Dollars	Per cent
Balance, beginning of year	$216,000	$189,500	$26,500	14.0
Net income	36,600	52,500	(22,800)	(43.5)
	$252,600	$242,000	$10,600	4.4
Less: Dividends on common stock ..	$ 24,000	$ 20,000	$ 4,000	20.0
Dividends on preferred stock .	6,000	6,000		
	$ 30,000	$ 26,000	$ 4,000	15.4
Balance, end of year	$222,600	$216,000	$ 6,600	3.0

Using the data in these statements, let us consider the kind of analysis that might be of particular interest to: (1) common stockholders, (2) long-term creditors and preferred stockholders, and (3) short-term creditors. Organizing our discussion in this way emphasizes the differences in the viewpoint of these groups; all of them have, of course, a considerable common interest in the performance of the company as a whole.

Analysis by common stockholders

Common stockholders and potential investors in common stock look first at a company's earnings record. Their investment is in shares of stock, so earnings data expressed in per share terms are of particular interest.

Return per share of stock. Earnings per share of stock are computed by dividing the income available to common stockholders by the number of shares of stock outstanding. Any preferred dividend requirements must be subtracted from net income to determine income available for common stock. The amount earned per share of common for the Weaver Company would be computed:

EARNINGS
RELATED TO
NUMBER OF
COMMON
SHARES
OUT-
STANDING

WEAVER COMPANY		
Earnings per Share of Common Stock		
	1963	1962
Net income	$36,600	$52,500
Less: preferred dividend requirements	6,000	6,000
Net income available for common ....(a)	$30,600	$46,500
Shares of common outstanding, end of year ..(b)	5,600	4,000
Earned per share (a ÷ b)	$ 5.47	$ 11.63

The relationship between per share earnings and dividends is also of interest to common stockholders. The Weaver Company paid dividends of $5 per share during 1962. During 1963 $2.50 per share was paid before the increase in shares, and $2 per share was paid after the increase in shares, or a total of $4.50 per actual share outstanding.

The relative importance of earnings and dividends varies among stockholders. Earnings reinvested in the business should produce an increase in the net income of the firm and thus tend to make each share of stock more valuable. Because the Federal income tax rates applicable to dividend income are at least twice as high as the rate of tax on capital gains from the sale of shares of stock, some stockholders may prefer that the company reinvest most of its earnings. Others may be more interested in immediate dividend income despite the tax disadvantage.

In comparing the merits of alternative investment opportunities, earnings and dividends per share should be related to market value. Dividends per share divided by market price per share determines the yield rate of the company's stock. Net income per share divided by market price per share determines the earning rate of the company's stock. In financial circles the earning rate is often expressed as a *price-earnings ratio* by reversing the computation and dividing the price per share by the net income per share. Thus, a stock selling for $100 per share and earning $8 per share may be said to have an earning rate of 8% ($8 ÷ $100); or a price-earnings ratio of 12.5 to 1 ($100 ÷ 8).

As a matter of historical interest, a stockholder might compute the earning or yield rates on his past investment, that is, the amount he actually paid for each share. For purposes of present decision making, however, this computation is not very useful. The decision to hold onto a share of stock represents a present investment of dollars equal to its market value, since the alternative is to sell the share, receive this amount, and reinvest it elsewhere. For this reason yield and earning rates on current market value are most useful. A comparison of the yield and earning rates on Weaver Company common stock at December 31, 1962, and December 31, 1963, using assumed market values at these two dates, would be:

EARNINGS
AND
DIVIDENDS
RELATED TO
MARKET
PRICE OF
STOCK

WEAVER COMPANY
Rates of Earnings and Dividends per Share on Common

Date	Assumed market value	Earnings per share	Dividends per share	Rates per share	
				Earnings	Dividend yield
Dec. 31, 1962	$100	$11.63	$5.00	11.6%	5.0%
Dec. 31, 1963	$ 80	$ 5.47	$4.50	6.8%	5.6%

The decline in market value during 1963 presumably reflects the lower earnings and dividends per share. An investor, appraising this stock at December 31, 1963, would consider whether an earning rate of 6.8% and a dividend yield of 5.6% represented a satisfactory return in the light of alternative investment opportunities open to him. Obviously he would also place considerable weight on his estimates of the company's prospective future earnings and their probable effect on the future market value of the stock.

Revenue and expense analysis. The trend of the return on common shares of the Weaver Company is unfavorable. Stockholders would want to know the reasons for the decline in net income. The comparative income statement (Schedule B) shows that despite a 20% increase in sales, net income of the Weaver Company fell from $52,500 in 1962 to $36,600 in 1963, a decline of 43.5%. The primary causes of this decline were the increases in selling expenses (56.0%), in administrative expenses (33.3%), and in the cost of goods sold (24.9%).

These observations suggest the need for further investigation. Suppose we find that the Weaver Company cut its selling prices in 1963. This fact would explain the decrease in gross profit rate and would also show that sales volume rose more than 20%, since it takes proportionally more sales at lower prices to produce a given increase in dollar sales. If reduced sales prices and increased volume had been accomplished with little change in expenses, the effect on net income would be favorable, in view of the increase of $33,800 in gross profit. Expenses, however, rose by $73,500.

The next step would be to find which expenses increased and why. An investor may be handicapped here, because detailed operating expenses are not usually shown in published statements. Some conclusions, however, can be reached on the basis of even the condensed information available in the comparative income statement that is shown in Schedule B:

ANALYSIS OF CHANGE IN OPERATING EXPENSES

	Amount of increase 1962 to 1963	Percentage increase 1963 over 1962	Per cent to net sales	
			1963	1962
Selling expenses	$42,000	56.0%	13%	10%
Administrative exp.	31,500	33.3%	14.0%	12.6%
	$73,500			

The $42,000 increase in selling expenses presumably reflects greater selling effort during 1963 in an attempt to improve sales volume. However, the growth in selling expenses from 10 to 13% of net sales indicates that the cost of this increased sales effort was not justified in terms of the fruit it bore. Even more disturbing is the change in administrative expenses. Some growth in administrative costs might be expected to accompany increased sales volume, but because of fixed elements the growth should be less than proportional to any increase in sales. An increase in administrative expenses from 12.6 to 14% of sales is, accordingly, an unfavorable development that is of serious concern to investors.

Return on total assets. An important test of management's ability to earn a return on funds supplied from all sources, without regard to variations in the method of financing, is found in the rate of return on total assets.

The income figure used in computing this ratio should be net income before deducting interest expense, since interest is a payment to creditors for the use of borrowed funds. Net income before interest reflects earnings throughout the year and therefore should be related to the average investment in assets during the year. The computation of this ratio for the Weaver Company is shown below.

EARNINGS RELATED TO INVESTMENT IN ASSETS

WEAVER COMPANY
Percentage Return on Total Assets

		1963	*1962*
Net income		$ 36,600	$ 52,500
Add back: interest expense		12,000	15,000
Net income before interest expense ...... (a)		$ 48,600	$ 67,500
Total assets, beginning of year		$860,000	$820,000
Total assets, end of year		950,000	860,000
Average total assets .... (b)		$905,000	$840,000
Return (a ÷ b)		5.4%	8.0%

This ratio shows that earnings per dollar of assets invested have fallen off in 1963. If the same ratios were available for other companies of similar kind and size, the significance of this decline could be better appraised.

Return on common stockholders' equity. Because interest and dividends paid to creditors and preferred stockholders is fixed in amount, a company may earn a greater or smaller return on the common stockholders' equity than on its total assets. For example, the computation of return on stockholders' equity for the Weaver Company is shown on page 806.

WEAVER COMPANY
Return on Common Stockholders' Equity

		1963	1962
Net income		$ 36,600	$ 52,500
Less: preferred dividend requirements		6,000	6,000
Net income available for common	(a)	$ 30,600	$ 46,500
Common stockholders' equity, beginning of year		$416,000	$389,500
Common stockholders' equity, end of year		502,600	416,000
Average common stockholders' equity	(b)	$459,300	$402,750
Rate of return $(a \div b)$		6.7%	11.6%
Rate of return on total assets (see page 805)		5.4%	8.0%

In both years the rate of return to common stockholders was higher than the return on total assets, because the average combined rate of interest paid to creditors and dividends to preferred stockholders was less than the rate earned on each dollar of assets.

This fact can be verified by computing the ratio of preferred dividends and interest expense to the total liabilities and preferred stock, as shown below. (Averages were not used in this computation, since the amount of liabilities and preferred stock was roughly the same for the two years.)

COMPARE WITH RATE EARNED ON TOTAL ASSETS

WEAVER COMPANY
Rate of Return Paid to Creditors and Preferred Stockholders

		1963	1962
Preferred dividends		$ 6,000	$ 6,000
Interest expense		12,000	15,000
Combined payment	(a)	$ 18,000	$ 21,000
Total liabilities, end of year		$347,400	$344,000
Preferred stock, end of year		100,000	100,000
Combined liabilities & preferred stock	(b)	$447,400	$444,000
Average combined rate of payment		4.0%	4.7%

The Weaver Company earned an average return of 5.4% on its total assets in 1963, and paid an average of 4.0% on the dollars contributed by creditors and preferred stockholders. This caused the return to common stockholders (6.7%) to exceed the average return on total assets (5.4%).

Financing with fixed-return securities is often called *trading on the equity.* Results may be favorable or unfavorable to stockholders:

1. If the rate of return on total assets is *greater* than the average rate of payment to creditors and preferred stockholders, the common stockholders will *gain* from trading on the equity. This was the case in the Weaver Company.

2. If the rate of return on total assets is *smaller* than the average rate of payment to creditors and preferred stockholders, the common stockholders will *lose* from trading on the equity.

Equity ratio. The equity ratio measures the proportion of the total assets financed by stockholders, as distinguished from creditors. It is computed by dividing total stockholders' equity by total assets (or the sum of liabilities and stockholders' equity, which is the same), as follows:

PROPORTION
OF ASSETS
FINANCED
BY STOCK-
HOLDERS

		1963	1962
WEAVER COMPANY			
Equity Ratio			
Total assets .... (a)		$950,000	$860,000
Total stockholders' equity .... (b)		602,600	516,000
Equity ratio (b ÷ a)		63.4%	60%

The equity ratio can of course be read directly from a schedule of component percentages (such as included in Schedule A, page 801). The Weaver Company has a higher equity ratio in 1963 than in 1962. Is this favorable or unfavorable?

From the common stockholders' viewpoint a low equity ratio (that is, a large proportion of financing supplied by creditors) will produce maximum benefits from trading on the equity if management is able to earn a return on assets greater than the interest paid to creditors. However, the loss that will result if the reverse is true (if interest is higher than return on assets) will be greater, the lower the equity ratio. Furthermore, if a business incurs more debt than it is able to repay, creditors may force liquidation or reorganization of the business, to the detriment of stockholders.

Because of these factors, the equity ratio is usually judged by stockholders in the light of the probable stability of the company's earnings, as well as the rate of earnings in relation to interest requirements. Public utilities, for example, which have a relatively stable earnings record, traditionally have lower equity ratios than industrial companies.

As we saw earlier in our analysis, trading on the equity from the common stockholder's viewpoint can also be accomplished through the issuance of preferred stock. If the preferred is nonparticipating, which is the typical case, the dividend requirements are fixed. Since preferred stock dividends are not deductible for income tax purposes, however, the advantage gained in this respect will usually be smaller than in the case of liabilities.

Analysis by long-term creditors

Bondholders and other long-term creditors are primarily interested in three factors: (1) the rate of return on their investment, (2) the firm's ability to meet its interest requirements over the life of the debt, and (3) the firm's ability to repay the principal of the debt when it falls due.

Yield rate on bonds. The yield rate on bonds or other long-term indebtedness cannot be computed in the same manner as the yield rate on shares of stock, because bonds, unlike stocks, have a definite maturity date and amount. The ownership of a 5%, 10-year bond represents the right to receive $1,000 at the end of 10 years and the right to receive $50 per year during each of the next 10 years. If the market price of this bond is $970, the yield rate on an investment in the bond is the rate of interest that will make the present value of these two contractual rights equal to $970. Determining the effective interest rate on such an investment requires the use of compound interest tables, a discussion of which is reserved to a more advanced coverage of this subject.

An estimate of annual bond yield rate may be made by dividing average annual interest by average amount invested. The average annual interest is the total cash interest plus any discount or minus any premium, divided by the number of years to maturity. The average investment is the average of the price paid for the bond and its maturity value. To illustrate, let us compute the approximate yield on a 10-year, 5%, $1,000 bond under two assumptions:

1. *The market price is $970.* The average interest is $53 per year [$50 cash interest + ($30 discount ÷ 10 years)]. The average investment is $985 ($970 cost + $1,000 maturity value ÷ 2). The approximate yield is 5.4% ($53 ÷ $985).

2. *The market price is $1,020.* The average interest is $48 per year [$50 cash interest − ($20 premium ÷ 10 years)]. The average investment is $1,010 ($1,020 cost + $1,000 maturity value ÷ 2). The approximate yield is 4.75% ($48 ÷ $1,010).

We may generalize the relation between yield rate and bond price as follows: the yield rate varies inversely with changes in the market price of the bond. For example, if the price of a bond is above maturity value, the yield rate is less than the bond interest rate. If the price of a bond is below maturity value, the yield rate is higher than the bond interest rate.

Number of times interest earned. Long-term creditors have learned from experience that one of the best indications of the safety of their investment is the fact that over the life of the debt the company has sufficient income to cover its interest requirements by a wide margin. A failure to cover interest requirements may have serious repercussions on the stability and solvency of the firm. Furthermore, since earnings retained in the business often are the source of funds for repayment of debt, a healthy earnings picture is a favorable sign in this direction.

A common measure of debt safety is the ratio of net income available for the payment of interest to the annual interest expense, called *times interest earned.* Net income available for interest is determined by adding back interest charges to the net income for the period, to get net income before interest charges, but after provision for income taxes. The computation for the Weaver Company would be:

LONG-TERM
CREDITORS
WATCH THIS
RATIO

WEAVER COMPANY
Number of Times Interest Earned

		1963	1962
Net income		$36,600	$52,500
Add back: interest expense	(a)	12,000	15,000
Income available for interest	(b)	$48,600	$67,500
Times interest earned (b ÷ a)		4.1	4.5

The slight decline in the ratio during 1963 is unfavorable, but a ratio of 4.1 for that year indicates that the earnings of the company could shrink to one-fourth of the present amount without impairing the company's ability to meet interest requirements out of current earnings.

It is sometimes argued that income before deducting income taxes should be used In this computation, since interest expense is deductible for income tax purposes. This is a logical alternative way of computing the ratio. The use of net income after taxes, however, seems a better reflection of the creditors' position, since income taxes must be paid out of current funds and taxes have a legal position superior to unpaid interest.

Debt Ratio. Long-term creditors also have an interest in the amount of debt outstanding in relation to the amount of capital contributed by stockholders. This may be measured in a number of ways. The ratio of owners' equity to total liabilities is one possibility. The equity ratio, discussed earlier in this chapter, is another. The most commonly employed test, however, is the ratio of total liabilities to total assets, or *debt ratio.* The debt ratio is the reciprocal of the equity ratio, that is, the sum of the two ratios will always add to 100%.

The debt ratio for the Weaver Company would be computed as follows:

HOW MUCH
DEBT?

WEAVER COMPANY
Debt Ratio

		1963	1962
Total liabilities	(a)	$347,400	$344,000
Total assets (or total liabilities and stockholders' equity)	(b)	950,000	860,000
Debt ratio (a ÷ b)		36.6%	40%
Equity ratio (100% − debt ratio)		63.4%	60%

From a creditor's viewpoint the lower the debt ratio (or the higher the equity ratio) the better, since this means that stockholders have contributed the bulk of the funds to the business, and therefore the margin of protection to creditors against a shrinkage of the assets is high. This view is often shared by management. The claim of creditors for payment of interest and ultimate repayment of principal is usually unqualified. When large amounts of debt fall due, repayment or settlement in some form must be made if the business is to continue in operation. On the other hand, the claims of preferred and common stockholders are contingent upon the profitability of the business, and there is no pressure for the ultimate repayment of these contributions. A low debt ratio, therefore, represents to management a certain freedom from worry and outside pressures.

Analysis by preferred stockholders

The analytical interests of preferred stockholders will vary, depending on whether the stock is entitled to participate in earnings above the fixed dividend rate or not. If preferred stock is convertible or participating, the interests of preferred stockholders are similar to those of common stockholders, previously discussed. If preferred stock is not convertible and is nonparticipating, the interests of preferred stockholders are more closely comparable to those of long-term creditors.

Yield rates. Preferred stockholders are interested first in the yield rate on their investment. Most preferred stock is callable, but call provisions are not often exercised. Unless there is some indication that a preferred stock will be called, it may reasonably be regarded as an investment without a maturity date. Therefore, the yield rate may be computed in a manner similar to that used for common shares, that is, the specified dividend per share divided by the market value per share. For example, the dividend per share of Weaver Company preferred is $6. If we assume that the market value at December 31, 1963, is $80 per share, the yield rate at that time is 7.5% ($6 ÷ $80).

Number of times preferred dividends earned. The primary measure of the safety of an investment in preferred stock is the ability of the firm to meet its preferred dividend requirements each period. The usual test of this factor is the ratio of income available for preferred dividends to the amount of dividends. For the Weaver Company this would be computed as shown below.

IS THE PREFERRED DIVIDEND SAFE?

WEAVER COMPANY *Times Preferred Dividends Earned*		
	1963	*1962*
Net income ....(a)	*$36,600*	*$52,500*
Preferred dividend requirements ....(b)	*6,000*	*6,000*
Times dividends earned (a ÷ b)	*6.1*	*8.75*

Although the margin of protection declined in 1963, the annual preferred dividend requirement appears well protected.

Analysis by short-term creditors

Bankers and other short-term creditors share the interest of stockholders and bondholders in the profitability and long-run stability of a business. Their primary interest, however, is in the current position of the firm: its ability to generate sufficient funds to meet current operating needs and to pay current debts promptly. Thus the analysis of financial statements by a banker considering a short-term loan, or by a major trade creditor investigating the credit position of a customer, is likely to center on the working capital position of the prospective debtor.

Amount of working capital. The amount of working capital is measured by the excess of current assets over current liabilities. The details of the working capital of the Weaver Company are shown below:

ELEMENTS OF WORKING CAPITAL

WEAVER COMPANY
Comparative Schedule of Working Capital
As of December 31, 1962 and 1963

	1963	1962	Increase or (decrease) Dollars	Increase or (decrease) Per cent	Per cent of total current items 1963	Per cent of total current items 1962
Current assets:						
Cash	$ 38,000	$ 40,000	$ (2,000)	(5.0)	9.8	13.9
Receivables (net) ...	117,000	86,000	31,000	36.0	30.0	29.9
Inventories	180,000	120,000	60,000	50.0	46.1	41.6
Prepaid expenses	55,000	42,000	13,000	31.0	14.1	14.6
Total current assets .	$390,000	$288,000	$102,000	35.4	100.0	100.0
Current liabilities:						
Notes payable	$ 50,000	$ 10,000	$ 40,000	400.0	33.9	10.7
Accounts payable	66,000	30,000	36,000	120.0	44.8	31.9
Accrued expenses	31,400	54,000	(22,600)	(42.0)	21.3	57.4
Total current liabilities	$147,400	$ 94,000	$ 53,400	56.8	100.0	100.0
Working capital	$242,600	$194,000	$ 48,600	25.0		

This schedule shows that current assets increased $102,000, while current liabilities rose by only $53,400, with the result that working capital increased $48,600, or 25%. There was a slight shift in the composition of current assets; cash dropped from 13.9 to 9.8% of current assets, and inventories rose from 41.6 to 46.1%. The increase in notes and accounts payable is significant both in amount and in percentage terms. We may surmise that the decline in accrued expenses was caused primarily by a reduction in income tax liabilities in 1963, due to the fall in net income, previously noted.

The current ratio. One means of further evaluating these changes in working capital is to observe the relationship between current assets and current liabilities, a test known as the *current ratio.*

The current ratio helps to place the amount of working capital in its proper perspective. To illustrate, compare the following assumed data for two companies:

	Company X	Company Y
Current assets	$20,000	$2,000,000
Current liabilities	10,000	1,990,000
Working capital	$10,000	$ 10,000

Although both companies have the same amount of working capital, the current position of Company X is clearly superior to that of Company Y. If the current ratio were computed for both companies the difference would be revealed.

The current ratios for the Weaver Company:

IS WORKING
CAPITAL
ADEQUATE?

WEAVER COMPANY
Current Ratio

		1963	1962
Total current assets	(a)	$390,000	$288,000
Total current liabilities	(b)	147,400	94,000
Current ratio (a ÷ b)		2.6	3.1

Despite the increase of $48,600 in the amount of working capital in 1963, current assets per dollar of current liabilities has declined from $3.10 to $2.60. The margin of safety, however, still appears satisfactory.

In interpreting the current ratio, a number of factors should be kept in mind:

1. Creditors tend to feel that the larger the current ratio the better; from a managerial view there is an upper limit. Too high a current ratio may indicate that current assets are in excess of the amount that can be profitably employed in the business.

2. Because creditors tend to stress the current ratio as an indication of short-term solvency, some firms may take conscious steps to improve

this ratio just before statements are prepared for submission to bankers or other creditors. This may be done by postponing purchases, allowing inventories to fall, pressing collections on accounts receivable, and using all available cash to pay off current creditors. To illustrate, suppose that by these devices, the Weaver Company had been able to reduce both its current assets and its current liabilities at the end of 1963 by $100,000. The amount of working capital would be unchanged at $242,600, but the current ratio would be 6.1 ($290,000 ÷ 47,400). This process is sometimes called *window dressing.* In general, it may be observed that any equal decrease in both current assets and current liabilities will raise a current ratio that is higher than 1.0 to begin with.

3. The current ratio computed at the end of a fiscal year may not be representative of the current position of the company throughout the year. This is true even though the amount of working capital does not change Assume, for example, that by the middle of 1964 both the current assets and the current liabilities of the Weaver Company had increased by $100,000 over the amounts at the end of 1963. The current ratio would then be $1.98 ($490,000 ÷ $247,400) rather than 2.6. Since many firms arrange their fiscal year to end during an ebb in the seasonal swing of business activity, the current ratio at year-end is likely to be more favorable than at any other time during the year. This reasoning indicates that an average of the current ratios computed at the end of each month during the year might be a more significant indication of the current position for any company experiencing a considerable seasonal variation in business activity.

A widely used rule of thumb is that a current ratio of 2 to 1 or better is satisfactory. Like all rules of thumb this is an arbitrary standard, subject to numerous exceptions and qualifications.

Quick ratio. Because inventories and prepaid expenses are further removed from conversion into cash than other current assets, a ratio known as the *quick ratio* or *acid-test ratio* is sometimes computed as a supplement to the current ratio. This ratio compares the highly liquid current assets (cash, marketable securities, and receivables) with current liabilities. The Weaver Company has no marketable securities; its quick ratio would be computed as follows:

A MEASURE
OF
LIQUIDITY

		1963	1962
WEAVER COMPANY			
Quick Ratio			
Quick assets (cash and receivables) .... (a)		*$155,000*	*$126,000*
Current liabilities .... (b)		*147,400*	*94,000*
Quick ratio (a ÷ b)		*1.1*	*1.3*

Here, again, the analysis reveals an unfavorable trend. Whether or not the quick ratio is adequate depends on the amount of receivables included among quick assets, and the average time required to collect receivables as compared to the average credit period extended by suppliers. If the credit periods extended to customers and granted by creditors are roughly equal, a ratio of 1.0 or better would be considered satisfactory.

The operating cycle. A business generates current funds through its operating cycle. Briefly, the operating cycle is the process of investing in inventories, converting these through sale into receivables, and transforming receivables by collection into cash, which is in turn used to pay current debts incurred for operating costs and the replacement of inventories. An important factor in evaluating the current position of any business is the average time required to complete this cycle, from cash to inventories and back to cash again. Two ratios are commonly used to estimate the approximate length of the operating cycle:

Inventory turnover. The cost of goods sold figure on the income statement represents the total cost of all goods that have been transferred out of inventories during any given period. Therefore the relationship between cost of goods sold and the average balance of inventories maintained throughout the year indicates the number of times, on the average, during the period that inventories "turn over" and must be replaced.

Ideally we should total the inventories at the end of each month and divide by 12 to obtain an average inventory. This information is not always available, however, and the nearest substitute is a simple average of the inventory at the beginning and at the end of the year. This tends to overstate the relationship, since many companies choose an accounting year that ends when business activity is at its lowest ebb and inventories are at a minimum.

WHAT DOES INVENTORY TURNOVER MEAN?

Assuming that only beginning and ending inventories are available, the computation of inventory turnover may be illustrated as follows:

WEAVER COMPANY
Inventory Turnover

	1963	1962
Cost of goods sold .... (a)	$585,000	$468,800
Inventory, beginning of year	$120,000	$100,000
Inventory, end of year	180,000	120,000
Average inventory .... (b)	$150,000	$110,000
Average inventory turnover per year (a ÷ b)	3.9 times	4.3 times
Average days to turnover (divide 365 days by inventory turnover)	94 days	85 days

The trend indicated by this analysis is unfavorable, since the average investment in inventories in relation to the cost of goods sold is rising.

Stating this another way, the company required on the average 9 days (94 — 85) more during 1963 to turn over its inventories than during 1962.

The relation between inventory turnover and gross profits per dollar of sales may be significant. A high inventory turnover and a low gross profit rate frequently go hand in hand. This, however, is merely another way of saying that if the gross profit rate is low, a high volume of business is necessary to produce a satisfactory return on investment. For example, the relatively low gross profit rate earned by the typical supermarket is usually accompanied by a fairly high rate of inventory turnover. Conversely, the lower rate of inventory turnover in a furniture store necessitates a higher average rate of gross profit to produce a satisfactory return on investment. Although a high inventory turnover is usually regarded as a good sign, a rate that is high in relation to that of similar firms may indicate that the company is losing sales by a failure to maintain an adequate stock of goods to serve its customers promptly.

Average age of receivables. The "turnover" of accounts receivable is computed in a manner comparable to that just described for inventories. The ratio between the total sales for the period and the average balance in accounts receivable is a rough indication of the average time required to convert receivables into cash, because any sales not represented in the receivables balance at any time have been collected. Ideally a monthly average of receivables should be used, and only sales on credit should be included in the sales figure. For illustrative purposes, we shall assume that Weaver Company sells almost entirely on credit and that only the beginning and ending balances of receivables are available:

ARE CUSTOMERS PAYING PROMPTLY?

WEAVER COMPANY
Average Age of Receivables

		1963	1962
Net sales	(a)	$900,000	$750,000
Receivables, beginning of year		$ 86,000	$ 80,000
Receivables, end of year		117,000	86,000
Average receivables	(b)	$101,500	$ 83,000
Receivable turnover per year $(a \div b)$		8.9 times	9.0 times
Average age of receivables (divide 365 days by receivable turnover)		41 days	41 days

There has been no significant change in the average time required to collect receivables. The interpretation of the absolute figures would depend to some extent upon the company's credit terms and policies. If the company grants credit on normal 30-day open account, for example, the above analysis indicates that accounts receivable collections are reasonably good. If the terms were net 15 days, however, there is evidence that collections are lagging.

A rough estimate of the average length of the operating cycle for the Weaver Company can now be obtained:

	1963	1962
Average days to turn over receivables	*41*	*41*
Average days to turn over inventories	*94*	*85*
Average days of operating cycle	*135*	*126*

This indicates that, on the average, it takes the Weaver Company between 4 and 4 1/2 months to convert a dollar invested in inventories into cash. The trend is unfavorable; a longer operating cycle means that current funds are tied up for longer periods of time. If this trend continues, a greater amount of working capital may be required. In view of the lack of precision in the computation, however, an increase of only 9 days (135 — 126) is probably not of material consequence.

STATEMENT OF SOURCES AND APPLICATIONS OF FUNDS

Further light may be thrown on the changes in the current position of a company through the use of a statement that shows the causes or sources of the change in working capital (current assets minus current liabilities) during any given period.

Such a statement is known as a *statement of sources and applications of funds.* A variety of other titles is also found in practice; for quick reference, it is commonly called simply a *funds statement.* A funds statement is extremely useful to management and credit grantors because it gives a picture of the flow of working capital in and out of the business.

If a business has an increase in working capital between two points in time, this means that more working capital was generated than was applied to various purposes. If there is a decrease in working capital, the reverse is true. The purpose of a funds statement is to show where working capital originated and where it was used during the period. The result will be an explanation of the net change in working capital that has occurred.

Meaning of term "funds"

One source of difficulty in understanding a funds statement is the use of "funds" in this particular connotation. The term funds, in ordinary usage, means cash. In the statement of sources and application of funds, however, the term funds means working capital, and the reader of such a statement must mentally shift gears to think in these terms.

Any transaction that operates to increase working capital is a *source* of funds. For example, the sale of merchandise for an amount greater than its cost is a source of funds, because the increase in receivables or cash is greater than the decrease in inventories; thus working capital is increased. Any transaction that decreases working capital is an *application* of funds. For example, either incurring a current liability for operating expenses, or paying expenses in cash represents a use or an application of funds, because the result is a decrease in working capital.

On the other hand, any transaction that affects current assets or current liabilities but does not result in a change in working capital is not a source or an application of funds. For example, the collection of an account receivable, or the payment of an account payable has no effect on the amount of working capital, and therefore these transactions are neither sources nor applications of funds.

Simple illustration

Let us begin with a very simple set of facts. Suppose that X Company is organized at the end of 1962. Capital stock is issued for $20,000 in cash; a building is rented. During 1963 it completed these transactions:

1. Sold additional capital stock at par for $10,000.
2. Purchased merchandise on credit for $50,000 and sold four-fifths of this, also on credit, for $75,000.
3. Collected $55,000 on receivables; paid $38,000 on accounts payable.
4. Paid rent of $6,000 and other operating expenses of $20,000.
5. In December, 1963, purchased a building site, with a view toward the construction of a store in which to operate. Gave $3,000 in cash and a six-month note for $5,000 in payment.
6. On December 31, 1963, declared a dividend of $4,000.

At the end of 1963, the financial statements for X Company (ignoring any provision for income taxes) would appear as follows:

STATEMENTS
COVERING
ONE YEAR'S
OPERATION

X COMPANY
Income Statement
Year Ended December 31, 1963

Sales		$75,000
Cost of sales:		
Purchases	$50,000	
Less: ending inventory	10,000	40,000
Gross profit on sales		$35,000
Operating expenses:		
Rent	$ 6,000	
Other	20,000	26,000
Net income for the year		$ 9,000

X COMPANY
Comparative Balance Sheets
As of December 31, 1962 and 1963

		December 31	
Assets		1963	1962
Cash		$18,000	$20,000
Receivables		20,000	
Inventory		10,000	
Land		8,000	
Total assets		$56,000	$20,000

Liabilities and Stockholders' Equity			
Notes payable		$ 5,000	
Accounts payable		12,000	
Dividend payable		4,000	
Capital stock		30,000	$20,000
Retained earnings		5,000	
Total liabilities and stockholders' equity		$56,000	$20,000

BALANCE SHEET CHANGES CLASSIFIED
Now let us prepare a schedule of the changes in balance sheet accounts, showing the details of the changes in working capital accounts separately from the changes in non-working capital accounts, as follows:

X COMPANY
Classification of Changes in Balance Sheet Accounts between December 31, 1962, and December 31, 1963

	1963	1962	Change in working capital accounts		Changes in non-working capital accounts	
			Debit	Credit	Debit	Credit
Cash	$18,000	$20,000		$ 2,000		
Receivables	20,000		$20,000			
Inventory	10,000		10,000			
Land	8,000				$ 8,000	
	$56,000	$20,000				
Notes payable	$ 5,000			5,000		
Accounts payable	12,000			12,000		
Dividends payable	4,000			4,000		

Capital stock	30,000	$20,000				$10,000
Retained earnings	5,000					5,000
	$56,000	$20,000	$30,000	$23,000	$ 8,000	$15,000
Net increase in working capital				7,000		
Net credits in non-working capital accounts .					7,000	
			$30,000	$30,000	$15,000	$15,000

UNDERLYING SOURCES OF INCREASE IN WORKING CAPITAL   The fact that the net credit change in non-working capital accounts is equal to the increase in working capital suggests that if we investigate the changes in noncurrent items we shall find the source of the $7,000 addition to working capital. This analysis might be scheduled as follows:

X COMPANY
Analysis of Changes in Non-working Capital Accounts and Their Effect on Working Capital

Changes during 1963		Explanation	Effect on working capital	
Debit	Credit		Increase	Decrease
$ 8,000		Land, acquisition of building site for which company gave: (a) Cash of $3,000, decrease in current assets (b) Note payable of $5,000, increase in current liabilities		$ 3,000 5,000
	$10,000	Capital stock, sale of capital stock for cash, resulting in an increase in current assets	$10,000	
	5,000	Retained earnings, caused by (a) Net income. Since all revenues increased current assets, and all costs either decreased current assets or increased current liabilities, the effect was a net increase in working capital (b) Dividend declared, increasing current liabilities	9,000	4,000
$ 8,000 7,000	$15,000	Net increase in working capital	$19,000	$12,000 7,000
$15,000	$15,000		$19,000	$19,000

From this analysis we can see the sources of additional working capital during the period, and the applications of working capital that were made. This information may be summarized in statement form as follows:

X COMPANY
Statement of Sources and Applications of Funds (Working Capital)
for the Year Ended December 31, 1963

Funds were provided by:		
Operations		*$ 9,000*
Sale of capital stock		*10,000*
Total funds provided		*$19,000*
Funds were applied to:		
Purchase of land	*$8,000*	
Declaration of dividends	*4,000*	*12,000*
Increase in working capital (see accompanying schedule)		*$ 7,000*

A schedule of the changes in individual current asset and current liability accounts, similar to that appearing on page 824, should accompany this statement. When examined together, these two statements provide a clear picture of the changes in working capital accounts and the underlying causes of the net change in working capital.

In collecting data for a funds statement, it will be seen that accounting transactions fall into three categories:

1. Transactions that affect only current asset or liability accounts but do not change the amount of working capital. These transactions produce changes in individual working capital accounts but are not a factor in explaining any change in the amount of working capital. For example, in the X Company illustration, the purchase of merchandise for $50,000 increased inventories and accounts payable but had no effect on working capital; it may therefore be ignored for funds statement purposes.

2. Transactions that affect a current asset or current liability account *and* a non-working capital account. These transactions bring about either an increase or a decrease in the amount of working capital. The issuance of long-term bonds, for example, increases current assets and increases bonds payable, a non-working capital account; therefore this is a source of funds. Similarly, the payment of such bonds at maturity reduces working capital and is an application of funds. By analyzing changes in non-working capital accounts, these events are brought to light, and their effect on working capital will be reported in the funds statement.

3. Transactions that affect *only* non-working capital accounts and therefore have no effect on the amount of working capital. There were no examples of this kind of transaction in the X Company illustration; they are discussed further below.

Transactions affecting only non-working capital accounts. Transactions of this type will be brought to light by an analysis of the changes in non-working capital accounts, but they are not relevant for funds statement purposes. To illustrate the procedures for handling such items, consider the following two examples:

1. Suppose that the X Company had acquired, near the end of 1963, a building worth $35,000 in exchange for 300 shares of its $100 par value capital stock. The entry to record this purchase would be:

EXAMPLE A:
TRANSAC-
TION

Building	*35,000*	
Capital stock		*30,000*
Capital in Excess of Par Value		*5,000*
Exchange of 300 shares of capital stock for		
building worth $35,000.		

EXAMPLE A:
FUND
ANALYSIS

Since these changes have no effect on working capital, they are not a part of any explanation of sources and applications of funds and therefore may be offset in the analytical schedule as follows:

Changes during 1963		Explanation	Effect on working capital		
Debit	Credit		Increase	Decrease	No effect
$35,000		Building, acquired in exchange for shares of capital stock			$35,000
	$30,000	Capital stock, shares issued in exchange for building			(30,000)
	5,000	Capital in excess of par value			(5,000)

2. Now suppose that during 1964 X Company operated in this building, and that its income statement at the end of the year showed:

EXAMPLE B:
YEAR'S
OPERATIONS

Sales		*$100,000*
Cost of goods sold		*60,000*
Gross profit on sales		*$ 40,000*
Operating expenses:		
Depreciation on building	*$ 1,000*	
Other expenses	*25,000*	*26,000*
Net income		*$ 14,000*

The change in working capital as a result of the operations of the period may be seen from the following analysis:

Sources of working capital:		
Sales, an addition to accounts receivable		*$100,000*
Uses of working capital:		
Cost of sales, a decrease in inventories	*$60,000*	
Other expenses, payments in cash or increases in current liabilities	*25,000*	*85,000*
No effect:		
Depreciation, a change in a non-working capital account, Allowance for Depreciation. The effect is to reduce the book value of the building from $35,000 to $34,000 and to reduce net income by $1,000		
Net increase in working capital resulting from operations		*$ 15,000*

Observe that the increase in working capital as a result of operations ($15,000) is greater than the amount of net income ($14,000) by the amount of depreciation expense ($1,000). This is because depreciation is an expense that reduces net income but does not involve the use of working capital during the current period.

The handling of nonfund expenses in the analysis of non-working capital accounts differs somewhat from the procedure illustrated in the previous example. The difference will be seen in the following partial schedule:

Changes during 1964		*Explanation*	*Effect on working capital*		
Debit	*Credit*		*Increase*	*Decrease*	*No effect*
	$ 1,000	*Accumulated depreciation on building. The addition to the valuation account representing depreciation for the year*	*$ 1,000 **		
	14,000	*Retained earnings. Net income for the year*	*14,000 **		

* Items will be combined on the funds statement.

If depreciation does not affect working capital, why is it shown on this schedule as an increase in working capital? The answer is that the amount of depreciation must be added back to the net income figure in order to reflect the increase of $15,000 in working capital as a result of operations.

Obviously, depreciation itself is not a source of funds. The net income figure, however, understates the amount of funds provided by operations because it is net of the nonfund depreciation charge. Thus when the change in retained earnings is analyzed and the net income for the year is extended as a source of working capital, this amount is short by the amount of the depreciation for the period. The change in the accumulated depreciation account, representing depreciation for the period, is therefore shown as an increase in working capital so that the effect of the depreciation deduction on the income statement will be canceled out.

Any charge to expense that does not stem from either a decrease in current assets or an increase in current liabilities must be treated similarly, that is, added back to the net income figure to show the amount of working capital provided by operations for the period.

In a funds statement prepared for the X Company, the working capital provided by operations might be shown as follows:

**EXAMPLE B:
PART OF
THE FUNDS
STATEMENT**

Funds were provided by:
   Operations:
      Net income for the period $14,000
      Add: expenses not requiring the use of current funds:
         Depreciation 1,000
   Total funds provided by operations $15,000

Illustration: the Weaver Company

Let us return now to the financial statements of the Weaver Company, which were used as a basis for our statement analysis in the earlier sections of this chapter, and demonstrate the preparation of a funds statement for this company for the year 1963.

The first step is to prepare a statement of the changes in working capital during the year. The following statement shows the detailed changes in the Weaver Company's current asset and current liability accounts that combine to make up the increase of $48,600 in working capital during 1963:

WEAVER COMPANY
Statement of Changes in Working Capital
Year Ended December 31, 1963

	1963	1962	Change in working capital	
			Debit	Credit
Current assets:				
Cash	$ 38,000	$ 40,000		$ 2,000
Receivables (net)	117,000	86,000	$ 31,000	
Inventories	180,000	120,000	60,000	
Prepaid expenses	55,000	42,000	13,000	
Current liabilities:				
Notes payable	50,000	10,000		40,000
Accounts payable	66,000	30,000		36,000
Accrued expenses	31,400	54,000	22,600	
			$126,600	$ 78,000
Net increase in working capital				48,600
			$126,600	$126,600

Analysis of changes in non-working capital accounts. The next step is to prepare an analysis of changes in non-working capital accounts, to show the effect of these transactions on working capital. The explana-
THIS FUND tions in the illustrative statement shown below are in more detail than is
ANALYSIS ordinarily necessary, in order to show clearly the reasoning behind the
BASED ON
STATEMENT treatment of each item. Note that the net decrease in all working capital
ON PAGES accounts exactly matches the previously computed increase of $48,600
800 AND in the Weaver Company's working capital.
801

WEAVER COMPANY
Analysis of Changes in Non-working Capital Accounts
For the Year Ended December 31, 1963

1963 changes		Explanation	Working capital effect		
Debit	Credit		Increase	Decrease	No effect
$ 68,000		**Plant and Equipment:** (a) Purchase of equipment on open account		$ 43,000	

WEAVER COMPANY (Continued)

1963 changes		Explanation	Working capital effect		
Debit	Credit		Increase	Decrease	No effect
		(b) Acquisition of land for parking lot. Land was turned over to company by officer in part settlement of amount owed to company (see loans to officers below)			$25,000
	$ 35,000	Accumulated Depreciation: represents a charge against net income which did not decrease working capital; therefore must be added to show the working capital resulting from operations for the period	$ 35,000 *		
		Other Assets:			
	45,000	Loan to Officers:			
		(a) Repayment of part of loan by transfer of land to the company (see plant & equipment, above)			(25,000) †
		(b) Repayment in cash	20,000		
50,000		Long-term Liabilities: repayment of the debt out of current assets		50,000	
	80,000	Capital Stock: sale of capital stock resulting in increase in current assets	80,000		
	6,600	Retained Earnings:			
		(a) Net income for the period	36,600 *		
		(b) Dividends on preferred and common stock		30,000	
$118,000	$166,600	Totals	$171,600	$123,000	000
48,600		Net increase in working capital		48,600	
$166,600	$166,600		$171,600	$171,600	

* Items to be combined on the funds statement.
† Parentheses indicate deduction.

On the basis of this information, the funds statement may be prepared as follows:

WEAVER COMPANY
Statement of Sources and Applications of Funds (Working Capital)
For the Year Ended December 31, 1963

Funds were provided by:
  Operations:
    Net income for the period .... $ 36,600
    Add: expenses not requiring the use of current funds:
      Depreciation 35,000
                                                           ————
    Total funds provided by operations .... $ 71,600
    Sale of capital stock 80,000
    Collection of officers' loan 20,000
                                                           ————
      Total funds provided $171,600

Funds were applied:
    To acquire plant and equipment $43,000
    To retire long-term liabilities 50,000
    To pay dividends:
      On preferred stock .... $ 6,000
      On common stock 24,000   30,000
                                        ————
      Total funds applied 123,000
                                                        ————
Net increase in working capital (see accompanying schedule) .... $ 48,600

The funds statement shows that working capital provided by operations ($71,600) is almost double net income because of the nonfund expense, depreciation. Of the total $171,600 funds available during the period, well over half came from nonrecurring sources. Available funds were used to expand plant, retire debt, pay dividends, and the balance was added to the working capital of the company.

QUESTIONS

1. What is the difference between a trend percentage and the percentage of increase or decrease? What are two situations in which a meaningful percentage of increase or decrease cannot be computed?

2. Net income for the J Company, expressed as a percentage of net sales, rose from 9.5 to 10.6%. Does this necessarily mean that the amount of net income increased? Why?

3. What are the advantages and disadvantages of analysis by observing past trends and analysis by comparing with an independent yardstick?

4. What single ratio or amount do you think is of greatest importance to

    a. a banker considering a short-term loan
    b. a common stockholder
    c. a bondholder?

5. G Company earned 5.3% on its total assets. Current liabilities are 10% of total assets, and 5% long-term bonds amount to one-fifth of total assets. There is no preferred stock. Would you expect that the rate of return earned on common stockholders' equity would be more or less than 5.3%? Why?

6. Why are yield rates computed on the basis of market values rather than cost or book value? If the market price of a bond rises, what effect does this have on its yield?

7. Why do creditors and stockholders take a different point of view in determining whether the equity ratio for a given company is favorable or unfavorable?

8. In the statement of source and application of funds, what is the meaning of the term *funds?* What are the primary ways in which a firm may generate funds in this sense of the term?

9. Assume that accounts receivable decreased by $15,000 during the current year. How would this decrease appear in a statement of the sources and applications of funds? How would it appear in a statement of cash receipts and disbursements?

10. Company A has a current ratio of 5.0 to 1. Company B has a current ratio of 3.0 to 1. Does this mean that Company A has a larger amount of working capital than Company B? Why?

11. Company F experiences a considerable amount of seasonal variation in its business. The high point in the year's activities comes during the month of November; the low point is in July. During which month would you expect the current ratio of the company to be higher? Why? If the company were choosing a fiscal year for accounting purposes, how would you advise them in this matter? Why?

12. Give an example of a transaction, other than depreciation, that reduces net income but that does not result in a use of working capital during the current period.

PROBLEMS

Group A

28A-1. The data shown below were taken from the financial records of the Seligman Company for the current year:

Accounts and notes payable	$ 56,300
Accrued liabilities (including income tax payable)	26,700
Cash	28,000
Inventories, beginning of year	42,300
Inventories, end of year	36,900
Marketable securities	15,000
Operating expenses	77,300
Prepaid expenses	17,300
Provision for income taxes (expense)	19,500
Purchases (net)	311,400
Receivables	85,400
Retained earnings	186,300
Sales	460,000
Sales returns and allowances	20,000

Instructions. On the basis of this information, determine the following:

a. Amount of working capital
b. Current ratio
c. Quick ratio
d. Inventory turnover
e. Rate of gross profit on sales
f. Rate of net income on sales

28A-2. Condensed comparative financial statements for the Hermco Manufacturing Company appear below:

HERMCO MANUFACTURING COMPANY
Comparative Balance Sheets
As of October 31
(In thousands of dollars)

	1962	1961	1960
Assets:			
Current assets	$ 680	$ 750	$1,000
Plant & equipment (net of depreciation)	4,200	3,600	3,000
Intangible assets	300	400	500
Total assets	$5,180	$4,750	$4,500
Liabilities and Stockholders' Equity:			
Current liabilities	$ 520	$ 500	$ 400
Long-term liabilities (net of discount)	980	960	940
Capital stock ($50 par)	2,400	2,000	2,000
Capital in excess of stated value	180	100	100
Retained earnings	1,100	1,190	1,060
Total liabilities and stockholders' equity	$5,180	$4,750	$4,500

HERMCO MANUFACTURING COMPANY
Comparative Income Statements
Years Ended October 31
(In thousands of dollars)

	1962	1961	1960
Net sales	$14,000	$12,000	$10,000
Cost of goods sold	10,500	8,700	7,000
Gross profit on sales	$ 3,500	$ 3,300	$ 3,000
Selling expenses	$ 1,380	$ 1,240	$ 1,000
Administrative expenses	1,470	1,440	1,400
Interest expense	49	48	47
Total expense	$ 2,899	$ 2,728	$ 2,447
Net income before income taxes	$ 601	$ 572	$ 553
Provision for income taxes	307	296	283
Net income	$ 294	$ 276	$ 270

Instructions
a. Compute the trend percentages for all balance sheet items, using 1960 as the base year.

b. Prepare "common-size" comparative income statements for the three-year period, expressing all items as percentage components of net sales.

c. Comment on the significant trends and relationships revealed by the analytical computations in (*a*) and (*b*)

28A-3. Certain financial information for two companies, A and B, as of the end of the current year, is shown below. (All figures are in thousands of dollars.)

	Company A	Company B
Current assets	$120,000	$110,000
Plant and equipment	508,000	385,000
Accumulated depreciation	(80,000)	(60,000)
Patents	2,000	
Goodwill		5,000
	$550,000	$440,000
Current liabilities	$ 65,000	$ 34,000
Bonds payable, 5%, due in 10 years	100,000	120,000
7% preferred stock, par $100	120,000	80,000
Common stock, par $25	200,000	150,000
Retained earnings	45,000	30,000
Reserve for contingencies	20,000	
Capital in excess of par		26,000
	$550,000	$440,000

Analysis of Retained Earnings:

Balance, beginning of the year	$ 45,600	$ 24,800
Net income for the year	37,400	19,800
Dividends: preferred	(8,400)	(5,600)
Dividends: common	(9,600)	(9,000)
Appropriation: Reserve for contingencies	(20,000)	—
	$ 45,000	$ 30,000
Market price of common stock, per share ...	$30	$30
Market price of preferred stock, per share ..	$105	$102

Instructions. Assuming that the two companies are generally comparable, write a brief answer to each of the following questions. Use whatever analytical computations you feel will best support your answer. Show the amounts used in calculating all ratios and percentages. (Carry computations to one place beyond the decimal point, for example, 2.5%.)

a. Market prices for the bonds are not given. On the basis of your analysis, which company's bonds do you think will sell at the highest price per $1,000 bond? Which company's bonds will yield the highest return? (You may assume that the safer the bonds, according to your analysis, the lower the yield rate.)

b. Which company's preferred stock is the safer investment?

c. To what extent is each company benefiting from the leverage factor inherent in the existence of bonds? Of preferred stock?

d. What are the dividend and net income yield rates for the common stock of each company?

28A-4. The adjusted trial balances of the Peterson Company at the end of two years appear below:

PETERSON COMPANY
Adjusted Trial Balance
December 31, 1962 and 1963
(In thousands of dollars)

Debits	1963	1962
Cash	$ 550	$ 440
Receivables (net)	830	700
Inventories	750	500
Prepaid expenses	210	250
Land	95	95
Buildings	1,050	915
Equipment	460	340
Cost of goods sold	1,600	1,500
Operating expenses	600	580
Provision for income taxes	180	90
Dividends paid	75	40
Interest expense	20	25
	$6,420	$5,475

Credits

Accumulated depreciation: buildings	$ 380	$ 340
Accumulated depreciation: equipment	200	170
Accounts payable	590	690
Accrued expenses payable	380	210
Bonds payable, 5%	400	500
Capital stock, par $20	1,100	800
Capital in excess of par	340	100
Retained earnings	430	365
Sales (net)	2,600	2,300
	$6,420	$5,475

Other data. Additional shares of common were issued on July 15, 1963. Of the dividends paid during 1963, $55,000 was paid after the issue of the new shares.

At the beginning of 1962, inventories were $440,000 and receivables (net) were $620,000. Terms of sale are net 90 days.

The market value of the common stock was $20 per share at the end of 1962 and $40 per share at the end of 1963.

Instructions

a. Make a comparative analysis of the working capital position of the Peterson Company for 1962 and 1963. Include in your analysis a comparative statement of working capital, showing the amount and per cent of increases and decreases. Compute whatever ratios you feel are necessary. Write a brief statement of your conclusions as to favorable or unfavorable trends.

b. Prepare a comparative income statement for the two years, showing dollar and percentage increases and decreases and component percentages to net sales. Also prepare a condensed comparative balance sheet (showing current assets and fixed assets in total only), computing dollar increases and decreases.

c. Using the information in (b) prepare an analysis of the Peterson Company from the viewpoint of a prospective investor in its common shares. Compute any ratios you feel would be helpful in your analysis.

Note: All dollar figures may be expressed in thousands. Carry all percentages and ratios to one decimal place, for example, 30.5%. Show clearly how all ratios were computed through the use of schedules similar to those appearing in the text.

28A-5. *Instructions.* Using the data for the Peterson Company, given in problem 28A-4, prepare the following:

a. A schedule showing the increase or decrease in working capital during 1963.

b. An analysis of the changes in non-working capital accounts during 1963.

c. A statement of sources and applications of funds.

All figures may be expressed in thousands of dollars, for example, $605,000 may be written $605.

28A-6. The information shown below is taken from the ledger of the Risinger Company:

	June 30, 1962 Dr	June 30, 1962 Cr	June 30, 1961 Dr	June 30, 1961 Cr	Amount of change
Accounts payable		$ 26,397		$ 24,376	$ 2,021
Accrued expenses		18,620		28,368	9,748
Accumulated depr.: bldgs..		52,100		45,700	6,400
Accumulated depr.: equip..		38,600		31,898	6,702
Allow. for doubtful accts. .		5,000		4,600	400
Buildings	$186,730		$156,280		30,450
Capital in excess of par ..		30,000		20,000	10,000
Cash	23,465		30,191		6,726
Common stock, par $50 ..		120,000		100,000	20,000
Convertible bonds payable		20,000		50,000	30,000
Equipment	96,494		98,542		2,048
Inventories	52,380		49,425		2,955
Land	21,000		30,000		9,000
Notes payable		22,500		15,000	7,500
Prepaid expenses	6,436		7,623		1,187
Receivables	36,420		33,276		3,144
Retained earnings		89,708		85,395	4,313
	$422,925	$422,925	$405,337	$405,337	

Analysis of Retained Earnings:

Balance, June 30, 1961	$85,395
Net income	7,313
Gain on sale of land	3,000
Dividends	(6,000)
Balance, June 30, 1962	$89,708

Other data. Land was sold on December 1, 1961, for $12,000. The bonds are convertible into common stock at the option of the owner. Bonds in the amount of $30,000 were converted on March 1, 1962. In June, 1962, certain equipment (original cost $2,048) that was fully depreciated was abandoned and written off. All other changes are the result of normal transactions.

Instructions. Prepare
a. A comparative statement of change in working capital
b. An analysis of changes in noncurrent accounts
c. A statement of source and application of funds

Group B

28B-1. *Instructions.* In the left-hand column below is listed a series of transactions; in the right-hand column a series of ratios. Explain the effect that each transaction would have on the ratio listed opposite to it; that is, as a result of this transaction would the ratio increase, decrease, or remain unchanged, and why?

Transaction	Ratio
(1) Declaration of a cash dividend	Current ratio
(2) Write-off of uncollectible account receivable	Receivable turnover
(3) Purchased inventory on open account	Quick ratio
(4) Issue of 10-year mortgage bonds	Rate of earnings on total assets
(5) Issue of additional shares of stock for cash	Debt ratio
(6) Decreased sales volume at higher unit price	Gross profit percentage
(7) Payment of stock dividend on common stock	Earnings per share
(8) Appropriation of retained earnings	Rate of earnings on stockholders' equity
(9) Purchased supplies on open account	Current ratio
(10) Net income increased 10%; interest expense increased 25%	Times interest charges earned
(11) Paid short-term creditor in full	Quick ratio
(12) Payment of accounts payable, taking the cash discount	Inventory turnover

28B-2. In the schedule below, certain items taken from the income statements of the Stillman Company have been expressed as a percentage of net sales:

	Percentage of net sales	
	1963	1962
Net sales	100%	100%
Beginning inventory	10	16
Net purchases	68	60
Ending inventory	8	12
Selling expenses	13	15
Administrative expenses	8	9
Provision for income taxes	2.7	3.6

Net sales were $200,000 in 1962 and increased by 20% in 1963. Average accounts receivable were $21,000 in 1963, and $20,000 in 1962. Credit sales were 80% of total sales in both years.

Instructions

a. Did the net income increase or decrease in 1963 as compared with 1962, and by how much? Prepare a comparative income statement to support your answer.

b. Compute the average length of the company's operating cycle in days for both years, showing the basis of your computation.

28B-3. Certain financial information relating to Companies P and Q, as of the end of the current year, is shown below. All figures (except market prices per share of stock) are in millions of dollars.

Assets:	Company P	Company Q
Cash	$ 96.0	$ 72.0
Marketable securities	118.0	500.0
Receivables (net)	134.0	121.0
Inventories	596.4	363.2
Prepaid expenses	19.6	13.8
Plant and equipment (net)	1,700.0	1,100.0
Other assets	40.0	20.0
	$2,704.0	$2,190.0

Liabilities & Stockholders' Equity:		
Bonds payable, 5%, due in 20 years	$ 200.0	$ 400.0
Accounts payable	380.0	260.0
Accrued liabilities	235.7	210.0
Reserve for guarantees	22.3	30.0
Reserve for future price declines	50.0	
Common stock (par $50)	700.0	500.0
Preferred stock ($100 par)	255.0	100.0
Capital in excess of par	140.6	60.0
Retained earnings	818.4	630.0
Treasury stock (100,000 shares at cost)	(98.0)	
	$2,704.0	$2,190.0

Analysis of Retained Earnings:		
Balance, beginning of the year	$ 763.0	$ 543.0
Net income	162.9	153.0
Dividends: preferred	(15.3)	(6.0)
Dividends: common	(67.2)	(60.0)
Appropriation: reserve for future price declines	(25.0)	
	$ 818.4	$ 630.0

Market price of common stock, per share	$140	$120
Market price of preferred stock, per share	$92	$96

Instructions. Companies P and Q are in the same industry and are generally comparable in the nature of their operations and accounting procedures used. Write a short answer to each of the following questions, using whatever analytical computations you feel will best support your answer. Show the amounts used in calculating all ratios and percentages. Carry computations to one place beyond the decimal point, for example, 13.6%.

a. What is the book value per share of stock for each company?

b. From the viewpoint of creditors, which company has the most conservative capital structure?

c. What are the rates of dividends and net income on the common stock of each company?

d. Which company is gaining the most from trading on the equity with respect to debt?

e. Which company's preferred stock yields the higher return to investors? Can you suggest a reason for the difference in yields?

f. Which company is covering its bond interest by the greater margin?

28B-4. The financial data for the Craig & Haig Co. given below is presented to you by Pegg, who is considering entering the firm. Pegg has been offered one-half of Craig's interest. It is proposed that he pay Craig personally an amount equal to the book value of the interest acquired as of December 31, 1963. By mutual agreement Craig and Haig pay themselves salaries of $15,000 and $10,000 per year, respectively, which amounts are paid in cash and deducted in the computation of partnership net income, since it is felt that these salaries are commensurate with the value of their personal services to the firm. It is agreed that upon Pegg's admission to the firm he would receive a salary of $10,000 per year and 30% (one-half of Craig's share) of the residual profits; and that Craig's salary would be reduced to $7,500 since he plans to devote only half time to the business in the future.

CRAIG & HAIG PARTNERSHIP
Balance Sheet Accounts
As of December 31, 1962 and 1963

Assets	1963	1962
Cash	$ 18,500	$ 25,200
Receivables	98,000	84,600
Less: allowance for uncollectible	(500)	(800)
Inventories	84,000	60,000
Total current assets	$200,000	$169,000
Land	30,000	30,000
Buildings	350,000	350,000
Allow. for depreciation: buildings	(84,000)	(70,000)
Equipment	180,000	120,000
Allow. for depreciation: equipment	(62,000)	(48,000)
Total assets	$614,000	$551,000

Liabilities & Owners' Equity		
Notes payable	$ 50,000	
Accounts payable	51,400	$ 60,000
Accrued liabilities	36,000	42,000
Total current liabilities	$137,400	$102,000
Mortgage payable, due Dec. 31, 1970	180,000	180,000
Craig, original capital	80,000	80,000
Craig, reinvested earnings	114,360	96,000
Haig, original capital	50,000	50,000
Haig, reinvested earnings	52,240	43,000
Total liabilities and owners' equity	$614,000	$551,000

CRAIG & HAIG
Statement of Partners' Reinvested Earnings
Year Ended December 31, 1962 and 1963

	Craig		Haig	
	1963	1962	1963	1962
Reinvested earnings	$ 96,000	$75,600	$43,000	$34,400
Net income (after salaries) *	18,360	20,400	12,240	13,600
	$114,360	$96,000	$55,240	$48,000
Drawings			3,000	5,000
Reinvested earnings	$114,360	$96,000	$52,240	$43,000

   * Craig, 60%; Haig, 40%.

CRAIG & HAIG PARTNERSHIP
Comparative Income Statements

	1963	1962
Net sales	$540,000	$600,000
Cost of goods sold	334,800	402,000
Gross profit on sales	$205,200	$198,000
Operating expenses:		
Sales force expense	$ 27,000	$ 28,000
Advertising and promotion	37,800	30,000
Occupancy expense	21,600	25,200
Buying expenses	10,800	6,600
Administrative expenses	40,100	38,400
Interest expense	12,300	10,800
Total expenses	$149,600	$139,000
Net income	55,600	59,000
Salaries to partners	25,000	25,000
Net income (return on investment)	$ 30,600	$ 34,000

Instructions

    a. Compute the following ratios for 1963. (Carry computations to one decimal place, for example, 10.4%.)

    (1) Current ratio
    (2) Quick ratio
    (3) Inventory turnover
    (4) Receivable turnover
    (5) Rate of earnings on invested capital
    (6) Equity or debt ratio
    (7) Rate of return on total assets
    (8) Times interest charges earned

b. Prepare a comparative common-sized income statement for 1962 and 1963, expressing all items as a percentage of net sales.

c. On the basis of the above analysis, write a report to Pegg commenting on your findings. Pegg is concerned with the firm's earning capacity and with its ability to meet short- and long-term debts as they fall due. He also asks that you compute for him the return he would earn on his investment if he became a member of the partnership on the proposed terms and if the partnership earnings for 1964 were equal to the average of 1962–1963 earnings.

28B-5. Comparative financial data for the Karenel Company appear below:

KARENEL COMPANY
Comparative Post-closing Trial Balances
December 31, 1962 and 1963

	December 31	
Debits	*1963*	*1962*
Cash	$ 50,000	$120,000
Marketable securities		80,000
Accounts receivable	110,000	140,000
Inventories	100,000	150,000
Prepaid expenses	25,000	20,000
Land	40,000	
Buildings	500,000	
	$825,000	$510,000

Credits		
Allowance for doubtful accounts	$ 15,000	$ 10,000
Accounts payable	125,000	85,000
Accrued expenses	75,000	65,000
Long-term note payable	200,000	
Common stock	300,000	300,000
Retained earnings	110,000	50,000
	$825,000	$510,000

Other data. The company operated in rented space during 1962. Early in 1963, it acquired suitable land and made arrangements to borrow money on long-term notes to finance the construction of a building. Construction was completed near the end of December, 1963.

The only entries in Retained Earnings other than the closing of annual net income were to record dividends of $18,000 in 1962 and $15,000 in 1963.

Instructions
a. Prepare a statement of change in working capital.
b. Prepare an analysis of changes in non-working capital accounts.
c. Prepare a funds statement.
d. Compute the current ratio and quick ratio for 1962 and 1963.

28B-6. The comparative data given below relate to the financial position of the Scott-Wilson Company as of May 31, 1961 and 1962. The figures for 1961 are dollar amounts; the figures for 1962 are percentages of increase or decrease over 1961 amounts.

	As of May 31	
	1962	*1961*
Debits	*Per cent of increase or (decrease)*	*Thousands of dollars*
Cash	(10%)	$ 15,800
Receivables (net)	(15%)	24,000
Inventories	(25%)	36,800
Prepaid expenses	(5%)	4,400
Land		19,000
Buildings	10 2/5%	250,000
Equipment	6%	360,000
Patents and development costs	(20%)	40,000
Total debits	3 1/3%	$750,000

Credits		
Accumulated depreciation: bldgs.	12 1/2%	$ 80,000
Accumulated depreciation: equipment	15%	120,000
Accounts payable	20%	30,000
Accrued liabilities	100%	10,000
Long-term debt	(33 1/3%)	90,000
Preferred stock ($100 par)		100,000
Common stock ($25 par)	5%	200,000
Capital in excess of par	15%	40,000
Retained earnings	(6 1/4%)	80,000
Total credits	3 1/3%	$750,000

Other data. There were no sales or retirements of plant and equipment during the year, and no additions were made to patent and development costs. During 1962 the company declared a stock dividend on its common stock, and the Board of Directors ordered that $16,000 be transferred from retained earnings. Cash dividends of $6,000 were declared and paid on preferred stock.

Instructions
a. Prepare a statement of changes in working capital during the year.
b. Prepare a statement of changes in non-working capital accounts.
c. Prepare a statement of sources and applications of funds.

29

Budgeting: a planning and control device

The term *budgeting* may be used broadly to describe the entire process of planning and controlling business operations. *Planning* is essentially a process of deciding what management wants to accomplish and how it can be done. *Control* is a matter of seeing to it that the organization does what management wants it to do. A budget is the expression of plans in quantitative terms.

A budget may be expressed in dollars, hours of time, units of production, or any other quantitative terms. Most college students have at one time or another drawn up plans for the effective use of limited amounts of time to secure a balance between scholastic and extracurricular activities. This is a budget in terms of hours of time. Similarly, a student with a limited amount of financial resources may draw up a plan for efficiently using the available money to see him through a semester or a year of schooling. This is a budget in terms of dollars.

The problem that plagues college students—planning for the efficient use of limited resources—also faces the management of organizations of every type. Business enterprises must plan future revenues and costs in order to attain profit objectives. Nonprofit organizations and governmental units at all levels must establish plans in order effectively to accomplish desired programs within the limits of the resources available to them. Whether or not such plans are formalized into a complete systematic budgeting program, it is clear that the central concept of budgeting is of almost universal application.

Many aspects of the broad subject of budgeting are beyond the scope of an introductory discussion. Because organizations of all types use budgets, however, even an introduction to the use of accounting data is not complete without giving some attention to the budgeting process.

Budgetary control

Budgetary planning for a business is done in terms of future revenues, future costs, and the financial position of the company at the end of some period if budgeted revenues and costs are attained. This kind of systematic forecasting is useful for control purposes in two primary ways:

First, by pointing up what results will be if present plans are put into effect, the budget will disclose areas that require special attention or corrective action before it is too late to adopt a remedy. The person who coined the phrase "forewarned is forearmed" was expressing this idea. For example, the college student whose budget shows potential expenditures of $1,000 for the year and who has only $700 in financial resources may, by knowing this in advance, take action to meet his educational objective by searching for ways either to cut expenses or to augment his resources. If he waits until his funds are gone in midyear, however, effective action may no longer be possible. Similarly, a business budget showing that profit objectives will not be met, or that working capital will not be sufficient to finance planned operations, may lead management to take action to alter the prospective revenue and cost picture or to obtain additional financing.

The second use of budgets for control purposes is as a yardstick against which actual performance may be compared. Plans in business organizations are carried out by people, and control is thus exercised not over operations, revenues, and costs, but over the persons responsible for various business functions and the revenue or cost results attained. If responsible personnel know that their performance will be compared with planned results, they will presumably be motivated to attempt seriously to carry out the plans represented by the budget. At the end of any given budget period, a comparison of budget objectives against results attained will not only provide a measure of performance, it will also point up areas that require particular managerial attention in the future.

Program versus responsibility budgets

In drawing up a set of plans for future business operations, there are at least two ways of viewing the problem. One is in terms of management's over-all program and its effect on the business as a whole. This type of budget (known as the *program* or *master* budget) is drawn in terms of revenue and cost objectives, the means of attaining them, and the effect that attaining these objectives will have on the properties and obligations of the business at the end of the budget period. Company plans are set forth in a series of forecasts of future income statements and balance sheets, backed up by schedules containing the detailed estimates on which the forecast is based.

The second way to view the planning process is in terms of responsibility centers. A responsibility center is simply some part of a business that is headed by a supervisor charged with responsibility for certain revenues or costs or both. In a large business responsibility may be centered at several levels. Top management is charged with the over-all successful operation of the business. Staff officers and operating heads are responsible for particular operating departments or staff functions. Foremen and department heads are responsible for the segment of operations under their supervision. For control purposes the program or master budget should be rearranged into a series of individual budgets prepared for each responsibility center. These are known as *responsibility budgets.*

A complete budgetary system involves both program and responsibility budgets. Since they represent merely two different ways of looking at total business operations, budgeted net income will be the same under either type of budget. Presumably every part of the total program is the responsibility of someone; responsibility budgets are merely subdivisions of the program budget into parts that can be traced to some responsibility center.

Participation in budgeting

A prerequisite for successful budgeting is that management be sold on the budgeting process. General objectives and over-all plans are set by top management. The detailed means of carrying out those objectives, however, should in general move from the bottom to the top of the organization. This principle of budgeting is merely a common-sense application of the idea that those who will be responsible for carrying out plans and whose performance will be checked against planned results should participate in formulating the plans. One of the essential benefits of budgeting stems from the educational process involved in planning. The greater the participation in the planning process, the greater the awareness of a company's objectives and problems throughout the organization.

Length of budget period

As a general rule, the period covered by budget planning should be long enough to show the effect of managerial policies, but short enough so that estimates can be made with reasonable accuracy. This suggests that various types of budgets may be made for varying time periods. For example, a broadly drawn program budget, with few detailed projections other than major revenue and cost relationships, might be made for 5 or even 10 years into the future. Similarly, a budget of planned capital expenditures or an expansion program might incorporate estimates of 5, 10, or 15 years in advance. On the other hand, detailed estimates of operations and operating results can be made with reasonable accuracy only for the near future.

Most companies that prepare detailed operating budgets do so on an annual basis. A common practice is to divide the annual budgeted amounts into quarterly or monthly budgets, and to revise these budgets as the year progresses in the light of any material changes in business conditions.

Preparing a program budget

The starting point in the preparation of a program budget is the *operating budget,* a forecast of the revenues and expenses that make up net income for the budget period. When the operating plans have been completed, the effect of these prospective operating results are reflected in a *financial budget,* which represents a forecast of the balances in the asset, liability, and equity accounts at the end of the budget period.

The forecast of operating results should start with an estimate of the most important variable on the income statement. Usually this will be sales volume. However, in some cases the starting point may be the desired level of net income, or the amount of unavoidable expenses that will be incurred. Sales volume is not the only variable on the income statement, since in some cases the volume of sales attained will be dependent upon decisions as to costs to be incurred. Variations in selling and promotional expenses, for example, may result in changes in planned sales volume. The decision to upgrade the quality of a product will affect costs first and then sales volume. In these instances, the amount of revenues realized will depend to some extent on expenses incurred, rather than the reverse.

We must not lose sight of the fact that the ultimate objective of business planning is to produce a satisfactory net income in relation to dollars invested. Return on investment thus becomes a test of operating performance to which planned sales volume and expenditure levels should be geared.

In a manufacturing concern, sales and production estimates should first be made in terms of physical units of product, in order to coordinate the sales program with purchasing and production activities. In a merchandising concern, where the variety of products sold is so great as to make budgeting in unit terms virtually impossible, it may be necessary to express budget estimates only in terms of dollars of revenues and costs.

Cost-volume relationships. Once sales and production goals have been set, the operating budget becomes essentially a problem of determining what costs and expenses should be incurred to enable the business to operate at the budgeted level of activity. In making this forecast, a knowledge of the way in which costs behave in response to variations in the volume of production or sales is essential.

In broad terms, operating costs may be classified in two behavior patterns with respect to volume: fixed and variable.

A *fixed cost* does not change significantly when the volume of business activity changes. Building rental, supervisory salaries, and property taxes are examples of fixed costs. A budget for fixed costs may thus be expressed as a definite total dollar amount for a given period of time. This might be shown graphically as on page 843.

A *variable cost* is one that changes directly and proportionately with changes in the volume of business activity. For example, as sales or pro-

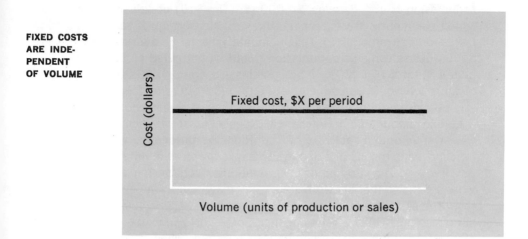

duction increases 10%, a cost that is variable with respect to sales or production will increase 10% also. Variable costs may thus be budgeted as a given dollar amount per unit of volume. Direct material costs, direct labor costs, and power used are examples of costs that vary with volume of production. Sales commissions, sales supplies used, and delivery expense are examples of costs that are likely to vary directly with volume of sales. If a variable cost is shown graphically in relation to volume of business, it will be represented by an upward slanting line, as shown below, since total variable cost increases as volume increases.

Many types of operating costs are in part variable and in part fixed in nature; that is, they vary directly, but less than proportionately, with changes in volume. The term *semivariable* is often used to describe this kind of cost-volume behavior. The compensation of salesmen under a salary plus commission arrangement is a clear example of a semivariable

VARIABLE
COSTS
CHANGE
PROPOR-
TIONALLY
WITH
VOLUME

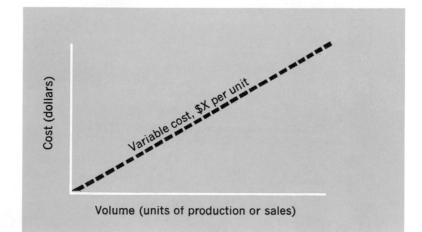

expense. If a company has 10 salesmen, each paid $400 per month plus a commission of 1% of sales, $4,000 ($400 × 10) of salesmen's compensation per month is a fixed cost; the variable portion of salesmen's compensation will amount to 1% of monthly sales. If budgeted sales were $100,000, salesmen's commission would be budgeted at $5,000 ($4,000 plus 1% of $100,000); if budgeted sales were $200,000, salesmen's commission would be budgeted at $6,000 ($4,000 plus 1% of $200,000).

Many operating costs exhibit a semivariable behavior. For example, a certain amount of maintenance expense must be incurred no matter what the volume of activity, but additional maintenance will vary largely in response to the volume of output. Thus a graph of maintenance expense, or any other semivariable cost, in relation to volume might appear somewhat similar to that shown below.

The assumption of *straight-line* fixed and variable cost behavior oversimplifies cost-volume relationships. Some costs increase in "lump-sum" steps rather than small amounts. For example, when production reaches the point where another foreman and crew must be added, a lump-sum addition to cost takes place at this point. Other costs vary along a curve rather than a straight line. For example, when overtime must be worked in order to increase volume, labor cost rises more rapidly than volume because of the necessity of paying overtime premium. These factors add to the complexity of cost analysis for budgeting purposes, and a discussion of such complications must be left to a more advanced coverage of this topic. Fortunately, the assumption that operating costs are composed

SOME COSTS EXHIBIT A MIXED BEHAVIOR

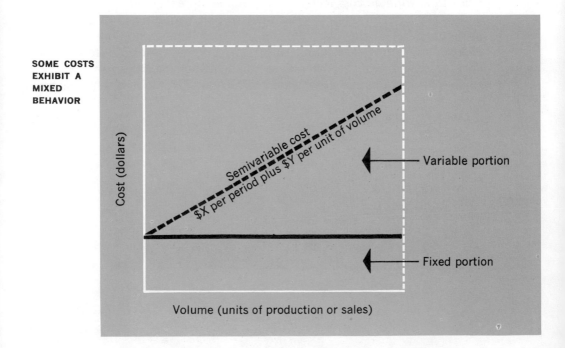

entirely of simple fixed and variable elements is a satisfactory working approximation for budgeting purposes in many situations.

Break-even chart. A useful means of expressing over-all cost-volume relationships graphically is the *break-even chart* (known also as an *income realization chart* or *profitgraph*). A simple version of a break-even chart, showing the relationship between revenues, fixed costs, and variable costs in three plotted straight lines, appears below.

The horizontal scale represents the volume of business activity expressed in units; the vertical scale represents dollars of revenue or cost. The area under the fixed cost line represents the dollar amount of fixed costs. The area between the fixed cost and variable cost lines represents dollar variable costs at different volumes. The area between the total cost line and the revenue line to the left of where these lines cross represents the net operating loss; the area between these lines to the right of the break-even point represents net operating income.[1] Various statistical techniques may be used to analyze cost and revenue data and obtain the information necessary to plot these lines graphically. When this analysis has been made, the information that forms the basis for the break-even chart will be of great value in forecasting costs and expenses at any given volume of activity that is budgeted.

[1] The break-even point in terms of dollar sales may be estimated by using the following formula: Break-even point (sales) equals dollar fixed expenses divided by (1 minus variable expenses, expressed as a percentage of sales).

RELATION OF COSTS, REVENUES, AND VOLUME

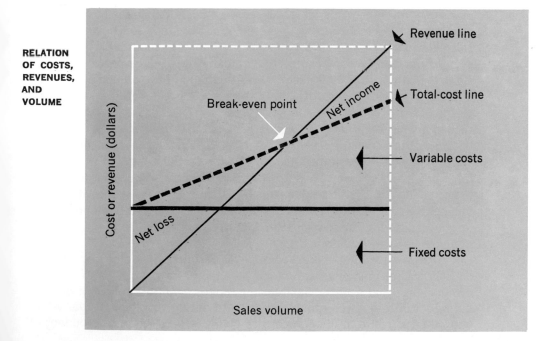

Setting budget estimates

If a budget is to be an effective forecast and control device, it is essential that estimates of future conditions be made with a reasonable degree of accuracy. There is no point in making plans that obviously cannot be realized. On the other hand, some of the incentive advantages of planning are lost if goals are set too low. The objective should be to establish revenue and expense goals that can be attained with good performance. A failure to meet the budget will thus represent something less than a good performance. If conditions arise that make it impossible to attain budgeted results, a revised budget should be prepared to reflect realistically the new conditions.

Period planning: an illustrative program budget

From an accounting standpoint, there are two steps involved in developing a program budget: (1) making estimates of sales and production and the effect of these on revenues and expenses, and (2) summarizing the estimated data in the form of budgeted income statements and periodic statements of financial position. In order to illustrate these two processes, let us consider a simple budgeting situation involving X Company, a manufacturing company that makes and sells a single product. In order to avoid undue complexity and detail in the illustrative budget, we shall make a number of simplifying assumptions where this can be done without losing the essential features of the budgeting process.

The financial position of X Company as of January 1 of the current year is shown in the balance sheet on page 847. Management has asked for a program budget showing net income for the first and second quarters of the current year and an estimate of the financial position at the end of each of the first two quarters. The company has a substantial loan outstanding with a local bank (see Notes Payable on the balance sheet) due in quarterly installments of $40,000 each. The sale of the company's product is subject to considerable seasonal variation; sales during the second quarter are expected to be larger than first-quarter sales. However, because of the economic advantages of stabilizing production throughout the first half of the year and because of a tight labor supply at the present time, management has set as its objective a stable production during the first and second quarters. Management is thus concerned with its ability to meet the quarterly obligation to the bank and to handle the increases in inventories during the first quarter that are necessary if a stable production volume is to be attained.

Operating budget expressed in physical units. The sales department, on the basis of market research and an analysis of past sales experience by customers and geographic areas, estimates 100,000 units will be sold during the first quarter and 150,000 units during the second quarter. In line with the desire of the company to stabilize production, the budget of

X COMPANY
Balance Sheet
January 1, Current Year
(Actual)

Assets

Current assets:

Cash		$ 75,000
Receivables		82,000
Inventories:		
Materials	$ 25,000	
Finished goods	52,000	77,000
Prepayments		21,000
Total current assets		$255,000

	Cost	Cumulative depreciation	Book value
Plant and equipment:			
Land	$ 70,000		$ 70,000
Buildings	600,000	$300,000	300,000
Equipment	300,000	120,000	180,000
	$970,000	$420,000	
Total plant and equipment			550,000
Total assets			$805,000

Liabilities and Equities

Current liabilities:

Notes payable *		$160,000
Accounts payable		46,000
Accrued expenses payable		32,000
Income taxes payable		50,000	$288,000
Stockholders' equity:		
Capital stock		$350,000
Retained earnings		167,000	517,000
Total liabilities and stockholders' equity		$805,000

* 6% serial note. Due in $40,000 installments on March 31, June 30, September 30, and December 31 of the current year.

physical sales and production is then drawn up as shown on the following page.

Schedule A1

X COMPANY
Budget of Sales and Production
(In units of product)

	Budget estimates	
	1st quarter	2d quarter
Planned production	120,000	120,000
Inventory at beginning of quarter	30,000	50,000
Units available for sale	150,000	170,000
Estimated sales	100,000	150,000
Inventory at end of quarter	50,000	20,000

The decision to reduce the inventory of finished goods from 30,000 units as of January 1 to 20,000 units at the end of June will minimize funds tied up in finished inventory at the end of the second quarter and thus help in meeting loan requirements. It is expected that sales during the third quarter can be met largely from production, since production can be increased during the summer months by hiring temporary employees available at that time. Thus the company will deliberately expand its finished goods inventory during the first quarter, and draw down on this inventory during the second quarter.

We now have an operating budget in very simple physical terms. If we had assumed a more realistic situation involving a number of different products, this would simply mean a multiplication of the physical budget estimates; that is, a similar estimate would have to be made for each product.

Operating budget expressed in dollars. In order to attach dollar figures to the budget data expressed in physical units, it is necessary to forecast selling prices and the costs that will be incurred in making and selling the product. The sales department has estimated that the unit selling price of X Company's product will remain relatively stable at $3 per unit during the next two quarters. In a company making a number of different products and subject to short-term changes in selling prices, the estimate of sales revenues would be considerably more difficult. X Company has made a careful study of its costs, based on an analysis of past experience and cost-volume relationship, and the estimates shown in Schedule A2 are available in preparing the budget for the first two quarters of the current year.

Note that the estimates of variable costs are made in terms of units manufactured or units sold. A strictly variable cost is constant per unit or product, but varies in total in proportion to the number of units sold or produced. On the other hand, fixed costs are budgeted in total at a dollar

Schedule A2

X COMPANY
Budget Estimates
For the First and Second Quarters of the Current Year

Sales price per unit	$3.00
Variable costs:	
Per unit manufactured:	
Materials	0.50
Direct labor	0.60
Variable manufacturing expense	0.30
Per unit sold:	
Selling expenses	0.20
Administrative expenses	0.10
Fixed costs (per quarter):	
Manufacturing expenses	$42,000
Selling expenses	20,000
Administrative expenses	50,000

amount per quarter. Per unit fixed costs will vary depending on the number of units of product sold or produced during a given period, that is, the larger the number of units of volume the smaller the per unit fixed cost.

The quarterly budget estimates for cost of goods manufactured, finished goods inventory, selling expenses, and administrative expenses may now be prepared on the basis of this information, as shown in the following schedules:

Schedule A3

X COMPANY
Budget Estimates
Cost of Goods Manufactured and Finished Goods Inventory

	1st quarter	2d quarter
Production budget (units)	120,000	120,000
Raw materials used ($0.50 × 120,000 units)	$ 60,000	$ 60,000
Direct labor ($0.60 × 120,000 units)	72,000	72,000
Variable manufacturing expense ($0.30 × 120,000 units) ..	36,000	36,000
Fixed manufacturing expense (per budget)	42,000	42,000
Budgeted cost of goods manufactured	$210,000	$210,000
Cost per unit ($210,000 ÷ 120,000 units)	$1.75	$1.75
Ending finished goods inventory:		
End of 1st quarter: 50,000 units @ $1.75	$ 87,500	
End of 2d quarter: 20,000 units @ $1.75		$ 35,000

Schedule A4

X COMPANY
Budgeted Selling Expenses

	1st quarter	*2d quarter*
Variable selling expenses ($0.20 × units sold)	$20,000	$30,000
Fixed selling expenses (per budget estimate)	20,000	20,000
Total budgeted selling expense	$40,000	$50,000

Schedule A5

X COMPANY
Budgeted Administrative Expenses

	1st quarter	*2d quarter*
Variable administrative expenses ($0.10 × units sold)	$10,000	$15,000
Fixed administrative expenses (per budget estimate)	50,000	50,000
Total budgeted administrative expenses	$60,000	$65,000

Diagram of budgeted costs. The budget estimates of costs and expenses may also be expressed graphically in a manner similar to that illustrated earlier in this chapter. The diagrams on page 852 are based on the X Company budget data for the first two quarters of the current year:

HERE IS
WHAT
QUARTERLY
INCOME
SHOULD BE

Budgeted income statement. We now have sufficient information to prepare a budgeted income statement for the first two quarters of the coming year:

Schedule A

X COMPANY
Budgeted Income Statement
First Two Quarters of Current Year

	1st quarter	*2d quarter*
Sales ($3 × units sold)	$300,000	$450,000
Cost of goods sold:		
Finished goods, beginning inventory	$ 52,000	$ 87,500
Cost of goods manufactured (A3)	210,000	210,000
	$262,000	$297,500
Less: finished goods, ending inventory (A3)	87,500	35,000
Cost of goods sold	$174,500	$262,500
Gross margin on sales	$125,500	$187,500

Expenses:		
Selling expenses (A4)	$ 40,000	$ 50,000
Administrative expenses (A5)	60,000	65,000
Interest expense	2,400	1,800
Total expenses	$102,400	$116,800
Net income before income taxes	$ 23,100	$ 70,700
Estimated income taxes (50% of net income)	11,550	35,350
Net income	$ 11,550	$ 35,350

Most of the items appearing on the income statement have been carried forward from previously illustrated budget schedules. Two exceptions require further comment:

At the beginning of the year X Company has outstanding a $160,000, 6% note that is to be paid in quarterly installments of $40,000. Therefore the interest expense will be 1 1/2% (6% ÷ 4) per quarter on the outstanding balance due. Interest expense for the first quarter is thus budgeted at $2,400 ($160,000 × 1 1/2%) and for the second quarter, $1,800 ($120,000 × 1 1/2%).

X Company estimates that income taxes for the current year will be approximately 50% of the reported net income for the year. The provision for income taxes has been budgeted on the basis of this assumption.

Financial budget. A forecast of X Company's financial position at the end of the first and second quarters of the coming year requires that assets and liabilities at January 1 (see page 847) be adjusted to reflect projected revenues and expenses during the two quarterly periods. The balance sheet items that will be affected by revenues and costs, together with a reference to the schedule on which financial budget data appear, are:

OUTLINE OF SUPPORTING BUDGET SCHEDULES

Balance sheet item	*Budget schedule*
Determined from operating budget:	
Finished goods inventory	A3
Entered directly on balance sheet:	
Allowance for depreciation on plant and equipment	(See B2 for amount of depreciation)
Retained earnings	(Reconciliation appears on Schedule C)
Schedules to be prepared:	
Materials inventory	B1
Accounts payable	B3
Accrued liabilities	B3
Prepaid expenses	B4
Income taxes payable	B5
Accounts receivable	B7
Cash	Schedule B

The inventory of finished goods has already been estimated in preparing the operating budget. The materials inventory was not required for operating budget purposes, however, because the figure for materials used was computed directly by multiplying the number of units produced by the raw material cost per unit. To convert materials used to materials purchased, an estimate of the materials inventories at the end of each quarter is needed.

**BUDGET IN
DIAGRAMS**

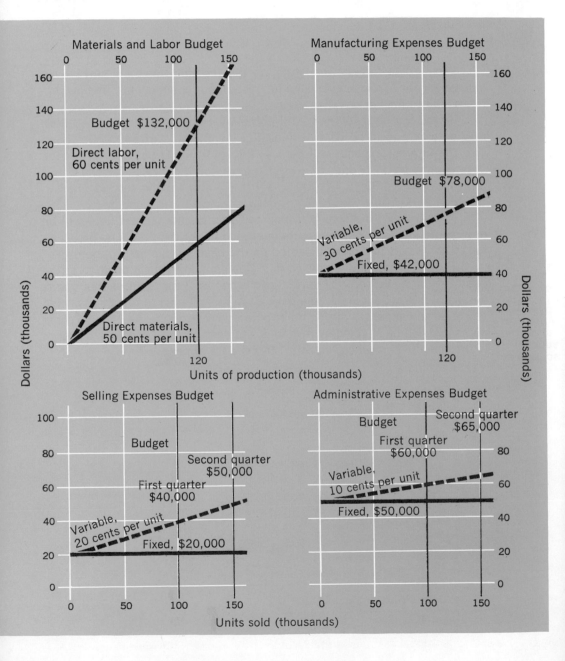

The production manager feels that the January 1 materials inventory of $25,000 is too low, and that it should be increased to approximately two-thirds of the material usage for one quarter. Since the estimate of materials used during the first two quarters is $60,000 each quarter, raw materials inventory should be increased to $40,000 (2/3 of $60,000). The budget for materials purchases reflects this decision:

Schedule B1

X COMPANY
Budgeted Materials Purchases and Inventories

	1st quarter	2d quarter
Materials used (A3)	$ 60,000	$ 60,000
Desired inventory at end of quarter	40,000	40,000
	$100,000	$100,000
Less: inventory at beginning of quarter	25,000	40,000
Budgeted materials purchases	$ 75,000	$ 60,000

The source of operating expenses. To determine the quarter-end balances of prepaid expenses and the various current liability accounts, it will be necessary to estimate the sources of the operating expenses that appear on the budgeted quarterly income statement. The following schedules show the estimates for X Company:

Schedule B2

X COMPANY
Source of Budgeted Expenses

	Total expenses	Accounts payable	Accrued liabilities	Write-off of prepaid expenses	Depreciation Bldg.	Depreciation Equip.
First Quarter:						
Materials purchases ...	$ 75,000	$ 75,000				
Direct labor	72,000		$ 72,000			
Manufacturing expense .	78,000	16,000	48,000	$4,400	$3,600	$6,000
Selling expense	40,000	13,000	25,100	1,000	500	400
Administrative expense .	60,000	11,000	45,500	2,000	400	1,100
Interest expense	2,400		2,400			
Totals	$327,400	$115,000	$193,000	$7,400	$4,500	$7,500

Second Quarter:						
Materials purchases ...	$ 60,000	$ 60,000				
Direct labor	72,000		$ 72,000			
Manufacturing expense .	78,000	16,000	48,400	$4,000	$3,600	$6,000
Selling expense	50,000	18,000	30,000	1,100	500	400
Administrative expense .	65,000	11,000	50,500	2,000	400	1,100
Interest expense	1,800		1,800			
Totals	$326,800	$105,000	$202,700	$7,100	$4,500	$7,500

The analysis of expenses by sources first supplies the budgeted amount of decrease in the book value of fixed assets each quarter. Since no acquisition of plant and equipment is contemplated by X Company during the first two quarters, the book value of the fixed asset accounts will simply decline by the amount of depreciation each quarter. Quarter-end balances of buildings and equipment may thus be entered directly on the budgeted balance sheets (see page 858).

An intermediate step is necessary in the case of prepaid expenses, accrued liabilities, and accounts payable. The analysis of expenses by sources shows the gross increase in the liability accounts and the gross decrease in prepaid expenses each quarter. In order to determine the budgeted ending balances in these accounts, it will be necessary to estimate cash outlays for these items during each quarter. In addition, the amount of cash required to meet income tax obligations must be estimated to arrive at a figure for quarterly income taxes payable.

The cash outlay for accounts payable and accrued liabilities may be determined by estimating the balances in these accounts at the end of the quarter. These estimates would be based on a study of each of the items and their due dates, and might be summarized as follows:

ESTIMATES OF LIABILITY BALANCES SHOW REQUIRED CASH OUTLAYS

Schedule B3

X COMPANY
Budget Estimates of Cash Outlays
on
Accounts Payable and Accrued Liabilities

	1st quarter	2d quarter
Accounts Payable:		
Balance at beginning of quarter	$ 46,000	$ 60,000
Payables increase during quarter (B2) ...	115,000	105,000
Total	$161,000	$165,000
Estimated balance at end of quarter	60,000	45,000
Cash outlay required during quarter	$101,000	$120,000

Accrued Liabilities:		
Balance at beginning of quarter	$ 32,000	$ 38,500
Expenses accrued during quarter (B2)	193,000	202,700
Total	$225,000	$241,200
Estimated balance at end of quarter	38,500	40,500
Cash outlay required during quarter	$186,500	$200,700

In the case of prepaid expenses and income taxes, the actual cash disbursements that would be required in each quarter may be estimated and the balance in each of these accounts then determined in the following manner:

NOTE REDUCTION IN PRE-PAYMENTS

Schedule B4

X COMPANY
Budget Estimate of Prepaid Expenses

	1st quarter	2d quarter
Balance at beginning of quarter	$21,000	$15,600
Estimated cash outlay during quarter	2,000	5,000
	$23,000	$20,600
Write-offs of prepayments (B2)	7,400	7,100
Balance at end of quarter	$15,600	$13,500

LAST YEAR'S INCOME TAX FULLY PAID BY END OF SECOND QUARTER

Schedule B5

X COMPANY
Budget Estimate of Income Taxes Payable

	1st quarter	2d quarter
Balance at beginning of quarter	$50,000	$36,550
Provision during quarter (Schedule A)	11,550	35,350
	$61,550	$71,900
Cash outlay (one-half of last year's tax)	25,000	25,000
Balance at end of quarter	$36,550	$46,900

Income taxes due on last year's income, as shown on the balance sheet at the beginning of the year, were $50,000. One-half of this amount is due on March 15 of the current year, and the remaining half is due on June 15. Thus $25,000 will be required for income taxes in each of the first two quarters.

Cash receipts. The primary sources of cash for any business are cash sales, collections on accounts receivable, the sale of operating assets (other than product), borrowing, and additional stockholder investment.

It is assumed that X Company contemplates no further borrowing or additional sale of capital stock during the first two quarters, and that all sales are made on open account. Therefore collections on receivables are the sole source of cash receipts for this company during the first two quarters covered by the budget. The estimate of cash collections would be based on past company experience. To simplify the illustration, two features, cash discounts on sales and the possibility that certain receivables will prove uncollectible, are not introduced in this example. We shall assume, therefore, that X Company does not grant cash discounts and that its collection experience is very good.

CASH INFLOW FROM REVENUES

The credit manager estimates, on the basis of past experience, that two-thirds of the sales in any quarter will be collected in that quarter, and that the remaining one-third of the sales of any quarter will be collected in the immediately following quarter. On the basis of this estimate, a forecast of cash collections on receivables for the first two quarters may be made as follows:

Schedule B6

X COMPANY
Budget of Cash Collections on Receivables

	1st quarter	2d quarter
Balance of receivables at beginning of year	$ 82,000	
Collections on first-quarter sales (2/3 in first quarter and 1/3 in second)	200,000	$100,000
Collections on second-quarter sales (2/3 in second quarter)		300,000
Total cash collections by quarter	$282,000	$400,000

RECEIVABLE ESTIMATE

The balance in accounts receivable at the end of each quarter may now be estimated as follows:

Schedule B7

X COMPANY
Budgeted Accounts Receivable

	1st quarter	2d quarter
Balance at the beginning of the quarter	$ 82,000	$100,000
Sales on open account during quarter (Schedule A)	300,000	450,000
	$382,000	$550,000
Less: estimated collections on accounts receivable (B6) ..	282,000	400,000
Estimated accounts receivable balance at end of quarter .	$100,000	$150,000

Cash forecast. On the basis of information accumulated in the budget
CASH FLOW schedules previously illustrated, it is now possible to prepare a cash fore-
AND ENDING cast for the first two quarters, as follows:
BALANCE

Schedule B

X COMPANY
Cash Budget
First Two Quarters of Current Year

	1st quarter	2d quarter
Balance at beginning of quarter	$ 75,000	$ 2,500
Receipts:		
Collections on receivables (B6)	282,000	400,000
Total cash available	$357,000	$402,500
Disbursements:		
Payment of accounts payable (B3)	$101,000	$120,000
Payments on accrued liabilities (B3)	186,500	200,700
Income tax payments (B5)	25,000	25,000
Prepaid expenses (B4)	2,000	5,000
Payments on notes (interest included in payments on accrued liabilities)	40,000	40,000
Total disbursements	$354,500	$390,700
Balance at end of the quarter	$ 2,500	$ 11,800

Budgeted financial position. We now have sufficient information to
forecast the financial position of X Company as of the end of each of the
quarters for which budget estimates have been made. The company's
budgeted balance sheets appear on page 858. Budget schedules from
which various figures on the balance sheet have been obtained are indicated in parentheses. In the very simple budget situation illustrated, the
balance sheets may be prepared directly from the budget schedules. In
a more complex situation, it might be desirable to set up the beginning
balance sheet amounts on a work sheet and trace through the budgeted
transactions for each quarter.

Using budgets effectively

The process of systematic planning would probably be of some value even
if the budget, once prepared, were promptly filed away and forgotten. The
primary benefits to be gained from a budget program, however, stem from
the uses that are made of the budgeted information. We have noted three
ways in which budgets can be useful to the management of an organization:
(1) as a forewarning of conditions that require remedial action; (2) as a
plan or blueprint for carrying out a given set of objectives; and (3) as a
yardstick in measuring the performance of company personnel.

Schedule C

X COMPANY
Budgeted Financial Position
As of the End of First Two Quarters of Current Year

	1st quarter	2d quarter
Assets		
Current assets:		
Cash (Schedule B)	$ 2,500	$ 11,800
Receivables (B7)	100,000	150,000
Inventories:		
Raw materials (B1)	40,000	40,000
Finished goods (A3)	87,500	35,000
Prepayments (B4)	15,600	13,500
Total current assets	$245,600	$250,300
Plant and equipment:		
Land	$ 70,000	$ 70,000
Buildings (net of depreciation, see B2)	295,500	291,000
Equipment (net of depreciation, see B2)	172,500	165,000
Total plant and equipment	$538,000	$526,000
Total assets	$783,600	$776,300
Liabilities and Stockholders' Equity		
Current liabilities:		
Notes payable (6%, $40,000 due quarterly)	$120,000	$ 80,000
Accounts payable (B3)	60,000	45,000
Expenses payable (B3)	38,500	40,500
Income taxes payable (B5)	36,550	46,900
Total current liabilities	$255,050	$212,400
Stockholders' equity:		
Capital stock, no par, 30,000 shares issued and outstanding	$350,000	$350,000
Retained earnings, beginning of quarter	167,000	178,550
Net income for the quarter	11,550	35,350
Total stockholders' equity	$528,550	$563,900
Total liabilities and stockholders' equity	$783,600	$776,300

Let us consider briefly the way in which the budget information compiled for the X Company in the preceding illustration might serve these three functions:

An advance warning of potential trouble. One of the major concerns of the management of X Company was the ability of the company to meet the quarterly payments on its note obligation. The cash budget for the first two quarters of the year indicates that the cash position of the company at the end of each quarter will be precariously low. A cash balance of $2,500 is forecast at the end of the first quarter, and a balance of $11,800 at the end of the second quarter (Schedule B). This indicates that if all goes well the payments *can* be met, but there is little margin for error in the estimates. Management, when confronted with such a forecast, should take steps in advance to prevent the cash balance from dropping as low as the budgeted amounts. It may be possible to obtain longer credit terms from suppliers and thus reduce payments on accounts payable during the first two quarters. The company may decide to let inventories fall below scheduled levels in order to postpone cash outlays. An extension of the terms of the note payable might also be sought. If any or all of these steps were taken, it would be necessary to revise the budget estimates accordingly. The fact that management is forewarned of this condition several months before it happens, however, illustrates one of the prime values of budgeting.

A plan for accomplishing desired objectives. A number of operating objectives were incorporated in the budget estimates of the X Company. A primary objective was to achieve management's profit goals. Secondary objectives were to stabilize production throughout the first two quarters and to reduce the inventory of finished goods by the end of the second quarter. The operating budget constitutes a set of plans for doing these things.

The budgeted income statement (Schedule A) shows an improved net income during the second quarter, reflecting the favorable effect of increased sales volume in relation to the existence of certain fixed costs. The responsibility for securing the volume of sales revenues budgeted in each quarter rests with the sales department. The problem of scheduling the production of 120,000 units each quarter and of seeing that production costs do not exceed budget estimates is the responsibility of the manufacturing department. General management is charged with maintaining control over administrative expenses.

In order to relate budgeted information to these various responsibilities, it will be necessary to rearrange the over-all program budget figures in terms of responsibility centers. In very broad outline, such a rearrangement might be accomplished by preparing quarterly budget estimates for major centers of responsibility as follows:

Responsibility Center	*Responsibility Budgets*
Sales manager	1. Sales quota in units of product
	2. Revenues for each quarter
	3. Selling expenses budgeted for each quarter
Production manager	1. Production schedule in units of product
	2. Cost of goods manufactured for each quarter

Financial manager 1. Cash budget for each quarter
2. Budgeted statements of financial position at the end of each quarter

General manager 1. Administrative expenses budgeted for each quarter
2. Over-all program budget for each quarter

Dividing the total budget plan into responsibility segments ensures that each executive knows the goals and his part in achieving them. Where possible, it is highly desirable to prepare monthly budgets for such purposes. The purpose of using quarterly figures in the illustrative budget for the X Company was merely to reduce the amount of detail in the illustration.

A yardstick for appraising performance. The effective use of budgets in gauging performance is not an easy task. It is not feasible to discuss all facets of this problem here, but let us consider briefly two points:

The heart of successful responsibility budgeting is to hold each supervisor accountable for the costs and revenues over which he can exercise significant control, and for which he is thus truly responsible.

For example, the foreman of a manufacturing department can influence labor costs in his department through his control over idle time, overtime hours, and the number of employees called to work. He may also exert some control over such items as equipment maintenance, supplies used, and power expenses. On the other hand, he probably has no influence on the salary of the plant superintendent or on the amount of building depreciation allocated to his department.

The view that a supervisor should not be charged with costs over which he has no control is gaining ground in modern budgeting practice, with the result that responsibility budgets commonly include only controllable costs. An alternative is to segregate noncontrollable costs in a separate section of a supervisor's budget and to use only the figures that are in the "controllable" section of the budget in appraising his performance.

The problem does not end here, however. Even controllable costs may be affected by factors over which a supervisor has little influence. A primary example is the effect of material differences between the volume of sales or production budgeted and the volume actually attained. The fact that attainment varied from budgeted volume will, of course, show up in comparisons with the over-all program budget. However, the effect of volume variations may lead to confusion when actual and budgeted results are compared for various responsibility centers.

Suppose, for example, a departmental operating budget is prepared under the assumption that 100,000 units of product will be manufactured. Direct labor cost, which is entirely variable, is budgeted at $50,000, or

IS PER-
FORMANCE
GOOD OR
BAD?

50 cents per unit. Now, under two different assumptions as to actual production, let us look at the responsibility budget for the production manager:

	Actual production	Actual per unit labor cost	Actual total labor cost	Budgeted labor cost	(Over) or under budget
Case 1	150,000	$0.40	$60,000	$50,000	$(10,000)
Case 2	50,000	0.60	30,000	50,000	20,000

A comparison between the actual labor cost and the budgeted labor cost in either of these two situations is meaningless as a measure of performance in controlling labor cost. In the first case it appears that the budget has been exceeded, yet the labor cost of 40 cents per unit represents a better performance than the 50 cents per unit budgeted. In the second case actual labor cost is under the budget, but the cost of 60 cents per unit compares unfavorably with the budgeted cost of 50 cents per unit. Charging the supervisor with a bad performance in the first case and with a good performance in the second is obviously unreasonable.

The heart of the matter is that departmental costs and expenses are influenced to varying degrees by the volume of output. If the volume of sales or production attained is outside the control of a given supervisor, a comparison of budget figures with actual figures when actual volume differs materially from that assumed in preparing the budget is of dubious value in judging the cost-control performance of a manager.

One solution to this problem is to revise the forecast budget to correspond with the actual volume of business attained during the period. To do this readily it may be desirable to establish responsibility budgets, not in terms of total dollar amounts, but in terms of fixed and variable components. This is sometimes called a *formula budget*. For example, a budget for factory supplies used might be stated as $4,000 plus 10 cents per unit of production. If production for the period were 100,000 units, the budget for factory supplies would be $14,000; if production for the period were 50,000 units, the budget for factory supplies would automatically be adjusted to $9,000.

The use of formula budgets to judge performance does not preclude the simultaneous use of forecast or program budgets as a means of comparing actual results with planned goals. A careful analysis of cost-volume relationship, however, is a key factor in developing budget figures that will be of real service to management in planning and controlling the operations of any organization.

QUESTIONS

1. Explain how budgetary planning is useful in controlling the operations of profit-making enterprises. Is it equally useful in the case of nonprofit organizations? Why?

2. What is the difference between a *program* budget and a *responsibility* budget?

3. In preparing a responsibility budget, how would you treat depreciation on building and equipment in the budget prepared for the factory superintendent? For the foreman of an operating department within the plant?

4. Explain why the relationship between sales and production is an important factor in forecasting financial position at the end of a budget period.

5. Manufacturing expense A is a variable cost, expense B is a fixed cost, and expense C is a semivariable cost. How would you expect each of these expenses to vary with changes in production? How would they vary with changes in production if they were expressed in dollars *per unit of product* produced?

6. What is a break-even chart? In general, what relationships does it show?

7. At the beginning of a budget period, the cost of raw materials used was estimated at $120,000. The actual cost of raw materials used during the period was $144,000. The plant superintendent concludes that this indicates a poor performance in either the buying or the use of materials. Is this conclusion valid on these facts? Why?

8. What is a "formula" budget estimate? In what way are formula budget estimates useful in appraising actual performance in relation to budgeted performance?

PROBLEMS

Group A

29A-1. The Pomeroy Manufacturing Company manufactures two products from a single raw material, "silco." From each 100 pounds of silco, 60 pounds of product A and 40 pounds of product B are produced. Silco costs 12 cents per pound and the variable manufacturing cost to process silco to the point where it becomes the raw material for products A and B is 8 cents per pound. Each pound of product A is separately processed at a variable manufacturing cost of 40 cents per pound, and each pound of B is separately processed at a variable manufacturing cost of 25 cents per pound. Product A then sells for $1.20 per pound; product B sells for $1.95 per pound. The finished product is shipped from the plant daily; therefore, ending inventories of goods in process and finished product are negligible.

The company's plant has a capacity of 60,000 pounds of A and 40,000 pounds of B per month. On an annual basis, fixed manufacturing costs are estimated at $192,000 and fixed selling and administrative expenses at $300,000. Variable selling and administrative expenses are budgeted at 10% of dollar sales.

Instructions
a. Prepare a break-even chart for the Pomeroy Manufacturing Company for

a month's operations, covering all ranges of production from zero to 100,000 pounds per month.

b. Prepare a budgeted income statement, showing the operating income that should be forecast if the plant operated during the month of September at 80% of capacity.

29A-2. The Babcock Company's fiscal year ends on March 31. The company prepares a monthly cash budget for a period six months in the future and extends this budget at the end of each three-month period. On July 1 a cash budget was prepared for the next six months, ending December 31. It is now nearing the end of September, and the time has come to extend the budget for the last three months of the current fiscal year, ending on March 31.

Sales for the current fiscal year, ending March 31, were budgeted at $2 million; the gross profit, on the average, has been 30% of sales. Experience indicates that annual sales will be distributed by months as follows:

Month	Per cent of total
October	9
November	10
December	16
January	4
February	6
March	8
April	7

Sales are made on 30-day open account. On the average 10% of sales are collected in the month of sale, 60% in the month following sale, 25% in the next month, 4% in the third month following sale, and 1% prove uncollectible.

Three-fourths of merchandise purchases are paid in the month incurred, and one-fourth in the month following purchase. The inventories at the end of each month are budgeted at one-half of the cost of the goods that will be sold during the following month.

Selling and administrative expenses for the year ended March 31 were budgeted as follows: Fixed expenses (including depreciation of $24,000), $192,000; variable expenses, 12% of sales. Expenses, other than depreciation, are paid on the average 40% in the month incurred and 60% in the following month.

Management is concerned about two matters: (1) The company has a bank loan dated July 31, which is due in two installments: $50,000 on January 31, and $50,000 on March 31. Interest at 6% of the unpaid balance will be paid with each installment. (2) The company is planning a major remodeling of one department during January and February. The lowest bid, on a cash basis, is $75,000. The company would prefer to pay for this work in February to avoid financing charges. However, if necessary, any amount up to one-half the cost may be financed and paid in monthly installments over a 12-month period. The company feels that it cannot allow its cash balance to fall below $13,000. The budget indicates a projected cash balance of $22,000 as of December 31, and expectations are that this will be met.

Instructions

a. Prepare a cash budget for the Babcock Company for the months of January, February, and March. Supporting schedules should be prepared for (1) estimated collections on receivables; (2) monthly purchases; (3) estimated cash payments on purchases; (4) estimated cash payments for expenses.

b. Determine from your budget estimates in (*a*) whether the company will be able to pay the cost of remodeling in February. Write a brief statement of your advice to the company as to whether they should plan to pay the $75,000 in full or finance some portion of this cost.

29A-3. The Bartel Company prepares a quarterly forecast budget for each of its operating departments. At the end of each quarter, department managers are requested to make a report comparing budgeted and actual results. For the second quarter of the current year, the report by the manager of Department K was as follows:

Second quarter, current year

	Budget	*Actual*	*Variance (over) or under*
Equivalent units of production	60,000	58,000	2,000
Direct materials	$108,000	$107,360	$ 640
Direct labor	132,000	132,170	(170)
Indirect labor	66,900	66,510	390
Factory supplies	18,200	16,900	1,300
Repairs & maintenance	14,100	13,750	350
Insurance & taxes	4,000	4,040	(40)
Depreciation	6,000	6,000	
	$349,200	$346,730	$2,470

The department manager, in forwarding his report, expressed pleasure over the fact that the results for the quarter were $2,470 under the budget and that all variances except direct labor and insurance and taxes were favorable. The controller of the Bartel Company, on receiving the report, called for the work sheets that had been used in preparing the forecast budget and found the following notations: Direct materials and direct labor are assumed to be variable costs. There is a fixed element of $6,300 per month in budgeted indirect labor. The variable portion in the budget for factory supplies is 25 cents per unit and for repairs and maintenance is 14 cents per unit. Insurance, taxes, and depreciation are regarded as fixed expenses.

You are requested by the controller to prepare a performance budget for Department K for the quarter, showing whether the performance in this department was favorable or unfavorable in relation to budget standards.

Instructions

a. From the information given, determine the quarterly budget formula for each element of cost in Department K.

b. Prepare a schedule showing the budgeted and the actual performance for Department K, and the budget variance, based on 58,000 units of production.

c. Explain briefly the reason for the difference between the budget figures you have arrived at and those shown in the forecast budget reported by the department manager.

29A-4. The post-closing trial balance of the Niven-Andrews Company, a partnership, as of January 31, the close of the current fiscal year, appears below:

POST-CLOSING TRIAL BALANCE
January 31

Cash	$ 47,000	
Receivables	152,000	
Allowance for uncollectibles		$ 3,600
Inventories	134,000	
Prepayments	8,000	
Land	25,000	
Buildings and equipment	380,000	
Allowance for depreciation		54,000
Vouchers payable		78,000
Portion of mortgage due within one year		18,000
Mortgage payable		162,000
Niven, capital		268,400
Andrews, capital		162,000
	$746,000	$746,000

The partners wish to prepare a forecast of operating results for the coming quarter (February, March, and April) and of their financial position on April 30.

Other data. The sales estimates for the current quarter are to be based on a review of sales during the first quarter of last year:

	Sales last year	1st quarter sales estimate this year	Estimated gross profit
Department A	$100,000	Down 10%	40%
Department B	220,000	Up 5%	30%
Department C	360,000	Up 12%	25%

After a careful study of operating expenses, the budget estimates shown below were made:

Expense	Estimated Quarterly Amount Fixed Variable	Source
Selling & Promotion	$18,000 + 7% of sales	$1,400 depreciation; provision for bad debts (1/4% of sales); the rest from vouchers payable
Occupancy Expense	12,000 + 2% of sales	$4,000 depreciation; $300 prepaid expense write-off; balance from vouchers payable

Buying Expense	10,000 + 4% of purchases	All from vouchers payable
Administrative Expense	40,000 + 1% of sales	$600 depreciation; $500 prepaid expense write-off; balance from vouchers payable
Interest Expense	5% per year on unpaid balance	Interest due is paid at the end of each quarter

It is estimated that vouchers payable will increase by $42,000 by the end of the first quarter. The company carries the amount due on the mortgage during the succeeding 12-month period as a current liability. Of the $18,000 shown on the balance sheet as current, one-fourth will be paid at the end of the first quarter. When this payment is made, an equal amount should be transferred from the long-term debt to the current liability classification. It is agreed that the partners will make monthly cash drawings during the year as follows: Niven, $2,000 per month; Andrews, $1,000 per month.

Of total sales, 80% are on open account, the balance are for cash. It is expected that 90% of the receivables on hand at January 31 will be collected by April 30, and that two-thirds of the charge sales during the first quarter will be collected prior to the end of the quarter. Inventories on April 30 are estimated to be $160,000, at cost.

No additional prepaid expenses or fixed asset purchases are contemplated during the first quarter. The partners share profits on the basis of 60% to Niven and 40% to Andrews.

Instructions. Prepare a budgeted income statement for the first quarter of the current year, ending on April 30, and a forecast balance sheet as of April 30. Round all figures to the nearest dollar. The following budget schedules should be prepared in support of these two statements:
   a. Budgeted operating expenses
   b. Estimate of merchandise purchases
   c. Source of budgeted expenses
   d. Analysis of changes in the accounts receivable and vouchers payable accounts for the quarter
   e. Estimate of cash receipts, cash disbursements, and April 30 cash balance
   f. Analysis of partners' capital accounts (This may be included in the balance sheet.)

Group B

29B-1. The Ziebarth Company manufactures a single product, and has prepared budget estimates for the first three months of the current year as follows:

	Units	
	Sales	Production
January	8,500	9,000
February	10,000	12,000
March	12,000	13,000

As of December 31, the inventory of finished product was 500 units, at a fifo cost of $8,500. The company estimates that material costs per unit of product manufactured will be $4 and that per unit direct labor will be $5. Factory overhead is budgeted at $45,000 per month plus $1 per unit manufactured. Operating expenses are estimated at $20,000 plus 10% of sales. The current selling price per unit is $20, and the company expects that it will be able to maintain this price throughout the first quarter. The work in process at the end of each month is negligible and may be ignored.

Instructions

a. Prepare in columnar form (using a column for each month) a statement showing the determination of the budgeted cost of sales for each of the three months. (Show how you determined the cost of the ending inventories on a fifo basis.)

b. Using a single cost of goods sold figure, as determined in (*a*), prepare a budgeted income statement for the three-month period, using one column for each month.

29B-2. Near the end of March, Victor Morris, the owner of Morris Supply Company, began negotiations with his bank for a loan. Morris estimates that his current position at March 31 will be as follows:

Cash in bank	$15,000
Receivables (net of $8,000 allowance for bad debts)	52,000
Inventories	30,000
Total current assets	$97,000
Current payables ($24,000 one month or more past due)	50,000
Net working capital	$47,000

Morris has applied for a 90-day bank loan of $50,000. The proceeds of this loan, $49,250, he plans to use on April 1 as follows:

Immediate increase in inventories	$22,000
Payment of past-due accounts payable	24,000
Add to cash balance	3,250

The loan officer asks Morris to prepare a forecast of his cash position at June 30, showing that the bank loan can be paid at this date. Morris has prepared estimates to be used as a basis for a three-month cash budget. Sales are estimated as: April, $80,000; May, $120,000; June, $90,000; and July, $60,000.

All sales are made on open account. Past experience indicates that 80% will be collected in the month following the sale, 19% in the following month, and 1% will prove uncollectible. On the average, cost of goods sold has been 65% of sales. Operating expenses are budgeted at $12,000 per month plus 8% of sales. With the exception of $1,000 per month depreciation, all expenses and merchandise purchases are on open account and are paid in the month following their incurrence.

Morris estimates that inventories at the end of each month should be sufficient to cover the sales of the following month. He expects to collect $40,000 of the March 31 receivables in April and $12,000 in May.

Instructions

a. Prepare a monthly cash budget showing estimated cash receipts and disbursements for April, May, and June, and the cash balance at the end of each month. Supporting schedules should be prepared for estimated collections on receivables, estimated merchandise purchases, and estimated payments of merchandise purchases and operating expenses.

b. On the basis of your cash budget, write a brief report to Morris explaining whether or not he will be able to meet his $50,000 loan at the bank on June 30.

29B-3. The management of the Jelnik Department Store has established the following budget estimates for costs during the coming year:

	Fixed per year	Variable per dollar of net sales
Cost of goods sold		$0.650
Sales and promotion expense	$85,000	0.080
Building occupancy	40,000	0.013
Buying expense	36,000	0.020
Delivery expense	28,000	0.030
Credit and collection expense	22,000	0.005
Administrative expense	39,000	0.002

On the basis of these estimates, the controller of the company prepared a break-even chart showing the operating profit (before taxes) that the company might expect to realize at various sales volumes up to $2 million.

At the end of the year, the actual results that had been achieved were as shown below.

Sales (net)	$1,800,000
Cost of goods sold	1,100,000
Selling and promotion	221,500
Building occupancy	62,100
Buying expense	73,400
Delivery expense	78,800
Credit and collection	28,700
Administrative expenses	43,000

Instructions

a. Construct a break-even chart as the controller might have prepared it at the beginning of the year. Label all lines on the chart.

b. Prepare a comparative income statement, showing the actual and budgeted revenues and expenses and the variations between actual and budgeted performance.

29B-4. The Snow Supply Company began business on July 1 with the following assets:

Cash	$ 20,000
Inventories	50,000
Land	25,000
Building & equipment	250,000

The management wishes to prepare budgets for the next two quarters (ending September 30 and December 31, respectively) showing the budgeted operating income for each quarter and the budgeted cash position of the company at the end of each quarter. These forecasts are to be based on the following estimates:

First-quarter sales are expected to be $150,000; the company expects to double sales during the second quarter and to triple first-quarter sales in the following quarter. It is estimated that 69% of sales will be collected in the quarter in which the goods are sold, 30% in the next quarter, and that 1% will prove uncollectible.

The cost of goods sold is expected to average 70% of sales. Selling expenses (excluding depreciation and bad debts) are budgeted at $21,000 plus 12% of sales. Administrative expenses (excluding depreciation) are budgeted at $15,000 plus 2% of sales. Depreciation on fixed assets will be at the composite rate of 5% per annum, of which 80% is a selling expense and 20% administrative. The inventory at the end of each quarter should be equal to one-third of the next quarter's requirements.

It is estimated that merchandise purchases will be paid 60% in the quarter purchased and 40% in the following quarter, and that two-thirds of operating expenses will be paid in the quarter incurred and one-third in the following quarter.

Management plans to purchase $30,000 of additional equipment near the end of the second quarter, and they are concerned about the ability of the company to pay for this at the time it is acquired. They feel that a minimum cash balance of $10,000 must be maintained.

Instructions

a. Prepare a budgeted statement of operating income for the first two quarters of the current fiscal year. Use a columnar form, with one column for each quarter.

b. Prepare a statement of budgeted cash receipts and disbursements for the first two quarters of the current fiscal year. It will be necessary to prepare a supporting schedule showing merchandise purchases during each quarter. Include the amount of the equipment purchase as a disbursement during the second quarter.

c. On the basis of the cash budget prepared in (*b*), write a short note to management stating your conclusions as to whether it will be necessary to arrange for a loan during either quarter, and the approximate amount you would recommend that the company borrow.

Index